# TOWN AND COUNTRY PLANNING IN BRITAIN

## Eleventh Edition

# TOWN AND COUNTRY PLANNING IN BRITAIN

Eleventh Edition

*J. Barry Cullingworth and Vincent Nadin*

London and New York

First published in 1964
Eleventh edition published 1994
by Routledge
11 New Fetter Lane, London EC4P 4EE

Simultaneously published in the USA and Canada
by Routledge
29 West 35th Street, New York, NY 10001

Typeset in Garamond by J&L Composition Ltd, Filey, North Yorkshire

Printed and bound in Great Britain by
Clays Ltd, St Ives plc

*British Library Cataloguing in Publication Data*
A catalogue record for this book is available from the British Library

*Library of Congress Cataloging in Publication Data*
Cullingworth, J. B.
Town and country planning in Britain / J. B. Cullingworth and
Vincent Nadin. – 11th ed.
p.    cm.
Includes bibliographical references and index.
1. City planning – Great Britain.    2. Regional planning – Great
Britain.    I. Nadin, Vincent.    II. Title.
HT169.G7C63    1994
361.6'0941 – dc20        93–35545

ISBN 0–415–10708–3

# CONTENTS

# FIGURES

# TABLES

# PREFACE

When this book was first drafted, in 1963, there seemed little difficulty in defining the British system of 'town and country planning'; it was a fairly straightforward activity of government. It was, therefore, a simple matter to decide what the coverage of the book should be, particularly since the modest objective was to describe the formal institutions and official policies which together constituted the system. Such simplicity is no longer to hand. The activities of government and the problems with which it deals have grown greatly during the post-war period. As a result, 'town and country planning' now merges with such a host of other governmental areas that it is difficult to determine where the boundaries of the system lie – if, indeed, there are any.

However, rather than agonising about definitions, this new edition follows its predecessors in building on (and taking away from) the issues which formed the basis of the original book. This may present conceptual problems, and it certainly gave the authors (of which there are now two) some practical difficulties about the matters which were to be excluded. (There were few difficulties in deciding what to *include*!) Though the difficulties were thus resolved (rather than solved) in a pragmatic way, there are some regrets that the discussion is clearly too shallow at many points. But the book is a long one, and it seeks only to introduce the field: it is in no way a comprehensive text.

Of course, after nearly thirty years, the book was showing indications of middle age, and was needing far more than an updating of facts and figures. In particular, the 'feel' of the 1990s is very different from that of earlier decades, and the book has been substantially rewritten in an attempt to reflect this. Some of the historical material has been reduced, though hopefully sufficient has been retained to illustrate the origins of policies and some of its meanderings. The biggest cuts have been made in the details of now superseded policies.

As with previous editions, the aim has been to provide an account of town and country planning over the whole of Britain. It has to be admitted, however, that this has been less than completely successful. This has been due in part to difficulties of logistics (and unpredictable transatlantic mail), and in part to the paucity of available material. The shortcomings are highlighted by the clear value of the intra-British comparisons that are presented in this edition. Work is continuing on this, and it is intended that a future edition will better fill the important gaps relating to Scotland and, to an even greater extent, Wales. (It would also be useful to extend the coverage to Northern Ireland.)

The basic structure of the book remains the same, though the chapter on regional planning (which became increasingly slender in former editions) has been deleted. Other deletions are the result of formerly current policies turning into history, as with the new towns. On the other hand, the material on the environment, the countryside, and the heritage has been expanded to reflect the increased interest and activity in these areas.

The book has also continued to change in character from a deadpan account of the planning system to a more critical discussion of policy issues. It is hoped that this will make the text more interesting to read: it certainly made it more interesting to write (particularly as the joint authorship led to preliminary debates before a final draft was ready).

A major change has been made in referencing. In addition to chapter notes, all published references have been consolidated in an extensive bibliography and a list of official publications. It is hoped that this change will make the references more accessible.

Acknowledgement is made with sincere gratitude to several colleagues who have commented on drafts of various chapters: Ian Dickins, Dave Hickling, Peter Larkham, Sue Manns, Janice Morphet, Dave Shaw, and Colin Wood. We also wish to thank Sally Jones and Steve Roddie for their work on the figures. The errors and blemishes which undoubtedly remain are the full responsibility of the authors.

Barry Cullingworth, Cambridge
Vincent Nadin, Birmingham

# ACRONYMS AND ABBREVIATIONS

Acronyms and abbreviations are a major growth area in public policy. The following list includes all that are used in the text and others that readers will come across in the planning literature. No claim is made for comprehensiveness.

| | | | |
|---|---|---|---|
| AAI | Area of archaeological importance | BC | British Coal |
| ACC | Association of County Councils | BIC | Business in the Community |
| ACCORD | Assistance for Coordinated Rural Development | BPEO | Best practical environmental option |
| | | BPF | British Property Federation |
| ACOST | Advisory Council on Science and Technology | BPM | Best practical means |
| | | BR | British Rail |
| ACRE | Association of Community Councils in Rural England | BRE | Building Research Establishment |
| | | BRF | British Road Federation |
| ADAS | Agricultural Development and Advice Service | BUD | British Urban Development |
| | | BWB | British Waterways Board |
| ADC | Association of District Councils | | |
| AESOP | Association of European Schools of Planning | CADW | Not an acronym, but the Welsh name for the Welsh Historic Monuments Agency. (The word means to keep, to preserve.) |
| AIS | Agricultural Improvement Scheme | | |
| ALURE | Alternative land use and rural economy | | |
| AMA | Association of Metropolitan Authorities | CAP | Common Agricultural Policy |
| | | CAT | City action team |
| AONB | Area of outstanding natural beauty | CBI | Confederation of British Industry |
| APRS | Association for the Protection of Rural Scotland | CC | Countryside Commission |
| | | CCP | Comprehensive Community programme |
| ARC | Action Resource Centre | | |
| ASNW | Area of semi-natural woodland | CCS | Countryside Commission for Scotland (now Scottish Natural Heritage |
| ATB | Agricultural Training Board | | |
| BACMI | British Aggregate Construction Materials Industries | CCT | Compulsory competitive tendering |
| | | CCW | Countryside Council for Wales |
| BATNEEC | Best available techniques not entailing excessive cost (Environmental Protection Act 1990, s.7 (10)) | CDA | Comprehensive development area |
| | | CDP | Community development project |
| | | CEGB | Central Electricity Generating Board |

| | | | |
|---|---|---|---|
| CES | Centre for Environmental Studies | DNH | Department of National Heritage |
| CFCs | Chlorofluorocarbons | DoE | Department of the Environment |
| CHAC | Central Housing Advisory Committee | DoT | Department of Transport (formerly DTp) |
| CIPFA | Chartered Institute of Public Finance and Accountancy | DPOS | District Planning Officers' Society |
| CLA | Country Landowners' Association | DRIVE | Dedicated road infrastructure for vehicle safety in Europe |
| CLRAE | Conference of Local and Regional Authorities of Europe (Council of Europe) | DTI | Department of Trade and Industry |
| | | DTp | Department of Transport (now DoT) |
| | | DWI | Drinking Water Inspectorate |
| CLES | Centre for Local Economic Strategies | | |
| CLEUD | Certificate of lawfulness of existing use or development | EA | Environmental assessment |
| | | EAGGF | European Agriculture Guidance and Guarantee Fund |
| CLOPUD | Certificate of lawfulness of proposed use or development | EBRD | European Bank for Reconstruction and Development |
| COBA | Cost–benefit analysis | | |
| COPA | Control of Pollution Act (1974) | EC | European Community |
| CoSIRA | Council for Small Industries in Rural Areas | ECSC | European Coal and Steel Community |
| | | ECTP | European Council of Town Planners |
| CORINE | Community Information System on the State of the Environment (EC) | ECU | European currency unit |
| | | EEC | European Economic Community |
| COSLA | Convention of Scottish Local Authorities | EFTA | European Free Trade Association |
| | | EIA | Environmental impact assessment |
| CPO | Compulsory purchase order | EIP | Examination in public |
| CPOS | County Planning Officers' Society | EIS | Environmental impact statement |
| CPRE | Council for the Protection of Rural England | EMA | Environmental management areas |
| | | EN | English Nature |
| CPRS | Central Policy Review Staff | EPA | Educational priority area |
| CPRW | Campaign (formerly Council) for the Protection of Rural Wales | EPA | Environmental Protection Act (1990) |
| CRE | Commission for Racial Equality | EPC | Economic planning council |
| CRRAG | Countryside Recreation Research Advisory Group | ERDF | European Regional Development Fund |
| CSO | Central Statistical Office | ERP | Electronic road pricing |
| CWI | Controlled Waste Inspectorate | ES | Environmental statement (UK) |
| | | ESA | Environmentally sensitive area |
| DAFS | Department of Agriculture and Fisheries for Scotland | ESF | European Social Fund |
| | | ESRC | Economic and Social Research Council |
| DBRW | Development Board for Rural Wales | | |
| DC | Development Corporation | ETB | English Tourist Board |
| DCC | Docklands Consultative Committee | EURATOM | European Atomic Energy Community |
| DEA | Department of Economic Affairs | | |
| DLG | Derelict land grant | EZ | Enterprise zone |
| DLGA | Derelict land grant advice note | | |
| DLT | Development land tax | FC | Forestry Commission |

| | | | |
|---|---|---|---|
| FCGS | Farm and Conservation Grant Scheme | IACGEC | Inter-Agency Committee on Global Environmental Change |
| FEOGA | Fonds Européen d'Orientation et de Garantie Agricole (European Agriculture Guidance and Guarantee Fund) | IAPI | Industrial Air Pollution Inspectorate |
| | | IAPs | Inner area programmes |
| | | ICE | Institution of Civil Engineers |
| | | IDC | Industrial development certificate |
| FIG | Financial Institutions Group | IEEP | Institute for European Environmental Policy |
| FMI | Financial Management Initiative | | |
| FoE | Friends of the Earth | IIA | Industrial improvement area |
| FTA | Freight Transport Association | INLOGOV | Institute of Local Government Studies (University of Birmingham) |
| FWAG | Farming and Wildlife Advisory Group | | |
| | | IPC | Integrated pollution control |
| FWGS | Farm Woodland Grant Scheme | IRD | Integrated Rural Development (Peak District) |
| GATT | General Agreement on Tariffs and Trade | | |
| | | ISOCARP | International Society of City and Regional Planners |
| GDO | General Development Order | | |
| GEAR | Glasgow Eastern Area Renewal (Scheme) | IWA | Inland Waterways Association |
| | | IWAAC | Inland Waterways Amenity Advisory Committee |
| GIA | General improvement area | | |
| GLC | Greater London Council | JPL | Journal of Planning and Environment Law (formerly Journal of Planning and Property Law) |
| GLDP | Greater London Development Plan | | |
| HAA | Housing action area | | |
| HAT | Housing action trust | | |
| HBF | House Builders Federation | LAW | Land Authority for Wales |
| HBMC | Historic Buildings and Monuments Commission | LAWDC | Local authority waste disposal company |
| HC | House of Commons | LBA | London Boroughs Association |
| HCiS | Housing Corporation in Scotland | LDDC | London Docklands Development Corporation |
| HIDB | Highlands and Islands Development Board (now HIE) | | |
| | | LEC | Local enterprise company (Scotland) |
| HIE | Highlands and Islands Enterprise | | |
| HIP | Housing investment programme | LEGUP | Local enterprises grants for urban projects (Scotland) |
| HL | House of Lords | | |
| HLCA | Hill Livestock Compensatory Allowances | LFA | Less favoured area (agriculture) |
| | | LGMB | Local Government Management Board |
| HMIP | Her Majesty's Inspectorate of Pollution | | |
| | | LNR | Local nature reserve |
| HMIPI | Her Majesty's Industrial Pollution Inspectorate (Scotland) | LPA | Local planning authority |
| | | LPAC | London Planning Advisory Committee |
| HMSO | Her Majesty's Stationery Office | | |
| HRF | Housing Research Foundation | LSPU | London Strategic Policy Unit |
| HSE | Health and Safety Executive | LWRA | London Waste Registration Authority |
| HWI | Hazardous Waste Inspectorate | | |

| | | | |
|---|---|---|---|
| MAFF | Ministry of Agriculture, Fisheries and Food | NFU | National Farmers' Union |
| MCC | Metropolitan County Council | NHMF | National Heritage Memorial Fund |
| MEA | Manual of Environmental Assessment (for trunk roads) | NII | Nuclear Installations Inspectorate |
| | | NNR | National nature reserve |
| | | NPA | National park authority |
| MEP | Member of the European Parliament | NPF | National planning Forum |
| MHLG | Ministry of Housing and Local Government | NPG | National Planning guidelines (Scotland) |
| MINIS | Management Information System for Ministers | NPPG | National planning policy guidance notes (Scotland) |
| MLGP | Ministry of Local Government and Planning | NRA | National Rivers Authority |
| | | NRTF | National road traffic forecasts (GB) |
| MNR | Marine nature reserve | NSA | Nitrate sensitive area |
| MPA | Mineral planning authority | NTDC | New town development corporation |
| MPG | Minerals policy guidance note | | |
| MPOS | Metropolitan Planning Officers Society | OECD | Organisation for Economic Co-operation and Development |
| MPP | Monuments protection programme (English Heritage) | OEEC | Organisation for European Economic Cooperation |
| MSC | Manpower Services Commission | OPCS | Office of Population Censuses and Surveys |
| MTCP | Ministry of Town and Country Planning | | |
| | | | |
| NAO | National Audit Office | PAG | Planning Advisory Group (1965) |
| NACRT | National Agricultural Centre Rural Trust | PAN | Planning advice note (Scotland) |
| | | PDR | Permitted development rights |
| NARIS | National Roads Information System | PEP | Political and Economic Planning (now PSI) |
| NCB | National Coal Board | | |
| NCBOE | National Coal Board Opencast Executive | PIA | Planning Inspectorate Agency |
| | | PIC | Planning inquiry commission |
| NCC | Nature Conservancy Council | PIEDA | Planning, Economic and Development Consultants |
| NCCI | National Committee for Commonwealth Immigrants | PLI | Public local inquiry |
| NCCS | Nature Conservancy Council for Scotland (now Scottish Natural Heritage) | PPG | Planning policy guidance note |
| | | PPP | Polluter pays principle |
| | | PRIDE | Programmes for rural initiatives and developments (Scotland) |
| NCVO | National Council of Voluntary Organisations | PSI | Policy Studies Institute |
| NDPB | Non-departmental public body | PTA | Passenger transport authority |
| NEDC | National Economic Development Council | PTE | Passenger transport executive |
| | | PTEG | Passenger transport executive group |
| NEDO | National Economic Development Office | PTRC | Planning and Transport Research and Computation |
| NERC | Natural Environment Research Council | PWR | Pressurised water reactor |

| | | | | |
|---|---|---|---|---|
| QUANGO | Quasi-autonomous non-governmental organisation | | SNH | Scottish Natural Heritage |
| | | | SMR | (County) sites and monuments records |
| RA | Renewal area | | SO | Scottish Office |
| RAC | Royal Automobile Club | | SOEnD | Scottish Office Environment Department |
| RCC | Rural community council | | | |
| RCEP | Royal Commission on Environmental Pollution | | SoS | Secretary of State |
| | | | SPA | Special protection area (for birds) |
| RCI | Radiochemical Inspectorate | | SPG | Supplementary planning guidance |
| RCU | Road construction unit | | SPZ | Simplified planning zone |
| RDA | Rural development area | | SSHA | Scottish Special Housing Association |
| RDC | Rural Development Commission | | SSSI | Site of special scientific interest |
| RDP | Rural development programme | | STB | Scottish Tourist Board |
| RIBA | Royal Institute of British Architects | | TCPA | Town and Country Planning Association |
| RICS | Royal Institution of Chartered Surveyors | | TCPSS | Town and Country Planning Summer School |
| RPG | Regional planning guidance note | | TEC | Training and Enterprise Council |
| RSA | Regional Studies Association | | TEST | Transport and Environment Studies |
| RSPB | Royal Society for the Protection of Birds | | TPPs | Transport policies and programmes |
| RTPI | Royal Town Planning Institute | | TRL | Transport Research Laboratory (formerly Transport and Road Research Laboratory) |
| SACTRA | Standing Advisory Committee on Trunk Road Assessment | | TSG | Transport Supplementary Grant |
| SAGA | Sand and Gravel Association | | UCO | Use Classes Order |
| SCLSERP | Standing Conference on London and South East Regional Planning (see also SERPLAN) | | UDA | Urban development area |
| | | | UDAG | Urban development action grant (USA) |
| SDA | Scottish Development Agency (now Scottish Enterprise) | | UDC | Urban development corporation |
| | | | UDG | Urban development grant |
| SDD | Scottish Development Department | | UDP | Unitary development plan |
| SDO | Special Development Order | | UNECE | United Nations Economic Commission for Europe |
| SERC | Science and Engineering Research Council | | UP | Urban Programme |
| SERPLAN | London and South East Regional Planning Conference | | URA | Urban Regeneration Agency |
| | | | URG | Urban regeneration grant |
| SHAC | Scottish Housing Advisory Committee | | VFM | Value for money |
| SI | Statutory instrument | | | |
| SLF | Scottish Landowners' Federation | | WCA | Waste collection authority |
| SME | Small and medium-sized enterprises (Europe) | | WDA | Welsh Development Agency |
| | | | WDA | Waste disposal authority |
| SNAP | Shelter Neighbourhood Action Project | | WDP | Waste disposal plan |

| | | | |
|---|---|---|---|
| WMEB | West Midlands Enterprise Board | WWF | World-Wide Fund for Nature |
| WO | Welsh Office | | (formerly World Wildlife Fund) |
| WRA | Waste regulation authority | | |
| WRAP | Waste reduction always pays | YTS | Youth Training Scheme |
| WTB | Welsh Tourist Board | | |

Grant: *Encyclopedia* refers to Malcolm Grant's *Encyclopedia of Planning Law and Practice*, London: Sweet and Maxwell, loose-leaf, regularly updated by supplements.

# 1

# THE EVOLUTION OF TOWN AND COUNTRY PLANNING

The first assumption that we have made is that national planning is intended to be a reality and a permanent feature of the internal affairs of this country.

Uthwatt Report, 1942

The town and country planning system has not changed in its essentials since it was established in 1947.

Planning Policy Guidance Note 1, 1988

## THE PUBLIC HEALTH ORIGINS

Town and country planning as a task of government has developed from public health and housing policies. The nineteenth-century increase in population and, even more significant, the growth of towns led to public health problems which demanded a new role for government. Together with the increase in medical knowledge, the realisation that overcrowded insanitary urban areas resulted in an economic cost (which had to be borne at least in part by the local ratepayers) and the fear of social unrest, this new urban growth eventually resulted in an appreciation of the necessity for interfering with market forces and private property rights in the interest of social well-being. The nineteenth-century public health legislation was directed at the creation of adequate sanitary conditions. Among the measures taken to achieve these were powers for local authorities to make and enforce building by-laws for controlling street widths, and the height, structure and layout of buildings. Limited and defective though these powers proved to be, they represented a marked advance in social control and paved the way for more imaginative measures. The physical impact of by-law control on

British towns is depressingly still very much in evidence; and it did not escape the attention of contemporary social reformers. In the words of Unwin:

> much good work has been done. In the ample supply of pure water, in the drainage and removal of waste matter, in the paving, lighting and cleansing of streets, and in many other such ways, probably our towns are as well served as, or even better than, those elsewhere. Moreover, by means of our much abused bye-laws, the worst excesses of overcrowding have been restrained; a certain minimum standard of air-space, light and ventilation has been secured; while in the more modern parts of towns, a fairly high degree of sanitation, of immunity from fire, and general stability of construction have been maintained, the importance of which can hardly be exaggerated. We have, indeed, in all these matters laid a good foundation and have secured many of the necessary elements for a healthy condition of life; and yet the remarkable fact remains that there are growing up around our big towns vast districts, under these very bye-laws, which for dreariness and sheer ugliness it is difficult to match anywhere, and compared with which many of the old unhealthy slums are, from the point of view of picturesqueness and beauty, infinitely more attractive.
>
> (Unwin 1909: 3)

It was on this point that public health and architecture met. The enlightened experiments at Saltaire (1853), Bournville (1878), Port Sunlight (1887) and elsewhere had provided object lessons. Ebenezer Howard and the Garden City Movement were now exerting considerable influence on contemporary thought. The National Housing Reform Council (later the National Housing and Town Planning Council) were campaigning for the introduction of town planning. Even more significant was a similar demand from local government and professional associations such as the Association of Municipal Corporations, the Royal Institute of British Architects, the Surveyors' Institute and the Association of Municipal and County Engineers. As Ashworth has pointed out,

> the support of many of these bodies was particularly important because it showed that the demand for town planning was arising not simply out of theoretical preoccupations but out of the everyday practical experience of local administration. The demand was coming in part from those who would be responsible for the execution of town planning if it were introduced.
> (Ashworth 1954: 180)

## THE FIRST PLANNING ACT

The movement for the extension of sanitary policy into town planning was uniting diverse interests. These were nicely summarised by John Burns, President of the Local Government Board, when he introduced the first legislation bearing the term 'town planning' – the Housing, Town Planning, Etc. Act 1909:

> The object of the bill is to provide a domestic condition for the people in which their physical health, their morals, their character and their whole social condition can be improved by what we hope to secure in this bill. The bill aims in broad outline at, and hopes to secure, the home healthy, the house beautiful, the town pleasant, the city dignified and the suburb salubrious.[1]

The new powers provided by the Act were for the preparation of 'schemes' by local authorities for controlling the development of new housing areas. Though novel, these powers were logically a simple extension of existing ones. It is significant that this

first legislative acceptance of town planning came in an Act dealing with health and housing. And, as Ashworth has pointed out, the gradual development and the accumulated experience of public health and housing measures facilitated a general acceptance of the principles of town planning.

> Housing reform had gradually been conceived in terms of larger and larger units. Torrens' Act (Artizans and Labourers Dwellings Act, 1868) had made a beginning with individual houses; Cross's Act (Artizans and Labourers Dwellings Improvement Act, 1875) had introduced an element of town planning by concerning itself with the reconstruction of insanitary areas; the framing of bylaws in accordance with the Public Health Act of 1875 had accustomed local authorities to the imposition of at least a minimum of regulation on new building, and such a measure as the London Building Act of 1894 brought into the scope of public control the formation and widening of streets, the lines of buildings frontage, the extent of open space around buildings, and the height of buildings. Town planning was therefore not altogether a leap in the dark, but could be represented as a logical extension, in accordance with changing aims and conditions, of earlier legislation concerned with housing and public health.
> (Ashworth 1954: 181)

The 'changing conditions' were predominantly the rapid growth of suburban development: a factor which increased in importance in the following decades.

> In fifteen years 500,000 acres of land have been abstracted from the agricultural domain for houses, factories, workshops and railways . . . If we go on in the next fifteen years abstracting another half a million from the agricultural domain, and we go on rearing in green fields slums, in many respects, considering their situation, more squalid than those which are found in Liverpool, London and Glasgow, posterity will blame us for not taking this matter in hand in a scientific spirit. Every two and a half years there is a County of London converted into urban life from rural conditions and agricultural land. It represents an enormous amount of building land which we have no right to allow to go unregulated.[2]

The emphasis was entirely on raising the standards of *new* development. The Act permitted local authorities (after obtaining the permission of the Local Government Board) to prepare town planning schemes with the general object of 'securing proper sanitary conditions, amenity and convenience', but only for land which was being developed or appeared likely to be developed.

Strangely it was not at all clear what town planning involved. Aldridge (1915: 459) noted that it certainly did not include 'the remodelling of the existing town, the replanning of badly planned areas, the driving of new roads through old parts of a town – all these are beyond the scope of the new planning powers'. The Act itself provided no definition: indeed, it merely listed nineteen 'matters to be dealt with by general provisions prescribed by the Local Government Board'. The restricted and vague nature of this first legislation was associated in part with the lack of experience of the problems involved: Nettlefold (1914: 179) even went so far as to suggest that 'when this Act was passed, it was recognised as only a trial trip for the purpose of finding out the weak spots in local government with regard to town and estate development so that effective remedies might be later on devised'.

Nevertheless, the cumbersome administrative procedure devised by the Local Government Board (in order to give all interested parties 'full opportunity of considering all the proposals at all stages')[3] might well have been intended to deter all but the most ardent of local authorities. The land taxes threatened by the 1910 Finance Act, and then the World War, added to the difficulties. It can be the occasion of no surprise that very few schemes were actually completed under the 1909 Act.

## INTER-WAR LEGISLATION

The first revision of town planning legislation which took place after the war (the Housing and Town Planning Act of 1919) did little in practice to broaden the basis of town planning. The preparation of schemes was made obligatory on all borough and urban districts having a population of 20,000 or more, but the time limit (1 January 1926) was first extended (by the Housing Act 1923) and finally abolished (by the Town and Country Planning Act 1932). Some of the procedural difficulties were

removed, but no change in concept appeared. Despite lip-service to the idea of town planning, the major advances made at this time were in the field of housing rather than planning. It was the 1919 Act which began what Marion Bowley (1945: 15) has called 'the series of experiments in State intervention to increase the supply of working-class houses'. The 1919 Act accepted the principle of state subsidies for housing and thus began the nation-wide growth of council house estates.[4] Equally significant was the entirely new standard of working-class housing provided: the three-bedroom house with kitchen, bath and garden, built at the density recommended by the Tudor Walters Committee (1918) of not more than twelve houses to the acre. At these new standards, development could generally take place only on virgin land on the periphery of towns, and municipal estates grew alongside the private suburbs: 'the basic social products of the twentieth century', as Asa Briggs (1952, vol. 2: 228) has termed them.

This suburbanisation was greatly accelerated by rapid developments in transportation – developments with which the young planning machine could not keep pace. The ideas of Howard (1898) and the Garden City Movement, of Geddes (1915), and of those who like Warren and Davidge (1930) saw town planning not just as a technique for controlling the layout and design of residential areas but as part of a policy of national economic and social planning, were receiving increasing attention; in practice, however, town planning often meant little more than an extension of the old public health and housing controls.

Various attempts were made to deal with the increasing difficulties. Of particular significance were the Town and Country Planning Act of 1932, which extended planning powers to almost any type of land, whether built-up or undeveloped, and the Restriction of Ribbon Development Act 1935, which, as its name suggests, was designed to control the spread of development along major roads. But these and similar measures were inadequate. For instance, under the 1932 Act planning schemes took about three years to prepare and pass through all their stages. Final approval had to be given by Parliament, and schemes then had the force of law, as a result of which variations or amendments were not possible except by a repetition of the whole procedure. Interim development control operated during the time between the passing of a resolution to prepare a scheme and its date of operation (as approved by Parliament). This enabled, but did not require, developers to apply for planning permission. If they did not obtain planning permission, and the development was not in conformity with the scheme when approved, the planning authority could require the owner (without compensation) to remove or alter the development.

All too often, however, developers preferred to take a chance that no scheme would ever come into force, or that if it did no local authority would face pulling down existing buildings. The damage was therefore done before the planning authorities had a chance to intervene (Wood 1949: 45). Once a planning scheme was approved, on the other hand, the local authority ceased to have any planning control over individual developments. The scheme was in fact a zoning plan: land was zoned for particular uses such as residential or industrial, though provision could be made for such controls as limiting the number of buildings and the space around them. In fact, so long as the developer did not try to introduce a non-conforming use he was fairly safe. Furthermore, most schemes did little more than accept and ratify existing trends of development, since any attempt at a more radical solution would have involved the planning authority in compensation which they could not afford to pay. In most cases the zones were so widely drawn as to place hardly more restriction on the developer than if there had been no scheme at all. Indeed, in the half of the country covered by draft planning schemes in 1937 there was sufficient land zoned for housing to accommodate nearly 300 million people (Barlow Report 1940: 113).

## ADMINISTRATIVE SHORTCOMINGS

A major weakness was, of course, the administrative structure itself. At the local level, the administrative unit outside the county boroughs was the district council. Such authorities were generally small and weak. This was implicitly recognised as early as 1919, for the Act of that year permitted the establishment of joint planning committees. The 1929 Local Government Act went further, by empowering county councils to take part in planning, either by becoming constituent members of joint planning committees or by undertaking powers relinquished by district councils. A number of regional advisory plans were prepared, but these were generally ineffective and, in fact, were conceived as little more than a series of suggestions for controlling future development, together with proposals for new main roads.

The noteworthy characteristic of a planning scheme was its regulatory nature. It did not secure that development would take place: it merely secured that if it did take place in any particular part of the area covered by the scheme it would be controlled in certain ways. Furthermore, as the Uthwatt Report (1942) stressed, the system was

> essentially one of local planning based on the initiative and financial resources of local bodies (whether individual local authorities or combinations of such authorities) responsible to local electorates . . . The local authorities naturally consider questions of planning and development largely with a view to the effect they will have on the authorities' own finances and the trade of the district. Proposals by landowners involving the further development of an existing urban area are not likely in practice to be refused by a local authority if the only reason against the development taking place is that from the national standpoint its proper location is elsewhere, particularly when it is remembered that the prevention of any such development might not only involve the authority in liability to pay heavy compensation but would, in addition, deprive them of substantial increases in rate income.[5]

The central authority, the Ministry of Health, had no effective powers of initiation and no power to grant financial assistance to local authorities. Indeed, their powers were essentially regulatory and seemed to be designed to cast them in the role of a quasi-judicial body to be chiefly concerned with ensuring that local authorities did not treat property owners unfairly.

The difficulties were not, however, solely administrative. Even the most progressive authorities were greatly handicapped by the inadequacies of the law relating to compensation. The compensation paid either for planning restrictions or for compulsory acquisition had to be determined in relation to the most profitable use of the land, even if it was unlikely that the land would be so developed, and without regard to the fact that the prohibition of development on one site usually resulted in the development value (which had been purchased at high cost) shifting to another site. Consequently, in the words of the Uthwatt Committee,

> an examination of the town planning maps of some of our most important built-up areas reveals that in many cases they are little more than photographs of existing uses and existing lay-outs, which, to avoid the necessity of paying compensation, become perpetuated by incorp- oration in a statutory scheme irrespective of their suitability or desirability.

These problems increased as the housing boom of the 1930s developed; 2.7 million houses were built in England and Wales between 1930 and 1940. At the outbreak of war, one-third of all the houses in England and Wales had been built since 1918. The implica- tions for urbanisation were obvious, particularly in the London area. Between 1919 and 1939 the population of Greater London rose by about two millions, of which three-quarters of a million was natural increase, and over one and a quarter million was migration (Abercrombie 1945). This growth of the metropolis was a force which existing powers were incapable of halting, despite the large body of opinion favouring some degree of control.

## THE DEPRESSED AREAS

The crux of the matter was that the problem of London was closely allied to that of the declining areas of the North and of South Wales, and both were part of the much wider problem of industrial location. In the South-East the insured employed population rose by 44 per cent between 1923 and 1934, but in the North-East it fell by 5.5 per cent and in Wales by 26 per cent. In 1934, 8.6 per cent of insured workers in Greater London were unemployed, but in Workington

the proportion was 36.3 per cent, in Gateshead 44.2 per cent and in Jarrow 67.8 per cent. In the early stages of political action these two problems were divorced. For London, various advisory committees were set up and a series of reports issued – the Royal Commission on the Local Government of Greater London (1921–3); the London and Home Counties Traffic Advisory Committee (1924); the Greater London Regional Planning Committee (1927); the Standing Conference on London Regional Planning (1937); as well as *ad hoc* committees and inquiries, for example, on Greater London Drainage (1935) and a Highway Development Plan (the Bressey Report, 1938).

For the depressed areas, attention was first concen- trated on encouraging migration, on training schemes and on schemes for establishing the unemployed in smallholdings. Increasing unemployment accompanied by rising public concern (especially after hunger marches on the one hand and articles in *The Times*[6] on the other) necessitated further action. Government 'investiga- tors' were appointed and, following their reports,[7] the Depressed Areas Bill was introduced in November 1934, to pass (after the Lords had amended the title) as the Special Areas (Development and Improvement) Act.

Under the Act, a Special Commissioner for England and Wales, and one for Scotland, were appointed, with very wide powers for 'the initiation, organisa- tion, prosecution and assistance of measures to facilitate the economic development and social improvement' of the special areas. The areas were defined in the Act and included the north-east coast, West Cumberland, industrial South Wales and, in Scotland, the industrial area around Glasgow. By September 1938, the Commissioners had spent, or approved the spending of, nearly £21 million, of which £15 million was for the improvement of public and social services, £3 million for smallholdings and allotment schemes, and £500,000 on amenity schemes such as the clearance of derelict sites.[8] Physical and social amelioration, however, was intended to be complementary to the Commissioners' main task: the attraction of new industry. Appeals to industrialists proved inadequate; in his second report, Sir Malcolm

Stewart, the Commissioner for England and Wales, concluded that 'there is little prospect of the special areas being assisted by the spontaneous action of industrialists now located outside these areas'. On the other hand, the attempt actively to attract new industry by the development of trading estates achieved considerable success, which at least warranted the comment of the Scottish Commissioner that there had been 'sufficient progress to dispel the fallacy that the areas are incapable of expanding their light industries'.

Nevertheless, there were still 300,000 unemployed in the special areas at the end of 1938, and although 123 factories had been opened between 1937 and 1938 in the special areas, 372 had been opened in the London area. Sir Malcolm Stewart concluded, in his third annual report, that 'the further expansion of industry should be controlled to secure a more evenly distributed production'. Such thinking might have been in harmony with the current increasing recognition of the need for national planning, but it called for political action of a character which would have been sensational. Furthermore, as Neville Chamberlain (then Chancellor of the Exchequer) pointed out, even if new factories were excluded from London it did not follow that they would forthwith spring up in South Wales or West Cumberland. The immediate answer of the government was to appoint the Royal Commission on the Distribution of the Industrial Population.

## THE BARLOW REPORT

The Barlow Report is of significance not merely because it is an important historical landmark, but also because, for a period of at least a quarter of a century, some of its major recommendations were accepted as a basis for planning policy.

The terms of reference of the Commission were

> to inquire into the causes which have influenced the present geographical distribution of the industrial population of Great Britain and the probable direction of any change in the distribution in the future; to consider what social, economic or strategic disadvantages

arise from the concentration of industries or of the industrial population in large towns or in particular areas of the country; and to report what remedial measures if any should be taken in the national interest.

These very wide terms of reference represented, as the Commission pointed out, 'an important step forward' in contemporary thinking. Reviewing the history of town planning it was noted that:

> Legislation has not yet proceeded so far as to deal with the problem of planning from a *national* standpoint; there is no duty imposed on any authority or government department to view the country as a whole and to consider the problems of industrial, commercial and urban growth in the light of the needs of the entire population. The appointment, therefore, of the present Commission marks an important step forward. The evils attendant on haphazard and ill-regulated town growth were first brought under observation; then similar dangers when prevalent over wider areas or regions; now the investigation is extended to Great Britain as a whole. The Causes, Probable Direction of Change and Disadvantages mentioned in the terms of reference are clearly not concerned with separate localities or local authorities, but with England, Scotland and Wales collectively: and the Remedial Measures to be considered are expressly required to be in the national interest.

After reviewing the evidence, the Commission concluded that

> the disadvantages in many, if not most of the great industrial concentrations, alike on the strategical, the social and the economic side, do constitute serious handicaps and even in some respects dangers to the nation's life and development, and we are of opinion that definite action should be taken by the government towards remedying them.

The advantages of concentration were clear: proximity to markets, reduction of transport costs and availability of a supply of suitable labour. But these, in the Commission's view, were accompanied by serious disadvantages such as heavy charges on account mainly of high site values, loss of time through street traffic congestion and the risk of adverse effects on efficiency due to long and fatiguing journeys to work. The Commission maintained that the development of garden cities, satellite towns and trading estates could make a useful contribution towards the solution of these problems of urban congestion.

The London area, of course, presented the largest problem, not simply because of its huge size, but also because 'the trend of migration to London and the Home Counties is on so large a scale and of so serious a character that it can hardly fail to increase in the future the disadvantages already shown to exist'. The problems of London were thus in part related to the problems of the depressed areas:

It is not in the national interest, economically, socially or strategically, that a quarter, or even a larger, proportion of the population of Great Britain should be concentrated within 20 to 30 miles or so of Central London. On the other hand, a policy:

(i) of balanced distribution of industry and the industrial population so far as possible throughout the different areas or regions in Great Britain;
(ii) of appropriate diversification of industries in those areas or regions;

would tend to make the best national use of the resources of the country, and at the same time would go far to secure for each region or area, through diversification of industry, and variety of employment, some safeguard against severe and persistent depression, such as attacks an area dependent mainly on one industry when that industry is struck by bad times.

Such policies could not be carried out by the existing administrative machinery: it was no part of statutory planning to check or to encourage a local or regional growth of population. Planning was essentially on a local basis; it did not, and was not intended to, influence the geographical distribution of the population as between one locality or another. The Commission unanimously agreed that the problems were national in character and required a central authority to deal with them. They argued that the activities of this authority ought to be distinct from and extend beyond those of any existing government department. It should be responsible for formulating a plan for dispersal from congested urban areas – determining in which areas dispersal was desirable; whether and where dispersal could be effected by developing garden cities or garden suburbs, satellite towns, trading estates, or the expansion of existing small towns or regional centres. It should be given the right to inspect town planning schemes and 'to consider, where necessary, in cooperation with the government departments concerned, the modification or correlation of existing or future plans in the national interest'. It should study the location of industry throughout the country with a view to anticipating cases where depression might probably occur in the future and encouraging industrial or public development before a depression actually occurred.

Whatever form this central agency might take (a matter on which the Commission could not agree), it was essential that the government should adopt a much more positive role: control should be exercised over new factory building at least in London and the Home Counties, that dispersal from the larger conurbations should be facilitated, and that measures should be taken to anticipate regional economic depression.

## THE IMPACT OF WAR

The Barlow Report was published in January 1940, some four months after the start of the Second World War. The problem which precipitated the decision to set up the Barlow Commission, that of the depressed areas, rapidly disappeared. The unemployed of the depressed areas now became a powerful national asset. A considerable share of the new factories built to provide munitions or to replace bombed factories were located in these areas. By the end of 1940, 'an extraordinary scramble for factory space had developed'; and out of all this 'grew a wartime, an extempore, location of industry policy covering the country as a whole' (Meynell 1959: 13). This emergency wartime policy, paralleled in other fields, such as hospitals, not only provided some 13 million square feet of munitions factory space in the depressed areas which could be adapted for civilian industry after the end of the war but also provided experience in dispersing industry and in controlling industrial location which showed the practicability (under wartime conditions at least) of such policies. The Board of Trade became a central clearing-house of information on industrial sites. During the debates on the 1945 Distribution of Industry Bill, their spokesman stressed:

We have collected a great deal of information regarding the relative advantage of different sites in different parts of the country, and of the facilities available there with regard to local supply, housing accommodation, transport facilities, electricity, gas, water, drainage and so on . . . We are now able to offer to industrialists a service of information regarding location which has never been available before.[9]

Hence, though the Barlow Report (to use a phrase of Dame Alix Meynell) 'lay inanimate in the iron lung of war', it seemed that the conditions for the acceptance of its views on the control of industrial location were becoming very propitious: there is nothing better than successful experience for demonstrating the practicability of a policy.

The war thus provided a great stimulus to the extension of town and country planning into the sphere of industrial location. And this was not the only stimulus it provided. The destruction wrought by bombing transformed 'the rebuilding of Britain' from a socially desirable but somewhat visionary and vague ideal into a matter of practical and defined necessity. Nor was this all: the very fact that rebuilding was clearly going to take place on a large scale provided an unprecedented opportunity for comprehensive planning of the bombed areas and a stimulus to overall town planning. In the Exeter Plan, Thomas Sharp urged that

to rebuild the city on the old lines . . . would be a dreadful mistake. It would be an exact repetition of what happened in the rebuilding of London after the Fire – and the results, in regret at lost opportunity, will be the same. While, therefore, the arrangements for rebuilding to the new plan should proceed with all possible speed, some patience and discipline will be necessary if the new-built city is to be a city that is really renewed.

(Sharp 1947: 10)

In Hull, Lutyens and Abercrombie argued that

there is now both the opportunity and the necessity for an overhaul of the urban structure before undertaking this second refounding of the great Port on the Humber. Due consideration, however urgent the desire to get back to working conditions, must be given to every aspect of town existence.

(Lutyens and Abercrombie 1945: 1)

The note was one of optimism of being able to tackle problems which were of long standing. In the metropolis (to quote from the *County of London Plan*)

London was ripe for reconstruction before the war; obsolescence, bad and unsuitable housing, inchoate communities, uncorrelated road systems, industrial congestion, a low level of urban design, inequality in the distribution of open spaces, increasing congestion of dismal journeys to work – all these and more clamoured for improvement before the enemy's efforts to smash us by air attack stiffened our resistance and intensified our zeal for reconstruction.

(Forshaw and Abercrombie 1943: 20)[10]

This was the social climate of the war and early post-war years. There was an enthusiasm and a determination to undertake social reconstruction on a scale hitherto considered utopian. The catalyst was, of course, the war itself. At one and the same time war occasions a mass support for the way of life which is being fought for and a critical appraisal of the inadequacies of that way of life. Modern total warfare demands the unification of national effort and a breaking down of social barriers and differences. As Titmuss (1958: 85) noted, it 'presupposes and imposes a great increase in social discipline; moreover, this discipline is tolerable if, and only if, social inequalities are not intolerable'. On no occasion was this more true than in the Second World War. A new and better Britain was to be built. The feeling was one of intense optimism and confidence. Not only would the war be won: it would be followed by a similar campaign against the forces of want. That there was much that was inadequate, even intolerable, in pre-war Britain had been generally accepted. What was new was the belief that the problems could be tackled in the same way as a military operation.[11] What supreme confidence was evidenced by the setting up in 1941 of committees to consider post-war reconstruction problems: the Uthwatt Committee on Compensation and Betterment, the Scott Committee on Land Utilisation in Rural Areas, and the Beveridge Committee on Social Insurance and Allied Services. Perhaps it was Beveridge (1942: 170) who most clearly summed up the spirit of the time, and the philosophy which was to underlie post-war social policy:

The Plan for Social Security is put forward as part of a general programme of social policy. It is one part only of an attack upon five great evils: upon the physical Want with which it is directly concerned, upon Disease which often causes Want and brings many other troubles in its train, upon Ignorance which no democracy can afford among its citizens, upon Squalor which arises mainly through haphazard distribution of industry and population, and upon Idleness which destroys wealth and corrupts men, whether they are well fed or not, when they are idle. In seeking security not merely against physical want, but against all these evils in all their forms, and in showing that security can be combined with freedom and enterprise and responsibility of the individual for his own life, the British community and those who in other lands have inherited the British tradition, have a vital service to render to human progress.

It was within this framework of a newly acquired confidence to tackle long-standing social and economic problems that post-war town and country planning policy was conceived. No longer was this to be restricted to town planning 'schemes' or regulatory measures. There was now to be the same breadth in official thinking as had permeated the Barlow Report. The attack on squalor was conceived as part of a comprehensive series of plans for social amelioration. To quote the 1944 White Paper *The Control of Land Use*:

Provision for the right use of land, in accordance with a considered policy, is an essential requirement of the government's programme of postwar reconstruction. New houses, whether of permanent or emergency construction; the new layout of areas devastated by enemy action or blighted by reason of age or bad living conditions; the new schools which will be required under the Education Bill now before Parliament; the balanced distribution of industry which the government's recently published proposals for maintaining employment envisage; the requirements of sound nutrition and of a healthy and well-balanced agriculture; the preservation of land for national parks and forests, and the assurance to the people of enjoyment of the sea and countryside in times of leisure; a new and safer highway system better adapted to modern industrial and other needs; the proper provision of airfields – all these related parts of a single reconstruction programme involve the use of land, and it is essential that their various claims on land should be so harmonized as to ensure for the people of this country the greatest possible measure of individual well-being and national prosperity.

## THE NEW PLANNING SYSTEM

The pre-war system of planning was defective in several ways. It was optional on local authorities; planning powers were essentially regulatory and restrictive; such planning as was achieved was purely local in character; the central government had no effective powers of initiative, or of coordinating local plans; and the 'compensation bogey', with which local authorities had to cope without any Exchequer assistance, bedevilled the efforts of all who attempted to make the cumbersome planning machinery work.

By 1942, 73 per cent of the land in England and 36 per cent of the land in Wales had become subject to interim development control, but only 5 per cent of England and 1 per cent of Wales was actually subject to operative schemes (Uthwatt Report 1942: 9); and there were several important towns and cities as well as some large country districts for which not even the preliminary stages of a planning scheme had been carried out. Administration was highly fragmented and was essentially a matter for the lower-tier authorities: in 1944 there were over 1,400 planning authorities. Some attempt to solve the problems to which this gave rise was made by the (voluntary) grouping of planning authorities in joint committees for formulating schemes over wide areas but, though an improvement, this was not sufficiently effective.

The new conception of town and country planning underlined the inadequacies. It was generally (and uncritically) accepted that the growth of the large cities should be restricted. Regional plans for London, Lancashire, the Clyde Valley and South Wales all stressed the necessity of large-scale overspill to new and expanded towns. Government pronouncements echoed the enthusiasm which permeated these plans. Large cities were no longer to be allowed to continue their unchecked sprawl over the countryside. The explosive forces generated by the desire for better living and working conditions would no longer run riot. Suburban dormitories were a thing of the past. Overspill would be steered into new and expanded towns which could provide the conditions people wanted, without the disadvantages inherent in satellite suburban development. When the problems of reconstructing blitzed areas, redeveloping blighted areas, securing a 'proper distribution' of industry, developing national parks, and so on, are added to the list, there was a clear need for a new and more positive role for the central government, a transfer of powers from the smaller to the larger authorities, a considerable extension of these powers and, most difficult of all, a solution to the compensation–betterment problem.

The necessary machinery was provided in the main by the Town and Country Planning Acts, the Distribution of Industry Acts, the National Parks and Access to the Countryside Act, the New Towns Act and the Town Development Act.

The 1947 Town and Country Planning Act brought almost all development under control by making it subject to planning permission. But planning was to be no longer merely a regulative function. Development plans were to be prepared for every area in the country. These were to outline the way in which each area was to be developed or, where desirable, preserved. In accordance with the wider concepts of planning, powers were transferred from district councils to county councils. The smallest planning units thereby became the counties and the county boroughs. Coordination of local plans was to be effected by the new Ministry of Town and Country Planning. Development rights in land and the associated development values were nationalised. All the owners were thus placed in the position of owning only the existing (1947) use rights and values in their land. Compensation for development rights was to be paid 'once and for all' out of a national fund, and developers were to pay a development charge amounting to 100 per cent of the increase in the value of land resulting from the development. The 'compensation bogey' was thus at last to be completely abolished: henceforth development would take place according to 'good planning principles'.

Responsibility for securing a 'proper distribution of industry' was given to the Board of Trade. New industrial projects (above a minimum size) would require the Board's certification that the development would be consistent with the proper distribution of industry. More positively, the Board were given powers to attract industries to development areas by loans and grants, and by the erection of factories.

New towns were to be developed by *ad hoc* development corporations financed by the Treasury. Somewhat later, new powers were provided for the planned expansion of towns by local authorities. The designation of national parks and 'areas of outstanding natural beauty' was entrusted to a new National Parks Commission, and local authorities were given wider powers for securing public access to the countryside. A Nature Conservancy was set up to provide scientific advice on the conservation and control of natural flora and fauna, and to establish and manage nature reserves. New powers were granted for preserving amenity, trees, historic buildings and ancient monuments. Later controls were introduced over river and air pollution, litter and noise. Indeed, the flow of legislation has been unceasing, partly because of increased experience, partly because of changing political perspectives, but perhaps above all because of the changing social and economic climate within which town and country planning operates.

The ways in which the various parts of this web of policies operated, and the ways in which both the policies and the machinery have developed since 1947, are summarised in the following chapters. Here a brief overview sets the scene.

## THE EARLY YEARS OF THE NEW PLANNING SYSTEM

The early years of the new system were years of austerity. This was a truly regulatory era, with controls operating over an even wider range of matters than during the war. It had not been expected that there would be any surge in pressures for private development but, even if there were, it was envisaged that these would be subject to the new controls. Additionally, private building was regulated by a licensing system which was another brake on the private market. Building resources were channelled to local authorities, and (after an initial uncontrolled spurt of private house building) council house building became the major part of the housing programme.

The sluggish economy made it relatively easy to operate regulatory controls (since there was little to regulate), but it certainly was not favourable to 'positive planning'. The architects of the 1947 system had assumed that most of this positive planning would take the form of public investment, particularly by local authorities and new town development corporations. Housing, town centre renewal and other forms of 'comprehensive development' were seen as essentially public enterprises. This might have been practicable had resources been plentiful, but they were not, and both new building and redevelopment proceeded slowly. Thus, neither the public nor the private sectors made much progress in 'rebuilding Britain' (to use one of the slogans which had been popular at the end of the war).

The architects of the post-war planning system foresaw a modest economic growth, little population increase (except an anticipated short post-war 'baby boom'), little migration either internally or from abroad, a balance in economic activity among the regions, and a generally manageable administrative task in maintaining controls. Problems of social security and the initiation of a wide range of social services were at the forefront of attention: welfare for all rather than prosperity for a few was the aim. There was little expectation that incomes would rise, that car ownership would spread, and that economic growth would make it politically possible to declare (as Harold Macmillan later did) that 'you have never had it so good'. The plans for the new towns were almost lavish in providing one garage for every four houses.

The making of plans went ahead at a steady pace, frequently in isolation from wider planning considerations, though the regional offices of the MTCP made a valiant attempt at coordination; but even here progress was much slower than expected, and it soon became clear that comprehensive planning would have to be postponed for the sake of immediate development requirements.

For a time, the early economic and social assumptions seemed to be borne out but, during the 1950s,

dramatic changes took place, some of which were the result of the release of pent-up demand which followed the return of the Conservative Government in 1951 – a Government which was wedded to a 'bonfire of controls'. One of the first acts of this Government in the planning sphere was a symbolic one: a change in the name of the planning ministry from 'local government and planning' to 'housing and local government'. This reflected the political primacy of housing and the lack of support for 'planning' (now viewed, with justification, as restrictive). The regional offices of the planning ministry were abolished: thus saving a small amount of public funds, but also dismantling the machinery for coordination. Though this machinery was modest in scope (and in resources), it was important because there was no other regional organisation to carry out this function.

The first change to the 1947 system came in 1953 when, instead of amending the development charge in the light of experience (as the Labour Government had been about to do) it was abolished. At about the same time, all building licensing was scrapped. Private housebuilding boomed; and curiously so did council house building, since the high building targets set by the Conservative Government could be met only by an all-out effort by both private and public sectors. The birth-rate (which – as expected – dropped steadily from 1948 to the mid-1950s) suddenly started a large and continuing rise.

The new towns programme went ahead at a slow pace, accompanied by a constant battle with the Treasury for resources which, so the Treasury argued, were just as urgently needed in the old towns. (The provision of 'amenities' was a particular focus of the arguments.) By contrast, public housing estates and private suburban developments mushroomed. Indeed, there was soon a concern that pre-war patterns of urban growth were to be repeated. The conflict between town and country moved to centre stage. This was a more difficult matter for the Conservative Government than the abolition of building controls, development charges and other restrictive measures. New policies were forged, foremost of which was the control over the urban fringes of the conurbations and other large cities where an acrimonious war was waged between Conservative counties seeking to safeguard undeveloped land and the urban areas in great need of more land for their expanding housebuilding programmes. On the side of the counties was the high priority attached to maintaining good quality land in agricultural production. On the side of the urban areas was a huge backlog of housing need. The war reached epic proportions in the Liverpool and Manchester areas where Cheshire fought bitterly 'to prevent Cheshire becoming another Lancashire'. Similar arguments were used in the West Midlands, where a campaign for new towns (led by the Midland New Towns Society) was complicated by the Government view that Birmingham was a rich area from which to move industry to the depressed areas. London, of course, had its ring of new towns, but these were inevitably slow in providing houses for needy Londoners, particularly since tenants were selected partly on the basis of their suitability for the jobs which had been attracted to the towns. The London County Council, therefore, like its provincial counterparts, built houses for 'overspill' in what were then called 'out-county estates'. Similarly, Glasgow and Edinburgh built their 'peripheral estates'.

The pressures for development grew as households increased even more rapidly than population (a little-understood phenomenon at the time), and as car ownership spread (the number of cars doubled in the 1950s and doubled again in the following decade). Increased mobility and suburban growth reinforced each other, and new road building began to make its own contribution to the centrifugal forces.

Working in the opposite direction was the implacable opposition of the counties. They received a powerful new weapon when Duncan Sandys initiated the green belt circular of 1955. Green belts had no longer even to be green: their function was to halt urban development. Hope that all interests could be appeased was raised by the Town Development Acts (1952 in England, 1955 in Scotland). These provided a neat mechanism for housing urban 'overspill' and, at the same time, rejuvenating declining small towns and minimising the loss of agricultural land. But though a number of schemes were (slowly) successful,

the local government machinery was generally not equal to such a major regional task.

## LOCAL GOVERNMENT REORGANISATION

It was this machinery which was at the root of many of the difficulties. Few politicians wanted to embark on the unpopular task of reforming local government, and even those who appreciated the need for change could not agree on why it was wanted — whether to resolve the urban–rural conflict, to facilitate a more efficient delivery of services, or to provide a system of more effective political units. These and similar issues were grist to the academic mill, but a treacherous area for politicians. Perhaps the biggest surprise here was the decision to go ahead with the reorganisation of London government. The legislation was passed in 1963: this followed — in sequence but not in content — a wide-ranging inquiry. The surprise was not that the recommendations were altered by the political process, but that anything was done at all. One important factor in the politics of the situation was the desire to abolish the socialist London County Council (though ironically the hoped-for guarantee of a permanent Conservative GLC was dashed by the success of the peripheral districts in maintaining their independence).

One effect of the London reorganisation was that further changes were taken very seriously. The writing was now on the wall for local government in the rest of the country, and campaigns and counter-campaigns proliferated. Three inquiries (for England, Scotland, and Wales) were established by the Labour Government which assumed office in 1964. These reported in 1969, but implementation fell to its successor Conservative Government. For Scotland, the recommendations were generally accepted (with a two-tier system of regions and districts over most of the country). The city-region recommendations for England, however, were unacceptable, and a slimmer two-tier system was adopted. Wales was treated in the same way. The result south of the border was that the boundaries for the urban–rural strife, though amended in detail, were basically unchanged in character.

## POPULATION PROJECTIONS

In the meantime, truly alarming population projections had appeared which transformed the planning horizon. The population at the end of the century had been projected in 1960 at 64 million; by 1965 the projection had increased to 75 million. At the same time, migration and household fission had added to the pressures for development and the need for an alternative to expanding suburbs and 'peripheral estates'. It seemed abundantly clear that a second generation of new towns was required.[12]

Between 1961 and 1971, fourteen new new towns were designated. Some, like Skelmersdale and Redditch were 'traditional' in the sense that their purpose was to house people from the conurbations. Others, such as Livingston and Irvine, had the additional function of being growth points in a comprehensive regional programme for Central Scotland. One of the most striking characteristics of the last new towns to be designated was their huge size. In comparison with the Reith Committee's optimum of 30,000 to 50,000, Central Lancashire's 500,000 seemed massive. But size was not the only striking feature. Another was the fact that four of them were based on substantial existing towns – Northampton, Peterborough, Warrington, and Central Lancashire (Preston–Leyland). Of course, town building had been going on for a long time in Britain, and all the best sites may have already been taken by what had become old towns. The time was bound to come when the only places left for new towns were the sites of existing towns. There were, however, other important factors. First, the older towns were in need of rejuvenation and a share in the limited capital investment programme. Second, there was the established argument that nothing succeeds like success; or, to be more precise, a major development with a population base of 80,000 to 130,000 or more had a flying start over one with a mere 5,000 to 10,000. A wide range of facilities was already available, and (hopefully) could be readily expanded at the margin.

No sooner had all this been settled than the population projections were drastically revised downwards. It was too late to reverse the new new towns programme, though it was decided not to go ahead with Ipswich (and Stonehouse was killed by the opposition of Strathclyde because of its irrelevance to the problems of the rapidly declining economy of Clydeside). However, the reduced population growth prevented some problems becoming worse, though little respite was apparent at the time. Household formation continued apace, as did car ownership and migration. The resulting pressures on the South-East were severe – and remained so into the 1990s, with little resolution of the difficulties of 'land allocation'.

## URBAN POVERTY

While much political energy was spent on dealing with urban growth, even more intractable problems of urban decay forced their attention on government. Every generation, it seems, has to rediscover poverty for itself, and the post-war British realisation came in the late 1960s (Sinfield 1973). As usual, there were several strands: the reaction against inhuman slum clearance and high-density redevelopment, the impact of these and of urban motorways on communities ('get us out of this hell' cried the families living alongside the elevated M4), fear of racial unrest (inflamed by the speeches of Enoch Powell). These issues went far beyond even the most ambitious definition of 'planning', and they posed perplexing problems of the coordination of policies and programmes. Not surprisingly, the response was anything but coordinated, and programmes proliferated in confusion.

Housing policy was the clearest field of policy development. Slum clearance had been abruptly halted at the beginning of the war, when demolitions were running at the rate of 90,000 a year. It was resumed in the mid-1950s, and steadily rose to over 80,000. Both the scale of this clearance and its insensitivity to community concerns, as well as the inadequate character of some redevelopment schemes, led to an increasing demand for a reappraisal of the policy. Added force was given to this by the growing realisation that demolition alone could not possibly cope with the huge amount of inadequate housing — and the continuing deterioration of basically sound housing. Rent control had played a part in this tide of decay, and halting steps were taken to ameliorate its worst effects, though not with much success. More effective was the introduction of policies to improve, rehabilitate, and renovate older housing: changing terminology reflected constant refinements of policy. Increasingly, it was realised that *ad hoc* improvements to individual houses were of limited impact: area rehabilitation paid far higher dividends, particularly in encouraging individual improvement efforts. A succession of area programmes (now *renewal areas*) have made a significant impact on some older urban neighbourhoods, but a considerable problem remains. Since the middle of the 1980s, renovations have averaged over 400,000 a year. By contrast slum clearance declined throughout the 1980s, falling to a mere 6,000 in 1990. The latest turn in policy is based on the belief that renovation policy has been overextended, and that a resumption of clearance is necessary.

But the housing policies were basically aimed at the physical fabric of housing and the residential environment. Their impact on people generally, and the poor in particular, was less than housing reformers had hoped (the lessons of earlier times being ignored). This realisation, followed a spate of social inquiries, of which *The Poor and the Poorest* by Brian Abel-Smith and Peter Townsend (published in 1965) was a landmark in raising public concern. A bewildering rush of programmes was promoted by the Home Office (including the urban programme in 1968, community development projects in 1969, comprehensive community programmes in 1974), the DoE (urban guidelines in 1972, area management trials in 1974, and 'the policy for the inner cities' in 1977), the Department of Education (educational priority areas in 1968) and the DHSS (cycle of deprivation studies in 1973). This list is by no means complete, but it demonstrates the almost frantic search for

effective policies in fields which had hitherto largely been left to local effort. Despite all this, the problems of the 'inner cities' (a misnomer since some of the deprived areas were on the periphery of cities) grew apace. The most important factors were the rapid rate of deindustrialisation and the massive movement of people and jobs to outer areas and beyond. Unlike the inter-war years, the problems were not restricted to the 'depressed areas': the South-East, previously the source for moving employment to the North, was badly affected. In absolute (rather than percentage) terms, London suffered severely — losing three-quarters of a million manufacturing jobs between 1961 and 1984 (Hall 1992a: 150).

There was initially little difference between the political parties here: both were searching for solutions which continued to evade them. Lessons from America indicated that more money was not necessarily the answer, and academic writers pointed to the need for societal changes, but there were few politically helpful ideas around. Following a period in which the problems were seen in terms of social pathology, attention was increasingly directed to 'structural' issues, particularly of the local economy. In the 1980s, the Conservative Government put its faith in releasing enterprise, though it was never clear how this would benefit the poor. New initiatives included urban development corporations, modelled on the new town development corporations but with a different private enterprise ethic. The London Docklands UDC seemed almost determined to ignore, if not override, the community in which it was located, but this attitude eventually changed, and both the LDDC and later UDCs have become more attuned to local needs and feelings.

## LAND VALUES

The issue of land values was addressed by both the two later Labour Governments. In the 1964–70 administration, the Land Commission was established to buy development land at a price excluding a part of the development value and to levy a betterment charge on private sales. Its life and promise were cut short by the incoming Conservative Government. Exactly the same happened with the community land scheme and the development land tax introduced by the 1974–79 Labour Government. Thus, there were three post-war attempts to wrestle with the problem, and none was given an adequate chance to work. With only the happy anomaly of the Land Authority for Wales, land transactions are now a matter for the market, for local government, and for land availability studies. The latter, as with speeding planning permissions, have become a time-demanding ritual for planners.

The abandonment of attempts to solve 'the betterment problem' (which may no longer even be regarded as a problem) is more than a matter of land taxation or even equity. The so-called 'financial provisions' of the 1947 Act underpinned the whole system, and made positive planning a real possibility. Though it seems unlikely that the issue will return to the political agenda in the foreseeable future, it should not be forgotten that this vital piece of the planning machinery is missing. (Holford once neatly called the half-dismantled legislation 'a set of spare parts'.) Planning is therefore essentially a servant of the market – in the sense that it comes into operation only when market operations are set in motion. This change, made some forty years ago, is far more fundamental than the high-profile changes made under the Thatcher regime.

## ENTREPRENEURIAL PLANNING

The Conservative Government since 1979 has voiced a commitment to 'releasing enterprise'. This has translated into a miscellany of policies which have little in the way of a coherent underlying philosophy. These may, however, be characterised in terms of removing particular barriers which are identified as holding back initiative. The identified problems range from inner-city landholding by public bodies (dealt with by requiring land registers which by publicising the lack of use of the land thereby 'brings it into the market'); to the 'wasteful' and 'unnecessary' tier of metropolitan government in London and the

provincial conurbations (simply abolished). Many areas of public activity have been privatised, large parts of government have been hived off to executive agencies, and compulsory competitive tendering has been imposed on local government. The emphasis on 'market orientation' and the concerted attack (regrettably the word is not an exaggeration) on local government has had some strange results. More power has been vested in central government and its agencies. Public participation has been reduced. But, though the planning system has been affected in tangible ways (Thornley 1991), in no sense has it been dismantled, or even changed in any really significant way. True, it has been bypassed (by urban development corporations); its procedures have been modified (by government circulars, and changes in the General Development and Use Classes Orders); development plans were, for a time, downgraded, and threatened with severe curtailment; and simplified planning zones have been introduced: a system in which 'simplification' means less planning control but may involve even more human resources in negotiation. The list can be extended, but the rhetoric which preceded and accompanied the changes was harsher than the changes themselves. Moreover, the language of confrontation which the politicians employed disguised the fact that previous governments had done similar things, even if more *sotto voce*. The development corporation initiative, for example, was essentially the brainchild of a much earlier period and, indeed, as applied to redevelopment (as distinct from new town development) had for long been proposed by socialists as a means of assisting local authorities. Some of the early days of the UDC flagship – the London Docklands Development Corporation – were characterised by an excess of zeal, a lack of understanding on the way in which the administration of government is different from the administration of business, (and an authoritarian style which has been widely – and justifiably – criticised). Time, however, has mellowed misplaced enthusiasm, and brought about a better understanding of the inherent slowness of democratic government. There has also been a keener awareness of the need to pay some attention to the 'social' issues of the locality as well as its physical regeneration.

More generally, an old lesson has been relearned: it is extremely difficult for one level of government to impose its will on another unless it has some broad and powerful support from outside, as well as willing cooperation inside. (There is, however, the draconian alternative of simply abolishing a wayward layer of local government, as was done with the Greater London Council and the metropolitan county councils.) Scotland's different approach (in crafting its urban policies to be operated in conjunction with local government) is now apparently finding favour in England.

The about-turn on structure plans illustrates the pragmatic nature (what some call the flexibility, and others the inconsistency) of recent Conservative thinking. The initial decision to abolish them was one option for dealing with a problem which dates back to 1947: how to ensure that plans provide (without overwhelming detail) sufficient guidance for the land-use planning of an area, while being adaptable to unforeseen changing circumstances. The option actually adopted was a 'streamlining' not unlike earlier attempts. The 1965 PAG report highlighted the problem: 'It has proved extremely difficult to keep these plans not only up to date but forward looking and responsive to the demands of change.' Twenty years later, the 1985 White Paper, *Lifting the Burden*, was in a similar key: 'There is cause for concern that this process of plan review and updating is becoming too slow and cumbersome.' More effective structure plans require a framework of regional policy. It is debatable whether, in a country like Britain, there is any alternative to this being a function of central government; but debate there will always be. The increased role of central government in providing regional guidance (most apparent in the introduction of regional policy guidance notes) can be represented as undue central interference with local planning, even though it has been considerably influenced (probably too much so) by local input. This again, is a part of a very lengthy debate on regional planning. Various stratagems have been tried: regional economic planning councils (which despite their name, found themselves absorbed in land-use matters); proposed constitutional devolution;

the establishment (by a Conservative Government) of metropolitan counties – and their later abolition (also by a Conservative Government). It is, however, unclear whether the current regional planning guidance system will work – not because of too much central government control, but because of too little. The guidance for the South-East is proving highly problematic and, though there do not appear to be similar difficulties in the provincial regions, it is at least arguable that this is because it is bland and inadequate: it hides the problems instead of facing them. [13] Nevertheless, further permutations on regional planning continue to be discussed on the political and academic sidelines.

A final point, in this somewhat tendentious overview, is that there is now probably more regional planning than ever before. This is undertaken by a wide range of public and private agencies. In addition to the regional offices of government departments such as Environment, Trade and Industry, and Transport, there are the regional organisations of the National Rivers Authority and British Waterways, regional advisory councils for education and training, regional boards of the Arts Council, and such like. Regionalism in various forms is thus a fact of contemporary administration though much of it, of course, is not the same as 'regional planning'. Even where activities justify the term, the crucial element of coordination is missing. The deficiency becomes of increasing importance as the number of separated planning activities grows: urban development corporations, enterprise zones, groundwork trusts, development agencies and enterprise boards, and new bodies for environmental protection and the administration of the national parks.

## THE ENVIRONMENT

All governments operate with some degree of pragmatism: electoral politics force this upon them. So it has been with the Conservative Government. After many years of relegating environmental issues to a low level of concern, there was a sudden conversion to environmentalism in 1988. This was heralded in a remarkable speech by Mrs Thatcher in which she declared that Conservatives were the guardians and trustees of the earth. At base, this reflected a heightening of public concern for the environment which is partly local (particularly in the shires) and partly global.

The action which followed looks impressive (though critics have been less impressed by the results). A 1990 White Paper *This Common Inheritance* spelled out the Government's environmental strategy over a comprehensive range of policy areas (untypically this covered the whole of the UK). An update is published each year reporting progress and consolidating policy advances. Environmental protection legislation was passed, 'integrated pollution control' is being implemented, 'green ministers' have been appointed to oversee the environmental implications of their departmental functions, and new environmental regulation agencies are to be established. The latter follow a spate of organisational changes which remind one of the old saying: 'when in doubt reorganise'. But there are difficult issues here which, though including organisational matters, go much deeper. Questions about the protection of the environment underline a perhaps (to the layperson) surprising ignorance of the workings of ecosystems at the local, national and global levels. Additionally, new questions of ethics have come to the fore. Difficult problems of deciding among alternative courses of action are rendered ever more complex. Cost–benefit analysis is of little help: indeed all forms of economic reasoning are being challenged. International pressures have played a role here as, of course, has the coming of age of the EC. This has added a new dimension to the politics of the environment (and much else as well).

Concern for historic preservation (now embraced in the term 'heritage') is of much longer standing. Though many historic buildings were destroyed during the war, the more effective stimulus to preservation came from the clearance, redevelopment, renewal and road building policies which got under way in the 1950s and accelerated rapidly. As with housing, the emphasis has been mainly on individual historic structures, but a conservation area policy was ushered in by the Civic Amenities Act 1967, sponsored by a private member (Duncan Sandys), though with wide support. This proved a popular measure, and there are now nearly 8,000 of them. Indeed, there has been mounting concern that too many areas are designated, and too few resources applied to their upkeep and management. A later Act, the Ancient Monuments and Archaeological Areas Act 1979, promised more in its title than it could provide, and only five *areas of archaeological importance* were designated. But the Act did more: it consolidated legislation dating back to 1882, and strengthened controls safeguarding ancient monuments. It was substantially amended by the National Heritage Act 1983, whose modern name signified a new and wider appreciation of the historical legacy. A new executive agency, English Heritage (formally called the Historic Buildings and Monuments Commission for England), was established and took over many of the functions previously housed within the DoE. In Scotland and Wales, rather different administrative solutions were devised, as befits the distinctive character of these two parts of Britain.

Surprisingly, the new environmental and historical awareness was late in raising sufficient concern about transport to bring about any significant change from a preoccupation with catering for the car.

## FROM ROAD POLICY TO TRANSPORT POLICY

Transport policy has for long been largely equated with road building policy, and protests that alternatives need to be considered have been unavailing until recently. On a number of issues, however, the protests could not be ignored. One has already been mentioned: the brutal impact of urban motorways on the communities through which they passed. The outcry against this led to a reassessment of both the location of urban roads and their necessity. Compensation for 'distress' caused by new roads was increased as part of a policy labelled (in a 1972 White Paper) *Putting People First*. Closely related was a growing concern about the inadequacy of the road inquiry process, which resulted in a significant improvement of the provisions for public participation. These and other changes curbed, but did not allay, the concerns: indeed, they are still vocal, though it seems that further changes can be expected. The turning point came in 1989 when new forecasts of huge increases in car ownership and use were published. It was widely considered to be impossible to satisfactorily accommodate the forecast amount of traffic. The results of this change in attitude are beginning to work through the political system. Traffic calming has become part of the contemporary vocabulary (and is now statutorily enshrined); road pricing is on the agenda for serious discussion; and road building has been hived off from the Department of Transport to an executive agency which, it is believed, may reduce the preoccupation of the Department with road building as the foremost means of meeting transport needs.

## THE COUNTRYSIDE

The countryside has always been dear to the hearts of Conservatives, though support for the protection and enjoyment of the countryside has traditionally cut across party and class lines. Increasing concern for the rural landscape, growing use of the countryside for recreation (and investment), and huge changes in the fortunes of the agricultural industry have transformed the arena of debate on rural land use. At the end of the war, and for many years afterwards, the greatest importance was attached to the promotion of British agriculture. There were, however, established movements for countryside conservation and recreation, some of which came together with the National Parks and Access to the Countryside Act of 1949 (but a separate Nature Conservancy Council was also established, thus dividing the conservancy function). The pressures for conservation and for recreation have varied over time, and the balance between them is inevitably an ongoing problem, particularly in areas of easy access (which now includes most of the country). Limited budgets held back incipient pressures in the early post-war years, but

increasing real incomes and mobility led to mounting pressures which were acknowledged in the 1966 White Paper *Leisure in the Countryside* and in the 1968 Countryside Act. This replaced the National Parks Commission with a Countryside Commission which was given wider powers and improved finance. At the same time, the powers of local authorities were expanded to include, for instance, the provision of country parks. Unlike national parks, these were not necessarily places of beauty but were intended primarily for enjoyment. They were also seen as having the added advantage of taking some of the pressure off the national parks and similar areas where added protection was needed. The 1972 reorganisation of local government was accompanied by a requirement that local authorities which were responsible for national parks should establish a separate committee and appoint a park planning officer. The modesty of this provision was clearly a compromise between concerns for local government and for the planning of national parks. It was a step forward, but an enduring case for *ad hoc* park authorities continued. Local authorities had too many local interests to satisfy to give adequate resources for national parks – whose very name indicated their much wider role. The growth of pressures on the parks continued, and the administrative knot was finally cut in 1992 when it was decided to establish national park authorities for all the parks (though, at the time of writing, legislation had not been introduced).

More widely, a long-standing debate continued on the divided organisational arrangements for nature conservation and amenity and for scientific conservation and wildlife. In England, that separation continues, but in Scotland and Wales the responsibilities are now vested in a single body: Scottish Natural Heritage and the Countryside Council for Wales. The arguments justifying this curious difference for England are not easy to follow. Of particular note is the first outcome of Scottish thinking on integrated countryside planning, which builds upon the simple (but rarely used) idea that all countryside activities 'are based on use, in one way or another, of the natural heritage'.[14]

There are many underlying concerns in the changes

which are taking place in countryside policy. The most salient is the remarkable change in the fortunes of the agricultural industry. With huge increases in productivity, competition from abroad, and the impact of the Common Market, the need now is to reduce agricultural production. It is never easy to change the course of a well-established policy, and still more difficult is it to reverse a policy, particularly one which has had such widespread support as agriculture. Nevertheless, changes are being made, and the thrust of these in reducing agricultural production is clear, though the policy instruments are less so and are in a state of flux. Given the dramatic changes involved, this is hardly surprising.

## WHITHER PLANNING?

It is now nearly half a century since the post-war planning system was put into place. Major changes have taken place during this time in society, the economy, and the political scene – some of which have been touched upon in this rapid review. In these shifting sands, 'town and country planning' has grown into (or been submerged by) a series of different policy areas which defy description, let alone coordination. Yet 'planning' is nothing if not a coordinative function, and the frenetic activity in reorganising machinery which has absorbed so much energy in the last fifty years must, at some point, give way to substantive progress. The difficulty lies in determining the direction in which this lies.

One thing is clear: some of the most important underlying problems are well beyond any conceivable scope of 'planning': for example, much urban change has been due to global forces which are currently beyond *any* political control. Multinationals and international finance were not in the standard vocabulary in the early post-war years. Planners find it easier to think in terms of 'need'. In recent years, they have been forced to recast some of their thinking in 'market' terms. But could they ever come to terms with the workings of the property investment market? As many studies have shown, 'the channeling of money to promote new urban development is

determined not by need or demand, but by the relative profitability of alternative investments'[15] – which may be in different sectors, such as industrial equities, or in quite different geographical locations. Much private sector development is now 'driven more by investment demand and suppliers' decisions than by final user demand – and even less by any sort of final user needs' (Edwards 1990: 175). This widening gap between land-use development and 'needs' throws considerable doubt on the adequacy of a planning system which is based on the assumption that land uses can be predicted and appropriate amounts of land 'allocated' for specific types of use.[16]

Overriding all other pressing considerations, of course, is the state of the economy. (It is little comfort that so many other countries share the same problem.) The result has been a strengthening of the 'partnership' philosophy which has gradually grown over the last two decades. The term now means more than coordination of the efforts of different agencies: it implies that planning has to embrace the agents of the market, and adapt a regulatory system of planning to the need for negotiation (a style which, as shown in Chapter 6, has traditionally characterised British pollution control).

The implications of all this are not clear, and though an obvious response may be to try harder to identify emerging trends this is more difficult to do than ever before. Economic and social trends seem as unpredictable as the weather or the course of scientific inquiry. It is perhaps not surprising that one planning analyst has commented that 'it appears now that almost everybody is working on chaos theory'.[17] This, of course, is an intended exaggeration, but the point is valid: comprehensive planning based on firm predictions of the future course of events is now clearly impossible. Incrementalism is the order of the day, and Burnham's famous aphorism has now been turned on its head: 'make no big plans'. But planners have always strained for unattainable planning goals, whether they be frankly utopian or simply over-enthusiastic. Contemporary plans are more realistic in this regard than many earlier plans. The plans prepared at the end of the Second World War were often quite unrealistic in the assumptions that were made about the availability (and control) of resources – though that did not prevent them being very influential in moulding planning ideas. Even as late as the 1960s, the Greater London Development Plan was replete with policies over which the GLC had no control.[18] It remains to be seen whether the lesson has been learned – or whether some currently unpredictable change will transform the future. Be that as it may, there seems little doubt that in the perpetual planning conflict between flexibility and certainty, the former is the clear winner.

## UPDATE

An interesting account of post-war reconstruction of the town centres of Bristol, Coventry, and Southampton is given in J. Hasegawa, *Replanning the Blitzed City Centre*, Buckingham: Open University Press, 1992. For a comparative study of German cities, see J.M. Diefendorf, *In the Wake of War: The Reconstruction of German Cities after World War II*, New York: Oxford University Press, 1993.

## NOTES

1 *Parliamentary Debates*, vol. 188, 12 May 1908, col. 949.
2 John Burns, President of the Local Government Board, in the second reading debates on the Housing, Town Planning, Etc. Bill 1908, *Parliamentary Debates*, vol. 188, col. 958, 12 May 1908.
3 'This necessity . . . involves considerable delay; the careful consideration of a case in all its aspects and the arrangements for holding of the necessary local inquiries must necessarily take a substantial amount of time.' Local Government Board, Circular 3, May 1910, Order No. 55373 (reprinted in Nettlefold 1914: 392).
4 Some local authorities, notably London, Liverpool and Manchester, had built houses under earlier legislation, but these were statistically insignificant. Generally, the

building of houses by local authorities was regarded as a step to be taken in the last resort – if at all.
5 Uthwatt Report: *Final Report of the Expert Committee on Compensation and Betterment*, Cmd 6386, HMSO, 1942, pp. 8–9, paras 13–14.
6 'Places without a future' (County Durham), *The Times*, 20, 21, 22 March 1934.
7 *Reports of Investigations into the Industrial Conditions in Certain Depressed Areas*, Cmd 4728, HMSO, 1934. The investigators were J.C.C. Davidson, Euan Wallace, Sir William Portal and Sir Arthur Rose.
8 This account is based on *Reports of the Commissioner for the Special Areas (England and Wales)* (1935–8); *Reports of the Commissioner for the Special Areas in Scotland* (1935–8); and Meynell 1959. See also Davison 1938; and Political and Economic Planning 1939.
9 *HC Debates*, vol. 409, 21 March 1945; the Minister of Production (Oliver Lyttelton) on the second reading of the Distribution of Industry Bill.
10 An account of the reactions of 'the man in the street' (drawing heavily on the reports of the Mass Observation team) is to be found in Calder 1971. See also Backwell and Dickens 1978; and Ambrose 1986: chapter 2.
11 Cf. the statement by Mr Tomlinson on the introduction of the first post-war housing bill: 'Housing should be tackled as a military operation', *HC Debates*, vol. 416, col. 901, 26 November 1945.
12 See the DoE study: *Long-term Population Distribution in Great Britain*, HMSO, 1971. An extract from this is reprinted in Cullingworth 1973.
13 See the symposium on 'Developing regional planning guidance in England and Wales', in *Town Planning Review* (1992) 63: 415–34.
14 Scottish Natural Heritage, *An Agenda for Investment in Scotland's Natural Heritage*, 1992.
15 Bateman 1985: 32.
16 Consider, for instance, the failure of the Government's Business Expansion Scheme, which was significantly affected by the preference for property investments.
17 Batty 1990: 6. This short article has an excellent discussion of 'changing fashions in urban and regional planning'.
18 Centre for Environmental Studies 1970. London presents particular problems for prediction, since the economy of the central area (with more than a million jobs) is more dependent upon global trends than on the course of the domestic economy (A.D. King 1990; Sassen 1991; Frost and Spence 1993).

# 2

# THE AGENCIES OF PLANNING

## (A) CENTRAL GOVERNMENT

Most entrepreneurial governments promote competition between service providers. They empower citizens by pushing control out of the bureaucracy, into the community. They measure the performance of their agencies, focusing not on inputs but on outcomes. They are driven by their goals — their missions — not by their rules and regulations. They define their clients as customers and offer them choices . . . They put their energy into earning money, not simply spending it. They prefer market mechanisms to bureaucratic mechanisms . . .

D. Osborne and T. Gaebler, *An American Perestroika*, 1992

The quotation is from an account of ways in which the American governmental system is changing. Though there are differences, the resemblance to the changes which have taken place in Britain over the last decade is striking. But change is not of recent origin: on the contrary, inquiries into the management of government, reorganisations of departmental and ministerial responsibilities, and innovations in the control of public expenditure and in management have been a long-standing feature of British government.[1] What has distinguished the recent past is the extent and pace of change, though whether this has increased the effectiveness of government is a debatable question.[2]

All arms of the state have been affected by these changes: central government, local government, and a multitude of *ad hoc* agencies — including those which have statutory responsibilities for aspects of land-use planning, development and environmental protection. Moreover, the experience of private sector and voluntary agencies has been similar, indicating that the forces for change are wider than those emanating

from the ideological stance of the Conservative Government to which they are often ascribed (Stoker 1989). Of particular relevance to this book is the establishment of executive 'agencies' both within and outside the governmental machine, and the promotion of local authorities as 'enablers' rather than direct service providers. The objective of these changes is to institute 'a quite different way of conducting the business of government'.[3]

Agencies external to government include English Heritage (established by the 1983 National Heritage Act) which has taken over many of the heritage functions of the DoE, and longer-established bodies such as the Countryside Commission and the Nature Conservancy (now English Nature). Agencies within the machinery of government, which (borrowing the subtitle of the Efficiency Unit's report) are known as *Next Steps Agencies*, include the Planning Inspectorate, the Historic Royal Palaces Agency, Historic Scotland, the Land Registry, the Training and Employment Agency, and Welsh Historic Monuments (*Cadw* in Welsh). In July 1992 there were 75 of these

Next Step agencies, employing some 300,000 civil servants.[4]

Since 'precision about the task to be done, coupled with greater individual responsibility for the results achieved is central to Next Steps', each agency has an 'agency framework document' which defines its role and functions. Importance is attached to the publication of these:

> Publication represents a significant change in the way Government has traditionally conducted its business. It introduces a new element of openness into the delivery of government services which the Government trusts will be welcomed by Parliament and the public alike. The Government sees no grounds for fearing that the traditional impartiality of the Civil Service will be impaired by these arrangements.[5]

The way in which aims and objectives are cast is illustrated by the case of the Historic Royal Palaces Agency:

> The aims of the Agency are to:
> – provide an educational and enjoyable experience for visitors consistent with the Royal status of the Palaces;
> – preserve the Palaces for future generations; and
> – achieve progressive improvements in the standard of service provided in terms of both efficiency and effectiveness.[6]

The establishment of agencies has important implications for the functioning of departments – as it is intended to do. In the words of the Efficiency Unit report:

> The setting up of agencies has substantial implications for the staff of departments, for Ministers, and for Parliament. Departments have two main functions – ministerial support including policy development and evaluation, and managing or influencing the delivery of government services. Where departments are directly responsible for service delivery their task will no longer be the detailed prescription of operational functions: it will be the definition of a rigorous policy and resources framework within which the agency management is set free to manage operations, and is held to account for results.

One of the implications for Parliament is to be seen from the Expenditure Committee's inquiry on historic buildings. The response of the DoE to several of the Committee's recommendations was that they were matters for English Heritage (which itself provided the answers).[7]

## THE DEPARTMENT OF THE ENVIRONMENT

The Department of the Environment (DoE) was established by the newly elected Conservative Government in 1971. This centralised housing, construction, transport, planning, local government and a number of other environmental functions under a Secretary of State for the Environment (Draper 1977). Except in Scotland and Wales, where the Scottish and Welsh Offices (together with their own Secretaries of State) have major responsibilities, the DoE became responsible for 'the whole range of functions which affect people's living environment'. These now include planning, environmental protection, countryside and wildlife, urban policy, local government, housing, construction, and the property holdings of government. The Secretary of State has final responsibility for all the functions of the Department. He is, however, concerned primarily with strategic issues of policy and priority, including public expenditure, which determine the operations of the Department as a whole. In 1992/93, the estimated expenditure of the Department was £41,000m, most of which is support to local government (£36,000m) or other bodies (£3,000m). Most of the financial support to the non-departmental public bodies sponsored by the DoE goes to the Housing Corporation (£2,500m) and the urban development corporations (£250m). The New Towns Commission has been a net 'earner' of income for the DoE because of the sale of new town assets.

Originally, the DoE was divided into three main parts, each under a separate Minister: housing and construction; transport industries; and local government and development. Several changes have taken place since 1970 including the re-establishment of transport as an independent department with its own Secretary of State in 1976 and, more recently, following the 1992 general election, the creation of a separate Department for National Heritage.[8]

Another recent change is the gathering together of the pollution regulation functions within Her Majesty's Inspectorate of Pollution (HMIP). Further reorganisation of pollution control has been announced, with the establishment of a new Environment Agency, which will combine the functions of HMIP and the National Rivers Authority, together with the waste regulation functions of local government.[9]

As at the beginning of 1993, ministerial responsibilities, under the Secretary of State, were divided among three Ministers of State: local government and inner cities, housing and planning, and environment and the countryside.

## THE DEPARTMENT OF TRANSPORT

As already indicated, transport was merged in the DoE in 1970, but was moved back into a separate Department in 1976 (though it remained physically in Marsham Street). This Department is responsible for central government transport responsibilities in England, and has additional responsibilities for airports policy, railways, major ports, and other licensing and taxation matters across Britain. It is the responsible authority throughout the United Kingdom (that is, including Northern Ireland) for civil aviation and merchant shipping.[10]

The DoT aims are to ensure the provision and maintenance of a high-quality transport system; to conserve the environment; to protect and improve transport safety; to ensure the provision of the standards of service set out in the Citizen's Charter; to promote adequate transport provision for people with disabilities; and to advance UK transport interests abroad. In more detail, the first aim is to be achieved by:

— improving efficiency and making the market for transport work better;
— providing for competition and private sector ownership;
— improving and maintaining national and local road systems;
— financing public transport where justified, through grants and loans.

There is a wide range of responsibilities undertaken by the various directorates: railways, public transport, shipping, civil aviation, the channel tunnel, road programmes, road safety, and so forth. Each of the directorates has a number of divisions dealing with smaller areas of policy: the disability unit, for example, addresses a growing concern 'to promote and encourage greater recognition of and more effective provision for the needs of people with mobility problems in public transport, special services, personal mobility and in the pedestrian environment'.[11]

The DoT works through the same network of regional offices as the DoE, and shares the same Regional Controller.

## THE DEPARTMENT OF NATIONAL HERITAGE

In May 1992, the Department of National Heritage (DNH) was created, taking important planning functions from the DoE. The DNH now has responsibility for heritage and tourism, historic and royal palaces, broadcasting and films, sport, and the arts. Its general aim is 'to conserve, nurture and enhance, and make more widely accessible the rich and varied cultural heritage of the countries of the United Kingdom'.[12] The Department is perhaps most widely known, however, as the home of the National Lottery. The development of this is its highest immediate priority, and a potential source of substantial additional financial support for its other work. Most of this is undertaken through sponsored bodies (which absorb 93 per cent of its total expenditure of £900m).

In the planning area, the Department has a specific remit 'to preserve ancient sites, monuments, and historic buildings, and increase their accessibility for study and enjoyment now and in the future', and 'to attract a wide range of people from this country and abroad to enjoy and enrich our national culture'. Thus the Department has taken over the heritage functions of the DoE and tourism from the Department of Employment.

The DNH is responsible for 440,000 listed buildings and an estimated 13,500 monuments. A review of ancient monuments is under way by the Royal Commission on the Historical Monuments of England, and it is anticipated that more than 2,000 scheduling recommendations will be made in each year up to 2003. The Royal Commission received £2.3m in 1992/93 from the DNH. The most significant of the sponsored bodies in the heritage area is the Historic Buildings and Monuments Commission, better known as English Heritage, which receives £102m to support its properties in care and its grant aid programme, which are discussed more fully in Chapter 7. Also now within the responsibility of the DNH are the Royal Fine Art Commission, which provides advice on major development proposals (£5.4m); the Redundant Churches Fund (£1.8m); the National Heritage Memorial Fund (£12m); and the Historic Royal Palaces Agency (£22m).

In the tourism field, the British Tourist Authority, which supports the development of overseas tourism to the UK, will continue to be strongly supported by the DNH (£31m), but the English Tourist Board (ETB) whose main spending is within the UK is to have its responsibilities devolved to the regional tourist boards. As in other areas of government spending, there is an increasing emphasis in heritage and tourism on levering partnership funding from the private sector and on focusing spending on economic regeneration.

## THE MINISTRY OF AGRICULTURE

Other departments of government have special status in respect of town and country planning, notably the Ministry of Agriculture, Fisheries and Food (MAFF). An overriding concern of government after the war was to protect agriculturally productive land. This secured a central place for the MAFF in land-use decisions. It has had to be consulted on important proposals, and the MAFF classifications of agricultural land quality are an important consideration in development control. The influence of the MAFF has waned somewhat in parallel with the decline of agriculture in the British economy, but it still retains a special status. For example, if the MAFF has an unresolved objection to a development plan, the LPA must refer the dispute to the DoE. The MAFF also has to be consulted on any planning application which involves the loss of 20 or more hectares of high quality agricultural land if the proposal is not in accordance with the development plan. Objections by the MAFF have fallen considerably over recent years. At the same time, it has assumed an increasing responsibility for countryside protection functions such as environmentally sensitive areas (discussed further in Chapter 8).

## SCOTLAND AND WALES

In Scotland, departmental changes were made as long ago as 1962, when town and country planning and environmental services were transferred from the Department of Health to the Scottish Development Department (now the Scottish Office Environment Department – SOEnD), which at the same time took over all the local government, electricity, roads and industry functions of the Scottish Home Department. A later reorganisation divided functions between the Scottish Office Environment Department and the Scottish Office Industry Department. The former is responsible for natural heritage, rural affairs, town and country planning, housing and local government, energy, water, waste, and pollution. The Industry Department is concerned with urban policy, new towns, industrial and regional economic development, and transport, including the Scottish aspects of regional policies in both a UK and EEC context.

In Wales, increasing responsibilities over a wide field have been transferred from Whitehall to the Welsh Office. This now has responsibility for health, community care, education, agriculture and fisheries, forestry, local government, housing, water and sewerage, environmental protection, town and country planning, nature conservation and the countryside, and (through the executive agency of Cadw) ancient monuments and historic buildings.

In the following account the term 'Secretary of State' is used for the sake of simplicity, but it should be interpreted to refer to the Secretaries of State for the Environment, for Scotland and for Wales. Similarly, references to the Department of the Environment should be read as applying, *mutatis mutandis*, to the Scottish Office and the Welsh Office.

## CENTRAL GOVERNMENT PLANNING FUNCTIONS

Relationships between central and local government vary significantly among various policy areas, 'reflecting, in part, the difference in weight and concern which the centre gives to items on its political agenda, and, in part, differences in the sets of actors involved in particular issue areas' (Goldsmith and Newton 1986: 103).

Under the 1947 Act, the Secretary of State was charged with the duty of 'securing consistency and continuity in the framing of a national policy with respect to the use and development of land'. Though this is no longer an explicit statutory duty, the spirit lives on,[13] and the SoS has very extensive powers. These, in effect, give the Department the final say in all policy matters (subject, of course, to parliamentary control). For many matters, the Secretary of State is required or empowered to make regulations or orders. These are subject to different levels of parliamentary control, but many come into effect automatically. This delegated legislation covers a wide field, including the Use Classes Orders and the General Development Orders. These give the Secretary of State wide power to change the categories of development which require planning permission.

The powers over local authorities are extensive. If a local authority fails to produce a plan, or a plan which is 'satisfactory', default powers can be used. These have never been used in the field of planning, though they have in some other policy areas (such as housing finance). Nevertheless, the SoS can require a local authority to make 'modifications' to a plan, or 'call in' a plan for his own 'determination'. Such powers are occasionally used, but gentler methods of better-mannered persuasion are preferred. Decisions of a local planning authority on applications for planning permission can, on appeal, be modified or revoked, even if the development proposed is contrary to the development plan. Proposals which the Secretary of State regards as being sufficiently important can be called in for his decision.

In spite of all these powers, it is not the function of the Secretary of State to decide detailed planning matters. This is the business of local planning authorities. The Secretary of State's function is to coordinate the work of individual local authorities and to ensure that their development plans and development control procedures are in harmony with broad planning policies. That this often involves rather closer relationships than might prima facie be supposed follows from the nature of the governmental processes. The line dividing policy from day-to-day administration is a fine one. Policy has to be translated into decisions on specific issues, and a series of decisions can amount to a change in policy. This is particularly important in the British planning system, where a large measure of administrative discretion is given to central and local government bodies. This is a distinctive feature of the planning system. There is little provision for external judicial review of local planning decisions: instead, there is the system of appeals to the Secretary of State. It is this broad area of discretion which brings the Department in close contact with local planning authorities (though, as is explained later, it is not the only factor). The Department in effect operates both in a quasi-judicial capacity and as a developer of policy.

The Department's quasi-judicial role stems in part from the vagueness of planning policies. Even if policies are precisely worded, their application can raise problems. Since local authorities have such a wide area of discretion, and since the courts have only very limited powers of action, the Department has to act as arbiter over what is fair and reasonable. This is not, however, simply a judicial process. A decision is not taken on the basis of legal rules as in a court of law: it involves the exercise of a wide discretion in the balance of public and private interest within the framework of planning policies.

Appeals to the Secretary of State against the refusal of planning permission are normally decided by the Planning Inspectorate, formerly a directorate of the DoE but, since 1992, an executive agency of the DoE and the Welsh Office. In Scotland, the same role is performed by the Scottish Office Inquiry Reporters Office:

> The role of the Inspectorate is to assist the Secretaries of State in resolving disputes between individuals and local authorities in matters relating to decisions under planning, housing, environment, highways and allied legislation, against a background of government policy in these areas.[14]

In the year 1991/92, the Inspectorate decided 22,553 appeals. This is about 4,000 less than in 1990/91 but 4,000 more than in 1987/88.

Inspectors make decisions on appeals against the refusal of planning permission, and other matters including enforcement and compulsory purchase. In decisions made by the Inspectorate and the Reporters Office, the final decision is the formal responsibility of the Secretary of State. There is no appeal against such a decision except on a question of law. Inspectors also consider objections made to local development plans, but in this case the recommendations are made to the local authority rather than the Secretary of State. The local authority is responsible for deciding how to act on the recommendations, but there are additional public safeguards allowing further objections and call-in by the Secretary of State.

Planning authorities, inspectors, and others are guided in their decisions and recommendations by government policy. Central government guidance on planning matters is issued by way of circulars and, since 1988, in *planning policy guidance notes* (PPGs), *minerals policy guidance notes* (MPGs), and *derelict land grant advice notes* (DLGA). Regional planning guidance and strategic planning guidance was initially published in the PPG series, but from 1989 there has been a separate series of RPG notes. A previous series of *development control notes* is being phased out, but a few are still in force.[15]

Since the introduction of PPGs in England and Wales, circulars have been concerned mainly with the further explanation and elaboration of statutory procedures. PPGs concentrate on the explanation of government policy in substantive areas, ranging from green belts to outdoor advertising.[16] A full review of DoE policy guidance was under way in 1993, and resulted in the revision of many PPGs. Circulars and guidance notes are generally subject to some consultation with local authorities and other organisations, prior to final publication, but the Secretary of State has the final word.

Most policy guidance relating to England and Wales is issued jointly by the DoE and the Welsh Office but, on occasion, separate advice is needed to reflect distinctive Welsh conditions (for instance on land for housing and strategic planning). In Scotland, the SOEnD introduced *national planning guidelines* (NPGs) long before its southern counterparts. The first national guidance on *North Sea Oil and Gas: Coastal Planning* was published in 1974. There is now a fairly comprehensive range of guidelines covering such matters as aggregate workings, housing, scenic areas, forestry, skiing, major retail development, and agricultural land.[17] The SOEnD is now replacing NPGs with *national planning policy guidance*: the character of these, and their implications, are discussed in Chapter 3 (footnote 46).

Circulars and guidance notes are recognised as important sources of government policy and interpretation of the law, although they are not the authoritative interpretation of law (this is the role of the courts), neither are they generally legally binding.[18] Furthermore, 'a local planning authority can, if it chooses, ignore the advice given in a circular. All that the law demands is that it is taken into account as a relevant consideration' (Nott and Morgan 1984: 628). Indeed, it may be that the advice in one circular or guidance note may contradict another, perhaps as a result of piecemeal revisions at different times. Nevertheless, circulars and guidance notes command a great deal of respect and are closely followed in development control and development planning. They exert significant influence in planning policy and decisions, and are quoted profusely, at least by professional planners.[19]

The Department's role in policy formulation is not easy to summarise. Policies are usually couched in very general terms such as 'preserving amenity' or 'restraining urban sprawl', which give local authorities considerable leeway. Formal guidance (as in the guidance notes) cannot always provide a clear indication of the action which should be followed in any particular case. Proposals have to be considered 'on their merits' within the broad framework of a set of principles. These principles can, and do, change, at least in emphasis. Usually the change is gradual, perhaps even coming without a conscious step. And the motivating power may well be the local authorities themselves rather than the Department. All this makes it very difficult to present a lucid picture of central–local relationships. The truth is that the position is not clear cut. Nevertheless, as is discussed in the following section, the character of central–local relationships has changed dramatically in recent years.

## (B) LOCAL GOVERNMENT

Local authorities are undergoing a fundamental transformation from being the main providers of services to having responsibility for securing their provision. The task of setting standards, specifying the work to be done and monitoring performance is done better if it is fully separated from the job of providing the services . . . As enablers, local authorities have greater opportunities to choose the best source of service and thus to provide local people with a greater choice. The aim should be to secure the best services at least cost. The private and voluntary sectors should be used to provide services where this is more cost-effective than direct provision by the authority.[20]

The map of local government areas in Britain has been radically redrawn in the last twenty years, and it is on the verge of a further major change. London government was reorganised by an Act of 1963, English and Welsh local government by an Act of 1972, and Scottish local government by an Act of 1973 (Richards 1973; Alexander 1982). A further reorganisation (if that is the right word) took place in 1986 when the Greater London Council and the metropolitan county councils were abolished: this was announced in a 1983 White Paper as 'streamlining the cities'.

The London Government Act of 1963 came into operation in 1965. In brief, it established a Greater London Council covering an area of about 1,600 square kilometres and a population, at that time, of nearly 8 million; and 32 new London boroughs, plus the unmolested Corporation of the City of London (which, for the purposes of this book, can be regarded as the 33rd borough). These replaced the London County Council, 28 metropolitan borough councils, the county council of Middlesex and the county boroughs of Croydon, East Ham and West Ham. Considerable parts of Essex, Hertfordshire, Kent and Surrey were transferred to the new Greater London area.

The GLC had the responsibility for preparing the strategic development plan for the whole of the Greater London area. (This was published in 1969.) It set out the policies relating to population, housing, employment, transport and, indeed, all major issues which came within the compass of strategic planning. Within this strategic framework, the London borough councils were responsible for preparing their own local development plans. Originally, it was intended that these would be structure plans, but this was changed in 1972 owing to the great length of time required to process the Greater London Development Plan. The boroughs, therefore, were required only to prepare local plans within the framework of the GLC structure plan.

With the abolition of the GLC in 1986, the London boroughs became unitary authorities, with responsibility for most planning functions. Each borough now has to prepare a unitary development plan, which is described in the following chapter. There is, in addition, a statutory joint committee which has the function of advising on matters of common interest relating to the planning and development of Greater London.[21] This is the London Planning Advisory Committee. Each borough is also the mineral planning authority and highway authority for its area. Public Transport is operated by London Regional Transport, which is responsible directly to the Secretary of State.[22] Responsibility for waste in London, as elsewhere, is complex, being divided among the statutory joint London Waste Regulation Authority, Waste Disposal Authorities (the boroughs either singly or jointly), and the Waste Collection Authorities (the boroughs).[23]

## LOCAL GOVERNMENT IN ENGLAND AND WALES FROM 1974

The Local Government Act of 1972 provided for the establishment of a two-tier system of counties and districts throughout England and Wales. This was brought into operation in 1974. Outside six metropolitan areas, England was divided into 39 counties and 264 districts. Wales, with no 'metropolitan' areas, was divided into eight counties and 37 districts. In the six English metropolitan areas (Greater Manchester, Merseyside, South Yorkshire, Tyne & Wear, West Midlands, and West Yorkshire) metropolitan county councils were established.

There was no difference between the planning powers of the metropolitan and non-metropolitan counties. Their responsibilities included structure planning, agreeing a framework for local plan preparation with the district councils, consulting on matters of common concern, and determining major development control issues.

In fields other than planning, the metropolitan districts had a much wider range of functions than the non-metropolitan districts: they were, for instance, the local authority for education, social services, and libraries (which elsewhere were county functions).

The overall picture, however, was – and remains – by no means as neat as this summary suggests. Some services (such as parks, museums and swimming baths) can be provided by either the county or the district. Highway maintenance is divided between counties and districts. Housing is a district function, but counties have reserve powers. Moreover, the legislation provides for the discharge of any local authority function 'by any other authority' (except for police, education and social services): this was mainly to allow districts which were formerly county boroughs to continue to operate, on an agency basis, services which were transferred to the counties. The final result is confusing and, with some services, the division of responsibilities is blurred. Nowhere is this more so than with planning.

## METROPOLITAN GOVERNMENT SINCE 1986

In 1986, under the banner of 'streamlining the cities', the Thatcher Government abolished the Greater London Council (GLC) and the metropolitan county councils (MCCs). This dramatic step, untraditionally, was preceded by no royal commission, committee of inquiry, or study.

The arguments put forward by the Government were ludicrously thin. Efficiency was cited as the main objective, and it was held that this was where the GLC and MCCs were particularly deficient. They had few functions, but they spent a great deal of money; they were inefficient and had poor and counterproductive relations with their constituent districts (which were often controlled by a different political party); and their autonomy was frequently annoying and embarrassing to the Thatcher Government, particularly after 1981 when all six MCCs returned Labour councils with huge majorities. Finally, in this abbreviated list, it was argued that efficiency could be improved and public resources saved by abolition. The details are too complex to spell out here, but the question arises: what really went wrong?

It is clear that the regions 'gained few friends since their establishment' (Flynn et al. 1985: 105). Partly, this was a matter of the previous history of local government in the regions, and the acrimonious town–county battle which had for so long bedevilled English local government. Partly, it was a matter of the lack of functional and political power of the regions. The matter of power is crucial. The new counties had the difficulty of establishing themselves between the well-established 'political arenas' of the district councils and central government; and (at least in the time available to them) they did not succeed (Healey *et al*. 1988: 209). In Ken Young's words, 'a metropolitan authority tends to have too little power to be effective, and too much to be acceptable' (Young 1984: 5).[24] The White Paper took up this point: whereas the shire counties were major providers of services in their areas, this was not the case with the metropolitan counties.

Given the predispositions of the Government, no argument about strategic planning was persuasive: indeed, since strategy in the two-tier system required the agreement of both tiers, this was 'a recipe for conflict and uncertainty'. Moreover, their 'search for a role' brought the GLC and the MCCs into conflict not only with the district councils but also with central government, both in terms of expenditure and policy. The conclusion was clear: the structure was 'fundamentally unsound' and had 'imposed heavy and unnecessary burdens on ratepayers'. The proposed reorganisation involved transferring as many services as possible to the districts; others were to be moved to joint authorities or other statutory bodies.

An extraordinarily wide debate ensued. Except for the London Boroughs (which, not unsurprisingly, supported the abolition of the GLC), the majority of arguments were strongly in favour of retaining the GLC and the MCCs as the important strategic planning tier.[25] All the arguments were unavailing: they had as little impact as Alan Norton's academic study of metropolitan governments in Europe and Canada (Norton 1983), and Ron Bailey's 1984 pamphlet attacking the abolition as 'a denial of civil liberties'. The only tangible result of the controversy was the publication by the DoE Library of a bibliography of publications on the debate (Lambert 1984).

Thus in 1986, all the metropolitan counties and the GLC were abolished, and the 36 metropolitan boroughs and the 32 London boroughs and the City of London became single-tier 'unitary' authorities. Functions transferred to these unitary districts

included highways and traffic management; minerals and derelict land reclamation; waste regulation and disposal; sport; historic buildings; recreation, parks and green belt land; and gypsy sites.[26] Additionally, and of prime importance, is the planning function. Here the major difficulty is that of strategic planning, and of establishing a substitute for the metropolitan county structure plans to provide a basis for coordinating the unitary plans of the individual districts. The metropolitan county areas have nothing to compare with the London Planning Advisory Committee. The Manchester experience is probably typical. There it is clear that there is little approaching a plan for the conurbation as a whole. Instead, there are 'ten largely isolationist visions born out of separate processes of plan development'.[27]

Some coordination is provided by non-statutory strategic guidance, prepared cooperatively by the districts. When agreed by the Secretary of State, this is issued as a regional planning guidance note. The products to date generally have been poor substitutes for the former metropolitan county structure plans. They have been described as 'bland, anodyne and non-controversial, emphasising statements upon which all districts could agree'.[28]

## LOCAL GOVERNMENT IN THE NON-METROPOLITAN AREAS

In the shire counties, the planning functions of local government are split between the tiers (though further reorganisation is in hand, with unitary authorities appearing to be the most likely outcome). The division of planning control functions has shifted in favour of the districts since 1974: a major reduction in the range of 'county matters' was made in 1980 following proposals for 'organic change'.[29]

The concept of 'organic change' was one of limited change enabling 'improvements to be made in a pragmatic way in the distribution of functions between county and district authorities'. A 1979 White Paper published by the Labour Government set out a range of proposals, of which those relating to planning were quite different from the remainder

*Figure 2.1* Local Authorities in Britain

# Resident Populations – England, Wales and Scotland

## England

| | | |
|---|---|---|
| 1 | Greater London | 6,679,699 |
| 2 | Greater Manchester | 2,499,441 |
| 3 | Merseyside | 1,403,642 |
| 4 | South Yorkshire | 1,262,630 |
| 5 | Tyne & Wear | 1,095,150 |
| 6 | West Midlands | 2,551,671 |
| 7 | West Yorkshire | 2,013,693 |
| | | |
| 36 | Avon | 932,674 |
| 28 | Bedfordshire | 524,105 |
| 39 | Berkshire | 734,246 |
| 27 | Buckinghamshire | 632,487 |
| 30 | Cambridgeshire | 645,125 |
| 14 | Cheshire | 956,616 |
| 13 | Cleveland | 550,293 |
| 33 | Cornwall & Isles of Scilly | 468,425 |
| 8 | Cumbria | 483,163 |
| 18 | Derbyshire | 928,636 |
| 34 | Devon | 1,009,950 |
| 38 | Dorset | 645,166 |
| 10 | Durham | 593,430 |
| 44 | East Sussex | 690,477 |
| 42 | Essex | 1,528,577 |
| 25 | Gloucestershire | 528,370 |
| 40 | Hampshire | 1,541,547 |
| 21 | Hereford & Worcester | 676,747 |
| 29 | Hertfordshire | 975,829 |
| 15 | Humberside | 858,040 |
| — | Isle of Wight | 124,577 |
| 45 | Kent | 1,508,873 |
| 11 | Lancashire | 1,383,998 |
| 23 | Leicestershire | 867,521 |
| 20 | Lincolnshire | 584,534 |
| 31 | Norfolk | 745,613 |
| 24 | Northamptonshire | 578,807 |
| 9 | Northumberland | 304,694 |
| 12 | North Yorkshire | 702,161 |
| 19 | Nottinghamshire | 993,872 |
| 26 | Oxfordshire | 574,584 |
| 16 | Shropshire | 406,387 |
| 35 | Somerset | 460,368 |
| 17 | Staffordshire | 1,031,135 |
| 32 | Suffolk | 636,266 |
| 41 | Surrey | 1,018,003 |
| 22 | Warwickshire | 484,247 |
| 43 | West Sussex | 702,290 |
| 37 | Wiltshire | 564,741 |

## Wales

| | | |
|---|---|---|
| 47 | Clwyd | 408,090 |
| 48 | Dyfed | 343,543 |
| 52 | Gwent | 442,212 |
| 46 | Gwynedd | 235,452 |
| 51 | Mid Glamorgan | 534,101 |
| 49 | Powys | 117,467 |
| 53 | South Glamorgan | 392,428 |
| 50 | West Glamorgan | 361,428 |

## Scotland

| | | |
|---|---|---|
| 61 | Borders Region | 104,100 |
| 57 | Central Region | 272,800 |
| 62 | Dumfries & Galloway Region | 147,800 |
| 58 | Fife Region | 346,500 |
| 55 | Grampian Region | 514,400 |
| 54 | Highland Region | 204,200 |
| 59 | Lothian Region | 750,500 |
| 60 | Strathclyde Region | 2,296,300 |
| 56 | Tayside Region | 391,900 |
| | | |
| 63 | Orkney Islands Area | 19,580 |
| 64 | Shetland Islands Area | 22,500 |
| 65 | Western Isles Islands Area | 29,420 |

in that they were to apply to all local authorities (in England). Essentially, the proposal was that responsibility for development control should lie almost entirely with districts: counties should retain responsibility for only a limited number of special categories such as applications concerning mineral working, and applications which straddled the boundaries of a national park.

Though conceived as limited in character, the proposals as a whole were seen by some as not going far enough and by others as constituting a radical and important change.[30] The Labour Government did not stay in power sufficiently long to come to any decision, but the proposals for changes in development control (for which there was a wide agreement)[31] came into force in 1981.

The development planning functions have continued to be split between the tiers, with the county preparing structure plans and many local subject plans; and the district preparing local plans. In practice, the counties have dominated development plan work, and structure plans have formed the only framework for control in the greater part of the shire counties where local plans have not been prepared.

In addition, a major function of counties has been in the planning and control of minerals and waste disposal. This has been strengthened under the Planning and Compensation Act 1991, with the mandatory requirement for minerals and waste plans. The counties also have additional statutory functions in archaeology and coast protection. Tourism, economic development, and off-street parking are split between the tiers.

The districts are responsible for local development plans and for most of development control, and they also have statutory functions in respect of building control, housing, parks and open spaces and playing fields.

The two-tier structure has been subject to continued dispute which, in some cases, has developed into outright conflict. Certainly, there is force in the argument that such a structure is inappropriate for some of the large provincial cities, such as Nottingham, Exeter, and Leicester. This conflict has risen to the surface in the early debate on the latest proposals for local government reorganisation, and many districts, large and small, have made claims for independent status.

## SCOTTISH LOCAL GOVERNMENT

The 1969 Wheatley Commission recommended that the four counties of cities, 21 large burghs, 176 small burghs, 33 counties and 196 districts of Scotland should be replaced by a two-tier structure of seven regional and 37 district authorities. With some modifications, this general structure was accepted by the Government. Following amendments made by Parliament (particularly the addition of Fife as a separate region, and the exclusion of several districts from the Glasgow District), the Local Government (Scotland) Act 1973 provided for a two-tier system except in the three island areas of Orkney, Shetland and the Western Islands (which became 'most-purpose' authorities).

There are 9 regional and 53 district councils. Together with the three island authorities, there are thus 65 local authorities of which 49 have planning powers. The fact that, unlike the situation in England, not all local authorities have planning powers is a result of the difficulties of devising a local government structure for those parts of the country which cover a large area but contain few people. By allocating planning powers in these areas of scattered population to the regional authority it was possible to increase the number of districts (and thereby also reduce their enormous geographical size). There are thus three different types of area:

1 in the Central, Fife, Grampian, Lothian, Tayside and Strathclyde regions, planning is divided between regional and district authorities;
2 in the Borders, Dumfries & Galloway and Highland regions, planning is allocated to the regions: the districts have no planning functions. These three regions are termed *general planning authorities*;
3 in the three island areas of Orkney, Shetland and the Western Islands, there are no districts: there is thus only one local authority which undertakes

the functions of both a regional planning authority and a district planning authority. These authorities are termed *island areas* (not regions) and are designated as *general planning authorities*.

In effect, therefore, there is a two-tier planning system in six regions, and a 'general' planning authority system elsewhere. The former includes nine-tenths of the population of Scotland.

The regions vary greatly in size: Strathclyde (with a population of over 2 million) has nearly half the country's population. Districts range in population from 10,630 in Nairn to 439,000 in Edinburgh and 688,000 in Glasgow (1991 figures).

There is a clearer distinction, at least in concept, between the functions of the regions and the districts than is the case south of the border. The regions were conceived as strategic authorities and are responsible for 'regional planning functions', all highways, public transport, education, social work and water (which in England and Wales has been allocated to *ad hoc* authorities). The districts are responsible for local planning, housing, refuse collection and disposal and a range of other local services. As is explained in the following chapter, the division of planning functions was, from the start, made on a better basis than in England and Wales.

Proposals for further change emerged north of the border in 1980. These came from the Stodart Committee (1981) which was established to review the working relationships in the reorganised Scottish system, and from the Montgomery Committee (1984) which was set up to review the remote communities of the Islands Councils and the impact upon them of major economic developments such as those associated with off-shore oil exploitation.

Most of the recommendations of the Stodart Committee were designed to allocate responsibility for individual functions specifically to one tier. Thus, it was recommended that regional councils should have sole responsibility for industrial development and promotion, while district councils should be solely responsible for leisure and recreation, tourism, countryside and nature conservation. For planning, however, it was concluded that the division between

the tiers should remain. This apparently surprising recommendation was related to the more sensible division of planning functions effected in the Scottish reorganisation.

The Montgomery Committee commended the success of the Islands Councils as all-purpose authorities, and made no substantial proposals for change. Now in the 1990s, and despite the relative success of the hybrid Scottish structure, the advantages of a single all-purpose authority are to be spread more widely throughout Scotland (Dawson 1981). Before discussing this, it is useful to consider the extent to which Scotland's structure of government and policy might be considered to be a special case, different from the English experience.

The cultural history and physical conditions of the country dictate that, to a degree, the administration of planning will be different in Scotland. Changes to the law in Scotland require specific legislation, and the Scottish Office has administrative discretion within which it will take account of the very special circumstances which exist in parts of the country. The pursuit of planning objectives, therefore, is sometimes distinctive. The reluctance to designate UDCs is one example. Nevertheless the broad thrust and impact of government policy are much the same (Carmichael 1992). Indeed, some of the Government's most fundamental attempts at reform have been tried and tested in Scotland first, including the community charge, rate capping and 'compulsory competitive tendering'.

## OTHER PLANNING AUTHORITIES

There are several circumstances where planning functions are transferred from a local authority to other bodies. The Secretary of State has the power to establish an independent joint board, and has used this in the case of the Lake District Special Planning Board and the Peak Park Joint Planning Board. These two Boards are effectively both the county and the district planning authority: they are responsible for the preparation of both the structure plan and the local plan, for development control, and for other local government functions. In the other national parks, outside the metropolitan areas, the county council is the sole planning authority, but it is required to operate through a national park committee. This has the responsibility for preparing the park-wide local plan, minerals and waste local plans, and also development control. Two-thirds of national park authority members are appointed by the constituent authorities.

The Broads Authority was established in 1988, with 18 of its 35 members appointed by the constituent authorities. It is effectively the district planning authority for the area of the Broads. It has responsibility for making the local plan, and determining planning applications, though not minerals or waste.

Since 1980, the Secretary of State has designated urban development areas in which non-elected corporations generally have planning functions. However, the detailed arrangements have varied and, in some cases, local authorities continue to carry out the planning function on an agency basis. In enterprise zones, the Secretary of State may make the zone authority the local planning authority. Similarly, the Secretary of State can make housing action trusts the local planning authority for the whole or part of an area. Neither of these powers has been used.

## PARISH, COMMUNITY AND TOWN COUNCILS

There are over 12,000 parishes (or their equivalent) in Britain, many of which are represented by a parish, community, or town council. They do not form part of the local government structure, and most have a very limited role. However, they can play a significant part in the democratic process in rural areas and small towns by providing an effective voice for local interests. Where they are active, planning issues will make up a significant part of their agendas.

In England, there are about 10,200 'parishes' ranging from no population at all up to 48,700 in Bracknell. They are represented by 70,000 parish councillors.[32] About 8,200 have parish or town councils; in the remainder an annual parish meeting should be called. Provision was made in the Local Government Act 1972 for additional parishes to be created where they do not exist (especially in urban areas), but little use has been made of this power.[33] Several non-statutory neighbourhood councils have been established in the larger urban areas of England.[34] Scotland and Wales have no statutory provision for such bodies.

The last reorganisation of local government in Wales abolished parish councils, and provided for statutory 'community councils' on which a Consultation Paper was issued in 1992.[35]

The statutory functions of parishes are very restricted, and are mostly shared with the district council. They include the management of allotment gardens and some local open spaces, footpath lighting and maintenance, and the nomination of a governor to local schools. Of particular importance (and widely used) is the right of parish councils to be consulted on planning applications in their areas. Parish councils can require the LPA to notify them of all, or specific classes of, local applications.[36] In practice, where there is an active parish council, it will usually be consulted by the LPA on all applications. It can also play a consultative role in the preparation of development plans.

The Scottish Act provides for the establishment of community councils where there is a demand for them, under schemes prepared by district (or islands) authorities. Their purpose is 'to ascertain, co-ordinate and express to the regional, district and islands councils, and other public bodies, the views of the community' and 'to take such action in the interests of the community as appears to its members to be desirable and practicable'. Some 'alternatives for community council schemes' were prepared by the Scottish Development Department in 1974, and a review of the 1,131 operational councils was undertaken in 1983/84.[37]

As in England and Wales, the councils vary enormously in population size (from less than 500 to over 20,000), in funding (some receive more than £10,000 per annum from the local authority), and in level of activity (some areas have no active community council at all.[38] Unlike English parishes, the Scottish Community Councils have no statutory right to be consulted on planning applications, although in practice this happens to a significant extent.

## CENTRAL–LOCAL RELATIONS

It used to be common to talk of central–local government relationships as constituting a 'partnership' but, for several reasons, this no longer seems an appropriate description. First, the extent of the central government's responsibilities and its 'power of the purse' has 'inevitable inherent contradictions'.

> [This] produces a situation where the role of the department in relation to planning, land conversion and development is essentially an ambiguous one. Policy choices and conflicts arise over, for instance, whether to adopt a responsive or interventionist role in relation to development pressures and the balance to be struck between concern for the development industry and sponsorship of local authorities whose interests may well conflict with those of the private sector.'
>
> (Barrett et al. 1978: 7)

Second, there has been a fundamental change in the place of local government within the British system of government. In its heyday, local government was largely concerned with the provision of 'public goods' rather than redistributive services. (Public goods are those that benefit all the public – streets, sewers, parks, lighting, etc. – while redistributive services confer benefits on some at the cost of others.) This is no longer the case:

> The prominence of income redistribution in modern economic policy has not only shifted attention from local government to central, but also altered the balance of local authority activities. The slum clearance and community health services that originally were seen as benefiting the community as a whole have been superseded by housing and social services that are designed to be redistributive. In many cases local authorities are trying to fill the gaps or general inadequacies of national cash redistribution programmes. This switch of emphasis from public goods to redistribution has played a part in the postwar tendency to treat local authorities as agents of central government that 'should' act in accordance with the political will of the centre.
>
> (Dawson 1985: 31)

The replacement of domestic rates by the flat rate community charge (itself now replaced by the Council Tax) represented 'a major change in the direction of local government finance back to the notion of *charging* for local authority services'.[39]

Third, many functions have been removed from local government: in the early post-war reorganisations, electricity and gas, trunk roads, 'poor relief' and hospitals were all removed. Other local health services and water and sewage disposal functions were removed in 1974/75. Despite strong opposition from local government, the building of new towns was entrusted to *ad hoc* government-appointed development corporations.

Most important, however, has been the dramatic attack on local government by the Thatcher administration.[40] This started as a reaction to 'overspending' by local authorities: central government wanted to divert expenditure from areas such as housing and education to defence and (in response to rising unemployment) social security. But this was not under their control: local authorities still had their own sources of revenue which, though limited, were significant. The result was a tightening of controls, 'caps' on local expenditure, and eventually drastic changes in the system of local taxation – including the notorious 'poll tax' (officially the *community charge*).[41] These controls resulted in a major transfer of power from the localities to the centre. They also led, first, to strained relationships between local and central government, and, later, to strife and virtual open warfare.[42] The original intention to restrain public expenditure evolved into a drive to make local authorities more accountable. In the words of *Paying for Local Government* (1986):

> Effective local accountability must be the cornerstone of successful local government. All too often this accountability is blurred and weakened by the complexities of the national grant system and by the fact that differences arise among those who vote for, those who pay for, and those who receive local government services.

It was to correct this that the community charge was introduced (payable by all adults). The uncooperative, and sometimes belligerent stance of some local authorities, particularly in the metropolitan areas, led to further draconian measures based on a firm belief that central government policies had to prevail over local ones. Local authorities were forced to sell council houses (tenants were given the 'right to buy' at heavily discounted prices), and local authority housebuilding programmes were slashed: these and similar measures amounted to the 'nationalisation' of housing policy (Murie 1985). These, and other policies (such as the deregulation of passenger transport) significantly reduced the role of local authorities and diminished their position in the overall machinery of government. Not least, a whole tier of local government disappeared with the abolition of the GLC and the metropolitan counties in 1985. More than fifty Acts of Parliament have been passed extending controls over the operation of local government.[43]

These forces, however significant for the role of local government, were not the product of a clear and coherent strategy from the centre. Rather were they a series of *ad hoc* reactions to individual problems, first of controlling expenditure; later, of reducing the discretion of local government; and then of transforming local government into a means of enabling other agencies to provide services to a standard which could not be achieved by traditional means. It was not until 1987 that there was 'some evidence that central government rethought the role of local government in a consistent way across the whole range of local functions'.[44] The impact of this is now being felt in the 1990s, with continued centralisation, but with greater emphasis on competition and the contracting-out of services to the private sector.

## THE ENABLING LOCAL AUTHORITY

Towards the end of the 1980s, more far-reaching changes began to take place across virtually all local government functions. The 1988 Education Reform Act introduced a centralised curriculum and the local management of schools. The 1988 Housing Act introduced *Housing Action Trusts* to take over the management of large council housing estates and gave groups of council tenants not exercising the right to buy the opportunity to opt out of council control and

into the tenancy of a housing association or other landlord. The 1988 Local Government Act obliged councils and other specified public bodies to contract-out manual services through compulsory competitive tendering (CCT).[45] In November 1991, the Government published plans to extend CCT and, in November 1992, it was announced that new regulations would be introduced to widen the application of CCT to construction-related and corporate services including architecture and property management.[46]

In sum, the direct services, responsibilities and powers of local government are being systematically and substantially reduced. Local government is being cast in a new enabling role: a broker between central policy, local demands, and contractors who provide the service. The main instruments of this policy are the requirement for CCT, the separation of client and contractor roles, the need to demonstrate value for money (VFM), and performance review. A clear exposition of central government's view of the role of local authorities in the 1990s is given in the 1991 DoE Consultation Paper: *Local Government Review: The Internal Management of Local Authorities in England* (a similar paper was published by the Welsh Office).

> The local authorities' role in the provision of services should be to assess the needs of their area, plan the provision of services and ensure the delivery of those services. There are also fields in which local authorities will continue to have important regulatory functions and providing roles. But councils should be looking to contract out work to whoever can deliver services most efficiently and effectively, thus enabling the authority to be more responsive to the wishes of their electorate. The people who run local councils increasingly need different skills to meet the challenge of their developing role as enablers rather than providers. The ability to manage large numbers of directly employed staff is becoming less important than the ability to set up and oversee contractual arrangements. The key skills will lie in:
> – setting standards where appropriate
> – specifying service requirements
> – awarding contracts
> – monitoring performance
> – taking action if performance falls short of the required level.

Proponents inside and outside government, including some local authority managers who have embraced the idea of 'enabling', identify significant benefits, including the clearer focus on objectives and monitoring of performance, and the decentralisation of service delivery. Opposing arguments focus on the loss of direct local council control over the delivery of services and a diminution of local democracy in this style of service provision. There are many concerns about the 'dangers of fragmentation, conflicts of interest', and the underlying 'depoliticising capacity of competition' (Local Government Management Board 1992b; Walsh 1991)

It is here that the contrast with trends in European local government are most interesting. Stoker (in Batley and Stoker 1991: 12) describes Britain as being 'out of step' with Europe: 'It is developing a more centralised political system with a diminished role for elected local authorities while elsewhere in Europe the agenda of change is favouring greater decentralisation and local autonomy.' Comparisons can be misleading of course, and the very different conditions and starting points for local government in other European countries must be taken into account. Crucially, the notion of 'enabling' is already the norm in much of Western Europe, with local government implementing its functions through a diverse range of agencies and often in partnership. This, Stoker argues, has had the very positive benefit of sustaining the involvement of local authorities in a much wider range of services. The debate about local government in the UK has been dominated by disputes about service delivery rather than government and, despite the very genuine concerns noted above, the impact on service delivery may have been overplayed.

At least one commentator has called into question the assumption on which arguments both for and against 'enabling local government' are based, arguing that the central attack on local government has been much less successful than either camp would have us believe (Cochrane 1991: 282). Cochrane argues that 'the market model of local government looks less like an assessment of what has happened and more like a picture of what some people would like to happen (or like to believe has happened)'. Certainly, the government's privatisation ideology has yet to bite deeply into the planning service.[47]

## LOCAL GOVERNMENT CHANGE AND PLANNING

For town and country planning, the apparent and seemingly paradoxical outcome of change in the 1980s has been a larger and stronger body of planners with widened statutory functions. The indirect effect of market deregulation, the increasing complexity of development issues, and the growing emphasis on environmental protection were bound to lead to a greater demand for planning skills (Healey 1989). The concept of an enabling local government, too, increases the need for strategic thinking and focuses attention on the corporate planning function (Carter, Brown and Abbot 1991). Planners have again begun to identify themselves as a central component in local government.

The direct impact on the way in which the planning service is delivered is less significant. So far, planning has been subjected to only minimal change in comparison to other services, and the concept of the local authority as enabler requires more attention to strategy and in-house planning, rather than less.

More dramatic changes in the delivery of the planning function have also been avoided, at least for the time being. Planning was excluded from the list of professional services to be subject to the extension of CCT. The proposals for extension were underpinned by an unpublished report into the feasibility of extending CCT to professional services, prepared by PA Consulting Group. On regulatory services such as planning and environmental health, the report concluded that there was little scope for CCT,[48] despite the clear evidence that a number of authorities had successfully contracted out elements of the plan making and control functions.

The conclusion has to be that, in contrast to most local services, planning as a statutory and regulatory function has been somewhat protected from the pressure for change.[49]

Nevertheless, there are significant implications for the planning service, not least the need to demonstrate 'value for money' (VFM). This is not an easy concept to define for planning because of the difficulty of assessing quality in plans and planning decisions.

The Audit Commission provide guidance for local authorities and district auditors on performance indicators for all services, including planning,[50] but these have been criticised for the reliance on quantitative measures, the classic example being the proportion of applications decided within eight weeks.

The Audit Commission's 1992 report, *Building in Quality*, addressed these criticisms and made a real attempt to introduce a wider assessment of performance, recognising that there were many ancillary tasks in providing advice and negotiating with applicants and making 'complex professional and political judgments'. At the beginning of 1993, after consultation, the Audit Commission settled on six key indicators. As with the earlier version, these concentrate on matters of efficiency rather than on the effectiveness of the system, though the added breadth to performance review will be a significant improvement on previous practice.[51]

The emphasis on VFM is being reinforced in two ways. First, there is the requirement for all local authorities to establish a 'transparent' internal accounting system. This will ensure that the real costs of services can be identified,[52] will help to bring about internal markets in local authorities, and will enable much closer investigation of 'value for money' and cost-effectiveness. The second is the Citizen's Charter: this is discussed in Chapter 11.

## LOCAL GOVERNMENT REORGANISATION IN ENGLAND

The driving force behind the further reorganisation of local government was Michael Heseltine. Hence the title of the INLOGOV report: *The Heseltine Review of Local Government: A New Vision or Opportunities Missed?* (Leach *et al.* 1992). Whatever Heseltine's original 'vision' was, it disintegrated in the political storms through which his ideas had to pass.

Consultation on local government reorganisation in Britain is being handled separately but concurrently by the DoE and the Scottish and Welsh Offices. The proposals for England were set out in a Consultation Paper on *The Structure of Local Government in England*.[53] The paper sets out the argument, widely accepted across the political spectrum, for a unitary structure of local government in the shires (reflecting the structure already in place in the metropolitan counties). It is argued that a single tier would reduce bureaucracy and costs, and improve coordination. It would clarify responsibility for services and, since taxpayers would be able to relate their local tax bills more clearly to local services, it would provide for greater accountability. It is also claimed that local democracy could be enhanced by increased involvement of local people in council affairs resulting from a better relationship of local authority boundaries to 'communities' with which people 'identify'. The potential to increase the limited role of parish and town councils is also on the agenda.

However, the way in which unitary status is to be achieved is left open, with the possibility of existing districts taking unitary status, the merging of authorities to create larger ones, or the creation of wholly new authorities. Moreover, the option to retain a two-tier structure has been conceded.

A Local Government Commission was established and, in June 1992, the DoE published a series of documents on the procedures to be followed by the Commission and policy guidance to be taken into account.[54]

The Government has reduced internal political conflict by allowing the possibility for shire counties to be retained and by setting criteria which, on the face of it, draw heavily on local opinion. The main criteria for the review includes responsiveness to local needs and 'sense of identity' as well as the ubiquitous 'cost-effectiveness'. Advice is given on the manner in which the Commission should measure the short- and long-term costs and benefits in financial terms, but special attention is to be given to the intangible factors: those that 'by their nature are impossible to quantify with any precision'.

The thrust of the policy, focusing as it does on a unitary structure and local criteria, raises questions about the importance to be attached to strategic matters, and the way in which local government in the shires will fit in with the new plan regime introduced by the 1991 Planning and Compensation Act. Since the resolution (if not the solution) of these issues may be evident by the time this book is published, there is no point in the authors guessing what might come to pass: that would be unnecessary jeopardy.

## LOCAL GOVERNMENT REORGANISATION IN WALES

Reorganisation in Wales is proceeding more quickly, and a new structure of unitary authorities is planned to be in place by April 1995. After a two-year period of consultation, first on preliminary ideas and later on a Consultation Paper, the Government published, in March 1993, a White Paper setting out its detailed proposals.[55] There was widespread agreement that the new structure should be unitary in character: the debate was focused on how many there should be and where their boundaries were to be drawn.

The underlying thinking included a restoration of authorities which had been swept up in the earlier reorganisation – Cardiff, Swansea, Newport, and some of the traditional counties, such as Pembrokeshire, and Anglesey. To fit into a unitary structure, however, the boundaries had to be stretched somewhat, and some counties had to be amalgamated. The result was 21 authorities, ranging in population from 67,000 in Cardiganshire to 295,000 in Cardiff.

The unitary system was commended for its administrative simplicity, the traditional base for its familiarity, and the relative ease with which residents could identify 'with their own communities and localities'. The intention was to create 'good local government which is close to the communities it serves'. The White Paper continued:

> Its aims are to establish authorities which, so far as possible, are based on that strong sense of community identity that is such an important feature of Welsh life; which are clearly accessible to local people; which can, by taking full advantage of the 'enabling' role of local government, operate in an efficient and responsive way; and which will work with each other, and with other agencies, to promote the well-being of those they serve.

These desirable objectives do not all work in the same direction, of course, and the result has to be a compromise. Some of the areas are very large: Powys has over 500,000 hectares. This makes the role of the community councils important, though it is stressed that they are not to form a second tier of local government: rather they are to work in partnership with the unitary authorities 'both through an enhanced representational role and, in keeping with the enabling concept, by contributing, where practicable to service delivery'.

Development plans will be prepared by the unitary authorities for their areas, excluding any part which is in a national park. (Separate legislation establishing independent national park authorities in both Wales and England is promised.) Consultation with adjacent authorities will be a requirement in the development plan process. Additionally, since some planning functions will require areas larger than those of the new authorities, arrangements for consultation are to be introduced. The Secretary of State will have default powers to intervene if strategic issues are not being adequately addressed.

## LOCAL GOVERNMENT REORGANISATION IN SCOTLAND

In parallel with the review of local government in England and Wales, the Scottish Office issued a consultation paper in 1991 outlining the case for reform in Scotland.[56] This was followed by a further paper setting out the criteria to be used in judging options, together with illustrations of alternative structures.[57] One matter however, was not open to discussion: the Government is committed in Scotland, as in Wales, to a unitary structure.

> By giving every area of Scotland a single local authority, a single-tier system will strengthen local government. At present, except in the islands, people have two levels of local authority to represent their views. The district and the region will not always see eye to eye on all issues, and in some cases they will be controlled by different political parties. Each therefore lacks authority in claiming to speak for the population of a particular area. It also, of course, lacks authority because it lacks

responsibility for the full range of local authority services. A single-tier authority will not suffer these handicaps, and will be much better placed to build strong links with all interests in its local community.

This is a much firmer direction than that given in England, where, as we have seen, the option to retain the two-tier system has been retained. One reason for this is that the problem of conflicting interests for the Conservative Party is much less in Scotland, with only a handful of the 65 Scottish local authorities in Conservative control. The consultation documents in Scotland are also more forthright about the relationship between local government reform and the reduction in direct service provision promoted through the concept of the enabling authority. Whilst the 1992 paper confirms the Government commitment to 'a strong and effective local authority sector' it also argues that using outside contractors to deliver services means that local authorities no longer have to 'maintain a comprehensive range of expertise within their own organisation'.

In considering the possible number and size of the proposed unitary authorities, the 1992 Consultation Paper gives four illustrative maps showing structures of 15, 24, 35 and 51 authorities, but makes clear that there are other options. The choice between mainly small or mainly large authorities has important implications for the planning function, especially structure plans. Only the 15–authority option would allow for unitary authorities to prepare their own structure plans. Even here there would need to be special arrangements for Glasgow to ensure effective strategic planning. Special arrangements would be needed across the country if there were 35 or 51 authorities. The potential fragmentation of the planning function across a larger number of authorities therefore threatens a recognised strength of the Scottish system. This is acknowledged: 'It is clear that as the number of unitary authorities increases there is a greater need to apply special arrangements for strategic planning.' Among the options for dealing with this are 'advisory strategic guidance' from the central government (as with the GLC and MCC areas in England); the establishment of a central planning commission; and joint arrangements among the new local authorities. The Consultation Paper argues against the first option. A planning commission would involve the loss of democratic control. Joint arrangements would safeguard this, though it could prove cumbersome. In either case, plan preparation could be contracted out: 'this could help avoid creating unnecessary bureaucracies for such work under the new system'.

## (C) THE EUROPEAN COMMUNITY

The Council acting unanimously on a proposal from the Commission and after consulting the European Parliament and the Economic and Social Committee, shall decide what action is to be taken by the Community.

*Single European Act 1986, Title VII: Environment*

The impact of the European Community on land-use planning in Britain is becoming substantial, particularly in the field of environmental controls. The introduction of environmental impact assessment is the most striking, but there is a range of other environmental and agricultural policies which are having an effect on parts of the planning system. These are discussed in later chapters; here, a brief and more general account is given of the EC.

It seems likely that the influence of the EC, both directly and indirectly, will increase. As Rose notes:

The nature of the physical, economic, social, and environmental systems which planning seeks to influence or regulate is in a state of radical change as a result of European integration. One basic example of this is the trend towards free competition and movement within the countries of the Community.

(Rose 1992: 8)

Other examples which Rose mentions are the encouragement by the Commission of 'cross-frontier networking and joint projects as a means of fostering best practice, mental learning and innovation', and also the promotion of strategic regional planning. There has been a marked increase of interest in the experience of other planning systems.[58] Though this may have no immediate direct effect on British planning policy and practice, it will surely influence attitudes, modify perceptions, and raise new questions about long-established approaches which may benefit from a different perspective.[59]

## BRITAIN IN THE EC

Britain (or to be more precise, the UK) was not an enthusiastic supporter of the post-war moves towards a federal Europe.[60] Though it favoured intergovernmental cooperation through such bodies as the Organisation for European Economic Cooperation (1948) and the Council of Europe (1949),[61] it was opposed to the establishment of organisations which would facilitate functional cooperation alongside nation-states. It therefore did not join the European Coal and Steel Community (1952), nor was it a signatory to the 1955 Treaty of Rome which established the EEC and the European Atomic Energy Community (EURATOM). However, along with the other members of the OEEC, it formed the European Free Trade Association in 1960. Britain envisaged that EFTA would form the base for the development of stronger links with Europe. When it became clear that this was not viable, Britain applied for membership of the EC. This was opposed by France and, since membership requires the unanimous approval of existing members, negotiations broke down. The opposition continued until a political change took place in France in 1969. Renewed negotiations finally led to membership at the beginning of 1973.

The Treaty of Accession provided for transitional arrangements for the implementation of the Treaty of Rome, which Britain agreed to accept in its entirety. The objectives include the elimination of customs duties between member states and restrictions on the free movement of goods; the free movement of people, services, and capital between member states; the adoption of common agricultural and transport policies; and the approximation of the laws of member states to the extent required for the proper functioning of the common market.

There are currently 12 members of the EC: Belgium, Denmark, France, Germany, Greece, the Irish Republic, Italy, Luxembourg, the Netherlands, Portugal, Spain, and the United Kingdom.

The organisational and political structure of the EC is complex and, like all such bodies, its actual workings are somewhat different from the formal organisation chart. But, in brief, there is an elected Parliament which operates as a deliberative body, a Council of Ministers which makes policy largely on the basis of proposals made by the European Commission. There is also a Court of Justice which adjudicates matters of legal interpretation and alleged violations of Community law. There is a large number of other organisations within or related to the EC.

## The Commission

The major work of the EC is undertaken by the Commission. This executive body has responsibilities for preparing proposals for decision by the Council, and for overseeing their implementation. (Only rarely can the Council make a policy decision without a proposal from the Commission.) The Community's decision-making process 'is dominated by the search for consensus among the member states' and this gives the Commission a crucially important role in mediation and conciliation (Hadjilambrinos 1993: 287). Of the same nature is the ethos of achieving compromise and of progressing in an incremental way. There is thus no challenging bold vision to which the participants aspire: that would inevitably lead to conflict.

Among the Commission's powers is that of dealing with infringements of Community law. If it finds that an infringement has occurred, it serves a formal notice on the state concerned requiring discontinuance or comments with a specified period (usually two months). If the matter is not resolved in this way the Commission issues a *reasoned opinion*, requiring the state to comply by a given deadline. As a last resort, the Commission can refer a matter to the Court of Justice whose judgment is legally binding. Most matters are dealt with informally, but Britain has been subject to reasoned opinions on environmental matters, some of which are noted in Chapter 6.[62]

The Commission is organised in 23 Directorates-General (which, in good bureaucratic style, are referred to by their numbers rather than their names).[63] These are further divided into directorates and divisions, but the complexity varies according to the importance of their function – and hence their size.

## The European Parliament

The European Parliament is a directly elected body consisting of 518 representatives of the member states who are elected every five years. Britain has 81 representatives: 66 elected in England, eight in Scotland, four in Wales, and three in Northern Ireland. (These are known as MEPs: Members of the European Parliament.) The Parliament is consulted on all major Community decisions, and it has powers in relation to the budget which it shares with the Council. The Single European Act of 1986 increased the legislative powers of the Parliament, and the Maastricht Treaty will further extend these. In particular, despite British disagreement, the powers of the Parliament would be strengthened in relation to the Council of Ministers. These increased powers would apply to a number of areas including the environment.

Despite these moves to achieve a more democratic system of control, the Parliament is still essentially a supervisory and advisory body, rather than a legislative one (Lasok and Bridge 1991: 196). It is organised along party political (not national) lines. The political groups have their own secretariats and

are the 'prime determiners of tactics and voting patterns' (Nugent 1989: 130). Much of their work is carried out by standing committees.

## The Council of Ministers

The policy-making body of the EC is the Council of Ministers. This is composed of the senior ministers of the twelve countries – usually the foreign minister and the minister most concerned with the matters to be discussed. (When environmental matters are under discussion, the Council is known informally as the Environment Council.) It has numerous committees and working groups with various functions and membership. Thus 'while a single institution under the treaties, the Council has many forms, as it is composed of the appropriate ministers for the policy area under discussion' (Hadjilambrinos 1993: 289).

It is the Council which makes Community laws (termed *regulations*) which are binding on member states. These are 'directly binding': they require no additional implementing legislation. They are used mostly for detailed matters of a financial nature or for the technical aspects of (for example) administering the Common Agricultural Policy. By contrast, *directives* are broad statements of policy which, though equally binding, are implemented by national legislation. This leaves the method of implementation to the member states. Environmental matters are typically dealt with in this way. The Council can also issue *decisions* which are binding on the member state, organisation, firm, or individual to whom they are addressed. Finally, there are *recommendations* and *opinions*, which have no binding force.

A 1993 report from the Law Commission (for England and Wales), devoted to judicial review and statutory appeals, lays considerable emphasis on the importance of considering EC law in any law reform exercise concerning administrative law. Some Directives of the EC give rights which can be relied upon in UK legal proceedings. Moreover, 'membership of the Community gives EC law a greater role as an indicator of possible avenues of reform than other systems of law which might be considered in a comparative manner'. The Law Commission is seeking views on this interpretation of EC law. By such routes will the impact of the EC be felt.

## Court of Justice

The European Court of Justice has thirteen judges, with at least one from each member state. It decides on the legality of decisions of the Council and the Commission, and it determines violations of Treaties. Cases can be brought before it by member states, organisations of the Community, and private firms and individuals.

## The EC: A Unique Institution

The EC is an international organisation unique in the scope of its functions and in its supranational character. It has developed as a hybrid organisation which is neither federal nor intergovernmental. Hadjilambrinos writes:

> While the latter, embodied in the Council, seem to have been most influential in shaping the EC structure, the former, embodied in the European Parliament, the Commission, and the Court of Justice, continue to capture the imagination of the public, not only within the Communities but, increasingly throughout Europe. In spite of their shortcomings, the Parliament and the Commission have been able to keep the process of integration going and, in spite of periods of stagnation and disappointment, the Communities today have competencies over a wider policy area, and their importance and visibility in the lives of the citizens of the member states is continually increasing.
>
> (Hadjilambrinos 1993: 303)

## UPDATE

For a discussion of the impact of the EC on local government (and vice versa) see S. Barber and T. Millns, *Building the New Europe: The Role of Local Authorities in the UK*, London: Association of County Councils, 1993.

## NOTES

1 See, for example, Hennessy 1989; and Drewry and Butcher 1991. There is a veritable library of government reports on *The Next Steps*: some of the more important recent ones are listed in *Improving Management in Government – The Next Steps Agencies: Review 1991*, Cm 1760, HMSO, 1991.

2 Effectiveness is a difficult concept: it can mean many different things. The Conservative Government has aimed at improving service delivery, even if this entails lessened public control. See Stoker 1991.

3 A major landmark in this development is the Cabinet Office Efficiency Unit's 1988 report, and its acceptance by Mrs Thatcher: Efficiency Unit, *Improving Management in Government: The Next Steps* (Report to the Prime Minister by Kate Jenkins, Karen Caines, and Andrew Jackson), HMSO, 1988. Mrs Thatcher's acceptance of the recommendations of the report were announced in the House of Commons on 18 February 1988. Her statement is reproduced in *Improving Management in Government – The Next Steps Agencies: Review 1990*, Cm 1261, HMSO, 1990. For a general discussion of Next Steps and its antecedents, see Drewry and Butcher 1991. See also Privy Council Office, *Improving Management in Government: The Next Steps Agencies: Review 1991*, Cm 1760, HMSO, 1991.

4 A list is given in *Civil Service Year Book 1992* (August edition), HMSO, 1992, and in *The Next Steps Agencies, Review 1992*, HMSO, 1992. For discussion on the Next Steps initiative see, for example, Flynn *et al.* 1988; Fry 1988; Hennessy 1989; Jordan 1992.

5 *Civil Service Management Reform: The Next Steps* (Government reply to the Eighth Report from the Treasury and Civil Service Committee, Session 1987–88), Cm 524, HMSO, 1988.

6 *DoE Annual Report 1992*: para. 4.46.

7 House of Commons Environment Committee, First Special Report, Session 1987–88, *Historic Buildings and Ancient Monuments* (Observations on the First Report of the Committee in Session 1986–87), HC 268 (1987–88), HMSO, 1988.

8 For a discussion of reorganisation in central government (between 1960 and 1983 there were twenty-nine births of departments and thirty-four deaths) see Pollitt 1984; Chapman and Greenway 1980. The separation of transport from DoE is dealt with at length in Radcliffe 1991; see also Painter 1980a and 1980b.

9 See O'Riordan and Weale (1989) for a discussion of the background to, and the implications of, the reorganisation of pollution control. This useful paper also considers the approaches taken in other European countries.

10 For an introduction to the Department and to transport issues in Britain, see DoT, *Transport: A Guide to the Department, DoT, 1989*, available from the Department.

11 DoT, *Disability Unit Annual Report 1991* (issued by the Department).

12 The quotations and figures in this section are taken from the *Department of National Heritage Annual Report 1993*, Cm 2211, 1993.

13 The duty was first established by the Minister of Town and Country Planning Act 1943. For later changes, see Grant 1982: 40, and Switzer 1984.

14 *Chief Planning Inspector's Annual Report, April 1991 – March 1992.*

15 They are gradually being replaced by the guidance notes. A list of all these is given on pp. 321–2.

16 The aim of PPGs is 'to provide concise and practical guidance on planning policies, in a clearer and more accessible form than in departmental circulars, the earlier series of development control notes, and other statements' (William Waldegrave, then Minister for Housing and Planning, *HC Debates, Written Answers*, col. 745, 20 January 1988).

17 A full list is given in the section on official publications at the end of this book. Lloyd and Rowan-Robinson (1992) have stressed the value of the NPGs in providing a strategic planning framework for Scotland. Like other features of the Scottish planning system they enjoy a 'considerable measure of acceptability'. See also Rowan-Robinson and Lloyd 1991.

18 Exceptionally, a circular may contain policy which is legally binding. Nott and Morgan 1984 discuss Circular 2/81 as an example. More recently, the DoT's Local Authority Circular 5/92 *Traffic in London: Traffic Management and Parking Guidance* contains 'determinations' by the SoS for Transport on the manner in which London local authorities should publish certain types of parking charges, and also on the uniforms that should be worn by local authority parking attendants.

19 Lloyd and Rowan-Robinson 1992. Elected members, it seems, are much less aware of and influenced by national planning guidance. Findings of a survey of chief planning officers, commissioned by the retailer J. Sainsbury plc (Insight Social Research 1989) suggests that councillors are generally poorly informed about central guidance. 'Government advice was seen as very important in only a third of authorities. It was less important than the views of local businesses (possibly retail competitors) . . . Particularly interesting is the revelation that the opportunity to secure planning gain from retail development was seen as very important . . . two-thirds of members see this as a key influence.'

20 *Local Government Review: The Structure of Local Government in England: A Consultation Paper*, DoE, 1991.

21 See, for example, the Committee's report *London: World City Moving into the 21st Century*, HMSO, 1991.

22 London Regional Transport was established by the London Regional Transport Act 1984, to replace the Transport Executive which was formerly responsible to the GLC.

23 This complicated division of functions is the result of the Environmental Protection Act 1990, which separated responsibility for regulation from disposal, and also increased the role of the private sector through Waste Disposal Contractors. Waste regulation is to be transferred to the proposed Environment Agency. For further discussion, see Chapter 6.

24 In another paper, Young (1986b) argues that the case for metropolitan government is a thin one. His perspicacious analysis is in striking contrast to much of the political debate on the abolition of the GLC and the metropolitan county councils. But see also Healey *et al*. 1988, especially pp. 205–9

25 See, for example, Coopers & Lybrand 1984; Greater London Group 1985; Leach 1984. See also Bramley 1984 who argues that what is 'strikingly missing from all the prescriptions' is a convincing set of arguments on how large and complex local and central organisations can be made to operate effectively and efficiently. He comments that 'since inefficiency seems to be the most potent charge against local government in the present climate, this is a serious omission'. Unfortunately, the debate which Bramley wished to advance was of no interest to the Government of the day.

26 Other 'specialist units' have been created in the metropolitan counties to deal with particular issues. For example, most now have Joint Planning and Transportation Units; South Yorkshire has a 'Mining Advisory Unit'.

27 Williams *et al*. 1992. For a wider review, see Leach and Game 1991.

28 Leach 1993: 8. For reviews of strategic planning guidance, see Leach and Game 1991; Leach 1992; Leach *et al*. 1992; Kidd and Kumar 1993, and Town Planning Review 1992. The role of strategic and regional planning guidance in the planning framework is considered further in Chapter 3.

29 The change was made by the Local Government, Planning and Land Act 1980. *Organic Change in Local Government* was the title of a White Paper issued by the Labour Government in 1979.

30 See for example Labour Party 1978; and Stewart *et al*. 1978.

31 See, for example, HC Expenditure Committee, *Planning Procedures*, HC 395 (1976–77), HMSO, 1977.

32 See *Parish Councils in England: A Survey*, commissioned by DoE and undertaken by the Public Sector Management Research Centre (Aston University), 1992.

33 DoE Circular 121/77 reiterated the duty of local authorities to review parishes in their areas.

34 See the Consultation Paper *Neighbourhood Councils in England* (DoE 1974) and the Advisory Group on Neighbourhood Councils 1977.

35 *The Role of Community and Town Councils in Wales: A Consultation Paper*, Welsh Office, 1992.

36 Town and Country Planning Act 1990, Schedule 1, para. 8; Schedule 14, para. 1.

37 SDD, *Community Councils: Some Alternatives for Community Council Schemes in Scotland*, HMSO, 1974, and D.M. Hart, *A Review of Community Councils in Scotland 1983–84*, SDD, 1986.

38 Figures are from the Scottish Office *Consultation Paper on Local Government in Scotland*, 1992: 95.

39 White Paper, *Paying for Local Government*, 1986: para. 3.36.

40 There is a large literature on this. See, for example, Duncan and Goodwin 1987, Leach and Stoker 1988, and Parkinson 1989.

41 Leach and Stoker 1988: 99; Travers 1986: 80; and Loughlin 1986: chapter 2.

42 Liverpool was the notorious case: see Parkinson 1985; Ridley 1986.

43 Hambleton 1986 and 1991; Blunkett and Jackson 1987; Stoker 1991; John 1991; Leach and Game 1991; Goldsmith 1992.

44 John 1991 cites the paper by Nicholas Ridley, *The Local Right* (London: Centre for Policy Studies) as evidence of this more coherent strategy.

45 For an explanation of the Act, see Flynn and Walsh 1988, and for a review of the impact of the first round of CCT (the first contracts were started in August 1989) see Painter 1991.

46 The 1992 announcement was accompanied by a DoE paper *Extension of Compulsory Competitive Tendering* (1992). Proposals to give the Minister more extensive powers in the extension of CCT to professional services were originally put forward in the Local Government Bill 1991, but the clause was defeated in the House of Lords on 2 December 1991 because of concern about changes being made to primary legislation through regulations.

47 Cochrane argues that whilst the changes in the management and provision of local services are obvious, they have not fundamentally changed the character of service provision. This is a particularly pertinent issue for planning which, perhaps for most councils, has been the least affected of all local authority functions and where the rhetoric of both attack on, and defence of, local government has far outstripped reality. Cochrane points also to innovation in local economic development strategies, decentralisation and growing concerns for equal opportunities and 'green issues' as indications of the very active state of local government. Painter (1991: 207) reviews the first round of CCT and comes to the conclusion that 'three-quarters of contracts were retained in-house', that external contracts were concentrated in the 'Conservative-dominated shires of England and Wales', and that 'Labour controlled authorities have overwhelmingly retained services in-house'.

48 The findings of the report were leaked to the press, see for example, 'The secret services', *Municipal Journal*, 17–23 January, 1992.

49 Some local authorities have contracted out parts of the planning function, but this has been in rather limited circumstances where, for example, consultants have expertise (as in retailing) which is not available in-house. Contracting-out part of the development control service became an issue at the time of peak demand for planning permissions when there was a shortage of qualified planners, but there are very few examples. Only one authority so far has used consultants to prepare and progress a full statutory local plan through to adoption. (See Nadin and Daniels 1992; Nadin 1992; and Maitland *et al.* 1991.)

50 Audit Commission, *Performance Review in Local Government: Planning and Transportation*, 1986.

51 The percentage of applications decided in eight weeks is retained, but added to this are the relationship between that percentage and the target for householder applications, the number of appeals and their success; the number of departures from the statutory plan, the net expenditure per head on development control; the proportion of householder as against other proposals, and the percentage of the authority's population covered by a unitary or local development plan. Only this final indicator relates to plan making – a function which has received far less consideration than development control.

52 Currently, local authorities supply information to the Chartered Institute for Public Finance and Accountancy who produce summaries of actual and projected spending for each service annually. See CIPFA, annual *Statistical Information Service, Planning and Development Statistics*.

53 Department of the Environment, *Local Government Review: The Structure of Local Government in England: A Consultation Paper*, April 1991, DoE. Additional papers were published on the new council tax, and on the internal management of local authorities.

54 DoE (1992) *Policy Guidance to the Local Government Commission for England*, and *Procedure Guidance for the Local Government Commission for England*.

55 Welsh Office, *The Structure of Local Government in Wales: A Consultation Paper*, 1991; White Paper, *Local Government in Wales: A Charter for the Future*, Cm 2155, 1993.

56 Scottish Office, *The Structure of Local Government in Scotland: The Case for Change*, June 1991.

57 Scottish Office, *The Structure of Local Government in Scotland: Shaping the New Councils, A Consultation Paper*, SO, 1992.

58 See, for example, the work of H.W.E. Davies and his colleagues at the University of Reading, and the series of tape cassettes issued by the RTPI on European planning.

59 Rose (1992) outlines the scope of a research study which has been commissioned by the RTPI.

60 The best concise summary is the CoI booklet (in the *Aspects of Britain* series) *Britain and the European Community*.

61 The Council of Europe, which has 26 member states, was responsible for the European Convention on Human Rights, as well as the European Campaign for Urban Renaissance (1980–82). The latter led to a programme of *ad hoc* conferences, various reports and 'resolutions' on such matters as health in towns, the regeneration of industrial towns, and community development. These were addressed to European municipalities, and were sponsored by the Council's Standing Conference of Local and Regional Authorities of Europe (CLRAE). In 1992, the Conference adopted *The European Urban Charter*. This 'draws together into a single composite text, a series of principles on good urban management at local level'. The 'principles' relate to a wide range of issues, including transport and mobility, environment and nature in towns, the physical form of cities, and urban security and crime prevention.

62 Haigh (1990), gives several other examples of a 'reasoned opinion' being issued against Britain. See, for instance, the case of the Directive on the disposal of PCBs (p. 153), and that on the disposal of waste oils (p. 160).

63 For example DG VI, Agriculture; DG VII, Transport; DG XI, Environment, Consumer Protection and Nuclear Safety; and DG XVI, Regional Policies.

# 3

# THE PLANNING FRAMEWORK

We are, I think, entering a new planning era . . . After a period of some uncertainty, we see planning emerging in a new light, and with a subtly changed role.

Sir George Young 1992[1]

My own view is that the 'new system' of plans is essentially a side show, a new and ill-thought out set of procedures derived from a way of thinking which wishes to devolve as much of the work of plan-making to the lowest tier of government, while keeping hold of the possibility of central control of content and procedures.

Healey (1990b: 34)

The British planning system is, in one sense, embodied in a huge library of statutes, rules, regulations, directions, policy statements, circulars, and such like. Much of this chapter discusses the more significant matters to be found in these documents. It is, however, important to appreciate that the formal system is one thing: how matters work in practice may be very different. The 'informal' planning system operates within the formal structure. It may continue with little modification even when major legislative changes are made; alternatively, there may be significant changes in practice within a stable formal system. Political forces, professional attitudes, and management styles will all affect the ways in which the system operates.[2]

It is also necessary to note that much 'development' (in the everyday, rather than the legal, sense of that word) takes place, without any help or hindrance from the planning system. Even where the development is clearly related to some action within the statutory framework for planning, typically through the granting of permission to undertake the development, the actual outcome is affected by 'extraneous' factors, and it may not be at all clear what effect planning has had on the outcome. The question of whether the same development would have taken place in the same way is equally problematic.[3]

Nevertheless, the framework for planning policy, and the procedures which are followed in its design and operation, provide important starting points for an understanding of the way in which the system works. It is the current Government policy to bring much more of the informal operation of planning and development within the statutory planning framework. The emphasis is on plan-led development control. This is intended to reduce the amount of *ad hoc* planning control, and thus provide a firmer foundation for the resolution of conflicts and investment decisions. Plans are seen as providing a more efficient means of conflict mediation than decision-making on a project-by-project basis, as well as a measure of certainty and coordination for the promotion of investment (Healey 1990b). There had been considerable lobbying for this from a range of interests, including developers, conservationists, investors, and Conservative Party supporters (Nadin and Doak 1991).

The principal instrument in the reorientation of the planning system is the 1991 Planning and Compensation Act which, with the shift to a plan-led system, is heralded as a watershed in the history of town and country planning. The intention is to replace the current patchwork of planning policies with a comprehensive and systematic hierarchy of development plan policies. Within a framework of regional guidance and updated, slimmer county plans guidance, there will be complete cover of detailed local development plans. It is envisaged that, once these plans are in place, they will be a more important factor than their predecessors in land-use decision-making.

The first of the quotations at the head of this chapter suggests that expectations are high. The second reflects some scepticism about any major shift in emphasis or impact. As we shall see, the fundamental principles of the system remain intact, and recent changes, whilst superficially significant, may have little effect on the patterns of land use and protection, or on who gains and loses from it. Plans may be more significant – and there is certainly a high level of activity in plan-making – but it is too soon to assess what changes, if any, may come about. For planners who experienced the introduction of the 1947 or the 1968 changes, there must be a sense of *déjà vu*. Many of the questions of those times bear a marked resemblance to the current debate:

– What framework will ensure the accountability of decision-makers and safeguard the interests of those affected by planning, yet be expeditious and efficient in operation?
– How can the framework provide a measure of certainty and commitment yet allow for flexibility to cope with changing circumstances, local conditions, and new opportunities?
– What objectives should plans pursue, and how will these shape their form and content?
– Who should have influence in the planning process and what should be the respective roles of central and local government and of local communities?

These perplexing questions have no easy answer: indeed, by their nature, they have to be addressed constantly. An acceptable answer rarely has stability since conditions and attitudes change over time.

## FROM ZONING TO PLANNING

The main instrument of land-use control in Britain during the first half of this century was the planning scheme.[4] This was, in effect, development control by zoning. The zones shown in planning schemes indicated the development which would be permitted. The scheme document and maps showed where land was zoned for industry, for open space, for residential development at no more than eight houses to the acre, and so on. Under the 1932 Act, planning schemes had to be approved by the Minister and by resolution of both Houses of Parliament. This was a very time-consuming process, but it gave schemes the force of law and, with it, the advantage of absolute certainty about what development would be permitted. But therein lay one of its gravest shortcomings: certainty for the developer meant inflexibility for the local authority.

One way of circumventing this was for planning authorities to take advantage of the lengthy and cumbersome procedure for preparing and obtaining approval to their schemes by remaining at the draft stage for as long as possible. Yet this had the opposite danger: the flexibility thereby attained could easily become mere expediency. This was an early example of an informal system which local authorities had to devise to circumvent the rigidities of the statutory system: planning flexibility was thus obtained at the sacrifice of accountability.

Whilst zoning flourished as the dominant form of planning in most of the rest of the world, Britain introduced in 1947 a system which is markedly different, and which attempts to strike a distinctive balance between flexibility and commitment.[5]

## DEVELOPMENT PLANS: 1947 STYLE

The approach adopted in Britain, which is in many important ways the same in the 1990s as it was in the 1950s, is fundamentally a discretionary one in which decisions on particular development proposals are made 'on their merits' against the policy background of a generalised plan. The 1947 Act defined a development plan as 'a plan indicating the manner in which a local planning authority propose that land in their area should be used'. It was intended to show, for example, 'the direction in which a city will expand; the area to be preserved as an agricultural green belt, and the area to be allocated to industry and to housing'.[6]

Unlike the pre-war operative scheme, the development plan did not of itself imply that permission would be granted for particular developments even if they appeared to be in harmony with the plan. Though a developer was able to find out from the plan where particular uses were likely to be permitted, his specific proposals had to be considered by the local planning authority. When considering applications, the authority was expressly directed to 'have regard to the provisions of the development plan', but the plan was not binding and, indeed, authorities were instructed to have regard not only to the development plan but also to 'any other material considerations'. Furthermore, in granting permission to develop, local authorities could impose 'such conditions as they think fit'.

However, though the local planning authorities had considerable latitude in deciding whether to approve applications, they had to be clear on the planning objectives for their areas; otherwise they had no adequate basis on which they could judge the merits and shortcomings of particular applications. This was the essential purpose of the development plan.

The development plan consisted of a report of survey, providing background to the plan but having no statutory effect; a written statement, providing a short summary of the main proposals but no explanation or argument to support them; and detailed maps at various scales depending on the type of authority. The maps indicated development proposals for a twenty-year period and the intended pattern of land use, together with a programme of the stages by which the proposed development would

be realised. The plans were approved by the Minister (with or without modifications) following a local public inquiry. Initially, a three-year target was set for submission of the plans, but only 22 authorities met this, and it was not until the early 1960s that they were all approved. By this time, the requirement to review plans on a five-yearly cycle had brought forward amendments, many taking the form of more detailed plans for particular areas. These had to follow the same process of inquiry and ministerial approval as the original plans. But the whole process of approval and review moved forward slowly, and many authorities were still engaged on the first review in the mid-1960s, reflecting the difficulties encountered in preparing plans quickly and processing them through the formal procedure.

Furthermore, although the system of development control guided by development plans operated fairly well for two decades without significant change, 1947-style plans did not prove flexible in the face of the very different conditions of the 1960s. The statutory requirement for determining and mapping land use led inexorably towards greater detail and precision. Increasingly, the system became out of tune with contemporary needs and forward thinking, and was bogged down in details and cumbersome procedures. The quality of planning suffered, and delays were beginning to bring the system into disrepute. As a result, public acceptability, which is the basic foundation of any planning system, was beginning to crumble.

It was within this context that the Planning Advisory Group (PAG) was set up in May 1964 to review the broad structure of the planning system and, in particular, development plans. In its report, published in 1965, PAG concluded that plans had 'acquired the appearance of certainty and stability which is misleading since the primary use zonings may themselves permit a wide variety of use within a particular allocation, and it is impossible to forecast every land requirement over many years ahead'.[7] Above all:

> It has proved extremely difficult to keep these plans not only up to date but forward looking and responsive to the demands of change. The result has been that they

have tended to become out of date — in terms of technique in that they deal inadequately with transport and the interrelationship of traffic and land use; in factual terms in that they fail to take account quickly enough of changes in population forecasts, traffic growth and other economic and social trends; and in terms of policy in that they do not reflect more recent developments in the field of regional and urban planning. Over the years the plans have become more and more out of touch with emergent planning problems and policies, and have in many cases become no more than local land-use maps.

The report proposed a further fundamental change to the planning system, one which would distinguish between strategic issues and detailed tactical issues. Only the former would be submitted for ministerial approval: the latter would be for local decisions within the framework of the approved policy. Following a White Paper published in 1967,[8] legislative effect to the PAG proposals was given by the Town and Country Planning Acts of 1968 (for England and Wales) and 1969 (for Scotland).

## DEVELOPMENT PLANS: 1968 STYLE

The essential features of the 1968 system are still in place today, though there have been numerous incremental changes and, in 1991, a more thorough revision.

Structure plans provide the strategic tier of the development plan and are prepared by the county planning authorities and the two national park boards in England and Wales, and by the regional or general planning authorities in Scotland. Until 1992, they had to be submitted to the Secretary of State for approval. They consist of a written statement and key diagram (not a map) setting out the broad land-use policies (but not detailed land allocations) for the area, measures for the improvement of the physical environment and policies for the management of traffic. Accompanying these is an explanatory memorandum in which the authority summarises the reasons which 'justify each and every policy and general proposal formulated in the plan, stating the relationship thereof to expected development and other use of land in neighbouring areas where

relevant'. The other notable feature of the structure plan system is the method of dealing with outstanding objections — the examination-in-public. This is a 'probing discussion' concerned with the major policies of the plan, and participation is by invitation only. This is discussed further in the final chapter.

The DoE's view of the functions of the structure plan has been fairly consistent over the years, but the scope of the structure plan has been narrowed considerably since the early years. The functions, as now set out in PPG 12, are to:

— provide the strategic policy framework for planning and development control locally;
— ensure that the provision for development is realistic and consistent with national and regional policy; and
— secure consistency between local plans for neighbouring areas.

Because of the different administrative structure and larger planning areas in Scotland, there is a slightly different emphasis in the functions of structure plans (PAN 37: 7):

— to indicate policies and proposals concerning the scale and general location of new development;
— to provide a regional policy framework for accommodating development.

The policies relating to the form, function, content and procedure of structure plans have evolved since they were first introduced: they now consistently emphasise their use as a strategic land-use planning instrument. The key diagram reinforces the strategic element, thus avoiding the identification of particular parcels of land. This limits debate to the general questions of strategic location rather than the use of specific sites. The overall land-use policies can thus be determined before detailed land-use allocations are made, albeit not always to the liking of those affected by later more detailed plans.

Local plans provide detailed guidance on land use. They consist of a written statement, a proposals map and other appropriate illustrations. The written statement sets out the policies for the control of development, including the allocation of land for specific purposes, measures for the improvement of the physical environment, and the management of traffic. The proposals map must be on an ordnance survey base, thus showing the effects of the plan on specific sites.

Under the 1968 system, there were three types of local plan: general plans, referred to as 'district plans' before 1982, action area plans, and subject plans. General local plans were prepared 'where the strategic policies in the structure plan need to be developed in more detail'.[9] Unlike the structure plan, which was prepared by all authorities for the whole of their area, local authorities were advised that local plans would not be needed in all areas – for example, where there was little pressure for development and no need to stimulate growth. This discretion was used: a small number of authorities prepared a single plan for the whole area, others prepared one or more plans for parts of their area, while some prepared none at all.

An action area local plan dealt with an area 'intended for comprehensive development, redevelopment or improvement by public authorities or private enterprise, and where the implementation is to be given priority over a comparatively short period of time'. Action areas replaced the comprehensive development areas (CDAs) of the 1947 legislation. Subject plans, as their name suggests, dealt with specific planning issues over an extensive area. Minerals and green belt local plans were numerous, but there were less common ones such as Humberside County Council's 'Coastal Camping and Caravans Local Plan', and its 'Intensive Livestock Units Local Plan'.

Under the 1991 Act, local authorities are required to prepare plans *for the whole of their areas*. However, many existing local plans will remain in force for some time to come. (Indeed, in some parts of the country, the pre-1968 development plan was still formally the operative plan in the early 1990s.)

Local plans do not require to be approved by the Secretary of State (although there are rarely used powers to call in plans and to require modifications). The original rationale for this was that a local plan would be prepared within the framework of a structure plan; and since structure plans would be approved by the Secretary of State, local authorities could safely be left to the detailed elaboration of local plans. This

went to the very kernel of the philosophy underlying the new legislation, namely that the central government should be concerned only with strategic issues, and that local matters should be the clear responsibility of local authorities.

This division of plan-making functions was predicated on the reorganisation of local government into unitary authorities, with a single authority being responsible for preparing both a broad strategic plan and any necessary detailed plans. Since the same authority was to be responsible for both plans, there was no need to make legislative provision to ensure that a local plan did in fact 'conform generally', or even to spell out what this meant. The Secretary of State, having approved the structure plan, could safely leave the detailed elaboration of its policies at the local level to the (same) local authority *without the necessity of further approval.*

The reorganisation of local government initiated by the Conservative Government was very different from that envisaged in the 1968 Planning Act. The 1972 Local Government Act established two main types of local authority in England and Wales, and divided planning functions between them. Thus, while counties were made responsible for broad planning strategy (structure planning), districts were independently responsible for local planning (and most matters of planning control). Clearly, once the responsibility for local plans was allocated to a different authority, the institutional (and political) link between the two levels of planning was in jeopardy. Counties and districts are independent political entities which may have very different ideas on the way in which the general policies in a structure plan are to be put into practice. Furthermore, there is an inevitable temptation for counties to formulate their 'policy and general proposals' in greater detail than would be the case if there were no division of functions. In this way, they may assume greater control over the implementation of policy.

The division of responsibilities has indeed given rise to considerable conflict which was compounded by the delays in the preparation of structure plans. This was in spite of the attempt to avoid the difficulties through a series of complex statutory provisions for defining the respective roles of the two types of authority.

Two devices were 'designed to promote effective co-operation in the planning field and to minimise delay, dispute and duplication' – the development plan scheme and the certificate of conformity. Following consultations between the county and its constituent districts, the development plan scheme had to be agreed (and submitted to the Secretary of State) setting out the allocation of responsibility and the programme for the preparation and amendment of local plans. The development plan scheme was replaced in 1986 with the more comprehensive local plan schemes. With the introduction of a mandatory requirement to produce district-wide local plans such schemes have been made redundant.[10] However, the 1986 Act introduced the need for local authorities to keep a register of development plan policies and the new regulations require a similar index of information in respect of the development plan.[11]

The other device designed to ensure compatibility between the structure plan and local plans was the certificate of conformity. After initial consultation and before deposit of the proposed plan, it was a requirement for the county council to issue, within one month, a certificate indicating that the plan conformed generally with the provisions of the approved structure plan. In most cases, certificates have been issued with little public debate, but there have been a number of cases where the Secretary of State was asked to intervene. In some cases disputes over conformity have given rise to delays in the adoption of local plans and demonstrate the difficulty of making a distinction between county strategy and district tactics. Again the 1991 Act has amended the provision for certification and now the county must issue a certificate of either conformity or non-conformity within 28 days, and in the latter case take the issue forward as an objection to the plan.

The procedure for the approval and adoption of local plans also contains other safeguards to allow for public consultation and objection, and to ensure that authorities exercise their freedom to adopt plans with responsibility. These are discussed in a later section on statutory procedures (see pp. 65–7).

## THE CONTENT OF PLANS

Another major shift in planning philosophy embraced by the 1968 Act was in the scope and content of plans although, as will be seen, this had only limited practical consequences. The 1947 legislation was largely concerned with land use: 'a development plan means a plan indicating the manner in which a local planning authority propose that land in their area should be used'. The survey required as a preliminary to this dealt predominantly with physical matters. Under the 1968 legislation, on the other hand, emphasis was laid on major economic and social forces and on broad policies or strategies for large areas. In formulating the structure plan, particular attention was to be paid 'to current policies with respect to the economic planning and development of the region as a whole' and to the likely availability of resources. It was held that land-use planning could not be undertaken satisfactorily in isolation from the social and economic objectives which it served. Thus the plans were to encompass such matters as the distribution of population and employment, housing, education and leisure.

Since 1968, there has been a major shift in central government policy regarding the scope of structure plans. Increasingly, the central department has stressed that structure plans should deal only with specific land-use problems, not with broad social objectives. This radical departure from the ideas of 1968, and the contraction of the scope of structure plans, has been widely documented.[12] Solesbury explains how both central government and local authorities found it difficult to give expression in structure plans to policies which were the responsibility of other agencies. The result was

> to narrow the range of structure plans to what are more clearly land use policies and to present other, related, non-land use policies – for example, on public transport fares, pollution control, or housing allocation – as part of the supporting reasoned justification.
>
> (Solesbury 1983: 14)

From 1982, 'reasoned justification' ceased to have statutory status, thus downgrading such policies even further. Central government also intervened to significantly restrict plan content. Thornley (1991: 124) provides a useful summary of what he describes as the 'attack on structure plans'. In the 1980 Manchester Structure Plan, for example, the Secretary of State 'deleted more than 40% of the policies, and a further 20% were substantially modified'. Thornley argues that such actions reflected the Government's intention to allow market forces to operate at the cost of social and other wider objectives. Amos (1987: 22) contended that, as a result, structure plans 'tended to be too generalised to give the clear concise guidance which is necessary. Yet at the same time their scope was too limited to provide an adequate and coherent account of government policies for their area.' The centralisation of policy-making has continued into the 1990s but, as structure plans no longer require central approval, LPAs will have more freedom, though they have been warned not to adopt policies which conflict with national guidance.[13] Departmental advice about plan content has thus become increasingly specific and restrictive. However, towards the end of the 1980s, some softening of attitude was detectable.[14]

More emphasis is now given to the need for greater integration of land use and transport, and to the environmental implications of both. Proposals for transport infrastructure, set out in the annual Transport Policies and Programmes, should be derived from structure and local plans. Moreover, from 1992, structure plans should include proposals for major road schemes, and these will be subject to consideration in the examination in public.[15] Environmental issues are now to figure prominently in plans: 'The challenge is to ensure that newer environmental concerns, such as global warming and the consumption of non-renewable resources, are also reflected in the analysis of policies that forms part of plan preparation' (PPG 12: para. 6.3). Development plans should pay particular attention to development impacts which may be irreversible, as well as to the need to reduce the level of car journeys and the distances driven. PPG 12 stresses the value of environmental appraisal: a process of identifying, quantifying, weighing up and reporting on the environmental and other costs and benefits of plan proposals.

Local plans are not subject to the formal constraints of central government but, in practice, they reflect them. From her extensive study of development plans, Healey (1983: 189) points out that whilst local plans have embraced wide-ranging social and economic objectives, their proposals nevertheless are 'primarily about land allocation'. Moreover, whilst local plans vary substantially in form, and 'appear local in orientation and specific to particular areas and issues', there is considerable consistency in scope and content.

It is interesting to inquire why local plans conform so consistently with central advice. Healey (1983: 208) discusses three reasons for this. First, it is important to recognise that what binds the local plan to central government policy is the need for central support when local plan policies are challenged at appeal, or when they are used to coordinate or attract investment, including central government funding. Second, although the form of plans has changed, the powers to implement them have remained the same. Third, the attitudes and values of planners themselves are important moderating influences: whilst UK planners espouse wider social and economic goals, their professional culture and training is rooted in land use and physical concerns.

> The 1968 Act claimed to introduce more concern with social and economic policies into planning policies, and the reorganisation of local government further fragmented the planning system. Yet the results in terms of land use policies do not look very different. The important point here is that while the economic climate and the format of plans have changed, the powers to implement planning policies are substantially the same as those available from the early 1950s onwards.

The forces for consistency are now growing stronger. Central government has stressed that it will uphold statutory planning policies on appeal. It is also giving more thorough scrutiny to draft plans to ensure that they are in conformity with national and regional guidance. Finally, there are four ways in which the Secretary of State can intervene:

1 At the pre-deposit stage, the SoS is one of the prescribed consultees.
2 At the deposit stage, the SoS has the right to object.

3 A direction to modify a plan can be issued.
4 A plan can be called in.

These are, of course, reserve powers, and it is hoped that 'any disagreements could be resolved as early as possible in the plan preparation process' (PPG 12: 4.17).

## EVALUATION OF THE 1968 DEVELOPMENT PLANS

There has probably never been a time when development plans, of whatever vintage, did not have their critics – and some of the criticisms have never changed. Three quotations taken at random are illustrative. In 1976, the RTPI lamented the 'apparent inability of the system to reach durable plans that work'.[16] In 1979, Edison argued that 'the present structure planning system is inflexible . . . it cannot adapt to the quick reversal of a strategy found to be unsuccessful . . . it militates against [local planning] initiatives and seems operationally unsuitable' (quoted in Bruton 1980a). In 1985, the County Planning Officers' Society succinctly noted that 'the machinery for planning is too slow'. It would not be difficult to find an apt quote from every year that the post-war planning system has been in operation. A decade after the start of the new system, Bruton (1980a: 135) summarised the problems as 'delay and lack of flexibility; an over-concentration on detail; [and] ambiguity in regard to wider policy issues'. As we shall see, the criticisms voiced by government in the second half of the decade were much the same.

Plans have certainly been very slow in coming forward to statutory approval and adoption. By 1977, only seven of the necessary 89 structure plans had been approved and seventeen submitted.[17] By 1980, the numbers had improved: of 79 English structure plans which were expected, 64 had been submitted and 38 approved. The first structure plan cycle took fourteen years to complete: over the years 1981 to 1985 the time taken from the submission of structure plans to their final approval averaged 28 months in England and 17 months in Scotland. One of the main

reasons for this long delay was that many of the written statements and explanatory memoranda were very lengthy: in the first round, several contained more than 100,000 words. They also contained too many policies – typically more than a hundred, many of which the DoE considered to be irrelevant to structure plans: 'building design standards, storage of cycles, the costs of waste collection, the development of cooperatives, racial or sexual disadvantage, standards of highway maintenance, parking charges, the location of picnic sites and so-called nuclear-free zones'.

The disputes and delays over structure plan approval also held back the adoption of local plans where only a very slow start was made in the first ten years of the new system; indeed, the first local plan was not adopted until 1975 (Williams 1978). However, the rate of deposit and adoption increased sharply after the initial round of structure plans was mostly completed and, by March 1987, 495 local plans had been adopted in England and Wales.[18] (Progress in Scotland, where there has been a mandatory requirement to produce local plans, is discussed on pp. 59–62.) Unfortunately, many of the plans were out of date by the time their processing was complete. This is not surprising when it is noted that the average time taken to prepare and adopt a local plan was about five years.[19]

It was against this background that the popularity of non-statutory planning (or 'informal policy') has to be viewed. The terms relate to policy documents which are prepared and used by a LPA for development control but which have not been processed through the full statutory procedures. The studies of Bruton and Nicholson (1983, 1984, 1985) estimated that non-statutory policy documents outnumbered statutory plans by about ten to one. This non-statutory policy took many forms, from single issue or area policy notes to comprehensive but informal plans. Some informal policy may have been subject to public consultation, and indeed have progressed through some stages of the statutory procedure, and some will have been prepared solely within the authority or department with no intention of being made public. Central government has increasingly pressed for the elimination of non-statutory policy, except where it might be legitimately described as supplementary planning guidance (SPG), intended to assist applicants.[20]

The challenge of Great Portland Estates to the Westminster City Council's use of non-statutory documents for development control,[21] led to some debate about whether development-control decisions must be based on statutory documents. However, if plans are to avoid excessive detail, SPG is essential, and central guidance supports its use, particularly 'when it has been the subject of public consultation and a council resolution' (PPG 12: 3.19). But a distinction is drawn between SPG and 'bottom drawer' plans and policies which have not been subject to proper procedures. These are 'unsatisfactory and incompatible with the 1991 Act'.

The attitude of central government to this issue has been vacillating and confusing. Though some statements indicate that statutory plans are clearly to be preferred, this has been contradicted elsewhere. The matter peaked in 1985 when the White Paper, *Lifting the Burden*, denigrated both structure and local plans:

> Inevitably plans become out-of-date and tend to lag behind current needs and conditions. In particular, the twin priorities of generating jobs and providing sufficient land for housing have not been reflected fully or quickly enough in structure plans and the planning decisions of local authorities. The new circular [14/85] . . . accordingly makes it clear that development plans are one, but only one, of the material considerations that must be taken into account in dealing with planning applications. It is also important that development plans should concentrate on the essential elements and the key planning issues, be well related to current trends in the economy and the factors that influence market demand, and be capable of rapid revision to meet changing circumstances. There is cause for concern that this process of plan review and up-dating is becoming too slow and cumbersome.

This call for more flexibility was somewhat at odds with previous advice which had sought to reduce administrative discretion in the system by a planning framework which offered more certainty, clarity, and consistency to private sector investors (Healey 1986a).

This attitude was not to last, even though there was a considerable support for the Government's negative attitude. Overall, the experience with structure plans had been disappointing, and there was at this time growing confusion about their role. Certainly, they had not lived up to the expectations of the PAG report. Grant provided a reasoned assessment:

> The reality of structure planning has failed to match the early rhetoric. The plans have achieved some coordination of public sector policy but have not provided the firm lead that had been promised. Attempts to advance the role of the structure plan as an overall corporate, or even semi-corporate plan, have failed because of the different planning timescales for different public sector activities, and particularly the uncertainty in recent years of long term investment planning . . . On the merit side, the introduction of structure planning has at least initiated a serious examination of planning strategy in county areas, and has provided the first opportunity for any comprehensive review and public debate that has been enjoyed in some counties for many years. This is no insignificant achievement. It has prompted a re-examination of received assumptions and a reformulation of policies.
>
> (Grant 1982: 115)

The uncertainties and complications of structure planning in practice carried over to local planning and contributed, in some areas, to a professional culture that was at best indifferent to statutory plans.[22] There were more positive attitudes in other areas. Where the stakes being played for in development control applications were high, as in London and counties such as Hertfordshire (where full statutory plan cover was completed during the 1980s), statutory plan-making was pursued with enthusiasm. Also, despite very turbulent economic conditions, the plans proved to be reasonably robust and certainly effective in implementing policy and defending council decisions at appeal.

Research carried out during the 1980s produced useful findings about the operation of development plans. One important study examined a series of plans in the South-East, the West Midlands and Greater Manchester.[23] This concluded that plans had proved to be effective in guiding and supporting decisions, and in providing a framework for the protection of land. They were particularly useful in shaping private sector decisions, especially in the urban fringe. Conversely, the difficulty encountered in controlling public sector investment in housing, economic development, inner-city policy and infrastructure provision, was shown to be an impediment to effective implementation of strategy. The research team argued that this criticism was not one that plans alone could address. In similar vein, Carter, Brown and Abbott (1991) highlighted the 'considerable confusion' about the relationship between development plans and expenditure-based plans, such as HIPs and TPPs.

Another significant project on the role of the planning framework in the 1980s was undertaken by Lyn Davies and colleagues at the University of Reading.[24] This focused on the relationship between development plans, development control and appeals. It is discussed in detail in the next chapter, but here it is interesting to note that their general conclusions have been prophetic of the way the system has been modified over recent years. They concluded that plans might play only a small part in guiding development control decisions overall, but were much more important when a case went to appeal – what they termed the 'pinch points' of the system. They suggested that this reflected the system's chief virtue: its ability to enable a sensitive response to local conditions. It was recommended (Davies *et al.* 1986a: 83) that the Department should encourage local authorities to provide better written policy cover; to reduce its complexity by incorporating as much as possible in statutory plans; and to facilitate more speedy adoption.

Further support has been lent to these arguments by subsequent research (Rydin *et al.* 1990, Collins and McConnell 1988). Together, these studies argued for recognition of the value of plans and for a stronger development plan framework, but also for flexibility for local variation in form and content.

## PLANNING IN LONDON AND THE METROPOLITAN COUNTIES SINCE 1985

The Thatcher Government's precipitate decision to abolish the GLC and the MCCs forced hasty action about the planning system in these areas. This was simple in the extreme: London boroughs and the metropolitan districts became 'unitary' planning authorities. Thus, in precisely those parts of the country where there is a particular need for a two-tier planning system, it was lost.

Initially, the Government proposed that the borough and district authorities should have responsibility for both structure and local plans, but later it was decided that this would be too cumbersome. Instead, a new 'unitary' development plan was proposed, together with a joint planning committee for Greater London (a role which was undertaken by the London Planning Advisory Committee). Legislative effect was given to this in the Local Government Act 1985. The intention was that, after consultations, the Secretary of State would provide strategic guidance to assist in the preparation of the unitary development plans.[25]

Little advice was given to the districts about their input to the development of strategic guidance except that it was to be produced on a cooperative and voluntary basis by the districts themselves.[26]

Unitary development plans (UDPs) are in two parts, as explained in PPG 12:

> Part I is analogous to the structure plan in non-metropolitan areas. It consists of a written statement of the authority's general policies for the development and use of land in their area. The broad development and land-use strategy of Part I provides a framework for the authority's detailed proposals in Part II, which is analogous to the local plan in non-metropolitan areas. Part II contains a written statement of the authority's proposals for the development and use of land; a map showing these proposals on an Ordnance Survey base; and a reasoned justification of the general policies in Part II of the plan. The proposals in Part II of a plan must be in general conformity with the policies in Part I.

Advice has made it clear that the plans will be prepared simultaneously, that they should be presented as one document, and that they should have a ten-year horizon. Furthermore, a UDP is 'adopted' by the district council, and is not subject to the approval of the Secretary of State (although reserve powers of central intervention have been maintained). This means that the UDP is adopted through the local plan process, including a public local inquiry. Whilst a UDP is being prepared, any existing plans which were in force on 1 April 1986 are to be treated as 'the development plan'.

There was a good deal of initial scepticism about these new arrangements, though they are more closely allied to the 1965 thinking of PAG than the system that was then put into place. There were particular concerns about the future of strategic thinking in the metropolitan areas, difficulties of cooperation between districts, and the problems of participation and coping with the statutory right to objection in plans which embrace such large areas (Nadin and Wood 1988). For the districts themselves, many of these worries have proved unfounded. It has been possible to accommodate policy and political differences between districts on topics, but this has been very much on a 'lowest common denominator' level (Hill 1991; Williams *et al.* 1992). It has also proved possible, perhaps even desirable, to produce the strategy and detail concurrently within the districts themselves. However, there remain serious concerns about the extent to which the public, interest groups, and even some professionals can engage effectively in such a complex process.

## THE FUTURE OF DEVELOPMENT PLANS

As early as 1977, proposals were being made for a review of the 1968 system but, at this time, review was considered premature since only 24 structure plans had been submitted, and only seven of these had been approved.[27] By 1985, prompted by the concern for 'freeing' enterprise from unnecessary restraints, a package of new measures (entitled *Lifting the Burden*) included an announcement that the Government was 'giving further consideration to whether there should be changes in the content and procedures of development plans and in the relationship between development plans and development control'. The following year a Consultation Paper was published on possible changes to simplify and improve the development plan system. The analysis this provided of the

weaknesses of the current system was decidedly thin, though it did make reference to the research mentioned above. The paper proposed, *inter alia*, the abolition of structure plans in England and Wales (but not in Scotland where they had 'not in general given rise to the same problems as have been experienced south of the Border'); a wider coverage of regional and sub-regional planning guidance to be issued by the Secretary of State after consultations and public comment; the introduction of 'statements of county planning policies' on a limited range of issues (to be specified by the Secretary of State) which would not form part of the statutory development plan; and new-style single-tier district development plans covering the whole of each district.

The context for preparation and discussion of these proposals centred on the growing dissatisfaction of many different interests about the operation of the planning system and, in particular, the making of many *ad hoc* and apparently inconsistent decisions by both the Secretary of State and local authorities. The lobby for change created some unusual bedfellows encompassing both development and conservation lobbies. Both were looking for more certainty in the system and a reduction in the growing number of speculative applications – the former because of the increased level of speculation and risk, the latter because of the erosion of important environments. There was also some dissatisfaction amongst Government supporters about decisions taken centrally which went against local (often Conservative) opinion. Local authorities were concerned that more of their decisions were being overruled, and complained at the lack of clarity in central policy. By comparison, matters looked better in Scotland and in the emerging, although as yet untried, system in the metropolitan counties.

There were nearly 500 responses to the Consultation Paper, some of which argued very strongly against the proposed abolition of structure plans and their replacement by unitary plans. However, progress on introducing the new system was slow, partly because of the usual difficulty of finding parliamentary time for new legislation. Other measures had priority: water privatisation, the community charge scheme (the 'poll tax'), and a new housing bill. However, in November 1988, PPG 12 was published urging local authorities to extend statutory plan coverage, normally by district-wide plans, and to replace non-statutory policy which it described as 'insufficient and weak'. Strategic green-belt boundaries were singled out as requiring further specification in detailed local plans. In return, the Government offered an enhanced status for plans.

Early in 1989, the White Paper *The Future of Development Plans* was published: this contained a set of proposals very similar to those which had been circulated earlier. The only difference in the plan framework was the addition of a mandatory provision for all counties to prepare minerals development plans. However, PPG 15, published in 1990, urged county councils to press ahead with the revision and updating of structure plans and to cooperate on the elaboration of regional guidance. It seemed at the time that the considerable lobbying by major pressure groups had been successful in bringing about a reprieve for structure plans.

The main purpose of PPG 15 was to encourage some simplification of structure plans, but it also marked a change in the Government's attitude to regional guidance, which was now fully accepted. The counties were encouraged to review their structure plans and to take them forward to 2006, with the promise that the delays after submission would be reduced. The counties, for their part, were to ensure that plans were less bulky and concentrated on strategic issues.

Concerted lobbying from virtually all sides of the planning debate, perhaps assisted by further changes in ministerial responsibilities at the DoE, were to have some further success later that year. Chris Patten's short tour of duty at the DoE will now be remembered for his announcement of the intention to retain a statutory strategic tier of development plan, and 'to end the requirement that the Secretary of State must himself approve all structure plans and alterations to them'.[28] Shortly afterwards, the Planning and Compensation Bill was published incorporating the necessary legislative changes. The bill, steered through Parliament by Michael Heseltine (returning to a post he held in the early years of the administration), had a difficult passage, although the provisions relating to the planning framework were widely welcomed. Indeed, in response to pressure from the Opposition and its own backbenchers, provisions were added to further increase the status of the statutory plans in development control.

## DEVELOPMENT PLANS SINCE 1992

The Planning and Compensation Act 1991 came hard on the heels of the Town and Country Planning Act 1990 which consolidated the law in England and Wales. (The Scots will be luckier in that their consolidating legislation will incorporate the changes made by the 1991 Act.) There were four significant changes made to the planning framework by the Act.[29]

The first, brought about by an Opposition amendment accepted by the Government in the last stages of the bill, was to make the plan the primary consideration in development control. In commending the amendment, Sir George Young coined a phrase in saying that 'the approach shall leave no doubt about the importance of the plan-led system'. This shift in the relationship between plans and control, enacted by the insertion of Section 54A into the 1990 Act (and insertion of Section 18A into the 1972 Act in Scotland) could have potentially far-reaching implications for the nature of the planning system, but it is too soon to be at all sure about this. (Some of the implications for the preparation of plans are discussed below; the relationship with development control is dealt with in Chapter 4.)

The second change, forecast long before the bill was published, was to make the adoption of district-wide local plans mandatory, although allowing for the completion of part-area plans where they were already past deposit stage. The third major change was to abolish the requirement for central approval of structure plans. Central government has retained its powers of intervention, and the examination in public is still to be used to debate the plan after deposit.

Finally, the Act introduced a mandatory requirement for counties to produce minerals plans and waste plans for the whole of their areas. (In Wales, the responsibility for minerals and waste has been allocated to the districts.) There will be no further small area local plans, action area plans[30] or subject plans other than for minerals and waste. There are transitional arrangements for existing plans.[31]

The nature of 'the development plan' varies between metropolitan and shire areas. In either case, it will for some time comprise elements of the pre-1991 system. Eventually, each local metropolitan authority will have one plan, the UDP, which should contain all its land-use policies. In the shires, there will be county-wide structure plans, minerals plans, and waste plans. The districts will have local plans covering the whole of their areas.

One of the welcome offshoots of the 1991 Act is the consolidated revision of policy guidance on development plans. This is set out in a 1992 revision of PPG 12, issued under the title *Development Plans and Regional Planning Guidance*.[32] This covers policy on both shire and metropolitan development plans, and also includes a number of annexes, including codes of practice on development plans, local plan inquiries and examinations in public, together with a very useful cross-reference to other government guidance. It has thus become the central reference for development planning policy in England.[33]

## THE IMPACT OF THE PLAN-LED SYSTEM

There are high hopes in official circles for the new planning regime. DoE anticipates that:

[It] should reduce the resources devoted to planning appeals to the Secretary of State. The planning system should become simpler and more responsive, reducing costs for both the private sector and local authorities and making it easier for people to be involved in the planning process.

Considerable efforts are being made by local authorities to produce the plans expeditiously, and early indications are that good progress is being made, though there

is some 'slippage'.[34] One reason for this is the increasing complexity of plans. In 1988, an Inspector would have spent an average of seven weeks in holding and reporting on a local plan inquiry (Planning Inspectorate 1992a). By 1991, that average had increased to 22 weeks. This is an indication of both the larger area covered by plans and the increasing participation of interest groups. Objections to plans are now counted in their hundreds (and sometimes even thousands), whilst few plans would have been subject to this level of objection ten years earlier.[35]

Development interest groups have voiced concern about the increased status of the plan because it may reduce opportunities for appeal. There is particular anxiety lest the plans may not be in complete conformity with national guidance on such important matters as making realistic provision for development: 'the Secretary of State must show a greater willingness and commitment to intervene where necessary'.[36] To alleviate the problems, the DoE has recruited additional staff to scrutinise plans for consistency with central government policy and regional guidance.

The increased scrutiny of plans and the expansion of advice during recent years has created problems with plans which were at such an advanced stage that they were unable to incorporate relevant policies. This has resulted in often lengthy correspondence between local authorities and the DoE regional offices, and an increasing number of departmental objections to plans.[37] The District Planning Officers' Society has issued guidance to its members to contact the Regional Office informally before deposit of plans to avoid the difficulty that would arise at inquiries if the DoE played the role of chief objector![38] All this represents a very high degree of central involvement in local planning.

## DEVELOPMENT PLANS IN SCOTLAND

The Scottish system differs in several significant ways from that in England and Wales,[39] but the two-tier system of development plans and the procedures for the adoption and approval, have been broadly

# The Planning Framework in England and Wales 1993

| COUNTY COUNCILS | NATIONAL PARK AUTHORITIES | BROADS AUTHORITY | DISTRICT COUNCILS | METROPOLITAN DISTRICT COUNCILS & LONDON BOROUGHS | THE SECRETARY OF STATE |
|---|---|---|---|---|---|
| 39 in England & 8 in Wales | 2 Board run Authorities / 5 Joint — Committe Authorities | | 264 in England 37 in Wales | 36 Met Districts 32 London Boroughs & The City of London | in England - the Secretary of State for the Environment in Wales - the Secretary of State for Wales |

The DoE consults all planning authorities and relevant organisations on draft guidance

**NATIONAL PLANNING GUIDANCE**
Issued as PPGs & MPGNs

REGIONAL PLANNING GUIDANCE : County Councils lead preparation of 'advice' through a conference of all authorities. Provides a framework for structure plans and context for UDP's and local plans for 20 year period or longer. RPG & Strategic Planning Guidance is to be brought together

Issued by Secretary of State as RPGs, target for completion end 1993.

**STRATEGIC PLANNING GUIDANCE**
Advice prepared by metropolitan districts or London Planning Advisory Committee

Issued by Secretary of State as RPGs - full cover 1991

**UNITARY DEVELOPMENT PLANS**
DISTRICT WIDE
Part I
Framework of general policies and proposals.

Part II
Detailed policies and proposals to guide control, 10 year horizon, longer for some policies such as green belt. action areas may be included.

The Secretary of State is a statutory consultee on all plans; may object formally; may direct modifications; may call-in all or part of plans for own approval or to quash.

**STRUCTURE PLANS**
Authority wide, mandatory, adopted by counties and two Board National Parks. Broad framework, 15 year horizon, longer for some policies, eg green belt. Cover complete but under review in many areas.

Statements of conformity are required from counties for district council local plans

**LOCAL PLANS**
Authority wide, mandatory plans. Detailed polices and proposals to guide development control; 10 year horizon, longer for policies of conservation and long term phased development. Target for complete cover end 1996. May include action areas.

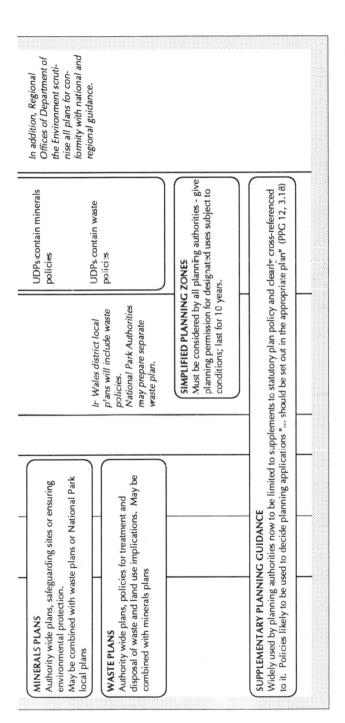

**MINERALS PLANS**
Authority wide plans, safeguarding sites or ensuring environmental protection.
May be combined with waste plans or National Park local plans

**WASTE PLANS**
Authority wide plans, policies for treatment and disposal of waste and land use implications. May be combined with minerals plans

In Wales district local plans will include waste policies.
National Park Authorities may prepare separate waste plan.

UDPs contain minerals policies

UDPs contain waste policies

In addition, Regional Offices of Department of the Environment scrutinise all plans for conformity with national and regional guidance.

**SIMPLIFIED PLANNING ZONES**
Must be considered by all planning authorities - give planning permission for designated uses subject to conditions; last for 10 years.

**SUPPLEMENTARY PLANNING GUIDANCE**
Widely used by planning authorities now to be limited to supplements to statutory plan policy and clearly cross-referenced to it. Policies likely to be used to decide planning applications "... should be set out in the appropriate plan" (PPG 12, 3.18)

NOTES

1  At the time of writing the Secretary of State for Wales has stated his intention to take forward reforms for a unitary structure in Wales and the Local Government Commission is expected to recommend unitary authorities in England. See the section on local government reorganisation in Chapter 2.

2  The Government have stated their intention to give all National Parks the same powers as the two 'Board' Authorities, the Peak District and the Lake District.

National Parks also prepare park-wide management plans.

3  The numbers of district councils is likely to change in response to recommendations from the Local Government Commission. See Chapter 2.

4  Urban development corporations may also designate simplified planning zones.

*Figure 3.1* The Planning Framework in England and Wales, 1993

similar.[40] Some differences can be attributed to the much more thoroughgoing nature of the Scottish local government reorganisation, and the particular geographical characteristics of Scotland; others may legitimately be attributed to a canny move to avoid some of the difficulties of the English system. (The structure of Scottish local government and the distribution of planning powers are outlined in Chapter 2.)

A significant difference in the plan regimes was introduced in 1973 when local plan coverage became mandatory.[41] Coon (1988, 1989) suggests that this requirement was instituted because of the introduction of regional reports and the subsequent 'doubts about whether full structure plan coverage would be essential – in which case local plans would become more necessary'. There is an interesting parallel here with the recent discussions on the English planning framework. However, as in England, the SDD recommended that 'priority should be given to those areas where development is expected and development pressures are likely to be greatest' (Thomson 1985).

The regional reports to which Coon refers were introduced in the 1970s. They provided a corporate policy statement for the regions and a framework for the preparation of structure plans. To facilitate speed, there were few formal procedures governing their preparation, and they did not require central government approval, but were simply published with the Secretary of State's observations. They were much admired (McDonald 1977) but, as the statutory development plan framework was put into place, they became regarded as redundant.[42]

Changes to the development plan system itself have followed closely those introduced south of the border. For example, the procedure for making alterations to structure plans and local plans has been made simpler. Also, certain adjustments have been made to the division of planning responsibilities between regions and districts. This was a matter of considerable discussion by the Stodart Committee (1981) who concluded that the broad distribution of planning functions between the strategic and the local levels was satisfactory. The changes had the objective, in the words of SDD Circular 29/1982, 'to clarify the division between regions and districts, and in particular to ensure that regions have all the powers necessary to them to fulfil their structure planning responsibilities, without introducing any element of concurrency'.

The 1991 Act will bring many of the same changes made in England and Wales to Scotland, notably the enhanced status of development plans in development control; calls for more succinct statements of policy; and the emphasis on 'physical land use development' (PAN 37, 1992). However, in a number of ways the Scottish development plan system remains distinctive. The structure plan still has to be approved by the Secretary of State. The survey still plays a part in the approval, and must be put on deposit and accompany the deposited plan in the submission to the Secretary of State.

Evaluation of the system also reveals similarity with the situation in England and Wales. Local government reorganisation delayed the production of plans, and it was not until 1989 that full structure plan cover was achieved. Progress on local plans has been better overall, mainly because of the mandatory requirement.[43]

## NATIONAL AND REGIONAL PLANNING GUIDANCE

One interesting feature of Scottish planning practice has been the publication by the Scottish Office of *National Planning Guidelines*. These were initially prompted by the need to have a strategy to deal with the unprecedented problems posed by North Sea oil and gas. Since these were considered to be of national importance, the Scottish Office decided to issue guidelines for use by local authorities, especially in relation to coastal development.[44] Following consultations, SDD issued, in 1974, *Coastal Planning Guidelines for North Sea Oil and Gas*. 'This was based on the concepts of preferred conservation zones, in which oil-related development could be justified only in exceptional circumstances, and preferred development zones, in which development should be encouraged.' Later guidelines were issued on large industrial sites, aggregate working, rural conservation, petrochemical developments, the location of major shopping developments, forestry, skiing developments, and high technology and individual high amenity sites. (A full list is given in the section on official publications at the end of the book.) Local authorities are required to notify SDD if they propose to grant permission for development which is contrary to the guidelines.

The benefits of this system soon became apparent (Diamond 1979). First, it enables local authorities to better establish the way in which their plans have taken account of national policies. Second, a higher degree of coordination and compatibility should emerge between the various branches of central government. Third, national interests in which the Secretary of State needs to be involved can be readily separated from local matters. Later assessments have continued to recognise the strengths of the NPGs (Nuffield Report 1986). Together with their accompanying 'land use summary sheets',[45] they set out the land use and locational priorities for development and conservation. Rowan-Robinson and Lloyd note that they have been used selectively:

> They are issued where a prognosis for change in the use of a land resource indicates that there is a client requirement from local authorities and developers for guidance. The themes which have helped to shape the Scottish guidelines are: the acceptance of a clear role for national physical land use planning; the need for information about the resource base; the importance of linkages with other agencies both at the national and local level; the selective approach (as opposed to a comprehensive approach) to issues which require guidance at the national level; the potential, not only for anticipating conflict, but for pointing up opportunities for development; and the need for any national statement to define areas for subjects requiring further work together with an indication of priorities.[46]
> (Rowan-Robinson and Lloyd 1991: 16)

In England and Wales, national and regional policy guidance has been much more piecemeal. It was noted in Chapter 2 that the planning policy guidance notes (PPGs) and minerals planning guidance notes (MPGs) have taken on the role of expressing national land use and development policy, leaving Circulars to be used

mainly for elaboration of procedural matters. The guidance notes have certainly clarified and extended the national policy framework, but they have tended to be more general than the NPGs in Scotland, being broader in scope and not location specific. However, some government policy is still to be found in circulars and also, from time to time, in ministerial statements. Major changes in policy are often published in White Papers. All of these documents can be regarded as material considerations in planning and thus the central government has an array of instruments in which national policy can be expressed. Indeed, the result can sometimes be confusing, if not actually contradictory.

In addition to the strengthening of national guidance, the Government has taken steps towards expanding regional policy guidance in England and Wales. The 1986 Consultation Paper on *The Future of Development Plans* noted the progress that had been made in some regions, such as East Anglia and the West Midlands, by local authorities cooperating voluntarily to produce regional strategies. Most prominent amongst these was the London and South East Regional Planning Conference (SERPLAN), which started life as the Standing Conference on London Regional Planning in 1962.[47] The Secretary of State had issued South East Regional Strategic Guidance in 1986 in response to advice from SERPLAN.

Official encouragement was given in the 1986 Consultation Paper to the formation of other regional groupings. As in the South-East, the Secretary of State would issue guidance after publishing a draft for comment. No precise procedures were suggested and a warning was given that 'such arrangements would not represent a formalised regional structure, nor would they be a return to the type of large-scale regional planning which was attempted in the 1960s and 70s'. The 1989 White Paper made similar comments and added the recommendation that business organisations and other bodies should be involved, as well as local authorities. Conservation and agricultural interests were added to this list later. The need to merge the strategic guidance produced by the metropolitan counties as part of the unitary development planning process (completed by December 1989) with the new regional guidance was also recognised.

At this stage, the production of advice by local authorities to the Secretary of State and the issuing of guidance was still thought not to be needed in all areas. In 1990, PPG 15 took a stronger line, and stated that 'the aim should be to have guidance in place for most regions during the early 1990s'. PPG 12 (1992) brought the target for completion forward to the end of 1993, and plans were to look ahead twenty or more years rather than fifteen. Flexibility in the process of production of advice has been retained, but local authorities are now expected to detail the results of the consultations they have undertaken, and also their responses. The conversion of the Government to a modicum of regional guidance, if not regional planning, is thus complete.

The outcome of this in terms of organisational arrangements and the character of the guidance produced is mixed, and the scale of the task should not be underestimated. Even where there are long-standing cooperative arrangements arising from old regional planning councils and boards, political conflict within the regions can be intense. The costs of producing the advice fall on the constituent authorities. It is unlikely that any will match the resources supporting SERPLAN, which has a full-time secretariat and an annual budget of £500,000 to support its 143 member authorities.

Early evaluation of some of the output raises the question as to whether the effort is worth while. An indication of the varying style and quality is given in a symposium in the *Town Planning Review* (1992).[48] From this, it appears that much of the guidance is no more than a further detailing of national guidance and restatement of current policies. The Regional Strategic Guidance for East Anglia (PPG 6) is described as:

> bland and incremental . . . it mostly describes existing situations and trends. It is very largely written as a substantive account of what has been happening in the region in recent years, informed mainly by topic PPGs (in other words, by national government policy) and specific programmes of road building and targets for housebuilding.

The East Midlands draft strategy is similarly criticised as consisting 'of little more than a shopping list of current proposals, pet projects and pious political expectations'. The proposed Strategic Guidance for the North-East, which absurdly excludes the metropolitan area, 'contains little that the Department of the Environment could not have extracted from existing structure plans'; and the counties 'have failed to address key issues and to define new approaches'. The South-West Regional Guidance gets a little better review by Coombes and her colleagues who describe the draft as being 'a genuine attempt to address the issues and concerns evidenced by the consultation responses' (T. Coombes *et al*. 1992).

In Wales, a series of guideline documents has been prepared as Strategic Planning Guidance in Wales by the Welsh Office.[49] The documents 'consolidate and re-present the wide range of available strategic guidance material in a consistent and accessible form'. They provide a base on which advice can be developed by the Welsh local authorities. The Welsh version of PPG 12 explains:

> The Assembly of Welsh Counties has taken the lead in assessing, in collaboration with the Council of Welsh Districts, the National Parks, and other interested bodies, the existing strategic framework and in providing advice on the main strategic planning issues likely to affect Wales over the next 10–15 years.

The latest national development on regional guidance is the publication of a Guidance Note on the regional planning process by the Royal Town Planning Institute. The Note has been published in a package, with the Institute's policy statement on the regional planning process in England and the final report of the South-West Branch Regional Planning Working Party, which was commissioned by the RTPI and HBF to identify good practice in the regional planning process. The note gives more advice about how to operate the current system, including what procedure is appropriate in the production of guidance, presentation techniques, and the topics to be covered. The policy statement reiterates and elaborates the RTPI's position on the need for a statutory tier of regional plans as opposed to guidance, to be prepared by a secretariat and technical staff independent of the constituent planning authorities.[50]

The RTPI view seems unlikely to prevail in the immediate future. What has been achieved has been little more than a tentative first step in developing a hazy notion of a regional planning process.[51] The situation could change when the next round of local government reorganisation is complete, but the current attempt and its outcome is not likely to satisfy anyone. The danger is that it may die of ennui, and make a later more serious initiative more difficult.

## THE STATUTORY PROCEDURES

A particularly helpful feature of the 1991 Act is that it brings the procedures for the various types of plans much closer into line with each other (though their complexities remain). Essentially, the procedures comprise 'safeguards' to ensure the accountability of government in the exercise of plan making. This is particularly important in the UK where there is no constitutional safeguard of private property rights, other than that provided by the European Convention on Human Rights, and where there is very wide administrative discretion in decision making (Grant 1992: 4). The procedures also provide for increased involvement of other organisations and the public in policy formulation. The process of open discussion and formal adoption lends authority and standing to plans, and provides an element of legitimacy even though the plans are not subject to direct ministerial approval (PAG 1965: 6.19).

The Planning Advisory Group recommended in 1965 that only strategic plans should be subject to approval by the Minister, while local plans would be 'adopted' by the local authority concerned. The acceptance of this principle proved to be an important watershed in planning practice, establishing the notion that local planning is essentially a matter for local authorities. Despite some strong criticism (Bridges 1979: 243), it has proved to be quite robust and, thus far, central government has not wished to intervene extensively. In the following discussion, the focus is on the key safeguards, the main criticisms

of the procedure, and recent amendments. The knotty questions about the extent to which the public and other objectors are effectively able to make use of the safeguards and how this influences plan content are dealt with in the final chapter on 'planning and the public'.

The main safeguards in plan adoption are the opportunity to be consulted in the formative stages of plan preparation; the need for authorities to consider conformity between plans, and regional and national guidance; the right to make objections to both strategic and detailed plans, and to have objections to the latter heard before an independent inspector; a further right to object to any proposed modifications or where the authority propose to reject the recommendation of an inspector or a panel; and the over-arching right of the Secretary of State to intervene and to direct modifications, and the right to challenge the plan in the courts.

The central focus of the formal adoption procedure is the hearing. In the case of a local plan or UDP, this is a public local inquiry; in the case of a structure plan, it is an examination in public. These have significant differences and strengths and weaknesses, many of which are discussed in a wider context in the final chapter. At the inquiry an independent inspector hears 'objections', whereas the examination in public (EIP) is a 'probing discussion' of selected matters which the authority (until 1992 it was the Secretary of State) needs to consider before taking the structure plan forward. Though the rights of individuals to object to a structure plan (and the duty of the local authority to consider all objections) are maintained, there has been no right for objectors to present their case at an inquiry since the EIP was introduced in 1972. The examination deals with only those matters which the authority considers need examination in public, and the planning authority determines who shall participate in the examination (whether or not they have made objections or representations).

Not surprisingly, such a system of controls has been criticised as being cumbersome.[52] The original PAG proposals were less onerous at the local level since no inquiry was needed. This was not acceptable to the Government of the day which wanted the procedure to be more open to scrutiny. The result, though subject to many criticisms from all sides, has proved very resilient. This is perhaps because the procedure nicely balances the concerns of local authorities (who typically call for more freedom of action in order to speed the process), and those of objectors of all kinds (who naturally desire more influence in the local planning process).

These points of view reflect the two major criticisms of the procedure: the time needed to navigate the apparently complex steps in adoption, and the principle that the authority is able to act as 'judge and jury in its own court'. The evidence suggests that both these criticisms have been overplayed.

The problem of delay is that it weakens the commitment of authorities to using statutory procedures, and effectively encourages them to make informal plans and *ad hoc* decisions. Piecemeal decision-making and non-statutory policy have been dominant over the last twenty years. The County Planning Officers' Society (CPOS 1985) have argued from this for a reduction in central government involvement; and the poor record of the DoE in approving plans promptly supports their claim, although the rejoinder could legitimately point to the excessive length and detail of structure plans. The District Planning Officers' Society have used the same argument to press for further simplification of local plan procedure, and thus more autonomy (DPOS 1982 and 1986).

But these criticisms perhaps focus too closely on the formal procedures. The average time to produce local plans (from start to formal adoption) is about five years, but the greatest amount of time is spent in preparation prior to formal deposit (Bruton and Nicholson 1987a). Furthermore, many authorities who get this far are able to negotiate the procedures without undue difficulty.[53] Thus, the problems with the statutory procedures have been exaggerated, although it is recognised that they are becoming more of a delaying factor with the increased level of objection following the enhanced status of plans.[54]

The second major criticism of the procedure is the right of authorities to reject recommendations made by inspectors after inquiries. At one time, this applied only to local planning but it now also applies to UDPs and, from 1992, to the panel reports from structure plan EIPs. It has always been difficult for some to understand that the inspector to a local plan inquiry (and now the panel to an EIP) is reporting, not to central government or the inspectorate, but to the local planning authority (which is responsible for adopting the plan, and organising the inquiry or examination, paying for the inspector, etc). Where local authorities have rejected recommendations and adopted the plan without amendment, there is naturally an outcry from those whose argument was accepted by the inspector. Some of these cases have been widely publicised, but the scale of the problem, if indeed it is a problem, is certainly not significant. Research throws some useful light on this issue. A study funded by the DoE on a sample of 76 plans adopted in the early part of the 1980s (Crispin *et al.* 1985; Nadin *et al.* 1985) showed that of 767 recommendations nearly 90 per cent were accepted without change. A further 3 per cent were accepted in part. Thus, only about 8 per cent of recommendations were rejected outright. In further examination, it was also found that the rejected recommendations reflected a cross-section of the various types of policy to which they applied. The reasons given were also mixed. Sometimes, the inspector simply got the facts wrong, although the authorities did report that there was often simply a difference of opinion about the best solution. The findings about the reasons for rejection of recommendations are less certain, not least because it is unlikely that 'poor reasons' would be reported. Nevertheless, the general point holds. Other smaller-scale studies, both before and after, have produced similar findings (Marsh 1983; Adams and Pawson 1991). The conclusion has to be that, in the main, local authorities have taken Inspectors' reports very seriously and acted responsibly in making decisions.

The fact remains, however, that this has been a much misunderstood principle of local planning, often because of the unwarranted comparisons with the procedure for Section 78 inquiries into refusal of planning permission and other inquiries where the decision of the Inspector or Secretary of State is binding on all parties. But misunderstanding also arises because many objectors anticipate the inquiry will be of a judicial nature (Bruton *et al*. 1982a and 1982b) which (as discussed in Chapter 11) it is not.

Some other procedural issues are worthy of note, since they reflect the way in which the procedures attempt to reach some balance between the basic tensions in the system. First, the relationship between the strategic and local plans, split between the two tiers of local government, have been a constant source of dispute. The 1980 Local Government and Planning Act introduced the expedited procedure in an attempt to free local plans from some of the delays of structure planning. This allowed the adoption of local plans in advance of the approval of a structure plan, on the strength of a certificate of general conformity with a structure plan that had been submitted to the Secretary of State. In practice, this had only a marginal effect: few districts used the procedure and, as late as 1989, structure plan alterations were still being cited as a principal reason for delays with local plans (Winter 1989). This problem has now been dealt with in a different way by altering the requirement for certificate of conformity (as previously discussed on p. 52).

Second, in 1980, local authorities were given greater freedom to modify plans for reasons other than those arising from objections and Inspectors' recommendations, where they will not materially affect the content of the plan.[55] Previously, some local authorities had been put in the position of objecting to their own plans in order to bring about sensible and uncontroversial modifications where, for example, further information had come to light following deposit. Again, this has raised little comment until recently when, in the light of the enhanced status of plans, it has been questioned whether a local authority is the best judge of what is material to the plan (CPRE 1991b).

Third, in 1986, the Secretary of State's powers of intervention were increased. It had always been possible for call-in to take place at any time, but this was regarded as a drastic step which was rarely exercised. The 1986 Housing and Planning Act made

provision for the Secretary of State to invite the authority to make modifications, with the indication that, if this did not happen, the next step would be call-in. This provision has assumed greater significance with the increased interest that the Secretary of State is now taking in the detailed expression of policy. Sir George Young (1992) has announced that he will be prepared to use these powers, although only as a last resort.

Taken together, these new provisions probably have more bark than bite; but Ministers are apt to make hortatory statements when they feel that local authorities need a stern warning. Nothing more may be required, at least until the next crisis.

## ENTERPRISE ZONES[56]

A major plank in the Conservative Government's response to economic recession in the early 1980s was the proposed reduction in the 'burden' of regulation on business and enterprise. In this and the next section two measures are discussed which were designed to promote business activity: enterprise zones, and simplified planning zones.

In enterprise zones (EZs), amendments to the planning regime were part of a much wider range of advantages offered, although the statement announcing their introduction was made with a strong side swipe at mainstream traditional town and country planning.

> Introducing his proposals, the Chancellor said that there were some parts of the economy, particularly in the older urban areas, where more and more public authority involvement had apparently led to less and less fruitful activity. The planning process had all too often allowed, or even encouraged, whole areas, at the heart of some of the most populous cities, to be laid waste for years. Even when development plans were finally made, the public purse was often unable to provide the funds or the enterprise to match the planners' aspirations. And when private initiative might have been ready to act, it had generally been stifled by rules and regulations.
> (HM Treasury 1980)

The same Conservative spokesperson, Sir Geoffrey Howe, had introduced the concept of the enterprise

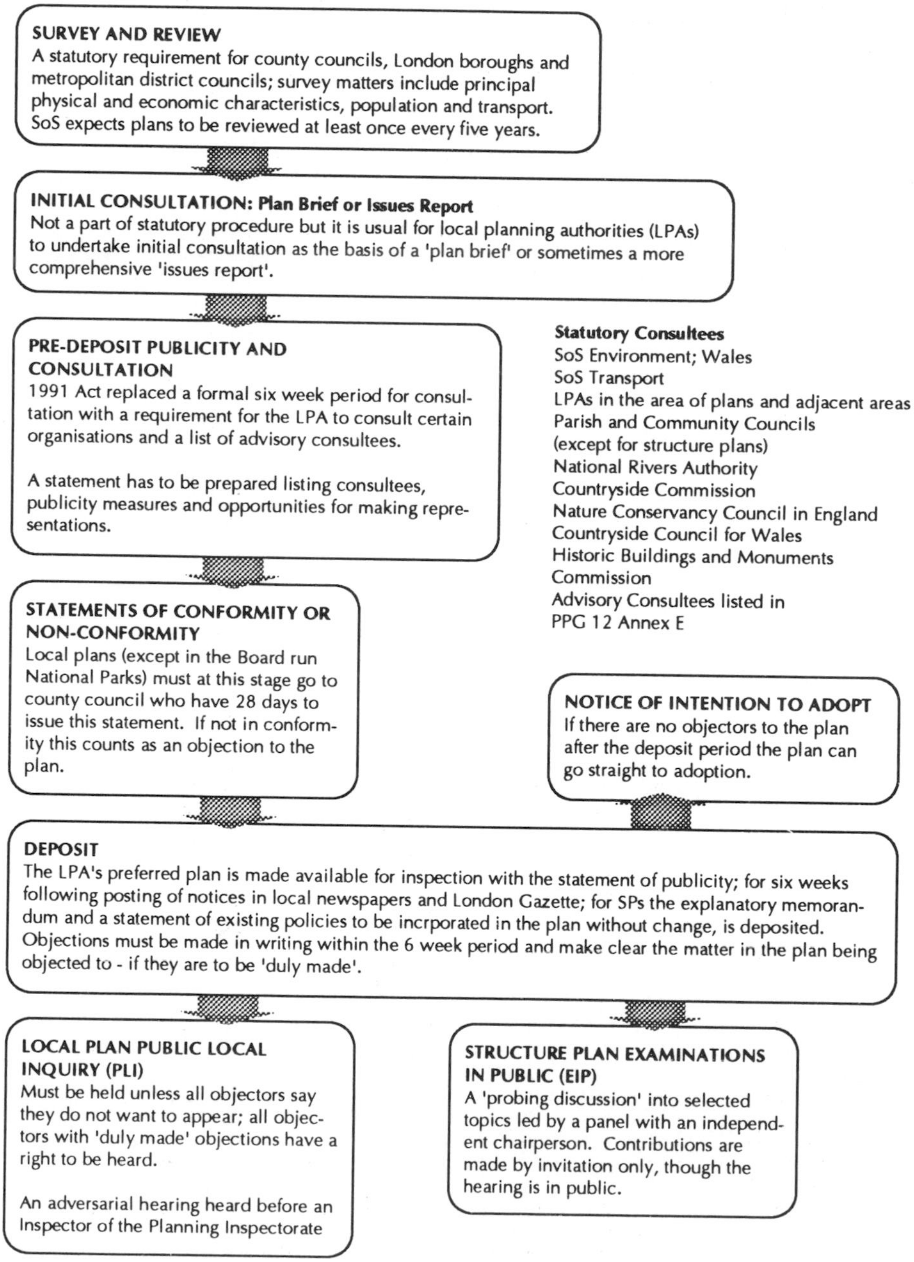

**SURVEY AND REVIEW**
A statutory requirement for county councils, London boroughs and metropolitan district councils; survey matters include principal physical and economic characteristics, population and transport. SoS expects plans to be reviewed at least once every five years.

**INITIAL CONSULTATION: Plan Brief or Issues Report**
Not a part of statutory procedure but it is usual for local planning authorities (LPAs) to undertake initial consultation as the basis of a 'plan brief' or sometimes a more comprehensive 'issues report'.

**PRE-DEPOSIT PUBLICITY AND CONSULTATION**
1991 Act replaced a formal six week period for consultation with a requirement for the LPA to consult certain organisations and a list of advisory consultees.

A statement has to be prepared listing consultees, publicity measures and opportunities for making representations.

**Statutory Consultees**
SoS Environment; Wales
SoS Transport
LPAs in the area of plans and adjacent areas
Parish and Community Councils
(except for structure plans)
National Rivers Authority
Countryside Commission
Nature Conservancy Council in England
Countryside Council for Wales
Historic Buildings and Monuments Commission
Advisory Consultees listed in PPG 12 Annex E

**STATEMENTS OF CONFORMITY OR NON-CONFORMITY**
Local plans (except in the Board run National Parks) must at this stage go to county council who have 28 days to issue this statement. If not in conformity this counts as an objection to the plan.

**NOTICE OF INTENTION TO ADOPT**
If there are no objectors to the plan after the deposit period the plan can go straight to adoption.

**DEPOSIT**
The LPA's preferred plan is made available for inspection with the statement of publicity; for six weeks following posting of notices in local newspapers and London Gazette; for SPs the explanatory memorandum and a statement of existing policies to be incrporated in the plan without change, is deposited. Objections must be made in writing within the 6 week period and make clear the matter in the plan being objected to - if they are to be 'duly made'.

**LOCAL PLAN PUBLIC LOCAL INQUIRY (PLI)**
Must be held unless all objectors say they do not want to appear; all objectors with 'duly made' objections have a right to be heard.

An adversarial hearing heard before an Inspector of the Planning Inspectorate

**STRUCTURE PLAN EXAMINATIONS IN PUBLIC (EIP)**
A 'probing discussion' into selected topics led by a panel with an independent chairperson. Contributions are made by invitation only, though the hearing is in public.

*Figure 3.2* Procedure for Adoption of Development Plans

**INSPECTOR'S REPORT**
Makes recommendations to local planning authority on how plan could be modified to meet objections, including written objections not heard at the inquiry.

**PANEL'S REPORT**
Makes recommendations to LPA on how plan could be modified in respect of matters selected for discussion at EIP only.

**STATEMENT OF DECISIONS AND REASONS**
LPA are not obliged to accept all recommendations (although 9 out of 10 ususally are) but they must give reasons for their decsions in each case paying special attention to recommendations rejected.

*If modifications recommended and accepted*

*If some or all recommended modifications not accepted*

*If no modifications recommended*

**LIST OF MODIFICATIONS AND REASONS**

**LIST OF MODIFICATIONS LIST OF RECOMMENDATIONS NOT ACCEPTED**

LPA can also make 'additional modifications' that do not materially affect plan content, for example to correct and update the content.

*Any modification which makes a material change to the plan must be listed.*

*Anyone may object to the absence of modifications recommended in the reports .*

**NOTICE OF INTENTION TO ADOPT**
If there are no objections the plan may be adopted after the six week period of deposit.

**DEPOSIT**
The Inspector's/Panel's Report and the statement of decisions must be placed on deposit for six weeks with any list of modifications and/or recommendations not accepted; notices are served on objectors.

Statement of decisions and reasons and Inspector's/Panel's Report is made available for inspection.

*If objectors raise new issues*

*If objectors do not raise new issues*

*If no objections*

**SECOND INQUIRY OR RE-OPENED EIP**
This will only take place where entirely new issues eg a new proposal or if LPA propose to withdraw a modification.

**STATEMENT OF DECISIONS**

**ADOPTION OF PLAN**
The plan is adopted by resolution of the Council, notices are published in the London Gazette and local newspapers and sent to those who asked to be notified.

**CHALLENGE IN THE COURTS**
There is a right challenge the plan but only on the grounds that the proposals are not within the powers of the 1990 Act or that regulations have not been complied with.

zone three years earlier, when in opposition. He credited the notion to Peter Hall, who in turn, identifies the origins of the concept in a 1969 article by himself and three others on 'Non-plan: an experiment in freedom' in *New Society* (Banham *et al*. 1969). The germ of the idea thus arises from the notion of virtually complete freedom from state control and intervention. Hall has more recently (1991) provided overviews of the way in which this notion was transposed and 'sanitised' into the enterprise zone initiative in Britain. He explains how the theoretical justification for such a proposal has itself been questioned (he cites Massey 1982, and Goldsmith 1982 as examples) and how, in its implementation, 'there has been a huge gap between the grand sweep of the original concept and the reality of what was actually achieved'.

The practical manifestation of the 'non-plan' concept was the enterprise zone, introduced by the 1980 Local Government Planning and Land Act. The actual 'freedoms' offered were exemption from rates on industrial and commercial property, 100 per cent tax allowances for capital expenditure, reduced demands for information from government, and simpler planning procedures. The planning element amounts to a rudimentary form of zoning. After designation by the Secretary of State, an enterprise zone scheme has the effect of granting planning permissions in advance for such developments as the scheme specifies.

EZ schemes are prepared by authorities invited to do so by the Secretary of State (district councils, London boroughs, and development corporations). Subject to any directions contained in the invitation, the authority is free to determine what planning concessions are to be offered. A draft scheme has to be given adequate publicity; 'persons who may be expected to want to make representations' are to be made aware of their entitlement to do so; and any representations have to be considered by the authority (but no public inquiry is required). The authority then proceeds to 'adopt' the scheme which may be approved by the Secretary of State after the expiry of a six-week period during which the validity of the scheme may be challenged. There is no requirement for conformity with existing plans. On the contrary, if any existing plans conflict with the scheme they have to be amended as necessary. Nor is there a requirement for an inquiry into objections to the scheme.

Twenty-seven enterprise zones have been designated, including eleven designated in 1981 which have now completed their ten-year lifespan. A second round of 14 designations followed in 1983/84, and extensions to some existing zones were made between 1983 and 1986. Since 1984, only two new designations have been made following exceptional circumstances in each case. In 1989 an EZ was designated in Inverclyde, and in 1990 a further zone was designated in Sunderland following shipyard closures. More designations are possible, and the Government announced in October 1992 that EZs might form one of a package of measures to tackle decline in the coalfields. This is a considerably larger number than originally envisaged. Enterprise zones have been designated in all the regions of the UK except East Anglia and the South-West. They range in size from the 110-acre zone at Inverclyde to the 1,121-acre zone at Tyneside and some have been designated on a number of separate sites (Table 3.1).

The enterprise zone initiative has been closely monitored, and findings show a dramatic increase in development activity in some cases. The Corby EZ, for example, was virtually fully committed after seven years with 5,600 jobs and 3.15m sq. ft of floorspace built (*Estates Gazette* 1990). Overall, however, it seems that most of the new development and employment in the zones would have occurred in any case, though not necessarily within the designated areas (PA Cambridge Economic Consultants 1987). Other studies have shown that the liberalisation of land-use planning controls made only a minor contribution to any success. The extent of the zone regimes amounts only to a total of about 36 sq. km or 14 sq. miles land area in Britain, and the simplified planning controls have not proved to be a major incentive (Roger Tym & Partners 1982–84). The reports certainly do not suggest that a bonfire of controls has released time-saving dynamic efficiency. Case-studies showed that a very considerable amount

*Table 3.1* Enterprise Zones in the UK, 1993

|  | Area (acres) | Year |
|---|---|---|
| **England** | | |
| Allerdale, Workington, Cumbria | 87 | 1983 |
| Corby, Northants | 113 | 1981 |
| Dudley, West Midlands | 263 | 1981 and 1984 |
| Glandford, Humberside | 50 | 1984 |
| Hartlepool, Cleveland | 109 | 1981 |
| Isle of Dogs, London | 147 | 1982 |
| Middlesborough | 79 | 1983 |
| NE Lancashire | 114 | 1983 |
| NW Kent | 125 | 1983 |
| Rotherham | 105 | 1983 |
| Salford/Trafford | 352 | 1981 |
| Scunthorpe, Humberside | 105 | 1983 |
| Speke, Liverpool | 138 | 1981 |
| Telford, Shropshire | 113 | 1984 |
| Tyneside | 454 | 1981 |
| Wakefield | 90 | 1981 and 1983 |
| Wellingborough, Northants | 54 | 1983 |
| Sunderland | 150 | 1990 |
| **Wales** | | |
| Delyn, Clwyd | 118 | 1983 |
| Milford Haven, Dyfed | 146 | 1984 |
| Swansea, West Glamorgan | 314 | 1981 and 1985 |
| **Scotland** | | |
| Clydebank | 230 | 1981 |
| Invergordon, Highland | 60 | 1983 |
| Tayside | 120 | 1984 |
| Inverclyde | 274 | 1989 |
| Lanarkshire | 507 | 1993 |
| **Northern Ireland** | | |
| Belfast | 207 | 1981 |
| Londonderry | 109 | 1983 |

of negotiation (whether it be termed 'planning' or not) still had to take place, both between the developers and local authorities and also between developers and other agencies. Moreover, it has become apparent that the zones are not as distinctive as had been envisaged: planning controls are often retained along zone boundaries; special industrial uses, including noxious and dangerous processes, are still subject to control; and, on occasion, environmental improvements are often written into declaration reports. Enterprise zones have not been environmentally harmful; in many cases standards have greatly improved (Lawless 1989: 65).

The positive advantage of a scheme is that it *can*

help a developer to get on site more quickly but, as the case-studies clearly show, it does not always do so. Developers have their own problems to sort out (with regard to finance, design, relationships with contractors and so on). Moreover, there are other statutory controls, and these still remain. Nevertheless, planning is *seen* as an important obstacle by developers partly because the outcome is never quite certain. What the scheme offers is the advantage of certainty. The conditions are set out and known from the beginning.

Much more important than any change in 'planning' has been the substantial financial benefits: tax allowances and the direct public investment in infrastructure and land reclamation.

## SIMPLIFIED PLANNING ZONES

Whatever the research on enterprise zones might have concluded, the Government was so enamoured of the idea that it introduced a new type of *simplified planning zone* (SPZ) based upon it. The general notion of zoning as an alternative to the development plan had been rejected, but the DoE did see a limited role for zoning in particular locations where greater certainty, and some flexibility in the detail of development proposals, would contribute to economic development objectives.[57] An SPZ is a local equivalent to a development order made by the Secretary of State. The objectives of the new measure were set out in a 1984 Consultation Paper *Simplified Planning Zones*:

> Instead of subjecting all development proposals to the uncertainty and delay of discretionary planning control, the SPZ scheme would specify types of development (including specified categories of outdoor advertising), allowed in the zone and the conditions and limitations attached. In so far as local planning authorities stated their objectives and requirements in advance, developers would thus be offered greater speed and certainty. Local planning authorities would be able to pursue a more positive approach than is possible with traditional development control.

In response to the Consultation Paper, the RTPI made a long and stinging criticism of the concept and the way that it was being promoted as an antidote to perceived problems of planning control. It suggested that the introduction of zoning 'would produce a more complex rather than a simplified planning system', and that the proposal was, in any case, 'based on a misapprehension that the need to seek planning permission is a significant delaying factor in the overall development process'. The response also pointed to a central finding of EZ monitoring, noted above, that the existence of 'advance planning permission' did not play a very significant role in promoting development.

The Institute proposed that, instead of SPZs, local authorities should be given wider powers to obtain planning permission themselves. This is currently limited to situations where the authority is landowner or developer; this effectively precludes the granting of planning permission in advance as a promotional tool.

The RTPI's paper is typical of the generally critical response to the SPZ concept in the early 1980s. Nevertheless, the Government pressed ahead, and the 1986 Housing and Planning Act made provision for local authorities to prepare schemes and designate zones. A stream of official guidance[58] dealt with the details of SPZ designation and the circumstances in which designation should be considered by local authorities and UDCs. Two broad types of scheme are possible, the *specific scheme* which lists certain uses to be permitted, and the *general scheme* which gives a wide permission but excludes certain uses. Conditions can be made in advance, and certain matters can be reserved for detailed consideration through the normal planning process. SPZs cannot be adopted in national parks, the Broads, AONBs, SSSIs, approved green belts, conservation areas, and other protected areas.

During the process of consultation there was a marked change in the focus of the SPZ proposal: in place of the concern for reducing the negative impacts of planning control there was a more positive concern for the potential advantages of SPZ designation for urban regeneration. Further emphasis was given in the Scottish Circular to the potential employment generating benefits of SPZs, their relationship to other grant-funded regeneration initiatives, and the need for schemes to be closely linked to the development

*Table 3.2* Simplified planning zones, 1992

| Authority and zone | Size (ha) | Status at 31.12.92 | Previous land use |
|---|---|---|---|
| **Adopted schemes** | | | |
| Derby (Sir Francis Ley Industrial Park) | 8.4 | Adopted June 1988 | Foundries |
| Corby (Willowbrook) | 178 | Adopted July 1988 | Steelworks |
| Highland (Dingwall) | 4.75 | Adopted 1989 | Agriculture |
| Monklands (Coatbridge) | 18 | Adopted September 1991 | Steelworks and industrial |
| Gedling (Victoria Park) | 32 | Adopted November 1991 | Railway sidings |
| Falkirk (Grangemouth Docks) | 50 (39 land and 11 water) | Adopted March 1992 | Docks |
| **Schemes in preparation** | | | |
| Birmingham (Saltley) | 110 | Consultations undertaken | Mixed vacant and industrial uses |
| Birmingham (Kings Norton) | 20 | Resolution to proceed | Industrial estate |
| Cleethorpes (North Promenade) | 13 | Consultations undertaken | Mixed leisure, retail and tourist related |
| Delyn | 65 | Deposit | Industrial plant |
| Derby (Spondon) | 41 | Draft agreed | Industrial plant |
| Rotherham | 20 | Draft agreed | Steelworks and industrial |
| Scunthorpe/Glanford | 141 | Draft | Steelworks |
| Slough | 164 | Consultations in progress | Business and trading estate |
| Enfield | 19.8 | Draft agreed | Gas works and industrial |
| Newcastle | n.a. | Draft agreed | Industrial |

*Source*: Department of the Environment.

plan. SPZs are now considered to be particularly appropriate for older industrial sites (especially those in single ownership) where there is a need to promote regeneration.[59]

The introduction of the SPZ provisions has excited very limited interest, and progress has been slow. According to a 1991 report by Arup Economic Consultants, such interest as there was tended to come from authorities with experience of (or failure to obtain) enterprise zones: these authorities had fewer fears about the loss of normal development control powers over the quality of development. The report evaluated the existing statutory procedures and guidance offered to local authorities which had already been the subject of some criticism in the earlier consultation exercises. The requirements for designation of an SPZ did not allow for as much local discretion as for EZs, but in all important respects the procedures were identical to those of local plan preparation and adoption, including preliminary public consultation, deposit for objections, a public local inquiry if necessary and further deposit of modifications. The prospect of taking a scheme through these lengthy procedures was daunting, and it rapidly became clear that they were (in the words of the research report) 'undoubtedly cumbersome'. Only three schemes had been adopted in England, Wales and Scotland by the time of the study (April 1990) with a further ten schemes in preparation and three under consideration. At the end of 1992, the adopted schemes had risen to only six (three in Scotland and three in England) with ten at some stage of preparation.

In 1990, in response to the consultants' report and the obvious lack of interest from local government, consultation papers on *Streamlining the Procedures* were published by the DoE, Welsh and Scottish Offices. The proposals followed recommendations in the consultants' report to make public consultation before deposit optional; to delete the specific 28-day period after the notice of disposition to adopt, and to allow the authority to consider objections in writing with or without the assistance of an inspector and dispense with the public local inquiry.[60] The recommended changes in procedure were enacted by Section 28 of the Planning and Compensation Act 1991 in parallel with the new procedures for local plans.[61]

As with local plans, the Secretary of State no longer prescribes the method of consultation before deposit but it has been made clear that publicity and consultation should be 'adequate'. The arrangements for consideration of objections, however, are different. The local authority now have a choice whether to consider objections themselves, to have an inspector consider objections in writing only, or to hold an inquiry. The latter option is anticipated only in circumstances 'where a scheme constitutes a departure which would significantly prejudice the implementation of the development plan or raises strategic planning issues, is the subject of substantial local controversy, covers a substantial area of land in the authority's ownership, or involves planning issues of more than local importance' (PPG 5, Annex B, para. 3.18). The thinking underlying this, which has some force, is that since the SPZ is the same as a planning permission it should not carry additional burdens for public involvement and objection. The right to an inquiry for the SPZ effectively extended third party rights in the planning decision process. In fact, now that local plan cover is to be extended to all areas, future SPZs will have been subject to the normal local plan preparation processes for public participation.

The evidence so far is that these changes have had little effect. Some of the reasons are perhaps obvious. There is little difference between the allocation of land in a development plan and an SPZ: both indicate the type of development that is acceptable. Moreover, the extra 'certainty' provided by an SPZ designation is to some extent illusory since formal relationships are replaced by informal discussions. Additionally, decisions on the fulfilment of conditions and negotiations on reserved matters may still be needed.[62] Furthermore, where a local authority is promoting urban regeneration it is likely that there will be a sympathetic approach to development proposals and a fast-track procedure for dealing with planning applications. Indeed, in situations where a developer has been identified, even the normal time-scale for grant of planning permission is likely to take less time than setting up an SPZ.

It might be argued therefore that SPZs offer little in the way of simplified planning, and the limited response from the private sector supports this view. There is only a very small number of zones, and these operate in a narrow range of circumstances.[63] The conclusion must be that the reintroduction of zoning into the British planning system through SPZs has had only very limited impact:

> Those SPZ schemes that have been adopted have harnessed the promotional value to the full. Where they have contributed to regeneration objectives it has been because they have focused efforts on achieving the new development, often in association with public sector grants. The perceived advantages have usually been more to do with promotion value and bringing together efforts to enable development to take place in physically difficult circumstances, than the inherent attraction of planning freedoms.
> (Arup Economic Consultants 1991: 71)

In promoting the zoning idea, the emphasis of government advice has shifted from the potentiality of removing 'planning red tape' to the advantages of promoting particular sites as part of wider urban regeneration strategies.

British planners view zoning as a rather strange and crude tool: they are accustomed to dealing with proposals 'on their merits'. The provision of 'planning permission in advance' has little role to play within the current planning system. The original intention to move the balance between flexibility and commitment more in the direction of the latter is now being served by the enhanced status of the development plan. Great efforts are being made to produce up-to-date plan cover and only limited interest has been shown in the SPZ concept by planners in the public and private sectors.

It would seem therefore, at least for the time being, that zoning is not likely to find fertile ground in Britain. There is, however, one factor which could alter the situation. As the UK engages more fully with the European Community there may be increasing demands for the harmonisation of planning systems.[64] Land-use planning in the other states of the EC is based on systems of zoning, and subject to the operation of subsidiarity. There could be some pressure for the British system to move in this direction.

## UPDATE

A useful note on the preparation of PPGs is given in R. Wakeford, 'Planning policy guidance: what's the use?', *Housing and Planning Review*, April/May 1993, pp. 14–18. A compact, up-to-date review of *Planning Law and Procedure* is to be found in the latest edition of the book with this title by A.E. Telling and R.M.C. Duxbury, Butterworth, 1993.

PPG 6 (*Major Retail Development*) has been revised and reissued under the title *Town Centres and Retail Development* (HMSO, 1993). This also cancels Development Policy Control Notes 5 (*Development in Town Centres*) and 11 (*Service Uses in Shopping Areas*). On the same subject, the London and South East Regional Planning Conference has published a report entitled *Planning a Future of Town Centre Shopping: A Survey of Experience in the South East*, SERPLAN, 1993.

## NOTES

1  Minister for Planning, Sir George Young, in an address to the Town and Country Planning Summer School, Exeter, September, 1992. This was published in the November 1992 issue of *The Planner*.
2  For discussions about 'what town and country planning is', see Healey *et al.* 1988, chapter 1. Grant (1992) gives an excellent overview of the planning system from a legal point of view.
3  For a critical discussion of the limitations of the understanding of the impact of planning on the pattern of land use, and on the wider social and economic consequences, see Reade 1987: chapters 1 and 3.
4  For a full explanation of planning schemes and the procedures for their approval, see Howard and Jennings 1946.
5  The differences between zoning and discretionary planning control are not as marked as they appear. For an exploration of this issue, see Cullingworth 1993.
6  White Paper, *Town and Country Planning Bill 1947: Explanatory Memorandum*, 1947, p. 5.
7  Planning Advisory Group, *The Future of Development Plans* (1965: 5). This is the traditional planning explanation in line with 'the heavy design bias in British town planning' (Jowell 1977b). Jowell quotes Foley's comment on British planners: 'They viewed the metropolitan community as having a special physical form that could be grasped and reduced to *maplike* graphic presentation' (Foley 1963: 53).
8  White Paper, *Town and Country Planning*, 1967.
9  The clearest explanation of the pre–1991 development plan system is to be found in the Memorandum on Structure and Local Plans attached to DoE Circular 22/84 (cancelled by PPG 12, 1992). The quotations in this section are from the Circular.
10  In practice, schemes were not always kept up to date, and in the early days were over-optimistic about likely progress (Bruton 1983).
11  *The Town and Country Planning (Development Plan) Regulations 1991*, SI No. 2794, para. 28.
12  For further discussion of the scope and content of structure plans see Jowell and Noble 1980; Jowell and Noble 1981; Jowell 1983; Cross and Bristow 1983; Healey 1986a; and the DoE 1986 Consultation Paper on *The Future of Development Plans*. For the central government position see PPG 12 (1992) and PAN 37

(1992). On the difficulties of addressing social policy and issues of need in statutory plans see Heycock 1991.

13  A recent example of government restrictions on structure plans are the DoE's objections to the Berkshire Structure Plan, which *Planning* headlined as: 'Department puts boot in over Berkshire draft structure plan' (12 February 1993: 1).

14  The 1988 version of PPG 12 accepted the need for phasing and density controls, but added that precise specification was not appropriate. PPG 15 (issued in 1990, but superseded in 1992) brought more guidance on scope and content, confirming that non-land-use matters should be excluded even in reasoned justification where they became a type of 'lower case policy' with indeterminate status. The main emphasis of this advice, however, was to further reduce the content and detail of structure plans. The latest PPG 12 (which replaces PPG 15) makes specific reference to the need to 'take account of the environment in the widest sense in plan preparation' (para. 6.3), though there is the ritualistic warning that 'policies for non land-use matters should not be included' (para. 5.6).

The DoE *Good Practice Guide* (1992) offers further advice on the level of detail in structure plans, and on the manner in which social and economic issues should be treated. For example, plan makers should 'be aware of the land use issues associated with "the needs of particular sections of the population" including ethnic minorities, religious groups and "perhaps children, women and homeless people"'. On the other hand, 'separate chapters on women and ethnic groups . . . is not considered good practice'.

The advice given by government at different times is a fascinating subject for textual analysis.

15  PPG 12. See also DoE/DoT, *Transport and the Environment Study* (Joint Memorandum to the Royal Commission on Environmental Pollution), DoE, 1992. Annex F of the latter gives a useful overview of 'Transport and Land Use Planning'.

16  See also Town Planning Review 1977, and Law 1977.

17  Sources used in this section are the 1978 White Paper, *Planning Procedures: The Government's Response to the Eighth Report from the Expenditure Committee Session 1976–77*; the 1985 White Paper, *Lifting the Burden*; the DoE 1986 Consultation Paper, *The Future of Development Plans*; SDD *Structure Planning* (PAN 37, 1992); and Bruton 1980a.

18  See Coon 1988. Of the English and Welsh local plans, 82 per cent were general (or district) plans, 10 per cent were subject plans and 8 per cent were action area plans. Over 700 local plans were in preparation. In population terms, about 20 per cent of the country was subject to an adopted plan in metropolitan and non-metropolitan districts, but substantially more, 60 per cent, in

London. The DoE estimated, at this time, that less than a quarter of the area of England and Wales had been covered by prepared plans. Coon's (1988) findings point to some interesting differences. Urban areas had greater coverage than rural areas, though provincial cities had produced less plan cover than the metropolitan areas. There was great variation in performance even between districts with similar characteristics, and half of non-metropolitan districts had no statutory local plans at all. By September 1992, there were 77 non-metropolitan districts with complete coverage of local plans, 41 of which were district-wide plans. Two metropolitan districts and 22 London boroughs had full coverage by adopted local plans. One London borough had an adopted unitary development plan.

19  This takes no account of plans that failed to complete the process through to adoption. Using a rule of thumb of five years life for a plan, Coon (1988) suggested that 'up to date coverage is provided for only 14% of the metropolitan population and only seven per cent of the non-metropolitan population'. Winter (1989) found, in his 1986 survey, that only about a quarter of authorities were actively engaged in review at that time, with over 40 per cent having no intention to review their adopted plan. It seems clear that, at that rate, the level of up-to-date statutory plan cover would increase only very slowly.

20  'Policies and proposals that are likely to provide the basis for deciding planning applications, or for determining conditions to be attached to planning permissions, should be set out in the appropriate plan, which is subject to statutory procedures' (PPG 12: 3.18). For further guidance on SPG, see the Department's *Good Practice Guide on Development Plans* (1992: 51).

21  *Great Portland Estates* v. *Westminster City Council*, Court of Apeal 1983; See *JPL* 1984: 510.

22  Shelton (1991: 46) describes attitudes in his authority, Leeds: 'In the mid and late seventies, statutory planning was off the menu, pending completion of the West Yorkshire Structure Plan . . . Since about 1980 local planning in inner city Leeds has increased but is now project and issue based – closer to implementation than to plan making . . . Because of their limited (land-use) role, the time they take and their formalised structure, statutory local plans can make very little contribution to inner areas.'

23  Healey *et al*. 1985; Healey *et al*. 1988; and Healey 1986b.

24  These are listed under the Davies, H.W.E. *et al*. references in the Bibliography.

25  For commentary on the early stages of strategic guidance and UDP preparation, see Hill 1991, and Wenban-Smith 1991.

26  The West Midlands (where there was an existing

framework of cooperation between the districts both at officer and member level) was the first area to produce strategic advice. Thew and Watson (1988) have set out the procedures followed. These included an initial meeting chaired by the DoE Regional Controller of Planning to set the agenda for the following technical work, followed by two conferences with an independent chair and 'public access'. The technical analysis was undertaken by 'lead authorities'. For example, Sandwell took responsibility for urban regeneration, Walsall and Solihull jointly led population and housing, and Coventry led transport. The process took sixteen months – including the time needed for the DoE to deliberate on the draft and to issue the final guidance as PPG 10 in February 1988. A similar procedure is being followed in the other metropolitan counties, although in some cases with more involvement of the surrounding shire authorities. (See Town Planning Review 1992.)

27 The first call came from the House of Commons Expenditure Committee in their 1976 report on *Planning Procedures*.

28 Secretary of State for the Environment Chris Patten's announcement, DoE Press Release, 24 September 1990.

29 In addition new enforcement powers were introduced (which apply also to Scotland): these are discussed in Chapter 4.

30 It is still possible for district-wide local plans and unitary development plans to designate action areas, PPG 12, 1992, paras 3.9 and 3.10.

31 The transitional arrangements are set out in DoE Circular 18/91.

32 The revised PPG 12 updated the advice contained in the previous PPG 12, PPG 15, the remaining sections of Circular 22/84, Circular 3/88 on UDPs, and Circulars 24/87 and 30/85.

33 There is a separate PPG 12 for Wales.

34 Association of District Councils, *Survey of Local Plan Progress and Intention*, ADC, 1990 and 1991. The DoE has a six-monthly survey. The results are not published although summaries are made available. The September 1992 survey showed signs of slippage with about 10 per cent of authorities suggesting that they would not be able to meet the December 1996 target. This prompted the Minister for Housing and Planning, Sir George Young, to urge the District Planning Officers' Society to make good progress saying 'I note with interest that those local authorities with full local plan coverage are able on average to decide a higher proportion of applications within the target. I suspect this is no coincidence' (Reported in *Planning*, 1001, 15 January 1993). See also McClenaghan and Blatchford 1993.

35 See, for example, the sample of plans in the study by Bruton *et al.* (1982a and 1982b). Adams and Pawson

(1991) found that the sample of plans adopted between September 1988 and September 1989 were subject to 7,579 representations, a mean of 474 per plan. Of these, 6,192 were considered by the Inspector (a mean of 387); 78 per cent were objections, and 22 per cent supporting representations. Interim results from a DoE-sponsored research project on a sample of local plan inquiries held between 1991 and 1993 give a mean of 578 objections for district-wide local plans, 909 for UDPs, and 173 for part-area plans.

36 Quoted in *Local Government News*, January 1991. The view of many in the development industry is reflected in the comment by RICS Chief Planning Spokesperson, Alan Cave, who said, 'The RICS has consistently argued for a strong strategic planning framework at county level . . . But we will want to examine in detail the impact of the new proposal for self-adoption of structure plans by counties . . . It is reassuring that the Secretary of State will retain reserve powers to ensure conformity between structure plans and regional guidance' (*Civil and Structural Weekly*, 4 October 1990).

37 Sir George Young's paper to the 1992 TCPSS. This gives a very clear statement of the Government's approach. The flavour is nicely given in another sentence: 'Sometimes, our objections have not been to the basic thrust of a policy but to the way it is expressed. If a plan as drafted seems to us to be defective as a development control tool, we shall say so.' See also *DoE Annual Report 1993*, para. 4.6.

38 Joint Chairman of the Development Plans Topic Committee, Andrew Wright, in a letter to members of the District Planning Officers' Society, 24 June 1992.

39 On the law of planning in Scotland generally see *Scottish Planning Law and Practice*, published three times a year by the Planning Exchange (186 Bath Street, Glasgow G2 4HG). Useful introductory accounts are given in Begg and Pollock 1991, and in Henderson 1989.

40 The provisions for development planning in Scotland are to be found in the Town and Country Planning (Scotland) Act 1972. The former provisions introduced by the Town and Country Planning (Scotland) Act 1947 were subject to a very similar set of criticisms to those made in England (see Coon 1981). Guidance on development plans in Scotland is given in Scottish Office PAN 30 *Local Planning* (1984) and PAN 37 *Structure Planning* (1992).

41 This was introduced by the Local Government (Scotland) Act 1973.

42 It should be noted, however, that regional reports had a wider purpose than structure plans and were, in effect, a substitute for them (Lloyd and Rown-Robinson 1988). When the statutory development plan framework was in place, no further purpose was seen for them. (See Gillett 1983: 61, and Gilg 1983: 23.)

43  The number of plans required to complete full coverage has fallen from over 400 in 1978 to an estimated 292 at August 1992, following the trend to larger area and complete district-wide plans (Draft NPPG 1, 1992). By 1985, 142 plans had been adopted; by 1989 the number had increased to 201, covering 65 per cent of the land area and 44 per cent of the population (Coon 1989). This is perhaps less than might be anticipated with a mandatory requirement in existence for sixteen years. At the end of 1992, three-quarters of the plans proposed had been adopted and about the same proportion of the land area covered. (The Scottish Office Environment Department's *Planning Bulletin*, which is published twice a year, gives reports on structure and local plan progress.) As in England and Wales, non-statutory plans have been widely used. This has been subject to criticisms by, for example, Coon 1989, and Lyddon 1985.

44  'Industrial development in the form of onshore terminals, pipeline landfalls, treatment plants or rig and platform construction yards was going to take place on an unprecedented scale and in considerable haste . . . Locally, the control of oil-related development rested with district and regional councils, but the view of the Scottish Office was that so many of the issues were of national importance that many of them would have to be determined by central government. It also followed, again in their view, that the central government should give some indication of the principles it would follow in the actions it took. The most immediate need was to draft a national policy on coastal development, since the greater part of oil-related industry needed a location on the coast for obvious reasons' (Gillett 1983: 23).

45  'The land use summary sheets report the current state and character of the land resource in question, define its national significance, review past changes and likely future demand, and address the implications for planning' (Rowan-Robinson and Lloyd 1991: 17).

46  In 1991, the Scottish Office's consultation paper *Review of Planning Guidance* proposed to replace the NPGs with National Planning Policy Guidance Notes (NPPGs) and to discontinue the land-use summary sheets. This latter decision, made on the assumption that local authorities can now get this information from a number of sources, and are in fact a major supplier of the information in the first place, has met with some concern (Lloyd and Rowan-Robinson 1992). The main proposal will lead to broader policy statements but (on the basis of the first two draft NPPGs) this has been welcomed since it 'should do much to reduce the confusion of purpose which presently exists between the various forms of guidance [and result in] the strengthening of the

framework for strategic planning in Scotland' (Lloyd and Rowan-Robinson 1992: 98).

47  For a discussion of SERPLAN see Marshall (1991); SERPLAN (1992b), and SERPLAN's regular newsletter.

48  'Developing regional planning guidance in England and Wales: a review symposium', *Town Planning Review* 63: 415–34, 1992. This consists of an introduction and concluding comments by C.L.W. Minay, and accounts of regional planning guidance for East Anglia (D. Cross), the East Midlands (D. Gillingwater), the North-East (T. Shaw), and the South-West (T. Coombes, P. Fidler, and A. Hathaway).

49  The reports were prepared for the authorities involved in the strategic planning process, but were not formally published. The relevant statistics are published in the annual *Environmental Digest for Wales* (Welsh Office).

50  A report from the TCPA (*Strategic Planning for Regional Development*, 1993) takes a more radical line, and argues for a regional tier of government which would have the power to prepare and to implement strategic development plans.

51  See also Leach 1992, and Williams *et al.* 1992.

52  See, for example, County Planning Officers' Society 1985: 5; British Property Federation 1986: 6.

53  Crispin *et al.* 1985. Of course, these figures do not include those plans which for one reason or another failed to reach the stage of formal adoption. However, research conducted for the SDD has shown that the major reason for failure to complete the process within a reasonable time is poor management and organisation within the authority itself (Thomson 1985).

54  The DoE has commissioned a report from Plan Local on 'the efficiency and effectiveness of local plan inquiries'. (Plan Local is a joint venture of Chesterton Consulting and the School of Planning, University of Central England in Birmingham.)

55  Introduced by the Local Government Planning and Land Act 1980.

56  In addition to the references given in the text the following is a selection of the literature on enterprise zones. For early general evaluations of the concept see Butler 1981; Catalano 1983; Hall 1982; Sorensen and Day 1981; Unger 1982. For later reviews, see Gunther and Leathers 1987; Hall 1991; Thornley 1991. For case-studies see, on Dudley: Latham 1982; on Inverclyde: Lloyd and Danson 1991; on Scunthorpe: Barnes and Preston 1985; on Tyneside: Talbot 1988; and on Swansea: Bromley and Morgan 1985, Bromley and Rees 1988, Sparks 1987, and Thomas and Bromley 1987.

57  The 1986 Consultation Paper on *The Future of Development Plans* rejected zoning, which had been indentified as an option in the 1976/77 Expenditure

Committee report, in favour of the existing system, arguing that 'development plans are an essential component of a rational land-use planning system. The Government's objective is to retain and strengthen the basic elements of the system and to improve its efficiency and effectiveness.'

58 In July 1987, draft regulations, a circular and an advice note were published by the Secretaries of State. Later in the same year several circulars were issued: DoE Circular 25/87, WO Circular 50/87, and SDD Circular 16/87. Scotland was the first with more specific guidance to local authorities with Planning Advice Note 31 (1987). Advice in England followed early in the following year with the publication in 1988 of PPG 5.

59 More controversial has been the proposed use of SPZs for residential areas. PPG 5 suggests that such a use of an SPZ scheme 'may have a useful role to play in encouraging good quality innovative design. The exact mix of dwelling types, layout and landscaping features can be left to developers. They can then respond more quickly to changing client preferences.' Such an idea goes well beyond normal zoning practices. In the event no action has been taken on it.

60 The response was much as before, with the RTPI, the CPRE, and the NHTPC being prominent amongst those who argued that the concept should be abandoned. In their view, the underlying assumption (that the planning system is an obstacle to development and regeneration) was false.

61 The DoE and Welsh Office have published a revised version of PPG 5 (November 1992) which provides further guidance on the new procedures and advice on the use of SPZs; and which also cancels Circulars 25/87 (WO 24/88) 24/88 (WO 48/88). The Scottish Office are proposing a new circular to replace SDD Circular 16/87 to give guidance on procedure which at the time of writing (April 1993) was not yet finalised; and to also update PAN 31 at a later date. The impact of the 1991 Act on SPZ procedure for Scotland is the same as for England and Wales, except that the list of consultees is different.

62 The point is illustrated by a quotation from a monitoring report of the first SPZ: 'The SPZ was designated to allow developers to establish on site without a further planning permission. This has occurred with the development of the vast majority of plots in the Zone. However, to allow this to happen, there has been regular informal liaison between the developers' site agents or interested companies themselves and officers of the Department of Development Services to clarify whether a particular proposal was within the terms of the SPZ scheme' (Derby City Council 1991: 4.1).

63 On the first SPZs, see Ross 1988, Jesper and Grass 1989, Derby City Council 1991. Only one private firm has had a significant involvement in promoting the SPZ initiative: Slough Estates promoted a scheme for the 450-acre trading estate at Slough and also for a second smaller scheme at Kings Norton, Birmingham. See *Planning* 625 (31 March 1989): 1.

64 See, for example, Davies 1992.

# 4

# THE CONTROL OF DEVELOPMENT

Development control is a process by which society, represented by locally elected councils, regulates changes in the use and appearance of the environment. As such it is of critical importance. Decisions taken in the planning process have long-term consequences and are usually irreversible. Well-considered decisions can enhance and enrich the environment. Poor decisions will be endured long after the decision-takers have died.

Audit Commission, *Building in Quality* 1992

## THE SCOPE OF CONTROL

Most forms of development (as statutorily defined) are subject to the prior approval of the local planning authority, though certain categories are excluded from control. Local planning authorities have considerable discretion in giving approval. Though they must 'have regard to the provisions of the development plan', they can take 'any other material considerations' into account. Indeed, they can approve a proposal which does not 'accord with the provisions of the plan'.

Planning decisions of a local planning authority can be one of three kinds: unconditional permission, permission subject to conditions, or refusal. The practical scope of these powers is discussed later; here it is necessary merely to stress that an applicant has the right of appeal to the Secretary of State against conditional permissions and refusals. If the action of the LPA is thought to be *ultra vires*, there is also a right of recourse to the courts. Furthermore, planning applications which raise issues which are of more than local importance, or are of a particular technical nature, can be 'called in' for ministerial decision.

Development control necessarily involves measures for enforcement. This is provided by procedures which require anyone who carries out development without permission or in breach of conditions to consult with the LPA and, in certain circumstances, to 'undo' the development, even if this involves the demolition of a new building. A *stop notice* can also be used to put a rapid end to the carrying out or continuation of development which is in breach of planning control, when serious environmental problems are being caused by the unauthorised activity.

These are very strong powers, and it is clearly important to establish the meaning of *development*, particularly since the term has a legal connotation far wider than in ordinary language.

## THE DEFINITION OF DEVELOPMENT

In brief, development is 'the carrying out of building, engineering, mining or other operations in, on, over or under land, or the making of any material change in the use of any buildings or other land' (and, since the 1991 Act, now covers some categories of demolition). There are many legal niceties attendant upon this definition with which it is fortunately not necessary to deal in the present outline. Some account of the breadth of the definition is, nevertheless, needed. 'Building operations', for instance, include rebuilding, structural alterations of or additions to buildings and, somewhat curiously, 'other operations normally undertaken by a person carrying on business as a builder'; but maintenance, improvement, and alteration works which affect only the interior of the building or which do not materially affect the external appearance of the building are specifically excluded.

The second half of the definition introduces a quite different concept: development here means not a physical operation, but a change in the *use* of a piece of land or a building. To constitute 'development', the change has to be *material*, that is, substantial: a concept which it is clearly difficult to define, and which, indeed, is not defined in the legislation. A change in *kind* (for example from a house to a shop) is material, but a change in *degree* is material only if the change is substantial. For instance, the fact that lodgers are taken privately in a family dwelling house does not of itself constitute a material change so long as the main use of the house remains that of a private residence. On the other hand, the change from a private residence with lodgers to a declared guest house, boarding house or private hotel would be material. Difficulties arise with changes of use involving part of a building; with ancillary uses; and with the distinction between a material change of use and a mere interruption.

This is by no means the end of the matter, but enough has been stated to show the breadth of the definition of development and the technical complexities to which it can give rise. Reference must, nevertheless, be made to one further matter. Experience has shown that complicated definitions are necessary if adequate development control is to be achieved, but the same tortuous technique can be used to exclude matters over which control is not necessary. First, there are certain matters which are specifically declared not to constitute development (for example, internal alterations to buildings, works of road maintenance, or improvement carried out by

a local highway authority within the boundaries of a road). Second, there are others which, though possibly constituting development, are declared not to require planning permission. Third, there is provision for the Secretary of State to make a *General Development Order* (GDO) specifying classes of 'permitted' development, a *Use Classes Order* (UCO) specifying groups of uses within which interchange is permissible, and *Special Development Orders* for specific locations or categories of development.

The distinction between the GDO and the UCO is that the former lists activities which, though constituting development, do not require permission from the LPA, while the UCO lists categories of use within which any changes do not constitute development. The distinction was of particular importance during the time when development charges were imposed, since if there was no 'development' then no development charge was payable, whereas development was, by definition, eligible for a charge. In fact, however, exemption from development charge was specifically made for many of these permitted developments. These complexities are now mainly of historical interest and are not discussed further (Home 1992).

## THE USE CLASSES ORDER AND THE GENERAL DEVELOPMENT ORDER[1]

The Use Classes Order prescribes sixteen classes of use within which change can take place without constituting development. Thus, class A1 covers shops used for all or any of a list of ten purposes, including the retail sale of goods (other than hot food); the sale of sandwiches or other cold food for consumption off the premises; for hairdressing; for the direction of funerals; and for the display of goods for sale. Class A3 covers 'use for the sale of food or drink for consumption on the premises or of hot food for consumption off the premises'. As a result of these classes, a shop can be changed from a hairdresser to funeral parlour or a sweet shop (or vice versa), but it cannot be changed (unless planning permission is obtained) to a restaurant or a hot food take-away which is in a different class. The classes, it should be stressed, refer only to changes of use, not to any building work, and the Order gives no freedom to change from one class to another. Whether such a change constitutes development depends on whether the change is 'material'.

The General Development Order gives the developer a little more freedom by listing classes of 'permitted development' – or, to be more precise, it gives advance general permission for certain classes of development, typically of a minor character. If a proposed development falls within these classes, no application for planning permission is necessary: the GDO itself constitutes the permission. The Order includes minor alterations to residential buildings, and the erection of certain agricultural buildings[2] (other than dwelling-houses). It also permits certain changes of use within the UCO, such as a change from an A3 use (the Food and Drink class) to an A1 use (shop), but not – because of the possible environmental implications – the other way round. While the use changes allowed by the UCO are all 'bilateral' (any change of use within a class is reversible without constituting development), the GDO builds upon this structure by specifying a number of 'unilateral' changes *between* classes for which permission is not required. The rationale here is that the permitted changes generally constitute an environmental improvement.

The cynic may perhaps be forgiven for commenting that the freedom given by the UCO and the GDO is so hedged by restrictions, and frequently so difficult to comprehend, that it would be safer to assume that any operation constitutes development and requires planning permission (though it may be noted with relief that painting is not normally subject to control, unless it is 'for purpose of advertisement, announcement or direction'). The legislators have been helpful here. Application can be made to the LPA for a *certificate of lawfulness* of a proposed use or development.[3] This enables a developer to ascertain whether or not planning permission is required.

The Orders were modified by the Conservative Government as part of its policy of 'lifting the burden'

on business. Some of the changes have proved to be very controversial. For example, it is now allowable to change a restaurant to a fast hot-food take-away, or to change a public house to more profitable uses such as professional offices, and other uses appropriate to a shopping area. The impact of these changes on such matters as local amenity and traffic generation is detailed in a 1992 report by Sandra Bell for the London Boroughs Association. The Government response to the representations of local government are set out in the report: it is maintained that 'the advantages of the present arrangements in terms of the certainty and flexibility they provide for the commercial sector, and the reduction in intervention and bureaucracy, far outweigh the disadvantages'. A clearer illustration of the political nature of planning would be difficult to find (though more persuasive are the photographs in this report depicting the detrimental effects of 'change of use').

## SPECIAL DEVELOPMENT ORDERS

While the GDO is applicable generally, Special Development Orders (SDOs) relate to particular areas or particular types of development. Thus, an urban development corporation SDO grants permission for the carrying out of development (approved by the Secretary of State) by an urban development corporation within the designated area. Other SDOs deal with development control in national parks, areas of outstanding natural beauty, and conservation areas, and with such special uses as the oxide fuel processing plant at Sellafield (Windscale), and sites for nuclear waste disposal.

SDOs (like other Orders) are subject to parliamentary debate and annulment by resolution of either House. This can provide an opportunity for testing opinion on controversial proposals such as the reprocessing of nuclear fuels at Windscale or the designation of Stansted as the site of the third London airport.

An unusual use of an SDO was the Vauxhall Cross proposal in London which, though receiving architectural acclaim, was fiercely opposed by the local authority. This granted planning permission for a very large development including more than 1 million square feet of offices and 260,000 square feet of dwellings on the eastern end of Vauxhall Bridge. Though, in fact, the development did not proceed, the use of the SDO procedure for such a purpose involves a high degree of central involvement in local planning decisions. The case submitted by the DoE was that 'the purpose of making fuller use of SDOs would not be to make any general relaxation in development control, but to stimulate planned development in acceptable locations, and speed up the planning process' (Thornley 1991: 163). This is tantamount to saying that the central government knows best.[4]

## CONDITIONAL PERMISSIONS

A local planning authority can grant planning permission subject to conditions.[5] This can be a very useful way of permitting development which would otherwise be undesirable. Thus a garage may be approved in a residential area on condition that the hours of business are limited. Residential development may be permitted in an area designated as a green belt subject to the condition that the houses are occupied only by agricultural workers.[6]

The power to impose conditions is a very wide one. The legislation allows LPAs to grant permission subject to 'such conditions as they think fit', but this does not mean 'as they please'. The conditions must be appropriate from a planning point of view:

the planning authority are not at liberty to use their power for an ulterior object, however desirable that object may seem to them to be in the public interest. If they mistake or misuse their powers, however *bona fide*, the court can interfere by declaration and injunction.[7]

DoE Circular 1/85, *The Use of Conditions in Planning Permission*, stresses that, in addition to satisfying the legal criteria for validity, 'conditions should not be imposed unless they are both necessary and effective, and do not place unjustifiable burdens on applicants'. Conditions should be 'necessary, relevant

to planning, relevant to the development to be permitted, enforceable, precise, and reasonable in all other respects'. As might be expected, there is considerable debate on the meaning of these terms.[8]

Up to 1968, there was no general time limit within which development had to take place: unless a specific condition was imposed, development for which planning permission had been given could take place at any time. The 1968 Act, however, made all planning permissions subject to a condition that development is commenced within five years. If the work is not begun within this time limit, the permission lapses. However, the Secretary of State or the local planning authority can vary the period, and there is no bar to the renewal of permission after that period has elapsed (whether it be more or less than five years).

The purpose of this provision is to prevent the accumulation of unused permissions and to discourage the speculative landhoarder. Accumulated unused permissions could constitute a difficult problem for some LPAs: they create uncertainty and could make an authority reluctant to grant further permissions, which might result in, for example, too great a strain on public services. The provision is directed towards the bringing forward of development for which permission has been granted, and thus to enable new allocations of land for development to be made against a reasonably certain background of pending development.

The provision relates, however, only to the beginning of development, and this has in the past been deemed to include digging a trench or putting a peg in the ground. But (if the permission is not a pre-1968 Act one) the trench-digger may be brought up against a further provision: the serving of a *completion notice*. Such a notice states that the planning permission lapses after the expiration of a specified period (of not less than one year). Any work carried out after then becomes liable to enforcement procedures.[9]

Planning 'conditions' of a different nature, involving *planning gain* and *planning agreements*, are discussed in the context of land values in Chapter 5.

It is sometimes convenient for an applicant or the

LPA (or both) to deal with an application in outline. *Outline planning permission* gives the applicant permission in principle to carry out development subject to *reserved matters* which are decided at a later stage. This is a useful device to enable a developer to proceed with the preparation of detailed plans with the security that they will not be opposed in principle (Davies *et al*. 1989).

## CONTROL OF DEMOLITION

Prior to the 1991 Act, it was generally accepted that demolition did not of itself constitute development, and local authorities typically assumed that demolition was outside the ambit of development control[10] (though there were some legal uncertainties). However, there was increasing disquiet in the early 1970s about the lack of clear and 'blanket' control of demolition. This was expressed by amenity societies, and also by local authorities who were concerned at some of the effects of commercial enterprise. Following the resulting parliamentary pressure, Mr George Dobry, QC, was commissioned to review the situation. This he did in a terse report, *The Control of Demolition*, published in 1974.

He concluded that there were several persuasive arguments in favour of subjecting demolition to control. These were, first, that 'there is a good deal of concern that the planning system should permit town centre and residential development that is sometimes strikingly out of scale or sympathy with the area affected'. Second, there was some uncertainty as to the law. Third, there was some inconsistency: here the argument, curiously, was that though there were powers for the control over the demolition of certain buildings, there was no 'overall system'. Fourth, 'and most importantly', there were several practical reasons for the general extension of control over demolition:

— *The aftermath of demolition*: barren sites, inadequately fenced, often become a dumping ground causing general deterioration of the neighbourhood.
— *Demolition as a 'fait accompli'* can be used by developers to force the grant of planning permission.

— *Premature demolition of houses*: premature demolition and vacancy of residential accommodation in anticipation of development causes public disquiet.
— *Need to preserve commercial and community use*: premature demolition of shops in a redevelopment area is clearly harmful. Many think that to prevent the demolition of useful residential buildings, theatres and cinemas is equally important.

No action was taken on Dobry's proposals until, following some contradictory court decisions, the Planning and Compensation Act 1991 introduced very limited planning control over demolition. This control relates mainly to the demolition of dwellinghouses and of buildings adjoining dwellinghouses.[11]

## FEES FOR PLANNING APPLICATIONS

Fees for planning applications were introduced in 1980. This represented a marked break with planning traditions, which had held (at least implicitly) that development control is of general communal benefit and directly analogous to other forms of public control for which no charges are made to individuals. The Thatcher administration had a very different view:

> We do not believe that the community as a whole should continue to pay for all sorts of things that it has paid for in the past . . . In the general review that has taken place to see where we can reduce spending from the public purse . . . we came to the conclusion that the cost of development control was an area where some part of the cost should be recovered.[12]

The 1980 bill provided additionally for fees for appeals but this was dropped in the face of widespread objections from both sides of the House.

The current regulations were made in 1989, and amended in 1991 and 1992. The fee structure is subject to change over time, and a detailed schedule is therefore not appropriate. However, to illustrate, under the current regulations the fee for residential development is £120 per dwelling (up to a maximum of £6,000 for fifty or more); applications relating to commercial and industrial buildings are charged according to the gross floor space to be created, with £60 for up to 40 sq. m, and £120 for each additional

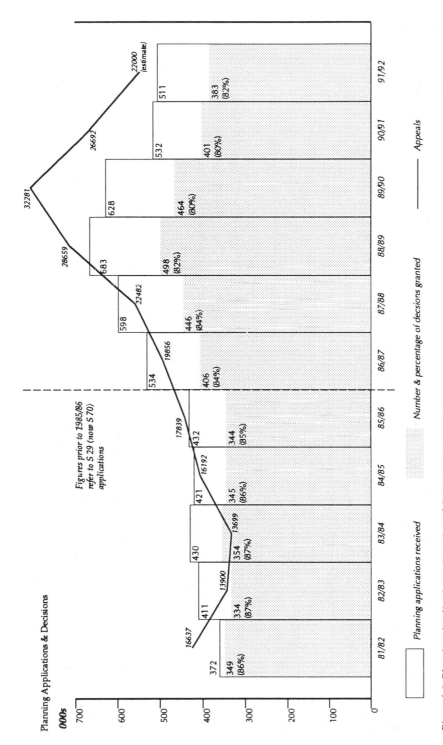

Planning Applications & Decisions

000s

Planning Applications and Decisions, England

Figure 4.1 Planning Applications, Appeals and Decisions, England

Figures prior to 1985/86 refer to S 29 (now S 70) applications

□ Planning applications received

▒ Number & percentage of decisions granted

── Appeals

75 sq. m, up to a maximum of £6,000.[13] The Government's ultimate aim is to recover the full administrative costs of dealing with planning applications. A working party has been established to undertake a comprehensive review of the fee structure.[14]

The power to charge fees for planning applications does not extend to the pre-application discussion stage. A decision of the Court of Appeal allowing such charges was reversed by the House of Lords in 1991.[15]

## PLANNING APPEALS

An unsuccessful planning applicant can appeal to the Secretary of State, and a large number in fact do so.[16] Appeals decided during 1991/92 (England and Wales) numbered 22,553 of which about a third were allowed.[17] Here the Secretary of State has wide powers. He may reverse the local authority's decision or subject it to conditions. He may quash or modify conditions which they have imposed. He may make those conditions more onerous, or he may even go to the extent of refusing planning permission altogether if he decides that the local authority should not have granted it with the conditions imposed.

Though each planning appeal is considered and determined on its merits, the cumulative effect is an emergence of the Department's views on a wide range of planning matters. The effect of these on the policy of individual authorities may be difficult to assess, but clearly they are likely to have a very real influence. Local planning authorities are unlikely to refuse planning consents for a particular type of development if they are convinced that the Department would uphold an appeal.

It is not, of course, every planning appeal that raises an issue of policy. Yet until 1969 all had to be dealt with by the Department's inspectorate, though the majority were settled by correspondence after an informal visit to the site and without a local inquiry. (This is *the written representations procedure.*) The Franks Committee on Administrative Tribunals and Inquiries argued that it was not satisfactory 'that a

government department should be occupied with appeal work of this volume, particularly as many of the appeals relate to minor and purely local matters, in which little or no departmental policy entered' (Franks Report 1957: 85). An analysis of the subject matter of appeals undertaken by the Department (and reported in the 1967 White Paper *Town and Country Planning*) confirmed this.[18]

In view of the delay which was inevitable in this appeals system and the huge administrative burden it placed on the Department, considerable thought was given to possible alternatives. The solution adopted by the 1968 Planning Act was for the determination of certain classes of appeals by inspectors. The classes are defined by regulation and can thus be amended in the light of experience. The trend has been to increase the range, and now the great majority of appeals are decided in this way. The Department has, in fact, divested itself of responsibility for adjudicating on all but a small number of planning appeals. Only matters of major importance are 'recovered' for decision by the Secretary of State.[19] Appeals that are recovered in this way include:

- residential developments of more than 150 homes;
- retail proposals of more than 100,000 sq. ft;
- cases giving rise to significant public controversy, legal difficulties, or novel issues of development control;
- proposals for significant development in the green belt;
- major proposals involving minerals;
- proposals to which another government department has objected;
- cases which can only be decided in conjunction with another case over which inspectors have no jurisdiction (so-called 'linked' cases).[20]

Since the beginning of the 1980s, the Government has been particularly concerned at 'freeing' the economy from unnecessary regulation. White Papers were issued with rousing titles such as *Lifting the Burden* (1985) and *Building Businesses . . . Not Barriers* (1986). Perversely, the number of appeals received rose during this decade, reaching a peak of 32,281 in 1989/90, since when there has been a significant fall. The increase in appeals had the effect of slowing down the appeals procedures. Since the Government was committed to speeding-up planning processes, this position was embarrassing (to put the matter no more strongly). In seeking ways to deal with this, reviews of the appeals system were undertaken within the Department, the first of which was completed in 1985 and published 'with action plan' in 1986.[21] This was an internal 'efficiency scrutiny' of the written representation system, which showed that some delays were the fault of the Department, while others were the result of factors outside the Department's control, including the way in which the applicant and his agent dealt with the appeal. In short, there was no simple answer to the problem, and the report made some forty detailed recommendations.[22]

In recent years, increased emphasis has been placed on ensuring that development plans provide a clear guide to applicants and a firm basis for planning decisions. This, in turn, requires that there is adequate input into the plan preparation process. It is envisaged that this will reduce the number of appeals. In the words of the Minister of State for Housing and Planning, Sir George Young:

> The ultimate success of the plan-led system will be measured by smaller proportions of refusals, because developers come to recognise the need to participate in plan preparation and then work within the framework it provides. Another key indicator will be the appeal success rate; we will be less likely to allow appeals if we have satisfied ourselves on the content of the plan, and the planning decision accords with the plan.
>
> (Sir George Young 1992)

## 'CALL-IN' OF PLANNING APPLICATIONS

The power to 'call in' a planning application for decision by the Secretary of State is quite separate from that of determining an appeal against an adverse decision of an LPA. This power is not circumscribed: the Secretary of State may call in *any* application. There are no statutory criteria or restrictions, and no prescribed procedures for handling representations from the public. Though there is no general statement of policy as to which applications will normally be called in, there are several categories which are particularly liable.

In the first place, all applications for development involving a substantial departure from the provisions of a development plan which the LPA intends to grant must be sent to the Secretary of State together with a statement of the reasons why it wishes to grant the permission.[23] This procedure enables the Secretary of State to decide whether the development is sufficiently important to warrant its being called in. Second, mineral workings often raise problems of more than local importance, and the national need for particular minerals has to be balanced against planning issues. Such matters cannot be adequately considered by local planning authorities and, in any case, involve technical considerations requiring expert opinion of a character more easily available to the Department. For these reasons, a large proportion of applications for permission to work minerals have been called in. Furthermore, there is a general direction calling in all applications for the winning and working of ironstone in certain counties where there are large-scale ironstone workings. Third, the power of call-in is generally used when the matter at stake is (as in the case of minerals) of more than local importance or interest. (The Royal Fine Art Commission has, in its terms of reference, the power 'to call the attention of any of our departments of state . . . to any project or development which [it considers] may appear to affect amenities of a national or public character'. The Commission has requested the use of call-in on a number of occasions, not always successfully.[24])

Dobry's review of development control noted that 'in recent years' (that is, recent to 1973) the call-in procedure had tended to be used only for the following kinds of applications:

(a) cases raising issues of national, regional, or otherwise more than local importance;
(b) cases which arouse more than local opposition, for example, the redevelopment of the Monico site in Shaftesbury Avenue;
(c) cases which, for any reason, it might be unreasonable to ask the local planning authority to decide, for example, involving development proposed by foreign governments (the decision on which could be diplomatically sensitive), or development raising unfamiliar problems on which adequate technical advice was not available to the local planning

authority, for example, the first application for a processing plant for North Sea Gas;

(d) cases associated with a different issue which can be decided only by the Secretary of State, for example, applications for town centre redevelopment associated with a compulsory purchase order.

(Dobry Report 1974b: 51)

Examples are sometimes given in the annual reports of the Chief Planning Inspector. Thus, in 1984, the applications which were called in included the proposed extension to the National Gallery, and the proposed redevelopment in Mansion House Square (which included a 290 feet high, eighteen-storey tower block designed by Mies van der Rohe). Both of these applications were refused. Similarly, proposals by the Property Services Agency to use an area of high landscape value at Gravesend, Kent for an army training ground were refused. On the other hand, the proposed Stolport (short take-off and landing airport) in London's Royal Docks was given conditional planning permission.

When an application is called in, the Secretary of State must, if either the applicant or the local planning authority so desire, hold a hearing or public inquiry. The public inquiry is more usual, particularly in important cases.

The power of call-in is only infrequently exercised. There has been considerable criticism about its modest use, and also about the haphazard way in which cases appear to be selected. The RTPI, in its evidence to the House of Commons Environment Committee,[25] suggested that 'failure to intervene on a number of occasions has been a dereliction of duty and indicated a partisan attitude to particular proposals by denying the objectors the right to a hearing by an independent inspector'. (Though there is no right of third parties to object to the grant of a planning permission, there is a right to object if the matter goes to public inquiry.) The Environment Committee agreed, and recommended 'radical change to place call-in on a more systematic footing'.[26]

Since 1968, the Secretary of State has had power to refer development proposals of a far-reaching or novel character to an *ad hoc* Planning Inquiry Commission. This power has never been used: the

Roskill Commission on the third London airport was set up under non-statutory powers, while the Greater London Development Plan Inquiry was established under the *general* powers to hold local inquiries provided by the Town and Country Planning Act (now section 320 of the 1990 Act). For major inquiries such as Windscale, Belvoir, Stansted, and Sizewell, this special form of inquiry might have been considered particularly apt: that it was not so considered gave rise to much debate (which is dealt with in the final chapter).

## ENFORCEMENT OF PLANNING CONTROL

If the machinery of planning control is to be effective, some means of enforcement is essential. Under the pre-war system of interim development control there were no such effective means. A developer could go ahead without applying for planning permission, or could even ignore a refusal of permission. He took the risk of being compelled to 'undo' his development (for example, demolish a newly built house) when, and if, the planning scheme was approved, but this was a risk which was usually worth taking. And if the development was inexpensive and lucrative (for example, a petrol station or a greyhound racing track) the risk was virtually no deterrent at all. This flaw in the pre-war system was remedied by the strengthening of enforcement provisions.

These are required not only for the obvious purpose of implementing planning policy but also to ensure that there is continuing public support for, and confidence in, the planning system. To quote PPG 18:

> The integrity of the development control process depends on the LPA's readiness to take effective action when it is essential. Public acceptance of the development control process is quickly undermined if unauthorised development, which is unacceptable on planning merits, is allowed to proceed without any apparent attempt by the LPA to intervene before serious harm results from it.

Development undertaken without permission is not an offence in itself, but ignoring an *enforcement notice* is, and there is a maximum fine, following conviction, of £20,000. (In determining the amount of the fine, the court is required to 'have regard to any financial benefit which has accrued'.)

There is a right of appeal against an enforcement notice to the Secretary of State. Appeals can be made on several grounds, for example, that permission ought to be granted, that permission has been granted (e.g. by the GDO), and that no permission is required. There is also a limited right of appeal on a point of law to the High Court.

Enforcement provisions were radically changed by the 1991 Planning and Compensation Act,[27] following a comprehensive review by Robert Carnwath, QC, published in 1989. In addition to the long-standing provision for enforcement notices, a LPA now has power to issue a *planning contravention notice*. This enables it to obtain information about a suspected breach of planning control and to seek the cooperation of the person thought to be in breach of planning control. This optional procedure is intended to enable discussions to take place on whether planning permission (with or without conditions) is required. If agreement is not forthcoming (whether or not a contravention notice is served) an enforcement notice may be issued, but only 'if it is expedient' to do so 'having regard to the provisions of the development plan and to any other material considerations'. In short, the local authority must be satisfied that enforcement is necessary in the interests of good planning. In view of the Government's commitment to fostering business enterprise (discussed further on pp. 100–101), LPAs are advised in PPG 18 to consider the financial impact on small businesses of conforming with planning requirements. 'Nevertheless, effective action is likely to be the only appropriate remedy if the business activity is causing irreparable harm.'[28]

Development 'in breach of planning control' (development carried out without planning permission or without compliance with a planning condition) might be undertaken in good faith, or ignorance. In such a case, application can be made for retrospective permission. It is unlikely that a local authority would grant unconditional permission for a development against which it had served a planning

contravention notice, but it might be willing to give conditional approval.

The 1991 Act also introduced a *breach of condition notice* as a remedy for contravention of a planning condition. This is a simple procedure against which there is no appeal, though there may be some legal complexities which will prevent its widespread use (Cocks 1991). Further, there is a new provision enabling a LPA to seek an injunction in the High Court or County Court to restrain 'any actual or apprehended breach of planning control'. In Scotland, the provision is for an interdict by the Court of Session or the Sheriff.[29]

Where there is an urgent need to stop activities that are being carried on in breach of planning control, a LPA can serve a *stop notice* (Bracken and Kingaby 1987). This is an attempt to prevent delays in the other enforcement procedures (and advantage being taken of these delays) resulting in the local authority being faced with a *fait accompli*. Development carried out in contravention of a stop notice constitutes an offence.[30]

The provisions for enforcement are complex, and the reader is referred to the discussion in Chapter 5 of the Carnwath Report. The position can be exacerbated by the lowly esteem in which the enforcement system — and those who staff it — are often held. Several commentators have termed enforcement 'the weakest link in the planning chain', both south and north of the border.[31] Fortunately, the majority of alleged contraventions of planning control are dealt with satisfactorily and without any recourse to legal action, but the minority have a disproportionate effect on the credibility of the enforcement process as a whole.

## REVOCATION, MODIFICATION AND DISCONTINUANCE

The powers of development control possessed by local authorities go considerably further than the granting or withholding of planning permission. They can interfere with existing uses and revoke a permission already given, even if the development has actually been carried out.

A *revocation order* or *modification order* is made when the development has not been undertaken (or before a change of use has taken place). The local authority must 'have regard to the development plan and to any other material considerations', and an opposed order has to be confirmed by the Secretary of State. Compensation is payable for abortive expenditure and any loss or damage due to the order.

Such orders are rarely made. One case which attracted some attention was that of the Eton Fish and Chip Restaurant.[32] This concerned an application for planning permission to use premises in Eton High Street as a fish and chip restaurant. The Eton Urban District Council granted permission, but after a petition, mainly from local shopkeepers, decided to seek a revocation order on the grounds that

> the existence of a fish and chip restaurant in the High Street would be detrimental to the amenities, would cause nuisance, offence and annoyance to occupiers of properties in the vicinity and to users of the public highway, and would adversely affect the general appearance of the High Street.

The order was confirmed by the Minister. In this particular case, it would seem that planning permission had been given after inadequate consideration or publicity. The revocation was therefore a rectification of a 'mistake'.

Quite distinct from these powers is the much wider power to make a *discontinuance order*. This power is expressed in extremely wide language: an order can be made 'if it appears to a local planning authority that it is expedient in the interests of the proper planning of their area (including the interests of amenity)'. Again ministerial confirmation is required and compensation is payable, for depreciation, disturbance, and expenses incurred in carrying out the works in compliance with the order. An order will be confirmed only if the case is a strong one. In rejecting a discontinuance order on a scrap metal business in an attractive residential area, for instance, the Minister said:

> the fact that such a business is out of place in an attractive residential area must be weighed in the light of an important distinction between the withdrawal of existing use rights, as sought in the discontinuance order, and the refusal of new rights.

In this particular case, the Minister did 'not feel justified in overriding the proper interests of the objector as long as his business is maintained on an inoffensive scale' (*JPL* 1962: 753). Other cases have established the principle that a stronger case is needed to justify action to bring about the discontinuance of a use than would be needed to warrant a refusal of permission in the first instance.

It needs to be stressed that British planning legislation does not assume that existing non-conforming uses must disappear if planning policy is to be made effective. This may often be the avowed policy, but the Planning Acts explicitly permit the continuance of existing uses.

## DEVELOPMENT BY GOVERNMENT DEPARTMENTS, STATUTORY UNDERTAKERS AND LOCAL AUTHORITIES

Development by government departments does not require planning permission, but there have been special arrangements for consultations since 1950. Increased public and professional concern about the inadequacy of these led to revised, but still non-statutory, arrangements culminating in DoE Circular 18/84. This asserts clearly that, before proceeding with development, government departments will consult LPAs when the proposed development is one for which specific planning permission would, in normal circumstances, be required.[33]

Development undertaken by statutory undertakers[34] and local authorities is also subject to special planning procedures. Where a development requires the authorisation of a government department (as do developments involving compulsory purchase orders, work requiring loan sanction, and developments on which government grants are paid) the authorisation is usually accompanied by *deemed planning permission*. Much of the regular development of statutory undertakers and local authorities (for example, road works, laying of underground mains and cables) is *permitted development* under the GDO. Statutory undertakers wishing to carry out development which is neither permitted development nor authorised by a government department have to apply for planning permission to the local planning authority in the normal way, but special provisions apply to *operational land*. The original justification for this special position of statutory undertakers was that they are under an obligation to provide services to the public and could not, like a private firm in planning difficulties, go elsewhere.

Until 1992, LPAs were also deemed to have permission for any development which they themselves undertook in their area, as long as it accorded with the provisions of the development plan; otherwise they had to advertise their proposals and invite objections. These 'self-donated' planning permissions are problematic: though local authorities are guardians of the local public interest, they can face a conflict of interest in dealing with their own proposals for development. In Grant's words, 'there is a pragmatism in local politics which is likely to result in the compromise of good planning'.[35] Because of these difficulties, new regulations were issued in 1992 which require LPAs to make planning applications in the same way as other applicants, and generally follow the same procedures.[36]

## CONTROL OF ADVERTISEMENTS

The need to control advertisements has long been accepted. Indeed, the first Advertisements Regulation Act of 1907 antedated by two years the first Planning Act. But, even when amended and extended (in 1925 and 1932), the control was quite inadequate. Not only were the powers permissive: they were also limited. For instance, under the 1932 Act, the right of appeal (on the ground that an advertisement did not injure the amenities of the area) was to the Magistrates Court – hardly an appropriate body for such a purpose. The 1947 Act set out to remedy the deficiencies. There are, however, particular difficulties in establishing a legal code for the control of advertisements. Advertisements may range in size from a small window notice to a massive hoarding; they vary in purpose from a bus stop sign to a demand

to buy a certain make of detergent; they could be situated alongside a cathedral, in a busy shopping street, or in a particularly beautiful rural setting; they might be pleasant or obnoxious to look at; they might be temporary or permanent; and so on. The task of devising a code which takes all the relevant factors into account and, at the same time, achieves a balance between the conflicting interests of legitimate advertising and 'amenity' presents real problems. Advertisers themselves frequently complain that decisions in apparently similar cases have not been consistent with each other. The official departmental view is that no case is exactly like another, and hard and fast rules cannot be applied: each case has to be considered on its individual merits in the light of the tests of amenity and – the other factor to be taken into account – public safety.

The control of advertisements is exercised by regulations.[37] The Secretary of State has very wide powers of making regulations 'in the interests of amenity or public safety'. The question of public safety is rather simpler than that of amenity, though there is ample scope for disagreement: the relevant issue is whether an advertisement is likely to cause danger to road users, and also to 'any person who may use any road, railway, waterway (including coastal waters), docks, harbour or airfield'. In particular, account has to be taken of the likelihood of whether an advertisement 'is likely to obscure, or hinder the ready interpretation of, any road traffic sign, railway signal, or aid to navigation by water or air'. Amenity includes 'the general characteristics of the locality, including the presence of any feature of historic, architectural, cultural or similar interest'.

The definition of an advertisement is not quite as complicated as that of development, but it is very wide:

> Advertisement means any word, letter, model, sign, placard, board, notice, awning, blind, device or representation, whether illuminated or not, in the nature of, and employed wholly or partly for the purposes of, advertisement, announcement or direction and . . . includes any hoarding or similar structure used, or designed or adapted for use, and anything else principally used, or designed or adapted principally for use, for the display of advertisements.

It is helpfully added that the definition excludes anything 'employed as a memorial or as a railway signal'.

Various classes of advertisement are excepted from all control: those displayed on a balloon; on enclosed land; within a building; and on or in a vehicle. Also excepted are traffic signs, election signs, and national flags. As one might expect, there are some interesting refinements of these categories, which can be ignored for present purposes (though we might note, in passing, that a vehicle must be kept moving or, to use the more exact legal language, must be normally employed as a moving vehicle). With these exceptions, no advertisements may be displayed without *consent*. However, certain categories of advertisement can be displayed without *express consent*; so long as the local authority takes no action, they are *deemed* to have received consent. These include bus-stop signs and timetables, hotel and inn signs, professional or business plates, 'To Let' and 'For Sale' signs, election notices, statutory advertisements and traffic signs.

It needs to be stressed that amenity and public safety are the only two criteria for control. The content or subject of an advertisement is not relevant, and a local authority cannot refuse express consent on grounds of morality, offensiveness or taste. Thus an advertisement which contained the words 'Chish and Fips' was considered by the Secretary of State, on appeal, to be questionable on grounds of taste, but not detrimental to amenity: the appeal was allowed (*JPL* 1959: 736). The display of all advertisements is subject to standard conditions relating to such matters as cleanliness, tidiness and safety.

If an advertisement displayed with deemed consent becomes unsafe, unsightly or in any way 'a substantial injury to the amenity of the locality or a danger to members of the public', the LPA can serve a *discontinuance order*. There is the normal right of appeal to the Secretary of State. Advertisements displayed with express consent can be subject to revocation or modification, again with the normal rights of appeal.

Complex though this may seem, it is not all that there is to advertisement control. In some areas – for example, conservation areas, national parks or areas of outstanding natural beauty – it may be desirable

to prohibit virtually all advertisements of the poster type and seriously restrict other advertisements including those normally displayed by the ordinary trader. Accordingly, local planning authorities have power to define *areas of special advertisement control* where special protection on grounds of amenity is thought desirable. Much of the open countryside is subject to this type of control. In urban areas special control can be operated only where the Secretary of State is satisfied that there is a need for 'special protection on grounds of amenity'. In 1989, rather more than 45 per cent of the total land area of England and Wales had been defined by local planning authorities as being within areas of special control. Within an area of special control the general rule is that no advertisement may be displayed; such advertisements as are given express consent are considered as exceptions to this general rule.

This has proved a very difficult field in which to obtain unanimity, but the effectiveness of the controls and agreements is very apparent to visitors from some foreign countries, particularly the USA.

## CONTROL OF MINERAL WORKING

The reconciliation of economic and amenity interests in mineral working is an obvious matter for planning authorities – in this case, mineral planning authorities (MPAs): county councils, London boroughs, and metropolitan boroughs.[38] It would, however, be misleading to give the impression that the function of planning authorities is simply to fight a continual battle for the preservation of amenity. Planning is concerned with competing pressures on land and with the resolution of conflicting demands. Amenity is only one of the factors to be taken into account. Thus MPG 1 sets out a general policy:

(a) to ensure that the needs of society for minerals are satisfied with due regard to the protection of the environment;
(b) to ensure that any environmental damage or loss of amenity caused by mineral operations and ancillary operations is kept at an acceptable level;
(c) to ensure that land taken for mineral operations is

reclaimed at the earliest opportunity and is capable of an acceptable use after working has come to an end;

(d) to prevent the unnecessary sterilisation of mineral resources.

These are the broad policy matters with which MPAs are concerned. The necessary powers are provided in the Planning Acts. Briefly, these are for the making of the essential survey of resources and potentialities, the allocation of land in development plans, and the control (by means of planning permission) of mineral workings. The MPA has to assess the amount of land required for mineral working, and this requires an assessment of the future demand likely to be made on production in their area. Obviously, this requires extensive and continuing consultation with mineral operators. All MPAs are now required to prepare *mineral subject plans* to accompany their structure plans, but there have been wide variations in the content of these.[39]

Powers to control mineral workings stem from the definition of development, which includes 'the carrying out of . . . mining . . . operations in, on, over or under land'. However, a special form of control is necessary to deal with the unique nature of mineral operations. Unlike other types of development, mining operations are not the means by which a new use comes into being, they are a continuing end in themselves, often for a very long time. They do not adapt land for a desired end-use: on the contrary, they are essentially harmful and may make land unfit for any later use. They also have unusual location characteristics: they have to be mined where they exist. For these reasons the normal planning controls are replaced by a unique set of regulations.

Two major features of the minerals control system are that it takes into account the fact that mineral operations can continue for a long period of time, and that measures are needed to restore that land when operations cease. It is, therefore, necessary for MPAs to have the power to review and modify permissions and to require restoration. Under current legislation, MPAs have a duty to review all mineral sites in their areas. This includes those which were 'grandfathered' in by the 1947 Act. These old sites,

of which there may be around a thousand in England and Wales, often lack adequate records. They present the particular problem that they can include large unworked extensions which are covered by the permission; if worked these could have serious adverse effects on the environment. The provisions relating to these sites is even more complicated than those pertaining to the generality of mineral operations; it is sufficient to note that the 1991 Act required them all to be registered within a specific period (failing which the permission lapses) and that compensation for any 'depreciation' is limited. All mineral permissions are now subject to a time limit condition, normally of not more than sixty years.

Policies for restoration (and what the Act quaintly calls 'aftercare') have become progressively more stringent, mainly in response to what the Stevens Report (1976) referred to as a great change in standards and attitudes to mineral exploitation. A lengthy guidance note fully explains restoration policies and options. In view of the ongoing nature of mineral operations, particular importance is attached to schemes of progressive restoration which are phased in with the gradual working out of the site. (A very effective policy is to make new working dependent upon satisfactory restoration of used sites.) A good idea of the current policy is gained from the following quotation from MPG7:

> Standards of reclamation have generally improved over recent years. Continuation of this trend will enable a wider range of sites to be restored to appropriate standards, leading to the release of land which has not so far been made available for mineral working. If there is serious doubt whether satisfactory reclamation can be achieved at a particular site, then there must also be a doubt whether permission for mineral working should be given.

Mineral deposits are frequently located on high-grade agricultural land or on sites of particular amenity or attraction. It is not surprising, therefore, that much restoration is for agricultural, amenity, and recreational uses.[40] However, with the changing agricultural scene in western countries, there is greater emphasis on measures which will diversify the rural economy: this is discussed in Chapter 8.

An official review of minerals policy has been under way for several years and, in January 1993 a draft revision of MPG 1 was issued together with a substantial consultation paper. The demand for aggregates, which has increased substantially in recent years, is expected to grow by about a half by the year 2011. There is dispute on the accuracy of the figures and on the adequacy of a range of possible options. These include the use of coastal 'superquarries', the potential contribution of waste and recycled materials, and the adoption of a supply policy which might increase prices. A major research programme on relevant issues is under way.

## CARAVANS

During the 1950s, the housing shortage led to a boom in unauthorised caravan sites.[41] The controversy and litigation to which this gave rise led to the introduction of special controls over caravan sites (by Part I of the Caravan Sites and Control of Development Act 1960). This legislation has remained as a separate code and is not consolidated in the Town and Country Planning Act of 1990. (The Caravan Sites Act 1968, which deals mainly with the protection from eviction of caravan dwellers and gypsies, is similarly separate.)

The 1960 Act gave local authorities new powers to control caravan sites, including a requirement that all caravan sites had to be licensed before they could start operating (thus partly closing loopholes in the planning and public health legislation). These controls over caravan sites operate in addition to the normal planning system: thus both planning permission and a licence have to be obtained. Most of the Act dealt with control, but local authorities were given wide powers to provide caravan sites.

Local authorities face strong pressure from their ratepayers 'to preserve local amenities and property values', to which caravans are seen as a threat. The DoE may be clear as to what 'planning policy recognises', but the reality differs considerably from the official statement.[42]

Holiday caravans are subject to the same planning and licensing controls as residential caravans. To ensure that a site is used only for holidays (and not for 'residential purposes'), planning permission can include a condition limiting the use of a site to the holiday season. Conditions may also be imposed to require the caravans to be removed at the end of each season or to require a number of pitches on a site to be reserved for touring caravans.

One group of caravanners is particularly unpopular: gypsies, or, to give them their less romantic description, 'persons of nomadic life, whatever their race or origin' (but excluding 'members of an organised group of travelling showmen, or persons engaged in travelling circuses, travelling together as such'). The basic problem is that no one wants gypsies around: 'all too often the settled community is concerned chiefly to persuade, or even force, the gypsy families to move on'.[43] In an attempt to deal with the problem, a Private Member's Bill was presented by Eric Lubbock and was passed as the Caravan Sites Act 1968. This gave local authorities in England and Wales (but not in Scotland) the duty to provide adequate sites for gypsies 'residing in or resorting to' their areas.

A 1977 report on the operation of the Act prepared by Sir John Cripps (stimulated by sporadic violence on gypsy encampments) underlined the lack of progress. Cripps's message was clear: the living conditions of many gypsies was scandalous, and no improvement in the slow rate of progress could be expected without a high level of commitment by central government. A major element in this was a proposed 100 per cent grant to local authorities on the capital cost of providing gypsy caravan sites. This was accepted and such grants have been available since 1979.

The problems, however, refuse to go away; indeed, despite significant increases in the provision of sites and in central government expenditure on gypsy-site grants (from £5.8m in 1988/89 to £12.5m in 1992/93) they have grown worse.[44] Reports continue to be produced,[45] but public opinion prevents effective action on the required scale. At the time of writing, a DoE consultation paper *Reform of the Caravan Sites Act 1968* is under consideration. This laments the fact that 'the problem has grown faster than its remedy', and that it is now compounded by 'new age travellers' (more popularly known as 'hippies'). It also suggests that the supply of sites may now be creating an artificial demand. The proposed remedies include a tightening of statutory controls; the replacement of the duty of local authorities to provide sites by an optional power; and the abolition of the present Exchequer grant system. It remains to be seen how far the new penal policy, if approved by Parliament, will meet the needs of either the gypsies themselves, or those to whom gypsy encampments are a nuisance. Unfortunately, 'the public visibility of gypsies has grown, while the tolerance of the settled community to them has declined' (Home 1993).

## PURCHASE AND BLIGHT NOTICES

A planning refusal does not of itself confer any right to compensation. On the other hand, revocations of planning permission or interference with existing uses do rank for compensation, since they involve a taking away of a legal right. In cases where, as a result of a planning decision, land becomes 'incapable of reasonably beneficial use' the owner can serve a *purchase notice* upon the local authority requiring it to buy the property. In all cases, ministerial confirmation is required. The circumstances in which a purchase notice can be served include:

– refusal or conditional grant of planning permission;
– revocation or modification of planning permission;
– discontinuance of use.

In considering whether the land has any *beneficial use*,

> relevant factors are the physical state of the land, its size, shape and surroundings, and the general patterns of land-uses in the area; a use of relatively low value may be regarded as reasonably beneficial if such a use is common for similar land in the vicinity.
> (DoE Circular 13/83)

A purchase notice is not intended to apply in a case where an owner is simply prevented from realising the full potential value of his land. This would imply

the acceptance in principle of paying compensation for virtually all refusals and conditional permissions. It is only if the existing and permitted uses of the land are so seriously affected as to render the land incapable of reasonably beneficial use that the owner can take advantage of the purchase notice procedure.

There are circumstances, other than the threat of public acquisition, in which planning controls so affect the value of the land to the owner that some means of reducing the hardship is clearly desirable. For example, the allocation of land in a development plan for a school or for a road will probably reduce the value of houses on the land or even make them completely unsaleable. In such cases, the affected owner can serve a *blight notice* on the local authority requiring the purchase of the property at an 'unblighted' price. These provisions are restricted to owner occupiers of houses and small businesses who can show that they have made reasonable attempts to sell their property but have found it impossible to do so except at a substantially depreciated price because of certain defined planning actions. These include land designated for compulsory purchase, or allocated or defined by a development plan for any functions of a government department, local authority, statutory undertaker, or the National Coal Board; and land on which the Secretary of State has given written notice of his intention to provide a trunk road or a *special road* (i.e. a motorway).

The subject of planning blight takes us into the much broader area of the law relating to compensation. This is an extremely complex field, and only an indication of three major provisions can be attempted here.

First, there is a statutory right to compensation for a fall in the value of property arising from the use of highways, aerodromes and other public works which have immunity from actions for *nuisance*. The depreciation has to be caused by physical factors such as noise, fumes, dust and vibration, and the compensation is payable by the authority responsible for the works. Second, there is a range of powers under the heading 'mitigation of injurious effect of public works'. Examples include sound insulation; the purchase of owner-occupied property which is severely affected by construction work or by the use of a new or improved highway; the erection of physical barriers (such as walls, screens, or mounds of earth) on or alongside roads to reduce the effects of traffic noise on people living nearby; the planting of trees and the grassing of areas; and the development or redevelopment of land for the specific purpose of improving the surroundings of a highway 'in a manner desirable by reason of its construction, improvement, existence or use'. Third, provision is made for *home loss payments* as a mark of recognition of the special hardship created by compulsory dispossession of one's home. Since the payments are for this purpose they are quite separate from, and are not dependent upon, any right to compensation or the *disturbance payment* which is described below. Logically, they apply to tenants as well as to owner-occupiers, and are given for all displacements whether by compulsory purchase or any action under the Housing Acts. These provisions were slightly extended in the 1991 Planning and Compensation Act.

Additionally, there is a general entitlement to a *disturbance payment* for persons who are not entitled to compensation. Local authorities have a duty 'to secure the provision of suitable alternative accommodation where this is not otherwise available on reasonable terms, for any person displaced from residential accommodation' by acquisition, redevelopment, demolition, closing orders, and so on.

## MANAGING DEVELOPMENT CONTROL

There has been a succession of attempts on the part of central government to 'streamline the planning process' and to make it more 'efficient'. The reasons for these have differed. In 1981, government concern was with the economic costs of control, with cutting public expenditure and with 'freeing' private initiative from unnecessary bureaucratic controls. In the early 1970s, the concern was with the enormous increase in planning applications and planning appeals. This, of course, stemmed from the property boom of the period. The resultant delay created a political situation which was dealt with in traditional style by setting up an inquiry. This was undertaken by George Dobry, QC (whose report on the control of demolition has already been discussed). Dobry's report[46] is now part of planning history, but it is live history: the issues are still very much with us in the 1990s, and there is no guarantee that the current resolution of them will prove sufficiently resilient to withstand the unpredictable changes in the context within which they operate. It is therefore useful to look briefly at Dobry's analysis.

The starting point for Dobry's inquiry was the lengthening delay in the processing of planning applications, but he was quick to point out that 'not all delay is unacceptable: it is the price we must pay for the democratic planning of the environment'. Moreover, his review took account of factors which were very different from those relevant to 'streamlining the planning machine': the increasing pressure for public consultation and participation in the planning process; and the 'dissatisfaction on the part of applicants because they often do not understand why particular decisions have been made, or why it is necessary for what may seem small matters to be the concern of the planning machinery at all'. Additionally, he noted that 'many people feel that the system has not done enough to protect what is good in an environment or to ensure that new development is of a sufficiently high quality'.

Dobry therefore had a difficult task of reconciling apparently irreconcilable objectives: to expedite planning procedures while at the same time facilitating greater public participation and devising a system which would produce better environmental results. His solutions attempted to provide more speed for developers, more participation for the public *and* better-quality development and conservation.

This was to be effected by the division of applications into minor and major. Despite the inherent difficulties of determining this in advance (at least to the satisfaction of the public and the local amenity societies) it is nevertheless a fact that some 80 per cent of all applications are granted, and that many of these *are* simple and straightforward. Dobry's proposal, in essence, was that the simple should be distinguished and treated expeditiously, though with the opportunity for some participation and with a safety channel to allow them to be transferred to the major category if this should prove appropriate. These Class A applications would be dealt with by officials acting under powers delegated to them by planning committees (or, if this is unacceptable, by small subcommittees of two or three members). Publicity would be restricted in time to twenty-one days and decisions would be reached within forty-two days, failing which an application would be deemed to be approved.

This, so Dobry believed, would relieve the overloaded planning machine to deal more thoroughly with the major and/or controversial applications (which he suggested would constitute less than a half and, hopefully, only a third of the total). These Class B applications would receive greater scrutiny than hitherto, and the period for decision would be increased from the current (impracticable) statutory two months to three months. They would receive greater public advertisement, and the more important applications would need to be accompanied by an impact study.

Dobry's scheme was an heroic attempt to improve the planning control system to everyone's satisfaction (Jowell 1975). Inevitably, therefore, it disappointed everybody. For example, though he made a number of proposals to increase public participation, his overriding concern for expediting procedures forced him to compress these into an impracticable time-scale. This is particularly so with his Class A applications, where twenty-one days is far too short a period for effective publicity, let alone considered public reaction. Moreover, it is open to question whether the Class A procedure would relieve planning administration or, in fact, overload it still further. In practice, the result might well have been either a collapse of the new procedure or a perfunctory and rapid processing which would have denied the public participation which Dobry sought to increase.

The Dobry inquiry was instigated by a Conservative Government at a time when the property market was booming. On its completion the boom had collapsed and a Labour Government had published their outline proposals for the community land legislation. Thus,

the planning scene had changed fundamentally. In purely administrative terms, it was thought that authorities concerned with distinguishing between applications for exempt development, excepted development, designated relevant development and non-designated relevant development could not also be expected to distinguish between Class A and Class B applications, and between outline, illustrative, detailed and guideline applications. The Government rejected all Dobry's major recommendations for changes in the system, though it was stressed that their objectives could typically be achieved if local authorities adopted 'the most efficient working methods'.[47] Dobry's view that 'it is not so much the system which is wrong but the way in which it is used' was endorsed, and his *Final Report* was commended 'to students of our planning system as an invaluable compendium of information about the working of the existing development control process, and to local authorities and developers as a source of advice on the best way to operate within it'.

The Conservative Government which was elected in 1979 lost no time in preparing a revised development control policy. A draft Circular was sent out for comment in mid-1980. It created alarm among the planning profession, partly because of its substantive proposals but also partly because of its abrasive style. 'The Most Savage Attack Yet' expostulated *Municipal Engineering*, while *Planner News* remonstrated that the results of the Circular 'could be disastrous'.[48]

An example of the matters to which objection was taken was the call for relaxation of controls over private sector housing: 'Local authorities should not lay down requirements on the mix of house types, provision of garages, internal standards, sizes of private gardens, location of houses on plots and in relation to each other, provision of private open space.'

The Circular also stated that planning authorities should not attempt to compel developers to adopt designs which were unpopular with customers or clients 'and they shouldn't attempt to control such details as shapes of windows or doors or the colour of bricks'. On density, the Circular played down its importance and commented that 'for many of the redevelopment and infill sites now to be brought into use, densities do not provide reliable performance indicators'.

The revised Circular, as published (22/80), was written with a lighter touch, but much of the message was very similar. The emphasis was on securing a 'speeding up of the system' and 'to ensure that development is only prevented or restricted when this serves a clear planning purpose and the economic effects have been taken into account'.

Regular publication of the percentage of planning application decisions taken within a period of eight weeks became the standard by which the efficiency of the development control system was operating. Quarterly figures have been published since 1979 and are used by both the Government and the development industry to bolster criticisms of the system.

The policy 'to simplify the system and improve its efficiency' (to use the words of the 1985 White Paper, *Lifting the Burden*) continued with revised circulars, new white papers, and the introduction of planning mechanisms which reduced or bypassed local government control such as simplified planning zones and urban development corporations. However, towards the end of the 1980s, a greater emphasis on 'quality' emerged as environmental awareness and concern increased. A particularly striking example is provided by the 1992 Audit Commission report on development control, significantly entitled *Building in Quality*. Though the major emphasis is still on the process of planning control rather than its outcome, there is a very clear recognition of the importance of the latter. It is noted that there had been a preoccupation with the speed of dealing with planning applications 'ignoring the mix of applications, the variety of development control functions, and the quality of outcomes'. But there had been no 'shared and explicit' concept of quality, yet: 'The quality of outcomes is more important than the quality of the process because buildings will be seen long after memories of the decision process have lapsed, but it is far harder to assess.' Quality of development control is seen as involving an 'adding of value' by the local authority. What that 'added value' may be is

dependent upon the authority's overall objectives: 'in areas under heavy development pressure or in rural areas, environmental, traffic, or ecological considerations may be paramount'; in Wales, 'the impact of the development on the Welsh language can be a consideration'.

This is a far cry from the character of the earlier pronouncements by Government spokespersons. At the least, it is refreshing to see a departure from the crude 'eight weeks' yardstick of quality.[49]

## DEVELOPMENT CONTROL AND DEVELOPMENT PLANS

How do planning authorities actually decide planning applications? Does the local development plan (if there is one) 'provide a detailed basis for development control and for the coordination of development and other land use'? (Grant 1982: 115.) What if there is no local plan (which was not uncommon under the pre-1991 legislation)? What if the local plan does not address an issue raised by a planning application? Answers to such questions have not been easy to obtain. Fortunately, since the early 1980s there has been a blossoming of research which considerably increases our understanding of how this part of the machinery of planning works. Of particular interest is a 1986 working paper from the Department of Land Management and Development at the University of Reading. This reports on research commissioned by the DoE on the relationship between development plans, development control, and appeals (Davies *et al*. 1986a).

The development control study reviewed the relationship between development plans and development control in a sample of twelve districts in England and Wales. It was found that the most significant characteristic is its variety, which in turn results from the wide variation in the conditions among different authorities, together with the wide area of discretionary power which they all have. Development plans (where they exist) are certainly used in development control, but many policies are not covered by the plans, and even when they are they are typically expressed in general terms requiring interpretation of their meaning and allowing a wide range of discretion. Districts rely not only on these plans but also on a range of non-statutory documents, including development control policy notes, design guides, development briefs, informal local plans, and 'policy frameworks'. The authors comment that the range of planning considerations fall into two broad categories:

> The practical planning considerations relate mainly to amenity and the form and layout of development. They have a long history of use in planning practice, there is a wide measure of consensus about their use in control and, where covered by policy, it tends to be as broad, flexible statements in structure or local plans, amplified in detail in supplementary planning guidance. The strategic and other planning considerations relate to the volume and timing of development and also more recent matters such as planning gain. They are of more recent origin in statutory planning and, apart from a few basic considerations, tend to vary in their incidence in different districts.

The appeals study comprised a random sample of one in ten (1,286) appeals determined in England and Wales in 1982, and an analysis of appeals during the same year in the twelve sample districts. This revealed that 'one third of all appeal decision letters contained no mention of policy, national or local, statutory or non-statutory'. These included a high proportion of the householder appeals and of the minor and change-of-use appeals, but comparatively few major proposals. In general, the main issues they raised concerned amenity, design and infrastructure. Such issues were not covered by policy, and these appeals tended to have a better than average chance of success (41 per cent as compared with an overall average of 31 per cent). Two-thirds of the appeal decision letters referred to some form of policy, and in these cases the policy usually became the main determinant of the outcome of the appeal: only 26 per cent were successful.

'Inspectors nearly always dismissed appeals, and supported the local authority, on proposals for which there was relevant cover in the development plan.' On the other hand, they 'more often allowed appeals which turned on practical appeal considerations lacking firm local policy coverage, but in which

national policies were invoked in favour of the appellant'. The final conclusion, in summary, was:

> The relationship between development plans and appeals is closer and less varied than that with development control. This largely reflects the different composition of the case load, with fewer householder proposals, which almost always lack policies. It also reflects the extent to which inspectors have a close regard to policies, whether it be those in the development plan or those in national sources.

In short, where there is an articulated policy which can clearly be applied to a case, development control and appeal decisions tend to abide by it. However, some areas do not have plans, some plans do not cover issues that arise in individual planning applications, and much development control has to rely on unwritten policy and professional skill and judgement.

Can the situation be improved? Obviously more written statements of policy would help, and this the authors recommend: for both central and local government. But there is a limit to which governments at any level wish to, or can, commit policies to paper. The more this is done, the more inflexible will planning become, the less will it be able to adapt to changing circumstances, the greater is the likelihood of conflict between policies, and the more confusing the situation will be. The great merit of the British development control system is its flexibility and adaptability to differing and changing situations.

The situation has been changed by a new provision in the 1991 Act, though it is not at all clear whether the change is substantial or minimal. The Act added these words:[50] 'Where, in making any determination under the planning acts, regard is to be had to the development plan, the determination shall be made in accordance with the plan unless material considerations indicate otherwise.' There has been considerable debate on the extent to which this really makes any difference. There has been much talk of a new 'presumption' in favour of development which accords with the provisions of the development plan and (a very different matter) a 'presumption' in favour of development.[51] It is, however, arguable whether there is anything new, apart from a desire for the planning system to become more 'plan-led'. This implies that the requisite plans have been prepared, are up to date, and accord with structure plans and national and regional policies as set out by the central government. Where this is not the case, other 'material considerations' come into play. But this has always been essentially the position where such plans were in place. The presumption in favour of development is of very long standing: it dates back to the beginnings of planning control.[52] The new policy (as spelled out in *Planning Policy Guidance Note 1*) simply stresses that a local authority has to give very good reasons for refusing planning permission; but this has always been the case, and the only differences lie, not so much in the law, as in planning policy: the extent to which planning appeals are decided differently, and the way in which draft plans are dealt with. With the 'plan-led' regime, the central departments will scrutinise plans (which, it must be remembered, are now mandatory) to ensure that they conform with national and regional guidance, and that planning decisions accord with them.[53] In short, the matter is not so much one of law as of practice. Law is only the framework for action.

## DEVELOPMENT BY SMALL BUSINESSES

The changing nature of 'town and country planning' is nowhere more apparent than in the importance attached in recent years, first, to business activity and, later, to environmental issues. DoE Circular 22/80 cancelled relevant previous circulars, and local authorities were 'asked to pick out for priority handling those applications which in their judgement will contribute most to national and local economic activity'. Particular emphasis was laid on small businesses which 'the Government are particularly keen to encourage'. Indeed, in striking contrast to earlier ideas about the separation of industry and housing,

> the characteristics of industry and commerce . . . have changed . . . There are many businesses that can be carried on in rural and residential areas without causing

unacceptable disturbance . . . The rigid application of 'zoning' policies (where indeed it continues) can have a very damaging effect.

Moreover, far from 'planning out' non-conforming industry (which was a worthy planning aim in earlier years) such industry

> substantially eases the problems of starting and maintaining small scale businesses if permission can be given for such uses to be established in redundant buildings such as disused agricultural buildings, industrial, warehouse, or commercial premises, on derelict sites, or in unsuitable housing.[54]

There are many generations of qualified town planners who would have failed their examinations had they suggested such a thing. Yet the Circular as published was a considerably milder version of one which was circulated among local authority associations in July 1980. This came under heavy fire for implying that small firms set up without planning permission should have enforcement orders issued against them only if alternative premises were available. A shadow of this remained in a section on enforcement and discontinuance. While stressing that nothing in the Circular should be taken as condoning a wilful breach of planning law, there is a highly significant qualification:

> the power to issue an enforcement notice alleging that there has been a breach of planning control is discretionary and is only to be used if the authority 'consider it expedient to do so having regard to the provision of the development plan and to any other material considerations'. This permissive power should be used, in regard to either operational development or material changes of use, only where planning reasons clearly warrant such action, and there is no alternative to enforcement proceedings. Where the activity involved is one which would not give rise to insuperable planning objections if it were carried out somewhere else, then the planning authority should do all it can to help in finding suitable alternative premises before initiating enforcement action.

Similarly, 'but with even more force', discontinuance orders were appropriate 'only if there appears to be an overriding justification on planning grounds'.

The theme was developed in later Circulars such as 14/85 on *Development and Employment*, and 2/86

*Development by Small Businesses*, and in the original 1988 version of PPG 4.[55] By the beginning of the 1990s, however, environmental issues had risen to prominence, and rather less emphasis was given to business. The revised PPG 4, issued in 1992, opens as follows: 'One of the Government's key aims is to encourage continued economic development in a way which is compatible with its stated environmental objectives. Economic growth and a high quality environment have to be pursued together.' Development control, so the argument continued, should not place 'unjustifiable obstacles' in the way of development, but 'nevertheless, planning decisions must reconcile necessary development with environmental protection and other development plan policies'.[56]

The point does not need labouring, though it is an important one: planning policies reflect the political concerns of the day. Economic development is still a priority, but it is now modified by an increasing regard for the quality of the environment. Just how far this has developed is the subject of Chapter 6.

## UPDATE

A rare exercise of the Secretary of State's power to issue a revocation order is reported in *JPL* 1993: 717.

The DoE have published the first issue of a new statistical series: *Comparative Performance of Local Planning Authorities in Deciding Planning Applications: Year Ending 31 March 1993*. The document is available from DoE (not HMSO).

In 'Welsh planners voice some lingering doubts' (*Planning* 1041, 22 October 1993, pp. 20–1), H. Thomas discusses the extent to which the use of the Welsh language within a particular community is a valid planning consideration.

## NOTES

1 The current versions of the UCO and the GDO were issued in 1987 and 1988 respectively. For a study of the effects of these revisions, see DoE, *An Examination of the Effects of the Use Classes Order 1987 and the General Development Order 1988*, 1991. Subsequently, various revisions have been made (and continue to be made) via statutory instruments issued by the Secretary of State.

2 See the study by Land Use Consultants, *Permitted Development Rights for Agriculture and Forestry*, 1991. The long argument for the extension of control to agriculture and forestry has been consistently rejected by the Government. See, for example, PPG 7 where it is stated: 'While the Government has no plans to extend planning controls to all farming activities, it has been ready to introduce new closely-targeted controls over agricultural development where necessary to deal with specific problems.'

3 Before the coming into operation of section 192 of the 1991 Planning and Compensation Act, the provision was for a 'determination' as to whether a proposed operation constituted development and, if so, whether planning permission was required. The 1991 Act also introduced a procedure for certifying the lawfulness of an *existing* use or development. Lovers of acronyms will note that the former are known as CLOPUDs (Certificates of Lawfulness of Proposed Use or Development), and the latter as CLEUDs (Certificates of Lawfulness of Existing Use or Development).

4 Rowan-Robinson and Lloyd (1986) give other examples of the use of SDOs: 'the granting of planning permission for a nuclear oxide reprocessing plant at Windscale in Cumbria' and 'the granting of planning permission to a consortium to lay a nework of telecommunication cables alongside railway routes'.

5 DoE Circular 1/85; Tym 1989b; and Davies *et al.* 1989.

6 More fully: 'the occupation of the houses shall be limited to persons whose employment is or was employment in agriculture . . . or in forestry, or in an industry mainly dependent upon agriculture, and including also the dependants of such persons'. A leading case on this (from which the preceding formulation is taken) is *Fawcett Properties* v. *Buckingham County Council* [1961] AC 636. This is summarised in Moore 1987: 138. Moore also instances *British Airports Authority* v. *Secretary of State for Scotland* [1980] JPL 260, which regarded as reasonable a condition attached to a planning permission for development at Aberdeen Airport that restricted the hours between which aircraft could take off and land.

7 *Pyx Granite Co. Ltd* v. *Ministry of Housing and Local Government* [1958] 1 QB 554, 572. This famous case is widely reported in legal texts.

8 A highly detailed account is given in *Encyclopedia of Planning*; a shorter treatment is to be found in chapter 8 of Morgan and Nott 1988, and in Little 1992. The

Deparment's views are set out clearly and in detail in DoE Circular 1/85. See also PPG 1.

9  Two planning officers of the Land Authority for Wales have commented that completion notices are difficult to enforce 'because when they are approved by the Minister (and this is not very often) builders usually have a lengthy period of grace to complete the development. They are usually successfully resisted on the basis that market conditions are unfavourable and that it would be unreasonable to require compliance, and this is now well-established by legal precedent' (Cuddy and Hollingsworth 1985: 174).

10  There are extensive powers to prevent the demolition of buildings of historic or architectural value: these are discussed in Chapter 7.

11  DoE Circular 26/92 explains the provisions relating to demolition. Circular 16/92 includes the Town and Country Planning (Demolition – Description of Buildings Direction) 1992. The latter lists works which do not constitute a building operation. (The GDO is amended to grant planning permission for demolition of all buildings that are *not* excluded by Direction.)

12  Speech by the Under-Secretary of State for the Environment (Marcus Fox), *Standing Committee Debates on the Local Government, Planning and Land (No 2) Bill*, col. 245, 22 April 1980.

13  The current fee schedule is summarised in DoE Circular 31/92 and SOEnD Circular 27/91.

14  House of Commons, Parliamentary Debates, Fourth Standing Committee on Statutory Instruments etc., *Draft Town and Country Planning (Fees for Applications and Deemed Applications) (Amendment) Regulations 1992*.

15  *R. v. Richmond upon Thames London Borough Council, ex parte McCarthy and Stone (Developments) Ltd.*, Times Law Report, November 13, 1991, HL; and *R. v. Richmond upon Thames London Borough Council, ex parte McCarthy and Stone (Developments) Ltd.* [1990] All ER 854, CA. See Taussik 1992.

16  This discussion relates particularly to appeals under section 78 of the Town and Country Planning Act 1990. It does not deal specifically with advertisement appeals, appeals against enforcement notices, appeals to determine whether in doubtful cases planning permission is required, or appeals in respect of a local authority's failure to give a planning decision within prescribed time limits – though the principles discussed are generally the same. Section 78 of the 1990 Act covers appeals against such matters as a decision of a LPA to refuse planning permission, or against conditions imposed on a grant of permission.

Details of the procedures for planning appeals and inquiries are to be found in DoE Circular 24/92.

17  DoE, *Chief Planning Inspector's Report, April 1991 to March 1992*. An account of 'Planning appeals in Scotland' is given in MacKinnon 1992.

18  About 60 per cent concerned small-scale development; many of these raised issues of purely local significance. They included such matters as minor residential development, small groups of shops, small caravan sites, betting shops, garages and minor changes of use. Rather more than a quarter related to single houses. Another relevant point was that, of all appeals made during the five years 1962 to 1967, 97.5 per cent were decided as the inspector recommended.

19  The regulations transfer (virtually all) appeals to inspectors, but the Secretary of State can 'recover' any appeal for his own decision.

20  COI, *Planning*, 1992: 43.

21  DoE, *Speeding Planning Permissions: A Review of the Handling of Transferred Written Representation Planning Appeals: Report of an Efficiency Scrutiny (Published with 'Action Plan')*, HMSO, 1986.

22  Another review, *Speeding Planning Appeals: A Review of the Handling of Inquiries Planning Appeals*, was completed in 1986 and published in 1987. A third, 'The Handling of Recovered Planning Appeals by DoE Regional Offices' was completed in 1986 but was not published.

23  There is, of course, a possible difficulty with the definition of 'substantial'. The Scottish Local Government Ombudsman has complained about 'the ease with which planning authorities breach their own plans, particularly considering the time, effort and con-sultation which goes into them' (Commissioner for Local Administration in Scotland, *Annual Report 1991*: 14).

24  Royal Fine Art Commission, *Twenty-Second Report, October 1971–December 1984*, 1985. See particularly p. 20.

25  HC Environment Committee, *Planning Appeals, Call-in, and Major Public Inquiries*, 1986, vol. 2, p. 130, para. 7.

26  Ibid., vol. 1, p. lviii, para. 128.

27  For a detailed exposition of the current law see Bourne 1992.

28  PPG 18: para. 17. A good illustration of the problem of small businesses is given in the Carnwath Report (1989: para. 2.5): 'The small business which starts in a backyard may not attract attention or cause problems until it begins to become successful. There is often a critical point when the business is beginning to outgrow its premises, but either there is no obvious alternative, or the business is not sufficiently established to be able to risk the expense and commitment of a formal business location. An inflexible approach to enforcement at this point will simply destroy the business.'

29  Sections 187A and 187B of the 1991 Act; and s. 260 of the 1972 Scottish Act.

30 There is no right of appeal against a stop notice. DoE Circular 21/91 advises LPAs to carry out a cost–benefit assessment for stop notices to ensure that there would not be unacceptable costs to the local economy and that prohibitions are restricted to those required 'to prevent serious or irreversible harm to the environment'.

31 See, for example, Samuels 1985; Jowell and Millichap 1987; Rowan-Robinson and Young 1987; and the Carnwath Report 1989: ch. 4.

32 *JPL* 1957: 783, and *JPL* 1958: 334 and 384.

33 A DoE Consultation Paper of November 1992, *The Removal of Crown Exemption from Planning Law*, proposes that all Crown bodies should be required to apply for planning permission (and listed building consent etc.) in the normal way.

34 'Statutory undertakers' are bodies authorised by legislation to carry on an undertaking defined in s. 262 of the Planning Act. With privatisation, the nationalised industries have lost this status, and most statutory undertakers are now concerned with transport operations. The current definition is 'persons authorised by any enactment to carry on any railway, light railway, tramway, road transport, water transport, canal, inland navigation, dock, harbour, pier or lighthouse undertaking, or any undertaking for the supply of hydraulic power and a relevant airport operator'. However, privatised statutory undertakers retain the development rights of their predecessor bodies.

35 Illustrations of the problem were given in evidence to the Environment Committee: 'attempts by authorities to dispose of surplus school playing fields with the benefit of permission for development; and competing applications for superstore development when one of the sites is owned by the authority themselves' (HC Environment Committee, *Planning Appeals, Call-in, and Major Public Inquiries*, 1986).

36 See DoE Circular 19/92.

37 The regulations are explained in DoE Circular 5/92; policy guidance is given in PPG 9. The fullest exposition of the law of advertisement control is given in Mynors 1992. For Scotland, SOEnD Circular 31/92 deals with *Control over Advertisements and Fish Farming*.

38 See DoE, *Environmental Effects of Surface Mineral Workings*, 1991.

39 For an analysis of two contrasting plans see Everton and Hughes 1987. A survey of *Mineral Policies in Development Plans* by Arup Economic Consultants was published by HMSO in 1990.

40 See DoE, *Amenity Reclamation of Mineral Workings*, 1992. A bibliography on reclamation for various uses is given in MPG 7.

41 Sir Arton Wilson's 1959 report, *Caravans as Homes*, highlighted the problems of residential caravanning. In 1959, about 60,000 caravans in England and Wales were being used as homes by some 150,000 people: mainly young married couples, often with small children. The report estimated that about 38,000 of the 60,000 caravans were on sites for which permission, usually conditional or temporary, had been given; about 12,000 had 'existing use' rights; and about 10,000 were on sites which appeared to contravene planning control. With some notable exceptions, local authorities tended to regard caravans as a substandard form of accomodation and, less debatably, difficult to control. The caravan interests, on the other hand, argued the case for recognition of caravanning as an acceptable way of life and pressed for more positive approaches by the local authorities.

42 The issues raised by mobile homes are similar: see DoE, *Report of the Mobile Homes Review*, HMSO, 1977. Following a spate of inquiries and studies, 1983 saw the passing of the Mobile Homes Act. This statute is outside the boundaries of 'town and country planning', and is nearer in spirit to landlord and tenant legislation. It provides some solid basis for 'mobile home agreements' between mobile-home occupiers and site owners. See Kenny 1983.

43 The appalling conditions in which the majority of the gypsies live in England and Wales were portrayed in the 1967 report of the DoE's Sociological Research Section, *Gypsies and other Travellers*. (The quotation is from the foreword to this report.) See also Adams *et al.* 1976, and the Scottish reports *Scotland's Travelling People*, 1971, and *Counting Travellers in Scotland*, 1992.

44 The *DoE Annual Report 1993*; p. 92 notes: 'There are now 288 local authority sites accommodating 5,494 caravans. 2,959 gypsy caravans are on private sites, which are not eligible for grant. The proportion of caravans on unauthorised sites has fallen from 50% to 34% since 1979, but in absolute terms has risen from 4,176 to 4,324.'

45 See DoE, *Management of Local Authority Gypsy Sites*, 1982; *The Accommodation Needs of Long-Distance and Regional Travellers: A Consultation Paper*, 1982; *Defining a Gypsy*, 1984; and *A Report on the Analysis of Responses to Consultation on the Operation of the Caravan Sites Act 1968 by Professor Gerald Wibberley*, 1986; all published by DoE. See also Hawes 1987, and H. Green 1991. There was a debate on gypsy sites in the House of Commons on 10 July 1990: see *House of Commons Debates*, vol. 176, cols 227–60.

46 In addition to the report on demolition control (1974), Dobry produced two reports entitled *Review of the Development Control System*: an interim report (1974) and a final report (1975).

47 See DoE Circulars 113/75 and 9/76.
48 *Municipal Engineering*, 29 July 1980, and *Planner News*, September 1980.
49 The report criticises the 'eight week figures' on several grounds and maintains that they have 'grave weaknesses'. Among the shortcomings are its crudity, its unreliability, and its perversity (see p. 20, para. 35). For reactions from the planning profession, see Fyson 1992, and Williamson 1992.
50 Section 54A of the 1990 Act; s. 18A of the Scottish Act.
51 See, for example, M. Harrison 1992. It has also been argued that the term 'presumption' is an inappropriate importation from civil litigation where the issue is one of dispute between parties: in planning cases the issue (though frequently cast in simple terms of a dispute between an applicant and the local authority) involves determining where the public interest lies (Graham 1990).
52 M. Harrison (1992) quotes a 1923 circular (issued at a time when controls were operated by way of 'interim development consent'): 'The presumption should always be in favour of the person seeking consent to interim development, and obstacles should not be placed in the way of such development, except in the case where it is clearly detrimental to local needs and interests.'
53 PPG 1: para. 29. At the 1992 TCPSS, the Minister of State for Housing and Planning, Sir George Young, made the point more strongly: 'Local authorities which have been preparing plans recently will have noticed that we have adopted a much more rigorous approach to the scrutiny of draft plans . . . Although we would naturally hope to resolve any difficulties at pre-deposit stage, the Department is quite prepared to object at deposit stage, if need be. And, of course, in the last resort there are reserve powers of direction and call-in . . . We will be less likely to allow appeals if we have satisfied ourselves on the content of the plan, and the planning decision accords with the plan.' See also Gatenby and Williams 1992.
54 PPG 7, *The Countryside and the Rural Economy*, stresses the positive need for fostering rural industries. Para. 2.13 states: 'In many rural areas, a lack of suitable workspace at affordable rent is holding back economic development. Re-use and adaptation of existing buildings . . . have an important role to play in meeting the demand for workspace. But provision needs to be made for new development as well. Sensitive, small scale development can be accommodated in and around many settlements.'
55 See also research report undertaken by Roger Tym & Partners (1989a) for the DoE, *The Effect on Small Firms of Refusal of Planning Permission*.
56 LPAs are advised, in PPG 18, *Enforcing Planning Control*, that enforcement action 'should be preceded by informal discussion about possible means of minimising harm to local amenity caused by business activity, and, if formal action will be needed, by discussion of the possible relocation of the business to another site'. Although it is not the responsibility of a LPA to provide or find an alternative site, 'if formal enforcement action is likely to compel a small business or self-employed person to relocate their trading activities, the LPA should aim to agree on a timetable for relocation which will minimise disruption to the business and, if possible avoid any permanent loss of employment as a result of the relocation'.

# 5

# LAND POLICIES

It is clear that under a system of well-conceived planning the resolution of competing claims and the allocation of land for the various requirements must proceed on the basis of selecting the most suitable land for the particular purpose, irrespective of the existing values which may attach to the individual parcels of land.

*Uthwatt Report* 1942

## THE UTHWATT REPORT

It was the task of the Uthwatt Committee, from whose report the above quotation is taken, to devise a scheme which would make the sentiments expressed in the quotation a reality. Effective planning necessarily controls, limits, or even completely destroys, the market value of particular pieces of land. Is the owner to be compensated for this loss in value? If so, how is the compensation to be calculated? And is any 'balancing' payment to be extracted from owners whose land appreciates in value as a result of planning measures?

This problem of compensation and betterment arises fundamentally 'from the existing legal position with regard to the use of land, which attempts largely to preserve, in a highly developed economy, the purely individualistic approach to land ownership'. This 'individualistic approach', however, has been increasingly modified during the past hundred years. The rights of ownership were restricted in the interests of public health: owners had (by law) to ensure, for example, that their properties were in good sanitary condition, that new buildings conformed to certain building standards, that streets were of a minimum width, and so on. It was accepted that these

restrictions were necessary in the interests of the community: *salus populi est suprema lex*, and that private owners should be compelled to comply with them even at cost to themselves.

> All these restrictions, whether carrying a right to compensation or not, are imposed in the public interest, and the essence of the compensation problem as regards the imposition of restrictions appears to be this — at what point does the public interest become such that a private individual ought to be compelled to comply, at his own cost, with a restriction or requirement designed to secure that public interest? The history of the imposition of obligations without compensation has been to push that point progressively further on and to add to the list of requirements considered to be essential to the well-being of the community.[1]

But clearly there is a point beyond which restrictions cannot reasonably be imposed on the grounds of good neighbourliness without payment of compensation — and 'general consideration of regional or national policy require so great a restriction on the landowner's use of his land as to amount to a taking away from him of a proprietary interest in the land'.

This, however, is not the end of the matter. Planning sets out to achieve a selection of the most suitable pieces of land for particular uses. Some land will therefore be zoned for a use which is profitable for the owner, whereas other land will be zoned for a use having a low, or even nil, private value. It is this difficulty of *development value* which raises the compensation problem in its most acute form. The expectations (or hopes) of owners extend over a far larger area than is likely to be developed. This *potential* development value is therefore speculative, but until the individual owners are proved to be wrong in their assessments (and how can this be done?) all owners of land having a potential value can make a case for compensation on the assumption that their particular pieces of land would in fact be chosen for development if planning restrictions were not imposed. Yet this *floating value* might never have settled on their land, and obviously the aggregate of the values claimed by the individual owners is likely to be greatly in excess of a total valuation of all pieces of land. As Haar (1951: 99) has nicely put it, the situation is akin to that of a sweepstake: a single ticket fetches much more than its mathematically calculated value, for the simple reason that the grand prize may fall to any one holder.

Furthermore, the public control of land use necessarily involves the shifting of land values from certain pieces of land to other pieces: the value of some land is decreased, while that of other land is increased. Planning controls, so it was argued, do not destroy land values: in the words of the Uthwatt Committee, 'neither the total demand for development nor its average annual rate is materially affected, if at all, by planning ordinances'. Nevertheless, the owner of the land on which development is prohibited will claim compensation for the full potential development of his land, irrespective of the fact that the value may shift to another site.[2]

In theory, it is logical to balance the compensation paid to aggrieved owners by collecting a betterment charge on owners who benefit from planning controls (Hagman and Misczynski 1978). But previous experience with the collection of betterment had not been encouraging. The principle had been first established in an Act of 1662 which authorised the levying of a capital sum or an annual rent in respect of the 'melioration' of properties following street widenings in London. There were similar provisions in Acts providing for the rebuilding of London after the Great Fire. The principle was revived and extended in the Planning Acts of 1909 and 1932. These allowed a local authority to claim, first 50 per cent, and then (in the later Act) 75 per cent, of the amount by which any property increased in value as the result of the operation of a planning scheme. In fact, these provisions were largely ineffective since it proved extremely difficult to determine with any certainty which properties had increased in value as a result of a scheme (or of works carried out under a scheme) or, where there was a reasonable degree of certainty, how much of the increase in value was directly attributable to the scheme and how much to other factors. The Uthwatt Committee noted that there were only three cases in which betterment had actually been paid under the Planning Acts.

The Uthwatt Committee concluded that the solution to these problems lay in changing the system of land ownership under which land had a development value dependent upon the prospects of its profitable use. They maintained that no new code for the assessment of compensation or the collection of betterment would be adequate if this 'individualistic' system remained. The system itself had inherent 'contradictions provoking a conflict between private and public interest and hindering the proper operation of the planning machinery'. A new system was needed which would avoid these contradictions and which so unified existing rights in land as to 'enable shifts of value to operate within the same ownership'.

The logic of this line of reasoning led to a consideration of land nationalisation. This the Committee rejected on the grounds that it would arouse keen political controversy, would involve insuperable financial problems, and would necessitate the establishment of a complicated national administrative machinery. In their view the solution to the problem lay in the nationalisation, not of the land itself, but of all development rights in undeveloped land.

## THE 1947 ACT

Essentially, this is precisely what the 1947 Town and Country Planning Act did. Effectively, development rights and their associated values were nationalised. No development was to take place without permission from the local planning authority. If permission were refused, no compensation would be paid (except in a limited range of special cases). If permission were granted, any resulting increase in land value was to be subject to a development charge. The view was taken that 'owners who lose development value as a result of the passing of the Bill are not on that account entitled to compensation'. This cut through the insoluble problem posed in previous attempts to collect betterment values created by public action. Betterment had been conceived as

> any increase in the value of land (including the buildings thereon) arising from central or local government action, whether positive, for example by the execution of public works or improvements, or negative, for example by the imposition of restrictions on the other land.

The 1947 Act went further: all betterment was created by the community, and it was unreal and undesirable (as well as virtually impossible) to distinguish between values created, for example, by particular planning schemes, and those due to other factors such as the general activities of the community or the general level of prosperity.

If rigorous logic had been followed, no payment at all would have been made for the transfer of development value to the state but this, as the Uthwatt Committee had pointed out, would have resulted in considerable hardship in individual cases. A £300m fund was therefore established for making 'payments' (as distinct from compensation) to owners who could successfully claim that their land had some development value on the appointed day — the day on which the provisions of the bill which prevented landowners from realising development values came into force. Considerable discussion took place during the passage of the bill through Parliament on the sum fixed for the payments, and it was strongly opposed on the ground that it was too small. The truth of the matter was that, in the absence of relevant reliable information, any global sum had to be determined in a somewhat arbitrary way; but in any case it was not intended that everybody should be paid the full value of their claims. Landowners would submit claims to a centralised agency, the Central Land Board, for *loss of development value*, that is, the difference between the *unrestricted value* (the market value without the restrictions introduced by the Act) and the *existing use value* (the value subject to these restrictions). When all the claims had been received and examined, the £300m would be divided between claimants at whatever proportion of their 1948 value that total would allow. (In the event the estimate of £300m was not as far out as critics feared: the total of all claims finally amounted to £380m.)

The original intention was to have a flexible rate of development charge. In some cases 100 per cent would be levied, but in others a lower rate would be more appropriate in order to encourage development 'on account of economic conditions in the country generally, or in particular areas where unemployment is above the average', or where it was important to secure 'a particular piece of development now, instead of in, say, twenty years'.[3] However, when the regulations came to be made, the Government maintained that the policy which had been set out during the passage of the bill through the House was unworkable. The only explanation given for this was that:

> The whole conception is that the value of land is divided into two parts — the value restricted to its existing use and the development value. The market value is the sum of the two. If, by the action of the State, the development value is no longer in the possession of the owner of the land, then all he has left is the existing use value. Moreover, the fund of £300 million is being provided for the purposes of compensating the owner of land for this reduced value . . . therefore the owner of land can have no possible claim to any part of the development value and it is logical and right that the State should, where development takes place, make a charge which represents the amount of the development value.

The whole idea of variable development charges (particularly for the depressed areas) was rejected, and a flat-rate 100 per cent levy introduced.

These provisions, of which only the barest summary has been given here, were very complex and, together with the inevitable uncertainty as to when compensation would be paid and how much it should be, resulted in a general feeling of uncertainty and discontent which did not augur well for the scheme. The principles, however, were clear. To recapitulate, all development rights and values were vested in the State: no development could take place without permission from the local planning authority and then only on payment of a betterment charge to the Central Land Board. The nationalisation of development rights was effected by the 'promised' payment of compensation. As a result landowners only owned the existing use rights of their land and it thus followed, first, that if permission to develop was refused no compensation was payable, and, second, that the price paid to public authorities for the compulsory acquisition of land would be equal to the existing use value – that is, its value excluding any allowance for future development.

## THE 1947 SCHEME IN OPERATION

The scheme did not work as smoothly as was expected. In their first annual report, the Central Land Board 'noted with concern some weeks after the Act came into operation that despite the liability for development charge land was being widely offered and, still worse, taken at prices including the full development value'. This remained a problem throughout the lifetime of the scheme, though the magnitude of the problem still remains a matter of some controversy. Nevertheless, it is clear that the conditions were such that developers were prepared to pay more than existing-use prices for land. This was largely due to the severe restrictions which were imposed on building. Building licences were very scarce, and developers who were able to obtain them were willing to pay a high price for land upon which to build.

It was to prevent such problems that the Central Land Board had been given powers of compulsory purchase at the 'correct' price. These powers were used, not as a general means of facilitating the supply of land at existing-use prices, but selectively, 'as a warning to owners of land in general'.[4] Furthermore, they were used only where an owner had actually offered his land for sale at a price above existing-use

value. Thus, purchases by the Board would have done nothing to facilitate an increase in the total supply of land for development even if they had been much more numerous. In fact, however, their very rarity served only to make the procedure arbitrary in the extreme and, indeed, may have added to the reluctance of owners to offer land for development at all.

The Conservative Government which took office in 1951 was intent on raising the level of construction activity and particularly the rate of private house-building. Though, within the limits of building activity set by the Labour Government, it is unlikely that the development charge procedure seriously affected the supply of land, it is probable that the Conservative Government's plans for private building would have been jeopardised by it.[5] This was one factor which led the new Government to consider repealing development charges. There is no doubt that these charges were unpopular, particularly since they were payable in cash and in full, whereas payment on the claims on the £300m fund were deferred and uncertain in amount.[6] The position was slightly eased after the announcement that the Central Land Board would accept claims as security for the charge up to 80 per cent of their agreed value. However, the basic difficulty remained: purchasers of land were compelled to pay a premium above the existing-use value in order to persuade an owner to sell. A development charge of 100 per cent therefore constituted a permanent addition to the cost of development.

Further problems began to loom ahead as the final date for payments from the £300m fund (1 July 1953) drew near. First, the payment of this sum of money over a short period would have a considerable inflationary effect. Second, all claimants on the fund would receive payment whether or not they had actually suffered any loss as a result of the 1947 Act. (Some would have already recovered the development value of the land by selling at a high price; others may never have wished to develop their land, and, indeed, might even have bought it for the express purpose of preventing its development.) But the main difficulty was that if compensation were paid out on this 'once for all' basis, it would be exceedingly difficult for any future Government ever to make radical changes in the financial provisions, however badly they were working. For all the holders of claims on the fund would have to be compensated for loss of development value – those who will be allowed to develop their land as well as those who will not.[7]

Some amendment of the 1947 Act was clearly desirable, but though there might have been agreement on this, there was no agreement on what the amendments should be. There was a real fear that an amendment which satisfied developers would seriously weaken or even wreck the planning machine: the scheme was part of a complex of planning controls which might easily be upset and result in a return to the very problems which the 1947 Act was designed to solve.

Various proposals were canvassed, but the most popular was a reduction in the rate of development charge. The intention was to provide an incentive to owners to sell their land at a price which took account of the developer's liability to pay the (reduced) charge. The Government took the view that this was not possible: 'vendors of land, like vendors of any other commodity, will always get the best price that they can, and the development charge, however small, would in effect be passed on, in whole or in part, to the ultimate user of the land'. Furthermore, the Government's objective was not merely one of easing the market in land: it was particularly concerned to encourage more private development, and even a low rate of development charge would act as a brake. On the (implicit) assumption that market prices for land would rise, the time would inevitably come when the charge would begin to greatly exceed the corresponding claim on the £300m fund. Finally, it was felt that once the rate of development charge was reduced there would be no clear principle as to the level at which it should continue to be levied – 'the process of reduction, once begun, would be difficult to stop'. In short, the Government held that the financial provisions of the 1947 Act were inherently unsatisfactory and could not be sufficiently improved by a mere modification: what was needed was a complete abolition of development charges.

## THE 1954 SCHEME

The abolition of development charges was made on the ground that they had proved 'too unreliable an instrument to act as the lynchpin of a permanent settlement'. But, at the same time, if the main part of the planning system was to remain, some limit to the liability to compensation for planning restrictions was essential. Otherwise effective planning controls would be prohibitively expensive: the cost of compensation for restrictions, if paid at the market value, would be crippling. The solution arrived at was to compensate only 'for loss of development value which accrued in the past up to the point where the 1947 axe fell – but not for loss of development value accruing in the future'.

There were some clear advantages in this scheme: not only was the state's liability for compensation limited, but it was to be paid only if and when the owner of land suffered from planning restrictions. The compensation would be the *admitted claim* on the £300m fund (plus one-seventh for accrued interest on the amount of the claim). But not all admitted claims were to be met, even where loss of development value was caused by refusal of planning permission or by conditions attached to a permission. The 1932 Act had clearly established the principle that compensation should not be paid for restrictions imposed in the interest of 'good neighbourliness' and this principle was extended. No compensation was payable for refusal to allow a change in the use of a building; or for restrictions regarding density, layout, construction, design, and so on; or for refusal to permit development which would place an undue burden on the community (for example, in the provision of services). Some of these matters clearly fall within the 'good neighbour' concept, while others are based on the principle that compensation is not to be paid merely because maximum exploitation has been prevented so long as development of a reasonably remunerative character is allowed.

The 1954 scheme[8] did not put anything in place of the development charge: the collection of betterment was now left to the blunt instruments of general taxation. Hence the attempt to 'hold the scales evenly between those who were allowed to develop their land and those who were not' was abandoned, but the use of 1947 development values as a 'permanent basis for compensation' safeguarded the public purse. But this created a dual market in land. Compensation both for planning restrictions (in cases where a claim had been admitted) and for compulsory purchase by public authorities was to be paid on the basis of existing use plus any admitted 1947 development value, but private sales would be at current market prices. The difference between these two values might be very substantial, particularly where development of a far more valuable character than had been anticipated in 1947 took place. Furthermore, with the passage of time land values generally would increase, especially if inflation continued. Whatever theoretical justification there might be for a dual market it would appear increasingly unjust.

Moreover, there is a real distinction between the hardships inflicted by a refusal of planning permission (that is, the loss of the development value of land) and that caused by the loss of the land itself (that is, compulsory purchase). In the first case, the owner retains the existing-use value of his land and is worse off only in comparison with owners who have been fortunate in owning land on which development is permitted and who can therefore realise a capital gain. But in the second case, compulsory acquisition at less than market price involves an actual loss since the owner is not only deprived of his property, he is also compensated at a price which might be less than he paid for it and which would almost certainly be insufficient to purchase a similar parcel of land in the open market.

To recapitulate, the effect of the complicated network of legislation which was now (1954) in force was basically to create two values for land according to whether it was sold in the open market or acquired by a public authority. In the former case, there were no restrictions and thus land changed hands at the full market price; but in the latter case, the public authority would pay only the existing (1947) use value plus any agreed claim for loss of 1947 development value. This was a most unsatisfactory outcome. As land prices increased, due partly to

planning controls, the gap between existing use and market values widened, particularly in suburban areas near green belt land. The greater the amount of planning control, the greater did the gap become. Thus, owners who were forced to sell their land to public authorities considered themselves to be very badly treated in comparison with those who were able to sell at the enhanced prices resulting in part from planning restrictions on other sites. The inherent uncertainties of future public acquisitions – no plan can be so definite and inflexible as to determine which sites will (or might) be needed in the future for public purposes – made this distinction appear arbitrary and unjust. The abolition of the development charge served to increase the inequity.

The contradictions and anomalies in the 1954 scheme were obvious. It was only a matter of time before public opinion demanded further amending legislation.

## THE 1959 ACT: THE RETURN TO MARKET VALUE

Opposition to this state of affairs increased with the growth of private pressures for development following the abolition of building licences. Eventually the Government was forced to take action. The resulting legislation (the Town and Country Planning Act 1959) restored *fair market price* as the basis of compensation for compulsory acquisition. This, in the Government's view, was the only practicable way of rectifying the injustices of the dual market for land. An owner now obtained (in theory at least) the same price for his land irrespective of whether he sold it to a private individual or to a public authority.

These provisions thus removed a source of grievance, but they did nothing towards solving the fundamental problems of compensation and betterment, and the result proved extremely costly to public authorities. If this had been a reflection of basic principles of justice there could have been little cause for complaint but, in fact, an examination of the position shows clearly that this was not the case.

In the first place, the 1959 Act (like previous

legislation) accepted the principle that development rights should be vested in the State. This followed from the fact that no compensation was payable for the loss of development value in cases where planning permission was refused. But if development rights belong to the State, surely so should the associated development values? Consider, for example, the case of two owners of agricultural land on the periphery of a town, both of whom applied for planning permission to develop for housing purposes – the first being given permission and the second refused on the ground that the site in question was to form part of a green belt. The former benefited from the full market value of his site in residential use, whereas the latter could benefit only from its existing-use value. No question of compensation arose since the development rights already belonged to the State, but the first owner had these given back to him without payment. There was an obvious injustice here which could have eventually led to a demand that the 'penalised' owner should be compensated.

Second, as has already been stressed, the comprehensive nature of the planning system has a marked effect on values. The use for which planning permission has been, or will be, given is a very important factor in the determination of value. Furthermore, the value of a given site is increased not only by the development permitted on that site, but also by the development not permitted on other sites. In the example given above, for instance, the value of the site for which planning permission for housing development was given might be increased by virtue of the fact that it was refused on the second site.

## THE LAND COMMISSION 1967–71

Mounting criticism of the inadequacy of the 1959 Act led to a number of proposals for a tax on betterment, by way either of a capital gains tax or of a betterment levy. The Labour Government which was returned to power in 1964 introduced both. The 1967 Finance Act introduced a capital gains tax, and the 1967 Land Commission Act introduced a new betterment levy. Broadly, the distinguishing principle was that capital gains tax was charged on increases in the current-use value of land only, while betterment levy was charged on increases in development value. Though the Land Commission was abolished by the Conservative Government in 1971, a summary account of its powers and operations is appropriate. The rationale underlying the Land Commission Act was set out in a 1965 White Paper:

> In the Government's view it is wrong that planning decisions about land use should so often result in the realising of unearned increments by the owners of the land to which they apply, and that desirable development should be frustrated by owners withholding their land in the hope of higher prices. The two main objectives of the Government's land policy are, therefore:
> (i) to secure that the right land is available at the right time for the implementation of national, regional and local plans;
> (ii) to secure that a substantial part of the development value created by the community returns to the community and that the burden of the cost of land for essential purposes is reduced.

To enable these two objectives to be achieved, a Land Commission was established (with headquarters located at Newcastle upon Tyne, in line with the dispersal of offices policy). The Commission could buy land either by agreement or compulsorily, and it was given very wide powers for this purpose. The second objective was met by the introduction of a betterment levy on development value. This was necessary not only to secure that a substantial part of the development 'returned to the community', but also to prevent a two-price system as existed under the 1954 Act. The levy was deducted from the price paid by the Commission on its own purchases and was paid by owners when they sold land privately. A landowner thus theoretically received the same amount for his land whether he sold it privately, to the Land Commission, or to another public authority.

Though the Commission could buy by agreement, it had to have effective powers of compulsory purchase if it was 'to ensure that the right land is made available at the right time'. There were two reasons for this. First, though the levy was at a rate (initially 40 per cent) thought to be adequate to leave enough of the development value to provide 'a reasonable incentive', some owners of land might still be unwilling to sell. Second, though the net price obtained by the owner of land should have been the same irrespective of whether the body to whom he sold it was private or public, some owners might have been unwilling to sell to the Commission.

The Act provided two sets of compulsory powers. One was the normal powers available to local authorities, with the usual machinery for appeals and a public inquiry. The second set of compulsory powers were not to become operative until the 'second appointed day' and were to be brought into effect only if it appeared 'that it is necessary in the public interest to enable the Commission to obtain authority for the compulsory acquisition of land by a simplified procedure'. They were intended to provide a rapid procedure under which objectors would have no right to state their case at a public inquiry, and the Commission was not required to disclose the purpose for which the land was needed. The purpose here was to deal quickly and effectively with landowners who were holding up development. In fact they did not become operative during the lifetime of the Commission.

The levy differed from the development charge of the 1947 Act in two important ways. First, it did not take all the development value. The Act did not specify what the rate was to be, but it was made clear that the initial rate of 40 per cent would be increased to 45 per cent and then to 50 per cent 'at reasonably short intervals'. (It never was.)

The second difference from the development charge was that though the levy would normally be paid to the seller, if 'when the land comes to be developed, it still has some development value on which levy has not been taken in previous sales, that residual value will be subject to levy at the time of development'. Thus (ignoring a few complications and qualifications), if a piece of land was worth £500 in its existing use but was sold for £3,500 with planning permission, the levy was applied to the difference, that is, £3,000; the levy, at the initial rate, was £1,200. If, however, the land were sold (at existing-use value plus a 'hope' value that planning permission might be obtained) at £1,000, while the full development value was £3,500, the levy would be paid by both seller and purchaser: £200 by the former and £1,000 by the latter.

The Land Commission's first task was to assess the availability of, and demand for, land for housebuilding, particularly in the areas of greatest pressure. In its first annual report, it pointed to the difficulties in some areas (particularly in the South-East and the West Midlands) where the available land was limited to only a few years' supply. Most of this land could not, in fact, be made available for early development. Much of it was in small parcels; some was not suitable for development at all because of physical difficulties; and, of the remainder, a great deal was already in the hands of builders. Thus there was little that could be acquired and developed immediately by those other builders who had an urgent need for land. All this highlighted the need for more land to be allocated by planning authorities for development.

The Land Commission had to work within the framework of the planning system, and was subject to the same planning control as private developers. The intention was that the Commission would work harmoniously with local planning authorities and form an important addition to the planning machinery. As the Commission pointed out, despite the sophistication of the British planning system, it was designed to control land use rather than to promote the development of land. The Commission's role was to ensure that land allocated for development was in fact developed, by channelling it to those who would develop it. It could use its powers of compulsory acquisition to amalgamate land which was in separate ownerships and acquire land whose owners could not be traced. It could purchase land from owners who refused to sell for development or from builders who wished to retain it for future development.

In its first report, the Land Commission gently referred to the importance of their role in acting 'as a spur to those local planning authorities whose plans have not kept pace with the demand for various kinds of development'. Though it hoped that planning authorities would allocate sufficient land, it warned that in some cases it might have to take the initiative and, if local authorities refused planning permission, go to appeal. In its second interim report, a much stronger line was taken. It pointed out that, in the pressure areas, they had only modest success in achieving a steady flow of land on to the market. This was largely because these were areas in which planning authorities were aimed at containing urban growth and preserving open country.

In 1969/70, the Land Commission purchased 1,000 acres by agreement and a further 240 acres compulsorily. But the use of these compulsory powers was on the increase, and a further 2,500 acres were subject to compulsory purchase at March 1970.

It is not easy to appraise what success the Land Commission achieved. It was only beginning to get into its stride in 1970 when a new Government was returned which was pledged to its abolition on the grounds that it 'had no place in a free society'. This pledge was fulfilled in 1971 and thus the Land Commission went the same way as its predecessor, the Central Land Board.

## THE CONSERVATIVE YEARS, 1970–74

Land prices were rising during the late 1960s (with an increase of 55 per cent between 1967 and 1970), but the early 1970s witnessed a veritable price explosion. Using 1967 as a base (100), prices rose to 287 in 1972 and 458 in 1973. Average plot prices rose from £908 in 1970 to £2,676 in 1973.[9]

Not surprisingly, considerable pressure was put on the Conservative Government to take some action to cope with the problem, though it was neither clear nor agreed what the basic problem was (Hallett 1977: 135). The favourite explanation, however, was 'speculative hoarding', and it was this which became the target for Government action (in addition to a series of measures designed to speed up the release and development of land). A 1973 White Paper, *Widening the Choice: The Next Steps in Housing*, set out

proposals for a *land hoarding charge*. This was to be levied 'for failure to complete development within a specified period from the grant of planning permission'. After this 'completion period' (of four years from the granting of outline planning permission or three years in the case of full planning permission), the charge was to be imposed at an annual rate of 30 per cent of the capital value of the land.

The scheme was clearly a long-term one and, to deal with the urgent problem ('urgent' in political if not in any other terms), a *development gains tax* and a *first letting tax* were introduced.

The development gains tax provided for gains from land sales by individuals to be treated not as capital gains but as income (and thus subject to high marginal rates). The first letting tax, as its name implies, was a tax levied on the first letting of shops, offices, or industrial premises. In concept, it was an equivalent to the capital gains tax which would have been levied had the building been sold.

Both taxes came into operation at the time when the land and property boom turned into a slump. Indeed, it has been suggested that they contributed to it (Hallett 1977: 137).

## THE 1974 WHITE PAPER

The Labour Government which was returned to power in March 1974 lost little time in producing its anticipated White Paper *Land*. The objectives of this were 'to enable the community to control the development of land in accordance with its needs and priorities' and 'to restore to the community the increase in value of land arising from its efforts'. The keynote was 'positive planning', which was to be achieved by public ownership of development land. In England and Scotland, the agency for purchasing development land was to be local government (thus avoiding the inter-agency conflict which arose between local authorities and the Land Commission). In Wales, however, with its smaller local authorities, an *ad hoc* agency was to be created (this became the Land Authority for Wales).

In order 'to restore to the community the increase

in value of land arising from its efforts', it was proposed that 'the ultimate basis on which the community will buy all land will be current use value'. Sale of the land to developers, on the other hand, would be at market value. Thus all development value would accrue to the community. Provisionally, however, development values were to be recouped by a development land tax.

## THE COMMUNITY LAND SCHEME

The ensuing legislation came in two parts: the 1975 Community Land Act provided wide powers for compulsory land acquisition, while the Development Land Tax Act 1976 provided for the taxation of development values. Thus the twin purposes of 'positive planning' and of 'returning development values to the community' were to be served.

The Community Land Scheme was complex, and became increasingly so as regulations, directions and circulars followed the passing of the two Acts. The intention was for it to be phased-in gradually, thus enabling programmes to be developed in line with available resources of finance, staff and expertise.

In the first stage, which started on the 'first appointed day' (6 April 1976), local authorities had a general duty 'to have regard to the desirability of bringing development land into public ownership'. In doing so, they had 'to pay particular regard to the location and nature of development necessary to meet the planning needs of their areas'. To assist them in carrying out this role, they had new and wider powers to buy land to make it available for development. Following the passing of the Development Land Tax of 1976, all land acquisitions by authorities were made at a price *net* of any tax payable by the sellers of development land.

The second stage was to be introduced as authorities built up resources and expertise. The Secretary of State would make orders providing that land for development of the kind designated in the order, and in the area specified by the order, would pass through public ownership before development took place.

These *duty orders* were to be brought in to match the varying rates at which authorities became ready to take on such responsibilities.

When duty orders had been made covering the whole of Great Britain, the 'second appointed day' (or SAD Day as critics dubbed it) could be brought in. This would have had the effect of changing the basis of compensation for land publicly acquired from a market-value (net of tax) basis to a current-use-value basis, that is, its value in its existing use, taking no account of any increase in value actually or potentially conferred by the grant of a planning permission for new development.

The scheme, like its two predecessors, had little chance to prove itself (Grant 1979; Emms 1980). The economic climate of the first two years of its operation could hardly have been worse, and the consequent public expenditure crisis resulted in a central control which limited it severely.

It is fortunate, however, that a thorough monitoring of the scheme, funded by the DoE, was undertaken by the School for Advanced Urban Studies at the University of Bristol. The reader is referred to reports of this study (Barrett *et al*. 1979; Barrett and Whitting 1983).

## PLANNING AGREEMENTS AND OBLIGATIONS

The abandonment of attempts to collect betterment was one of a number of factors which, in the early 1980s, stimulated an already established trend for increasing the levying of charges on developers. Other influences included a general move from a regulatory to a negotiatory style of development control, increased delays in the planning system, and the financial difficulties of local authorities.[10]

Planning authorities have had power to make 'agreements' since 1932, but it was not until the property boom of the early 1970s that they became widely used – or, as some argue, abused. The term *planning gain* is popularly used, but with two different meanings. The term can denote facilities which are an integral part of a development; but it can also mean 'benefits' which have little or no relationship to the development, and which the local authority require as 'the price of planning permission'. There has been very extensive debate on this issue, and the list of relevant publications is very long; there is even a *Planning Gain Newsletter*, published bi-monthly.[11] Unfortunately, neither these publications nor statutory changes and ministerial exhortations have done much to settle the arguments. The extremes range from the Property Advisory Group's (1981) categorical statement that planning gain has no place in the planning control system, to Mather's (1988) proposal that planning gain should be formalised by allowing local authorities to sell or auction planning consents. Essentially, the issue is the extent to which local authorities can legitimately require developers to shoulder the wider costs of development: the needed infrastructure, schools and other local services.

The extremes are easy to identify: the cost of local roads in a development are clearly legitimate, while financial contributions to the cost of running a central library are not. But, of course, most items fall well within these extremes. S. Byrne (1989) provides a useful selection of agreements, and concludes that the majority are legitimate – a view corroborated by studies commissioned by DoE (Grimley J.R. Eve 1992) and by the Scottish Office (Rowan-Robinson and Durman 1992a). These studies effectively demolish the argument that there is widespread extortion by way of planning gain. In England, less than 1 per cent of planning decisions involve planning agreements; the largest proportion are concerned with regulatory matters (contracts, plans and drawings, building materials, etc.),[12] and over a half deal with occupancy conditions (for example, restrictions required for sheltered housing, agricultural dwellings, social housing). Agreements serve an important function in securing the provision of infrastructure necessitated by a development (particularly local roads), and in environmental improvement (such as landscaping). Only a very small number of agreements are concerned with wider planning objectives. In Scotland,

> most agreements are a useful adjunct to the development control process; abuse of power does not present a

problem; and for the most part, the benefits secured by agreements have been related to the development proposed: where they have not, the benefits have been of a relatively minor order.
>
> (Rowan-Robinson and Durman 1992a: 73)

The statutory provisions relating to agreements were amended by the Planning and Compensation Act 1991. Agreements have become 'obligations' and may be unilateral – not involving any 'agreement' between a local authority and a developer at all:

> Any person interested in land in the area of a local planning authority may, by agreement or otherwise, enter into an obligation (referred to . . . as a *planning obligation*) . . .
> (a) restricting the development or use of the land in any specified way;
> (b) requiring specified operations or activities to be carried out, in, on, under or over the land;
> (c) requiring the land to be used in any specified way;
> (d) requiring a sum or sums to be paid to the authority on a specified date or dates or periodically.[13]

Though the wider debate has been on the ethics of planning gain, this new provision in fact deals only with a narrow legal difficulty. A DoE Consultation Paper issued in August 1989 explained that a log-jam could arise where the Secretary of State decided that a planning appeal should be allowed if a certain condition were met, but there was no legal basis for imposing the condition (typically because it involved off-site infrastructure). The new provision allows a developer to make an agreement to provide the necessary off-site works even if the local authority are not prepared to be a party to the agreement.[14] This seems a small point on which to base the change from 'agreements' to 'obligations': it is possible that a more important function of the new provision is to give the appearance of a change in policy which will curb the alleged excesses of planning gain.

In fact, nothing could be further from the reality. DoE Circular 7/91 had already made it clear that local authorities could negotiate with developers for the provision of social housing. This represented a major extension of the arena of planning agreements. But, in the debates on the 1991 bill, the Minister (Sir George Young) went further:

I think we are all agreed that planning gain is a useful part of the planning system and should be preserved and even encouraged . . . A planning gain would do more than merely provide facilities that would normally have been provided at public expense. It would provide facilities that the public would never have afforded.[15]

Similarly, the RICS in their response (1991) to the White Paper *This Common Inheritance* expressed the hope that agreements would be extended:

It is hoped that consideration can be given to an increased use of agreements where major developments are proposed so that the community can gain some off-setting benefit, particularly when there is a loss of amenity.

As the report on the Scottish study notes,[16] these views (from such eminent sources) amount to a major change in opinion since the Property Advisory Group (1981) declared the pursuit of planning gain to be unacceptable.

At the root of this is a significant change in the expected roles of the private and public sectors in land development. Whereas it used to be the case that the responsibilities of developers were clearly limited, it has become generally (even if not unanimously) accepted that the public sector is financially unable to meet the associated costs in the traditional way.[17] The move from a regulatory to a negotiatory style of control is another aspect of this, as has been the willingness of developers to shoulder these costs. This is to be seen even more clearly in relation to charges imposed by other agencies for off-site works such as water, sewers, and highways. Recent proposals on the latter are particularly striking. Following an *Efficiency Scrutiny Report*, the Department of Transport issued a consultation paper on *Developers' Contributions to Highway Works* (1992). This proposes that the Department should take 'a more positive approach to development proposals': this involves acting 'in a more pro-active way, giving developers greater certainty and better advance notice of the Department's requirements in respect of highway works and contributions'. Contributions would vary according to road capacity, the traffic to be generated by a development, and the plans for future highway construction. In a *red line case*, where

there was no spare road capacity, the developer would pay the full costs of any improvement made necessary by the development. In a *yellow line case*, where a road was not at capacity but might become so within the life of the development plan, contributions would be allocated according to the amount of traffic growth for which individual developments were forecast to be responsible. The *green line case* would be one where a highway improvement was planned but needed to be brought forward to meet the traffic requirements of the development: here the developer would pay the extra cost involved in bringing the improvement forward.

The detailed proposals are more complex than this summary suggests, but it does give an indication of what is expected from developers. In intention, the proposals are only a codification of existing policy, but with the advantage that developers will be able to establish in advance what liabilities would flow from new development. (There is also the major benefit of a closer link between land-use planning and highway planning.)[18]

The effect of all these imposts (to use an American term) is to significantly increase the costs which are borne by developers. There is an underlying factor: the way in which attitudes on the character and scope of planning have changed. Economic and social factors now loom large, and can be seen as being of greater importance than purely land-use matters. The courts have clearly stated that financial issues can be 'material considerations' in planning, as long as they are secondary to planning matters.[19] Thus, in the case of office development granted (contrary to the local plan) to enable the redevelopment of the Covent Garden Opera House to be financially viable, it was argued:

Financial constraints on the economic viability of a desirable planning development are unavoidable facts of life in an imperfect world. It would be unreal and contrary to common sense to insist that they must be excluded from the range of considerations which may properly be regarded as material in determining planning applications . . . Provided that the ultimate determination is based on planning grounds and not on some ulterior motive, and that it is not irrational, there would be no basis for holding it to be invalid in law solely on the ground that it has taken account of, and adjusted itself to, the financial realities of the overall situation.[20]

Social factors may present greater difficulties as when Lord Widgery held that the London Borough of Hillingdon could not impose a condition that the occupants of a private housing development should be people on the council's waiting list.[21] Nevertheless, the matter is not settled – as is instanced by the debate on the role of planning policies (as distinct from housing policies) in the provision of affordable housing.[22] The stance of the DoE on this matter is far from clear. On the one hand 'planning conditions and agreements cannot normally be used to impose restrictions on tenure, price or ownership', but they 'can properly be used to restrict the occupation of property to people falling within particular categories of need'. Both statements are from Circular 7/91 on *Planning and Affordable Housing*. Even more curious (during the regime of a Conservative Government) is the policy of 'exceptional release' of land, outside the provisions of the development plan, for 'local needs' housing.[23] This is an explicit 'use of the planning system to subsidise the provision of low cost housing through containment of land value' (RTPI 1992a: 5).

The extent to which authorities can achieve planning benefits depends, of course, on their bargaining power, which in turn may be related to current (and local) economic conditions. The situation varies over time and by region. In some circumstances, 'getting a developer to build anything is, in our eyes, a planning gain' (quoted in Jowell 1977a: 428); in others, the local pressures for development are so strong that local authorities can secure considerable benefits.

The growth of planning agreements gives rise to a number of concerns. The ethics of bargaining are debatable; there is scope for unjustifiable coercion; and equal treatment as between applicants can be abandoned in favour of charging what the market will bear at any particular time. Additionally, bargaining is a closed, private activity which sits uneasily astride the current emphasis on open government and public participation.

Much of the difficulty in this area may arise from the discretionary nature of the British planning control system in which negotiation is an important feature. However, studies of US land-use regulation (which supposedly emphasises property rights and reduces development uncertainties) show that negotiation is equally prevalent there (Cullingworth 1993). An essential issue is that, while development rights in land are nationalised, their associated values are privately owned. Much of the case for 'planning gain' is that it is a means of capturing some of this value for the public benefit.[24]

## LAND POLICIES SINCE 1980

Though the Community Land Act was repealed by the Local Government, Planning and Land Act 1980, local authorities still retained considerable powers of compulsory acquisition of land. They could acquire, with the consent of the Secretary of State:

> any land in their area which –
> (a) is suitable for and required in order to secure the carrying out of development, redevelopment, or improvement; or
> (b) is required for a purpose which it is necessary to achieve in the interests of the proper planning of an area in which the land is situated.

These powers (which are still possessed by local authorities under section 226 of the 1990 Act) specifically provided for compulsory acquisition of land for disposal to a private developer. Indeed, the Government made it clear that these 'planning purposes' powers (which could be of particular importance in bringing land on to the market) were generally to be used to assist the private sector.

Additionally, the Secretary of State has some formidable powers himself. First he has the reserve power to direct a local authority to make an assessment of land available and suitable for residential development. Second, his powers to acquire any land 'necessary for the public service' include the authorisation of acquisitions 'to meet the interests of proper planning of the area, or to secure the best or most economic development or use of land'. (Ironically these provisions are a modified re-enactment of a section of the repealed Community Land Act.) However, little use has been made of these powers; instead reliance has been placed on ensuring that LPAs make sufficient land 'available'.

Considerable debate has taken place on the adequacy of 'land availability' policies. The problems are partly financial (providing the necessary infrastructure), but mainly political. This is particularly the case for a Conservative Government aiming at privatisation and the reduction in controls, an ample supply of land for private development, and the retention of land-use planning at the local level.

Patsy Healey has argued that the crux of the political dilemma lies in the traditional Conservative support in the shire counties:

> This support combines a concern to preserve the attractive environments in which they live and a commitment to local democracy at the smallest scale. The 1972 Local Government Act ensured continuing Conservative control of suburban and rural areas. Conservative Governments thus face a dilemma. At national level they may be concerned to shift land policies more towards production than consumption purposes. Yet they must not lose the support of the environmental lobby or local Conservative councillors. In other words, the ideology of limited intervention which the current Conservative administration espouses sits uneasily with its need to respond to the demands of industrial and property production and to those for environmental conservation and local control over land policy.
>
> (Healey 1983: 269)

Of course, the debate is not carried on in these terms. Instead there are numerous surveys and a barrage of figures. The calculation of land availability, in particular, has moved to centre stage.

## LAND AVAILABILITY STUDIES

It was a major objective of the architects of the post-war planning system to ensure that land required for development would become available – if necessary by the use of compulsory purchase powers. As previous discussion has shown, things did not work out like this despite three attempts (in 1947, 1967, and 1975). Except in special cases, such as new towns

and comprehensive development areas, there has been little use of compulsory purchase powers. Thus the land 'allocations' in plans remained just that – allocations on paper. There is no necessary relationship between the allocation of land and its *availability*.[25] It is therefore not surprising that there has been considerable controversy over the extent to which allocated land is in fact available for development. In Hooper's words:

> The planning system and the house building industry operate not only with a different definition, but with a different conception, of land availability – the former based on public control over land use, the latter on market orientation to the ownership of land.
>
> (Hooper 1980)

The early land availability studies foundered on this difference, but the Government continued to press their importance.[26] The 1980 Local Government, Planning and Land Act even gave powers to the Secretary of State to *direct* a local authority to 'make an assessment of land which is in its area and which is in its opinion available and suitable for development for residential purposes'. Circular 9/80 sets out a detailed methodology for studies and urged cooperation between local authorities and housebuilders in establishing the local situation.

Dissatisfied with the quality of many land availability studies, the DoE commissioned Coopers & Lybrand to carry out a study

> to assess and report on the varying assessments and assumptions about new housing made by the planning authorities and house builders, and to assess the extent to which both the provision in plans and land which is made available for housing takes account of the requirements of the market for new private sector housing.
>
> (Coopers & Lybrand 1985)

Their conclusion is clear:

> there is no doubt that most of the structure plans of the 1970s paid little attention to the market demand for housing. The structure plans tended to be based on a *survey–analysis–plan* approach which required a rather determinist view of the issues which they examined.

But there is a deeper issue: 'market demand for housing was not *and probably cannot* [emphasis added] be estimated in an area and over time; this precludes its incorporation into structure plans and prevents any meaningful quantitative comparisons to be made with plan figures'.

This constitutes a fundamental challenge to the basis of the British planning system, and raises a host of thorny questions about the nature and efficacy of the system. Surprisingly, the nine members of the steering group for the Coopers & Lybrand study were not members of the Conservative Party Central Office or the Adam Smith Institute but, with one exception (the representative of the House Builders Federation), were government officials, mostly from the Department of the Environment. Moreover, they had no hesitation in stressing the point that builders do not operate or think in terms familiar to planners: instead they look to 'market signals'. It follows, so they argued, that the planning system should concern itself with ways of improving the process of responding to demand. Three types of change were proposed. First, there should be clearer signals from the market. (A working paper includes a list of possible indicators, together with the suggestion that those operating in the market should work with planners to develop useful indicators.) Second,

> the plans themselves should consciously take note of such demand factors and, of critical importance, the plans should be sufficiently flexible to be able to respond to demand in the course of implementation – including the identification of criteria which, when met, should signal a need for a review. Plans should ensure that sites of varying size and location are available.

Finally, the report maintained that clearer guidance from central government was required, and that appeal decisions should be consistent with exhortations. Review of structure plans should be simplified and accelerated, and other major aspects of the planning process should be strengthened – 'including some possible limit on the extent of public participation'. The 'rationale for some of the more rigid land constraints which flow from national policies' also needs review, particularly the planning presumption against development of agricultural land.

This is one of the most important reports since the Planning Advisory Group's 1965 *The Future of*

*Development Plans.* Unfortunately, it has two incidental weaknesses. First, it is too brief (a rare complaint!); second, the fact that it is published by the consultants and not by the DoE or HMSO reduces its ease of accessibility. This may suit some since, as the authors note at the end of their hard-hitting proposals, 'none of these suggestions offers easy solutions'.

A study by Duncan Maclennan (1986), commissioned by the SDD was equally critical of Scottish practice. In estimating demand, Scottish authorities had used inadequate techniques: in particular, they had omitted economic factors. Builders' estimates, whilst stressing economic considerations, lacked a sound quantitative basis. Maclennan continued:

> The importance of current omissions is clearly illustrated by recourse to some basic economics. In the short run, say a single year, quantity demanded is largely determined by market price. Over the longer period changes in population, income, etc., shift this relationship in measurable ways. Price and income effects on housing demand are demonstrably important but they are ignored in structure plans. In consequence 1981 Census based demand estimates could understate 1990 demand by as much as one quarter. Supply side estimates ignore long term changes in land and construction costs and in consequence probably overestimate the long run level of effective demand. Thus the omission of economic factors leads to a divergence of demand estimates between builders and regions thus increasing the potential for unnecessary conflict.
>
> (Maclennan 1986)

Maclennan was more optimistic about improvements in forecasting than the Coopers & Lybrand team, partly because of Scotland's unique source of house price information (known as the Register of Sasines). Nevertheless, speedy results were not to be expected, since much research remained to be done.

In reviewing the controversy over land-availability studies, one is struck by their curious remoteness from the real world of land assembly and development. Though a greater understanding was probably achieved between planners and builders, the studies themselves proved to be of less value than the DoE had envisaged. Hooper (1985: 126) concluded that 'whilst preserving a facade of cooperation between the main agents involved in the land conversion process' the approach in fact only served 'to obscure the fundamental issues underlying land policy in relation to residential development'. Cuddy and Hollingsworth (1985), however, while noting that land policy tended to be of a 'stable door' character (with major changes taking place before a policy was fully implemented) conclude that the land-availability exercises were worth while since they promote a dialogue on uncertain futures where 'bargains' are struck between local authorities and housebuilders. The 'bargains' cannot be firm since both the parties face uncertainties, but the outcome is of less importance than the process of negotiation itself. In Barrett's words:

> [They] see what is going on in such studies as a process of negotiation in which neither party to the negotiation has control over its own delivery system. It is not a simple win/lose game, but a strategic negotiation for flexibility of manoeuvre in an uncertain environment. Both parties stand to gain from not committing themselves to a firm outcome 'contract' yet maintaining the negotiation process . . . the main value of the studies lies in the process itself as a basis for reviewing performance and as a means of learning more about the short/medium term flow of land through the development process.[27]

This may be the latent function of land-availability studies, but the DoE remain focused on their manifest function, as is evident from the 1992 Planning Policy Guidance Note on *Housing*.[28] Since a commissioned report from Roger Tym & Partners (1991) repeats the long-standing criticisms that the studies take insufficient account of ownership and marketability constraints, it seems that history is repeating itself. The studies now seem to be a part of the planning system, whether they have any tangible use or not![29] Whether they have any effect on restraining land price increases is yet another question.[30]

## THE LAND AUTHORITY FOR WALES

A surprising anomaly in the institutional arrangements for land policy is the survival of the Land Authority for Wales (LAW), an *ad hoc* body originally established under the Community Land Act. This provides precisely what is missing from the English scene: a body with a long-term and wide-ranging view of the land situation complete with powers to act positively in order to solve land-availability problems.

It 'makes land available for development in the Principality, particularly where the private sector experiences difficulties in acquiring land' (LAW 1992). It can also acquire land (compulsorily if necessary). The Authority obtains planning permission for development and, in many cases, provides the necessary infrastructure. By virtue of its powers and financial position, it is able to purchase large sites and phase their development. Though its main function is to make land available for private housing, it also promotes the regeneration of town centres. It plays a major role in Welsh land-availability studies. Its land-assembly activities are illustrated by the figures for 1991/92: in that year it acquired 207 hectares at a cost of £5.487m and disposed of 130 hectares for £8.822m. Its gross profit for the year was £5.614m.

Grant has commented that this represents 'the clearest and least restrictive legislative authorisation for positive planning that now exists'. He also explains why LAW exists:

> Two factors in particular contributed to the Authority's success . . . and prevented their abolition. First, they are a single purpose authority, and, unlike the local planning authorities of England and Scotland, were able, and indeed required, to pursue positive planning as their first priority. Second, the authority are not themselves a planning authority. They operate within the confines of the planning policies administered by the Welsh local planning authorities, and, where their planning applications are refused they have the usual right of appeal to the Secretary of State for Wales. They have managed therefore to avoid the suspicion of conflict of interest which has often attached to the positive planning efforts of local planning authorities. In practice they have also assisted Welsh local authorities in land availability studies and with advice on land disposal for development.
>
> (Grant 1982: 521)

Praise has come from other quarters. For example, Chubb (1988: para. 6.6) points to LAW's advantage in being able to 'pursue its objectives single mindedly, without conflicts of priority . . . which cause diffi-culties for local authorities'. The House Builders' Federation (1987) commends LAW's success in obtaining land for development and securing plann-ing permissions for private builders, often on appeal against local authorities. It argues that there is a strong case for a similar land development agency for London and perhaps other areas.

## NEW SETTLEMENTS

The conclusion of the new towns programmes, coupled with increasing concern with the 'land for housing' problem naturally prompted debate on additional new towns. The TCPA had traditionally maintained that these should be a major plank in regional policy, but, during the 1980s, against the background of a buoyant housing market, proposals came from the private sector for private enterprise new towns that would fill the gap left by the completion of the existing new towns (Amos 1989 and 1991). The best known of these came from the now disbanded Consortium Developments (Hebbert 1992). This was a group of housebuilders who were advised by Conran Roche, a privatised group of officials from the Milton Keynes Development Corp-oration. They proposed a ring of new villages around the South-East which would form 'balanced com-munities' developed to high standards of design.

> Consortium Developments Ltd, by working on a relatively large scale, can negotiate a keen price that allows investment in a quality product. High quality infrastructure in the paving and road surfaces, high quality landscaping, sensitive design of public spaces, variety in both form and tenure of housing provision, and a wide range of supporting facilities.
>
> (Roche 1986: 312)

These were words in the direct tradition of the new towns movement (Hardy 1991a and 1991b), but their spokespersons now had to contend with a sophisti-cated planning machine. Proposals for 'Foxley Wood' in Hampshire, 'Stone Bassett' in Oxfordshire, 'Westmere' in Cambridgeshire, and Tillingham Hall in Essex were all rejected on appeal. As Hebbert

(1992: 178) comments, their experience 'demon-strated that even the presence of the most radical free enterprise British Government of recent times is no guarantor of profitable large scale private develop-ments in green field sites'. However, they have not been completely ruled out, and PPG 3 provides a list of the requirements for proposals (which it is noted 'have almost invariably been deeply controversial').[31] Politically, the importance attached to 'local choice' effectively means that any proposal for a new settlement is likely to be killed. Nevertheless, there is still deep interest in the idea as is illustrated by the *Tomorrow's New Communities* competition organised by the Joseph Rowntree Foundation and the TCPA (Darley *et al*. 1991). Cloke (1992: 285) has suggested that 'new settlement proposals will be included by beleaguered local authorities in their development plans over the next decade'. The latest proposal to come from the private sector, which has royal support, is for *urban villages*.[32]

Nevertheless, perhaps the final death knell of new settlements policy is the comment by Sir George Young, the Minister of State for Housing and Planning, on the commissioned study of the relation-ship between land use and transport, 'and the part which different measures could play in reducing the need to travel'. The research results

> confirm that our current planning policies are on lines that help keep transport emissions to a minimum. They aim to focus development in urban areas, rather than in villages and new settlements, and maintain and revitalise towns and city centres . . .

The decision, announced in March 1993, to reject the 'Micheldever Station Market Town' proposal put for-ward by Eagle Star underlines the position being taken on new settlements. This proposal was accompanied by a major public relations drive and excellent publicity.[33] It seems clear that the Government will look with favour on new settlements only when they emerge directly from the plan-making process (Fyson 1993.)

## GREEN BELTS

The policy of maintaining an adequate supply of land for housing can be difficult to reconcile with policies relating to green belts and the safeguarding of agricultural land. Though 1987 saw a major policy shift on the latter (which is discussed on pp. 124–5), green belts have, for a variety of reasons, remained a strong policy issue for both central and local government, as well, of course, for the environmental lobby. A wealth of material is available in the House of Commons Environment Committee's 1984 report *Green Belt and Land for Housing* and in Martin Elson's detailed study (1986).

Green-belt policy emerged in 1955 after the expression of considerable concern (for example by the TCPA)[34] at the implications for urban growth of the expanded housebuilding programme. Unusually, the policy can be identified with a particular minister – Duncan Sandys (who later made another contribution to planning with the promotion of the Civic Trust and the Civic Amenities Act). Sandys' personal commitment involved disagreement with his senior civil servants who advised that it would arouse opposition from the urban local authorities and private developers who would be forced to seek sites beyond the green belt. Experience with the Town Development Act (which provided for negotiated schemes of 'overspill' from congested urban areas to towns wishing to expand) did not suggest that it would be easy to find sufficient sites. Sandys, however, was adamant,[35] and a circular was issued asking local planning authorities to consider the formal designation of clearly defined green belts wherever this was desirable in order to check the physical growth of a large built-up area; to prevent neighbouring towns from merging into one another; or to preserve the special character of a town.

The policy had widespread appeal, not only to county councils who now had another weapon in their armoury to fight expansionist urban authorities, but also more widely. One planning officer commented that 'probably no planning circular and all that it implies has ever been so popular with the public. The idea has caught on and is supported by people of all shades of interest'. Another noted that

the very expression *green belt* sounds like something an ordinary man may find it worthwhile to be interested in who may find no appeal whatever in 'the distribution

of industrial population' or 'decentralisation' . . . Green belt has a natural faculty for engendering support.
(Elson 1986: 269)

The green belt also formed a tangible focal point for what is now called the environmental lobby. However, initially, its biggest support came from the planning profession which in those days still saw planning in terms of tidy spatial ordering of land uses. Desmond Heap, in his 1955 presidential address to the (then) Town Planning Institute, went so far as to declare that the preservation of green belts was 'the very *raison d'etre* of town and country planning'. Their popularity, however, has not made it any easier to reconcile conservation and development.[36] The land availability studies are an attempt to do precisely this.

The green-belt policy commands even wider support today than it did in the 1950s (and it is noteworthy that the 1988 DoE booklet on *Green Belts* is basically the same as its 1962 predecessor).[37] Elson concludes his study with the reason why this is so:

It acts to foster rather than hinder the material and non-material interests of most groups involved in the planning process, although it may be to the short term tactical advantage of some not to recognise the fact. To *central government* it assists in the essential tasks on interest mediation and compromise which planning policy-making represents . . . To *local government* it delivers a desirable mix of policy control with discretion. To *local residents* of the outer city it remains their best form of protection against rapid change. To the *inner city local authority* it offers at least the promise of retaining some economic activities that would otherwise leave the area; and to the *inner city resident* it offers the prospect, as well as often the reality, of countryside recreation and relaxation. To the *agriculturist* it offers a basic form of protection against urban influences, and for the *minerals industry* it retains accessible, cheap, and exploitable natural resources. *Industrial developers* and *housebuilders* complain bitterly about the rate at which land is fed into the development pipeline, yet at the same time are dependent on planning to provide a degree of certainty and support for profitable investment.

Planning may be an attempt to reconcile the irreconcilable, but green belt is one of the most successful all-purpose tools invented with which to try.
(Elson 1986: 264)

The latest policy statement on green belts (PPG 2 of 1988) confirms the validity and permanence of the

*Table 5.1*  Green Belts

| | Acres |
|---|---:|
| **Approved Green Belts in England 1987** | |
| Tyne and Wear | 200,000 |
| Lancaster and Fylde Coast | 5,750 |
| York | 50,000 |
| South and West Yorkshire | 800,000 |
| Greater Manchester, Central Lancs, Merseyside, Wirral | 750,000 |
| Stoke-on-Trent | 125,000 |
| Nottingham, Derby | 200,000 |
| Burton-Swadlincote | 2,000 |
| West Midlands | 650,000 |
| Cambridge | 26,500 |
| Gloucester, Cheltenham | 20,000 |
| Oxford | 100,000 |
| London | 1,200,000 |
| Avon | 150,000 |
| SW Hampshire/SE Dorset | 220,000 |
| **Total England** | **4,495,300** |
| **Green Belts in Scotland 1993** | |
| Aberdeen | 58,475 |
| Ayr/Prestwick | 7,050 |
| Falkirk/Grangemouth | 8,636 |
| Glasgow | 296,526 |
| Lothian/Edinburgh | 36,077 |
| **Total Scotland** | **370,658** |

*Sources*:  PPG 2 and The Scottish Office.

green-belts policy which now covers 4.5 million acres (14 per cent) of England. (There is no formal green-belt policy in Wales; Scotland is discussed separately on p. 124.) Five purposes are listed for green belts:

1 to check the unrestricted sprawl of large built-up areas;
2 to safeguard the surrounding countryside from further encroachment;
3 to prevent neighbouring towns from merging into one another;
4 to preserve the special character of historic towns; and
5 to assist in urban regeneration.

Only the fifth of these is relatively new. The major policies remain as they were when Sandys insisted on promoting the green-belt policy:

> The essential characteristic of green belts is their permanence, and their protection must be maintained as far as can be seen ahead . . . Inside a green belt, approval should not be given, except in very special circumstances, for the construction of new buildings or for the change of use of existing buildings for purposes other than agriculture and forestry, outdoor sport, cemeteries, institutions standing in extensive grounds, or other uses appropriate to a rural area.

The changing role of agriculture in the British economy has not altered the essential point of this policy though, as is shown in the next section, it has affected the character of policies in relation to agricultural land.

In Scotland, green belts have been established around Aberdeen, Ayr/Prestwick, Edinburgh, Falkirk/Grangemouth, and Glasgow. Interestingly, the Dundee green belt has been replaced by a general countryside policy (Regional Studies Association 1990: 22). Scottish green belts have somewhat wider purposes than those in England: these include maintaining the identity of towns by establishing a clear definition of their physical boundaries and preventing coalescence; providing for countryside recreation and institutional uses of various kinds; and maintaining the landscape setting of towns. There is a greater emphasis on the environmental functions of the green belts, and recreation is included as a primary objective. The title of the Scottish circular is significant: *Development in the Countryside and Green Belts* underlines the links between general countryside policies and green belts. 'As a result, a much more integrated approach to the planning of green belt and non-green belt areas is achieved in Scotland.'[38] A Regional Studies Association (1990) study commends the Scottish approach, arguing that 'green belts have become an outmoded and largely irrelevant mechanism for handling the complexity of future change in the city's countryside'. Less drastic proposals have come from the Countryside Commission which, while commending the Government's policy statement that 'green belts also have a positive role in providing access to open countryside for the urban population' argue that this does not go far enough:

> Where green belts have been defined, they should serve two further purposes:
> — to enhance and improve the natural beauty of the countryside adjoining the major centres of population;
> — to increase opportunities for the quiet enjoyment of the countryside.
> (Countryside Commission 1989: 12)

Around the towns which do not have green belts (which, of course, are the great majority) the Commission argues for 'planning on green belt principles'. The stage is thus set for a transformation of green-belt policies into much wider countryside policies. These are the subject of Chapter 8.

## DEVELOPMENT INVOLVING AGRICULTURAL LAND

The 'loss' of agricultural land has been an issue of debate throughout the post-war period. The valiant work of the late Robin Best (1981) has failed to dispel popular images, yet his figures showed that the annual average transfer of agricultural land to urban land use in England and Wales was only 9,300 hectares between 1975 and 1980 (compared with 17,500 between 1945 and 1950, and 25,100 between 1931 and 1939). The total urban area is about 1.64 million hectares: about 11 per cent of the total. More recent estimates from the DoE show (for England) an annual rate of transfer of agricultural land to urban, industrial and recreational use of 14,000 hectares between 1950 and 1969, falling to 12,000 in the decade 1970–79, and still further to 5,000 hectares in the 1980s (though alternative estimates by the CPRE put the figure much higher).[39]

Nevertheless, concern about the 'loss of agricultural land' has had a major impact on development plans, on planning decisions, and on appeal decisions. This stems partly from local resistance to change, and partly from the post-war approach to agricultural policy. The decision was taken to develop a strong and healthy agricultural sector. The 1947 Agriculture Act demanded 'a stable and efficient industry, capable of providing such part of the nation's food as in the national interest it is desirable to produce'. It was against this background that farming was largely exempted from planning control.

The 1976 DoE circular (75/76) on the safeguarding of agricultural land defined the general policy as being

> to ensure that, as far as possible, land of a higher agricultural quality is not taken for development where land of a lower quality is available, and that the amount of land taken should be no greater than is reasonably required for carrying out the development in accordance with proper standards.

This was based on the 1975 White Paper, *Food from our Own Resources*, which proposed a significant increase in home food production to reduce dependence on imports which had risen sharply in cost. It also drew a graphic picture of the continuing loss of agricultural land, estimated at 144,000 acres a year which, if continued, 'would imply a substantial reduction in the available agricultural land'.

Times change, and Circular 16/87 noted that 'at present, by contrast, there are substantial surpluses of the main agricultural products in western countries. The need now is to foster the diversification of the rural economy so as to open up wider and more varied employment opportunities'. The Circular continued:

> The agricultural quality of the land and the need to control the rate at which land is taken for development are among the factors to be considered [in assessing planning applications affecting agricultural land], together with the need to facilitate development and economic activity that provides jobs, and the continuing need to protect the countryside for its own sake rather than primarily for the productive value of the land.

The circular was a mere twelve paragraphs long, but it represented a dramatic change in policy. This change was due, of course, to the increasing agricultural overproduction – in Europe generally as well as in Britain.[40]

This is further underlined by several initiatives of the Ministry of Agriculture, Fisheries and Food (MAFF). First, section 17(1) of the Agriculture Act 1986 places a duty on the Minister of Agriculture to

have regard to and endeavour to achieve a reasonable balance between the following considerations –
(a) the promotion and maintenance of a stable and efficient agricultural industry;
(b) the economic and social interests of rural areas;
(c) the conservation and enhancement of the natural beauty and amenity of the countryside (including its flora and fauna and geological and physiographical features) and of any features of archaeological interest there; and
(d) the promotion of the enjoyment of the countryside by the public.

Second, the same Act makes provision for *environmentally sensitive areas* (ESAs) where annual grants are payable by this ministry to farmers to enable them to follow farming practices which will achieve conservation objectives.[41] The first ESAs were designated in 1987/88. In 1990 there were seventeen ESAs (ten in England, two in Wales, and five in Scotland), and a considerable expansion of the scheme was in hand.[42]

In addition to the ESAs, the Ministry's diversification policies include a *Farm Woodland Scheme* to encourage farmers to plant new woodland on productive agricultural land, and a *Farm Diversification Grant Scheme* to promote ancillary businesses on or adjacent to farms.[43]

## VACANT AND DERELICT LAND

Much land that was once useful and productive has become waste land, particularly in the inner cities and in mining areas. It is unsightly, unwanted and, at worst, derelict and dangerous. The planning system is not designed to deal with such land easily: its essential characteristic is to allocate land between competing uses. Where there are no pressures for development, there is a severe limit to what a local authority can do, especially when the amount of waste land is large, as it is in older industrial areas. Until 1986, powers were limited to dealing with the 'proper maintenance' of land which was 'seriously injured by the condition of any garden, vacant site, or other open land', and planting trees or carrying out works for the improvement of derelict, neglected or unsightly land.[44] The wording was changed by the Housing and Planning Act 1986 to an area 'which is adversely affected by the condition of the land'. As is apparent from the wording, these powers were not intended to deal with the vast areas of dereliction. For these there are the much wider provisions (and more extensive grant aid) of the Derelict Land Act.[45] Indeed, there is now a wide range of policy instruments available for dealing with waste land.

Some of the attempts have been made as part of broader policies in relation to urban regeneration such as the establishment of urban development corporations, enterprise zones, and simplified planning zones. The urban programme, and the urban development and urban regeneration grants (replaced in 1988

*Table 5.2* Reasons for Sites Remaining Vacant

| Principal reason | 1979 sample % | 1984 sample % | Case study sites % |
|---|---|---|---|
| Physical constraints | 31 | 9 | 19 |
| Institutional factors | 12 | 24 | 16 |
| Owners' intentions | 32 | 40 | 36 |
| Poor demand | 19 | 25 | 19 |
| Sites in pipeline | 6 | 2 | 10 |

*Source*: Whitbread, Mayne and Wickens 1991, Tables 2.31 and 3.3.

by the city grant), can also be used incidentally for promoting the development of vacant urban land. All these are discussed in Chapter 9. Additionally, and more specifically concerned with urban land, are the land register and the derelict land grant.

## Registers of Unused Publicly Owned Land

Policies can be founded on myths as well as on adequate understanding of problems. So it was with the land registers established by the 1980 Local Government, Planning and Land Act. The myth was that one of the major causes of urban dereliction was the hoarding of land by public authorities. By requiring local authorities and other public bodies to 'register' their land, it was expected that it would find its way into the development process. In the words of the Secretary of State:

> The publication of land registers for the greater part of the country represents a major opportunity to secure the better use of massive acreages of underused land. Given the resources also available for dealing with dereliction, it is important that action should be taken to dispose of the land to the best advantage as soon as possible . . . It is up to builders and developers to examine registers and seek out the owners to make an offer for any sale in which they are interested.[46]

In fact, with the reality being much more complicated than the perception, the registers have been of little effect. Indeed, an evaluation undertaken for the DoE (Whitbread *et al*. 1991: 57) concluded that the registers were 'an ineffective instrument which was

not used in a single case [in the sample studied] to help bring land forward for development'.[47]

The legislation provides that the Secretary of State may designate an area where he may 'compile and maintain a register, of land . . . owned by a public body' which, in his opinion, 'is not being used or not being sufficiently used'. Owners of land so registered can be directed by the Secretary of State to dispose of it.[48] The two objectives of land registers are to encourage the disposal of unused or underused land in public ownership and to provide information for potential purchasers.

Research shows that land vacancy is typically a transient feature of the environment.[49] Though much of it has been vacant for a long time (two-thirds of a sample had been vacant for more than twelve years)[50] some of this idle land – perhaps a third – can be used when subsidies are paid to overcome physical constraints. However, some vacant land – perhaps two-thirds – is so because of institutional factors, owners' intentions, or poor demand. As the evaluation study explained:

> Many sites remain vacant for non-physical reasons. Some are delayed by the legitimate workings of the planning system, and by legal and other institutional difficulties. Existing policy instruments can do little to overcome these difficulties. Others are delayed by owners', particularly private sector owners', intentions that they should remain vacant for various (largely obscure) reasons.[51]

Much of this land is in private ownership and, short of compulsory acquisition (which is unpopular with a Conservative Government), there is little that 'policy' can do to speed up the reuse of the land.

But these are the failures: more striking are the undoubted successes of other policy instruments, of which the evaluation study counted thirteen (ranging from grant aid to planning and promotional action by local authorities). Foremost among these is the derelict land grant.

## Derelict Land

Though there is no statutory definition, derelict land is generally regarded as 'land so damaged by industrial or other development that it is incapable of beneficial use without treatment'. (This is the definition used in connection with the payment of government grants for reclamation.)[52] Derelict land is commonly thought of as a legacy of the Industrial Revolution, but this is only part of the picture: of the 43,000 hectares of 'inherited dereliction' in England recorded in 1974, some 10,000 hectares represented an *increase* since the end of 1971. Making allowance for land which had been reclaimed, the net increase over the period was around 4,000 hectares. Greater expenditure on reclamation during recent years has reversed the trend. The 1988 survey showed that the total amount of derelict land in England had declined from 45,700 hectares in 1982 to 40,500 hectares, a reduction of 11 per cent.[53]

Much derelict land (particularly waste tips and abandoned industrial land) is concentrated in relatively small parts of the older industrial areas of the North, the Midlands and South Wales. The Hunt Committee (1969) called for a national programme and the establishment of a derelict land reclamation agency. Both Scottish Enterprise (formerly the Scottish Development Agency) and the Welsh Development Agencies have powers in relation to land reclamation. In England, the responsibilities lie with the local authorities and with urban development corporations.

Great advances in reclamation techniques have been made since the 1930s. Slow and costly 'pick and shovel' methods have now given way to modern earth-moving machines which can move mountains of material at relatively low cost. Techniques of 'making soil' have been refined, and it is now possible to make grass and trees grow in the most uncongenial conditions. For a time, rising land values and the need for sites for open space, playing fields and all types of urban development added a welcome impetus to reclamation in or near urban areas, but this is less so now that the abandonment and deterioration of urban land has accelerated.

Local authorities have no statutory duty to reclaim derelict land or to improve its appearance. Their powers are purely permissive and, as is too often the case, much depends on the energy of individual local

*Table 5.3* Derelict Land Reclaimed in England

| Year | Hard end use hectares | Soft end use hectares | Total hectares |
|---|---|---|---|
| 1986–87 | 381 | 522 | 903 |
| 1987–88 | 588 | 697 | 1,285 |
| 1988–89 | 912 | 575 | 1,487 |
| 1989–90 | 618 | 565 | 1,183 |
| 1990–91 | 627 | 456 | 1,083 |
| **Target** | | | |
| 1991–92 | 540 | 780 | 1,320 |
| 1992–93 | 600 | 875 | 1,475 |
| 1993–94 | 600 | 930 | 1,530 |
| 1994–95 | 620 | 980 | 1,600 |

*Source: Department of the Environment Annual Report 1992: The Government's Expenditure Plans 1992–93 to 1994–95, Cm 1908, HMSO, 1992, Figure 71, p. 67.*

authorities. Some good illustrations are given in a report from the University of Liverpool Environmental Advisory Unit (1986). Another report, by Johnson *et al* (1992) sets out *The Strategic Approach to Derelict Land Reclamation.*

The powers available to local authorities (in addition to those relating to the provision of housing, open spaces and schools under which they can acquire derelict land and reclaim it during the normal course of development) were consolidated in the Derelict Land Act 1982. The National Parks and Access to the Countryside Act gives specific powers for the reclamation or improvement of land which is derelict, neglected or unsightly, whether or not it is owned by the local authority. They can also acquire land compulsorily for this purpose.[54]

Government grants towards the cost of acquisition and reclamation of derelict land were originally introduced to assist industrial growth in development areas, but have been extended to all areas (though there is a higher rate of grant in the assisted areas and in *derelict land clearance areas* – areas where the economic situation in the locality is such that it is 'particularly appropriate with a view to contributing to the development of industry in the locality' that grants should be paid).[55] Currently (1993), in these areas, the grant is 100 per cent for local authorities and 80 per cent for other bodies. Elsewhere it is 50 per cent for both local authorities and others, except in national parks and areas of outstanding natural beauty where local authorities may receive 75 per cent grants.[56]

Reclamation policies have changed over the years. Originally, the objective was to remove eyesores and potential dangers caused by spoil heaps and other waste. Much of this was located in rural areas, and the policy was to return the land to agriculture or forestry, or to make it available for public open space (known in the jargon as 'soft end use'). Since 1981, emphasis has shifted to 'hard end uses' such as industrial, commercial or residential development, particularly in older urban areas. There has also been an explicit commitment (originally set out in the 1983 White Paper *Coal and the Environment*[57]) to funding reclamation in coalfield areas, as well as in

limestone mining areas of the Black Country.[58] In 1991, following an extensive and lengthy review, a broadening of the grant scheme was announced.[59] The objectives now are to support the reclamation of sites for both development and environmental improvement, to promote nature conservation, historic preservation and community forests, and to give priority to areas which can be made more attractive, especially where local policies can be fostered. Thus, from being focused on eyesores, the grant programme has become a broad national policy with environmental and development aims. Annual central government expenditure is expected to increase by about a third (to £100 million) between 1992 and 1995.[60]

Dereliction, unfortunately, is a continuing process in both urban and rural areas. In some cases operations, such as mineral working, can be subjected to special controls but, as explained earlier, safeguarding environmental quality is only one of the several relevant considerations. The National Audit Office examined, but did not pronounce on, the proposal (espoused by local authorities, but condemned by industry) that operators might be required to contribute to a restoration fund by a levy on production which could be used to finance the reclamation of land following the default of an individual operator or to tackle the backlog of dereliction – which had worked successfully with the Ironstone Restoration Fund (Sheail 1983).

Problems of derelict land, at least in the older industrial areas, require a more comprehensive approach than is typical today. It is Government policy to give priority to 'the treatment of land which in its present condition reduces the attractiveness of an area as a place in which to live, work or invest' (DLGA 1). This requires more than getting rid of dereliction, important though this is: removing dereliction needs to be part of a wider strategy for urban regeneration – in economic and social terms in addition to the physical. A report of the Aston University Business School has proposed that local authorities with substantial areas of dereliction should adopt a strategic approach, both for their own planning purposes and for their bid for derelict land grant. A *derelict land policy statement* would set out plans for dealing with derelict land (and preventing future dereliction) within the context of other local policies and programmes:

> The policy statement should clearly explain how the strategy will contribute to the implementation of the statutory development plans for the area including identifying the potential for recycling derelict land for housing and industrial purposes. Other, more specific policies, relating for example to inner city areas, economic development, recreation, tourism and nature conservation may also have a part to play in defining the direction of the strategy, together with plans relating to the future pattern of infrastructure.
>
> (Johnson *et al*. 1992: ix)

Perhaps another way of looking at this is to regard the removal of dereliction, waste land, and other 'invasions of amenity' as integral elements in local planning.

## Contaminated Land

There is no clear line between vacant, derelict, and contaminated land (or neglected, underused, waste, and despoiled land). The terms are used in different ways, sometimes for different purposes, sometimes with the same or similar meanings. Contaminated land is particularly difficult to define, but the term is commonly used to imply the existence of a hazard to public health. Clearly, there is an overlap with 'derelict' land (which, as already noted, is defined administratively for the purpose of reclamation grants); but there are important differences. A chemical waste tip may be both derelict and contaminated; a disused chalk quarry may be derelict but not contaminated; an active chemical factory may be contaminated but not derelict.[61] It is the additional health danger which is the characteristic feature of contaminated land; and this also implies a severe degree of pollution and, typically, an increased difficulty in abating it. However, the health risk arises only in relation to the use to which the land is to be put. A piece of land may pose no risk if used for one purpose, but a severe risk if it is used for another. The site of an oil refinery may be contaminated, but that is of no consequence if no other use is intended

(and assuming that there are no effects beyond the site). 'A scrapyard contaminated by metal traces would constitute a hazard for subsequent agricultural use, but the contamination would be of no account in the construction of an office block . . .'[62]

Partly because of this pragmatic approach, there has never been an attempt to quantify the amount of contaminated land in Britain. Instead of identifying contaminated land and then determining appropriate policies for dealing with it, the British approach has been to regard contamination as a general concept which is given substance only in relation to particular sites and particular end-uses. The nature of policy flows from this:

> Policy is to ensure that the quality of land is fit for the purpose to which it is being or will be used. There is no requirement for land to be brought up to a minimum quality standard regardless of use, unless that land poses a threat to the public health or the environment.

The House of Commons Environment Committee considered this approach to be inadequate since (in its judgement) there is land which is so contaminated that it is 'a threat to health and the environment both on site and in the surrounding area'. The Committee also recommended that local authorities should be given a duty 'to seek out and compile registers of contaminated land'.

There was a remarkably swift response to this: the Environment Protection Bill was amended to place such a duty on district councils and London boroughs. The implementation of this duty, however, rapidly ran into severe difficulties, and the initial proposals had to be drastically changed. The crux of the problem lay in the concept of 'contamination'. Instead of referring to land that is contaminated, the Act relates to 'land which is being or has been put to any use which may cause that land to become contaminated with noxious substances'. This very inclusive definition was made particularly onerous in the initial draft regulations because of the very large number of contaminative uses which were specified. There was strong criticism that the registers would create widespread blight and, as a result of extensive lobbying, the number of specified uses was reduced to such an extent that (in the words of the revised consultation paper), 'the area of land covered by the registers will be some 10–15% of the area previously envisaged'.[63]

The problem underlying all this is that it is relatively simple to register land that is possibly contaminated, but extremely laborious and costly to identify land that is in fact contaminated. Even at the low rate of £15,000 per hectare, it would cost around £600m merely to investigate the 40,000 hectares of land identified in the 1988 Derelict Land Survey. To cover all relevant land would cost many times this amount, and would take many years to complete (Thompson 1992: 22).

Another objection to the initial regulations was that they prohibited the deregistration of sites. The second consultation draft defended this provision on two grounds:

> One is that factual information on the site's history (which cannot by definition change) will be necessary when any future change of use is proposed. The other is that contamination from the site may have migrated to adjacent sites; owners, regulatory authorities and developers are expected to use registers to identify such sources of contamination.

It was because of difficulties such as these that the consultation period was extended; and, at the time of writing, no final decisions had been announced (see UPDATE at the end of this chapter). The difficulties of changing from the traditional British reactive approach to a genuinely pro-active approach are manifest (A. Harrison 1992: 809).

## The Urban Regeneration Agency

In 1992, the Government published its proposals for a new agency to deal with the problems of vacant and derelict land.[64] The Housing and Urban Development Bill (now the 1993 Act) provides the necessary statutory powers. The main purpose of the URA is to implement 'a new approach to vacant land' – which includes unused, under-used or ineffectively used urban land, land which is contaminated, derelict, neglected or unsightly, or land which is likely to be affected by subsidence. The agency will facilitate a 'targeted' approach, 'speed up the provision of good

quality land', and 'act entrepreneurially to encourage redevelopment by bringing together all parties with a role to play'. Since about a half of vacant urban land is owned by public bodies (and 'is not always subject to the normal incentives and disciplines of the market that apply to private sector land'), the Secretary of State is given power to vest such land in the URA 'where this would help to promote its development'. The Agency has extensive powers of land assembly and preparation, and is intended to draw together the existing activities and funding of English Estates[65] with the derelict land and city grant regimes of the DoE. (The DoE retains responsibility for other urban policy funding through *City Challenge*, the urban programme and other initiatives.)

It is clear from this summary of the role and power of the URA that it is envisaged essentially as a redevelopment agency. Its name is therefore misleading, since the term 'regeneration' implies a much wider role. Of course, it remains to be seen how it develops.

In line with current philosophy, the new agency is to concentrate on 'enabling' activities. It will act primarily as a 'one stop shop' for grant aid, and facilitate development by land assembly. Though it will have compulsory purchase powers, it will generally acquire land on the open market. It is not intended that the agency will maintain a long-term interest in any development, though it will have the power to manage the estates it develops.

The intention to combine and simplify the funding support to land reclamation and urban development and, moreover, to concentrate responsibilities within one agency has been welcomed,[66] though this is at the cost of a further reduction in local authority responsibilities. Critics will argue that the land reclamation activities of local authorities are well established, especially in areas such as the Black Country of the West Midlands and the North-East where local authority in-house teams have considerable experience of putting together land reclamation projects for derelict land grant funding. Of perhaps even more concern is the provision in the Housing and Urban Development Bill for the Secretary of State to designate areas 'of widespread dereliction' where the URA may take over the development control function.

## UPDATE

The relationships between land-use planning, transport, and pollution is the subject of a research report commissioned jointly by the Departments of the Environment and Transport: *Reducing Transport Emissions through Planning* (HMSO 1993) and DoE *Draft Revised PPG 13* (DoE 1993).

The Government has decided to abandon the proposed registers of contaminated land. (This will require legislation.) At the time of writing, it was unclear what would take its place. Nevertheless, as this chapter demonstrates, there are many other statutory provisions in force which relate to contaminated land. Moreover, as Highman has commented, 'demonstrating that a site has a clean bill of health could become important for attracting purchasers to a development' (G. Highman, 'Laws of nature', *Building*, 14 May 1993, p. 42). Indeed, another commentator has stated unequivocally that 'with up to 100,000 contaminated sites in the UK, finding out whether land is contaminated before buying or developing it is essential' (J. Macneil, 'Digging for dirt', *Building*, 14 May 1993, p. 44). A review of the current legislative position is provided by R. Langham, 'Contaminated land – the legal aspect', *JPL* 1993: 807–15.

The *Report of the Scottish Vacant and Derelict Land Survey 1990* (Scottish Office Environment Department, Edinburgh, 1992) shows that over 12,000 hectares of land in Scotland are derelict (8,300 ha) or vacant (3,900 ha). Forty-five per cent had been derelict or vacant for more than ten years, half is in private ownership, and the most common previously recorded use was mineral activity.

On planning gain, see R. Fordham, 'Planning gain in ten dimensions', *JPL* 1993: 719–31. Fordham concludes that planning gain 'is a process whereby an increasing proportion of the infrastructure consequences of new development are paid for by the landowners whose land is to be developed. As such

it is not a tax, but has the virtue denied to previous attempts at land tax, that it is site specific. As a result it is always affordable. If it were not, then the proposed development could not bear the proper costs of mobilising the site and so the scheme should be regarded as unacceptable. The claim of insupportable cost is familiar in planning gain negotiation but, as with claims of impropriety, is much more often heard than established.'

On the use of the planning system to facilitate the provision of affordable housing, see G. Kirkwood and M. Edwards, 'Affordable housing policy – desirable but unlawful?', *JPL* 1993: 317–24.

On the 1993 Act (which provides, *inter alia*, for the establishment of the Urban Regeneration Agency), see P. Matthews and D. Millichap, *A Guide to the Leasehold Reform, Housing and Urban Development Act 1993*, Butterworths, 1993.

An extensive study of green belts commissioned by the DoE has now been published: M. Elson, S. Walker, and R. Macdonald, *The Effectiveness of Green Belts*, HMSO, 1993.

## NOTES

1 Uthwatt Report, p. 20, para. 33. In a footnote there is a reference to a dictum of J. Wright [1927] (1 KB 458): 'A mere negative prohibition, though it involves interference with an owner's enjoyment of property, does not, I think, merely because it is obeyed, carry with it at common law any right to compensation. A subject cannot at common law claim compensation merely because he obeys a lawful order of the State.' However, full acceptance of this common-law rule would necessarily result in hardship and inconsistent treatment between individuals (for example, between the owners of land zoned for agriculture and land zoned for building): ibid., p. 22.

2 Extraordinarily little analysis has been made of these concepts. Leung (1979) however, has noted: 'Many commentators recognised the fallacy of the shifting value argument. They pointed out that when planning permission for development is refused there is no necessary shift of development value and, in Sir Arnold Plant's words, no law of conservation of value.' Munby (1954) suggested that the original concept of shifting value was an attempt to rebut the argument that town

planning would lead to an actual loss of land values. Parker (1954) criticised the basic assumptions in the shifting value concept that a particular form of development would give rise to the same development value wherever it occurred, and argued that there was 'no special relationship between the development value of land and the gross rental value of the building standing on it.'

3 *HL Debates*, vol. 432, col. 983, 29 January 1947; see also *HC Debates*, vol. 451, cols 294–5, 26 May 1948.

4 An example given in the 1949/50 report of the Central Land Board was a plot of land offered for private purchase at £300 and compulsorily acquired by the Board for £10. It was resold, inclusive of development charge for the erection of a house, at £180.

5 The Labour Government repeatedly stressed that a great deal of land (estimated to be enough for 100,000 houses) had been made available for development without payment of development charge under the 'dead-ripe' scheme. (MHLG, *Town and Country Planning 1943–1951 Progress Report*, Cmd 8204, HMSO, 1951, p. 13.)

6 It was originally expected that claims on the £300m would be worth very little. Even in January 1951 a claim for £4,193 was sold by auction for £220; other sales took place at 2s 6d (12.5 per cent) in the pound (Turvey 1957: 140).

7 White Paper, *Town and Country Planning Act 1947: Amendment of Financial Provisions*, Cmd 8699, HMSO, 1952. Unless otherwise indicated, the quotations are from this White Paper.

8 There were two Acts: the Town and Country Planning Act 1953 abolished development charges, while the Town and Country Planning Act 1954 limited compensation for loss of development value to those sites for which a claim had been approved, and then only under defined circumstances when an application to develop was actually refused.

9 DoE, *Housing Policy: A Consultative Document* (1977) Table 11; and DoE, *Housing and Construction Statistics 1969–1979* Table 3.

10 Jowell 1977a. For a listing of the factors which affected 'the rise of planning gain', see Jowell and Grant 1983.

11 See, for example, (listed in order of year published): Grant 1975 and 1978a: Jowell 1977a and 1977b; Hawke 1981; Rowan-Robinson and Young 1989; Keogh 1985; S. Byrne 1989; Elson 1990; Callies and Grant 1991; Redman 1991; Grimley J.R. Eve 1992; Healey, Ennis, and Purdue 1992; Healey, Purdue, and Ennis 1992; Rowan-Robinson and Durman 1992a and 1992b. The *Planning Gain Newsletter* is published by Planning Negotiators/Planning Gain Consultants, 91 Ledbury Road, London W11 2AG.

12 Eve comments that many of these requirements probably do not need to be made the subject of an agreement, but could be secured by planning conditions (para. 4.19). However, despite central government advice (DoE Circular 1/85; SDD Circular 18/86) against replicating conditions in an agreement, LPAs sometimes feel that conditions are an inadequate safeguard, particularly in relation to user restrictions. The Planning and Compensation Act 1991 strengthens the provisions relating to enforcement of conditions (DoE Circular 16/91).

13 Section 12 of the Planning and Compensation Act 1991, amending section 106 of the Town and Country Planning Act 1990. By comparison, the former provision is a model of simplicity: 'A local planning authority may enter into an agreement with any person interested in their land for the purpose of restricting or regulating the development or use of the land, either permanently or during such period as may be prescribed by the agreement.'

14 Where needed off-site works could not be achieved by a planning condition, an agreement could be made under the former section 106. However, if the local authority was unwilling to enter into an agreement, the Secretary of State was forced to dismiss the appeal. Grant (*Encyclopedia*: notes to section 106) comments that by providing a unilateral obligation, the developer is able to overcome the authority's recalcitrance to some extent, but it remains a second-best option. It cannot, for example, secure the authority's consent actually to undertake the necessary off-site works, nor to use its compulsory purchase powers to acquire the necessary land.'

15 *HC Standing Committee F Debates*, cols, 115–16.

16 Rowan-Robinson and Durman 1992a: para. 27.12.

17 There is a useful wide ranging discussion in Rowan-Robinson and Lloyd 1988. See also Rowan-Robinson and Young 1989.

18 But not *transport* planning in its wider sense. As the RTPI point out in its observations on the proposals: 'The question needs to be asked as to whether developer's contributions should only apply to major highway works. The Department should not only consider whether the existing highway network should be improved in this way, but should also be considering whether other solutions are more appropriate. These might include traffic suppression methods, e.g. by restriction on car parking or provision of park-and-ride, or the development of other public transport solutions . . .' This well illustrates how the framework of debate is changing.

19 There is, however, little consideration of who gains and who loses by the financial implications.

20 *R. v. Westminster City Council ex parte Monahan*, JPL 1989: 107 – better known as the Covent Garden case.

An edited version of this case is given in *Journal of Environmental Law*, vol. 1, 1989, pp. 221–44. Though the case mainly revolved around 'material considerations', it also included an agreement, and the judgment is highly relevant to the validity of financial agreements in planning. See also Heap 1989.

21  *R.* v. *London Borough of Hillingdon ex. p. Royco Homes Ltd* [1974] 2 All ER 643.

22  See, for example, SERPLAN 1990a; Scottish Homes 1991; Barlow and Chambers 1992; DPOS 1992.

23  DoE Circular 7/91 (replaced by PPG 3, revised version 1992); Bishop and Hooper 1991 (which contains a good bibliography); DPOS 1992; RTPI *Planning Policy and Social Housing* (1992a).

24  The point is nicely illustrated by the way in which 'some planning authorities, consultants and community groups have used development appraisal methods to explore how much profit they think they can reasonably extract, given estimates of likely developers' profits'. See Healey, Purdue, and Ennis (1992: 26).

25  Indeed, there is an ongoing debate about 'windfall sites'. These are sites which are not 'allocated', but which nevertheless make a significant contribution to the supply of development land. See Tym 1991: 19; and CPRE 1988.

26  There is a considerable literature on land availability studies: The important early DoE Circulars were 10/70, 102/72, 44/78, 9/80, 22/80, and 15/84 (all now cancelled). The current policy statement is PPG 3 and the regional planning guidance notes.

The *Journal of Planning and Environmental Law* is a good source of relevant articles: Hooper 1979; Humber 1980; Hooper 1982. Later publications include Hill 1987; Hooper *et al.* 1988. The School for Advanced Urban Studies at the University of Bristol has published several important studies including: Barrett *et al.* 1978; Barrett and Whitting 1983. See also Rydin 1984 and 1986; Bramley 1989; Coopers & Lybrand 1985 and 1987. A useful overview by Cuddy and Hollingsworth is to be found in Barrett and Healey, *Land Policy: Problems and Alternatives*, 1985 (a volume which contains much other useful material for the student of land policy). More recent publications include Bramley 1993; Breheny 1993; and RTPI 1992a.

27  Barrett, in Barrett and Healey 1985.

28  Previously issued under the title *Land for Housing* in 1988, a revised version, *Housing*, was published in 1992. The new version (which also supersedes Circular 22/84 *Memorandum on Structure and Local Plans*) places 'increased emphasis on re-using urban land, particularly derelict or under-used land as a means of relieving pressure on the countryside'. The sections on land availability studies have not changed significantly, though they are longer.

29  For a recent study of the Scottish situation, see Pacione 1991.

30  There is a long-standing debate on this, and on the wider question of the impact of planning on the land market. Recent examples of the heated debate include A.W. Evans 1988 and 1991 (the latter characterises the effect as being to produce 'rabbit hutches on postage stamps'). Less tendentious (and therefore less interesting) is the study commissioned by the DoE on *The Relationship between House Prices and Land Supply* (Gerald Eve 1992). There is a huge American literature on the subject which is referred to in chapter 6 of Cullingworth 1993.

31  The TCPA issued a spoof PPG on *New Settlements* in 1992: not suprisingly this takes a much more positive line. One of the major policy arguments against new settlements is that they would discourage redevelopment in older urban areas. This argument is put forward with force in Eversley 1986.

32  One group of builders (including Grand Metropolitan Estates, Barratt Developments, John Laing Holdings, and Regalian Properties) produced a handsome volume entitled *Urban Villages* (published by Urban Villages Group, 1992). Subtitled *A Concept for Creating Mixed-use Urban Developments on a Sustainable Scale*, it is much more than a concept: it is a campaign by a group of developers, builders, architects, and planners, formed on the initiative of the Prince of Wales, to promote a new form of mixed-use urban development. The concept is in line with the EC's 1990 *Green Paper on the Urban Environment* – so much so in fact that the EC was one of the report's financial sponsors. The proposal envisages a development of some 40 hectares, with 'a combined resident and working population of perhaps 3,000 to 5,000'. It must be 'small enough for any place to be in easy distance of any other; also small enough for people to know each other – by sight, by name, or by association – and to have that working basis of common experience and common assumptions which gives strength to a community'. It must also be 'large enough to support a wide range of activities and facilities, to attract firms and individuals who will give it life and prosperity'. It will foster 'a real sense of belonging', and provide a convenient, efficient, and pleasing place in which to live. There is no set of prescriptions for an urban village. Each will have its own master plan and, to ensure that 'the carefully balanced mixture of uses and tenure will not be upset by short-term opportunism', each will be designated as a distinct land-use category. Each will have an environmental action plan. Highly attractive illustrations are given of the ideas in practice. An enclosed 'poster' details an imaginary urban village. Though in the grand tradition of utopian town planning, the concept is espoused

by practitioners (and *International Business in the Community*), and seven developer-members have formed a separate Urban Village Company whose shares are held by the companies with which they are associated. They are stated to be currently seeking suitable sites.

33  The campaign included the usual public meetings, but also a conference in the Grand Committee Room of the House of Commons, a public opinion survey on public attitudes to the provision and location of housing in Hampshire, the distribution of 'preferential share [*sic*] certificates' to Hampshire residents for priority viewing of houses in the development, and highly attractive publications including *Micheldever Station Market Town: A Vision for Hampshire*, and *Micheldever Station Market Town: A Strategy for the Environment – Towards a Sustainable Development*.

34  TCPA, *Dispersal: A Call for Action*, 1955. See also Nairn 1955, and Laws 1955. Green belts have a longer history than this suggests. The Greater London Regional Planning Committee adopted a green-belt policy in 1935, and purchased land for this purpose. The London and Home Counties (Green Belt) Act 1938 led to further acquisitions. Green-belt land was also purchased by Birmingham and Sheffield. A sketch of this early history is given in Elson 1986: ch. 1. Green belts of earlier times are discussed in an anonymous article entitled 'Ye Olde Englishe Green Belt', *Journal of the Town Planning Institute*, 1955, and in Ginsburg, 'Green Belts in the Bible', *Journal of the Town Planning Institute*, 1956. Other studies on green belts include Thomas 1970, and Munton 1983. For a bibliography see Grayson 1990.

35  See Sandys' statement in the House of Commons, 26 April 1953; reproduced as an annex to Circular 42/55 (and significantly also as an annex to Circular 14/84). It is also significant, as Elson notes (1986: 15), that on the same day that Sandys made his statement on green belts, he also announced increased financial assistance to local authorities operating town development schemes for 'overspill'. More generally on the latter see Cullingworth 1960, and Self 1961a.

36  Just how difficult the reconciliation can be is seen by the conflicts created by the draft (and redrafted) 1984 Circulars on *Green Belts* and *Land for Housing* (DoE Circulars 14/84 and 15/84.) The story is set out in Elson's book but, in brief, there was widespread concern that the government were intending to relax the green-belt policy (see Elson, 1986, chapter 10: 'The politics of the 1984 circular').

37  The Secretary of State's foreword explicitly stresses that the green-belts policy has remained unchanged: 'This booklet was first published in 1962. I have decided to publish a new edition of it, not because our green belt policy has changed but because it demonstrates the continuity of that policy and our strong commitment to the green belts.'

38  Regional Studies Association 1990. (This section on Scottish green belts is based on this source.) See also P. Jones 1987.

39  The official figures are given in PPG 7: para. 2.6. The latest relevant figures are given in DoE Statistical Bulletin (92)4: *Land Use Change in England No. 7*, 1992. This shows a continuing transfer of agricultural land to urban uses (in England) of about 5,000 hectares a year. The CPRE estimates are set out in detail in Sinclair 1992.

40  For Scotland, see SDD Circular 16/87.

41  See MAFF, *Environmentally Sensitive Areas*, 1989; MAFF, *Our Farming Future*, 1991; Baldock *et al.* 1990.

42  *This Common Inheritance: The Second Year Report*, 1992: 80.

43  See the annual MAFF Departmental Report published in the series of *The Government's Expenditure Plans*. (The 1992 report was issued as Cm 1903.)

44  National Parks and Access to the Countryside Act, as amended.

45  The Derelict Land Act 1982 consolidates and amends earlier legislation. Among other changes, it extended the powers to encompass land which is likely to become 'derelict, neglected or unsightly' by reason of subsidence.

46  *HC Debates*, vol. 21, col. 40, 29 March 1982.

47  Chubb (1988: para. 6.4) maintains that 'land registers have been successful in stimulating public bodies to review and reconsider their reasons for keeping land unused and in encouraging them to release surplus sites onto the market. Registered land sold or brought into use up to 1 July 1987 runs to some 15,000 hectares, equivalent to about one quarter of the area registered since mid-1981, including 32 hectares on 19 sites which have been sold as a result of the Secretary of State's resort to statutory powers under section 98 of the 1980 Act.' What this rosy account neglects is the likelihood that this land would have been brought into use even had there been no land registers: there is no evidence that the registers have made any difference. The point is that the development process is very slow-moving, and vacant land may remain so for a very long while.

48  Local Government, Planning and Land Act 1980, section 93–100. (The Act does not apply to Scotland.) The public bodies are listed in Schedule 16; in addition to local authorities, the list includes new towns, development corporations, urban development corporations, the Housing Corporation, the British Airports Authority, the Civil Aviation Authority, British Shipbuilders, the British Steel Corporation, the National Coal Board, the British Broadcasting Corporation, the Independent Broadcasting Authority, the Post Office and statutory undertakers (authorities for electricity,

gas, water, railways, etc., etc.). The Secretary of State has made use of the powers to require disposals: see previous note and Chubb 1988: para. 5.29.

49 The research on vacant land includes: Bruton and Gore 1981; Howes 1984; Nicholson 1984; Ibbot 1984; Cameron *et al.* 1988; and Whitbread *et al.* 1991. The latter provides a review of previous research. For a broader overview of urban land policies, see Chubb 1988. A *National Survey of Vacant Land in Urban Areas of England 1990* (Shepherd and Abakuks 1992) estimated a total of 59,800 hectares in these areas. For a study of vacant industrial *buildings*, see Ball 1989; see also Fothergill *et al.* 1987.

50 Whitbread *et al.* 1991: viii.

51 Ibid., para. 3.147. An earlier report suggested a long list of reasons why vacant land is not put to temporary uses: expenditure by the owner in meeting fire, safety and insurance requirements, in providing access, and in site clearance; temporary tenants tend to be unreliable and to cause environmental problems; demand from temporary users is deficient and uncertain, and often provides landowners with a very low financial return; there are often problems in securing vacant possession; landowners may be unaware of the potential of temporary uses; or they may think that keeping sites vacant preserves existing use rights, or puts pressure on local authorities to grant planning consent for development. (See Cameron *et al.* 1988; this is also summarised in Chubb 1988: para. 4.21.)

52 Derelict Land Grant Advice Note 1 (1991) Annex, para. 4.

53 Detailed figures are given in DoE statistical reports on the *Survey of Derelict and Despoiled Land in England 1974* (1975); in DoE Pollution Paper 16, *The United Kingdom Environment 1979: Progress of Pollution Control*, 1979, and in *Survey of Derelict Land in England 1988*, (1991). A summary of the latter is available from the DoE.

54 National Parks and Access to the Countryside Act 1949 (section 89) as amended by the Local Authorities (Land) Act 1963 (which itself was amended by the Derelict Land Act 1982).

55 These were introduced by the Local Employment Act 1970, following the report of the Hunt Committee (1969). The areas are specified in the Derelict Land Clearance Areas Order 1982 (SI 1982, No. 935).

56 A study of derelict land grant schemes was carried out by Roger Tym and Partners in association with Land Use Consultants, see DoE, *Evaluation of Derelict Land Grant Schemes*, HMSO, 1987. Details of the grant scheme are set out in DLGA 1.

57 White Paper, *Coal and the Environment*, Cmnd 8877, HMSO, 1983. This was the Government's response to the 1981 Flowers Report.

58 DoE Circular 28/85, *Reclamation and Re-Use of Derelict Land*. This has now been superseded by DLGA note 1.

59 *HC Debates*, vol. 192, col. 588, Written Answers, 12 June 1991. See DoE, *A Review of Derelict Land Policy*, DoE 1989, and *Derelict Land Grant: Developments and Achievements: Report 1988–1992*, HMSO, 1992.

60 The *DoE Annual Report 1992* (fig. 69, p. 66) gives the following figures of net government expenditure on derelict land grant: 1990/91 (outturn) £61.7m; 1991/92 (estimated outturn) £75.6m; 1994/95 (plans) £101.3m.

61 HC Environment Committee, *Contaminated Land*, 1990, Vol. II, para. 3.1.

62 This, and other quotations, are from the Environment Committee report on *Contaminated Land*, ibid.

63 DoE, *Environmental Protection Act 1990: Section 143 Registers* (31 July 1992).

64 DoE, *The Urban Regeneration Agency: Consultation Paper*, DoE July 1992; *Housing and Urban Development Bill 1992*.

65 English Estates is a non-departmental body, sponsored by the Department of Trade and Industry, which builds factories in the assisted areas.

66 Peter Hall (1992b) argues that the proposal is 'pragmatic and workable': 'The URA is surely destined to represent the major venture of this Government in the field of urban development; indeed, it will surely become the major venture of the 1990s, as the Urban Development Corporations were of the 1980s. [The proposal] enshrines a central principle that the URA, an independent agency reporting to the DoE, should act as a facilitation to existing local government (and where appropriate, to existing UDCs), helping them to clear and prepare difficult land but not, in all normal circumstances, seeking to appropriate powers of planning, which are properly left where they belong. It makes available substantial funds for the purpose, not previously available through a single agency; and this change should ensure a more flexible and above all a more focused approach to solving particular problems.'

# 6

# PLANNING AND THE ENVIRONMENT

There are moments in history when apparently disparate forces or issues come together and take shape. Almost half a century ago that was true of arguments about the welfare state . . . Today it is the environment that captures headlines and excites public concern.

White Paper, *This Common Inheritance*, 1990

## THE ENVIRONMENT

In one sense, all 'town and country planning' is concerned with 'the environment'. However, the reverse is not true, and it is difficult to decide where to draw the boundaries. The difficulty is increased by the shifting of responsibilities from local government to *ad hoc* bodies, and by the flood of new legislation, prompted in part by the EC. Further complications arise because of the rate of organisational change which has taken place in recent years – including the establishment of Her Majesty's Inspectorate of Pollution and the National Rivers Authority – and, at the time of writing, the proposals for Environmental Agencies for England and Wales and for Scotland. But the most important factor of all has been the increased concern for the environment which has brought about changes such as these.

The implications for 'town and country planning' are still working themselves out, not always with clarity.[1] Thus, it has been a long-standing feature of planning control that permission is given unless there are good reasons for refusal. It is for the local planning authority to demonstrate (to the Secretary of State if necessary) that an application should be refused. With 'environmental' procedures, however, the onus shifts somewhat: the developer's proposals have to be demonstrably acceptable, and permission can be refused if they are not. Though official pronouncements and advice are coy in acknowledging this, it is clear that environmental factors can be decisive in a planning decision and that applicants may even be required to discuss the merits of alternative sites.[2] The immediate stimulus for this change (which could become more substantial in time) was the EC though, with the 1991 Act extension of the requirements for environmental impact statements, the Government has now, uncharacteristically, gone further than required by the EC Directive.[3]

The scope of the requirements for environmental assessment go beyond the developments covered by the planning legislation. Local authorities have specific powers in relation to some environmental issues such as certain aspects of pollution, waste, and noise, but they are not environmental planning authorities. Other specific 'pollution control regimes' exist for this purpose, but there is no clear dividing line:

While pollution controls seek to protect health and the environment, planning controls are concerned with the impact of development on the use of land and the appropriate use of land. Where the potential for harm to man and the environment affects the use of land (e.g. by precluding the use of neighbouring land for a particular purpose or by making the use of that land inappropriate because of, say, the risk to an underlying aquifer), then planning and pollution controls may overlap. It is important to provide safeguards against loss of amenity which may be caused by pollution. The dividing line between planning and pollution control consideration is therefore not always clear-cut. In such cases, close consultation between planning and pollution control authorities will be important at all stages, in particular because it would not be sensible to grant planning permission for a development for which a necessary pollution control authorisation is unlikely to be forthcoming.[4]

A related issue here is the concept of *sustainability*. Like many such terms, this has a variety of meanings. Shiva (1992: 192) has pointed to two very different uses of the concept. One ('the real meaning') relates to the primacy of nature: 'sustaining nature implies maintaining the integrity of nature's processes, cycles and rhythms'. This is to be contrasted with 'market sustainability' which is concerned with conserving resources for development purposes, and, if they become depleted, finding substitutes. On this approach, sustainability is convertible into substitutability and hence a cash nexus. The distinction is given eloquent expression in the words of a native American elder who, in epitomising the non-convertibility of money into life said: 'Only when you have felled the last tree, caught the last fish, and polluted the last river, will you realize that you can't eat money' (Shiva 1992: 193). The easiest way round the difficulty, of course, is to define the term in very general terms, as does PPG 12:

> The Government has made clear its intention to work towards ensuring that development and growth are sustainable. It will continue to develop policies consistent with the concept of sustainable development. The planning system, and the preparation of development plans in particular, can contribute to the objectives of ensuring that development and growth are sustainable. The sum total of decisions in the planning field, as elsewhere, should not deny future generations the best of today's environment. This should be expressed through the policies adopted in development planning.

Presumably, it is hoped that such assuasive words will appease all interests.[5]

The framework for planning is now broad and unclear. The boundaries between land-use planning, environmental planning, and sustainability (and many other issues as well) are now blurred. As the interrelated nature of the increasing complexities of the modern world become more apparent, attempts to surmount them will continue, though by their very nature the problems will always remain political. It seems possible that the bewildering changes in governmental organisation which have characterised recent years also will continue: to borrow a phrase, there is now little likelihood of a 'stable state' (Schon 1971). Two of the factors which will propel this require some discussion before detailing current environmental policies and programmes: the growth of environmental politics in Britain, and the impact of the European Community (McCormick 1991).

## ENVIRONMENTAL POLITICS

Environmental politics has only recently become an energetic force on the British scene.[6] Its rise has been prompted by a miscellany of matters, including the oil crises of the 1970s which prompted a new look at resource depletion; fears of environmental disasters (global warming, the ozone layer, etc.) which seemed more credible after catastrophes such as Seveso, Bhopal, Chernobyl, and at home, Windscale, and Flixborough.[7] Environmental tragedies became eminently newsworthy and received constant press attention. There was (and remains) a constant apprehension that catastrophe is likely to strike at any time: as in California, where 'the big one' (the forecast earthquake of enormous power) is confidently expected. Almost suddenly, the environment became part of the political coinage, and the parties vied with each other in producing convincing statements not only of their concern but also of their workable programmes of action. Even the National Front climbed on the bandwagon: 'The war which man is now waging against nature is not only foolhardy, it is downright dangerous. We can't go on polluting the atmosphere and poisoning the sea, we can't go on slaughtering our wildlife forever . . .' (Robinson 1992: 1). The impact of the new environmental concern was even more pronounced when, in 1989, the Greens gained 15 per cent of the vote in the European elections.

*This Common Inheritance* and its annual successors include, on the inside cover, an erudite statement which makes a declaration of the Government's environmental sanctity:

> This White Paper is printed on recycled paper comprising about 50% de-inked fibre and about 50% unbleached best white unprinted waste, depending on availability. Up to 15% virgin pulp from managed forests may have been used to strengthen the stock, depending on the quality of the recycled material. The latex bonding in the coating of the paper is fully recyclable.

Such statements, though usually briefer and simpler, are now commonplace: 'recycled', 'recyclable', 'environmentally friendly', are now part of the advertising stock-in-trade – and not always justifiably.

Curiously, part of the growth of environmental consciousness was due initially to the lack of government concern. The environment was rarely the subject of political battles. Yet, England has been a world pioneer on a number of environmental issues. The Alkali Inspectorate, which was established in 1863, was the world's first environmental agency.[8] Some of the earliest voluntary organisations had their origin in England: for example, the Commons, Open Spaces and Footpaths Preservation Society in 1865, and the National Trust in 1895 – an organisation that (with over 2 million members) has grown to be the largest conservation organisation in Europe. The 1947 Town and Country Planning Act introduced a remarkably comprehensive land-use planning system (even though, in the circumstances of the time, much of rural land use was purposely omitted). Legislation on clean air has a long history, with its major landmark being the 1956 Act, passed following the killer smog of 1952. England also had the first cabinet-level environment department (the Department of the Environment was established in 1970) though its name was, for many years, more impressive than its achievements. Yet these historical events stand as lonely peaks in an otherwise flat plain: until recently, the environment has not been

a salient political issue (McCormick 1991; Robinson 1992).

Part of the reason for this has been the idiosyncratic nature of British pollution control (Scotland shares the same style): instead of the formal, legalistic, and adversarial styles common elsewhere, Britain has traditionally operated a system of comfortable negotiation between government technicians and industry. This curiously informal and secretive system avoids confrontation and legalistic procedures.[9] The objective has been to achieve the *best practicable means* (affectionately known as BPM) of dealing with pollution problems – means that will go as far as seems reasonable towards meeting desirable standards but which do not involve too great a strain on the polluter's resources.[10] This system of voluntary compliance is a striking feature of other British regulatory systems.[11] (It also appears in a different guise in countryside policy where, to quote from *This Common Inheritance* (1990: para. 7.3), 'the Government works in partnership with [countryside] owners and managers to protect it through voluntary effort'.) This approach has a long history: indeed, it has been the cornerstone of industrial air pollution control since the Alkali Act of 1874. Its modern version has been expanded to BPEO: *best practicable environmental option* which retains the element of negotiation but involves a wider consideration of environmental issues and an openness which was foreign to its predecessor.[12]

Environmental groups do not have the clout of the major economic interests, and therefore are not involved in the initial stages of policy-making, but they do have some powers of reaction to proposals that governments may have worked out with the more powerful interests. The Control of Pollution Act 1974, for example, 'was essentially shaped by industry and local government'; and the Countryside and Wildlife Act 1981 was similarly the result of the efforts of 'powerful farming and landowning lobbies' (McCormick 1991: 12). In both these cases, environmental groups fared badly, but they did have some effect – and they were accepted as legitimate actors on the political stage. Another success was achieved in 1986 when the environmental lobby prevailed upon the Minister of Agriculture to exempt conservation advice from the charges being introduced generally for agricultural advice: the consequence was that 'this previously peripheral role of the Ministry's advisory staff has become much more central' (Lowe and Flynn 1989: 278).

Mention also needs to be made of the importance of the relatively new system of parliamentary select committees. Though these committees are often regarded as ineffectual, they have been of great value to environmental groups (Drewry 1989). They have provided a new public platform and a route for exerting pressure on Parliament. In particular, the Environment Committee, under Sir Hugh Rossi's chairmanship, has become a respected source of alternative wisdom and relatively accessible information.

Another feature of British environmental politics is the active character of many of the interest groups. Many of them are not merely interest groups: they own and manage extensive areas of land, and they fulfil a range of executive responsibilities. The National Trust and the Royal Society for the Protection of Birds, for instance, own and manage large areas of protected land. Such bodies are also characteristically charities and therefore debarred from overt political activity. Lobbying is thus not only well mannered: it is also discrete. The emphasis may be more on education than propaganda.

Governments may try to outflank the environmental groups, but increasingly they cannot ignore them, particularly with their new access to power via the EC. Some thirty British groups, together with eighty from other countries, are members of the European Environmental Bureau which gives them easy access to the European Commission and the Council of Ministers. The British groups have been able to make good use of their experience in lobbying. According to Lowe and Flynn (1989: 272), they 'have adapted more easily than many of their counterparts to the successive rounds of consultation and detailed redrafting of directives and regulations that characterise Community decision-making'. One illustration of their activity within Britain was the role they played in thwarting the Conservative Government's original proposals for the privatisation of the regional water authorities. Initially, it was

envisaged that the privatised water companies would take over responsibilities for pollution control. The CPRE took legal advice on this, and it was submitted that it would be illegal under EC law for water pollution control to be the responsibility of private organisations. The Government was obliged to radically change its plans: the solution adopted was to set up a new body, the National Rivers Authority, to protect water quality. CPRE have since published a *Campaigners' Guide to Using EC Environmental Law* (1992a), which is one of the clearest, most succinct, and easily accessible guides to EC environmental law.

Mrs Thatcher was initially averse to environmental concerns which she viewed as a brake on enterprise. On this, as with much of what she sought to do, she neither obtained nor sought consensus. Nevertheless, her administrations have followed traditional British practice in responding 'pragmatically and flexibly, even opportunistically, when environmental issues have threatened to become too contentious' (Lowe and Flynn 1989: 273). And, of course, there was her remarkable conversion to the environmental cause in 1988 when she surprised everybody by testifying her personal 'commitment to science and the environment'. With resounding words, she rallied her followers to environmentalism, declaring that Conservatives were 'not merely friends of the earth' but also 'its guardians and trustees for generations to come'. She continued:

> The core of Tory philosophy and the case for protecting the environment are the same. No generation has a freehold on the Earth. All we have is a life tenancy – with a full repairing lease. And this Government intends to meet the terms of that lease in full.[13]

Whatever might have been the reasons for Mrs Thatcher's conversion, it moved environmental policy to centre stage (Robinson 1992: 178). It did not, however, resolve the dilemma faced by the Conservative Government: how to reconcile its enterprise philosophy with a concern for good environmental management. The former is characterised by a market orientation, with profits as the reward; the latter revolves around much broader ideas. Market forces do not necessarily work well with environmental protection. Quite the contrary, individuals may be rewarded for actions which harm the environment (and, indeed, they may be subsidised to do so – as with some agricultural policies). Attempts can be made to adjust or influence the market (for example, with devices such as environmentally sensitive areas, woodland schemes, or other financial mechanisms), but there is a limit to the extent to which a Government wedded to market ideals can provide incentives for actions which protect the environment – and certainly incentives at the level necessary to provide adequate rewards (Milton 1991). An increasingly accepted solution is a firmer use of the *polluter pays principle* – officially embraced by the EC.[14] Other alternatives involve increased regulation; and here again there is the very handy excuse of the EC.

## THE IMPACT OF THE EC

There can be no doubt that the EC has had a major impact on British environmental policy. Indeed, it is not a great exaggeration to say that much of the Government's policy has been 'dictated by EC directives' (Milton 1991: 11). This is so despite the fact that the Treaty of Rome imposed no environmental obligations on member states, and the EC initially had no environmental policies. Indeed, 'sustained rather than sustainable growth was the aim: a continuous and balanced expansion'.[15] The international scene changed in the late 1960s and early 1970s, with a significant influence being the UN Conference on the Human Environment which was held in Stockholm in 1972. In the same year, the EC determined that economic expansion should not be 'an end in itself', and that 'special attention will be paid to protection of the environment'.[16] In 1973, the first EC *Action Programme on the Environment* was agreed, covering the period 1973–76. Further programmes followed: at the time of writing, the most recent (the fourth) covered the period 1987–92.[17] The Single European Act of 1987 placed this activity on a firm constitutional basis and, significantly, added the important provision that 'environmental protection requirements shall be a

component of the Community's other policies' (Haigh 1990: 11).

The EC action programmes are couched in general terms. They are also far too wordy to reproduce, but the following gives some flavour of their character:

> While it is true that there can be no sound environmental policy unless, at the same time, there is progress on the economic and social front, it is equally true that there can be no lasting economic and social progress unless environmental considerations are taken into account . . . It will accordingly be a central part of the Commission's efforts during the period of the Fourth Environmental Action Programme to make major progress towards the practical realization of this objective – initially at the level of the Community's own policies and actions; secondly at the level of the policies implemented by Member States; but as soon as possible in a more generalized way so that all economic and social developments throughout the Community, whether undertaken by public or private bodies or of a mixed character, would have environmental requirements built fully into their planning and execution.

However, these are general policy statements. The workhorses of the EC are its regulations and directives. Regulations become law throughout the EC as soon as they become operative. They create legal rights and obligations without any further action by national governments, though they may be implemented by domestic legislation.[18] An example of the binding effect of regulations is provided by the dispute in the Tachograph case. There the British Government contended (unsuccessfully) that a regulation regarding the installation of recording equipment in certain vehicles was not compulsory. The European Court held that it was: a member state could not implement a regulation 'in an incomplete or selective manner . . . so as to render abortive certain aspects of Community legislation which it has opposed or which it considered contrary to its national interest'.[19]

The great majority of EC environmental laws are in the form of *directives*. These are 'binding as to the result to be achieved, upon each member state to which they are addressed'. This leaves the individual states free to choose the manner in which directives are translated into national law. Since different countries have different legislative and administrative styles (and, of course, their particular political situations) it is not surprising that this gives rise to difficulties. Indeed, it is unusual for directives to be transposed into national legislation by the due date – which is typically two months after adoption by the Council of Ministers.[20] Nevertheless, they must be implemented 'in a way which fully meets the requirements of clarity and certainty in legal situations'. States cannot rely on administrative practices carried out under existing legislation (Wägenbaur 1991). Moreover, if a directive is not implemented by national law, it is possible for legal action to be taken by private parties to seek enforcement. A case in point is the action taken by Friends of the Earth alleging that the water supplied by Thames Water Utilities did not comply with the requirements of the directive on drinking water.[21] Furthermore, EC law must be followed even if national law contradicts it (Krämer 1992: chapter 7).

In spite of these apparently very strong powers, it seems likely that much more is to come: 'the environment is still regarded as a peripheral issue for the Community'. Only 0.1 per cent of the EC budget is spent on environmental projects. Whereas the agriculture directorate has a staff of over 1,000, the environment directorate has less than 150 (Robins 1991: 8). The advent of the European Environment Agency will presumably expand the Commission's activities (when the deadlock over its location is broken); but current agreements limit its responsibilities to monitoring: it will have no enforcement powers.[22] It also needs to be noted that, as with much on the national scene, EC environmental policy has often been 'disaster driven' – as with the introduction of measures on sea pollution following the wreck of the Amoco Cadiz (Freestone 1991: 138).

The constraints placed on the British Government must be stressed. It is particularly striking when a Conservative Government is in power:

A number of factors have combined to imprint on European environmental policy a temper of progressive reform somewhat at odds with the outlook of the Thatcher Government. These factors include the regulatory and integrating inclinations of the European Commission, the corporatist interests of transnational

business, the strength of the environmental and consumer movements across Western Europe, the pro-environmental stance of some of the leading member states, and the imperative need for community safeguards over sensitive aspects of public welfare to foster popular confidence in the process of economic integration.

(Lowe and Flynn 1989: 277)

In the following sections, several of the major issues in environmental regulation are discussed, and the influence of the EC noted. First, however, it is worth noting how the British approach differs from other countries in Europe – particularly Germany. An important difference in principle (differences in practice may be less marked) is that of 'anticipation' as distinct from reaction. Whereas Britain has taken the view that environmental problems should be defined in terms of their measurable impacts, other countries have gone beyond this, and anticipated problems before the degree of environmental damage can be ascertained.

A particularly striking example of the latter is the German *vorsorgeprinzip*. The term is not easily translatable: it is commonly taken to mean the principle of 'prevention' or 'anticipation', but this fails to capture its full meaning, as do the terms 'precaution' or 'foresight'. The German word connotes a 'notion of good husbandry which represents what one might also call best practice'.[23] *Vorsorgeprinzip* is also different from the principle of prevention which forms the basis of the EC policy. To quote from the *Second Action Programme of the Environment*:

The best environment policy consists in preventing the creation of pollution or nuisances at source rather than subsequently trying to counteract their effects. To this end, technical progress must be conceived and directed so as to take into account the concern for the protection of the environment and for the improvement of the quality of life, at the lowest cost to the Community.

Moltke comments that this principle, though

practicable and generally also economically the most reasonable approach . . . gives no guidance as to the degree of prevention, whereas this is an essential aspect of the *vorsorgeprinzip* . . . *Vorsorgeprinzip* is more than just prevention as an efficient means to an end but rather prevention as an end of itself.

(Moltke 1988: 58)

The aim is therefore, to establish pollution-control policy, not merely as a means of reducing economic or social cost but also as a means of preserving wider ecosystems. The principle has no economic qualifications attached to it, although these tend to appear in practice.[24] Typically, the European approach involves the avoidance of 'excessive cost'. This, of course, is no easier to define than concepts such as 'reasonable cost', but it is clearly intended to be more demanding. Shed of its more philosophical overtones, the issue is fundamentally 'whether to protect environmental systems before science can determine whether damage will result, or whether to apply controls only with respect to a known likelihood of environmental disturbance' (O'Riordan and Weale 1989: 290).

The currently favoured concept in the EC is BATNEEC: *best available technology not entailing excessive costs*. The term has been adopted in the English Environmental Protection Act 1990, but there are differences of interpretation among European countries. Also in currency, in this directory of acronyms, is the BPEO (*best practicable environmental option*) concept proposed by the Royal Commission on Environmental Pollution.[25] This was seen as an extension of the concept of *best practicable means* (BPM) which dates back to the Alkali Act 1874 'and which has been the cornerstone of industrial air pollution control in England and Wales since that time'.[26] Central to this principle is the recognition of the need for a coordinated approach to pollution control – an approach that takes into account the danger of the transfer of pollutants from one medium to another, as well as the need for prevention. It is defined by the Royal Commission in these terms:

A BPEO is the outcome of a systematic consultative and decision-making procedure which emphasises the protection and conservation of the environment across land, air and water. The BPEO procedure establishes, for a given set of objectives, the option that provides the most benefit or least damage to the environment as a whole, at acceptable cost, in the long term as well as in the short term.

Costs in environmental protection are elusive, complex, and controversial. The Conservative Government lays great stress on deregulation and, in harmony with the EC, on the *polluter pays principle*. It is an article of faith (which has considerable economic support) that 'economic instruments are an inherently more flexible and cost effective way of achieving environmental goals'.[27] Charges are under consideration for the discharge of effluent; a system of recycling credits to reduce landfill wastes has been introduced; and a scheme for tradeable permits for $SO_2$ is under consideration. Urban road pricing has been under discussion for many years (Smeed Report: 1964). Nevertheless, there are areas where there is no alternative to regulation, such as requiring catalytic converters to reduce car emissions. Sometimes, a combination of regulation and pricing is used, as with the regulation of the lead content of petrol and the lower tax rate on unleaded petrol.

## THE CONTROL OF POLLUTION

Concern about pollution is not new: it was as early as 1273 that action in Britain was taken to protect the environment from polluted air: a royal proclamation of that year prohibited the use of coal in London. (It was not effective, despite the dire penalties: it is recorded that a man was sent to the scaffold in 1306 for burning coal instead of charcoal.)

Those who pollute the air are no longer sent to the gallows, but, though gentler methods are now preferred, it was not until the disastrous London smog of 1952 (resulting in 4,000 deaths) that really effective action was taken. The Clean Air Acts of 1956 and 1968 prohibited the emission of dark smoke, provided for the control of the emission of grit and dust from furnaces, and established a system for local authority approval of chimney heights. However, the principal source of air pollution at the time was domestic smoke, and it was in connection with this that the most extensive powers were introduced. Local authorities are empowered to establish *smoke control areas* in which the emission of smoke from chimneys constitutes an offence. About two-thirds of the premises in the conurbations are covered by smoke control orders (of which over 6,000 are in force).

So far as industrial emissions to the atmosphere are concerned, there are two systems of control in Britain. Local authorities are responsible for certain industrial emissions, but there are processes which, because of their nature or the specialised and complex methods necessary to minimise emissions, have been controlled for many years by an expert and centralised inspectorate, originally (in 1864) the Alkali Inspectorate, and now Her Majesty's Inspectorate of Pollution (HMIP). It is estimated that whereas some 5,000 plants will require authorisation under the latter system, the number of the less complex processes subject to local authority authorisation may be up to 27,000 (Tromans and Clarkson 1991: 512).

In line with the British tradition of dealing with one problem at a time, responsibilities for dealing with different types of pollution have grown piecemeal. Local authorities had many of the earlier responsibilities which have now moved to *ad hoc* agencies such as HMIP and the National Rivers Authority (NRA). In addition to smoke control, local authorities now have functions in relation to vehicle emissions, waste, registration of contaminated land, and noise control. A number of these are discussed in the following pages.

Following the Clean Air Acts of 1956 and 1968, came the Protection of the Environment Bill, introduced by the Conservative Government in 1973, but passed as the Control of Pollution Act 1974 by a Labour Government. In its first guise, there was an interesting debate (in the House of Lords) on a proposal to introduce a 'general standard' for environmental protection: this would have required all public bodies to have regard to the impact of any major development (whether public or private) on the environment. This was explicitly based on American legislation (the National Environment Protection Act), with its requirement that any federal project has to be preceded by an 'environmental impact statement'. This proposal made no progress, and the title of the Act is more accurate than that of the

initial bill. It dealt with four main issues: the deposit and disposal of waste on land; water pollution; noise; and atmospheric pollution. More recent is the Environmental Protection Act of 1990. This major landmark in environmental policy deals with a wide range of environmental matters, from genetically modified organisms to abandoned shopping trolleys. Of particular significance is its introduction of *integrated pollution control* (IPC).[28] This is the administrative apparatus for implementing the *best practical environmental option* (BPEO). It contrasts with the customary British method of operating different controls in isolation, with separate approaches to individual forms of pollution. The crucial problem with this is that pollution does not abide by the boundaries of air, land and water: pollution is mobile. In the jargon, it is a 'cross-media' problem.[29] Thus:

> Substances discharged into one medium may have damaging effects in another. For example, chemical fertilizers and sewage sludge spread on agricultural land, or toxic waste buried in land-fill disposal sites, may leach into watercourses. Sulphur dioxide and oxides of nitrogen emitted into the atmosphere from conventional power stations, large industrial combustion plants, and motor vehicles can produce acid rain that erodes buildings and kills trees and fish. Likewise, atmospheric emissions of carbon dioxide from the burning of fossil fuels contribute to the greenhouse effect, which may lead to global warming and a consequent rise in sea level . . . Moreover, unless pollutants can be eliminated altogether, they are simply transformed or transferred elsewhere, and measures taken to reduce pollution in one environmental medium may create problems for another. For instance, when flue gas desulphurization equipment is fitted to power stations in order to reduce air pollution from emissions of sulphur dioxide, the 'scrubbing' process produces by-products of contaminated water and lime that must be discharged into the aqueous environment or disposed of as waste on land.
> (Gibson 1991: 19)

Using BPEO involves choosing the best way of dealing with pollution, and this can be done only if there is an administrative organisation with sufficiently broad powers to take an 'integrated' approach. The 1990 Act made provision for HMIP to fulfil this purpose (now to be merged into an even more integrated Environment Agency). Under the Act, certain prescribed polluting processes require author-isation by HMIP. To obtain this, the operator must show that the *best available techniques not entailing excessive cost* (BATNEEC) are being used:

1 for preventing the release of prescribed substances into an environmental medium, or, where that is not practicable, for reducing the release to a minimum; and
2 for rendering harmless any other substance which could cause harm if released into any environmental medium.[30]

Where a process involves the release of harmful substances to more than one medium, BPEO must be adopted. Additionally, certain statutory environ-mental standards ('quality objectives') have to be met.

Local authority air pollution control over simple, less-polluting processes continues (and, if current proposals are implemented, will not be affected by the establishment of the Environment Agency). The 1990 Act revises this system of control, and also requires that controlled operators use BATNEEC and meet statutory standards. The Act also introduces a new regime for waste which is discussed later. It does not, however, deal with water pollution (unless this is subject to an IPC authorisation): this is covered separately by the Water Resources Act 1991.

Clearly, environmental controls and their admini-stration are complex. Moreover, since more change will take place with the legislation establishing the Environment Agency, any detailed discussion could be overtaken by events.

A striking feature of the recent environmental legislation is the severity of the penalties for polluting (Harris 1992a). One feature in particular is note-worthy: the use of 'strict liability'. Generally, under English law, the prosecution has the burden of proving that a defendant is guilty beyond reasonable doubt. The 1990 Act, however, provides that where it is alleged that BATNEEC has not been used in a prescribed operation, 'it shall be for the accused to prove that there was no better available technique not entailing excessive cost than was in fact used'. This makes an offence one of 'strict liability', in contrast to the traditional one of 'fault-based'. Though its use

is likely to be rare, it is indicative of the change in official attitudes to pollution. (It will also involve highly technical matters which – in the absence of a specialised court – may present real difficulties for the existing courts.[31])

## ACID RAIN

Acid rain was the subject of a literally sensational report by the House of Commons Environment Committee in 1984:

> The Central Electricity Generating Board (CEGB), despite its being the major burner of fossil fuels in this country, has made virtually no reduction in its $SO_2$ emissions. By following a tall stacks policy the CEGB has lessened the acid deposition falling near to power stations but has caused it to be transported over long distances; thus, it can be assumed, increasing the amount of deposition falling in rural areas and even in areas as remote as Scandinavia.

Neither the Government nor the CEGB accepted the basis for this conclusion, and herein lies a major difficulty with the subject: that of determining where the scientific truth lies. As with the arguments between Canada and the United States, different scientists can interpret the same data in varying ways (Cullingworth 1987: 14.)

There is also difficulty with the term 'acid rain' since it is used in different ways. The Environment Committee decided to use the words

> in their widest and most inaccurate sense, deliberately so, because they most readily cover the areas which are of major concern: namely, the consequences to water-life, the forests, buildings and human health of the chemical changes in the atmosphere to emissions from combusted fossil fuels.[32]

These problems operate on an international scale: British-created acid rain falls across the North Sea. Pollution knows no boundaries and, to the Scandinavian countries, Britain is the 'dirty man' of Europe.[33] These international difficulties do not appear likely to be easy of solution. (Even basic facts are at dispute: Britain argues that the link between sulphur dioxide and acid rain has yet to be proved; but Scandinavia has no doubts.)[34]

## WASTE: THE DUTY OF CARE

The UK produces about 500 million tonnes of waste each year.[35] Most of this is agricultural and mining and quarrying waste. Much of the remainder is 'controlled waste', i.e. waste that is controlled by the provisions of the Environmental Protection Act.[36] The definition of waste gives rise to problems of a Byzantine character: the lengthy DoE Circular 14/92 explains all.

Before the 1990 Act, the statutory responsibility for both waste management and waste disposal was vested in the English county councils, the Welsh district councils, and the Scottish district and island councils.[37] Generally the quality of service was judged to be related to the size of authority: the larger authorities had a greater range of competence and also were less subject to parochial pressures.[38] There was also a wider concern that waste regulation and disposal was the responsibility of the same authority. The situation was generally accepted as being unsatisfactory, a view which the House of Commons Environment Committee confirmed with force: 'Never, in any of our inquiries into environmental problems, have we experienced such consistent and universal criticism of existing legislation and of central and local government as we have during the course of this inquiry.'[39] The 1990 Act separated these waste regulatory and operational functions and introduced a new regime of waste control. Administratively, 'the poacher will no longer be the gamekeeper' (R.P. Lewis 1992) or, to use the words of a DoE Circular 10/91:

> The decisions by a waste regulation authority about policies, standards and enforcement are to be taken free from the pressures arising from the authority's position as a waste disposal authority . . . The other purpose of separation is to increase public and industry confidence in waste regulation so that regulatory policies and practices can be seen to be directed solely towards achieving the highest practicable environmental standards in all waste management.

The separation of functions between *waste regulation authorities* (WRAs) and *waste collection authorities* (WCAs) is a statutory one, though the same local authorities can be involved. The position is complicated by all the changes which have taken place in the organisation of local government – and more changes are on the way. The 1990 Act imposes a *duty of care* on all who are concerned with controlled waste.[40] This duty, similar to that imposed on employers by the Health and Safety at Work Act 1974, is designed to ensure that waste is properly managed. In particular, it aims at making fly-tipping more difficult. The duty requires anyone who has control of waste at any stage, from its original production to its final disposal, to take responsibility for its safe and legal handling. Control operates by way of conditional licensing (*waste management licences*). Before a licence is issued, the WRA must be satisfied that the operation will not cause pollution of the environment, harm to human health, and severe detriment to the amenities of the locality. The *duty of care* is more than a code of honour: as already indicated, there are severe penalties for failing to abide by it.

In the same way that energy conservation is an important feature of energy policy, so waste minimisation is of waste management. HMIP is giving increased attention to this as well as to the potential for recycling.[41] A new recycling scheme was introduced in 1992, based on the principle that recycling avoids the cost of collecting what would otherwise have been waste. The recycling credit is a payment by the local authority to a recycler for the amount saved. The Government's target (for the year 2000) is for 25 per cent of household waste to be recycled. (At present, only 1 million tonnes a year is recovered from some 20 million tonnes of household waste.[42]) It seems, however, that existing measures are not sufficient to enable this target to be reached, and new economic instruments are being considered, such as charging householders for the amount of waste they throw away. This might lead to an increase in fly-tipping, as would increases in the cost of landfilling waste. These and similar issues are 'under study'.[43]

## WASTE PLANS

Before the Planning and Compensation Act 1991, policies for waste formed part of county structure plans (and, in some cases, separate 'subject' waste plans). The 1991 Act introduced 'waste local plans': these contain 'detailed policies in respect of development which involves the depositing of refuse or waste materials other than mineral waste'. Minerals come under a different provision, but, since a significant proportion of waste arises from mineral workings, waste and mineral plans can be combined. Waste policies deal with all types of waste, including scrapyards, clinical and other types of waste incinerator, landfill sites, waste-storage facilities, recycling and waste-reception centres, concrete crushing and blacktop-reprocessing facilities, and bottle banks. Responsibilities for waste lie with *local waste authorities*: county councils, metropolitan district and London borough councils in England, district councils in Wales, and national park authorities in England and Wales.

Waste plans prepared by local authorities should not be confused with *waste disposal plans* which are required under the Environmental Protection Act 1990. These are the responsibility of waste regulation authorities (the same local authorities which are responsible for waste local plans, except in the metropolitan areas). The proposed relationship between waste disposal plans and waste local plans was explained in the DoE Consultation paper *Waste Disposal and Development Plans*:

> E.P. [Environmental Protection Act] waste disposal plans will cover issues such as the kinds and quantities of waste to be disposed of, methods of disposal and the authority's policy on the granting of licences for waste disposal. While E.P. plans may include information about existing sites and sites which are expected to be developed, they will not address land use issues fully in the way that a development plan would . . . While it would be open to planning authorities and planning inspectors to take E.P. waste disposal plans into account as a material consideration in dealing with planning applications and appeals, the fact that they will not provide a full land use framework will mean that they will not convey the degree of certainty on planning issues that a development plan would.

In Scotland, district and islands councils are both waste regulation and waste disposal authorities. As disposal authorities, they own and operate sites, and

as regulation authorities they regulate all sites, including those belonging to the private sector. Planning guidance is being prepared on development plans and land for waste disposal.

## WATER POLLUTION

As already noted, the protection of water quality in England and Wales is the responsibility of the National Rivers Authority (NRA).[44] This is an independent agency established under the Water Act 1989. It has taken over many of the regulatory powers of the former regional water authorities but, unlike those authorities, it has no operational responsibilities (these are carried out by ten water service companies). It has statutory functions in relation to water resources, and the control of pollution in inland, underground and coastal waters.[45] It can take preventive action to stop water pollution, take remedial steps where pollution has already occurred, and recover the reasonable costs of doing so from a polluter. It also has certain powers to prevent flooding, as well as responsibilities for the licensing of salmon and freshwater fisheries, for navigation, and for conservancy and harbour authority functions (Ball and Bell 1991: 32).

The NRA prides itself as being 'the strongest environmental protection agency in Europe, and a very effective *Guardian of the Water Environment*'.[46] It has a sophisticated and relatively public regulatory system which involves the setting of water-quality objectives and a requirement that consent is obtained for discharges of trade and sewage effluent to controlled waters (Ball and Bell 1991: 295). It is a statutory consultee on planning applications and development plans. In 1992/93, it spent £445m, and employed nearly 8,000 staff. Its corporate plan involves the spending of almost £2bn over the four years to 1995/96.[47]

To complete this account of water pollution control in England and Wales, mention needs to be made of the Drinking Water Inspectorate which was established within the DoE following the Water Act 1989. This small unit (supplemented by consultant services) monitors the quality of drinking water supplied by the water companies in England and Wales.

There is a different system in Scotland. The nine regional councils and three islands councils are responsible for water supply, sewerage and sewage disposal. Water pollution is the responsibility of the seven river purification boards, except in the areas of the three islands councils. The river purification boards have a bigger role in relation to IPC than the NRA: they have joint responsibility for operating the system with Her Majesty's Industrial Pollution Inspectorate (the Scottish equivalent of HMIP). A consultation paper *Investing for our Future*, issued in 1992, sets out a range of options for reorganisation.

## NOISE

'Quiet costs money . . . a machine manufacturer will try to make a quieter product only if he is forced to, either by legislation or because customers want quiet machines and will choose a rival product for a lower noise level.' So stated the Wilson Committee in 1963. This, in one sense, is the crux of the problem of noise. More, and more powerful, cars, aircraft, portable radios and the like must receive strong public opprobrium before manufacturers – and users – will be concerned with their noise level. Similarly, legislative measures and their implementation require public support before effective action can be taken.

As with other aspects of environmental quality, attitudes to noise and its control have changed in recent years, partly as a result of the advent of new sources of noise such as portable music centres, personal stereos, and electric DIY and garden equipment, as well as greatly increased traffic. (Developments in electronics have also provided easier methods of obtaining data on noise.) The increased concern about noise is reflected in the prominence given to the issue in *This Common Inheritance* and its annual successors, all of which devote a chapter to it. A review by a working party (the Batho Report) was published in 1990, a report on *Railway Noise and the Insulation of Dwellings* (the Mitchell Report) followed

in 1991, and a draft PPG on *Planning and Noise* and legislative proposals have been circulated for comment. It has also been announced that new guidance is under discussion on noise from mineral sites, local authority powers over noisy parties, and noise barriers alongside roads; new legislation is in preparation for the regulation of various types of noise.[48]

There are three ways in which noise is regulated: by setting limits to noise at source (as with aircraft, motorcycles, and lawnmowers); separating noise from people (as with subsidised double glazing in houses affected by serious noise from aircraft or from new roads); and exercising controls over noise nuisance. Where intolerable noise cannot be reduced and reduces property values, an action can be pursued at common law or, in the case of certain public works, compensation can be obtained under the Land Compensation Act 1973.

Noise from neighbours is the most common source of noise nuisance and complaints. The number of such complaints increased by six times over the ten years from 1976 (Batho Report 1990: para. 3.3). This is a difficult problem to deal with, and official encouragement is being given to various types of neighbourhood action, such as 'quiet neighbourhood', 'neighbourhood noise watch', noise mediation and similar schemes (Oliver and Waite 1989). There is provision under the Control of Pollution Act 1974 for the designation by local authorities of *noise abatement zones*, though the statutory procedures for these are cumbersome and, in any case, they are not well suited to dealing with neighbourhood noise in residential areas (though they are useful for regulating industrial and commercial areas).

Transportation noise takes many forms and is being tackled in various ways.[49] Road traffic noise is the most serious in the sense that it affects the most people. Here emphasis is being put on the development of quieter road surfaces and vehicles. The Batho Report also proposed extending the compensation scheme for people affected by high noise levels, including those resulting from traffic management schemes. Aircraft noise has long been subject to controls both nationally and (with the UK in the

Transport noise.

lead) internationally. The principal London airports are required by statute to provide sound insulation to homes seriously affected by aircraft noise, and similar non-statutory schemes apply to major airports in the provinces. Older jets are being phased out, and controls are also exercised over flight paths and times.[50]

## THE PROPOSED ENVIRONMENT AGENCY

On 8 July 1991, the Prime Minister announced the Government's intention 'to create a new agency for environmental protection and enhancement'. This was a major change in policy: until this time the Government had rejected the mounting arguments (led by the House of Commons Environment Committee) for such an agency. The Environment Committee – in appropriate parliamentary language, of course – wondered why there had been such a change of heart: 'in just two years, the Government's policy had shifted from outright rejection of the notion of such an agency, to enthusiastic acceptance'.[51] In reply, the Secretary of State, Michael Heseltine, referred to 'evolutionary change' and the fresh views of a new minister (i.e. himself), but he laid stress on the importance of relationships with industry:

> The relationships that we are developing with our industrial base, particularly through the advisory committee chaired by Mr John Collins of Shell with industry and commerce, has brought home to us very forcibly that industry is deeply affected by these increasingly comprehensive regulatory processes. The concept of a one-stop shop, where one group of experts is available for discussion and negotiation with the industrial and commercial world is particularly evident as we see the consequences of integrated pollution control flowing through.[52]

Heseltine's point was echoed in the evidence submitted by business and commerce: there was considerable support for the 'one-stop shop' for businesses whose activities involve pollution. The Institute of Directors, for example, saw the Agency as 'a step towards overcoming the administrative nightmare

that would otherwise have resulted from businesses having to seek a multiplicity of permits to transport and dispose of waste'. In its view, the local authority powers over air pollution control should be similarly integrated. The Environment Committee itself argued that the Agency should have more functions than proposed by the Government. The TCPA went further and argued the need for integration between environmental planning and land-use planning: the new Agency should be introduced in conjunction with the latest reorganisation of local government.[53]

Another factor in the debate was the importance of having an agency that was able to negotiate from a position of strength with the EC. There were dangers that there would be pressures for the new European Environmental Agency to have enforcement (as well as monitoring) powers. The HC Committee considered that it was 'imperative that the United Kingdom's Environmental Agencies be seen to be effective at an early stage in order to maintain a high degree of subsidiarity and to avoid any further attempts to erode United Kingdom sovereignty in this regard'.

*Subsidiarity* is a Eurospeak term meaning that the responsibility for policy should be exercised at the lowest level of government which can be effective for the particular purpose.[54] A Consultation Paper issued in October 1991 had discussed several options, all of which involved consideration of the relationship between HMIP, the NRA, and the waste regulatory functions currently carried out by local government. The option chosen combines all three of these in a single organisation.[55] Local authorities will retain their responsibilities for controlling air pollution from the less-polluting industrial processes, and the Drinking Water Inspectorate will remain separate from the new Agency. The advantage of the proposed amalgamation which was considered to be overwhelming was that 'it would secure the integrated approach to pollution control which the Government wishes to achieve whilst retaining the framework of integrated river basin management within one organisation'. The argument against the favoured option was that it might blur the pollution-control focus of the new body and create 'a large heterogeneous organisation with the major part of its resources dedicated to functions other than pollution control'. It was also feared that its huge size (with over 9,000 mostly regionally-based staff, and an annual budget of over £500m) could give rise to serious management problems.

The Scottish Environment Protection Agency is to take over the functions of main regulatory bodies: the river purification authorities, the district and islands councils, HM Industrial Pollution Inspectorate and the Hazardous Waste Inspectorate.

At the time of writing, legislation is promised.

## ENVIRONMENTAL ASSESSMENT

As environmental issues have become more complex, ways have been sought to measure the impacts of development. Cost–benefit analysis was at one time seen as a good guide to action. By taking into account non-priced benefits such as the saving of time, and the reduction in accidents, it can 'prove' that developments such as the Victoria underground line are justified. Useful though this technique is for incorporating certain non-market issues into the decision-making process, it has serious limitations. In particular (quite apart from the problems of valuing 'time'), some things are beyond price, while others have quite different 'values' for different groups of the population. Reducing everything to a monetary price ignores factors such as these. Alternatives such as Lichfield's *planning balance sheet* and Hill's *goals achievement matrix* attempt to take a much wider range of factors into account.[56]

Environmental assessment (EA) is a procedure introduced into the British planning system as a result of an EC Directive.[57] Though it might appear that environmental assessment is nothing new on the British planning scene (hasn't this always been done with important projects?), it is in fact conceptually different in that it involves a highly systematic quantitative and qualitative review of proposed projects – though early indications suggest that the practice is somewhat different.[58] Nevertheless, unlike some European countries, Britain has had, since the 1947 Act, a relatively sophisticated

system which involves a case-by-case review of development proposals. Indeed, there has been some controversy between the UK Government and the EC on some major projects about the need for formal EA in addition to the extensive reviews under the standard system.[59] A good statement of the particular character of EA is given in a DoE guide to procedures:

> What is new about EA is the emphasis on systematic analysis, using the best practicable techniques and best available sources of information, and on the presentation of information in a form which provides a focus for public scrutiny of the project and enables the importance of the predicted effects, and the scope for modifying or mitigating them, to be properly evaluated by the planning authority before a decision is given.[60]

It is important to appreciate that EA is a *process*. The production of an *environmental statement* (ES) is one part of this.[61] The process involves the gathering of information on the environmental effects of a development by the LPA and the developer. This information comes from a variety of sources: the developer, the LPA, statutory consultees (such as the Countryside Commission and HMIP), and third parties (including environmental groups).

For some types of development an EA is mandatory. These are listed in schedule 1 of the regulations (and are therefore inevitably known as 'schedule 1 projects'). These include large developments such as power-stations, airports, installations for the storage of radioactive waste, motorways, ports, and such like. Projects for which EA *may* be required ('schedule 2 projects') are those which have *significant* environmental impacts. There are three main types of development where it is considered that an EA is needed:

1 for major projects which are of more than local importance, principally in terms of physical size;
2 'occasionally' for projects proposed for particularly sensitive or vulnerable locations, for example, a national park or a SSSI; and
3 'in a small number of cases' for projects with unusually complex or potentially adverse effects, where expert analysis is desirable, for example, with the discharge of pollutants.[62]

There is a marked resemblance between this and the circumstances in which the Secretary of State may exercise his powers of 'call-in'.[63]

## UPDATE[64]

There is a rapidly expanding literature on sustainability: see, for example, DoE *UK Strategy for Sustainable Development: Consultation Paper*, DoE 1993; Royal Society for Nature Conservation, *Stepping Stones: The BT Environment City Review of Sustainability*, RSNC 1993.

A critical discussion of the 'polluter pays principle' is to be found in R. English, 'No fault liability: the *Cambridge Water* case', *JPL* 1993: 409–16. See also Organisation for Economic Cooperation and Development, *Taxation and the Environment: Complementary Policies*, Paris: OECD, 1993.

The Secretary of State for Transport (John MacGregor) announced on July 7, 1993 that it had been decided not to proceed with the East London River Crossing proposal that involved damage to Oxleas Wood. However, it was stressed that this decision was 'quite independent of the infraction proceedings instigated by the European Commission. The Government remains clear that the Environmental Impact Assessment Directive should not apply to projects which were in the pipeline when it came into force, and it will continue to contest the proceedings brought by the Commission.' (See *JPL* 1993: 823.)

In response to the EC's Habitats Directive the government propose to remove permitted development rights where the proposal, if not permitted development, would require environmental assessment, and/or 'likely to have a significant effect on a Special Protection Area (SPA) or Special Area of Conservation' (DoE Consultation Paper, *The Town and Country Planning General Development Order: Permitted Development, Environmental Assessment and Implementation of the Habitats Directive*, 1993).

The 17th report of the Royal Commission on Environmental Pollution is entitled *Incineration of Waste*, Cm 2181, HMSO, 1993. The Government's responses to the 13th and 14th reports (on the release of genetically altered and engineered organisms to the environment) have been issued by DoE (Biotechnology Unit, Toxic Substances Division, 1993).

A 1993 report to the DoE by ECOTEC Research and Consulting Ltd presents *A Review of UK Environmental Expenditure*. This is the final report on the project, and is published by HMSO.

## NOTES

1  See the study commissioned by DoE on the relationship between planning controls and pollution and waste management controls: *Planning, Pollution and Waste Management*, 1992. A useful review of the situation at the end of the 1980s is given by Miller 1990. An earlier paper by Wood (1986) reports on a number of case-studies. See also Tromans and Clarkson 1991.

2  The Draft PPG on *Planning Control and Pollution* states: 'Applicants do not normally have to prove the need for their proposed development, or discuss the merits of alternative sites, except in the case of an application which must be accompanied by an environmental statement . . . Environmental statements, which must accompany particular applications, can identify matters that will be relevant to the determination of the application; they may – and as a matter of practice should – include an outline discussion of the main alternatives studied by the developer and an indication of the reasons for choosing the development proposed, taking account of environmental effects.'

3  The EC Directive (85/337 of 27 June 1985) is implemented by regulation. The 1991 Planning and Compensation Act extended the regulatory powers, and a DoE Consultation Paper of June 1992 proposed extending the requirements of EIA to water treatment plants, wind generators, motorway service areas, coast protection works, golf courses, and privately financed toll roads. (See *This Common Inheritance: The Second Year Report*, 1992: para. 7.21.)

4  Draft PPG, *Planning and Pollution Control*, 1992: para. 1.26.

5  For some recent discussion on sustainability, see Amundson 1993, CPOS 1993, and Williams 1993a and 1993b.

6  But see Newby 1990; also Lowe and Goyder 1983.

7  Seveso is a town in northern Italy where, in 1976, a factory released a cloud of poisonous chemicals; this led to the EC 'Seveso Directive' of 1982. In the massive 1974 explosion at Flixborough, 28 workers were killed. For a succinct account of the change in attitudes to the environment, see Taylor 1992.

8 For a history of this and much else on the origins of English 'environmental policy', see Ashby and Anderson, *The Politics of Clean Air*, 1981. Also strongly recommended is Ashby's reflective *Reconciling Man with the Environment*, 1978.

9 Some interesting and important implications of this are brought out by McAuslan 1991. He argues that 'the law is coming to play a more and more central role in the management of the environment', and that 'we seem to be moving away slowly but surely from the old style of regulation, private and the product of bargaining, to a more public style, the product of public debate and differences'.

10 To quote the Chief Alkali Inspector in 1957 (quoted in Vogel 1986: 79): 'There must be compromise between (1) the natural desire of the public to enjoy pure air, (2) the legitimate desire of manufacturers to meet competition by producing their goods cheaply and therefore to avoid unremunerative expenses, (3) overriding national interests. The answer to these opposing interests lies in the honest use of the best practicable means . . .'

11 There is an extensive literature on this. See, for example, Hawkins 1984; Richardson, *et al.* 1982; Vogel 1986; and R.A.W. Rhodes 1981. See also Hutter 1989: 161, who gives a good illustration of a general attitude in a quotation from the annual report of the former industrial air pollution inspectors: 'Discussion, persuasion and cooperation leading to mutually agreed solutions, are preferred to coercion. In consequence, the inspectorate has made only limited use of the full enforcement powers.'

12 See Royal Commission on Environmental Pollution (RCEP), 5th Report: *Air Pollution Control: An Integrated Approach*, 1976, and 12th report: *Best Practicable Environmental Option*, 1988.

13 Mrs Thatcher's initial statement was made in a speech to the Royal Society on 17 September 1988. The second quotation is from her keynote speech to the Conservative Party conference in Brighton in the following month.

14 This was one of the general principles adopted in the First Action Programme: 'The cost of preventing and eliminating nuisances must in principle be borne by the polluter. However, there may be certain exceptions and special arrangements, in particular for transitional periods, provided that they cause no significant distortion to international trade and investment.' See Johnson and Corcelle 1989: chapter 10.

15 Article 2 of the Treaty of Rome; see Robins 1991: 7. For a discussion of the development of EC environmental policies, see Hughes 1992.

16 The 1972 Paris Heads of State summit; quoted in Robins 1991: 7.

17 A summary of these is given in Lasok and Bridge 1991: 545–47. See also Johnson and Corcelle 1989. At the time of writing, the Fifth Programme is under discussion: see the report of the House of Lords Select Committee on the European Communities: *Fifth Environmental Action Programme: Integration of Community Policies*, 1992.

18 *Treaty Establishing the European Economic Community*, 25 March 1957, article 189.

19 Case 128/78: *EC Commission* v. *United Kingdom* [1979] ERC 419, [1979] 2 *Common Market Law Reports* 45; quoted in Lasok and Bridge 1991: 132.

20 See *Implementation and Enforcement of Environmental Legislation*, HL Select Committee on the European Communities, 1992: 11–15. For a succinct discussion of EC directives and their implementation see Wägenbaur 1991.

21 Directive 80/778. See 'Friends of the Earth sue over U.K.'s drinking water', *Mealey's European Environmental Law Report*, 12 June 1991: 12.

22 It was originally conceived on the lines of the US agency. See Johnson and Corcelle 1989: 341, and also HC Environment Committee, *The Proposed European Environmental Agency*, 1989.

23 Moltke, 'The *vorsorgeprinzip* in West German environmental policy', printed as an appendix to the 12th report of the Royal Commission on Environmental Pollution, *Best Practicable Environmental Option*, 1988. See also Weale *et al.* 1991.

24 Moltke 1988: 58; see also chapter 3 of Haigh 1990.

25 Royal Commission on Environmental Pollution (RCEP) *Air Pollution Control: An Integrated Approach*, 1976.

26 RCEP, 12th Report, *Best Practicable Environmental Option*, 1988: para. 1.3.

27 *This Common Inheritance: The Second Year Report*, 1992: para. 3.44. The examples quoted in the subsequent sentence are from p. 34 of this report. Generally on market pricing of pollution, see Dales's classic *Pollution, Property and Prices*, 1968. Also well worth reading is Beckerman 1990. A recent study commissioned by the DoE is *The Potential Role of Market Mechanisms in the Control of Acid Rain*, 1992.

28 In addition to the RCEP reports, there is a useful technical publication of DoE: *Integrated Pollution Control: A Practical Guide*, 1992. See also Spooner *et al.* 1992.

29 There is debate on the extent to which a 'cross-media' approach is required. The RCEP stated its belief that 'most of the present and future problems in environmental pollution will be of this cross-media type and will therefore demand a broad consideration for which BPEO provides the correct framework'. (RCEP, 10th Report, *Tackling Pollution – Experience and Prospects*, 1984: para. 6.35). For a critical discussion, see Owens 1990.

30 A succinct explanation of the provisions is given in Layfield 1992.

31  On the need for a specialised court, see Carnwath 1992.
32  The Committee continued: 'These emissions may be sulphur dioxide, nitrogen oxides or hydrocarbons. Their major products are sulphuric acid and nitric acids, nitrogen dioxide, and also ozone. Hydrocarbons are produced by both motor vehicles and refineries/petrochemical works, and play a significant role in the process by which ozone is formed from nitrogen oxides. All fall within the sense in which we use the term "acid rain".' HC Environmental Committee, *Acid Rain*, 1984: para. 4.
33  Rose 1990. See also Wetstone and Rosencranz 1983a and 1983b; Hawkins 1984; Blowers 1984 and 1986.
34  See the detailed consideration of these issues in DoE, *Acid Rain: The Government's Reply to the Fourth Report from the Environment Committee, Session 1983–84*, 1984 (also reprinted in the Environment Committee's *Air Pollution*, 1988).
35  A useful collection of essays on the 'spatial aspects of waste management, hazards and disposal' is to be found in Clark *et al.* 1992.
36  Draft PPG: *Planning and Pollution Control*, Annex 4.
37  This ignores the complicated situation in London and the metropolitan counties after the abolition of the GLC and the metropolitan county councils.
38  RCEP, *Managing Waste: The Duty of Care*, 1985: para. 9.10.
39  House of Commons Environment Committee, *Toxic Waste*, 1989: para. 1
40  The term was the title of the RCEP's eleventh report, *Managing Waste: The Duty of Care*, 1985. See also DoE, *Waste Management: the Duty of Care: A Code of Practice*, 1991.
41  HMIP *Annual Report 1990–91*: 40.
42  *This Common Inheritance*, 1990: para. 14.21.
43  *This Common Inheritance: The Second Year Report*, 1992: 121.
44  For the position before the establishment of the NRA, see House of Commons Environment Committee, *Pollution of Rivers and Estuaries*, 1987. See also Hawke and Himan 1988b: and Watchman *et al.* 1988.
45  HMIP takes over whenever a process is subject to IPC.
46  National Rivers Authority, *Annual Report 1991/92*. See also Bowman 1992.
47  NRA, *Corporate Plan 1992/93*. See also *Sea Defence Survey, Weather Radar and Flood Warning Services*, and *Policy and Practice for the Protection of Groundwater*, all published by the NRA.
48  An elderly DoE circular *Planning and Noise* (10/73) will presumably be replaced by the forthcoming PPG; similarly with the SDD circular 23/73 which bears the same title.
49  See *Joint Memorandum by the Departments of Environment and Transport to the Royal Commission on Environmental Pollution: Transport and the Environment Study*, 1992: 33–36.
50  New legislative proposals were issued by the DoE in a Circular Letter of 9 June 1992: *Proposed Legislative Response to Recommendations in Noise Review Report*. The three proposed provisions discussed in this letter are: (1) the extension of the statutory nuisance abatement procedure, contained in the Environmental Protection Act, to include noise in the street; (2) improved controls over loudspeakers in the street; and (3) an adoptive power enabling local authorities to require the fitting of cut-out devices to intruder alarms.
51  The proposals were later outlined in consultation papers issued by the DoE and the Scottish Office: *Improving Environmental Quality: The Government's Proposal for a New Independent Environment Agency* (DoE 1991), and *Improving Scotland's Environment: The Way Forward* (SO 1992). The Environment Committee's report was published in 1992: *The Government's Proposals for an Environment Agency*. The DoE consultation paper is summarised in paragraphs 14–17 of the Committee's report.
52  The quotation is from the Environment Committee's report (Q.1). 'The advisory committee chaired by Mr John Collins' is the Advisory Committee on Business and the Environment. Its reports are published by the DoE; see, for example, *Second Progress Report to and Response from the President of the Board of Trade and the Secretary of State for the Environment*, DoE, 1992.
53  *The Environment Agency: Response by the Town and Country Planning Association*, TCPA, January 1992.
54  Under the subsidiarity principle, the EEC is 'limited to taking environmental action only by the extent to which this can be attained better at Community level than state level . . . it appears in practice that this means it is up to the Council of Ministers to decide who shall do what in relation to which environmental issue' (Hughes 1992: 90).
55  See *HC Debates*, 15 July 1992, Vol. 211, Written Answers cols 857–8. The later quotations are from the Consultation Paper.
56  There is an enormous literature in this field. A standard text on cost–benefit analysis is Mishan (1976). Lichfield's work is easily accessible through Lichfield *et al.* (1975). A useful report (which endorses a modified version of Lichfield's *planning balance sheet*) is the study commissioned by DoE: *Evaluating the Effectiveness of Land Use Planning*, 1992. An invaluable broader discussion is to be found in Self 1975.
57  The full title of the Directive is: *Council Directive of June 27, 1985 on the Assessment of the Effects of Certain Public and Private Projects on the Environment* (85/337/EEC). It is reproduced in full in Haigh 1987. There is a summary in Haigh 1990.

58 Wood and Jones 1991. See also Lambert and Wood 1990.

59 The Commission has considered taking legal proceedings against the UK for failure to comply with the detailed requirements of the Directive. Salter 1992a has argued that part of the difficulty lies with the EC drafting. There were originally seven projects involved in this dispute; five of them were later accepted by the Commission as meeting their requirements, but two remain (at the time of writing) at issue: the East London River Crossing (which passes through the Oxleas Wood SSSI), and the extension of the British Petroleum gas separation plant at Kinneil, near Falkirk. On the remaining cases, Secretary of State Michael Howard has forcefully maintained that 'there has been no breach of EC law. There can be no doubt that the environmental issues were thoroughly examined in the lengthy and rigorous approval procedures to which these projects were subject.' See also two further articles: Salter 1992b and 1992c.

60 DoE, *Environmental Assessment: A Guide to Procedures*, HMSO, 1989: 3. Haigh (1987) suggests that the EC Directive has been considerably influenced by the UK: 'the Directive has in effect been subtly modified in the process of negotiation so that it now accords very closely with existing British development control procedures'.

61 The common term *environmental impact statement* (EIS) is, in fact, an American import, though the meaning is the same.

62 This list is a composite of those given in DoE Circular 15/88, para. 20, and the *Guide*, para. 10.

63 See Chapter 4.

64 For space reasons, some major aspects of environmental planning have been necessarily omitted from this account. For example, the discussion of waste omitted reference to radioactive waste. On this, see White Paper, *Radioactive Waste Management*, 1982; Advisory Committee on the Safe Transport of Radioactive Materials, *The Transport of Low Level Radioactive Waste in the UK*, 1988; HMIP, *Radioactive Waste Management and Radioactivity in the Environment*, 1989; Radioactive Waste Management Advisory Committee, *Annual Reports*, HMSO, and Bond 1992. For Scotland, see *Waste Inspectorate Scotland: Report 1987–90*, SO 1991.

On landfill, see House of Commons Environment Committee, *The EC Draft Directive on the Landfill of Waste*, 1991; and the Government's response, issued as a White Paper, *The EC Draft Directive on the Landfill of Waste*, 1992. (See also DoE Circular 17/89: *Landfill Sites: Development Control*, and PPG 14: *Development on Unstable Land*.)

On environmental audit and environmental accounting, see Elkington 1990, Civic Trust 1991, United Nations 1992 (which has an international bibliography).

On climate change, see *The Potential Effects of Climate Change in the United Kingdom*, HMSO, 1991; *Climate Change: Report on United Kingdom National Programme for Limiting Carbon Dioxide Emissions*, DoE, 1992; *Climate Change: Our National Programme for $CO_2$ Emissions – A Discussion Document*, DoE, 1992; Owens and Cope, *Land Use Planning Policy and Climate Change*, HMSO, 1992.

More generally, the DoE have issued an extremely useful statistical report: *The UK Environment*, HMSO, 1992.

# 7

# HERITAGE PLANNING

Buildings, towns, monuments and other historic sites give us a sense of place. They remind us of our past, of how our forebears lived, and how our culture and society developed. They tell us what earlier generations aspired to and achieved.

White Paper, *This Common Inheritance*, 1990

'Heritage' is the fashionable word for the national inheritance of historic buildings and features of the landscape. Much has happened in heritage planning in recent years in addition to the acclamation of the term. In keeping with tradition, the first and most obvious changes were institutional: the establishment of the Historic Buildings and Monuments Commission (English Heritage) by the National Heritage Act of 1983; and the different arrangements for Scotland and Wales, with executive agencies being located in the Scottish Office (Historic Scotland) and the Welsh Office (Cadw: Welsh Historic Monuments). The latest change has been the move of responsibilities for heritage property, in 1992, from the DoE to the newly established Department of National Heritage.[1]

Major institutional change is often a politically adept technique of seeming to be doing something substantive while only giving the appearance of so doing. In this case, however, the institutional change has been part of a new commitment to preserving and enhancing the historic legacy. Perhaps the clearest evidence of this is the doubling of heritage expenditure by the central government between 1986 and 1994.[2]

Many governmental and voluntary organisations play a role in heritage planning. At the central level, in addition to government departments and the main heritage agencies (listed above) there are the National Heritage Fund, the Royal Armouries, the Historic Royal Palaces Agency, and the Royal Commission on the Historical Monuments of England. Scotland and Wales both have an Ancient Monuments Board, and a Historic Buildings Council which act as advisory bodies to the departments, and a Royal Commission on Historical Monuments. Current programmes aim to:

- promote the enjoyment and understanding of historic buildings and places;
- identify the more significant examples of the nation's heritage;
- protect and, so far as practicable, preserve the built heritage;
- maximise the private sector contribution to the conservation of the built heritage, and to get good value for the public money invested; and
- improve the management and public enjoyment of the Royal Parks.[3]

## CONSERVATION

Britain has a remarkable wealth of historic buildings, but changing economic and social conditions often turn this legacy into a liability. The cost of maintenance, the financial attractions of redevelopment, the need for urban renewal, the roads programme, and similar factors often threaten buildings which are of architectural or historic interest.

This is a field in which voluntary organisations have been particularly active. The first of these dates back to 1877 when William Morris (horrified at the proposed 'restoration' of Tewkesbury Abbey) inspired the founding of the Society for the Protection of Ancient Buildings.[4] In 1895, another prominent figure in Victorian history, Octavia Hill, founded the National Trust (its full name is the National Trust for Places of Historic Interest or Natural Beauty). Other organisations were established as threats to the heritage developed. The Georgian Group was founded in 1937, after the Commissioners for Crown Lands demolished Nash's Regent Street and threatened to do the same with Carlton House Terrace. The widespread destruction of Victorian and Edwardian buildings led to the creation of the Victorian Society in 1958. The Thirties Society, which was set up in 1979 to safeguard inter-war architecture, nearly saved the Firestone factory on the Great West Road, but was thwarted by the developers (Trafalgar House) which moved the bulldozers in over the August 1980 holiday weekend before the procedure for 'spot listing' had been completed. There are now numerous such heritage organisations, several of which have statutory consultee status on proposals to demolish listed buildings.

The first state action came in 1882 with the Ancient Monuments Act, but this was important chiefly because it acknowledged the interest of the State in the preservation of ancient monuments. Such preservation as was achieved under this Act (and similar Acts passed in the following thirty years) resulted from the goodwill and cooperation of private owners. A major landmark in the evolution of policy in this area was the establishment, in 1908, of the three Royal Commissions on the Historical Monuments (of England, Scotland, and Wales). They had (and still have) the same purpose,[5] exemplified by the original terms of reference of the English Commission:

> to make an inventory of the Ancient and Historical Monuments and constructions connected with or illustrative of the contemporary culture, civilisation and conditions of life of the people of England, from the earliest times to the year 1700 and to specify those that seem most worthy of preservation.

The quotation is instructive: the emphasis is on preservation and on 'ancient'. There was no concern for anything built after 1700: a prejudice which M. Ross (1991: 14) notes was typical of the time. Changing attitudes were reflected in 1921 when the year 1714 was substituted for 1700! The date was advanced to 1850 after the end of the Second World War, and in 1963 an end-date was abolished. The Commissions were established to record monuments, not to safeguard them. It was not until 1913 that general powers were provided to enable local authorities or the Commissioners of Works to purchase an ancient monument or (a surprising innovation in an era of sacrosanct property rights) to assume 'guardianship' of a monument, thereby preventing destruction or damage while leaving 'ownership' in private hands.

Major legislative changes were made in the 1940s, though in practice the most important innovation was the establishment of a national survey of historic buildings. This was a huge job (quite beyond the capabilities of the slow-moving Royal Commissions). It was undertaken, county by county, by so-called 'investigators'. (Ross gives an interesting account of how this mammoth job was done, often on a voluntary or near-voluntary basis.) The survey took 22 years and, even then, it was incomplete. This first survey, which ended in 1969, gave statutory protection to almost 120,000 buildings, and non-statutory recognition (but not protection) to a further 137,000 buildings.[6] Given the attitudes of the time, Victorian architecture was almost totally neglected. (The Victorian Society did not come into existence until 1957, after the demolition of the Euston Arch.)

Statutory protection, however, is not sufficient by itself: the owners of historic buildings often need financial assistance if the cost of maintaining old structures is to be met. The issue was highlighted by the Gowers Committee which was appointed in 1950.[7] The Historic Buildings and Ancient Monuments Act of 1953 followed. This established Historic

Building Councils for England, Scotland, and Wales, and introduced grants for preserving houses which were inhabited or 'capable of occupation'.

Further big changes were made in 1983, and later most of the provisions relating to heritage properties were consolidated in the Planning (Listed Building and Conservation Areas) Act 1990, though curiously those relating to ancient monuments are still separate in the Ancient Monuments and Archaeological Areas Act 1979. Responsibility for this area of policy now largely rests with English Heritage, Historic Scotland, and Welsh Historic Monuments.

## ENGLISH HERITAGE (HBMC)

Until the passing of the 1983 National Heritage Act, responsibilities for heritage policy and its execution rested with the DoE. Much the greater part of the work was of an executive character and was, therefore, an obvious candidate for hiving off.[8] The moving spirit behind the establishment of the Historic Buildings and Monuments Commission (generally called English Heritage) was the then Secretary of State for the Environment, Michael Heseltine. Its separate existence gives the field a higher profile and a more effective voice. Its official functions include:

1 making grants to individuals and bodies in respect of historic buildings, conservation areas, town schemes, ancient monuments and for archaeological investigation ('rescue archaeology');
2 acquiring or becoming guardian of ancient monuments and historic buildings;
3 advising the Secretary of State on the selection of buildings for inclusion in the list of buildings of special architectural or historic interest, on the monuments to be added to the schedule of monuments of national importance, and on the designation of areas of archaeological importance;
4 advising the Secretary of State on applications for permission to carry out works to listed buildings and to scheduled monuments;
5 carrying out, or contributing towards the cost of,

research in relation to ancient monuments, historic buildings and conservation areas in England;
6 undertaking archaeological investigation and publishing the results;
7 providing educational facilities and services, instruction and information to the public in relation to ancient monuments, historic buildings and conservation areas in England;
8 making and maintaining records in relation to ancient monuments and historic buildings in England;
9 advising any person in relation to ancient monuments, historic buildings and conservation in England.

Additionally, following the abolition of the GLC, English Heritage has assumed all the special powers previously operated by the Council's Historic Buildings Division. This gives the Commission powers in London that it does not have for the rest of the country, where listed building controls are exercised by district councils or the Secretary of State.[9] The Commission is advised by the Ancient Monuments Advisory Committee and the Historic Buildings Advisory Councils which have taken over the role previously carried out by the Ancient Monuments Board for England and the Historic Buildings Council for England.

## ANCIENT MONUMENTS

The term *ancient monument* is defined very widely: it is 'any scheduled monument' and 'any other monument which in the opinion of the Secretary of State is of public interest by reason of the historic, architectural, traditional, artistic or archaeological interest attaching to it'.[10] This is so broad a definition that it could include almost any building, structure, or site of archaeological interest made or occupied by man at any time.

The legislation requires the Secretary of State to prepare a schedule of monuments which appear to him to be 'of national importance'. In this he is advised by English Heritage and the Ancient Monuments

Boards for Scotland and Wales. This 'scheduling' is a selective and continuing process.[11] It has been in operation for 100 years and, until recently, was proceeding at a very slow rate. English Heritage now has a *Monuments Protection Programme* (MPP) which is evaluating all known archaeological remains. This is expected to significantly increase the number of scheduled monuments.

In 1990, there were 13,000 scheduled sites in England, 5,000 in Scotland, and 2,600 in Wales. It is expected that the unprecedented effort of scheduling all appropriate monuments will be completed by the end of the century. Estimates differ on the number of sites which are worthy of scheduling. The Environment Committee, in their 1987 report, quoted a figure of 600,000, and this is the figure envisaged by the DoE.[12] Others have suggested that the figure should be much higher, and since there is such a huge number of known archaeological sites and monuments, it is not surprising that estimates differ.[13]

It is recognised that the present schedule is not only very incomplete, but also an inadequate and unrepresentative sample of the archaeological heritage. English Heritage's Monuments Protection Programme involves surveying all known archaeological remains in England, and determining which may be suitable for scheduling. It is expected that this will take some ten years. By no means will all remains be scheduled: the criteria are stringent. The DoE comments (in PPG 16) that whether or not these unscheduled sites are preserved 'will depend upon the value of the remains, the commitment of owners of monuments and of the public, and the policies of local authorities'.

The fact that a monument is scheduled does not mean that it will automatically be preserved under all circumstances. It simply ensures that full consideration is given to the case for preservation if any proposal is made which will affect it. Any works have to be approved by the Secretary of State (who receives advice from English Heritage). Such approval is known as *scheduled monument consent*. Where consent is refused, compensation is payable (under certain limited circumstances) if the owner thereby suffers loss. In practice, the great majority of applications for consent are approved, often with conditions attached. The issue here is seen as one of balancing the need to protect the heritage with the rights and responsibilities of farmers, developers, statutory undertakers and other landowners.[14] The legislation also empowers the Secretary of State to acquire (if necessary by compulsion) an ancient monument 'for the purpose of securing its preservation' – a power which applies to any ancient monument, not solely those which have been scheduled.

The Commission manages some 400 monuments on behalf of the Secretary of State; a further 330 are managed by Historic Scotland, and 127 by Welsh Historic Monuments. These are of important historical, archaeological and architectural significance. A very high proportion are of great antiquity, including prehistoric field monuments such as Maiden Castle, prehistoric structures such as Stonehenge, Roman monuments such as Wroxeter and parts of Hadrian's Wall, and a large number of medieval buildings.

## ARCHAEOLOGY

The *areas of archaeological importance* (AAIs) in the title of the 1979 Act represented a new concept. These are areas which the Secretary of State considers 'to merit treatment as such': no further definition is provided. In these areas, developers are required to give six weeks' notice (an *operations notice*) of any works affecting the area, and the 'investigating authority' (e.g the local authority or a university) can hold up operations for a total period of up to six months. The powers are used very sparingly and, to date, only five areas have been designated, comprising the historic centres of Canterbury, Chester, Exeter, Hereford, and York.[15]

On a wider scale, there are similar (though less stringent) provisions which provide an opportunity for the investigation and recording of archaeological remains prior to proposed development. This is known as *rescue archaeology*.[16] It is very different from the scheduling of ancient monuments where the essential aim is preservation. Rescue work in central London has been well publicised. Interest in archaeology has grown greatly in recent years, as has understanding, competence and professionalism. A major indication of the current status is given by PPG 16 which clearly sets out the importance of archaeology:

> Archaeological remains should be seen as a finite and non-renewable resource, in many cases highly fragile and vulnerable to damage and destruction. Appropriate management is therefore essential to ensure that they survive in good condition. In particular, care must be taken to ensure that archaeological remains are not needlessly or thoughtlessly destroyed. They can contain irreplaceable information about our past and the potential for an increase in future knowledge. They are part of our sense of national identity and are valuable both for their own sake and for their role in education, leisure and tourism.

The PPG goes on to make it clear that there is a presumption in favour of the preservation of important remains, whether or not they are scheduled. There is thus a measure of protection over the large number of unscheduled sites which are on the lists maintained by county archaeological officers. (These are known as SMRs: *County Sites and Monuments Records*.) Such sites are a 'material consideration' in dealing with planning applications.

Many local authorities make provision in their development plans for the protection of archaeological interests (Redman 1990: 89), often with good cooperation from large developers. The image of archaeological excavations in areas undergoing redevelopment is one of outright war. Given the conflicting interests involved this is not surprising. What is perhaps surprising is the extent to which some developers are prepared to go to assist rescue archaeology, and even to fund it. Sometimes, this goes far beyond any statutory requirement (Hobley 1987: 25). A useful mechanism for liaison is provided by the British Archaeologists and Developers Liaison Group. This is an organisation promoted by the British Property Federation and the Standing Conference of Archaeological Unit Managers (itself a representative body of some 75 professional archaeological units). This has issued a code of practice.

However, rescue archaeology is, at best, of limited benefit: it is certainly far inferior to preservation *in situ*. The cost of this, however, can be enormous and, given the incredible range of archaeological remains in Britain, some selection is inevitable.

## LISTED BUILDINGS

Under planning legislation, and quite separate from the provisions relating to monuments, the central departments maintain lists of buildings of *special architectural or historic interest*.[17] The preparation of these lists has been a mammoth task which has progressed slowly because of inadequate funding and (the underlying factor) a lack of public interest. Added impetus, however, was given by events such as the declaration of European Architectural Heritage Year in 1975 and, less joyfully but perhaps more effectively by the already-mentioned demolition of the Firestone factory. The latter precipitated action by the Secretary of State, Michael Heseltine, to accelerate the survey – including the employment of private architectural firms. 'It is no exaggeration to say that Firestone was a sacrificial lamb' (M. Ross 1991: 44).

Listing is a continuing process, not only for additional buildings but also for updating information on existing listed buildings, particularly in terms of their condition. In addition to the ongoing survey programme, individual buildings can be spot-listed. This arises because of individual requests, often precipitated by the threat of alteration or demolition. English Heritage and the DoE regard the number of spot-listing requests as an indicator of the completeness of the lists. At the beginning of the 1990s, around 3,000 requests for spot-listing were made each year. This number is expected to decrease as progress is made with making the lists more comprehensive.

There are two objectives in *listing*. First, it is intended to provide guidance to local planning authorities in carrying out their planning functions. For example, in planning redevelopment, local authorities will take into account listed buildings in the area. Second, and more directly effective, when a building is listed, no demolition or alteration which would materially alter it can be undertaken by the owner without the approval of the local authority. This is technically termed *listed building consent*.

In considering the role of this regulatory system, it is important to appreciate what is meant by the term 'conservation'. Though often used synonymously with 'preservation', there is an important difference. Preservation implies maintaining the original in an unchanged state, but conservation embraces elements of change and even enhancement. To provide an economic base for the conservation of an old building, new uses often have to be sought. It is quite impossible to conserve all buildings in their original state irrespective of cost, and there frequently has to be a compromise between 'the value of the old and the needs of the new' (M. Ross 1991: 92). Thus 'new uses for old buildings' is a major factor in conservation, and it necessarily implies a degree of change, even if this is restricted to the interior.[18] (It was no doubt with this necessity for change in mind that the CPRE altered the second word in its name from 'preservation' to 'protection'.) Again, for conservation purposes it may be necessary to enhance a site to cater for public enjoyment. (Stonehenge is a good example.) The difference is more than one of name.

Applications for listed building consent have to be advertised, and any representation must be taken into account by the local authority before it reaches its decision. Where demolition is involved, English local authorities have to notify English Heritage, the appropriate local amenity society, and a number of other bodies, namely, the Ancient Monuments Society, the Council for British Archaeology, the Georgian Group, the Society for the Protection of Ancient Buildings, the Victorian Society, and the Royal Commission on Historical Monuments. Scottish and Welsh authorities are required to notify their respective Royal Commissions on Ancient and Historical Monuments. Again any representations have to be taken into account when the application is being considered.

If, after all this, the local authority intends to grant consent for the demolition (or, in certain cases, the alteration) of a listed building, it has to refer the application to the DoE so that it can be considered

for 'call in' and decision by the Secretary of State. English Heritage advise on this, and in most cases DoE accept its advice. It is the Department's policy that consent applications should generally be decided by local authorities: in 1991/92, 2,346 applications for consent were referred, of which only 20 were called in (National Audit Office, HC 132, 1992: 14).

Conditions can be imposed on a listed building consent in the same way as is done with planning permissions. Indeed, the legislation requires that all consents be subject to a time limit for implementation (again as is done with planning permissions). The type of conditions that can be imposed are set out in Circular 8/87, and include the preservation of particular features, the making good of damage caused by works of alteration, and the granting of access (before work commences) to a named body to enable a photographic record or measured drawings to be made.

All these provisions apply to listed buildings, but local authorities can serve a *building preservation notice* on an unlisted building. This has the effect of protecting the building for six months, thus giving time for the DoE to consider (on the advice of English Heritage) whether or not it should be listed. For owners and developers who wish to be assured that they will not be unexpectedly made subject to listing, application can be made to the LPA for a *certificate of immunity from listing*.[19]

With a listed building, the presumption is in favour of preservation. It is an offence to demolish or to alter a listed building unless listed building consent has been obtained. This is different from the general position in relation to planning permission where an offence arises only after the enforcement procedure has been invoked. Fines for illegal works to listed buildings are related to the financial benefit expected by the offender.[20]

The legislation also provides a deterrent against deliberate neglect of historic buildings. This was one way in which astute owners could circumvent the earlier statutory provisions: a building could be neglected to such an extent that demolition was unavoidable, thus giving the owner the possibility of reaping the development value of the site. In such cases, the local authority can now compulsorily acquire the building at a restricted price, technically known as *minimum compensation.* If the Secretary of State approves, the compensation is assessed on the assumption that neither planning permission nor listed building consent would be given for any works to the building except those for restoring it to, and maintaining it in, a proper state of repair; in short, all development value is excluded.

The strength of these powers (and others not detailed here)[21] reflect the concern which is felt at the loss of historic buildings. However, they are not all of this penal nature. Indeed, ministerial guidance has emphasised the need for a positive and comprehensive approach. Grants are available towards the cost of repair and maintenance.[22] Local authorities can also purchase properties by agreement, possibly with Exchequer aid. Furthermore, an owner of a building who is refused listed building consent can, in certain circumstances, serve a notice on the local authority requiring it to purchase the property. This is known as a *listed building purchase notice.* The issue to be decided here is whether the land has become 'incapable of reasonably beneficial use'. It is not sufficient to show that it is of less use to the owner in its present state than if developed.

## CONSERVATION AREAS

Of particular importance in heritage planning is the emphasis on areas, as distinct from individual buildings, of architectural or historic interest. Statutory recognition of the area concept was introduced by the Civic Amenities Act 1967 (promoted as a private member's bill by Duncan Sandys, President of the Civic Trust, and passed with Government backing). Local planning authorities have a duty 'to determine which parts of their area are areas of special architectural or historic interest, the character of which it is desirable to preserve or enhance', and to designate such areas as *conservation areas.* When a conservation area has been designated, special attention has to be paid in all planning decisions to the preservation or enhancement of its character or appearance. Demolition is controlled, and there are special provisions for preserving trees. There is an important (though inadequately implemented) duty to seek 'the preservation and enhancement' of conservation areas (Reade 1992).

The statutory provisions relating to the establishment of conservation areas are remarkably loose: there is no formal designation procedure, there is no requirement for a formal public inquiry (though proposals have to be put before a public meeting), and there is no specification of what qualifies for conservation area status. Circular 8/87 notes that 'these areas will naturally be of many different kinds':

> They may be large or small, from whole town areas to squares, terraces and smaller groups of buildings. They will often be centred on listed buildings, but not always. Pleasant groups of other buildings, open spaces, trees, and historic street patterns, a village green or features of historic or archaeological interest may also contribute to the special character of an area. Areas appropriate for designation as conservation areas will be found in almost every town and many villages. It is the character of areas, rather than individual buildings, that [section 60 of the Planning (Listed Buildings and Conservation Areas) Act 1990] seeks to preserve or enhance.

In practice, conservation areas are often dealt with in the preparation of development plans, and a DoE Consultation Paper has proposed that this 'integration' with the plan-making process should be formalised.[23]

The number of conservation areas has grown dramatically: in 1991, there were over 7,000 in England, 350 in Wales, and 550 in Scotland.[24] Over a million buildings are in these areas. Indeed, one commentator has suggested that perhaps a 'saturation point' has been reached in that the resources are simply not available for 'enhancing' such a large number of areas,[25] and there seems to be a widespread view that less attention should be given to designating conservation areas, and a lot more to managing them.[26]

A special type of conservation area is that covered by a *town scheme.* This is an historic area in which conservation and improvement is jointly funded by a local authority and English Heritage. While other grant schemes focus on buildings, this form of grant aid serves wider environmental purposes.

Town schemes cover not only the centres of the classic historic towns but also hundreds of smaller towns, and range from small domestic terraces to large warehouses. Increasingly, additional demands are coming from the run-down inner city areas, where grants at a comparatively low level can give a significant stimulus to urban regeneration and improve the quality of life for those living or working there.[27]

English Heritage grants are also sometimes combined with funding from other sources, such as City Grant (discussed in Chapter 9). Currently, English Heritage (1992b) have a policy of making conservation area grants only in 'areas which combine townscape quality with financial, material and social need'.

In spite of all these powers, many listed buildings are at risk. An English Heritage report showed that 36,700 listed buildings (7 per cent of the total) are at risk from neglect, and twice as many are in a vulnerable condition and need repair if they are not to fall into the 'at risk' category.[28] Of course, most listed buildings are in private ownership, and the owners may well not feel the respect for their buildings which preservationists do; or they simply may be unable to afford to maintain them adequately. Advice, grants, and default measures cannot achieve all that might be hoped and, though a precious building can be taken into public ownership, this is essentially a matter of last resort.

## CRITERIA FOR LISTING HISTORIC BUILDINGS

Criteria for listing historic buildings are divided into four groups:

1 All buildings built before 1700 which survive in anything like their original condition are listed;
2 Most buildings of 1700 to 1840, though selection is necessary;
3 Between 1840 and 1914, only buildings of definite quality and character are listed and the selection is designed to include the principal works of the principal architects;
4 Between 1914 and 1939, selected buildings of high quality are listed.

In choosing buildings, particular attention is paid to 'special value within certain types, either for architectural or planning reasons or as illustrating social and economic history'; to technological innovation or virtuosity (for instance, cast-iron prefabrication or the early use of concrete); to any association with well-known characters or events; and 'group value', especially as examples of town planning (for instance, squares, terraces or model villages).[29]

The buildings are classified in grades to show their relative importance as follows:

– *Grade I*: buildings of exceptional interest (only about 2 per cent of all listed buildings).
– *Grade II\**: particularly important buildings of more than special interest (some 4 per cent of the total; the asterisk distinguishes this small group of buildings from the remainder).
– *Grade II*: buildings of special interest which warrant every effort being made to preserve them (the majority).[30]

Scotland has for long had a rolling thirty-year rule under which any building of that age could be considered for listing. This was initially thought to be too problematic in relation to the much larger number of buildings that would be covered by such a rule in England. How was the quality of buildings to be assessed over such a short time period? Would apparent 'successes' soon be seen as 'failures' – and vice versa. There have been marked changes in attitudes to different architectural styles. Perhaps the most famous comes from Paris, where the Eiffel Tower was once described in terms of 'the grotesque mercantile imaginings of a constructor of machines', but is now 'the beloved signature of the Parisian skyline and an officially designated monument to boot' (Costonis 1989: 64). Many buildings have been demolished which would today attract vociferous defence.[31] On the other hand, much more modern architecture would have difficulty in finding a place in the hearts of those who support the protection of good inter-war buildings. Clearly, this an area where attitudes differ and firm guidelines are far from easy to determine – as is also the case with contemporary design and amenity guidelines. The DoE, however, hit upon an ingenious solution: in 1987, it announced that the thirty-year rule would be adopted, but that the first candidates would be selected by public competition. At the same time, going one better than the Scots, it was agreed to list outstanding buildings that were only ten to thirty-years old if there was an immediate threat to them. The results are interesting:

> The first modern building was listed ahead of the competition because of the threat of redevelopment. This was Sir Alfred Richardson's Bracken House, the *Financial Times* building in central London, which was listed in August 1988. Following the competition, and with the agreement of English Heritage, 18 further postwar buildings were added to the list, among them the Royal Festival Hall, Coventry Cathedral, and the Stockwell Bus Garage.
>
> (M. Ross 1991: 49)

There is an enormous range in the character of listed buildings, of which one of the most novel is the beloved old red telephone kiosk. British Telecom is replacing these with models of contemporary design. Opposition and lobbying resulted in a number of kiosks of unusual design being listed. Listings were later extended, but with strict criteria of special architectural or historic interest. There are now well over a thousand listed kiosks.

As these examples show, public opinion (when aroused) can play an important part in this planning field. The same is true with listed buildings under threat, of which St Pancras Station is perhaps the most renowned. By 1990, there were 400,000 listed buildings in England, 37,000 in Scotland, and 14,000 in Wales. It seems clear that both official policy and the public support that is essential to this is developing significantly — both for ancient monuments and for listed buildings: in short, for the heritage.[32]

Some questions remain, however, and they are likely to come to the fore as local planning authorities continue to develop their competencies in the area. One question is the justification for the existence of two regimes: one for the listing of historic buildings and the other for the scheduling of ancient monuments and archaeological remains. With historic buildings, some categories are automatically protected,

while ancient monuments are protected only if they accord with some concept of national importance. (Some buildings may be both scheduled and listed!) Other questions relate to the division of responsibilities between planning authorities and the central government and, in particular, the degree of the integration between heritage planning and the other functions of local planning authorities. This is not the place to enter into these issues, but they should be noted. They may well assume greater importance in the future.[33]

## CHURCHES

The situation regarding 'ecclesiastical buildings' is exceptional and also complicated. In essence, there is what is technically termed 'the ecclesiastical exemption' from listed building control.

By way of background, it is worth noting the statistics which were given to the Environment Committee during its 1986–87 inquiry: the Church of England owns 16,700 churches, of which no less than 8,500 are pre-Reformation, and 12,000 are statutorily listed (2,675 in the highest grade). The Church introduced measures to control demolition over 700 years ago, and has been regularly inspecting churches for 300 years. It spends at least £55m a year on the upkeep and maintenance of its buildings (mainly funded by its congregations) compared with about £4m which comes through state aid. The result is that 'a listed Church of England church has a chance of avoiding demolition nearly three times better than a listed secular building'.

There are two parallel statutory systems of control over Church of England churches: the Church's system, and the secular system. The Church's system is much stricter and more comprehensive. It involves regular inspection of every church, and embraces not only the fabric of the buildings, but their contents and churchyards. There are two separate statutory procedures applying to parish churches (whether listed or unlisted), according to whether they are in use or redundant.

Churches in use are subject to an elaborate system

of inspecting and reporting at the local level, and to monitoring at higher levels: by Diocesan Advisory Committees at diocesan level, and by the Council for the Care of Churches at the national level.

Redundant churches are safeguarded by the Pastoral Measure 1983 which provides procedures for deciding whether a church is still required for worship, and, if not, what the future of the building should be. A Redundant Churches Fund finances the management, maintenance and repair of churches judged of sufficient architectural or historic importance. The fund receives 70 per cent of its grant from the DoE, and the remainder from the Church Commissioners. In 1992, 270 churches were vested in the Fund.[34] A review of the operation and financing of the Fund was published in 1990 (Wilding 1990). Grant aid for churches in use is provided by English Heritage.

Until recently, cathedrals were outside any planning procedure and, despite their huge popularity with visitors (and contribution to tourism), were not eligible for grant aid. A separate system of controls over building works was introduced by the Care of Cathedrals Measure 1990.[35] This is administered by the individual cathedrals jointly with a Cathedrals Fabric Commission in consultation with English Heritage. Grant aid was also introduced in 1990, when English Heritage was allocated an extra £11.5m per year for three years for this purpose. English Heritage carried out a survey of the 61 Church of England and Roman Catholic cathedrals in England to assemble information on the care and management of the fabric and to facilitate a plan for grant-aid.[36]

All church buildings are subject to normal planning control over, for example, changes of use and significant alterations. They are also listed in exactly the same way as other buildings of special historic or architectural interest. However, because of the Church's separate statutory procedure, listed building consent is not required for churches in use. Such consent is required, however, for alterations to redundant churches, though not if demolition is carried out pursuant to a scheme under the Pastoral Measure 1983.

Under an agreement with the Secretary of State, the Church Commissioners do not proceed with the demolition of a listed redundant church, or an unlisted one in a conservation area, without providing the opportunity for the Secretary of State to hold a non-statutory public inquiry. The findings and the Secretary of State's views are taken into account by the Commissioners.

A government review of the ecclesiastical exemption completed at the beginning of 1993 led to a decision to restrict the exemption to churches for which there is a willingness to subscribe to a proposed code of practice. The code includes the requirement that all works to a listed church building which would affect its character should be submitted for the approval of an independent body, and that there should be consultation with the LPA, English Heritage, and national amenity societies.[37]

## THE NATIONAL HERITAGE MEMORIAL FUND

In 1946, a National Land Fund was established from the sale of war stores as a memorial to those who lost their lives during the war. Some £50m of Exchequer moneys were allocated to the fund for use to assist organisations whose purpose was to promote appreciation and enjoyment of the countryside. The money was used for the purchase by the Secretary of State of buildings of outstanding architectural or historic interest, together with their contents. The fund was raided by the Exchequer in 1957 and became moribund.

> The folly of this was illustrated by the controversial sale of the assets of the Mentmore estate in 1977 which exposed the need for a fund which could exercise similar powers to those of the Secretary of State, with sufficient resources, and without excessive central government control.[38]

This is what the National Heritage Act of 1980 does: 'There shall be a fund known as the National Heritage Memorial Fund, to be a memorial to those who have died for the United Kingdom'. In addition to normal Exchequer payments into the fund, further payments can be made in relation to property accepted in satisfaction of tax debts. The fund can make loans or grants for any property (in the widest sense of the term) which is 'of outstanding scenic, historic, architectural or scientific interest'.

In 1991/92, the Trustees spent some £15m on a hundred projects. These included £5.4m for the establishment of a new charitable foundation to own and run Burton Constable Hall in Humberside. A further £1m was used for the acquisition of the Fortescue Estate (4,260 acres) in the Exmoor national park. This adjoins previously acquired land, and results in the majority of Exmoor now being 'in the safe hands of the national park authority'.[39]

## PRESERVATION OF TREES AND WOODLANDS

Trees are a delight in themselves; they also have the remarkable quality of hiding developments which are best out of sight. Trees are clearly, so far as town and country planning is concerned, a matter of amenity. Indeed, the powers which local authorities have with regard to trees can be exercised only if it is 'expedient in the interests of amenity'. Where a local authority is satisfied that it is expedient, it can make a *tree preservation order*, applicable to trees, groups of trees, or woodlands. Such an order can prohibit the cutting down, topping, or lopping of trees except with the consent of the local planning authority.

Mere preservation, however, can lead eventually to decay and thus defeats its object. To prevent this, a local authority can make replanting obligatory when it gives permission for trees to be felled. The aim is to avoid any clash between good forestry and the claims of amenity. But the timber of woodlands always has a claim to be treated as a commercial crop, and though the making of a tree preservation order does not necessarily involve the owner in any financial loss (isolated trees or groups of trees are usually planted expressly as an amenity), there are occasions when it does.

Yet, though woodlands are primarily a timber crop from which the owner is entitled to benefit, two principles have been laid down which qualify this. First, 'the national interest demands that woodlands should be managed in accordance with the principles of good forestry', and second, where they are of amenity value, the owner has 'a public duty to act with reasonable regard for amenity aspects'. It follows that a refusal to permit felling or the imposition of conditions on operations which are either contrary to the principles of good forestry or destructive of amenity ought not to carry any compensation rights. But where there is a clash between these two principles, compensation is payable.

Thus, in a case where the 'principles of good forestry' dictate that felling should take place, but this would result in too great a sacrifice of amenity, the owner can claim compensation for the loss which he suffers. Normally, a compromise is reached whereby the felling is deferred or phased. The commercial felling of timber is subject to licence from the Forestry Commission, and special arrangements exist for consultation between the Commission, the central department and the local planning authority.

Planning powers go considerably further than simply enabling local authorities to preserve trees. Planning permission can be made subject to the condition that trees are planted, and local authorities themselves have power to plant trees on any land in their area. With the increasing vulnerability of trees and woodlands to urban development and the needs of modern farming, wider powers and more Exchequer aid have been provided by successive statutes. Local planning authorities are now *required* to ensure that conditions (preferably reinforced by tree preservation orders) are imposed for the protection of existing trees and for the planting of new ones.

Coordination of voluntary effort in relation to the promotion of tree planting and the protection of trees is effected through the Tree Council. This is 'a forum for some twenty-five national voluntary organisations and professional associations with a central aim to promote the conservation, planting and good maintenance of amenity trees and woodlands'.[40]

## AMENITY

'Amenity' is one of the key concepts in British town and country planning: yet nowhere in the legislation is it defined. The legislation merely states that 'if it appears to a local planning authority that it is expedient in the interests of amenity', they may take certain action, in relation, for example, to unsightly neglected waste land[41] or to the preservation of trees. It is also one of the factors that may need to be taken into account in controlling advertisements and in determining whether a discontinuance order should be made. It is a term widely used in planning refusals and appeals: indeed the phrase 'injurious to the interests of amenity' has become part of the stock-in-trade jargon of the planning world.[42] But like the proverbial elephant, amenity is easier to recognise than to define, with the important difference that, though all would be agreed that an elephant is such, there is considerable scope for disagreement on the degree and importance of amenities: which amenities should be preserved, in what way they should be preserved and how much expense (public or private) is justified.

The problem is relatively straightforward in so far as trees are concerned. It is much more acute in connection with electricity pylons, yet the Central Electricity Generating Board is specifically charged not only with maintaining an efficient and co-ordinated supply of electricity but also with the preservation of amenity. Here the question is not merely one of sensitivity but also of the enormous additional cost of preserving amenities by placing cables underground.

Apart from problems of cost, there is the problem of determining how much control the public will accept. Poor architecture, ill-conceived schemes, mock-Tudor frontages may upset the planning officer, but how much regulation of this type of 'amenity-injury' will be publicly acceptable? And how far can negative controls succeed in raising public standards? Here emphasis has been laid on design bulletins, design awards and such ventures as those of the Civic Trust, a body whose object is 'to promote beauty and fight ugliness in town, village and countryside'. Nevertheless, LPAs have power not only to prevent developments which would clash with amenity (for example, the siting of a repair garage in a residential area) but also to reject badly designed developments which are not intrinsically harmful. Indeed, outline planning permission for a proposal is often given on the condition that detailed plans and appearances meet the approval of the authority.

Since the 1950s, there has been a marked sharpening of interest in amenity, caused partly by the rapid rate of development, and an awareness of the inadequacy of the planning system automatically to preserve and enhance amenity. The Transport Act of 1968, for instance, enables the use of a road by vehicles to be prohibited on amenity grounds for certain periods of the day. Perhaps the most striking provision, found in the Countryside (Scotland) Act 1967 and the Countryside Act 1968, is that which requires every minister, government department and public body to have regard to the desirability of conserving the natural beauty and amenity of the countryside in all their functions relating to land. Lawyers may rightly point out that this does not constitute, of itself, an effective restriction on any statutory power or discretion, but it is an important statement of policy, and one which the statutory and voluntary guardians of amenity will seize upon whenever it is infringed. There is more to planning than law.

## GOOD DESIGN

The national heritage is created in part by good design. Much of the built heritage is worth preserving because it is well designed. It is therefore of more than contemporary concern that new buildings should be well designed. Nevertheless, the extent to which 'good' design can be fostered by the planning system (or any other system) is problematic.

Good design is an elusive quality which cannot easily be defined. In the words of Sir William Holford (1953),

> design cannot be taught by correspondence; words are inadequate, and being inadequate may then become misleading, or even dangerous. For the competent designer a handbook on design is unnecessary, and for the incompetent it is almost useless as a medium of instruction.

Yet local authorities have to pass judgement on the design merits of thousands of planning proposals each year, and there is continuous pressure from professional bodies for higher design standards to be imposed.

There is a long and inconclusive history to design control (well set out by John Punter, in various publications between 1985 and 1992). A 1959 statement by the MHLG stressed that it was impossible to lay down rules to define good design.[43] Developers were recommended to seek the advice of an architect (presumably a 'good' one!). The policy should be to avoid stifling 'initiative or experiment in design'; but 'shoddy or badly proportioned or out of place designs' should be rejected – with clear reasons being given. The Ministry added:

> Two questions arise on design. The first is whether the design is bad in itself: fussy or ill-proportioned, or downright ugly. The second is whether, if the design is not bad in itself, it would be bad on a particular site: right out of scale with close neighbours (which does not mean that it need be similar to neighbouring designs), an urban design in a rural setting, or a jarring design or the wrong materials in a harmonious scene.

The reader is referred to Punter's work for the fascinating details of the continuing story, recounting the personal achievements of Duncan Sandys, particularly in founding the Civic Trust in 1957, and later in promoting the Civic Amenities Act; the high buildings controversy ('sunlight equals health'); the problem of protecting views of St Paul's Cathedral; the arguments over the Shell Tower (which prompted the quip that the best view of the Shell Tower was to be obtained from its roof); the publication of Worskett's *The Character of Towns* (1969); the Matthew–Skillington Report on *Promotion of High Standards of Architectural Design* which led to the appointment of a Chief Architect in the Property Services Agency; the property boom and a spate of books bearing titles such as *The Rape of Britain* (Amery and Cruikshank 1975) and *The Sack of Bath* (Fergusson 1973); the Essex *Design Guide for Residential Areas* (1973) – 'the most influential local planning authority publication ever'; and (in 1978) the attempt to prevent the building of the National Westminster Tower; and so on.[44]

New contexts emerged with the return of the Conservative Government in 1979, and there was the unprincely attack in 1984 by Prince Charles on the 'monstrous carbuncle' of the proposed extension to the National Gallery, and the 'giant glass stump' of the Mies van der Rohe office block adjacent to the Mansion House (described by one architect – whose name I will not repeat – as a building which would be 'unsurpassed in elegance and economy of form'). The Prince followed up his criticisms with 'a personal view of architecture' spelling out, with telling illustrations, how 'we can do better'.[45]

In his case-study of office development control in Reading, Punter (1985) demonstrates the interesting point that it is only since the late 1970s that the local authority 'have begun to influence the full aesthetic impact of office buildings, though they have controlled height, floorspace and functional considerations since 1947'. Other conclusions are that the study shows that:

> aesthetic considerations do not operate in a vacuum: they are merely one set of considerations amongst many in deciding whether a development gets planning permission. In the case of office development, despite its visual impact, the control of floorspace and the provision of associated facilities and land uses have been higher order goals in Reading . . . aesthetic considerations are inevitably the first to be sacrificed in the cause of 'speed and efficiency' in decision-making, by clients, developers, architects and planners . . . There is a lack of design and architectural skills within the control section of the planning authority, but while its presence would strengthen the planning effort, its scope would be severely constrained by wider policy constraints, by general manpower shortages and, most of all perhaps, by the relevant circulars and the appeal process.
>
> (Punter 1985)

This dismal conclusion is corroborated by the studies of Booth and Beer (1983). They found that nearly two-thirds of all permissions granted (86 per cent in the case of residential permissions) 'carried conditions that were intended to modify the landscape design, layout and architectural detailing of the developments'. However, the conditions were frequently vague and not site-specific. Enforcement was lax. Many applications were considered 'without anybody fully trained in design having been involved in their processing'. The suggestion is made that 'this may well be a factor in the generally poor quality and particularly the monotony of the new environments which can be observed in many parts of Britain'.

The Conservative administration of 1979 started off with a strong bias against design controls, and the views of the Secretary of State (Michael Heseltine), which had been expressed at the Town and Country Planning Summer School, were reproduced in (the now withdrawn) DoE Circular 22/80:

> Far too many of those involved in the system – whether the planning officer or the amateur on the planning committee – have tried to impose their standards quite unnecessarily on what individuals want to do . . . Democracy as a system of government I will defend against all comers but as an arbiter of taste or as a judge of aesthetic or artistic standards it falls short of a far less controlled system of individual, corporate or institutional patronage and initiative.

Mr Heseltine may have been expressing a strong personal view here, but the official policy clearly reflects it. The 1980 Circular continued:

> Planning authorities should recognise that aesthetics is an extremely subjective matter. They should not therefore impose their tastes on developers simply because they believe them to be superior. Developers should not be compelled to conform to the fashion of the moment at the expense of individuality, originality or traditional styles. Nor should they be asked to adopt designs which are unpopular with their customers or clients.

The debate continued, however, and the DoE prepared a draft Circular which attempted to steer a middle course. This came to little: when published (as Circular 31/85) it consisted largely of sections of the 1980 Circular, accompanied by an emphasis on the fact that 'a large proportion of planning appeals involve detailed design matters' and that 'far too many planning applications are delayed because the planning authority seeks to impose detailed design alterations'.

The latest instalment is an annex to the revised PPG 1 (based on a draft prepared jointly by the RIBA and RTPI) which tries to square the circle by advising that, on the one hand:

> The appearance of proposed development and its relationship to its surroundings are material considerations, and those who determine planning applications and appeals should have regard to them in reaching their decisions.

On the other hand:

> Good design should be the aim of all involved in the development process, but it is primarily the responsibility of designers and their clients . . . Planning authorities should reject obviously poor designs [which are out of scale or character with their surroundings]. But aesthetic judgments are [to some extent] subjective, and authorities should not impose their taste on applicants for planning permission simply because they believe it to be superior.

This statement went through several versions before being finalised. (The phrases in square brackets were added after the consultation stage.)[46]

## UPDATE

A report by the Association of County Archaeological Officers (1993) criticises the shortcomings of the present legislation and argues that it is deficient in emergency powers for scheduling, compulsory repair and compulsory acquisition; in the lack of provision for a county class on monuments (which though not of national significance, are of county importance); in ineffective means of dealing with areas as well as sites; in prosecution and enforcement procedures; in class consents; and in its relationship with other legislation. It recommends major amending legislation which would also bring scheduled monument control within the scope of the Planning Acts.

An extensive review of historic preservation policy in Wales is to be found in HC Welsh Affairs Committee, *The Preservation of Historic Buildings and Ancient Monuments: 2nd Report of the Welsh Affairs Committee, Session 1992–93*, HC 403 (1992–93), HMSO, 1993.

Three English agencies have collaborated in publishing *Conservation Issues in Strategic Plans* (Countryside Commission, English Heritage, and English Nature, 1993). A report has been published by the RTPI on *Conservation in the Built Environment* (1993).

The Secretary of State for National Heritage has for the first time issued a compulsory purchase order for a listed building: the St Ann's Hotel in Buxton, Derbyshire (Grant, *Encyclopedia: Monthly Bulletin*, April 1993, p. 4).

## NOTES

1 To ensure the necessary coordination of conservation with planning policy, formal jurisdiction for certain types of heritage casework (such as decisions on call-in of listed buildings and conservation area consents) remain with the DoE. For details, see DoE Circular 20/92.

2 *DoE Annual Report 1992*: part A.4.

3 *DoE Annual Report 1992*: 39.

4 This and subsequent references to the history of preservation are based on M. Ross 1991. Ross was former head of the Listing Branch of the DoE. His book is an excellent, sympathetic and informative account of heritage planning.

5 Revised Royal Warrants were issued in 1992.

6 Many of these are now statutorily protected, and form part of a total of around a half-million.

7 The terms of reference of the Gowers Committee were to consider 'what arrangements might be made for the preservation, maintenance and use of houses of outstanding historic or architectural interest which might not otherwise be preserved, including, where desirable, the preservation of a house and its contents as a unity'.

8 See the discussion on *The Next Steps* programme in Chapter 2.

9 English Heritage announced in 1992 that it was proposing to transfer its powers with respect to Grade II buildings to the London boroughs under an agreed phased programme. See *Managing England's Heritage: Setting our Priorities for the 1990s*; and the *Consultation Paper on the Implementation of Changes in the Role of English Heritage in Greater London*, both issued by English Heritage in 1992.

10 Ancient Monuments and Archaeological Areas Act 1979, section 61(12). The term 'schedule' originates from the Ancient Monument Protection Act 1882 which provided for the protection of 29 monuments which were set out in a *schedule* to the Act. The term has persisted.

11 The information in this section is taken from the annual reports of English Heritage; DoE PPG 16; the National Audit Office report *Protecting and Managing England's Heritage Property* (1992), the evidence given to the HC Committee of Public Accounts on *Protecting and*

*Managing England's Heritage Property* (1992), and M. Ross 1991.

12 House of Commons Environment Committee, *Historic Buildings and Ancient Monuments*, 1987. See also the statement by David Trippier, then Minister of State for the Environment and Countryside, in the House of Commons, 29 January 1989. English Heritage recommended 840 sites for scheduling in 1990, and 1,416 in 1991 (*English Heritage Report and Accounts 1991–1992*).

13 See, for example, DoE, *The Past under the Plough*, 1980, and the two reports of the Royal Commission on Historical Monuments of England, *A Matter of Time*, 1960, and *Monuments Threatened or Destroyed*, 1963. For a statement of the criteria used for assessing whether a monument is worthy of scheduling, see PPG 16 (which also quotes the figure of 600,000 sites and monuments).

14 The limitations of the scheduling as a means of protecting ancient monuments are currently under review in Scotland: see *Ancient Monuments Board for Scotland Thirty-Eighth Report, 1991*, 1992, para. 7.

15 The Environment Committee pressed for more AAIs to be established but, apart from discussions with Winchester on the possible designation of an AAI in that city, the DoE has argued that 'further areas should not be designated until there has been a review of the effectiveness of the procedure' (Environment Committee, *Historic Buildings and Ancient Monuments: Observations on the First Report of the Committee in Session 1986–87 (HC 146)*, 1988, para. 33). A further review was announced in 1990, with the publication of PPG 16: 'As this PPG has been framed to deal with archaeological interests more comprehensively than the provision for AAIs allows, the Secretary of State has decided that no more AAIs should be designated until an assessment of the effectiveness of the PPG has been undertaken which it is planned should begin some 12 months following publication of this PPG.' (That is November 1991.)

16 See Hobley 1987, and Redman 1990. (Earlier works include Rahtz 1974, and Fowler 1977.) For a well-reported case (the Rose Theatre) which illustrates the problems involved, see Harte 1990.

17 See DoE Circular 8/87; for Scotland see SDD Circular 17/87 and *Memorandum on Listed Buildings and Conservation Areas*, SDD, 1987 (amended 1988). There is a mammoth amount of material on this subject in the Environment Committee's 1987 report on *Historic Buildings and Ancient Monuments*. Ranging more widely is Dix and Tarn 1985. See also Esher 1981.

18 See two DoE publications: *New Life for Old Buildings* (1971) and *New Life for Old Churches* (1978).

19 Section 6 of the Planning (Listed Buildings and Conservation Areas) Act. See DoE Circular 8/87, paras 41–45.

20 M. Ross (1991: 112) argues that the courts are too

lenient: 'Unfortunately, as with so many such environmental offences, the courts, and in particular magistrates courts, seem reluctant to impose the maximum penalties allowed even in the most serious cases. A fine of a few hundred or even a thousand pounds is scarcely likely to deter a builder or a developer who may stand to make many tens of thousands by clearing an awkwardly-sited listed building out of the way. But such penalties are likely to deter planning authorities from launching prosecutions: and this could well be the reason why so few cases reach the courts each year.' Elsewhere, a case has been made for a special court for environmental regulation: see Carnwath 1992.

21  A detailed exposition of the powers is given in DoE Circular 8/87. As is apparent from the frequent references, *Planning and the Heritage*, by M. Ross (1991) is invaluable. For changes brought about by the Planning and Compensation Act 1991, see DoE Circular 14/91, SOEnD Circular 8/92, and Historic Scotland Circular (HS)1/92.

22  A useful discussion is to be found in the National Audit Office report, *Protecting and Managing England's Heritage Property*, 1992.

23  See the 1989 White Paper, *The Future of Development Plans*: para 2.20, and the DoE 1989 Consultation Paper, *Listed Buildings and Conservation Areas*: paras 6–10. (The necessary legislation has not yet been brought forward.) See also *Development Plan Policies for Archaeology*, English Heritage, 1992a.

24  An inventory of conservation areas is published by English Heritage in a national and four regional volumes of *The Conservation Areas of England*, 1990. See also English Tourist Board, *English Heritage Monitor 1992*; this is an annual publication of the Board.

25  Morton, 1991, and Suddards and Morton 1991. Nicholas Ridley, when Secretary of State for the Environment (in an address to the National Association of Conservative Graduates) went much further: 'I have a recurring nightmare, that sometime in the next century the entire country will be designated under some conservation order or other. The people actually living there will be smothered with bureaucratic instructions limiting their freedom. We will have a sanitised, bureaucratised and ossified countryside out of something which has always been, and should always be, a product of the interaction of man and his environment as time goes by' (quoted in Suddards 1988: 523).

For a discussion of the threats to conservation areas (from ill-considered alterations) see English Historic Towns Forum, 1992. This recommends planning controls over such matters as roof materials, external doors and windows, and 'all development which materially affects the external appearance of the building'. The photographs in the report are far more eloquent than any words.

26  There is a useful review in Larkham and Jones 1993.

27  HC Expenditure Committee, *Historic Buildings and Ancient Monuments*, 1987: 230.

28  English Heritage, *Annual Report and Accounts 1991–1992*, p. 11. See also Association of Conservation Officers, *Listed Buildings Repair Notices*, 1992.

29  DoE Circular 8/87, Appendix I.

30  Originally there was a *Grade III* category: this was a non-statutory grade which is now obsolete. Grade III buildings were those which, whilst not qualifying for the first statutory list when compiled from 1949 to 1969, were considered nevertheless to be of some importance. Many of these buildings are now considered to be of special interest by current standards – particularly where they possess 'group value' – and are being added to the statutory lists as these are revised. M. Ross (1991: 74) notes that most of the former Grade III buildings have been upgraded to Grade II in the course of resurveying.

31  For a tragic tale of municipal vandalism, see Fergusson, *The Sack of Bath: A Record and an Indictment*, 1973, and Curl, *The Erosion of Oxford*, 1977.

32  See, for example, the study commissioned by English Heritage: Lane and Vaughan 1992.

33  See Scrase 1991.

34  DoE *Annual Report 1992*, para. 4.41.

35  *Care of Cathedrals Measure*, HC 383 and HL 52 (1989–90), HMSO 1990.

36  *English Heritage Annual Report and Accounts 1991–1992*, English Heritage, 1992, p. 11.

37  The proposals are set out in the February 1993 *Monthly Bulletin* of Grant's *Encyclopedia of Planning Law and Practice*.

38  See *Third Report from the Expenditure Committee, Session 1977–78: National Land Fund*, 1978; White Paper, *A National Heritage Fund*, 1979.

39  National Heritage Memorial Fund, *Accounts 1991–1992*, HC 139 (1991–92): 2.

40  *Tree News* (The Tree Council Newsletter). A bibliography on trees and woodlands can be obtained from the Tree Council, 35 Belgrave Square, London SW1X 8QN.

41  Local planning authorities have power to take action in relation to land which 'adversely affects' the amenity of an area: section 215 of the Town and Country Planning Act 1990.

42  The 1991 Planning and Compensation Act provides that unitary development plans shall include policies for the conservation of the natural beauty and amenity of the land; the improvement of the physical environment; and the management of traffic. It is claimed, in *This Common Inheritance: The First Year Report* (para 4.3), that 'this will help ensure a positive role for the

environment in plans and local decisions. New planning policy guidance on development plans will offer advice on these topics.'

43  In the 1959 *Bulletin of Selected Planning Appeals*.

44  Others included Aldous, *Goodbye Britain*, 1975; Booker and Green, *Goodbye London: An Illustrated Guide to Threatened Buildings*, 1973; Curl, *The Erosion of Oxford*, 1977; and MacEwen, *Crisis in Architecture*, 1973.

45  Charles, HRH The Prince of Wales, *A Vision of Britain – A Personal View of Architecture*, 1989. The book aroused strong feelings: Martin Pawley, the architectural critic of *The Guardian* complained that the Prince 'is exercising benevolent totalitarianism over the mini-kingdom of architecture', while Peter Conrad of *The Observer* declared that 'The Prince doesn't have a vision of Britain: he has a fantasy about it, nurtured at a lofty distance from the facts of national life.' On the other hand, Chris Shepley, writing in *The Planner* (8 September 1989, p. 8), praised it and suggested that it deserved to be 'one of the most influential books on design and planning of recent years'.

46  For a critical account of the RIBA–RTPI agreed statement, see Tugnutt 1991.

# 8

# COUNTRYSIDE PLANNING

The countryside is changing. The simple assumptions of the past no longer hold good.

*Action for the Countryside*, 1992

## THE CHANGING COUNTRYSIDE

There have been great changes in the British countryside since the early post-war policies were forged. Suburban commuter residential development, roads and transport, people seeking recreation, the changing economy, forestry, conservation, and a host of other pressures have grown beyond any expectation. The changes show no sign of abating: they never have. The British countryside has been subject to continual change: the 'natural' scenery which is now the concern of preservationists is the human-made result of earlier economic change. The changes continue, and the current ones are more far-reaching than those of the past. The most recent are those which come with telecommunications and agricultural surpluses.[1] Above all, new problems of land management – in both the countryside and the urban areas – have arisen for which the post-war planning system is inadequate. This system was designed to deal with land use, not its management; and it was restricted to urban land, not the countryside. It was assumed that a prosperous agriculture would by itself deal with any problems of the rural economy. One implication of this was that there appeared to be no problem about the division of central government countryside responsibilities between departments concerned with planning and those concerned with agriculture. Other divided responsibilities, particularly between country-side conservation and nature conservation, seemed more problematic: these later gave rise to several organisational changes.

New problems require new tools, but the changes in the countryside and, indeed, in the character of 'rural' society have been so far-reaching as to demand more than marginal changes in the planning system. This chapter sketches some of the main features of the contemporary countryside scene, starting with access and conservation (where progress has been steady but slow), and finishing with the agonies of policy change necessitated by the latest agricultural revolution.

## NATIONAL PARKS AND ACCESS TO THE COUNTRYSIDE

The demand for public access to the countryside has a long history (Eversley 1910), stretching from the early nineteenth-century fight against enclosures, James Bryce's abortive 1884 Access to Mountains Bill and the attenuated Access to Mountains Act of 1939, to the promise of the National Parks and Access to the Countryside Act of 1949: an Act which, among other things, poetically provides powers for 'preserving and enhancing natural beauty'. Many battles have been fought by voluntary bodies such as the Commons, Open Spaces and Footpaths

Preservation Society and the Council for the Protection of Rural England (whose reports clearly indicate that their continued activity is still all too necessary), but they worked largely in a legislative vacuum until the Second World War.[2] The mood engendered by the Second World War augured a better reception for the Scott Committee's emphatic statement that 'the establishment of national parks is long overdue' (Scott Report 1942: para 178). The Scott Committee had very wide terms of reference, and for the first time an overall view was taken of questions of public rights of access to the open country, and the establishment of national parks and nature reserves within the context of a national policy for the preservation and planning of the countryside. Government acceptance of the necessity for establishing national parks was announced in the series of debates on post-war reconstruction which took place during 1941 and 1943, and the White Paper on *The Control of Land Use* referred to the establishment of national parks as part of a comprehensive programme of post-war reconstruction and land-use planning. Not only was the principle accepted but, probably of equal importance, there was now a central government department with clear responsibility for such matters as national parks. There followed the Dower (1945) and Hobhouse (1947) reports on national parks, nature conservation, footpaths and access to the countryside, and, in 1949, the National Parks and Access to the Countryside Act which established the National Parks Commission and gave the main responsibility for the parks to local planning authorities.[3]

Great changes have taken place since the national parks were established: standards of living and the demand for recreation have risen, car ownership has increased tenfold giving rise to enormous pressures on the countryside, new attitudes to the environment have evolved, and the agricultural base of the countryside has changed dramatically. These changes have been mirrored in legislative changes (and, currently, debate on further changes). Under the provisions of the Countryside Act 1968, the National Parks Commission was superseded by the Countryside Commission, with enlarged powers. A Countryside Commission for Scotland was established under the Countryside (Scotland) Act 1967. The local government reorganisation of 1972 required county councils to establish single national park committees with wider responsibilities; in the Lake District and the Peak District planning boards replaced joint boards. The Wildlife and Countryside Act 1981 strengthened the provisions for management agreements and introduced compensation for farmers whose rights were restricted (a major change in principle). The turn of the decade saw major structural changes in the organisation of agencies responsible for countryside matters, including the establishment of a separate Countryside Council for Wales (CCW), and the merging of the Countryside Commission for Scotland with the Nature Conservancy Council for Scotland in Scottish Natural Heritage (SNH).[4]

From their inception, the national parks have had two purposes: 'the preservation and enhancement of natural beauty', and 'encouraging the provision or improvement, for persons resorting to national parks, of facilities for the enjoyment thereof and for the enjoyment of the opportunities for open air recreation and the study of nature afforded thereby'.[5] There is inevitably some conflict between these twin purposes, and the National Parks Review Panel (Edwards Report 1991) set up by the Countryside Commission recommended that they be reformulated to give added weight to conservation.[6] The favoured wording is:

> The purposes of national parks should be defined in a new National Park Act as:
> 1. to protect, maintain and enhance the scenic beauty, natural systems and land forms, and the wildlife and cultural heritage of the area;
> 2. to promote the quiet enjoyment and understanding of the area, insofar as it is not in conflict with the primary purpose of conservation.

This appears to have been accepted by the Government.[7]

The administration of the national parks has been a matter of controversy throughout their history. Dower had envisaged that there would be *ad hoc* committees with members appointed in equal numbers by the Commission and the relevant local authorities. Local representation was necessary since the well-being of the local people was to be the first consideration; but the parks were also to be *national*, and thus wider representation was essential. The lengthy arguments on this issue were eventually resolved by the 1949 Act in favour of a local authority majority, with only one-third of the members being appointed by the Secretary of State. (In line with his conception of truly national parks, Dower had proposed that the whole cost of administering them should be met by the Exchequer – an idea which was never accepted.)

In cases where a park lay in the areas of more than one local authority, the legislation provided that a joint board was to be the normal organisation. In fact, due to the strenuous opposition of local authorities (who were particularly worried about the financial implications) only two joint boards were set up – for the Peak District and the Lake District parks. Four parks had joint advisory committees, and the remaining four (which were entirely within the boundaries of a single county) were administered by a single local authority committee. In the local government reorganisation of 1972, significant changes were made to the administration of national parks. Joint boards were replaced by stronger planning boards, each park had to have a national park officer, and a national park plan was required.

The matter was not allowed to rest, however, and the Edwards Report recommended that independent authorities should be established for all national parks. Though strongly opposed by the local authorities, this has been accepted by the Government and,

in the words of the Association of County Councils (1992a: 6), 'priority must now be given to ensuring that the new arrangements are made to work in practice'. Legislation for the new system is awaited.

National parks vary greatly in their character and the ways in which they interrelate within the surrounding areas. There is thus a diversity of planning arrangements.[8] The Peak District is a separate structure planning authority; the Lake District prepares its structure plan in conjunction with Cumbria County Council; in other parks, the national park is part of a wider structure plan area. Development control is to become the clear responsibility of the new National Park Authorities (NPAs). (National parks, like Areas of Outstanding Natural Beauty and Heritage Coasts, have restricted development rights under the General Development Order.)

In addition to the normal plans, a NPA is required to prepare a *national park plan*. The distinguishing feature of this is that it is concerned with management.[9] In this it goes beyond the scope of development plans. In addition to policies, the plan spells out both short-term and long-term proposals, and programmes for action to achieve the purposes for which the park was designated.[10]

## THE BROADS

Though proposed by the Dower Report for a national park, the Broads was rejected as such because of its

**Table 8.1** Statutory Protected Areas in the UK, 1991

|  | Number | Sq. km |
|---|---|---|
| National Nature Reserves | 286 | 1,725 |
| Local Nature Reserves | 241 | 171 |
| SSSIs | 5,671 | 17,785 |
| Areas of Scientific Interest | 46 | 634 |
| Areas of Special Scientific Interest | 26 | 69 |
| Special Protection Areas | 40 | 1,344 |
| Biosphere Reserves | 13 | 443 |
| 'Ramsar' Wetland Sites | 44 | 1,377 |
| Environmentally Sensitive Areas | 19 | 7,856 |
| National Parks | 10 | 14,011 |
| AONBs | 40 | 20,449 |

deteriorated state and the anticipated cost of its management.[11] However, the need for some type of special protection continued to be debated, and the proposal surfaced again in the late 1970s. The local reaction was against this and, instead, a voluntary consortium, called the Broads Authority, was formed by the relevant public authorities (with powers and financial resources under the provisions of the Local Government Act 1972, and with 75 per cent Exchequer funding).

Discussions continued over several years among the large number of interested bodies and, in 1984, the Countryside Commission (CC) published a review of the problems of the area and the progress that had been made by the Broads Authority (CC 1984b). In the Commission's view, despite its achievements, the authority had not made significant improvements in water quality. 'An effective framework for the integrated management of water-based and land-based recreation has not been established. Loss of traditional grazing marsh has continued throughout the period, and further threats are in evidence.' The designation of the area as a national park was rejected in favour of 'a body of equivalent status . . . but with a constitution, powers and funding more appropriate to local circumstances'. This was accepted by the Government, and a new Broads Authority (with the same name as its predecessor) was established by the Norfolk and Suffolk Broads Act 1988.[12] The duties of the authority are extensive. It is the local planning authority and the principal unit of local government for the area. It has strong environmental responsibilities. The Broads Authority is required by the Act to produce a plan which has a wider remit than those required under the planning acts: it is more akin to a national park plan.

## THE NEW FOREST

While it took many years to devise an acceptable system for administering the Broads, it took even longer to do so for the New Forest. The New Forest was 'new' in 1079 when William the Conqueror appropriated it as his new royal hunting ground.

Situated in South Hampshire, close to a large urban population, it has unique qualities of landscape and habitats, and a singular set of administrative arrangements.[13] The Crown land, of some 27,000 hectares, is managed by the Forestry Commission. A third of this is enclosed, and the remainder is open forest. The so-called Perambulation is a wider area of about 38,000 hectares which embraces additional manorial and private land. It is defined in the New Forest Act of 1964 (one of several Acts relating to the area). A larger area is the New Forest Heritage Area which, though lacking statutory designation, was adopted in 1985 by the New Forest District Council, and is reflected in local development plans. An even larger heritage area was proposed in 1992 by the New Forest Committee.[14]

In addition to the public authorities in the area, there is a corporate body of Verderers which is responsible for managing the grazing and commoning within the forest. This exercises its powers through institutions such as the Court of Swainmote. It acts as a guardian of commoners' rights, and makes bylaws for controlling and charging fees for the number of animals allowed to graze. It also administers the Filly Premium Scheme (funded by English Nature) which aims to safeguard the well-being of the New Forest ponies. As well as the protection provided in these ways, much of the Crown land in the New Forest is designated as sites of special scientific interest (SSSI), and has also been listed as a potential Special Protection Area under the EC Birds Directive, and a Wetland of International Importance under the Ramsar Convention. The southern fringe of the forest is within the South Hampshire Coast AONB, and the whole of the heritage area is within the South-West Hampshire Green Belt. It might thus appear that the New Forest is adequately (even if confusingly) protected. However, quite apart from questions of coordinating all these protectors of the forest, there is a further need to safeguard the surrounding grazing lands which are under pressure for development, and also to ensure that adequate provision is made for recreation in a manner which is in harmony with conservation requirements.

The New Forest has for long been a candidate for

designation as a national park, but it has been generally agreed that, like the Broads, it has features which require special treatment. The Government decision on this was announced in early 1992.[15] The New Forest Committee which was set up in 1990, with government encouragement following the Forestry Commission's review, is to be the foundation for the new authority. This will provide a planning mechanism similar to that operating in the Broads. The functions of the new body will be essentially for planning and coordination. The local authorities will retain their planning responsibilities, as will the Verderers. The new authority will operate in a consultative way to ensure the adequacy and consistency of planning in the area. Following final consultations, the government will be introducing the necessary legislation 'when a suitable parliamentary opportunity presents itself'.

## ACCESS AGREEMENTS

The 1949 Act introduced the concept of access agreements. The hope was that local authorities and the national parks would negotiate these agreements over wide areas of land. This was not to be and, as Blunden and Curry (1989: 136) note, access agreements in England and Wales cover only 34,000 hectares. One reason in the early days was simply that such agreements were entirely new to local authorities, and that there was a reluctance to do battle with influential major landowners.[16] Even in the national parks — with the outstanding exception of the Peak District (where nearly 60 per cent of the land is covered by access agreements) — they attracted little enthusiasm. Moreover, since landowners are worried about the increasing numbers of people using access areas, original agreements which are expiring may be difficult to renew (Blunden and Curry 1989: 140). The clash of interests on access has become increasingly acute, and the Edwards Report (1991: 39) argued that circumstances had changed dramatically since the Hobhouse Report (1947) had pressed for a public right of access to all open country:

With greater mobility, greater numbers visiting the national parks for outside activity, a diminishing conservation resource, and the economic importance of upland land uses, the Panel conclude that a wholly unqualified right to roam would be difficult to justify. Rather, the aim should be to increase access opportunities whilst recognising the need to safeguard other interests where necessary.

As in the USA, there is a danger of people 'loving their national parks and historic sites to death' (Hunt 1988). The problem is well known; the difficulty lies in resolving it. At the time of writing, the Countryside Commission is preparing a consultation paper on the subject.[17]

Access agreements formed a major subject of debate in the Countryside and Wildlife Bill which is discussed later in this chapter.

## AREAS OF OUTSTANDING NATURAL BEAUTY

Both the Dower and Hobhouse Reports proposed that, in addition to national parks, certain areas of high landscape quality, scientific interest and recreational value should be subject to special protection. These areas were not considered, at that time, to require the positive management which it was assumed would characterise national parks, but 'their contribution to the wider enjoyment of the countryside is so important that special measures should be taken to preserve their natural beauty and interest'. The Hobhouse Committee proposed that these *conservation areas* should be the responsibility of local planning authorities, but would receive expert assistance and financial aid from the National Parks Commission. Advisory committees (with a majority of local authority members) would be set up to ensure that they would be comprehensively treated as a single unit. A total of fifty-two conservation areas, covering some 26,000 sq. km, was recommended, including, for example, the Breckland and much of central Wales, long stretches of the coast, the Cotswolds, most of the Downland, the Chilterns and Bodmin Moor (Cherry 1975: 55).

The 1949 Act did not contain any special provisions for the care of 'conservation areas', the power under the Planning Acts being considered adequate for the purpose. It did, however, give the Commission power to designate *areas of outstanding natural beauty* (AONBs), and provided for Exchequer grants on the same basis as for national parks. Thirty-nine areas have been designated covering some 20,000 sq. km (12 per cent of the total area of England and Wales). Two additional areas proposed for designation are the Tamar Valley (Devon–Cornwall), and Nidderdale (North Yorkshire).

Areas of outstanding natural beauty are, with some notable exceptions, generally smaller than national parks. They are the responsibility of local planning authorities who have powers for the 'preservation and enhancement of natural beauty' similar to those of park planning authorities. In contrast to national parks, however, the emphasis in areas of outstanding natural beauty is on the conservation of landscape beauty. They also receive less grant-aid than the national parks (Smart and Anderson 1990: chapter 10).

There has been continuing debate on the question as to whether the designation of areas of outstanding natural beauty serves any useful function. Several reviews have concluded that it does, but that there is inadequate funding. The latest (Smart and Anderson 1990) echoes the complaint of earlier reviews that the AONBs are starved of resources.[18]

## LOCAL AUTHORITY LANDSCAPE DESIGNATIONS

In addition to AONBs, there are many local authority designations designed to assist in safeguarding areas of the countryside from inappropriate development. Some of these have been given additional status through inclusion in structure and local plans. Though these are like AONBs in that they involve the application of special criteria for control in sensitive areas, they do not imply any special procedures for development control (for example, in terms of restrictions on permitted development). The

DoE Consultation Paper on *The Future of Development Plans* (1986) made reference to *areas of landscape quality, areas of great landscape value, landscape conservation areas, coastal preservation areas*, and *areas of semi-natural importance*. The same paper proposed a new statutory designation, the *rural conservation area* which, it was suggested, would provide a more coherent framework. This idea, however, found little favour during the consultation process, and it was dropped. There was a suggestion that the desired objectives could be achieved through statements of policy in development plans.[19]

The current advice simply makes reference to 'locally devised' designations, and notes that: 'It is for local authorities to determine the more specific policies that reflect the different types of countryside found in their areas.'[20]

## SCOTTISH POLICIES[21]

Scotland contains large areas of beautiful unspoilt countryside and wild landscape. It has the majority of Britain's highest mountains, with nearly 300 peaks over 3,000 ft (913 m). The northern highlands extend from the central lowlands to the north of the mainland, and are divided by the Great Glen which stretches from Inverness to Fort William and contains Loch Ness, Loch Oich, and Loch Lochy. The Grampians cover the southern highland area, and include Ben Nevis, the highest point in the British Isles (4,400 ft; 1,343 m). Scotland has the great majority of the UK islands. Its coast is over 10,000 km in length. Much of the west coast consists of fjord-type lochs of which the longest is Loch Fyne (67 km).

Despite expectations to the contrary, there are no national parks in Scotland. Though a Scottish committee (the Ramsay Committee) recommended, in 1945, the establishment of five Scottish national parks,[22] no action followed. The reasons for this inaction were partly political and partly pragmatic (Cherry 1975). An essential element of the latter was that (with the exception of the area around Clydeside and, in particular, Loch Lomond) the pressures which were so apparent south of the border were absent.

Nevertheless, the Secretary of State used the powers of the 1947 Planning Act to issue *national parks direction orders*. These required the relevant local planning authorities to submit to the Secretary of State all planning applications in the designated areas (which included Loch Lomond/Trossachs, the Cairngorms, and Ben Nevis/Glencoe). In effect therefore, in an almost Gilbertian manner, while Scotland at this time did not have any national parks, it had an administrative system which enabled controls to be operated as if it did! But, of course, this approach was inherently negative, and it was not until the Countryside (Scotland) Act of 1967 that positive measures could be taken on a significant scale.

This Act provided for the establishment of the Countryside Commission for Scotland – recently joined with the Nature Conservancy Council for Scotland in Scottish Natural Heritage (SNH). It also enabled the establishment of regional parks and country parks. A policy framework for these was set out in the Commission's 1974 report, *A Park System for Scotland*. The report also recommended the designation of national parks in Scotland, though the term *special park* was used. This has never been accepted by the Government, but objectives similar to those of national parks have been achieved under other designations.[23]

There are forty national scenic areas, four regional parks, and thirty-five country parks. The *national scenic areas* are of similar status to the AONBs. They extend over an area of a million hectares, and include such marvellous sites as Ben Nevis and Glencoe, Loch Lomond, the Cairngorms, and the World Heritage Site of the islands of St Kilda.[24] Development control in these areas is the responsibility of the local planning authorities, who are required to consult with SNH for certain categories of development. As in England and Wales, there is an increasing concern for 'positive action to improve planning and land use management' in the areas, and for dealing with the erosion of footpaths. There is also a similar complaint about the lack of resources.[25]

A *regional park* is statutorily defined simply as 'an extensive area of land, part of which is devoted to the recreational needs of the public'. The four parks are Clyde–Muirshiel, Loch Lomond, the Pentland Hills, and Fife. These parks are primarily recreational areas, and each has a local plan which sets out management policies. Emphasis is laid on *integrated land management* schemes to ensure that public access is in harmony with other land uses. In this, they give effect to Abercrombie's green-belt philosophy, articulated in the Clyde Valley Regional Plan. He conceived these *outer scenic areas* not only as recreational areas but also as a means of protecting the rural setting of the conurbations (Smith and Wannop 1985).

Since the passing of the 1967 Act, Scottish local authorities have provided thirty-five country parks spread across the central belt and the north-east. The parks are 'registered' with SNH which makes grants for capital development expenditure and also towards the cost of a ranger service. Country parks are not only of direct benefit to their 11 million annual visitors, they also have a conservation objective of 'drawing off areas that are sensitive due to productive land uses and fragile wildlife habitats'. Over 200 rangers are employed 'to help visitors understand what they see in the countryside, and to encourage responsible behaviour' (Fladmark 1988: 6).

The Scottish legislation mirrors the English provisions in allowing planning authorities to make management agreements with private landowners.

> Under such agreements, land uses can be modified on occasion in the interests of scenic conservation, and steps designed to promote the enjoyment of the countryside by the public. In return, the planning authority or the Commission may make a payment to the owners in recognition of the public benefit secured by the agreement.
>
> (CCS 1987)

The Natural Heritage (Scotland) Act 1991, which provided for the establishment of Scottish Natural Heritage also introduced *natural heritage areas*:

> Where it appears to SNH, after consultation with such persons as it thinks fit, that an area is of outstanding value to the natural heritage of Scotland, and that special protection measures are appropriate for it, it may recommend to the Secretary of State that the area be designated as a Natural Heritage Area.

The Scottish Office stresses that natural heritage areas are not a substitute for national parks; they are an alternative designed to meet the particular situation in Scotland.[26] They will be designated for a wide range of situations in both upland and lowland Scotland. They will typically cover wide areas where there is both a landscape and a nature conservation interest, and where there is therefore a need for integrated management. Examples are the Flow Country, where there are areas of international conservation interest within a much larger area of national landscape interest, and areas of lowland Scotland where there has been considerable damage to the landscape and there is a pressing need for rejuvenation. At present there is no unified designation which deals with both nature and landscape conservation and which also provides for access and enjoyment. This unified approach neatly reflects the merger of nature conservation and landscape protection and enjoyment in Scottish Natural Heritage. It is in striking contrast to the well-established approach in England where the separate existence of English Nature continues a division hallowed in the early post-war legislation (and reinforced by the division of countryside responsibilities between the DoE and the MAFF).

## THE COASTLINE

A few figures underline the particular significance of the coast, and therefore of coastal planning: nowhere in the UK is more than 135 km from the sea; the coastline is 18,600 km in length, and the territorial waters extend over about a third of a million square km.[27]

About a third of the coastline of England and Wales is included in national parks and areas of outstanding natural beauty. Large areas of the coast are owned or protected by the National Trust. Following the fund-raising *Enterprise Neptune* appeal, the Trust's ownership has increased to 760 km; it protects a further 84 km by covenant. Nevertheless, the pressures on the coastline are proving increasingly difficult to cope with. Between a quarter and a third of the coastline

of England and Wales is developed (PPG 20: Annex 1). Growing numbers of people are attracted to the coast for holidays, for recreation and for retirement. There are also economic pressures for major industrial development in certain parts, particularly on some estuaries. The National Trust has instanced road schemes, offshore fish farming, wind farms and radar stations, sewage treatment works, and tourist marinas.[28]

The problem is a difficult one which cannot be satisfactorily met simply by restrictive measures: it requires a positive policy of planning for leisure.[29] This has long been accepted, and the heritage coast designation, introduced in 1972, implies recreational provision as well as conservation. The Countryside Commission has urged that every heritage coast should have a management plan. This is seen as being an important means 'to enhance and protect all heritage coasts, and to manage effectively their enjoyment by the public'.[30] The Commission has also established the *Heritage Coast Forum* as 'a national body to promote the heritage coast concept and to act as a focus and liaison point for all heritage coast organisations'. This is seen as a needed addition to the activities of the Commission, whose capacity to promote all the initiatives that are necessary is limited.

By 1992, forty-four heritage coasts had been defined, extending laterally over 1,486 km. In Scotland, 26 *preferred coastal conservation zones* have been defined with a total length of 7,546 km, covering three-quarters of Scotland's mainland and islands coastlines.[31]

The Environment Committee complained of the lack of coordination among the host of bodies concerned with coastal protection, planning and management. (There are over 80 Acts which deal with the regulation of activities in the coastal zone, and as many as 240 government departments and public agencies involved in some way.[32]) Not surprisingly, there have been suggestions that action is required to simplify, rationalise, coordinate, or consolidate matters. Though an apparently obvious and sensible idea, it is remarkably difficult to see how the situation can be significantly changed; and the

Environment Committee contented itself by asking for a review of legislation and responsibilities. The Government response was negative. It was pointed out that, though there were many Acts relating to the coast, the same could be said about the land! Indeed, it was neither possible nor desirable to treat the coast separately from the adjoining land or from the territorial and international waters. Moreover, the suggestion that the town and country planning system might be extended seaward was not persuasive, though it was agreed that 'it is now time to take this debate further', and a discussion paper was promised.[33]

## PUBLIC RIGHTS OF WAY

The origin of a large number of public rights of way is obscure. As a result, innumerable disputes have arisen over them. Before the 1949 Act, these disputes could have been settled only by a case-by-case procedure, often with the evidence of 'eldest inhabitants' playing a leading role. The unsatisfactory nature of the situation was underlined by the Scott, Dower and Hobhouse Reports, as well as by the Special Committee on Footpaths and Access to the Countryside.[34] All were agreed that a complete survey of rights of way was essential, together with the introduction of a simple procedure for resolving the legal status of rights of way which were in dispute. The 1949 Act attempted to provide for both.

This Act has been amended several times;[35] under the current provisions, county councils have the responsibility for surveying rights of way (footpaths, bridleways, and 'byways open to all traffic') and preparing and keeping up to date what is misleadingly called a *definitive map*. The maps are supposedly conclusive evidence of the existence of rights of way but, in fact, they are not necessarily either complete or conclusive. They are incomplete because inadequate resources have been devoted to undertaking the necessary surveys, and they can be inconclusive because the map may wrongly identify a right of way. The latter is a legal matter which is not discussed here,[36] but the former is a continuing problem of planning policy and administration.

The definitive maps show some 225,000 km of rights of way in England and Wales. Most of these are 'existing': few new recreational paths have been designated, though they are certainly needed in some parts of the country. Moreover, there has been a loss of access by both neglect and deliberate obstruction. Each year some 1,500 formal proposals, affecting 500 km of the network, are made to change rights of way (by creation, diversion or extinguishment). Of these, about three-quarters are unopposed. The net change is negligible. It is difficult to establish what the overall effect is, though the Ramblers' Association maintain that over a half of the public rights of way 'are unavailable to all but the most determined and agile person' (Blunden and Curry 1989: 135).

The Rights of Way Act 1990 (sponsored as a private member's bill by Edward Leigh) made a significant change in that it requires the restoration of footpaths and bridleways after ploughing. The Act is being monitored by the Countryside Commission and the County Surveyors' Society. First indications are that there has been a marked improvement in public path conditions.[37]

Another footpath problem arises from their popularity: this is the wear and tear caused by a great intensity of use. The Pennine Way in particular has suffered from this, and 'damage limitation' experiments are under way with, for example, the laying of boardwalk and revegetation.[38] The Pennine Way is one of the long-distance routes which now stretch over some 2,700 km. The designation of these hikers' highways has been laborious, but they have had the attention and backing of the Countryside Commission, which has official responsibility for their establishment.

The Commission has set itself the target of putting the whole of the rights-of-way network into good order by the end of the century. As an aid to this, the Countryside Commission has launched a *parish paths partnership*. This aims to stimulate local improvement schemes through parish councils and other local groups. Exchequer assistance amounting to £900,000 has been made available for 1992/93.[39]

In Scotland, the position in relation to rights of way and access to the countryside is different from that south of the border. The legal system is distinct, and the pressures on the countryside are, with some exceptions, fewer. There is relatively free access to the Scottish countryside: there is 'a well-established system of mutual respect between walker and landowner'.[40] Nevertheless, this is not so in areas close to the towns where access is severely restricted. The Countryside Commission for Scotland initiated a review of access to the countryside; this is being continued by its successor, Scottish Heritage.

The first designated long-distance footpath in Scotland was opened in 1980. This is the West Highland Way which runs for 152 km from Milngavie (a suburb of Glasgow) to Fort William at the foot of Ben Nevis. The Way is used by an estimated 90,000 walkers a year, and also injects some £3.5m into the communities along the route. Unfortunately, this has also led to the same severe erosion that is experienced on some of the English footpaths. There has also been similar erosion on sections of the 328-km Southern Upland Way which stretches from Portpatrick on the south-west coast to Cockburnspath on the east coast. Negotiations for other long-distance footpaths are at various stages of negotiation, including an extension of the Speyside Way and the development of a new route, the Great Glen Way. The three approved long-distance routes in Scotland extend over some 580 km.

## RECREATIONAL FACILITIES

In the early post-war years, national recreation policy was largely concerned with national parks (and their Scottish shadow equivalents), areas of outstanding natural beauty, and the coast. Increasingly, however, there has developed a concern for positive policy in relation to metropolitan, regional and country parks.[41] In London, a very large and well-administered park has been established in the Lee Valley under special legislation. The Lee Valley Regional Park Authority was set up in January 1967 with members appointed by fifteen local authorities and with powers to precept on the relevant local authorities (in Essex, Hertfordshire, and London). This particular area (amounting to some 4,000

hectares) had been largely derelict for many years. (It is now over a third of a century since Abercrombie's *Greater London Plan* envisaged the valley as 'an opportunity for a great piece of regenerative planning'.) It has been graphically described by the Civic Trust as 'London's kitchen garden, its well, its privy and its workshop . . . London's back door'. The Lee Valley Regional Park Master Plan proposed a very wide range of facilities for recreation and education including twelve major multi-purpose recreation centres as well as four major centres for youth activity, water sports, motor sports and industrial archaeology. These are to be linked by river, canal, parkland and a park road (with tolls), footpaths and bridleways. Much progress has been made along these lines, and a new plan was adopted in 1986.[42]

The Lee Valley project is an ambitious scheme. It is an exercise in 'regeneration' as well as in recreational planning. It is perhaps unique. But the concept of major out-of-door recreational facilities has attracted considerable discussion in recent years and is embodied as part of contemporary wisdom in the legislation. The Countryside Act 1968 (which followed a White Paper with the significant title *Leisure in the Countryside*) gave additional powers to the new Countryside Commission (taking the place of the more restricted National Parks Commission) for 'the provision and improvement of facilities for the enjoyment of the countryside', including experimental schemes to promote countryside enjoyment. At the same time, local authorities were empowered to provide *country parks*, including facilities for sailing, boating, bathing and fishing. These country parks are not for those who are seeking the solitude and grandeur of the mountains, but for the large urban populations who are 'looking for a change of environment within easy reach'.[43] There is now a wide range of country parks, picnic sites, visitor-interpretive sites, recreation paths, interpretive trails, cycleways and similar facilities provided by local authorities and the Countryside Commission.[44]

## WATERWAYS

There are some 3,700 miles of waterways in Britain, of which the British Waterways Board (BWB) is responsible for about 2,000.[45] Most of the latter are canals; the others are stretches of river navigation. The Board's waterways are divided (under the Transport Act 1968) into three categories: commercial (350 miles) which are principally for the carriage of freight; cruising (1,100 miles) which are principally for cruising, fishing and other recreational purposes; and 'remainder waterways' (500 miles). Commercial and cruising waterways have to be maintained in a navigable condition, while remainder waterways are maintained to a level consistent with public health, amenity, and safety. Remainder waterways can be upgraded to cruising standard, retained, or eliminated. (The Board's annual reports give details of restoration work carried out with assistance from a range of bodies including local authorities, development agencies, and the European Regional Development Fund.) The Board has an annual turnover (1991/92) of £80m, of which £51m is met from a DoE grant. A considerable proportion of expenditure (£14m in 1991/92) is on major works, such as channel lining, embankments, aqueducts, and bridges. BWB is planning to eliminate a backlog of major works to the fabric of the canals which has accumulated during years of underfunding.

An important source of funding for improvements to the waterways is the Board's property portfolio. Several major developments have formed a focus for urban renewal, such as in the development of Sheffield Basin, Paddington Basin, and the comprehensive development of the Gas Street Basin in Birmingham. The BWB cooperates with other agencies such as the Birmingham Urban Development Agency and the Black Country Development Corporation. Some BWB development has attracted criticism from the Association of Pleasure Craft Operators because it has been seen as destroying the ambience of the canals and thus making them less attractive for cruising. As with many leisure pursuits, there is a problem of satisfying conflicting interests. Much of the use of the waterways brings no income, and there is a limit to the amount that can be raised by charges to boaters and anglers. Another conflict arises between the use of the waterways for leisure and their function as an aquatic habitat.

The canal network has been described as a country park which is 2,000 miles long by 10 yards wide; but it is much more than that: the BWB owns 2,185 listed structures and ancient monuments and 62 SSSIs.[46] Over 8 million people use the waterways in the course of a year, mainly for informal recreation rather than boating. In the view of the BWB this informal recreation 'offers the greatest prospect for increased use of the waterways', and this is recognised in the Board's initiative in seeking joint study and action with local authorities and a host of other relevant agencies. Its discussion paper on development plans states:

> British Waterways encourages joint preparation of 'corridor studies' with local authorities. These studies provide a useful means of exploring the potential of waterways, and provide a clear indication of the scope and priorities for environmental improvement, conservation and development relating to a specific stretch of waterway. They can provide a particularly effective framework for the formulation of policies and proposals. British Waterways welcomes the opportunity to co-operate with other landowning interests which are or can be associated with the waterways. It is also involved in joint activities with such organisations as the Countryside Commission, English Nature and the Groundwork Trust.

Though direct charges cannot be imposed, related leisure facilities are income-generating: for example, shops, public houses, hotels, restaurants and museums. A good example is the National Waterways Museum at Gloucester which had over 100,000 visitors in its first year of operation (1988/89). The Board is required by the DoE to 'run its affairs on a commercial basis' — so far as is practicable. In a consultation document prepared for local authorities and other relevant agencies, the Board has noted that 'further provision of leisure and tourism facilities and improved access for recreation will often need to be underpinned by enabling development'.[47] It is fortunate that national parks do not have to operate on the same basis.

## NATURE CONSERVATION

The concept of wildlife sanctuaries or nature reserves is one of long standing and, indeed, antedates the

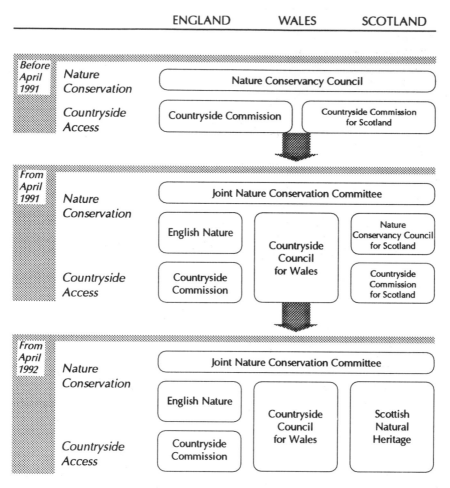

*Figure 8.1* Organisation for Nature Conservation and the Countryside
*Source: Britain 1992: An Official Handbook.*

modern idea of national parks. In other countries, some national parks are in fact primarily sanctuaries for the preservation of big game and other wildlife, as well as for the protection of outstanding physiological features and areas of outstanding geological interest. British national parks are somewhat different in concept: the emphasis is on the preservation of amenity and providing facilities for public access and enjoyment. The concept of nature conservation, on the other hand, is primarily a scientific one concerned particularly with research on problems underlying the management of natural sites and of vegetation and animal populations.

The Huxley Committee argued, in 1947, that there was no fundamental conflict between these two sets of interest:

> their special requirements may differ, and the case for each may be presented with too limited a vision: but since both have the same fundamental idea of conserving the rich variety of our countryside and sea-coasts and of increasing the general enjoyment and understanding of nature, their ultimate objectives are not divergent, still less antagonistic.

However, to ensure that recreational, economic and scientific interests are all fairly met presents some

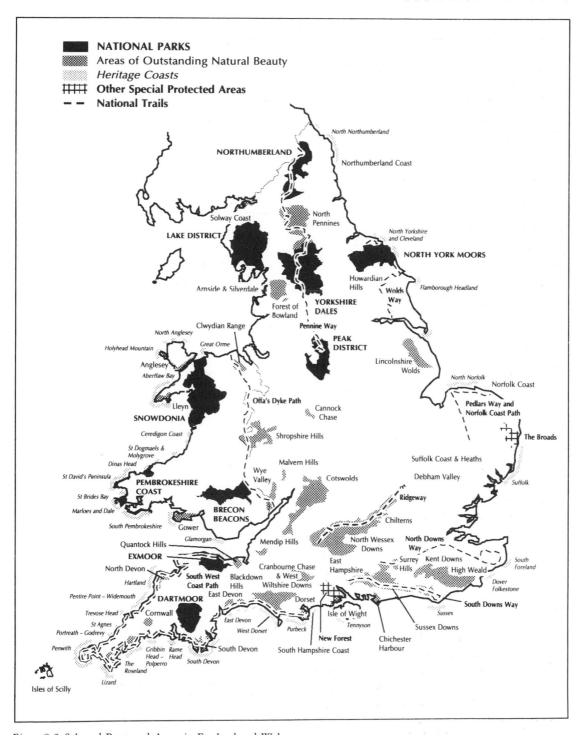

*Figure 8.2* Selected Protected Areas in England and Wales

difficulties. Several reports dealing with the various problems were published shortly after the war (Dower Report 1945; Huxley Report 1947; Hobhouse Report 1947). The outcome was the establishment of the Nature Conservancy, constituted by a Royal Charter in March 1949 and given additional powers by the National Parks and Access to the Countryside Act. As already noted, the Conservancy has now been replaced by English Nature (EN), Scottish Natural Heritage (SNH), and the Countryside Council for Wales (CCW). In Scotland and Wales, nature conservation and access to the countryside are the responsibility of a single body, but in England they remain separate.[48] Some implications of this are discussed later (see p. 191).

Nature conservation takes two main forms: the protection of particular species of flora and fauna, and the designation and protection of conservation sites. It is the latter which is of particular relevance to this book.[49] Statutory designations for conservation include nature reserves, sites of special scientific interest (SSSIs), marine nature reserves, bird sanctuaries, and limestone pavement areas. Protection is provided by agreements with owners and occupiers, or through acquisition by local authorities or English Nature.

There are 305 *local nature reserves* and 253 *national nature reserves*. The latter are, by definition, sites of national importance. Nature reserves are not sanctuaries: they are preserves where the conditions provide 'special opportunities for the study of, and research into, matters relating to the fauna and flora'. Most of these are in private ownership subject to a management agreement, but voluntary organisations such as the Royal Society for the Protection of Birds and county wildlife trusts own and manage their own reserves.

*Sites of special scientific interest* number around 5,600, and cover 1.7 million hectares (about 8 per cent of the land area of Britain). In these protected areas, occupiers must obtain permission before certain listed activities can be carried out; there is also strict planning control. (This control was strengthened in 1992.)[50] A small number of particularly important SSSIs are given even more stringent control by a *nature conservation order*. There were 29 of these in 1991.[51]

The designation of *marine nature reserves* was introduced by the Wildlife and Countryside Act 1981. Two such reserves had been designated by 1991: Lundy Island (off the coast of Devon), and Skomer, Dyfed. Three others were under negotiation: Loch Sween, Argyll; Menai Straits, Gwynedd; and Bardsey and Lleyn Peninsula, Gwynedd. The Crown Estate also has its own category of *very sensitive areas* for marine fish farming. (The Crown Estate is the legal authority for the management of the territorial sea-bed around the UK and most of the foreshore between high and low water mark.)[52] In Scotland, there are also *marine consultation areas* which, though without statutory authority, are regarded by SNH as areas with particular quality and sensitivity of the marine environment. The DoE has issued a Consultation Paper on proposals for a similar scheme in England and Wales.[53]

As required by the EC Directive on the Conservation of Wild Birds, special measures are taken to conserve certain habitats. These bird sanctuaries (termed *areas of special protection*) are designated to ensure the survival and breeding of certain species of vulnerable birds and also all regularly occurring migratory species. A 1990 report by the Commission identifies some 250 sites as meeting the EC requirements, of which 35 had been designated by March 1991.[54] Another EC Directive, on habitats, which was adopted in 1992, was welcomed in *This Common Inheritance: Second Year Report*, and legislative changes are being considered (1992: 76).

Provisions relating to *Limestone Pavement Areas* were introduced by the 1981 Wildlife and Countryside Act. These cover no more than 5,000 acres in England and Wales, but are 'of great natural beauty and scientific interest'. They are popular with gardeners looking for stone for rockeries: hence the need for protection.[55]

This bewildering (though incomplete)[56] recital of conservation instruments suggests that the time may well be near when some rationalisation may be considered appropriate. However, they are testimony to a heightened regard for 'this common inheritance'. This has been evolving for some time. It was in 1968 that the Countryside Act provided that 'in the exercise

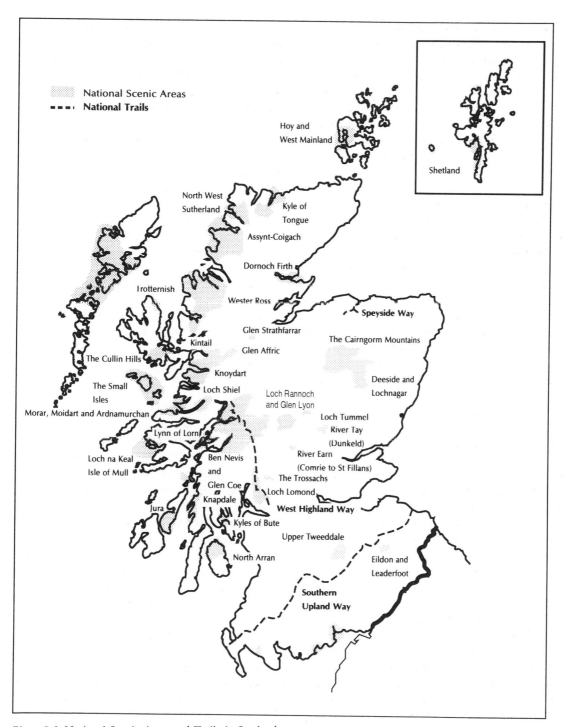

*Figure 8.3* National Scenic Areas and Trails in Scotland

of their functions relating to land under any enactment, every minister, government department and public body shall have regard to the desirability of conserving the natural beauty and amenity of the countryside'. Since 1986, there has been a statutory duty to balance the interests of agriculture with rural and environmental interests, 'agri-environmental regulation' has entered the planning lexicon, and a wide range of countryside initiatives are being made. Indeed, as the following pages illustrate, it is difficult to keep pace with the changing policies and programmes.

## PRESSURES FOR CHANGE: THE WILDLIFE AND COUNTRYSIDE ACT 1981

Legislation often emerges as a response to new perceptions of problems; but sometimes legislation itself fosters such perceptions. So it was with the Wildlife and Countryside Act 1981. Introduced as a mild alternative to the Labour Government's aborted Countryside Bill (and stimulated by the need to take action on several international conservation agreements[57]), the Conservative Government expected little trouble over the bill. It was very wrong. Preceded by a series of unadventurous Consultation Papers (on such issues as the adequacy of voluntary management agreements for moorland conservation orders, and the temporary diversion of footpaths to enable bulls to run in a field in order to get their cows in calf), the bill acted as a lightning rod for a host of countryside concerns that had been building up over the previous decade or so – moorland reclamation, afforestation and 'new agricultural landscapes', loss of hedgerows, damage to SSSIs, and such like. The bill had a stormy passage through Parliament, with an incredible 2,300 proposed amendments. Though most of these failed, the bill was considerably amended during the process.[58] The major focus of argument (with the strong NFU and the CLA holding the line against a large but diffuse environmental lobby) was the extent to which voluntary management agreements could be sufficient to resolve conflicts of

interest in the countryside. The Government steadfastly maintained that neither positive inducements nor negative controls were necessary. Indeed, it was held that controls would be counterproductive in that they would arouse intense opposition from country landowners.

Three issues aroused particular concern: the rate at which SSSIs were being seriously damaged; the rate at which moorland in national parks was being converted to agricultural use or afforestation; and the adverse impact of agricultural capital grants schemes both on landscape and on the social and economic well-being of upland communities. On the first issue, the Government finally made a concession and provided for a system of 'reciprocal notification'. This requires the NCC to notify all landowners, the local planning authority and the Secretary of State of any land which, in their opinion, 'is of special interest by reason for any of its flora, fauna, or geological or physiological features', and 'any operations appearing to the [NCC] to be likely to damage the flora or fauna or those features'. For the landowner, there is a requirement that three months' notice be given of intentions to carry out any operation listed in the SSSI notification. This three months provides the NCC with an opportunity 'to discuss modifications or the possibility of entering into a management agreement'.[59]

On the issue of moorland loss, the Act requires county planning authorities in national park areas to publish maps identifying 'any areas of moor or heath the natural beauty of which it is, in the opinion of the authority, particularly important to preserve'.

The third issue, that of agricultural grants, is a complex one on which the Government only narrowly scraped a sufficient majority. Capital farm grants are available for a very wide range of activities, from land drainage to fencing. Under the Act, notification of capital works and application for capital grants in national parks and SSSIs can trigger a number of provisions for objection to and refusal of grants, and for the offer of management agreements. This is intended to control the damage that might be caused by major agricultural improvements (Jenkins 1990).

During the debates, attempts to extend grants from

'agricultural business' to countryside conservation were defeated, and a host of amendments divided the Opposition and confused the issues. The amendments did little more than exhort the Minister of Agriculture, when considering grants in areas of special scientific interest, to provide advice on 'the conservation and enhancement of natural beauty and amenities of the countryside' and suchlike, 'free of charge'. There is, however, power to refuse an application for an agricultural grant on various 'countryside' grounds, but such a refusal renders the objecting authority (the county planning authority in national parks and the NCC in SSSIs) liable to pay compensation. This is a return to the pre-1947 planning system (even though it applies to only a small part of the country), and it has, not surprisingly, given rise to a considerable amount of debate.

The Minister for the Environment, Countryside and Local Government (William Waldegrave) has argued:

> I think that the moral and logical position of the farmer who finds that his particular bit of flora or fauna is now rare is such that there should be no hesitation in saying that he deserves public money if he is asked to do better than those who have been allowed to extinguish their bits, and if it is expensive for him to do so. I believe such flows of money, from taxpayer to land-user, for conservation expenses, are thoroughly justified and should become a useful and permanent adjunct to farm incomes for quite a considerable number of farmers, often in the rather more marginal farming areas where the inherent difficulty of farming has prevented our predecessors from extirpating species which may have gone for good elsewhere.[60]

As will be apparent from later discussion, the issue here goes much further than appears at first sight.

## FORESTRY AND LANDSCAPE

Forests cover some 2.34 million hectares in Britain: about 7 per cent of England, 13 per cent of Scotland, and 12 per cent of Wales. There has been a steady increase in the forest area; during the 1980s the increase was of some 300,000 hectares. About two-fifths of productive forestry is managed by the Forestry Commission. Productive forestry is essentially a very long-term enterprise, and there is a need 'to have regard to a number of broadly drawn secondary objectives [which] can produce conflicts with and constraints upon the Commission's primary aim of increasing the supply of timber'.[61] One of these secondary objectives is recreational provision: there are eleven forest parks in Britain, covering some 244,000 hectares. Another is the effects of forestry on the countryside and wildlife.

Much of the controversy both before and after the 1981 Act centred on the effects of hill farming and forest policies. For example, both a report by the Tourism Recreation Research Unit at Edinburgh University and a book on national parks by Ann and Malcolm MacEwen concluded that these policies, far from sustaining the economies and landscapes of the uplands of England and Wales, were major factors in their decline.[62] There was a large body of evidence to support this. In an attempt to bring about a change in policy, the Council for the National Parks commissioned Malcolm MacEwen and Geoffrey Sinclair (1983) to study the impact of current hill-farming policies, including those of the EEC, on the upland remoter areas of Britain, and to propose alternative policies which would retain such areas as viable rural communities. Their report was critical of both forestry and agricultural policies because of their predominant concern for *production* rather than the vitality of rural communities and the conservation of the countryside. They argued that much more employment could be created by coordinated policies sensitively directed to the problems of the uplands as a whole, rather than separate aspects of them. A similar message came from the Countryside Commission's *A Better Future for the Uplands*, published in 1984. This led to a provision in the 1985 Wildlife and Countryside (Amendment) Act that the Forestry Commission should try to achieve a reasonable balance between the interests of forestry and the conservation and enhancement of the countryside and conservation of wildlife.[63]

In the debate on the effects of forestry on the landscape, there has been particular concern about insensitive planting, particularly of conifers, and

*Table 8.2* Nature Conservation

### Sites of Special Scientific Interest

|  | No. | hectares |
|---|---|---|
| England | 3,675 | 809,525 |
| Scotland | 1,350 | 816,600 |
| Wales | 841 | 195,951 |
| Great Britain | 5,866 | 1,822,076 |

### National Nature Reserves

|  | No. | hectares |
|---|---|---|
| England | 135 | 46,804 |
| Scotland | 69 | 112,288 |
| Wales | 49 | 12,965 |
| Great Britain | 253 | 172,057 |

### Local Nature Reserves

|  | No. | hectares |
|---|---|---|
| England | 278 | 12,599 |
| Scotland | 8 | 2,866 |
| Wales | 19 | 3,423 |
| Great Britain | 305 | 18,888 |

of the destruction of wildlife habitats. The CPRE has stressed that 'the health and beauty of the English landscape depends critically on its broad-leaf tree cover', vast acreages of which have been lost. The need for a radical review of current forestry policy is eloquently set out in a 1986 report by S.C. Tompkins, belligerently entitled *The Theft of the Hills: Afforestation in Scotland*. With telling photographs, Tompkins (who had previously worked for the Forestry Commission and a major private forestry company) argues the case for a wide-ranging review of forestry policy. Like Marion Shoard, he argues that all major forestry operations should come under planning control.[64]

## THE TRANSFORMATION OF AGRICULTURE

A major plank of post-war policy was that a prosperous agriculture would be not only of strategic economic value but also would provide the best means of preserving the countryside. Aided by the policies of the EC, and by technological advances, the promotion of agricultural production has been a huge success. Unfortunately, as so often happens to policy successes, the solution of one problem gave rise to another one. In place of the need for increased agricultural production is the problem of dealing with enormous surpluses and finding ways of reducing output. Matters are further complicated (throughout Europe) by more productivity increases resulting from a number of factors including continuing technological advances (including biotechnological developments), and agricultural development in Eastern Europe (historically a major food producing region).

The pressures for change in agricultural policy have been increased by mounting concern over the rural landscapes which have changed in response to newer productive methods, and by growing demands for

*Table 8.3* Non-statutory Protected Areas

### Non-statutory protected areas 1991

|  | No. | Sq. km |
|---|---|---|
| Royal Society for the Protection of Birds | 118 | 756 |
| Royal Society for Nature Conservation and Local Nature Conservation Trust | 1,900 | 600 |
| National Trust | 74 | 100 |
| National Trust for Scotland | 101 | 44 |
| Woodland Trust | 465 | 61 |
| Wildfowl and Wetlands Trust | 9 | 17 |
| Field Studies Council | 3 | 15 |

*Source*: DoE, *Digest of Environmental Protection and Water Statistics*. No. 14, 1991, HMSO 1992, Table 7.5, p. 75. Some areas may be included in more than one category. There is also overlap with statutorily designated areas.

conservation and recreation. This has led to an 'erosion of the traditional view of farming as benevolent and benign'. In Brotherton's words:

> From the mid-1970s on the farming image has become increasingly tarnished. The spread of institutional ownership and industrialised units, the agribusiness, and the costly Common Agricultural Policy, the surpluses that suggest the environment has suffered for nought, all progressively and cumulatively take their toll.[65]

A major reversal of long-established, and previously popular policies, does not come easily; and the difficulties are increased when so many interests benefit from the subsidised regime. It is highly improbable that any political party could devise a policy that would bring about rapid and fundamental change to the traditional preoccupation with increased supply. For a Conservative Government, the political difficulties are obviously compounded (Cloke 1992: 279).

As a result, change is taking place gradually. The 1986 Agriculture Act required Agricultural Ministers to maintain a balance between the interests of agriculture and wider rural and environmental interests. These included:

— the economic and social interests of rural areas;
— the conservation and enhancement of the natural beauty and amenity of the countryside;
— the promotion of the enjoyment of the countryside by the public.

Such formal statements may invite scepticism, but it is wrong to belittle them. They constitute a political statement of which the Government can be constantly reminded. (This is reinforced by the appointment of a Cabinet Committee on the Environment and the allocation of environmental responsibilities for 'Green Ministers' in twenty government departments.)[66] Moreover, the Act went beyond rhetoric: for example, the powers of the Minister to provide agricultural services and goods were widened to encompass conservation, amenity, and enterprises of benefit to the rural economy. More dramatically, the same Act makes provision for *environmentally sensitive areas* (ESAs) where annual grants are given by MAFF to enable farmers to follow farming practices which will achieve conservation objectives.[67] These have developed into the main plank of the Ministry's countryside protection policy.[68] There were nineteen ESAs in the original scheme introduced in 1987. A revised scheme, covering a further twelve areas was being introduced in 1992 and 1993.

The Ministry of Agriculture also operates grant schemes for farm diversification and for farm woodlands. The former (now partly amalgamated with the EC-funded *Farm and Conservation Grant Scheme*) is mainly aimed at encouraging environmentally beneficial investments. The latter (the *Farm Woodland Scheme*) began as an experiment in 1991, but the results were disappointing and a comprehensive review led to the introduction of a new *Farm Woodland Premium Scheme* in 1992. The objectives are to enhance the farmed landscape and environment and to encourage a productive land-use alternative to agriculture. Additionally, a pilot *extensification scheme for beef and sheep* provides payments to farmers who reduce output by 20 per cent and, at the same time, maintain environmental features such as hedges, grassland, and moorland.

Successive measures have reflected the changed priorities, and there has been 'increased emphasis on the role of farmers as stewards of the countryside [which] has led to a greater concentration of funds on environmental schemes'.[69]

The Countryside Commission has been in the lead in promoting conservation and recreation as explicit objectives of agricultural policy. Its 1989 policy statement *Incentives for a New Direction in Farming* argued that the diminishing need for agricultural production provided an opportunity for 'environmentally friendly' farming. It presented a menu of incentives for farmers and landowners to provide environmental and recreational benefits. These ideas were translated into the *Countryside Premium*: an experimental scheme which gave incentives for land to be set aside for recreation. It has been followed by *Countryside Stewardship*: launched in 1991, this experimental scheme provides incentives for the protection and enhancement of valued and threatened landscapes. The scheme is 'market led'; in the words of the *Second Year Report* (1992: 80):

Its incentive rates have been set as a result of market research to determine the level of payments which would attract the greatest environmental benefits for least cost, and those rates may be adjusted – up or down – according to market response to the scheme.

In addition to the conservation incentives, payments are made for increased public access.

New schemes are being introduced at a bewildering rate. The glossy *Action for the Countryside* includes a new *hedgerow incentive scheme, wildlife enhancement scheme, parish paths partnership*, and the Development Commission's *countryside employment programme* and *redundant building grant*. A planning policy guidance note on nature conservation 'is also promised.

Diversification is the theme of much of current policy. In the words of PPG 7 (para 2.3): 'The priority now is to promote diversification of the rural economy so as to provide wide and varied employment opportunities for rural people, including those formerly employed in agriculture and related sectors.' This leads to the issue of integrated countryside planning.

## INTEGRATED COUNTRYSIDE PLANNING

This proliferation of initiatives underlines the need for some integration of policies. As PPG 7 states:

> The Government seeks to integrate its policies for the countryside in a number of ways, for example, by including environmental objectives in agricultural and forestry policies, and by encouraging high environmental standards in the implementation of rural development policies. The planning system is an important component of this policy.

A remarkable indication of what this might involve is provided by the new Scottish Natural Heritage (which, it will be remembered, combines responsibilities for conservation, amenity, and recreation). SNH points out that, currently, each economic activity related to the countryside is dealt with independently: agriculture, fisheries, forestry, mineral extraction, recreation and tourism, country sports, rural industries. Yet 'all of these activities are based

on use, in one way or another, of the natural heritage: *the natural heritage is the common resource*'. It is also a declining resource, since many of these uses contribute to 'a draw-down of Scotland's natural capital'. The deterioration is substantial and 'calls into question the capacity of the natural heritage to sustain the range of uses to which it is subjected'. All this (and more) clearly indicates the need for an integrated approach to the rural environment; how this is to be implemented remains to be determined (the publication from which these quotations are taken is a mere four pages long!). However, common objectives are required, and:

> SNH believes that the restoration, maintenance and management of Scotland's natural heritage – a common resource of great and diverse value – should be a primary aim of public policy. It should indeed provide one focus for the harmonisation of policies affecting the rural environment, a focus which should provide long-term benefit to the rural economy and to rural society.[70]

Encouragingly, the Scottish Office is now on record as stating that 'tackling rural issues in a sectoral manner does not work', though it remains to be seen whether the development of 'new partnership arrangements' will be sufficient.[71]

Experience with urban planning warns that good intentions and a belief in the efficacy of coordination are not enough. They do not necessarily bring about a 'balance'. Agriculture, for instance, in its modern guise, 'is incompatible with almost everything else' (Bowers and Cheshire 1983: 27). An honourable list of acute observers, from Rachel Carson to Howard Newby and Marion Shoard, testify in their different ways to the centrality of agriculture in this complex of issues.[72]

Part of the political difficulty (underlined by the quotation from William Waldegrave given earlier) is that, while the post-war planning legislation nationalised development rights, it effectively excluded agriculture and forestry. The owner of a listed building receives no compensation for the restrictions which are imposed, and may even be charged for repairs deemed necessary and undertaken by the local authority in default. The farmer, on the other hand, expects – and obtains – payment for 'profits forgone' in 'desisting from socially undesirable activity or merely for departing from what is conventionally regarded as good agricultural practice'.[73] The future agenda for action on the countryside seems likely to be even fuller than in the past.

## UPDATE

The MAFF Consultation Papers collectively entitled *Agriculture and England's Environment* (1993) must set a record for coverage and size! It contains the following papers: *Environmental Schemes under the Common Agricultural Policy, New Public Access in ESAs, New Nitrate Measures, Moorland Scheme, Set-Aside Management, Habitat Improvement Scheme,* and *Organic Farming.*

For a review of the current situation regarding 'Coastal zone protection and planning', see the article with this title by G. Stoker, *JPL* 1993: 521–6. The London and South East Regional Planning Conference has produced *Coastal Planning Guidelines for the South East*, SERPLAN, 1993. A discussion paper was issued by DoE in October 1993 on *Development below Low Water Mark: Managing the Coast*. The Ministry of Agriculture, Fisheries and Food has published *Strategy for Flood and Coastal Defence in England and Wales*, MAFF, 1993.

British Waterways' Consultation Paper on development plans has been revised and published under the title *The Waterway Environment and Development Plans*, Watford: British Waterways, 1993.

## NOTES

1 On telecommunications, see PPG 8, and Economic and Transport Planning Group 1989.
2 By the end of the 1920s the campaign for public access to the countryside became concentrated on the need for national parks such as had been established in Europe and North America but, though an official National Park Committee (the Addison Committee) reported in 1931 in favour of a national policy, no action was taken.
3 For accounts of the background to and the implementation of the 1949 Act, see Cherry 1975; and Blunden and Curry 1989. See also MacEwen and MacEwen 1982b and 1987.

4 See HL, Select Committee on Science and Technology, *Nature Conservancy Council*, 1990, and the Government response, 1990.
5 National Parks and Access to the Countryside Act 1949, section 1. The actual wording of the subsection on the preservation and enhancement of natural beauty relates to the duties of the National Parks Commission throughout England and Wales 'and particularly in the areas designated' as national parks. The Environmental Protection Act 1990 reworded the subsection to read: 'the preservation and enhancement of natural beauty in England, both in the areas designated under this Act as national parks or as areas of outstanding natural beauty'.
6 Edwards Report 1991. An earlier review, the Sandford Report (1974), recommended similarly. A lengthy response to the Sandford Report was issued in DoE Circular 4/76. Though this report is now largely of historical interest, the term 'Sandford principle' is still used as a shorthand for the policy of giving priority to natural beauty over recreation.
7 In a written answer of 21 January 1992, the Minister of State for the Environment and Countryside (David Trippier) announced: 'The Government intend to restate national park purposes to refer to quiet enjoyment and understanding, and to conservation of the wildlife and cultural heritage; to take steps to ensure that responsibility for detailed planning in their area should rest with national park authorities; and to invite local highway authorities, where they have not already done so, to delegate rights of way responsibilities to national park authorities.' (*HC Debates*, Written Answers, 21 January 1992, Vol. 1202, cols 108–9; the statement is reproduced in *JPL* 1992: 229–30.)
8 See Association of County Councils 1992a: 11–12 and 24; and Edwards Report 1991: chapter 12.
9 The requirement for a national park plan was introduced by section 18 of Schedule 17 of the Local Government Act 1972. This remains the operative Act: it has not been consolidated in later legislation.
10 The national parks have a surfeit of plans. The Edwards Report (1991: 93) recommended that the number should be reduced, and that an attempt should be made to obtain 'complementarity of purpose'.
11 The Broads is a unique area, subject to the contrary forces of flooding and (as a result of flood prevention) of conversion of grazing to arable farmland. Dower was personally opposed to the inclusion of the Broads in the list of proposed national parks, claiming that the area did not fit in with his definition. (He also commented that it might have been more suitable if the motor boat had never been invented!) However, the weight of opinion on the Committee was in favour of recommending the Broads as a national park. See Cherry 1975: 54.

12 See Shaw 1989. Earlier relevant publications include: Nature Conservancy Council 1965; Broads Consortium 1971; Countryside Commission 1976; Broads Authority 1982.

13 The following section is based on the summary contained in the Consultation Paper, *New Forest: The Government's Proposals*, DoE 1992.

14 *A New Boundary for the New Forest*, New Forest Committee, 1992. The New Forest Committee is a non-statutory body established in 1990 with Government encouragement. It was formerly termed the New Forest Heritage Area Committee.

15 *HC Debates*, Written Answer, 21 January 1992: see note 7 above.

16 In responding to the requirements of the 1949 Act, 38 English and *all* the Welsh LPAs stated that no agreements were necessary. With the change to a Conservative Government in 1951, 'the mood became even more compliant' (Blunden and Curry 1989: 136). Blunden and Curry provide a useful discussion of access: see their chapter 6.

17 Announced in the Countryside Commission's *Action for National Parks*, 1992.

18 See also the policy statement of the Countryside Commission that was published at the same time: *Areas of Outstanding Natural Beauty: A Policy Statement* (1990a). Earlier reviews published by the Countryside Commission include *Areas of Outstanding Natural Beauty: Report of a One Day Conference* (1978), and Himsworth 1980.

19 White Paper, *The Future of Development Plans*, 1989: para 1.17.

20 PPG 7: para 1.2. The reference to locally devised designations is in para 3.17.

21 A useful review of 'Rural planning in Scotland' is given in Shucksmith and Lloyd 1983.

22 Ramsay Report: *Report of the Scottish National Parks Survey Committee*, 1945. See also *National Parks and the Conservation of Nature in Scotland*, 1947. This report was produced by a further committee chaired by Sir Douglas Ramsay.

23 The CCS continued to press for the designation of national parks. In its 1990 report *The Mountain Areas of Scotland*, it proposed that four areas be designated as national parks: the Cairngorms, Loch Lomond, Ben Nevis/Glencoe/Black Mount, and Wester Ross.

24 The spectacular plateau of the Cairngorms (which is the greatest area of high land in Britain) has been proposed by the Government for inclusion in the World Heritage List (CCS *Annual Report 1990*: 13).

25 Countryside Commission for Scotland, *Twenty-third Annual Report 1990*, 1991: 11. See also the Commission's original proposals for 'areas of national scenic importance', in *Scotland's Scenic Heritage*, 1978.

26 Consultation Paper on *National Heritage Areas*, Scottish Office, 1991, and *The Implementation of Natural Heritage Areas: Statement of Government Position Following Consultation*, Scottish Office, 1992.

27 The figures are from the Environment Committee's report, *Coastal Zone Protection and Planning*, 1992: xvi.

28 Evidence of the National Trust to the Environment Committee, *Coastal Zone Protection and Planning*, 1992: 88.

29 Early initiatives included DoE Circular 56/63 on *Coastline Preservation and Development*, which asked authorities with coastal boundaries to make a study of their coastal areas; DoE Circular 7/66, *The Coast*, which asked for clear statements 'of each planning authority's policy for their coastal area in standard cartographic form'; a series of Countryside Commission reports on the coastline, culminating in *The Planning of the Coastline* (1970a) and *The Coastal Heritage* (1970b); and, in DoE Circular 12/72, Government endorsement of (non-statutorily) designated 'heritage coasts'. Current policy is set out in PPG 20 *Coastal Planning*, issued in 1992. Recreational provision is spelled out in PPG 17 *Sport and Recreation*. Other planning guidance, on issues which directly affect the coast, include PPG 2 on green belts, PPG 7 on the countryside, PPG 14 on development on unstable land, and PPG 16 on archaeology.

30 Countryside Commission, *Heritage Coasts: Policies and Priorities*, 1991: 17.

31 The Scottish figures are from DoE, *Digest of Environmental and Water Statistics 14*, 1991: 73.

32 HC Environment Committee, *Coastal Zone Protection and Planning*, 1992: 312 and 90.

33 DoE Response to the Environment Committee, *Coastal Zone Protection and Planning*, 1992: para 38. Another report, dealing with sea defences and coastal protection, was also critical of the complexity of the arrangements for this aspect of coastal planning. See National Audit Office, *Coastal Defences in England*, 1992.

34 This was a subcommittee of the Hobhouse Committee. It published a separate report in 1948 (Cmd 7207, HMSO).

35 Amendments were made by the Countryside Act 1968, the Highways Act 1980, and the Wildlife and Countryside Act 1981.

The Gosling Report (*Report of the Footpaths Committee*, 1968) dealt with 'the present system of footpaths, bridleways and other comparable rights of way in England and Wales and the arrangements for the recording, closure, diversion and maintenance of such routes as are suitable for present and potential needs in the countryside, and to make recommendations'. The majority of the recommendations were implemented in 1968.

The Sandford Committee, which reported six years later (*Report of the National Park Policies Review Committee*, 1974), maintained that the existing system was not suited to current needs: yet little was being done to improve it. Further legislative provisions were included in the Highways Act 1980 and the Wildlife and Countryside Act 1981.

36  See DoE Circular 18/90; Garner 1989; and Chesman 1991.

37  Countryside Commission, *Annual Report 1990–1991*: 16. A summary of the powers relating to the maintenance of public rights of way is given in *Planning Tools: Implementing Countryside Planning Policies in Metropolitan Areas through the Planning System*, Countryside Commission, 1990b.

38  Blunden and Curry 1989: 144. In the proceedings of the HC Employment Committee's inquiry on *Tourism* (1990: Q. 392), mention was made of a technique which (so it is believed) has not so far been used in Britain: supplying visitors with outsize slippers for walking!

39  DoE, *Action for the Countryside*, 1992: 21.

40  Blunden and Curry 1989: 152. For a very different (and persuasive) perspective see Shoard 1987: 360.

41  The Countryside Act 1968 confers powers on local authorities to provide 'opportunities for the enjoyment of the countryside by the public'. Specifically identified are country parks, which are 'primarily intended to meet the demand resulting from the increased leisure and mobility of large numbers of the population living in cities and urban areas, and looking for a change of environment within easy reach. The location of parks in relation to urban areas and alternative recreational facilities is of prime importance' (MHLG Circular 44/68).

42  Lee Valley Regional Park Authority, *Lee Valley Park Plan*, 1985. The publications of the Authority are obtainable from its offices at Myddelton House, Bulls Cross, Enfield, Middlesex EN2 9HG.

43  DoE Circular 44/68. See now PPG 17, 1991.

44  In 1988 there were 220 country parks and 264 picnic sites in England and Wales (Blunden and Curry 1989: 169). More generally, see two publications of the Countryside Commission: *Enjoying the Countryside: Priorities for Action* (1987), and *Enjoying the Countryside: Policies for People* (1992).

45  There is extensive documentation on the waterways in the HC Environment Committee's report *British Waterways Board*, 1989. This section draws freely from this source. See also the Government response to the HC report (1990).

46  BWB *Report and Accounts 1991/92*: 19 and 17.

47  *British Waterways and Development Plans: Consultation Document*, BWB, 1992. 'Many remainder canals have

been upgraded to cruising waterways following restoration and the negotiation of maintenance agreements with the relevant local authorities to meet the cost of maintenance above the remainder waterway standards' (*Government Response to the Report of the Environment Committee, British Waterways Board*, 1990, para 54).

Considerable support is also made by voluntary organisations. For example, the Kennet and Avon Canal Trust raised over £2m towards the cost of restoration.

48  The division reflects the separation of 'landscape conservation for amenity and habitat conservation for science: the former is about access and the latter is about exclusion'. This 'false distinction . . . is hardly to be found anywhere else in the world' (Blunden and Curry 1989: 49).

49  Protection of particular species of flora and fauna is provided, in the main, by Part I of the Wildlife and Countryside Act 1981.

50  DoE Circular 1/92, *Planning Controls over Sites of Special Scientific Interest*. More generally, see DoE Circular 27/87, *Nature Conservation*, and PPG 7, *The Countryside and the Rural Economy*, 1992.

51  A list is given in the annual reports of the Nature Conservancy Council: see its last report (before the reorganisation), *Nature Conservancy Council, 17th Report 1990–1991*, English Nature, 1991: 83–4.

52  A House of Commons inquiry deals with fish farming: see HC Select Committee on Agriculture, *Fish Farming*, 1990. See also Lloyd and Livingstone 1991.

53  DoE, *Consultation Paper on Marine Consultation Areas*, 1992.

54  Nature Conservancy Council 1990: 14. The EC Directive on the Conservation of Wild Birds is reproduced as an annex to DoE Circular 27/87.

55  Lord Bellwin, during the second reading of the bill in the House of Lords (*HL Debates*, vol. 415, col. 986, 16 December 1980) quoted in Grant *Encyclopedia*, para 2–1986, p. 20808.

56  Among the omissions are the Ramsar Convention on Wetlands (see *Ramsar Convention: Convention on Wetlands of International Importance*, 1976); the *Species Recovery Programme* which aims to increase populations of plants and animals that are threatened with extinction (see *English Nature: Progress Report 1992*: 25–7); *Regionally Important Geological/Geomorphological Sites* (in *English Nature: Progress Report 1992*: 23); controls over the conversion of moorland and heathland (see section 42 of the Countryside and Wildlife Act 1981).

The memorandum prepared by the Royal Society of Birds for the HL Select Committee inquiry on the *Nature Conservancy Council* (1990: 94) gives a summary of several international treaties and conventions.

57  These were the Berne Convention on the Conservation of European Wildlife and Natural Habitats, the

Convention of International Trade in Endangered Species, the Convention on the Conservation of Migratory Species, the EC Directive on the Conservation of Wild Birds, and the Ramsar Convention on Wetlands.

58  A detailed account of the passage of the bill is given in Cox and Lowe 1983b. An excellent succinct analysis of the political forces which gathered around the bill (and its aftermath) is to be found in the epilogue of the updated edition of Newby (1985). See also MacEwen and MacEwen 1982a. The Act is discussed in a wider context in Roome 1986.

59  The quotation is from a slender booklet entitled *Codes of Guidance for Sites of Special Scientific Interest*, 1982. A useful article on SSSIs is Ball 1985. The much vaunted 'voluntary principle' did not survive its test: the Wildlife and Countryside (Amendment) Act 1985 closed a loophole in the 1981 Act which allowed farmers to damage sites while required consultations were in progress (see Adams 1986).

60  Waldegrave *et al.* 1986; for a different view see, for example, Mowie 1986.

61  NAO, *Review of Forestry Commission Objectives and Achievements*, 1986: 1.

62  MacEwen and MacEwen 1982b; see also Tourism Recreation Research Unit 1981, and Sinclair 1983.

63  See Samuels 1986, and Gilg 1986: 127.

64  Note should be taken of the introduction of *Indicative Forestry Strategies*, first in Scotland (Circular 13/91), and later in England and Wales (DoE Circular 29/92). Essentially, these concern the identification of preferred areas for new woodlands.

65  Brotherton 1986: 157. Newby (1985: 299) remarks that the furore over the 1981 Act made it clear 'that the hitherto unquestioned belief that farmers were the trusted custodians of the countryside was now in tatters'.

66  *This Common Inheritance: The Second Year Report*, 1992: 29 (para 3.24). A list of the departments and the Green Ministers is given on p. 190 of this report.

67  The Agriculture Act 1986, which introduced ESAs, also required the Minister to publish a report on their effects. The first such report was MAFF, *Environmentally Sensitive Areas*, 1989. It was British pressure which resulted in the EC Council of Ministers giving authorisation for member states to make payments to farmers in designated areas of high conservation value

to encourage them to follow environmentally favourable practices: see p. 4 of the aforementioned MAFF report.

68  Cloke 1992: 278. Cloke explains the background to the new policy: 'In February 1987, the Thatcher administration issued two sets of proposals which emanated from a group established to look at alternative land use and rural economy (ALURE) in Britain. The immediate context of these proposals was a short term concern over gaining middle class votes from those who were interested in green issues, although the longer term issues of the CAP were also important here. One package of proposals came from the MAFF and proposed some £25m per annum of new expenditure on farm diversification . . . The other proposals came from the DoE and consisted of removing the presumption that agricultural use of rural land should be paramount for the purposes of town and country planning, and promoting three equal concerns for rural land use planning – agriculture, the environment, and rural economic revival . . . The notion of this dual ALURE was to present an integrated and coherent policy initiative which would appeal to farmers, conservationists, middle class rural residents, and even house building interests – the Thatcher juggling act personified.'

69  *The Government's Expenditure Plans 1992–93 to 1994–95: Departmental Report by the Ministry of Agriculture, Fisheries and Food*, 1992: 1.

70  SNH, *An Agenda for Investment in Scotland's Natural Heritage*, 1992.

71  Scottish Office, *Rural Framework*, 1992.

72  For instance, Newby (in a passage which refers to Rachel Carson's contribution to the debate) comments that 'agriculture, by definition, involves a disturbance of the natural ecology. Indeed, most forms of agriculture do not so much disturb the natural environment as destroy it by a manmade artefact' (Newby 1985: 205).

73  Jenkins 1990: 15. See also Hodge 1989 and 1991. Both these articles give useful references to other literature. The Association of National Park Officers (1988) has proposed a system of *environmentally favoured areas* under which farmers would become environmental managers as well as food producers. Environmental management would be treated as a crop, and the producers rewarded accordingly. This is a logical development of the present arrangements (the term 'environmentally favoured areas' is a play on words – combining the present *less favoured areas* and environmentally sensitive areas which are designations for much of the land in national parks).

# 9

# URBAN POLICIES

If local politicians cannot normally be expected to provide the visionary leadership required, neither can central government . . . Solutions imposed from the centre without the support and involvement of the local community are unlikely to succeed.

Confederation of British Industry, 1988

Urban regeneration must, if it is to have a lasting effect, involve the active commitment of local authorities in adapting their policies and spending programmes to assist areas of need. Local authorities are essential partners in the urban regeneration process, and often play a leading role.

Scottish Office, 1990[1]

The quotations would have been unremarkable in the 1970s but, in the following decade, much of urban policy denied their validity: indeed, local government was sometimes seen, not as part of a solution, but as part of the problem. This had significant implications for urban policy which are discussed in this chapter. Two preliminary points, however, need to be made. First, the title may be somewhat misleading in that a number of the policies discussed extend to rural areas (housing, for example) or may have non-spatial dimensions (for example, economic development). Nevertheless, the focus of the discussion is on urban areas in general and inner cities in particular. Second, the title is in the plural since there is no such thing as a single urban policy or a set of policies which are so cohesive as to justify the use of the word *policy* in an omnibus way. Moreover, it is highly unlikely that there could be, as experience elsewhere has shown.[2]

As these points suggest, it is not a simple matter to define what are, and what are not, urban policies. (Social security and housing benefits may play a more significant role than urban aid or urban regeneration policies.) Indeed, there is an important question as to whether there is – or should be – a distinct area of *urban* policy; this is a matter which is briefly discussed at the end of the chapter. Nevertheless, there is a group of policies which are officially labelled 'urban' in the *DoE Annual Report,* and which have sufficient urban identity to justify discussing them together.[3]

The chapter opens with a discussion of inadequate housing: the starting point of 'urban policy' in the nineteenth century, and the major concern of policy until at least the end of the 1960s. The focus then shifted from physical conditions to the social aspects of housing and, later, to 'areas of social need'. A further shift took place in the late 1970s when economic issues were seen as being the key to urban regeneration. By the mid-1980s this had become the conventional wisdom, with an accent on large-scale property development projects undertaken in 'partnership' with the private sector. In the early 1990s, the value of these large projects (often modelled on the supposed successful experience in the USA) was increasingly being questioned.[4]

## INADEQUATE HOUSING

Britain has a very large legacy of old housing which is inadequate by modern standards. This results from the relatively early start of the Industrial Revolution in this country and the rapid, unplanned and speculative urban development which took place in the nineteenth century. (The contrast with, for example, the Scandinavian countries, whose industrial revolutions came later when wealth was greater and standards higher, is marked.) As a result, British policies in relation to clearance and redevelopment are of long standing, though it was the Greenwood Housing Act of 1930 which heralded the start of the modern slum clearance programme. Over a third of a million houses were demolished before the Second World War brought the programme to an abrupt halt.

By 1938 demolitions were running at the rate of 90,000 a year: had it not been for the war, over a million older houses would (at this rate) have been demolished by 1951. The war, however, not only delayed clearance programmes: it resulted in enforced neglect and deterioration. War damage, shortage of building resources and (of increasing importance in the period of post-war inflation) crude rent restriction policies increased the problem of old and inadequate housing.

It was not until the mid-1950s that clearance could generally be resumed, and well over 2 million slum houses (in Great Britain) have been demolished since then. But the problem is still one of large dimensions. The 1986 House Condition Survey showed that, of the 22.5 million dwellings in England, 909,000 were 'unfit' (according to the pre-1989 Act standards), 436,000 lacked one or more of the basic amenities, and 2.4 million were in poor repair. Some progress had been made since 1981: in particular there had been a fall in the number of dwellings lacking basic amenities; but there had been little change in the number of dwellings in serious disrepair. This may have been related to the marked decline in slum clearance since the mid-1970s. This has continued into the 1990s and, in 1991/92, the number of houses demolished or closed in Britain was less than 4,000,

compared with 54,000 in 1974/75, and 90,000 in 1969.

## FROM CLEARANCE TO RENEWAL

Though an improvements grants policy was introduced in 1949, it was not until the mid-1950s that it got under way. Since then, the emphasis gradually shifted from individual house improvements, first to the improvement of streets or areas of sub-standard housing, and later to the improvement of the total environment.

Initially, it was assumed that houses could be neatly divided into two groups: according to the 1953 White Paper *Houses: The Next Step*, there were those which were unfit for human habitation and those which were 'essentially sound'. As experience was gained, the 'improvement philosophy' broadened, and it came to be realised that there was a very wide range of housing situations related not only to the presence or otherwise of plumbing facilities and the state of repair of individual houses, but also to location, the varying socio-economic character of different neighbourhoods and the nature of the local housing market. A house 'lacking amenities' in Chelsea was, in important ways, different from an identical house in Rochdale: the appropriate action was similarly different. Later, it was better understood that appropriate action defined in housing market terms was not necessarily equally appropriate in social terms. A middle class 'invasion' might restore the physical fabric and raise the quality (and 'tone') of a neighbourhood, but the social costs of this were borne largely by displaced low-income families. The problem thus became redefined.

Growing concern for the environment also led to an increased awareness of the importance of the factors *causing* deterioration. It became clear that these are more numerous and complex than housing legislation had recognised. Through-traffic and inadequate parking provision were quickly recognised as being of physical importance. The answer, in appropriately physical terms, was the re-routing of traffic, the closure of streets and the provision of parking spaces (together with cobbled areas and the planting of trees). Most difficult of all is to assess the social function of an area, the needs it meets and the ways in which conditions can be improved for (and in accordance with the wishes of) the people living in an area.

For a considerable time, this issue of the social function of areas was dealt with largely by ignoring it, although a strong shift towards improvement rather than clearance was heralded by the 1969 Housing Act. This increased grants for improvement, and introduced *general improvement areas* (GIAs), which were envisaged as being areas of between 300 and 800 'fundamentally sound houses capable of providing good living conditions for many years to come and unlikely to be affected by known redevelopment or major planning proposals'.[5] The enhanced grants and the GIAs made a significant contribution to the reduction in the number of unfit properties, though in some areas gentrification unexpectedly took place, reducing the amount of privately rented housing, and affecting the existing communities (Wood 1991: 52).

The 1974 Housing Act, however, which represented a major reorientation of policy, brought social considerations to the fore. There was a new emphasis on a comprehensive strategy on an area basis implementing a policy of 'gradual renewal'.

> Gradual renewal is a continuous process of minor rebuilding and renovation which sustains and reinforces the vitality of a neighbourhood in ways responsive to social and physical needs as they develop and change. Rehabilitation should take place to varying standards to match the effective demand of individual occupiers . . . It must be accepted, and willingly, that some houses of low quality meet a real need for cheap accommodation, a need which might not otherwise be satisfied . . .[6]

The powers (and duties) conferred by the 1974 Housing Act focused upon areas of particular housing stress. Local housing authorities were required to consider the need for dealing with these as *housing action areas* (HAAs). Though these were conceived in terms of housing conditions, particular importance was attached to 'the concentration in the area of households likely to have special housing problems – for instance, old-age pensioners, large families, single-parent families, or families whose head is unemployed or in a low income group'.[7]

The intention was that intense activity in HAAs would significantly improve housing conditions within a period of about five years. In the event, HAA designation has lasted much longer in many cities. Various additional powers were made available to local authorities within HAAs, for compulsory purchase, renewal, and environmental improvement; and grant aid for renewal has been targeted to HAAs.

The novel feature of HAAs was the statutory provision which made the well-being of those living in them one of the requirements for, and objects of, declaration. This meant that residents had to be involved in the 'nature and timing of action programmes'. Thus HAA implementation has in some cases involved the setting up of new residents' groups with the help and advice of the local authority, and quite extensive communication exercises to inform residents, often in many languages.

## HOUSING RENEWAL AREAS

The area-based approach has been retained, although substantially altered, in the major revision of the urban renewal and renovation grant systems made by the Local Government and Housing Act 1989. In addition to individual income-related house renovation grants, the Act introduces *renewal areas* (RAs), which have replaced GIAs and HAAs. There are also powers for local authority support for group repair schemes to renovate the exteriors of blocks of houses.

Detailed explanation and guidance is given in the lengthy DoE Circular 6/90.[8] The thrust of the changes reflects a concern for a broader strategic approach including economic and social regeneration as well as housing renewal. It involves the resumption of clearance; the use of partnerships to bring together the initiatives of local authorities, housing associations, property owners, and residents; and a system of grants which are mainly both mandatory and income related.[9] In discussing the changes, Circular 6/90 heralds a significant change in policy:

> [Some authorities] have been using resources for improvement where this seems not to have been cost-effective in terms of securing the life of the stock and

where there were no good social reasons why redevelopment should not have taken place. In future, therefore, authorities will be required to carry out a thorough appraisal of the various options available to them for dealing with areas of poor quality private sector housing before declaring an RA. Furthermore, RAs will normally be larger than previous statutory areas to allow for a comprehensive approach covering renovation and redevelopment of the housing alongside action on social, economic and environmental problems . . .

Clearance is thus firmly back on the agenda. Moreover, it is suggested that the declaration of RAs 'may not necessarily mean tackling the worst areas first'. Rather 'it may be better to concentrate on "turning around" areas which have not yet reached the bottom of the spiral of decline in order to improve market confidence, and thus be able to make the maximum use of private sector inputs'.

In determining local strategies, importance is placed on a *neighbourhood renewal assessment*. This is, in effect, a plan-making and implementation programme combined. Designation has to be preceded by an assessment of conditions, an estimate of the resources available, and the selection of the preferred options. The procedure goes much further than the typical land-use planning process to incorporate a cost–benefit analysis of different alternative policies. This is to include the costs (private as well as public) over a thirty-year period. The qualitative social and environmental implications of different strategies are also to be measured. Examples of factors which might be relevant are: 'maintaining the existing community', 'private sector attractiveness', 'security and safety', 'anti-social behaviour elimination', and 'litter and refuse reduction'.

Stress is laid on publicity and consultation, both during and after the declaration process. This includes press statements and site notices, and the delivery of an explanatory summary of the proposals to every address in the area. A period of up to 28 days is to be allowed for responses. An interesting requirement is that all who make representations which are not accepted must be provided with a written explanation. These extensive publicity requirements are considered to be necessary to underpin action in the area (including compulsory purchase and clearance, if this is deemed desirable).

The options which are open to a local authority in an RA are constrained by a set of detailed conditions. The number of properties in an area is to be at least 300, though it is advised that a more usual minimum will be 500. (The lower figure is to allow declaration in smaller towns and villages, such as in the coalfield areas.) There is no maximum, but it is suggested that a figure of more than 3,000 dwellings would be difficult to manage. More than 75 per cent of the dwellings must be privately owned, and at least 75 per cent must be considered unfit or qualify for the mandatory or discretionary grants. At least 30 per cent of the households must be in receipt of specified state benefits, thus ensuring that 'a significant proportion of residents in an RA should not be able to afford the cost of the works to their properties'. In addition, RAs cannot include Housing Action Trust properties (discussed on pp. 199–200) or substantial local authority stock: these are dealt with under different powers. Nevertheless, RA strategies will have to take into account housing, planning, economic development, and other programmes in the area, or adjacent to it. In line with the 'comprehensive approach', areas of derelict land may be included in an RA where its improvement needs to be considered as part of the wider strategy, and where the extra powers might help to bring about its improvement.[10]

Among the many other provisions of the 1989 Local Government and Housing Act, is a revision of the criteria for determining whether a dwelling is 'unfit'. Previously, the statutory definition (in England and Wales) was related to structure, physical condition and plumbing. These nineteenth-century public health factors certainly could affect health and safety, but there was considerable scope for differing judgements, and some more modern essentials (such as hot water) were not included. The approach was altered in Scotland following the 1967 Cullingworth Report.[11] The 1969 Housing (Scotland) Act introduced the concept of a 'tolerable standard', and this was followed in the 1989 Act for England and Wales.[12] Dwellings which fail to meet the new statutory fitness standard qualify for mandatory grants, but this is subject to a means test for both owner-occupiers and private landlords. Another important change is that, whereas compensation for unfit houses was formerly based on site value (since, by definition, a slum house had no value),[13] full market value compensation is now payable. This has facilitated another change: 'the presumption against the confirmation of compulsory purchase orders . . . in respect of fit properties *and properties which the owners are prepared to improve* will no longer apply' (emphasis added).

In addition to the mandatory renovation grants, there are mandatory grants for 'common parts' (as in the case of shared spaces in flats), houses in multiple occupation where repairs are needed to comply with an Order; and for making houses fit for occupation by people with disabilities. Discretionary grants are available for 'minor works' for several purposes such as adapting facilities to enable the elderly to remain in their homes, or to adapt houses for the use of people with disabilities.

Group schemes have been introduced to replace 'enveloping'. This approach, which was pioneered in Birmingham, involves the renovation of the external fabric and curtilage of deteriorated dwellings. The most significant change is the introduction of means testing, with maximum contributions from households of 25 per cent of the costs in RAs, and 50 per cent elsewhere. This may well act as a brake, particularly since it will take only one objecting owner to hold up a scheme.

## ESTATE ACTION

In 1979, the DoE set up the *priority estates project* to explore ways in which problem council estates could be improved. These estates varied in their problems, but all had become neglected and run down; some had been vandalised. A 1981 report[14] considered three experiments in the improvement of such estates, and concluded that the task of improvement involved a great deal more than mere physical renovation: social and economic problems needed to be addressed at the same time. In 1985, the DoE established an *Urban Renewal Unit* (now called *Estate Action*) to encourage and assist local authorities to develop a range of measures to revitalise run-down estates. These measures include transfers of ownership and/or management to tenants' cooperatives or *management trusts* involving tenants; sales of tenanted estates to private trusts or developers; and sales of empty property to developers for refurbishment for sale or rent. Estate Action funding is allocated on a competitive basis. A wide range of factors is taken into account: the provisions for tenant participation; the devolution of management to tenants; increases in 'tenant mix', and right-to-buy activity; and the role of the private sector. In 1993/94, Estate Action was programmed to deal with 60,000 dwellings and 3,750 'disposals' to the private sector. One part of the funding (which increased from £75m in 1987/88 to an estimated £364m in 1992/93) is set aside for the *Design Improvement Controlled Experiment*. Budgeted at a total cost of £42m, this experiment has been mounted to test the controversial thesis of Alice Coleman (1985/1990) that design improvements can in themselves result in social as well as physical improvements. Seven estates are involved in the experiment which is being evaluated by consultants: a report is expected in 1994.

## HOUSING ACTION TRUSTS

The 1987 White Paper, *Housing: The Government's Proposals*, announced the creation of *housing action trusts* (HATs) to tackle the management and renewal of badly run-down housing estates that have 'problems that are beyond the capacity of authorities to remedy with existing resources'.[15] HATs are the housing equivalent of the urban development corporations, but they can be introduced only with the consent of a majority of the tenants. They are non-departmental public bodies, responsible directly to the Secretary of State for improving the physical conditions of estates by renovations and improvements to the houses and the environment. They are intended to secure more diverse tenure, essentially by involving private and voluntary housing agencies, and they also aim to improve economic and social conditions.

Although funding was allocated for HATs as early as 1988, there was considerable delay in getting the first ones started because of fierce opposition by affected local authorities and tenants. Rao (1990) has documented two areas in Lambeth and Sunderland that were initially identified for designation. The dilemma facing local authorities is that HATs involve a loss of control to the private sector, but a potential source of very substantial extra funding. Tenants fear increased rents and reduced availability of housing if it is sold to private owners after improvement.

Following the embarrassing rejection of HAT designation in the first ballots, much greater care was taken with subsequent proposals to involve tenants in early discussions. The first HATs to be designated were at Waltham Forest and North Hull.[16] In 1992, 82 per cent of the tenants of a Liverpool tower block voted in favour of the third HAT. Others have since been designated in Birmingham and Tower Hamlets.[17]

## SCOTTISH HOUSING

Scottish housing is different from that south of the Border in significant ways. There is a high proportion of tenemental properties; dwellings tend to be smaller; rents are lower; and a higher proportion of the housing stock is owned by public authorities. These and other differences reflect history, economic growth and decline, local building materials, and climate. Above all, Scotland faces a major problem of poor-quality tenemental housing. Despite the large amount of clearance in the post-war years, there still remains much poor-quality housing in both the private and the public sectors.

No house condition survey was conducted at the time of the 1986 English survey, but one was completed in 1992 (and was due for publication in 1993). Previous evidence suggests that, because of the dominance and relatively young age of much of the public housing stock, a high proportion of housing has the basic amenities, but the condition is often poor, and requires high levels of expenditure.

Scottish housing is distinctive in important ways. First, there is the scale and character of public housing. The low council rents of the past contributed to the relatively low demand for private housing

which, coupled with massive public house building programmes, gave Scotland the highest proportion of public sector housing in Western Europe – and made Glasgow City Council the largest public sector landlord (McCrone 1991). (It should be noted that the Scots use the term 'house' in the English sense of 'dwelling', i.e. it embraces a flat or tenement.) The Right to Buy has shifted the balance somewhat between the owner-occupied and public housing sectors: owner-occupation rose from 35 per cent in 1979 to 53 per cent in 1991, while public sector renting fell from 54 per cent to 38 per cent. Nevertheless, in spite of the sale of nearly a quarter of the public housing stock, the level of public renting in Scotland is still much higher than in England and Wales.

The Conservative Government believes that the large-scale public ownership of housing is at the root of much of the Scottish housing problem. The 1987 White Paper, *Housing: The Government's Proposals for Scotland*, sets out the argument:

> Municipal housing was an effective means of increasing the total housing stock and of clearing the slums, but it has created problems which arose from the single mindedness with which these problems were pursued. In some areas, the system has provided good quality housing and management. In others, there are major problems of unsuitable housing types, disrepair, and management failure. In some parts of Scotland, the public landlording operations are on such a vast scale that there is an inevitable risk that they become too distant and bureaucratic to respond well to individual tenants' wishes and needs. The provision of housing in the public sector can all too easily result in inefficiencies and bureaucracy, producing queuing and lack of choice for the consumer, made worse by the existence of some housing which people do not want to live in. Poor housing conditions, just as much as tenant dissatisfaction are the result of bad management, as well as insensitive and misconceived design. Low rents in many areas have contributed to inadequate standards of management and repair, against tenants' long term interests.

The Government's strong desire to reduce the public housing sector (and particularly to break up the public ownership of the large peripheral estates) is an important background issue in Scottish housing policy.

Equally distinctive is the institutional context of Scottish housing policy. The relationship between the Scottish Office and Scottish local authorities has always been much closer than in England, and there has been much easier coordination. This has resulted in what Carley (1990: 51) describes as 'a much more clearly defined and integrated housing-neighbourhood renewal policy, which covers housing and planning issues together'. Though the term may have come into use only recently, the idea of partnership has been a long-standing feature of Scottish urban renewal. The Scottish Office has tended to work with local authorities (which have a single local authority association), rather than exerting central control through such mechanisms as UDCs and HATs. Instead, there have been centrally sponsored bodies which have worked in cooperation with local government. In addition to the Scottish Development Agency (discussed on pp. 213–15), there is a housing agency, now Scottish Homes. Established by the Housing (Scotland) Act 1988, this incorporates the former Scottish Special Housing Association (SSHA), which dates from 1937 and the Housing Corporation in Scotland (HCiS). The SSHA has been a major housing authority which has worked alongside local authorities in the implementation of housing policies. There is no equivalent body in England and Wales.

Scottish Homes has contributed to the pursuit of privatisation policies, including the disposal of its own stock. During 1991/92, it assisted in the sale of 4,349 homes to owner-occupiers, and the transfer of 2,908 homes to community ownership; it also transferred 4,164 of its own stock to different landlords. In 1992 there were 61,000 houses remaining in its ownership. It has also made a substantial contribution to the four Partnership Areas in the large peripheral estates of Dundee, Edinburgh, Glasgow, and Paisley (which are discussed later in this chapter). Additionally, Scottish Homes is involved in *smaller urban renewal initiatives* in seven towns. It spent £8m on housing renewal in 1992/93, in the provision of new or improved homes in partnership with local authorities and alongside programmes for economic and environmental improvement.

As in England and Wales during the 1980s, policy in relation to the older private housing stock placed more emphasis on rehabilitation than on clearance. But with much of the older tenemental properties the scope for improvement is severely restricted by the decayed fabric of the buildings, their internal layout, and the high cost of alteration, as well as the practical problems of multiple ownership. Some of these difficulties have been met by the use of powers of *compulsory improvement* of a whole tenemental structure, and by the establishment of *ad hoc* housing associations. However, the Scottish legislation has long provided for more flexibility than the English. The *housing action areas* are of three types: for demolition, for improvement, and for a combination of the two. This enables the most appropriate action to be taken according to area conditions.

Scottish practice also has involved residents in housing renewal. There is a requirement for a two-month period of consultation with local residents before an HAA is declared, and small community-based housing associations are established to lead renewal. This has been part of the policy of HCiS:

> Operating with local authorities, the Corporation identified a set of adjacent Housing Action Areas. Housing associations were informed or were created to manage the rehabilitation programme in areas containing 1,000 to 2,000 units. Management committees consisting almost entirely of local residents were formed.
> (Maclennan 1989: 698)

Given the distinctive Scottish style of implementing HAAs, there has not been the need for the new legislation equivalent to the Local Government and Housing Act 1989. However, proposals for a means-tested scheme for improvement grants were issued in 1988, though no action has yet followed.[18]

## THINKING ON AREA POLICIES

Several major elements can be identified in the development of thinking on deprived areas in Britain: inadequate physical conditions, the presence of a 'large' number of 'immigrants' (many of whom were born in Britain), educational 'disadvantage', and a multiplicity of less-easily measurable social problems.

For a very long time, there was a preoccupation with inadequate physical conditions (particularly in relation to plumbing). Indeed, British housing policy developed from sanitary policy (Bowley 1945), and it still remains a significant feature of it. Area policy in relation to housing was almost entirely restricted to slum clearance until the late 1960s when concepts of housing improvement widened, first to the improvement of areas of housing and then to environmental improvement. Despite a number of social surveys[19] the policy was unashamedly physical: so much so that increasing powers were provided to *compel* reluctant owners and tenants to have improvements carried out. Not until the 'seventies was attention focused on the social character and function of areas of old housing.[20]

A further area of policy in the field of housing developed as a response to the problems of controlling multi-occupation and overcrowding in areas of 'housing stress'. The Milner Holland Committee (1965) looked favourably on the idea of designating the worst areas as *areas of special control* in which

> some authority might be set up, with responsibility for the whole area and armed with wide powers to control sales and lettings, to acquire property by agreement or compulsorily over the whole area or part of it, to demolish and rebuild as necessary, to require improvements to be carried out or to undertake such improvements themselves, and to make grants on a more generous and flexible basis than under the present law.

Similarly, the National Committee for Commonwealth Immigrants, starting from a concern for the socioeconomic problems facing local authorities with substantial numbers of immigrant families, argued for the designation of *areas of special housing need*.[21] Again, the crucial issue was the control of overcrowding, exorbitant rents, insanitary conditions, disrepair and the risk of fire. The NCCI, however, noted that it was not possible to consider areas such as these 'without considering the deficiencies in all other social services that exist within such an area, and the need to rehabilitate these services at the same time as examining housing problems'.

These proposals were not accepted by the Government, though increased powers to control multi-occupation and abuses were provided. Part of the reason for this was that there was considerable doubt as to the efficacy of measures designed to *control*. The NCCI report had referred to the need for treating the problems of the stress areas 'patiently and tactfully', for giving the public 'every opportunity to understand the steps which are being undertaken' and for seeking the 'active and willing cooperation' of voluntary organisations and community groups. Indeed, without this they saw the likelihood of their proposed solution creating 'problems almost as serious as those which are being alleviated'. It was left to the Plowden, Seebohm, and Skeffington reports to probe more deeply into this area.

The Plowden Committee was appointed in 1963, 'to consider primary education *in all its aspects*', it reported four years later in very broad terms. The Committee appreciated and underlined the complex of factors which produced seriously disadvantaged areas. Researchers are faced with attempting to abstract and measure the importance of individual factors when 'all other things are equal'. Policymakers and administrators, on the other hand,

> must act in a world where other things are never equal; this, too, is the world in which children grow up, where everything influences everything else, where nothing succeeds like success and nothing fails like failure. The outlook and aspirations of their own parents; the opportunities and handicaps of the neighbourhood in which they live; the skill of their teachers and the resources of the schools they go to; their genetic inheritance; and other factors still unmeasured or unknown surround the children with a seamless web of circumstances.[22]

This web of circumstances is neatly illustrated in the following quotation which is as relevant today as it was in 1967.

> In a neighbourhood where the jobs people do and the status they hold owe little to their education, it is natural for children as they grow older to regard school as a brief prelude to work rather than an avenue to future opportunities . . . Not surprisingly, many teachers are unwilling to work in a neighbourhood where the schools are old, where housing of the sort they want is unobtainable, and where education does not attain the standards they expect for their own children. From some

neighbourhoods, urban and rural, there has been a continuing flow of the more successful young people. The loss of enterprise and skill makes things worse for those left behind. Thus, the vicious circle may turn from generation to generation and the schools play a central part in the process, both causing and suffering cumulative deprivation.

The Plowden Committee recommended a national policy of 'positive discrimination', the aim of which would be to make schools in the most deprived areas as good as the best in the country. Additional resources were necessary to achieve this: extra teachers and special salary increases; teachers' aides; priority for replacement and improvement in the school-building programme; extra books and equipment; and expanded provision for nursery education.

The Seebohm Committee (1968) had wider terms of reference than the Plowden Committee: 'to review the organisation and responsibilities of the local authority personal social services in England and Wales, and to consider what changes are desirable to secure an effective family service'. Of relevance to the present discussion is the Committee's concern for 'social planning' (which is dealt with largely in terms of administrative organisation) and their recommendations in relation to *areas of special need*. Unfortunately, the Committee did not suggest how these should be identified, in spite of a recommendation that the areas should be accorded priority in the allocation of resources.

More helpful was its reference to citizen participation, which underlined a point hardly recognised by the Skeffington Committee (1969) even though it was specifically concerned with it. It was Seebohm, not Skeffington, who clearly saw that, if area action was to be based on the wishes of the inhabitants and carried out with their participation, 'the participants may wish to pursue policies directly at variance with the ideas of the local authorities . . . Participation provides a means by which further consumer control may be exercised over professional and bureaucratic power'.

This is an issue which will be discussed in a broader context in the final chapter. Here, we need briefly to survey some of the ways in which the development of thinking on 'deprived areas' was translated into policy.

## THE URBAN PROGRAMME

Area policies in relation to housing improvement, however inadequate they may have been, were based on long experience of dealing with slum clearance and redevelopment. With other area policies there was no such base upon which to work, and both legislation and practice were hesitant and experimental. The approach, however, has remained consistently a spatial one, focusing on particular cities and areas within cities.

Legislatively, the important landmarks (though modest) were the Local Government Act 1966 (section 11) and the Local Government (Social Need) Act of 1969. These constituted the statutory basis for the *educational priority areas programme* and the *urban aid programme*. The 1966 Act provided for grants in aid of staff costs involved in 'dealing with some of the transitional [*sic*] problems caused by the presence of Commonwealth immigrants'. The Urban Aid Programme was broader in concept, 'designed to raise the level of social services in areas of acute social need, and thus help to provide an equal opportunity for all citizens'.[23]

*Areas of special social need* were not defined in the legislation, but Home Office circulars referred to

> localised districts, within the boundaries of an urban authority, which bear the marks of multiple deprivation, such as old, overcrowded, decrepit houses without plumbing and sanitation; persistent unemployment; family sizes above the average; a high proportion of children in trouble or in need of care; or a combination of some or all of these.[24]

The *urban aid programme* (later recast as the *urban programme*) funded mainly social schemes, but it was progressively widened in scope to embrace voluntary organisations, and to cover industrial, environmental and recreational provision. In 1977, its expenditure was increased, and the major coordinative responsibility was transferred from the Home Office to the Department of the Environment. The 1977 White

Paper *Policy for the Inner Cities* and the Inner Urban Areas Act 1978 brought about more significant changes. The new policy was 'to give additional powers to local authorities with severe inner area problems so that they may participate more effectively in the economic development of their areas'.[25] The provisions effectively designated three types of districts: seven *partnerships* in the most severely deprived large urban areas; 23 *programme authorities* for local authority districts with severe, but less extensive, problems; and 16 *other designated areas* with problems of lesser severity.

It is difficult to give a coherent account of this programme since its objectives were never clearly spelled out, and its extreme flexibility gave rise to a great deal of confusion. Indeed, it was even suggested at one time that it was 'simply an extremely versatile ministerial weapon whose very flexibility allows its use to be extended into any social field in which at any particular time the government is accused of being insufficiently involved' (McBride 1973). With the development of inner-city partnerships and programme authorities, the position became even more confused. It is not easy to keep pace with the proliferation of programmes which, by 1990 numbered 34 (NAO 1990).

The *urban programme* was the major plank of the 'deprived area policy' stage. Additionally there were the *community development projects* (CDPs) These produced a veritable spate of publications ranging from carefully researched analysis to neo-marxist denunciations of the basic structural weaknesses of capitalist society, though the original aim was 'to overcome the sense of disintegration and depersonalisation felt by residents of deprived areas'.[26] There were twelve CDPs in all: in Birmingham, Coventry, Cumbria, Glamorgan, Liverpool, Newham, Newcastle, Oldham, Paisley, Southwark, Tynemouth, and West Yorkshire. Additionally, 1974 saw the introduction of a small number of *comprehensive community programmes* (CCPs) in areas of 'intense urban deprivation'. In the wake of these, large numbers of studies were undertaken.[27]

The urban programme continued with an increasing emphasis on economic development. It has been a valuable source of funding for the many thousands of projects and organisations that have been supported. The *DoE Annual Report 1993* noted that some 9,800 projects have been funded each year in the 57 urban programme areas, costing in 1992/93 an estimated £267m. Almost half the expenditure is devoted to economic objectives, and the rest is shared roughly equally between social and environmental objectives. The DoE estimates that this funding will provide 74,000 training places; create or preserve 34,000 jobs; support 3,700 projects, workshop units, and building improvements; and help the start-up of 788 new businesses.

With the increased importance being attached to the other programmes (particularly *City Challenge*), the urban programme is being phased out.[28]

## URBAN REGENERATION

Economic regeneration has now taken pride of place in urban policy. The transition has been gradual but clear.[29] The 1977 White Paper spoke of local authorities needing 'to stimulate investment by the private sector, by firms and by individuals, in industry, in commerce, and in housing'. The return of the Conservative Government led to a review of inner-city policy which concluded that a much greater emphasis needed to be placed on the potential contribution of the private sector. One of the initiatives taken was the establishment of the *Financial Institutions Group* (FIG). This was started in July 1981 by the Secretary of State (Michael Heseltine) when he invited the chairmen or chief executives of twenty-six financial institutions to accompany him to Merseyside to review the conditions in the inner city. He then requested each of them to second, at their own expense, a manager to work with his departmental officials on inner-city problems for a year. 'Their objective was to develop new approaches and ideas for securing urban regeneration, to examine existing programmes, and to provide advice direct to the Secretary of State.'[30] Twenty-five agreed, and over the following year produced a total of 35 reports (which were not published).

Among the proposals were recommendations for a selective employment grant; a rating and rate support grant; deferred payment mortgages; improvements to the business start-up scheme; better use of redundant buildings; longer shopping hours; and additional public expenditure on capital investment in the cities. These proposals fell on stony ground, but others were acted upon: for example, a proposal for building society involvement in house repair and improvement agency services, where a pilot scheme was undertaken in Birmingham. Another was a recommendation that banks should take specific measures to assist small businesses in inner-city areas: this led to the appointment of 'special inner city business development officers'. The most important proposal, however, was for an urban development grant on the lines of the American *urban development action grant* (UDAG). This was implemented by the introduction of the *urban development grant* (UDG) in 1982. Modelled on the American UDAG, the objective of the UDG was 'to promote the economic and physical regeneration of inner urban areas by levering private sector investment into such areas'. It was flexible in terms of the area covered, but the private sector contribution to a project had to be significant.[31]

## URBAN DEVELOPMENT CORPORATIONS

The 1977 White Paper on inner cities considered the idea of 'using new town style development corporations to tackle inner areas'.[32] Though such an agency 'could be expected to bring to bear single-minded management, industrial promotional expertise and experience in carrying out development', the Labour Government concluded that it was inappropriate for the inner cities:

> The task in inner areas is quite different to green field development where there is only a small existing population. Development will be needed, but it will also be a matter of modifying the provision of local authority services and of working with residents to secure the improvement of housing, the environment, and community facilities. In these circumstances, it is

important to preserve accountability to the local electorate.

The Conservative Government thought differently, mainly because it had little faith in the capabilities of local government. The manifest argument, however, was that the regeneration of areas such as the Docklands was 'in the national interest, effectively defining a broader community who would benefit from the regeneration' (Oc and Tiesdell 1991: 313).

The 1980 Local Government, Planning and Land Act made the necessary legislative provisions, and defined the role of an urban development corporation (UDC) as being:

> to secure the regeneration of its area . . . by bringing land and buildings into effective use, encouraging the development of existing and new industry and commerce, creating an attractive environment and ensuring that housing and social facilities are available to encourage people to live and work in the area.

Though their structure and powers are based on the experience of the new town development corporations (NTDCs), the urban development corporations are different in several important respects. Since their task is a limited one, it is envisaged that they will have a relatively short life of ten years or so. Partly because of this, their designation procedure is rapid. In the case of the new towns, there was a pre-designation stage during which a consultant's report was prepared, a draft designation order published, and a public inquiry held (if there were any objections – as there usually, but not always, were). Only after the completion of these stages, was the final designation order made. This process could take up to two years. In urban areas such a time-consuming process 'would be an unaffordable luxury, since so long a period of delay would lead to excessive uncertainty and to blight'.[33] Instead, the designation of an area, known as an *urban development area* (UDA), is by way of a statutory instrument. This requires parliamentary approval under a procedure which allows a petition to be made to a select committee against the confirmation of the Order. In this manner, a curious route is provided for some limited public input. Though no objection was sustained against the

*Table 9.1* Urban Development Corporations

| | | | Total planned expenditure 1992–3 £m |
|---|---|---|---|
| First generation | London Docklands | 1981 | 293.9 |
| | Merseyside | 1981 | 42.1 |
| Second generation | Trafford Park | 1987 | 61.3 |
| | Black Country | 1987 | 68.0 |
| | Teeside | 1987 | 34.5 |
| | Tyne and Wear | 1987 | 50.2 |
| | Cardiff Bay | 1987 | NA |
| Third generation | Central Manchester | 1988 | 20.5 |
| | Leeds | 1988 | 9.6 |
| | Sheffield | 1988 | 15.9 |
| | Bristol | 1989 | 20.4 |
| Fourth generation | Birmingham Heartlands | 1992 | 5.0 |
| | Plymouth | 1993 | NA |

first Order which was made in 1991 (for Merseyside), there was a number of petitions against the much more controversial Docklands Order in the same year.[34]

Since then, eleven more designations have been made, and a further designation is planned for the Plymouth Dockyards in 1993. Except for the London Docklands, the UDAs are not large. Indeed, in Bovaird's (1992) words, they can be seen merely as replacing local authority development programmes 'for small areas with especially severe derelict land or plant closure problems'. There are no UDCs in Scotland, since the Scottish Development Agency (now merged in Scottish Enterprise) already has the relevant powers, and can operate anywhere in the country, unrestrained by the boundaries of a designated area.

UDCs have extraordinary powers of land acquisition: land may be acquired simply if it is within the designated area. Additionally, 'to reduce uncertainty', there is a provision which allows for public sector land to be transferred to the corporation by means of a *vesting order*.[35] They also (unlike the NTDCs) usurp the local planning authority's development control functions, not only for determining planning applications (including their own proposals) but also for enforcement, tree preservation, conservation areas, advertisements, wasteland, and listed building

controls. In short, the UDCs have very wide planning responsibilities and freedom from local authority controls. This is not accidental or incidental: it is an essential feature of their conception. The organisational ethos of the UDCs is described by Lawless (1990):

> UDCs were to be run by Boards of Directors drawn primarily from business who were ultimately responsible to central government through the Secretary of State for Environment. Using business attitudes and acumen UDCs were to seek out market opportunities and private sector investment. Broader strategic planning was to play a limited role in UDCs. The market instead was to become the primary instrument through which change was to be effected.

These market opportunities have been teased out, however, only at some considerable public expense. Expenditure rose to an annual rate of over £600m in 1990/91, declined to £514m in 1992/93, and is planned to fall to just under £300m by 1995/96.[36] The need for this level of public investment reveals that UDCs are 'de facto interventionist, seeking to shape, influence or induce the market, rather than simply to follow it' (Brayshaw 1990). The major share of public funding, and similarly high levels of private investment, has gone to London Docklands.

There are differences in style and approach among the UDCs, reflecting their time of designation, local circumstances, and management. In the early years, the UDCs operated very independently of their corresponding local authorities, sometimes ignoring existing plans, and thereby generating great conflict. Over recent years, there has been more cooperation between the UDCs and the local authorities, with the latter retaining certain functions such as elements of development control, on an agency basis. This is most marked in the case of the LDDC: 'from being the target of considerable local abuse for its neglect of any but the commercial development of Docklands, it now openly speaks the language of community development' (N. Lewis 1992: 10). The most recent designation, Birmingham Heartlands, has incorporated a significant role for the City Council in the UDC's affairs through representation on the Board.

All UDCs have been asked to incorporate 'exit strategies' in their corporate plans for 1992/93 to 1993/94, as a start to the winding-down process which, for most of them, will come in the middle of the 1990s. It is also intended that the legislation will be amended to allow for the partial de-designation of UDCs and the return of these areas to local authority control.

The UDCs take by far the largest share of spending from the Government's expenditure on the inner cities. In 1992/93, this was expected to be just over £600m, or 51 per cent of inner-city spending, a fall from the 1990/91 peak of 61 per cent.[37] Across all urban policy spending there has been a significant shift since 1984 to the centrally directed UDCs and urban development grants and away from Urban Programme funding directed through local authorities. In 1984/85, the Urban Programme accounted for about three-quarters of inner cities' spending. In 1992/93, the proposed spending on the Urban Programme at £243m was less than half the funding for UDCs. Total spending on UDCs was more than £1bn by the end of 1989/90 (NAO 1990: 23). In 1992/93, spending by the LDDC on roads, transport and other infrastructure accounted for £237m (80 per cent of its total expenditure) almost equal to all spending on the Urban Programme, and more than the annual funding projected for all the 31 City Challenge areas.

## CITY ACTION TEAMS – INNER-CITY TASK FORCES

Following Michael Heseltine's 1981 visit to Merseyside, in the wake of the Toxteth riots, the Merseyside Task Force Initiative was created. Initially, this was a task force of officials from the DoE and the then Department of Industry and Employment, established to support him 'to bring together and concentrate the activities of central government departments and to work with local government and the private sector to find ways of strengthening the economy and improving the environment in Merseyside'.[38]

With such a remit, from such a source, it was clear that problems of Merseyside were regarded as being particularly severe, and that the Government intended to tackle them with vigour. The omens were not good, however: Liverpool had (in the words of the select committee) 'a sad history of past initiatives'. The new one ran true to form.

The implementation of urban policy in Merseyside, as in other cities, was characterised by a proliferation of small area schemes, which in the view of the Environment Committee, resulted in a 'complex patchwork of overlapping areas, disparate powers . . . constituting an unduly "fragmented" system of urban governance'. Conflicts between the various authorities, and between them and central government, led to the breakdown of any genuine partnerships. In reviewing the Merseyside Initiative, the Environment Committee considered the task force to have been a useful device which should be continued, though they regretted that it became preoccupied with the details of individual projects, and failed to adopt 'a broader strategic approach'.

As a result of the criticisms of the lack of coordination in inner-city policy, action teams and task forces were used more widely from 1985. *City Action Teams* (CATs) take a broad, even regional, view of the problems of coordinating programmes of government, business and the voluntary sector. Task Forces, on the other hand, have been created to coordinate and stimulate economic development and job opportunities in small sections of the inner city.

*Figure 9.1* Urban Policy Initiatives

CATs were first set up in 1985 with the aim of providing more coordination between government departments in the implementation of Government policy in the inner cities. Each team is chaired by the regional director of one of the main departments involved. These are the DoE, the DTI, and the Training Agency. There are now eight City Action Teams[39] under the general responsibility of the DoE, which took this over from the DTI in 1989.

The funding of the CATs is small, reflecting their role as coordinators rather than direct providers, although they do have a fund available for small projects. In 1991/92 this was £8.4m, which the DoE claims 'helped to create or safeguard around 2,300 jobs, 2,700 training places and supporting 1,000 small to medium businesses'.[40] In fact, the National Audit Office report *Regenerating the Inner Cities* (1990: 11) concluded that too much attention was paid to how the funds were spent on particular projects and not enough on 'their effectiveness and results in coordinating programmes'.[41]

Eight task forces were established in February 1986, and their number was increased following the *Action for Cities* initiative in 1987. Task forces now operate in 16 locations. The first Task Forces were expected to have a life of two years, but in the event the lifespan has been treated with flexibility. They are, however, temporary arrangements only. The locations are decided on the basis of measures of urban deprivation and responses to specific problems. The task forces have the general objective of increasing the effectiveness of central government programmes in meeting the needs of the local communities. They also have resources to develop innovative approaches to the employment problems of local residents, and to support schemes that might not otherwise be covered by main programme activities. In 1992/93, the task forces' funding was £23m which, together with £6.4m attracted from the private sector, is expected to create 8,000 jobs and 29,000 training places, and to support 6,300 businesses.[42]

The limited funding of task forces reflects their primary role as coordinators, trying to bend existing programmes and private sector investment (and attitudes) towards the inner cities. Their staffing is typically made up of secondees from local business, central government and local authorities, including planners, together with some local recruitment.[43] The Department of Employment oversaw task forces in the early stages but responsibility quickly moved to the Department of Trade and Industry; in 1992 responsibility was transferred again, this time to the DoE.

## ACTION FOR CITIES

After the 1987 General Election, Margaret Thatcher, then Prime Minister, announced her intention to 'do something about those inner cities'. The immediate result was the publication of a glossy brochure entitled *Action for Cities* (Cabinet Office 1988). This maintained that, though the UK had benefited during the 1980s by embracing the ethic of 'enterprise', this change in attitudes had not reached into the inner city. The aim of urban policy therefore was to establish 'a permanent climate of enterprise in the inner cities, led by industry and commerce'. This was to be achieved through creating confidence for business to grow, improving people's motivation and skills, and making inner cities safer and more attractive. Twelve specific initiatives were announced, including the extension of the UDC and CAT measures, the replacement of UDG by *city grant*, facilitating the market in under-used land, the Safer Cities Project, extra provision for managed workshop premises, business support services, and compacts between inner-city schools and employers providing training places.

At the same time, and following some encouragement from the Prime Minister, the private sector came forward with its own modest package of measures, *Business in the Community*, to promote business involvement in regeneration,[44] *Investors in Industry*, to provide venture capital for inner-city schemes, and *British Urban Development* (BUD), a consortium of the eleven largest construction companies who together would seek urban regeneration opportunities.

*Action for Cities* programmes were said to have

cost the Government £3bn in 1988/89 and £4bn in 1990/91 but, in fact, little additional money was involved. The package gave the appearance that the Government was making a determined effort to come to grips with the problems. However debatable this might be (Lawless 1989: 155), it did indicate some reorientation of thinking on urban policy.

## CITY GRANT

*City Grant* was launched by the *Action for Cities* initiative in 1988, and replaced several existing grants including the Urban Development Grant (UDG) which had been in place since 1982. City Grant has aims similar to those of the UDG, although it is paid directly to the private sector developers.[45] It operates in the areas of the 57 English programme authorities. It supports private sector projects costing more than £200,000 which would not be viable without assistance. Projects can include the provision of new or converted property for industrial or commercial development, and the erection, conversion or refurbishing of housing.

Government funding for UDG and now City Grant has expanded steadily, from £26.8m in 1987/88 to £59.6m in 1992/93, and a projected £83m in 1995/96. More money could have been spent in the earlier years, but there was a general 'lack of good implementable schemes' (Lawless 1989: 77). The demand for City Grant is buoyant: 89 applications were approved during 1991/92, and between May 1988 when City Grant was introduced and November 1992, £261m of grant aid had been approved for 300 schemes. This has levered £1,163m of private investment, a ratio of about 1:4.4. The DoE claim that the 'outputs' over the period total 39,000 jobs, 8,000 homes and 1.18 million sq. m of commercial and industrial floorspace.[46] How far such figures provide a realistic assessment of the impact of urban policy is discussed on pp. 215–18.

## CITY CHALLENGE

A major switch in funding mechanisms was announced in May 1991, in the form of *City Challenge*. It is too early to assess the impact of this but, at least in principle, it marks a significant change in policy. The emphasis on land and property development remains, but there is now a recognition that this should be more closely linked to the needs of local communities. It is also

*Table 9.2* Inner City Expenditure by the DoE, 1987/88 to 1995/96

| | 1987–88 | 1988–89 | 1989–90 | 1990–91 | 1991–92 | 1992–93 estimate | 1993–94 plans | 1994–95 plans | 1995–96 plans |
|---|---|---|---|---|---|---|---|---|---|
| City challenge | – | – | – | – | – | 63.5 | 213.5 | 213.5 | 213.5 |
| Urban programme | 245.7 | 224.3 | 222.7 | 225.8 | 237.5 | 243.1 | 175.6 | 90.7 | 79.5 |
| City grants | 26.8 | 27.8 | 39.1 | 45.4 | 40.8 | 59.6 | 71.0 | 71.0 | 83.0 |
| Derelict land | 76.7 | 67.9 | 54.2 | 61.7 | 77.3 | 94.6 | 93.0 | 92.9 | 120.5 |
| Urban Regeneration Agency set up costs | – | – | – | – | – | – | 2.0 | 2.0 | 2.0 |
| UDCs and DLR | 160.2 | 255.0 | 476.7 | 607.2 | 601.8 | 514.5 | 337.4 | 292.7 | 283.7 |
| Manchester Olympics bid | – | – | – | – | 0.8 | 13.1 | 35.0 | 25.0 | – |
| Inner City Task Forces | 5.2 | 22.9 | 19.9 | 20.9 | 20.5 | 23.0 | 18.0 | 16.0 | 15.0 |
| City Action Teams | – | – | 4.0 | 7.7 | 8.4 | 4.4 | 3.4 | 1.3 | 1.2 |
| Special grants programme | – | – | – | – | – | – | 1.3 | 1.3 | 1.3 |
| Other | –0.1 | – | –1.6 | –4.4 | –7.2 | –1.9 | 2.2 | 7.0 | – |
| Total | 514.4 | 597.9 | 814.9 | 964.2 | 979.8 | 1,013.9 | 952.3 | 813.5 | 799.8 |

*Source*: *Department of the Environment Annual Report 1992: The Government's Expenditure Plans 1992–93 to 1994–95*, Cm 1908, HMSO, 1992, Fig. 45, p. 53. (Minus figures indicate income.)

intended that City Challenge should encourage a long-term perspective on change; that it should integrate the work of different programmes and agencies; that this will require some effort in setting up new institutional arrangements or 'partnerships', and that the local authority should be the initiating body. In this, it follows the models for partnerships coming forward throughout the 1980s, and it addresses some of the criticisms noted above. However, City Challenge is to run parallel with the UDCs and other centrally controlled initiatives, and the most dramatic immediate impact has been on the largely local-authority-run Urban Programme, from which substantial resources have been transferred. The property development theme is also very evident, and thus City Challenge follows the general trend of the late 1980s, but it is still seen as a marked and unexpected turnaround in the Government's approach, due at least in part to the views of the then Secretary of State, Michael Heseltine.[47]

The explicit objectives of City Challenge emphasise physical change through land and property development, but these are to be linked with the provision of opportunities for disadvantaged residents. The aim is to enable 'winners' of the financial assistance 'to provide major impetus to area improvement, leading to self-sustaining economic regeneration'.[48] The mechanisms for achieving this are competitive bidding for funds; concentrated regeneration on small areas, an emphasis on devising new and long-standing institutional arrangements, and comprehensive programmes of renewal including social objectives. Much of this has been welcomed by practitioners, not least because it confirms the role to be assumed by local authorities in initiating and coordinating regeneration.

Only 15 authorities were invited to bid for funds in the first round, 11 of which were selected to begin implementation of programmes in April 1992.[49] During 1992, a second round of City Challenge bidding was opened up to all 57 urban programme areas, and a further 20 were chosen to develop programmes from April 1993.[50]

Most projects are in inner-city locations, a few are on the urban fringe. The Dearne Valley is unique in being 20 square miles in area, covering a number of smaller settlements in the South Yorkshire conurbation. City Challenge encourages an integrated approach focusing on property development but cutting across a range of topic areas, including economic development, housing, training, environmental improvements, and social programmes including such matters as crime, and equal opportunities.

The competition prize appears substantial, £7.5m for each area for each of five years' funding, which, including a total of £19m per year earmarked for City Challenge from the Housing Corporation, is costing the government £232.5m a year from 1993/94. But this was not new money: City Challenge is a different approach to spending rather than an allocation of new funds. Funding comes wholly from 'top-slicing' of seven other urban and housing budgets, notably, the Urban Programme, and many of the existing rules governing individual projects remain. Spending for those authorities which win a City Challenge bid can begin only after an action programme is agreed. Projects within the action programme effectively continue to be funded through existing programmes, with similar, if simplified, procedures for making and considering applications. The private sector is expected to play a significant role, and its involvement needs to be demonstrated before projects are agreed. This has forced a quickening in the trend towards partnership arrangements and their institutional management structures.

> What is new about City Challenge is that it requires councils to obtain money for inner city regeneration on the basis of a highly politicised competitive bidding process which has no objective relationship to need or even ability to deliver. The rules of the competition and the whole ethos behind the process has prioritised skills, alliances and attitudes not traditionally associated with either local or central government! It has also required from both councillors and officers a flexibility and intensity of activity which has not previously been associated with urban regeneration work.
>
> (de Groot 1992: 197)

Local communities, too, are seen to be important partners, but their place in the management structures is more variable. Sometimes they are represented at the policy-making level, while in others they are involved only as consultees or in the detailed implementation of projects. Tower Hamlets intends to have a 'regeneration corporation', a limited company in which the local authority has only a minority holding; other board members will be drawn from 'the private sector, the community, the voluntary sector and the other statutory agencies' (Forsyth 1992: 20). Such a commitment is perhaps feasible in an authority such as Tower Hamlets where partnerships and 'targeted action plans' have been evolving over several years, but elsewhere the great speed needed to respond to invitations to bid (only six weeks in the first round) has worked against much meaningful community participation in the early stages. Nevertheless, it is the impetus that City Challenge gives in bringing together different sectors and creating new and positive relationships between them, shifting attitudes and 'mainstream investment', that offers the greatest potential.

Whilst local authorities play the primary role in coordination, leadership, and contact with central government, an essential feature of City Challenge is a devolution of both control and responsibility to the 'partnership'. For many councils, this may constitute a significant political challenge. The 'partnership boards' have no statutory status or powers and cannot receive money directly from Government: their funds are channelled through existing local government structures, sometimes requiring the same committee and council approval as mainstream spending programmes. There is thus considerable potential for conflict between the lead authorities and 'partnership boards'.

The need to secure short-term tangible indications of success also works against the long and difficult process of forming real coalitions around shared objectives. Healey points to the problems that may arise with implementation:

> A tension between the objectives of the programme and the mode of central control has developed focused around the specification of *output targets and measures* on which performance is to be judged (with the threat of funds withheld if targets are not reached). These latter emphasize material outputs — jobs and training places provided, stock built and refurbished, trees planted;

rather than qualitative changes relating to building up the links in routes to jobs, or transforming institutional capacity.

(Healey 1992a)

## EMPLOYMENT, TRAINING AND ENTERPRISE AGENCIES

Employment is, of course, one of the principal economic considerations in town and country planning, and its importance has increased as the general state of the economy has worsened. Yet, it cannot be said that employment policies have ever been successfully integrated with physical planning policies. In part, at least, this is due to organisational separatism and the fact that local authorities have little responsibility for employment and training policies. Under the Conservative administration what influence they did have in this area has waned.

Employment and training policy and services have been functions largely of central government, managed from 1973 by the Manpower Services Commission (MSC). The responsibilities and initiatives of the MSC were widespread. Its Vocational Education and Training Group, managed the *youth training scheme*, providing work-based training for school-leavers who would otherwise be unemployed. The Employment and Enterprise Group ran the national network of *job centres* and provided schemes to support small businesses. The MSC also provided some training directly through the Skills Training Agency.

Many of these schemes have had a planning or environmental dimension. Training schemes have been of particular interest to planners engaged in economic development or urban regeneration. Some employment schemes have directly implemented environmental improvements. The MSC *community programme* provided short-term employment and training for the long-term unemployed on projects of benefit to the community. Local authorities, other public sector agencies and large businesses have made the most use of these funds. Examples include the clearance of derelict sites; 'drainage, construction of footpaths and removal of debris in country parks; clearing canals and footpaths, stabilising sand dunes; tree planting to replace dead elms; and creating conservation areas for rare animals and birds'. Thus by a curious route a new environmental improvement programme emerged.[51]

This is only an indication of the many and varied employment and training schemes which, at the end of the 1980s, were managed by a complex web of government-sponsored agencies. This was a situation which the Conservative Government considered to be in need of radical change. The MSC first lost some of its responsibilities in becoming the Training Agency, and a further reorganisation was announced in the 1990 White Paper, *Employment in the 1990s*. There are now networks of 82 *Training and Enterprise Councils* (TECs) in England and Wales, and 22 *Local Enterprise Companies* (LECs) in Scotland. This new system is aimed at providing 'value for money' through a privatised organisation, linked, in this case, to the additional objectives of 'localism and decentralisation' (Meager 1991).

Copied from the USA (where TECs are known as Private Industry Councils), the underlying rationale is that if local businesses take a central place in guiding the support programmes for employment and training, the results would be superior to those of the former system: a better response to local employers' needs, a more business-like mode of operation, and increased leverage of private-sector support for training.[52]

TECs have taken over youth and employment training, and business support and growth initiatives, again with the objective of tailoring these to local conditions. Their activities include maintaining a knowledge base of local labour markets and training needs and provision, providing information to employers, employees and the unemployed; encouraging employers to meet training needs; promoting collaborative ventures; and directly providing or commissioning training for employees or the self-employed, and providing counselling services.[53] All this (to the extent that it is actually done) is decided, in the manner of private board meetings, behind closed doors. As with other current urban policies,

accountability has been sacri' of efficiency. N. Lewis (1⁣ concluding that 'the emergⵁ be seen as an articulate and coherent problems of the inner cities'.

## SCOTTISH URBAN POLICIES

Scottish urban policies have evolved differently from those in England and Wales. There are several reasons for this, including the different urban history of Scotland, its distinctive governmental organisation, and the close relationship that exists between local and central government. Glasgow and its extreme urban problems have been highly significant in determining the course of urban policy. Of particular note was the establishment of the Scottish Development Agency (SDA) in 1975, and its role in the *Glasgow Eastern Area Renewal* (GEAR) project.

The rationale for the SDA was twofold. First, since it had become clear that economic regeneration could not depend on the traditional policy of enticing mobile manufacturing industry, measures were needed to promote local growth, non-manufacturing activities, and overseas investment. Second, the lesson of the Scottish new towns was that environmental quality was an important aspect of economic growth, and that both required managerial expertise and dynamism (which was generally not to be found in local government). But, unlike the case with the later UDCs in England, importance was attached to retaining the role of local authorities as well as the many other agencies involved. The Scottish approach therefore placed emphasis on joint schemes, with the SDA acting as the lead agency:

> It was felt that this was more likely to be effective, that it was not appropriate simply to override local democracy if cooperation could be obtained and that, given the important functions local authorities would retain in any event, cooperation between willing partners, rather than a provoked antagonism, was the best approach.[54]

The GEAR project had economic, environmental, and social objectives. Despite initial teething problems associated with a lack of clarity about the scope of the project and consequent delays, the physical impact on the area was massive. Economic revitalisation, however, proved much more elusive, as was underlined in an unpublished 1988 report by PIEDA.[55] Though up to 2,000 jobs were retained or created, the benefits to the resident disadvantaged population were limited.

> This illustrates one of the most difficult aspects of any renewal project . . . It is as important to find a means of equipping local labour to compete for the jobs available as it is to increase the total quantum of jobs.
> (McCrone 1991: 927)

The experience of the GEAR project was used subsequently in tackling disadvantaged areas facing the additional problem of a severe local employment crisis resulting from the closure of a dominant firm: the steel-making plant at Glengarnock in North Ayrshire, the Singer sewing machine factory in Clydebank, and the Leyland plant at Bathgate. In each case, a strategy was agreed by a working party involving the local authorities, the SDA, the Industry Department for Scotland, and other agencies. Chaired by a senior Scottish Office official, these working parties provided a framework for local action which was implemented by a Task Force led by the SDA (or, in the case of Bathgate, by the constituent local authorities). Their accomplishments were impressive, in terms of job creation, the provision of new infrastructure, and widespread environmental improvement.

The success of these projects (which were, of course, more limited in scope and therefore less complex than GEAR) is attributed to several factors, First, a strategy was established in advance of action. Second, the approach was an integrated one, with environmental recovery, job creation, and retraining all working together. Third, the local authorities agreed to actively participate in the scheme (in the knowledge that, if they did not, the scheme would not go ahead). Finally, 'it was recognised that in this type of renewal work a substantial part of the battle is psychological, involving both morale in the area and perceptions from outside' (McCrone 1991: 929). It was in recognition of this, that a key physical project was used to symbolise the advent of a positive renewal programme.[56]

Also benefiting from experience, the SDA assumed a coordination role in later projects in Leith, Dundee, Motherwell, Monklands, and Inverclyde. Most of these projects involved 'issues that were socially related in that the areas suffered from decay and deprivation of long standing', but they all included an objective of economic regeneration. Moreover, the SDA, the local authorities, and other bodies, committed themselves in advance to a 'project agreement' which spelled out who was to do what, where, and when. A more ambitious scheme was undertaken jointly by SDA and the City of Glasgow in the old Merchant City area, with the aid of housing improvement grants and the SDA's *local enterprise grants for urban projects* (LEGUP). The outcome has been judged a success, with a transformation of a large area. Together with other initiatives in the City, there has been an about-turn in both the City's morale and outside perceptions of Glasgow as an attractive place for investment. The extent of the change was epitomised by the designation of Glasgow in 1990 as European City of Culture. The Scottish statements *New Life in Urban Scotland* (1988) and *Urban Scotland into the 90s: New Life—Two Years On* (1990) reviewed the achievements and the priorities for further urban action. Much attention is devoted to the large housing estates on the periphery of Scottish cities. Those of Paisley, Glasgow, Edinburgh, and Dundee (which are the most problematic) are now undergoing regeneration with Partnerships established by the Scottish Office. These involve the local authorities, the local community organisations, the Scottish Office, Scottish Enterprise, and other agencies operating in the areas.[57] There is a justified emphasis on the physical improvement of these monuments to old problems (all were built by local authorities to cater for their horrendous post-war housing shortages), but it is now accepted that physical improvements must be carried out as part of an integrated strategy of economic, social, educational and training measures. Above all, there has to be sensitive concern for local needs and a commitment to the involvement of local people in the regeneration process. In the words of *New Life for Urban Scotland*:

plans for the regeneration of problem areas must have the full understanding, involvement and commitment of the local community . . . The Government's central aim is to renew the self-confidence and initiative of local people, and to help them to assume increased responsibility for their communities.

It is this which is the major advance made in Scottish urban policy. To put the matter in the lowest terms, 'experience has shown that unless tenants can be encouraged to take more responsibility for their living conditions through being involved more closely in management, the areas will quickly deteriorate again'.[58] Participation is thus seen to be good economics as well as good politics. The other major ingredient is the crucial importance of training: a problem on which it is hoped that greater success will be achieved by the formation, in 1991, of Scottish Enterprise. This brings training into the same administrative organisation as development. Some of the problem areas have little hope of attracting much new employment, and thus emphasis is placed not only on training, but also on improved transport in a wider travel to work area. Each area has its own problems, and so 'tailor-made local programmes and objectives will be required for each place'.[59]

The Enterprise and New Towns (Scotland) Act 1990 restructured Scotland's economic development and training agencies by creating two new bodies, Scottish Enterprise and Highlands and Islands Enterprise (HIE).[60] These are effectively mergers of the Training Agency with the Scottish Development Agency and the Highlands and Islands Development Board (HIDB). The legislation lists the functions of Scottish Enterprise as being to develop the Scottish economy; to enhance the skills of the workforce; to promote the efficiency and competitiveness of Scottish industry; and to improve the environment. Merger effectively brings these activities under one umbrella.[61]

## EVALUATION OF URBAN POLICY

One remarkable change in government policy over the last decade or so has been the embracing of research

as an essential part of the policy-making process. There has been a huge expansion of research studies, as the list of official publications at the end of the volume demonstrates. This is, at first sight, surprising, since governments typically find it easier to express their goals in broad terms which encompass the widest possible range of outcomes. Modern management techniques, however, have raised to the fore the formulation of specific objectives which can be monitored and evaluated. This has made the easy option of vagueness unacceptable in principle; but practice is a different matter, as illustrated by the emphasis laid on undefined 'regeneration'. Much of the recently commissioned research is limited to the evaluation of specific programmes, as the NAO report (1990: 3.19) pointed out: 'Most of the [evaluation] measures so far developed are intermediate measures related to activities rather than effectiveness.' These 'intermediate measures' include a plethora of numbers relating to matters such as training places, jobs, visitors, roads, and reclaimed land. Nevertheless, many of the projects have produced conclusions that have wider import, and some of them have clearly demonstrated that urban issues are so complex that it is very difficult to devise effective policies to deal with them. Indeed, there is an extraordinary difficulty at the outset: how to define clearly what the objectives of policy are (though this does not justify the complexity of the current plethora of programmes). The problem is very familiar to policy analysts,[62] but it has to be constantly tackled anew by policy-makers. A good example (and this discussion has to be illustrative rather than comprehensive) is the apparently simple matter of increasing employment.

A major problem in evaluating programmes aimed to increase employment is that of finding a satisfactory definition (or even concept) of the term 'new employment'. There is a surprising range of possibilities.[63] Some are obviously inadequate: the total employment in a grant-aided development, for example, or the increase in employment since the scheme was started. Both of these ignore all other factors, including those which would have operated in the absence of the scheme: 'i.e. whether the programme has produced more of an effect than would have occurred without the programme'.[64] More sophisticated approaches have attempted to deal with this problem by such techniques as shift–share analysis. Such methods, however, cannot be used for small areas, where the popular approaches have been to ask the firms concerned about the effect of grant-aid on their employment levels; to compare firms which have received assistance with those which have not (using selected indicators such as turnover, profitability, and employment); and to investigate the characteristics of employees who have taken up jobs with the assisted firms.[65] As this incomplete list of possibilities indicates, it is important to be clear precisely what is intended to be measured. The effectiveness of policy, as measured by the cost per job created, is greatly affected by the definition used: in the Aston University evaluation of the UDG programme, the cost per new job ranged from £3,100 to £18,300 on different definitions.[66]

Other complications arise when account is taken of the 'life' of new jobs created: many of the jobs created in the course of regional development programmes later disappeared.[67] Moreover, there may be a lag in the growth of jobs which might be difficult to take into account. Again, policy may be directed 'not to the objective of short term job creation, but towards increasing the long term competitiveness of the area in a changing national and world economy'. This poses obvious difficulties of evaluation. Going further, if the aim of policy is 'wealth creation' (a term that was popular for a short time in the mid-1980s), any thought of evaluation becomes mind-boggling. How is 'wealth' to be defined (particularly in these environmentally conscious days); is the object to raise the average level of wealth, or the level of those who are the poorest? Such questions quickly banished the term from general use.

Despite all the conceptual and practical difficulties, researchers have been able to draw some important conclusions from their evaluations. Above all, job creation is much more problematic and costly than had been assumed. Many of the jobs that have been 'created' would have arisen without any intervention (in the jargon of the trade, there is a significant amount of 'deadweight' in the UDG programme).[68] Indeed, if the projects that have been evaluated are typical, 'such programmes are unlikely to make more than a modest contribution to the economic regeneration of the inner cities' (S. Martin 1989: 638). On reflection, this is perhaps unsurprising. In a complex interdependent society (and, increasingly, an interdependent world) 'local' issues are elusive. In Kirby's words (1985: 216), 'we cannot attempt to understand the complexities of local economic affairs *in situ*'. Much research corroborates this view.[69]

Another issue in which difficulties of assessment abound (and in which myths live on) is that of the impact of property-led development. It is frequently assumed that property development will somehow or other stimulate economic growth. Indeed, this is a central plank of Government policy (typically concentrated in small areas).

> Property development offers the potential to achieve visible results, changing the appearance if not the underlying characteristics of places . . . Precisely how property development is intended to bring about the economic revival of urban areas has not been officially articulated. In practice, it is often simply assumed that private sector property development is synonymous with economic development, or that there is an inevitable one-way process leading from physical to economic regeneration and community prosperity.
>
> (Turok 1992: 363)

Though 'the links between property development and economic regeneration are universally poorly understood, there has been little detailed research on the subject'.[70] Such research as has been undertaken offers no clear conclusions, though recent studies 'suggest that access to markets, management abilities, and the availability of finance are more important than buildings' and 'levels of investment in product development and production technology, together with differences in the way human resources are managed, are most significant'.[71] The experience of the Scottish new towns underlines the importance of factors other than property (such as the availability of a skilled labour force, ready finance, and an attractive environment).[72] The experience of the SDA in the GEAR project (discussed on p. 214) showed that, though the provision of premises attracted some firms to the area, this was 'at the expense of other parts of the city, and most jobs were filled by inward commuters anyway'.[73] Moreover, property development can present its own problems: this became clear in 1990, when rental values began to fall as the economy dipped. The slowing down of property investment in 1990 quickly turned into a spectacular collapse, with catastrophic effects on the construction industry and local economies.

Above all, the speculative approach of UDCs has failed to consider the relationship between the local economy and property development. This is especially so in terms of the variable nature of local conditions which affect the value of property development as an economic development tool. In some cases, urban policy can have a detrimental effect on local economic activity when, for example, the precarious position of small local firms is challenged with competition from outside the locality. Urban policy has been characterised by short-term thinking, centred on getting the best return from particular sites (CLES 1992b).

Although social, community and employment objectives have been secondary for urban policy in the 1980s, the assumption has been that property-led urban regeneration will produce a 'trickle down' of benefits for the local disadvantaged community as the local economy improves. The first report of the CLES monitoring project on UDCs reported little evidence of 'trickle down'. Edwards and Deakin support this view:

> Evidence for any extensive penetrative effects of trickle-down from economic regeneration is thin, and such as there is suggests that benefits extend no further than to individual households in which a previously unemployed member gains employment as a result of job growth from regeneration. The piling of virtually all the policy eggs into the enterprise basket therefore, and the relative absence − or at least, inadequacy − of alternatives must seriously circumscribe the reach of inner city policy if the trickledown effect is as limited as we suspect.
>
> (Edwards and Deakin 1992: 365)

The rationale for the concentration of urban policy on property development and the private sector is not simply that this creates more physical development and infrastructure. It is argued that it is cost-effective in that long-standing revitalisation of the local economy is stimulated by involving and encouraging renewed private investment; that benefits eventually 'trickle down' to local communities in the form of jobs, facilities and quality of life; and, more recently, that such an approach generates an 'enterprise culture' and results in 'moral regeneration'.

> In shorthand terms, this policy could be labelled 'privatism': the attracting into the Inner City of private developers, whose activities can in turn demonstrate that regeneration is taking place. Such regeneration should be tangibly evident, in the form of 'cranes on the horizon'; but also extend to the intangibles − the putting to rout of dependency.
>
> (Edwards and Deakin 1992: 362)

A critical examination of the assumptions underlying this approach, together with illustrations of how it has worked in practice, is given in *Rebuilding the City: Property-Led Urban Regeneration* (Healey, Davoudi, O'Toole, Tavsanoglu, and Usher 1992). They explain how the urban regeneration tools used by Government focus on improving the supply of land and property in run-down parts of cities. The principal problems addressed have been blockages in the property market caused by the physical problems of derelict sites, and by public sector landowners who, lacking market orientation, are unwilling to engage in and promote the local property market. Urban policy has been directed to removing the blockages. The problem of demand, on the other hand, has not been viewed as significant in national policy. Instead, areas are aggressively marketed. Promotion, image building or 'place marketing' is central to the approach. The object is to generate confidence in the area for private investment and to create an active property market.[74]

Despite the rhetoric about the private sector leading regeneration efforts, the public sector in fact has continued to play the dominant role in urban regeneration, though the style of intervention has changed. This is most marked with the UDCs, but local authorities have been urged to adopt an entrepreneurial approach. This implies a significant change in the character of planning. In the words of Healey, Davoudi *et al.* (1992: 282): '[There has been] a shift from planning frameworks to *ad hoc* projects, and to short-term preoccupations with flagship schemes and leverage ratios, rather than providing a stable framework within which markets could again become active.'

The approach involves the creation of a corporate identity, a marketing strategy, infrastructure improvements, flagship schemes, early environmental improvements, and intensive promotion (CLES 1990). These are the hallmarks of 'urban regeneration' in the late 1980s and into the 1990s. The strategies adopted by the UDCs have been 'much looser than local authority plans, much more concerned with "concepts" and promotion of opportunities for private development'.[75]

However, there has been no systematic evaluation of the UDCs comparable to that done for the enterprise zones. (Perhaps it is considered sacrilegious to investigate the Government's leading policy prescription?) Independent assessments have been highly critical, though they have been made from very different perspectives.[76]

## URBAN PROBLEMS AND POLICY

Underlying the transition from a physical policy concerned with deteriorated housing to a social policy in aid of deprived areas and then to an economic policy for strengthening the base for local growth, is the dramatic change which has taken place in the character of inner cities. There has been a relentless decline of population and employment in the urban areas generally, and particularly in the inner areas. (The other side of the coin is the growth in smaller towns and rural areas.) The economy of the older industrial British cities has been transformed: their manufacturing base has been eroded, and there has been little of the expanding tertiary industries to take its place. Peter Hall (ed.) (1981: 138) has suggested that it may well be that 'certain kinds of area no longer represent an appropriate milieu for the expanding kinds of economic activity'. There are many possible reasons for this, ranging from climate and infrastructure to the local political culture.

Cameron (1990: 486) goes further: 'The aggregate decline of many major British cities is inevitable and indeed desirable. Probably a growing percentage of British consumers and producers will seek locations for living and producing outside such cities.'

Currently, explicit inner-city policies are restricted to selected areas. It is not clear whether this is for experimental reasons (we are not sure *how* to go about solving the problem) or, more simply, for financial reasons (there is not enough money to go round). But it is clear that to attempt to explain, or even describe, the inner-city problem is to fall into a major trap. There is no such thing as *the* inner city, still less a conceivable set of plans for it. The historian has the luxury of looking backwards and attempting to explain what happened why, when and where (Checkland 1981) but those concerned with current issues have no such privilege. They have to wrestle with the pressing, and perhaps misleadingly articulated, problems of today.

Cities (and still less inner cities) are not islands: they are part of the wider dynamic of change. Traditionally, urban populations have improved their conditions by moving out to suburban locations and, in the process, have made room for newcomers who have chosen the central cities because of the opportunities which they have provided. The situation is now more complex. There are few newcomers, there have been changes in the economic structure of cities (and the regions of which they form a part), in the ease of mobility (which greatly increased the area of job markets), in the difficulties of access to good-quality housing (considerably exacerbated by housing policies which have strangled the private provision of rental housing and made inner-city owner-occupation prohibitively expensive for the majority), in new laws of settlement (operated through the council housing system and through bureaucratic and political stances in relation to 'homelessness'), and, more generally, in the character of the post-industrial city.

These are but some of the changes which have transformed the functions of the inner cities. When other factors such as education, urban roads (and parking), the impact of public and private forces on 'community', the spread of urban blight and dere-liction, the concentration of families with children in high flats (thereby raising 'child densities' to unmanageable levels), teenage unemployment, and so forth are added, the list becomes frightening to contemplate. And overshadowing such features are fears of racial (or sectarian) violence, of a general run-down in the quality of life and in the concentration of self-exacerbating social problems.

It is questionable whether there is any useful validity in the notion of an inner-city economy as a spatially and economically discrete entity (Edwards and Deakin 1992). There are important interrelation-ships between the local, national and international economy. Major new employment-generating uses will frequently be determined by national and international corporate decisions. They do not grow out of the inner city. Employment uses do not have to be located in the inner city to serve those residents. The direct benefits of urban regeneration in economic development are therefore questionable.

The basic 'problem' with current urban policies is that they assume that the issue to be tackled lies in a particular part of particular cities: but 'inner city' problems is a misleading abstraction. Adapting a passage from Marc Fried (1969) (who was com-menting upon the concept of poverty), 'the inner city [is] an empirical category, not a conceptual entity, and it represents congeries of unrelated problems'. The problems posed in the inner city 'are not readily accessible for study or resolution in the name' of the inner city.

Progress will not be made by 'comprehensive action' but by identifying priority fields in which effort should be concentrated. (This, of course, is precisely what the Conservative Government has done, even if its choice of focus is debatable.) Most of the problems identified in inner cities are matters of national policy relating to all areas. (Thus, though poverty is undoubtedly a problem which arises in inner cities, most of the residents are not in poverty: and most poverty is not in inner areas.)

The arguments *against* inner-city, or indeed any area-based, policy are strong.[77] To the extent that the problems relate to the deprived, it makes more sense to channel assistance to them directly, irrespective of where they live. Only to the extent that the problems are locationally concentrated, should remedies focus on specific locations – as in the case of *housing action areas* and *renewal areas*.

None of this is to deny the importance of directly tackling those problems of decay and disadvantage which are all too apparent in many inner areas. Nor is there any argument against the desirability of attempting better organisation of services at local levels, or improved coordination both within and between agencies. What is crucial is to identify the forces which have created the problems and to establish means of stemming or redirecting them. This certainly means a reorganisation of urban policy and implementation processes. Currently, both suffer from the multiplicity of agencies, the project-led nature of policy, the absence of any strategic view (or even the machinery for preparing one), and the secrecy with which the many *ad hoc* agencies surround themselves.[78] The only agency which overcomes these problems is the much-maligned local government. But local authorities need a framework of central policy and finance geared to assist them 'to improve the process of adjustment to new economic structure and to avoid welfare losses by those who suffer during the process' (Cameron 1990: 486).

## UPDATE

Some major reports on the English and Scottish house condition surveys were published during 1993: Department of the Environment, *English House Condition Survey 1991*, London: HMSO; and Scottish Homes, *Scottish House Condition Survey 1991*, Edin-burgh: Scottish Homes.

The Government has confirmed its intention to create three new enterprise zones to counter the impact of pit closures in the coalfield communities of Easington (County Durham), the Dearne Valley (South Yorkshire) and Mansfield (East Midlands).

The DoE's 1993 report *Enterprise Zone Information*, estimates the total public cost of enterprise zones as £1,167m (excluding public sector construction).

*British Urban Policy and the Urban Development Corporations*, edited by R. Imrie and H. Thomas (Paul Chapman Publishing, 1993) includes case studies of eight of the thirteen urban development corporations. The National Audit Office has reported on *The Achievements of the Second and Third Generation Urban Development Corporations* (HMSO, 1993). The report warns about the difficulties of interpreting output measures, and notes that the DoE plans to commission research evaluating the UDCs.

An East Thames Task Force is to be set up to prepare a framework for development in the East Thames corridor. The DoE has published a consultation paper *The East Thames Corridor: The Government's Approach* (DoE, 1993), following publication of the consultant's report *The East Thames Corridor: A Study of Development Capacity and Potential* (HMSO, 1993).

Other publications include: N. Deakin and J. Edwards, *The Enterprise Culture and the Inner City*, London: Routledge, 1993; S. Mackintosh and P. Leather: *Home Improvement under the New Regime*, School for Advanced Urban Studies, University of Bristol, 1992; P. Willmott and R. Hutchinson, *Urban Trends 1: A Report on Britain's Deprived Urban Areas*, London: Policy Studies Institute, 1993; Scottish Office, *Progress in Partnership – Consultation Paper on the Future of Urban Regeneration Policy in Scotland*, SOEnD, 1993.

## NOTES

1 *Urban Scotland into the 90s: New Life – Two Years on*, Scottish Office 1990: 6.
2 See, for example, Cullingworth 1986 and 1987. On the other hand, there is a strong case for 'a national strategy to shape the process of urban adjustment' to economic change (Cameron 1990: 487).
3 For a fuller discussion see Lawless 1989. A broader theoretical framework is included in Lawless 1986.
4 See, for example, Hambleton 1990 and 1991.
5 For England and Wales, see the Denington Report 1966 and the 1968 White Paper *Old Houses into New Homes*. For Scotland, see the 1973 White Paper *Towards Better Homes: Proposals for Dealing with Scotland's Older Housing*. Later White Papers on *Home Improvement: A New Approach* were published for both countries in 1985.

6 See DoE Circular 13/75, *Renewal Strategies*.
7 DoE Circular 14/75. See also DoE Improvement Note 10, *The Use of Indicators for Area Action*, HMSO, 1975.
8 DoE Circular 6/90, *Local Government and Housing Act 1989: Area Renewal, Unfitness, Slum Clearance, and Enforcement Action*. Unattributed quotations are from this source.
9 Since the renovation grants scheme is largely mandatory and therefore demand-led, a growing number of local authorities were experiencing financial difficulties in 1992. Possible changes in the renovation grant system were therefore under consideration in 1993. See *DoE Annual Report 1993*, para 6.108, p. 91.
10 Derelict land is discussed in Chapter 5.
11 Committee on Unfit Housing in Scotland, *Scotland's Older Houses*, HMSO, 1967. This was the Scottish equivalent of the Denington Report.
12 The matters included in the tolerable standard are: structural stability; freedom from serious disrepair; freedom from dampness prejudicial to health; adequate provision for lighting, heating, and ventilation; adequate supply of wholesome water; satisfactory facilities for the preparation and cooking of food, including a sink and supply of hot and cold water; suitably located WC; exclusive use of a suitably located fixed bath or shower, and basin each provided with hot and cold water; and an effective system for the draining of foul, waste, and surface water.
13 However, as a result of strong opposition to this nineteenth-century rule, provision was made for 'well maintained' payments. The rule could be particularly harsh because of the subjective nature of the former unfitness standard.
14 DoE, *Priority Estates Project 1981: Improving Problem Council Estates*, HMSO, 1981.
15 *DoE Annual Report 1993*: 85.
16 The Waltham Forest HAT is particularly well known because it was included in the Prince of Wales's *Vision of Britain* exhibition. The tenants had been campaigning for some action on the four system-built estates for many years. The HAT has taken over responsibility for more than 2,500 dwellings (Wilson 1993).
17 The Citizen's Charter gives tenants the right to put forward proposals for HATs. The *DoE Annual Report 1993* states that a number of proposals were made during 1992. These will be considered along with those received from local authorities.
18 *Private Housing Renewal: The Government's Proposals for Scotland: A Consultation Paper*, Scottish Office, 1988. However, means-testing was introduced for the 'lead plumbing' and 'radon works' programmes.
19 See, for example, MHLG, *The Deeplish Study: Improvement Possibilities in a District of Rochdale*, HMSO, 1966; and MHLG, *Barnsbury Environmental Study*, The Ministry, 1968.

20 See particularly, DoE, *New Life in Old Towns*, HMSO, 1972.
21 National Committee for Commonwealth Immigrants, *Areas of Special Housing Need*, NCCI, 1967.
22 Plowden Report: *Children and their Primary Schools* (1967), vol. 1, para. 131. This must not be interpreted as a lack of concern for research. On the contrary, it reinforces the need for research, to which volume 2 of the report is eloquent testimony.
23 Home Office, *Urban Needs in Britain*, Home Office, 1970.
24 Educational Priority Areas were defined in similar terms. See A.J. Halsey (ed.) *Educational Priority: Vol. 1: EPA Problems and Policies* (1972), especially ch. 4, 'The definition of EPA'.
25 DoE Circular 67/78, para 1.
26 Three of the last community development reports were reviewed by L. Howes in *The Planner* 67 (January–February 1981): 24–8.
27 There is a considerable library of reports from these years. The Urban Guidelines and the Inner Area Studies are particularly important. The Urban Guidelines Studies were published by HMSO in 1973 under the general heading, *Making Towns Better*. Their full titles are: *The Oldham Study: Environmental Planning and Management; The Rotherham Study, Vol. 1: Improving the Physical Environment; Vol. 2: Technical Appendices; The Sunderland Study, Vol. 1: Tackling Urban Problems: A Basic Handbook, Vol. 2: Tackling Urban Problems: A Working Guide*. The Inner Area Studies were published by HMSO in 1977: Birmingham: *Unequal City*; Lambeth: *Inner London: Policies for Dispersal and Balance*; Liverpool: *Change or Decay*. Additionally a summary was published earlier in 1977: *Inner Area Studies: Liverpool, Birmingham and Lambeth – Summaries of Consultants' Final Reports*. See also the reviews of these three studies by Amos *et al.* 1978. Among the many other studies, a particularly influential one was the Shelter Neighbourhood Action Project (Shelter 1972). Reference can also be usefully made to the broader paper by Stewart *et al.* 1976. See also McConaghy 1978.
28 However, two new programmes which are organised on Urban Programme lines were introduced in 1992. The *Urban Partnership Fund* is intended to promote urban regeneration with funding from the DOE, local authorities' usable capital receipts, and levered private sector investment. The 57 Programme authorities are eligible to bid for a share of £20m which has been set aside in 1993/94. The *Coalfield Areas Fund* was set up in 1992 to help in the alleviation of the effects of colliery closures. Local authorities can bid for funding for both revenue (100 per cent grant) and capital projects (75 per cent grant) in support of suitable local economic development. The programme cost is £5m over two years.

A much more substantial package, amounting to a total of £55m, has been allocated to support the *Manchester Olympic Bid* to host the Olympic Games in 2000. This will make substantial contributions to the construction of a velodrome, a private-sector-led arena development, and the Olympic Stadium.
29 For a discussion of earlier policies, see Edwards and Batley 1978; and Hambleton *et al.* 1980.
30 HC Environment Committee, *The Problems of Management of Urban Renewal*, 1983. Other unattributed quotations are from this source.
31 The Urban Regeneration Grant had the same provenance. This grant, introduced by the Housing and Planning Act 1986, was directed at large schemes, and was paid direct to the developer. DoE *Urban Regeneration Grant: Guidance Notes*, 1987. In its lifetime, the UDG supported 296 projects at a cost of £136m with a corresponding private sector investment of £555m. This represents a leverage ratio of about 1:4. The URG supported ten schemes at a cost of £46.5m, with private sector investment of £208m – a leverage of about 1:4.5. Together, the Government estimated that they contributed 31,966 jobs, 6,750 new homes and 1,456 acres of land brought back into use (Brunivells and Rodrigues 1989: 66).
32 The TCPA had argued the case for special development agencies for the inner cities: see TCPA, *Inner Cities* (1979).
33 DoE, *Urban Development Corporations: Summary of Legislative Provisions*, The Department, 1981.
34 The Select Committee, consisting of five Lords, had the task of assessing the justification for the Government's proposals for the area together with the alternative proposed by the London Boroughs involved. The Docklands Joint Committee, established by the GLC and the London Boroughs, had produced the 1976 *Docklands Strategic Plan*, and submitted that they were the democratic body responsible for the area and that they were capable of redeveloping it. After 50 days of hearing and argument, the Select Committee accepted the government's view that an urban development corporation was the most appropriate agency (adding that it considered the select committee procedure unsuitable for an inquiry of this nature). *Report from the Select Committee of the House of Lords on the London Docklands Development Corporation (Area and Constitution) Order 1980*, HL 198 (1980–81), HMSO 1981. For detailed accounts of the history of planning in the London docklands see Ledgerwood 1985, and Brownill 1990.
35 This has to be agreed jointly by the Secretary of State and the appropriate Minister, and it is subject to affirmative parliamentary resolution.
36 *DoE Annual Report 1993*: 62 (Figure 58).

37 These figures may give a false impression since spending disproportionately favours London Docklands and, within that area, major projects: particularly the Limehouse Link, part of the Docklands Highway. The Limehouse Link is a cut and cover tunnel which 'involved the demolition of over 450 dwellings . . . the loss of 274 local jobs' and 'would, at £120m at 1989 prices cost £163,500 per yard (£150,000 per metre) the most expensive stretch of road built in the country' (Brownill 1990: 139).

38 HC Environment Committee, *The Problems of Management of Urban Renewal*, 1983.

39 The first five CATS were set up in 1985 in the Partnership areas of Birmingham, Liverpool, London, Manchester/Salford, and Tyne and Wear. Later the same year another was set up in Cleveland. In 1988, two more teams were set up in Leeds/Bradford and Nottingham/Leicester/Derby.

40 *DoE Annual Report 1993*: 67.

41 Lawless (1989: 61) argues that CATs have been 'unable to devise anything that might be termed a corporate central-government strategy towards inner-city areas'.

42 *DoE Annual Report 1993*: 67.

43 For a description and critique of a task force and its projects see Tibbs 1991, and Hillier 1991.

44 Business in the Community emanated from a conference held in 1980 at which British representatives from industry and government met with American counterparts to discuss their experience of corporate social responsibility. This led to the establishment of a working party, under the chairmanship of Sir Alastair Pilkington, to examine ways in which major British companies could become involved in community affairs. The group recommended the formation of BIC. This is a limited company whose objectives are:

> To encourage industry and commerce to become more involved on a local basis with the economic, social, training and environmental needs of the communities in which they operate;
> To bring together local authorities, organisations and business, to assist in the development of effective action;
> To collect and disseminate information about successful local initiatives so that others can learn rapidly and effectively; and to work through and support existing initiatives and organisations.
> (Quoted in Keating and Boyle 1986: 141)

N. Lewis (1992: 36) comments that the BIC 'is as confused as most observers on how to tackle the problems of inner city regeneration although it has made suggestions from time to time on how business can help'.

45 Applications for UDG and the payments were made through local authorities, who had to contribute 25 per cent of the total grant aid. The process of appraising applications was slow, even in the case of URG which was paid directly to developers, and considerable (occasionally abortive) work was required on applications before any indication of success was forthcoming. Nevertheless, the grants were generally considered to be effective, and there were only a few planned projects which failed to materialise. (See Public Sector Management Research Unit 1988a; Pearce 1988; and Johnson 1988.) There has been considerable streamlining of the procedures for City Grant. Local authorities are not involved directly, although they are able to encourage applications from developers, and their support can be an important consideration.

46 *DoE Annual Report 1993*: 59 and 60.

47 The change of direction has been largely credited to Michael Heseltine by the Head of the DoE Inner Cities Directorate (Gahagan 1992: 3): 'While out of office, he has spent much time travelling around the world looking at urban regeneration not only in Europe but also in the United States and Far East. He had come to a number of conclusions about how urban regeneration ought to be managed. First, that local authorities should be in the lead by acting as a broker, not doing everything itself. Second, that the urban programme needed reorganisation because it had become moribund and too diffuse. Third, that the urban programme needed a kick-start, and the most effective way to do this was through competition.'

48 *DoE Annual Report 1993*: 55.

49 The winners in the first round of City Challenge bids were, Bradford, the Dearne Valley Partnership (led by Barnsley, but also working with Doncaster and Rotherham), Lewisham, Liverpool, Manchester, Middlesbrough, Newcastle, Nottingham, Tower Hamlets, Wirral and Wolverhampton.

50 The winners of the second round of City Challenge were, Barnsley (the only authority to win in both rounds), Birmingham, Blackburn, Bolton, Brent, Derby, Hackney, Hartlepool, Kensington & Chelsea, Kirklees, Lambeth, Leicester, Newham, North Tyneside, Sandwell, Sefton, Stockton-on-Tees, Sunderland, Walsall and Wigan.

51 An interesting report on this programme was published in 1987 under the title *Alternative Manpower for the Scottish Countryside: The Role of MSC and the Voluntary Sector*, Centre for Leisure Research, Dunfermline College of Physical Education (Countryside Commission 1987).

52 'The original intention, exploded by the experience of [the American Private Industry Councils] was that private sector funding would begin to match the public funding in a short time, but that requirement seems to have been quietly dropped' (N. Lewis 1992: 40).

53 Amongst the 82 TECs in England and Wales, there

are differences in area covered, organisation, approach, and in the vigour with which they pursue the Government's philosophy. A glowing account of the success of one TEC in meeting the Government's objectives is given by Groves (1992). A different view is expressed in the Centre for Local Economic Strategies 1992a.

In a review of the weaknesses of the TEC initiative, Meager (1991) questions many of the assumptions about employer involvement and local needs. He points to the short-term nature of the thinking, and the potential bias towards large firms, and the manufacturing sector. The Government has ensured a preponderance of employer interests in TECs by insisting that two-thirds of the membership of the Boards should be made up of chairmen, chief executives, or top operational managers at the local level of major companies. There is little direct role for local authorities, even where there have been strong links between councils and employer. See also Bovaird 1992: 354.

54  McCrone 1991: 926. This section leans heavily on McCrone's invaluable account. It is interesting to note that the success of the SDA (and the WDA) has been seen by some as being the result of being given unfair advantages over other depressed regions (N. Lewis 1992: 42).

55  Referred to in McCrone 1991: 927.

56  These included the speedy removal of the abandoned steel works in Glengarnock, the demolition and redevelopment of the Singer site in Clydebank, and the reopening of the passenger railway in Bathgate (McCrone 1991: 929).

57  For example, the members of the Edinburgh Wester Hailes Partnership (in 1990) were: Scottish Office, Wester Hailes Community, Lothian Regional Council, Edinburgh District Council, Scottish Homes, Department of Employment, Edinburgh Venture Enterprise Trust Business Support Group, and the two agencies which were later merged in Scottish Enterprise (Scottish Development Agency, and the Training Agency).

58  McCrone 1991: 936, and Scottish Office, *New Life for Urban Scotland* (1988) and *Urban Scotland into the 90s: New Life – Two Years On* (1990).

59  *New Life for Urban Scotland*, p. 14.

60  The proposals were first announced in the 1988 White Paper, *Scottish Enterprise: A New Approach to Training and Enterprise Creation*.

61  For a critical review of this change, see Danson *et al.* 1989, and Hayton 1992 and 1993. Lloyd (1990) argues that the SDA changed its priorities over time, from direct intervention to support for local initiatives, and from employment generation to property development.

62  There is a large literature on this. See, for example, Rittel and Weber 1973; Levy *et al.* 1974; Wildavsky 1979; Pressman and Wildavsky 1984; and Coulson 1990.

63  See, for example, Belbin 1985, and S. Martin 1989.

64  S. Martin 1989: 628. Generally, see the well-known text on evaluation methods: Rossi *et al.* 1979.

65  This is a summary of S. Martin 1989: 628, which also gives the appropriate references. This is a useful paper to which the reader is referred.

66  Public Sector Management Research Unit, Aston University, 1988a. See also S. Martin 1989.

67  See Hughes 1991 on which this section is based. Unattributed quotations are from this source.

68  Cf. Molotch (1976: 320): 'local growth does not make jobs: it distributes jobs'.

69  One good illustration is Turok's study of the financial aid given to industry in Southwark, which concluded that: 'The provision of financial assistance did not address many of the external problems and internal constraints facing firms, so in most cases the initiative failed to moderate the impact of contraction processes, let alone to stimulate growth' (Turok 1989: 591). The study is reported also in Turok 1988.

70  Turok 1992, on which this discussion is based. Turok quotes Edwards (1990: 176): 'the role of building and property development in the economy is a crucial area of ignorance'.

71  Turok 1992; Bovaird, Gregory and Martin 1991; Turok 1989; Advisory Council on Science and Technology 1990; Porter 1990.

72  See Industry Department for Scotland (1989), *The Scottish New Towns: The Way Ahead*, Cm 711.

73  Turok 1992: 372; PIEDA 1987b.

74  Healey and her colleagues argue that the Government has failed to understand the crucial role played by local government in providing the conditions to facilitate urban development through site assembly, coordination, infrastructure provision and promotion. The approach also ignores the real problems of lack of demand which consistently confront local regeneration efforts.

75  CLES 1990: 40. Thornley (1991: chapter 8) compares the North Southwark Local Plan with the flexible planning framework adopted by the LDDC. The North Southwark Plan was later quashed by the Secretary of State.

76  See for example, Ambrose 1986; Audit Commission 1989; Brownill 1990; CLES 1990 and 1992b; Lawless 1990; N. Lewis 1992; *Urban Development Corporations*, National Audit Office, 1988; Parkinson and Evans 1990; Thornley 1991, chapter 8.

77  For an early critique see Townsend 1976.

78  'A failure in policy integration prevents us from

grasping that an exceedingly complex urban problem is compounded by the fact that government departments which make policy, like the social sciences themselves, are subdivided into discrete specialisations (housing, transport, employment) while the life experience of cities is holistic.' (N. Lewis 1992: 58, quoting Carley, *Housing and Neighbourhood Renewal: Britain's New Urban Challenge*, 1990.)

# 10

# TRANSPORT PLANNING

What nobler agent has culture or civilisation than the great open road made beautiful and safe for continually flowing traffic, a harmonious part of a great whole life?

Frank Lloyd Wright, 1963

There is a growing realisation that totally unrestrained vehicle ownership and use could destroy the improved lifestyle and freedom of movement that the car has brought to millions.

Sir Ralph Ellison, Chairman, Automobile Association, 1990[1]

Transport is many things: it is a means of getting from one place to another; it includes a range of very different forms of travel – walking, cycling, travelling by car, bus, or train, or flying. A journey to work on the London underground is very different from a country holiday tour. Except perhaps for the latter type of journey, transport is unlike other goods in that it is a means to an end: it is not an end in itself. Indeed, much transport is an impediment to the enjoyment of something else. It is a means of providing access. Mobility is not important of itself: its importance is in providing access. Yet the debate on transport often forgets this elementary point, and focuses on mobility: faster roads, faster trains, and more frequent buses. The advantage of focusing on accessibility rather than mobility is that it opens up the possibility of alternative means: changing land-use relationships for example. As an advert on a condominium tower above a Toronto metro station neatly pointed out, 'if you lived here, you would be home now'. The greater the accessibility, the lower the need for 'transport'. Thus, transport planning is much more than the building of roads, even though this does not always appear to be the case. It should

involve a consideration of the relationship between different land uses, and between land uses and transport feasibilities, as well as the relationships between different transport modes and their relative effectiveness in meeting economic, financial, social, and environmental goals.

There is nothing profound in these observations but, until recently, transport policy appeared to deny their validity. Roads have formed the major focus of policy. It is therefore fitting that we start by considering road traffic.

## THE GROWTH OF TRAFFIC

Between 1950 and 1960, the number of vehicles on the roads of Britain more than doubled, from 4.4 millon to 9.4 million. The number more than doubled again by the end of 1980, to 19.1 million. In the following decade, there was a further increase of a quarter. The figure for 1991 was 24.5 million. The most dramatic increase was in cars, from 5.7 million in 1960 to 19.7 million in 1990. The proportion of households owning a car has grown from about a third at the end of the 1950s to around two-thirds today. In terms of total road 'traffic' – measured in vehicle kilometres – the increase was about a third between 1975 to 1985, and about another third in the following five years. Despite a massive road-building programme, including some 3,000 km of motorway, the increase in the length of the road network has been far less than the increase in traffic. There were 358,000 km of road in 1990: an increase of about a seventh over the 1965 figure of 313,000 km. The consequence, of course, has been that roads have become far more crowded.[2]

The increase in traffic shows little sign of abating,[3] and a major increase is currently forecast. Traffic forecasts are, of course, only estimates, and no more reliable than weather forecasts – less so in fact. (Forecasts based on other forecasts are particularly suspect: the traffic forecast is based mainly on economic growth.) The Buchanan Report of 1963 referred to the prospect (a carefully chosen word) of 27 million vehicles by 1980, whereas the actual figure in that year was 19 million. Since then, forecasts of population growth have been drastically reduced, and this was a main factor in the reduction of later traffic forecasts.[4] However, the 1984 forecast proved to be far too low, and a revised forecast was made in 1989 (DoT, *National Road Traffic Forecasts, Great Britain, 1989*). This (NRTF) reflected more optimistic views on the future rate of economic growth and the level of fuel prices (both of which, it should be noted, could change dramatically). The 1989 forecast, which is the latest available, is for an increase in total traffic of between 27 per cent and 47 per cent by 2000, and between 83 per cent and 142 per cent by 2025. The increase for car traffic is forecast at between 29 per cent and 49 per cent by 2000, and between 82 per cent and 134 per cent by 2025.

With the emphasis which is so often placed on increases in cars and traffic, it is easy to forget that a third of households do not have a car. The proportion is higher in the north (42 per cent) and in Scotland (45 per cent). It is also higher for the retired (69 per cent) and for unskilled manual workers (57 per cent).[5] Even in the USA, where 34 per cent of households have one car, and 54 per cent have two or more, there remain 12 per cent without.[6] This is in spite of the fact that families are often compelled to use a car (or two if there are two workers) in order to get to work (Rosenbloom 1992). The hardship for the poorest families can be very great indeed. A car (even if a low value, expensive-to-run gas-guzzler) is a necessity in many areas of the USA.

The car-ownership forecasts have two components: car ownership and car use. In 1986, car ownership was at a rate of 310 per thousand people. By contrast, the rate in the USA was 552 per thousand; and it is still increasing. The 'saturation' level has not yet been reached in any country. It is therefore not easy to guess what this level may be, and, of course, it may well differ among countries. For the purpose of forecasting, the saturation level is assumed to occur when 90 per cent of the driving age-group (17–74) own a car. This works out at 650 cars per thousand people. Official forecasts are, therefore, estimates of how quickly the saturation level is reached. Factors taken into account include income, the cost of buying and running cars (including the after-tax price of cars and petrol), the availability and quality of public transport, and changes in attitudes to car ownership. Clearly, these are not simple matters to evaluate and, in practice, the greatest weight is given to income.

Car use is also difficult to predict. It fell during the period 1973–76 when GDP fell and real fuel prices rose, but there was no fall when similar conditions applied during 1979–82. Use of second and third cars is not lower than the use of first cars: in fact it is higher.

Of the vehicles on the road, four-fifths are cars. Most of the remainder are goods vehicles. The forecasts for these are calculated separately for light vans (not exceeding 30 cwt unladen weight) and heavy goods vehicles. Light goods traffic is forecast to increase by between 101 per cent and 215 per cent by 2025. Heavy goods traffic is more problematic. Previous forecasts were proved to be far too low (the high forecast for the period 1982 to 1987 was 4 per cent; the actual was 22 per cent). In fact, there are no obvious trends on which to base a forecast. The Channel Tunnel may divert some heavy goods traffic to rail, but the impact on domestic road movement is not expected to be significant.[7] The Single Market may increase international road transport, but it is difficult to predict how great this might be. For these and other reasons, the DoT forecast is based on a simple ratio of tonne/km to GDP.[8] This gives an increase of between 67 per cent and 141 per cent by 2025.

Buses and coaches account for only 1 per cent of total vehicle miles. Though there has been some increase in recent years ('possibly reflecting the effects of deregulation', according to NRTF), there is no way of determining whether this will continue. Consequently, the forecast assumes no change in this mode of travel.

Since the forecasts relate to road use, they do not deal with rail traffic. Passenger traffic increased from a total of 30,300m kilometres in 1980 to 34,100m in 1990. Freight traffic by rail has fallen (while freight traffic by road has increased greatly). Well over half of freight (measured in freight tonne/miles) goes by road, and the official view is that, since road and rail serve mainly different markets, there is little scope for transferring road freight to the railways.[9]

The huge increase in car traffic and the relative decline in bus and rail travel, both in the past and in the future (as forecast), does not signify a massive transfer from public to private transport. On the contrary, the figures show that most of the increase in car usage is newly generated traffic. Though the issue has not been subject to research (incredible though this seems) some of the increase must have resulted from the dispersed pattern of activities and the increased separation of home and work. This itself has been facilitated by road improvements, thus illustrating the impact of 'transport supply' on demand. Moreover, since this new traffic is based on dispersal, it may be very difficult to change it to a public transport mode. Though Britain is far from being as car-dependent as the USA, much new development is of this American character.[10]

## TRANSPORT POLICIES

Public policy on transport has a long history (Barker and Savage 1974), but post-war policy began with a plan for a network of new trunk roads (which was not implemented) and a plan for the nationalisation of road haulage and the railways (which was). Much energy was dissipated in the nationalisation and denationalisation processes, and more attention was paid to ownership and control than to transport policy. Experience with the centralised and, later, the decentralised British Railways left a legacy of

*Table 10.1* Cars and Car Ownership (Great Britain)

|  | 1981 | 1990 |
|---|---|---|
| % of households without regular use of a car | 40 | 33 |
| % with regular use of 1 car | 45 | 44 |
| % with regular use of 2 or more cars | 15 | 23 |
| Cars per 1,000 population | 281 | 363 |

*Source*: Social Trends 23, HMSO, 1993, Table 13.9, p. 183.

*Table 10.2* Motor Vehicles, 1960–91 (Great Britain)

| Year | Private cars | Motor cycles | Public transp. vehic. | Light goods Thousands | Heavy goods | Other | Total |
|---|---|---|---|---|---|---|---|
| 1960 | 5,717 | 1,796 | 93 | 565 | 641 | 627 | 9,439 |
| 1970 | 11,328 | 1,048 | 103 | 1,120 | 683 | 668 | 14,950 |
| 1980 | 14,772 | 1,372 | 110 | 1,461 | 507 | 910 | 19,132 |
| 1985 | 16,454 | 1,148 | 120 | 1,708 | 486 | 1,147 | 21,063 |
| 1991 | 19,737 | 750 | 109 | 2,214 | 476 | 1,189 | 24,475 |

*Source*: Transport Statistics, Great Britain (various issues).

*Table 10.3* Forecasts of Increase in Traffic (%), 1988–2025

| | Per cent increase from base year 1988 | | | |
|---|---|---|---|---|
| | *2000* Low | *High* | *Low* | *2025* High |
| Cars | 29 | 49 | 82 | 134 |
| Light goods vehicles | 26 | 46 | 101 | 215 |
| Heavy goods vehicles | 17 | 31 | 67 | 141 |
| Buses and coaches | 0 | 0 | 0 | 0 |
| All Traffic | 27 | 47 | 83 | 142 |

unease about railway spending in the Transport Department which persists to this day (Truelove 1992: 4; Kay and Evans 1992: 34). With road haulage, the role of government since denationalisation has been largely restricted to safety controls, though there has been acrimonious argument over axle weights (or, in popular parlance, juggernauts).[11] Bus services have been particularly affected by conflicting political philosophies. Indeed, fights over fares policy were a significant factor in the Conservative Government's decision to abolish the GLC and the MCCs.

Cycling and walking get relatively little attention, though their importance is increasingly being acknowledged. But the major focus of transport policy has always been on roads, and only in recent years has it become generally accepted that they have to be considered within a wider framework. The starting point for any discussion of this must be the Buchanan Report.

## THE BUCHANAN REPORT 1963

It is traffic in towns which forcibly demonstrates that the motor car is a 'mixed blessing', to borrow the title of an earlier book by Buchanan (1958). As a highly convenient means of personal transport it cannot, other things being equal, be bettered. But its mass use restricts its benefits to car users, imposes severe penalties (in congestion, pollution and reduction of public transport) on non-motorists, involves huge expenditure on roads, and at worst plays havoc with the urban environment.

A major landmark in the development of thought in this field was the 1963 Buchanan Report. This eloquent survey surmounted the administrative separatism which prevented the comprehensive co-ordination of the planning and location of buildings on the one hand, and the planning and management of traffic on the other. With due acknowledgement to the necessarily crude nature of the methods and assumptions used, the report proposed, as a basic principle, the canalisation of larger traffic movements on to properly designed networks, servicing areas within which environments suitable for a civilised urban life could be developed. The two main ideas here were for primary road networks and environmental areas.

> There must be areas of good environment – urban rooms – where people can live, work, shop, look about and move around on foot in reasonable freedom from the hazards of motor traffic, and there must be a complementary network of roads – urban corridors – for effecting the primary distribution of traffic to the environmental areas.

The simplicity of this concept is in stark contrast to the complexity and huge cost of its application. But what of the alternatives? Buchanan stressed that the general lesson was unavoidable: 'if the scale of road works and reconstruction seems frightening, then a lesser scale will suffice *provided there is less traffic*'. The accompanying report of the Steering Committee argued that the scope for deliberate limitations on the use of vehicles in towns would be almost impossible to enforce, even if a car-owning electorate were prepared to accept such limitations in principle. Not all would agree and, as traffic has grown, the practical possibilities of the various forms of control have assumed an increased significance.

The great danger, in Buchanan's view, lay in the temptation to seek a middle course between a massive investment in replanning and a curtailing of the use of vehicles 'by trying to cope with a steadily increasing volume of traffic by means of minor alterations resulting in the end in the worst of both worlds: poor traffic access and a grievously eroded environment'. (This, of course, is precisely what has happened.)[12]

An improvement of public transport is no answer to these problems, though it must be an essential part of an overall plan. Indeed, it is quite impossible to dispense with public transport. The implication is that there must be a planned coordination between transport systems, particularly with regard to the work journeys in concentrated centres. On this, Buchanan recommended that transportation plans should be included as part of the statutory development plans. This was accepted and passed into legislation by the 1968 Town and Country Planning Act.

## TRAFFIC PLANNING MACHINERY

Traffic policies and planning have evolved (and continue to evolve) over a long period of time. Initially, the main, if not the only, relevant matter was a road network plan. There have always been differing views on this. During the 1930s, there was rivalry between the highway engineers championing a 2,800-mile motorway system and the county surveyors favouring a more realistic 1,000–mile network – which became the basis for the motorway building programme (Kay and Evans 1992: 18). But there was little interest in plans for transport as a whole.

A major change came with the Labour Government's 1967 White Paper, *Public Transport and Traffic*. This heralded a new approach to transport planning: 'our major towns and cities can only be made to work effectively and to provide a decent environment for living by giving a new dynamic role to public transport as well as expanding facilities for private cars'. Since local authorities were responsible for 'planning' they were obviously the appropriate authorities for transport. All forms of transport, it was argued, needed to be planned together in a coordinated way. However, in major urban areas, existing local governments were too numerous and too small. Moreover, the traffic situation was so bad and was deteriorating so rapidly that reorganisation could not await general legislation on local government. Thus some kind of *ad hoc* system was necessary.

This was the background to the establishment of Passenger Transport Authorities (under powers provided by the 1968 Transport Act) in Greater Manchester, Merseyside, West Midlands, Tyneside and Greater Glasgow. The original intention had been to give these PTAs wide powers to coordinate different forms of transport but, as a result of local government objections, they were limited to public transport (including local rail services).

Subsequent local government reorganisation gave PTA status to all the English metropolitan county councils (including South Yorkshire and West Yorkshire) and the Strathclyde Regional Council. (Following the abolition of the metropolitan county councils, the PTAs have been resuscitated as *ad hoc* authorities.) County councils in the non-metropolitan counties were given parallel duties in relation to 'a coordinated and efficient system of public transport'. There was corresponding provision in the Scottish Local Government Act for the regional and islands authorities. In London, the Greater London Council was the PTA (until 1984, when London Regional Transport was established).

A major feature of this new organisation was that it facilitated the preparation of comprehensive public transport plans, as well as providing a mechanism for channelling financial support not only to roads but also to public transport services. This was particularly attractive to a number of Labour councils which wished to strengthen, and indeed favour, public transport. Unfortunately, a period of financial stringency followed, and this, together with the fragmented nature of the grant system (despite original aims of 'integration'), killed the rational basis of the new system (Skelcher 1985). Nevertheless, TPPs survived in an attenuated form, and they still operate. Their present function is spelled out in DoT Circular 3/92:

> The main purpose of TPPs is to enable the Government to assess local authorities' proposed programmes of capital expenditure on roads and parking, and to decide the way in which annual capital guidelines, supplementary credit approvals, and Transport Supplementary Grant should be distributed among authorities.

The complexities of Transport Supplementary Grant (TSG) need not be discussed here. (In any case, they are subject to change.) It is, however, necessary to indicate its broad outlines and the policy which it embodies. The grant is termed 'supplementary' since it is additional to the general grant (formerly the rate support grant, now the revenue support grant). Up to 1985, TSG was paid on a proportion of eligible transport expenditure. Since 1985, only capital expenditure on roads of more than local importance has been eligible for TSG; any other assistance to transport is given through the revenue support grant. Thus, in financial terms, there is not even a pretence of comprehensive transport planning.

Unlike development plans, TPPs are not statutory documents; nor are they subject to any formal inquiry procedures. Nevertheless, they obviously must be closely related to development plans. The 1992 PPG on development plans includes the following:

> Development plans should include land-use policies and proposals relating to the development of the transport network and related services, such as public transport interchange facilities, rail depots, harbours and airports, including safeguarding zones. They should include an indication of the timescale and priorities for the proposed developments, especially major roads and railway projects. And they should reflect national guidance on transport and environmental considerations. Plans should also include land-use policies and proposals relating to the management of traffic (including the coordination of public transport services, the movement of freight, the control of car and lorry parking, and the improvement of cyclist and pedestrian safety).

However, development plans are not an adequate vehicle for a comprehensive local transport policy. An example of what this might entail is well illustrated by a plan prepared by the Central Regional Council

(1992). This Scottish council has been spending almost £5m a year on new transport schemes, of which over 80 per cent has been devoted to new roads and town centre car parks. Only 5 per cent has been targeted at public transport and helping cyclists and pedestrians. In 1992, the Regional Council adopted a policy of redirecting investment 'towards facilities which provide alternatives to the car'. The objectives are to reduce road accident casualties; to promote public transport; to control traffic growth; and to meet the needs of those who do not use cars. To achieve this, expenditure is planned to be:

- 32 per cent on roads schemes;
- 18 per cent on improvements for pedestrians;
- 16 per cent on traffic calming;
- 10 per cent on facilities for buses;
- 8 per cent on rail facilities;
- 4 per cent on cycling facilities;
- 4 per cent on parking provision (mainly park and ride);
- 7 per cent on various other schemes.

The policy is elaborated in plans for the region as a whole and for its constituent towns.

## PUBLIC TRANSPORT PLANNING

The Labour Government of 1974–1979 laid emphasis on the development of public transport, and the Transport Act 1978 was intended 'to provide for the planning and development of public passenger transport services in the counties of England and Wales'.[13] All non-metropolitan counties were required by the Act 'to develop policies which will promote the provision of a coordinated and efficient system of public passenger transport to meet the country's needs . . . and to prepare and publish a passenger transport plan'. This plan was to have a five-year time-scale and be revised each year.

This statutory requirement for a further plan (that is, in addition to the TPP and the structure plan) may have been more symbolic than substantive. Be that as it may, it was part of a strongly held belief by the Labour Government of the time that there were serious deficiencies in transport planning and policy. Part of this, it was felt, could be met by additional statutory plans (and a range of specific provisions relating, for example, to concessionary fares, community bus services and car-sharing). But matters went deeper, and a better basis was needed for coordinated pricing and investment decisions.

That there was also public concern on some transport issues was apparent from opposition to specific highway proposals – particularly at Airedale, Winchester and Archway. Though the anti-road lobbies took up an extreme stance (eloquently justified by Tyme 1978), there was clearly a more broadly based lack of confidence in the system by which highway needs and routes were assessed. In addition to the new Act, therefore, a more effective and flexible approach to transport planning was promised, with more systematic and open public participation in policy formulation, annual white papers and, in the longer run, policies geared 'to decrease our absolute dependence on transport and the length and number of some of our journeys'. An independent assessment of the Government's methods of appraising road schemes and forecasting needs was established, and a review of highway inquiry procedures was set up. (This is discussed on pp. 234–7).

The Conservative Government, elected in 1979, had a very different approach to public transport: it strongly believed that it should be subject to the discipline of market forces (or, to use different terminology, consumer preferences). The main initial focus of debate was on the subsidisation of fares. The issue could be argued at length, but the 1982 White Paper *Public Transport Subsidy in Cities* concluded, in succinct terms, that there was a need for 'legislation which will provide for a reasonable, stable and lawful subsidy regime'. What this meant was that central government would take unto itself greater powers to control local government in its transport policies. Legislative effect to the proposals was provided by the Transport Act 1983.

Another White Paper, *Buses*, published in 1984, argued that it was inappropriate for county councils to coordinate public transport: 'it is for passengers to demonstrate what they want and for operators to

respond'. In this way, greater efficiency would be secured. The White Paper estimated that there was the potential for a reduction of up to 30 per cent in the cost of public operators. Many of the cost comparisons presented were made in terms of costs per vehicle mile and thus ignored the wide variation in traffic operating conditions. There were many similar debatable statistical inferences (for example, that subsidy payments leak substantially into higher operating costs). A major policy issue, of course, was that of cross-subsidy: the practice of using surpluses from some parts of the system to offset deficits in others. The Government argued against this on two main grounds. First, users of good routes were being penalised 'by being made to pay excessive fares in relation to the cost of providing the service they use'. Second:

> It leaves to operators for decision, matters which should not be so left. Services which the market does not provide and which therefore need subsidy if they are nevertheless to continue, should get that subsidy only by decision of elected representatives after proper testing that they constitute good value for public money and are within the resources available to them.

These and other arguments are more complex than they appear. Estimating cross-subsidy is difficult with the particular costing conventions used, and revenue attribution is problematic, particularly with return trips and linked trips. Moreover, as the HC Transport Committee's 1985 report noted, bus travellers are buying a transport *network*:

> Availability of services at unpopular hours and in less highly demanded parts of the network are part of a package. Reliance on the incremental adjustments which would result from the operations of an entirely free market would eliminate, or make more costly, a number of elements in the package.

## PUBLIC TRANSPORT IN LONDON

In the 1983 White Paper, *Streamlining the Cities*, the Government proposed that in the metropolitan counties the former system of passenger transport authorities (PTAs) should be resuscitated. This was provided for in the Local Government Act 1985. The PTAs are in effect joint boards of elected representatives from the relevant district councils. Their responsibility is for major policy, including decisions on revenue support, and hence on fares and service levels (subject to financial controls by the central government). London, however, was treated differently.

One of the more curious aspects of the new system is that it excludes London. The HC Transport Committee commented that it was 'very suspicious of the Government's justification for treating London separately'. The crux of the matter was that, however much the Conservative Government disliked the GLC generally, it disliked London Transport even more. The proposals for London were issued in a separate White Paper, *Public Transport in London* (1983). The fact that this paper was issued separately, and in advance of *Streamlining the Cities*, demonstrates how London was regarded as a distinct political issue.

In thirty-five paragraphs, the White Paper crisply surveyed the field, berated the GLC for its inadequacies, and (with no in-depth analysis) concluded that a new appointed body should be set up with responsibility solely for public transport – but excluding British Rail. This was established by the London Regional Transport Act 1984. Officially termed London Regional Transport, it is now known simply as London Transport. As the RTPI (1983) were quick to point out, this implies the divorce of land-use planning and transport planning 'by removing the control of the major public transport operator from the strategic planning authority for London'. But, since the strategic planning authority has also been abolished, this argument is hardly likely to carry much weight. The real responsibility has shifted to the central government.[14]

## RAPID TRANSIT

It is the central government which also has the main power in relation to rapid transit systems – almost inevitably so given their huge cost. Financial procedures virtually ruled out new rapid transit

systems until 1989. Until that year, central government grants[15] had to be justified mainly on the grounds of time savings to existing passengers and benefits arising from generated trips. Since then, it has been a requirement of grant that, where practicable, users should pay for the benefits they obtain. Subsidies are payable for the benefits accruing to non-users (for example, through reductions in road congestion). Rapid transit systems tend to be very expensive (particularly if they use a fixed rail), and they have been out of favour for the last quarter of a century. Schemes had been approved earlier for Glasgow, Tyne and Wear, Merseyside, and London (the Jubilee Line), but many more were shelved. Increased road congestion (and prospects of much more in the future), the model of the London Docklands Light Railway (promoted as part of the Docklands renewal strategy), and increasing experience of foreign systems has reawakened political interest in rapid transit.

The HC Transport Committee's 1991 report on rapid transit (*Urban Public Transport: The Light Rail Option*) noted that there were some forty urban areas with proposals for rapid transit. (The report lists 22 of the schemes which are well advanced: their total cost is estimated at £2,700m.) Underlining the change in the Government's attitude to these schemes (which, though costly, are less so than alternative road works) the Minister of State for Transport is quoted by the Committee as saying that, within ten years, 'based on the track record (*sic*) so far, we may be looking perhaps at up to a dozen schemes in operation'. The Committee's conclusion was: 'it is clear that, even if all the current plans are not realised, light rail represents a significant trend rather than a flash in the pan'.

Britain does not compare well with other European countries on rapid transit, and this may in part be due to the fact that public transport generally is expected to cover a large proportion of its operating costs. In a useful 1992 'state of the art review', Walmsley and Perrett note that 'even before deregulation, bus services in the major cities typically achieved revenue-cost ratios of 70%, and only in the most highly subsidised were the ratios as low as the systems abroad'. This makes the outlook for rapid transit in Britain less certain, though there is some comfort in the fact that most foreign public transport networks have improved their 'revenue-operating cost ratio'. There is, however, the added difficulty in Britain that any rapid transit system would find itself in competition with deregulated bus services. On this, Walmsley and Perrett comment that 'it could be argued that if a bus system is able to compete successfully, the case for rapid transit must be weak anyway, especially as it will inevitably cost a great deal more than a bus system'. As for promoting private enterprise, the authors have some pithy things to say. In particular, private development is likely to be stimulated only if there is a comprehensive planning framework:

> There are many different types of planning regimes. The least successful are those without any positive development powers, for such authorities can do little to make things happen. The most successful in terms of rapid transit will be those that have similar powers (and money) to those of the current development corporations. There also need to be supporting policies to limit development elsewhere.

Though the report is from the government Transport Research Laboratory, and it naturally has the usual disclaimers, its publication is significant nevertheless. Even the most rigid governments find that changing electoral attitudes demand flexibility in policy.

## ROAD POLICIES SINCE 1980

Whatever reservations the Conservative Government has had about public transport, it had no doubt as to the economic and social value of roads. During most of the 1980s, however, its concern for reducing public expenditure took priority. The Thatcher Government's White Papers on the trunk road system all stressed the importance of roads for economic growth, but 'national economic recovery' demanded a close rein on public expenditure. Within a programme smaller than that of the previous Labour Government, the top priority was for 'roads which aid economic recovery and development' (foremost

among which was the M25). Other priorities were for environmental improvement (by the building of by-passes), road maintenance ('preserving the investment already made'), and improved road safety. It was expected that the balance of the programme was likely to change as the major inter-urban routes were completed. Increasingly (so it was thought) the emphasis would shift to schemes which were required to deal with specific local problems. This perception was dramatically altered by the 1989 traffic forecasts, and a White Paper of that year, *Roads for Prosperity*, announced a massive increase in road building.

Between 1980 and 1990, the road network increased by 18,400 km. By 1989, investment in trunk roads was nearly 60 per cent higher in real terms than ten years earlier. The current policies follow earlier ones in emphasising the importance of roads to economic growth (despite little evidence on the matter[16]). The M25 is now the most heavily used road in Britain. Far more traffic uses it than was forecast (though at the planning stage, the Transport Department's forecast was fiercely attacked as being too high). This 'immediate success' (to use the Department's eccentric description) has led to a major *M25 Action Plan* (1990). This includes increased lighting, improved signalling, and widening the road to dual four lanes, with a later possibility of five lanes in certain sections. The 1989 *Roads for Prosperity* and the 1990 *Trunk Roads, England: Into the 1990s* set out a programme which consists mainly of widening existing inter-urban roads (including some 600 miles of motorway). This involves a doubling of the cost of the forward road programme to around £12bn. This 'massive' investment (as it was advertised by the Government), is of course a response to the 1989 traffic forecasts,[17] although the Government stresses that the forecasts are not really forecasts at all:

> They are in no sense a target or an option; they are an estimate of the increase in demand as increased prosperity brings more commercial activity and gives more people the opportunity to travel, and to travel more frequently and for longer distances.[18]

On the other hand, the DoT's NRTF report (see 'Official Publications' at the end of the volume) suggests a more tangible use for the forecasts:

Traffic forecasts are important in assessing whether the benefits from a road improvement, over its lifetime, justify the initial cost and in determining the standard of provision. They enable a balance to be struck between providing extra capacity before it is needed and the cost of adding to capacity at a later stage.

(NRTF Report 1989: 1)

But, if the Government is not to use the NRTF as a basis for policy, what alternative base is being employed? The forecasts are based on the assumption that the demand for roads will be met with an appropriate supply, that there will be no significant policy of traffic restraint, and that attitudes towards motoring (and its cost) will not change. Though the official stance on such questions has been a coy one, the question has been – and continues to be – widely debated.[19] An illustration of the imprecise character of current policy statements is given in a 1992 Circular:

It will not be possible to increase road capacity throughout London to meet all future demand. The Secretary of State's aims are to cater more efficiently for existing overall levels of traffic, to cater for growth associated with increasing economic activity, and to make optimum use of the existing network.[20]

If this is thought to be rather vague, that is because it is. The Government's uncertainties are underlined by its decision to commission 'a wide ranging study into urban traffic congestion, both its cause and possible cures'. In the meantime, it seems that policy will be incremental and pragmatic.

Underlying decisions on road programmes are ideas about 'need'. Successive governments have discovered that this is an elusive concept, and many have tried to find ways of giving it an objective basis. Not only is this appealingly rational: it also changes the nature of the debate. Argument can be settled by recourse to the 'facts'. In a democracy, such nonsense encounters stiff resistance. The history of assessing the need for roads is a good illustration of this.

## ASSESSING THE NEED FOR ROADS:
## Trunk Road Assessment (1977)

The independent assessment (the 1977 Leitch Report) was highly critical of the conventional methodologies.

These were judged to be essentially 'extrapolatory', 'insensitive to policy changes', and partly self-fulfilling. Public concern about road planning was shown to be well founded. There were, however, no easy solutions: indeed the issues were inherently complex. The way forward lay in a more balanced appraisal process, 'ongoing monitoring arrangements' and more openness – with no attempt 'to disguise the uncertainties inherent in the whole process'.

The Labour Government's response was positive, and the 1978 White Paper, *Report on the Review of Highway Inquiry Procedures*, represented a marked change in approach.[21] National policies were to be set out for parliamentary debate in White Papers: these would 'also serve as an authoritative background against which local issues can be examined at public inquiries into particular road schemes'. It was hoped that this would avoid the confusion at local inquiries between national policies and their application in specific areas. It was pointed out, however, that this would work only if the methods of assessing national needs (what the Leitch Committee termed 'a highly esoteric evaluation process') were acceptable. Since these methods could not be properly examined at local inquiries (or, indeed, by Parliament), they were to be subject to 'rigorous examination' by the independent Standing Advisory Committee on Trunk Road Assessment. The Committee's report was published in 1979, under the title *Trunk Road Proposals – A Comprehensive Framework for Appraisal*.

This SACTRA Report (as it came to be known) examined the techniques used to evaluate the economic value of proposed road schemes. The Department's system of cost-benefit analysis (the COBA programme) was criticised for the narrowness of its approach, and certain changes followed. For example, instead of using only one traffic forecast, high and low levels were introduced.

The report also made short shrift of the pervasive belief that road building stimulates the local economy.[22] A dramatic illustration of this is the lack of impact of the huge road investment in areas of economic decline, particularly in the North-East and in the Glasgow region.

## Urban Road Appraisal (1984)

The 1979 SACTRA report dealt with inter-urban roads; in 1984 it was given the task of assessing the traffic, environmental, economic and other effects of road improvements within urban areas. Some urgency for a review was added by the abolition of the GLC and the metropolitan county councils: this gave the Secretary of State, the London boroughs, and the metropolitan district councils new responsibilities for tackling the transport problems of major urban areas. The SACTRA report, *Urban Road Appraisal*, together with the Government response, was published in 1986.

Much of the report sets out recommendations as principles rather than as detailed prescriptions, and it thus seems to have more than a fair share of platitudes. As a result, though the Government accepted many of these, they 'can only be applied once detailed guidance on their application has been prepared'. Moreover, 'where further development or research is needed, the detailed guidance required to implement them will take some time to prepare, and progress must be subject to the availability of resources'. The Committee could hardly have found this a very helpful response!

There were four broad areas which the Committee saw as contributing to the nature and extent of change needed:

1 concern about the way in which the Department develops, assesses and justifies major schemes, particularly in urban areas;
2 expectations about public involvement;
3 the importance of integration between transport proposals and broader land-use planning and environmental considerations; and
4 the complexity of the planning, assessment and decision-making processes, especially in their application to urban areas.

Interestingly (in view of the common contention that public participation adds to delay), the Committee maintained that one reason why many road schemes took so long to bring to completion was that 'the opportunity to debate their justification comes too late in the procedural chain'. This was accepted, as was a recommendation that national and local objectives should be treated separately 'so that conflicts and common denominators can be readily seen'. However, a recommendation that there should be a two-stage assessment and public inquiry process for the larger and more complex schemes 'presented difficulties'. Though it was regarded as 'a constructive proposal', the Government was 'not convinced of the practicality of separating the examination of policy options from consideration of detailed design and local issues'.

Some of the SACTRA recommendations received equivocal answers. Thus one recommendation was that 'all the travel implications of a scheme, such as redistribution, changes of mode of transport, and generation of new trips' should be included in assessing the impact of a road improvement. To this, the response was that, although the recommendation was accepted, there were 'particular difficulties' involved, 'especially in congested urban areas where congestion may discourage some desired journeys'. Similarly, with the recommendation that 'where schemes are expected to affect the potential for development such effects generally merit inclusion in the environmental assessment': this was agreed in principle, 'but it is doubtful whether this can go beyond judgement and description in the present state of knowledge'. Finally (in this selection from 64 recommendations) there were some which the Committee recognised needed further research, such as night-time traffic noise and the severance of communities. For both, the Department simply reiterated the point about further research, though adding that 'research into night-time noise has already begun, but in general these are all difficult topics and it is not yet clear whether usable results will be forthcoming'. On this, as on a number of points, one has the impression that the Department was not at all enthusiastic!

The *Urban Road Appraisal* report also echoed the widespread unease about the methods used to assess the economic value of road schemes, but its recommendation was couched in such broad terms that the Government had no difficulty in side-stepping it by maintaining that it reflected existing practice: 'The economic evaluation is only a partial assessment and should never be used as the only or predominant criterion for deciding whether or not a scheme is justified.'

## Environmental Impact (1992)

The issues, which successive governments might have hoped would be settled by the various inquiries, refused to disappear: in fact, they became more problematic as public attention widened to encompass more and more matters which had not traditionally been regarded as pertaining to roads. Above all, concern has grown enormously about the environmental effects of roads and, indeed, of all forms of traffic. (The impact of the EC is discussed in Chapter 6.) Inevitably, further inquiries were commissioned and, among these is another SACTRA Report (*Assessing the Environmental Impact of Road Schemes*), which was published together with the Government's response in 1992.

By this date, the arguments about the limitations of COBA had intensified. Not only were environmental considerations now at the forefront of the debate (particularly after the shock of the 1989 traffic forecasts), but it was being argued that any sharp distinction between economic and environmental impacts was false (Pearce *et al.* 1989). Earlier reports had advised that environmental benefits and costs should not be evaluated in money terms but should be subject to 'professional judgement'. The rationale for this is a simple one: there is no acceptable way to estimate the 'value' of a cathedral, a marvellous view, or other such 'non-economic goods' – though this has not stopped economists from trying (Schofield 1987). But this leads to a host of mind-boggling questions. What is the value of land which is safeguarded from development? Is it the 'economic' value for development, or the lower 'social' value which is determined by planning controls? Which value should be used in evaluating alternative routes for a road? Other questions are equally baffling: if environmental factors are important, which should be taken into account and which should be ignored?

(The SACTRA Report has a long list of local, regional, national, and global factors.) How are the cumulative effects of a multiplicity of apparently unimportant decisions to be dealt with? Will future increases in traffic increase environmental damage, or will technological innovations more than offset these? The range and number of questions seem endless. No wonder that cost-benefit analysis is having a hard time!

The report deals at length with such issues, and it emphasises the importance of clear policy objectives and 'strategic' and long-term effects. These, of course, are precisely the policy issues with which the political process has difficulty, though the *Government's Response* is eloquent in listing good intentions, including a continuing research programme. The problem will never be 'solved' – it isn't that sort of problem. Instead, it falls into that class of which Rittel and Webber (1973) have neatly termed 'wicked problems': problems that are unique to a specific place and time, which defy definitive formulation, and which can only be 'resolved' by political judgement. The last sentence in the SACTRA report poses the issue, though it has an optimistic view of the assistance which can be given to decision makers by 'facts':

> The decision on any scheme will always be an exercise in political judgement in the end, but the quality of that decision is critically dependent upon the quantity, quality, and accuracy of the material on which it is based.

One modest way in which some 'environmental' factors have for long been taken into account (though not necessarily acted upon) is through the advice of a Committee concerned with the siting and landscaping of roads.

## SITING AND LANDSCAPING OF TRUNK ROADS

The planting of trees on highways has a long history. The 1925 Roads Improvement Act gave local authorities powers to acquire land on the side of highways 'for the purpose of planting and amenity'.

Lack of technical expertise led to some unhappy results, and the Road Beautifying Association was established in 1928 to rectify this. Though a voluntary body, this Association did notable work, for example on the Kingston and Dorking bypasses, the Dorking-Leatherhead road, the Denham-Rickmansworth section of the North Orbital Road, the Basingstoke and Romsey bypasses, the Woodbridge and Colchester bypass and the Market Harborough bypass. Following the 1937 Trunk Roads Act, the Association was officially appointed as adviser on trunk road planning to the Ministry of Transport. This work is now carried out directly by the Department, with advice from an expert Landscape Advisory Committee.

The Committee's name is somewhat misleading since it deals with more than beautification. Its terms of reference are:

> To advise the Secretary of State for Transport and the Secretary of State for Wales on the relative acceptability of alternative routes and, where the Department deems appropriate, alternative standards for proposed major new and improved trunk roads and motorways, having regard to the features and qualities of the landscape which would be affected and to other related environmental considerations; the general landscape treatment of trunk roads and motorways, including lighting, roadside planting and the siting of service areas; and such other questions as either Secretary of State may refer to them from time to time.

There were six ministerial decisions during 1991 concerning preferred and final routes on which the Committee had advised.[23] Amongst these, the preferred route for the A259 Hastings Eastern bypass was the route favoured by the Committee, but its advice on the A259 Winchelsea bypass was not accepted 'thus jeopardising the best solution'. The Committee has started to review the schemes involved in the upgrading of the A1 to motorway standard and in the programme of motorway widening. It often faces acute difficulties in its work, as the following quotation from its 1991 report indicates:

> We have been more aware than ever of the numerous problems involved in the siting of modern multi-lane highways in landscapes of great aesthetic appeal and historic interest and/or value. Again and again we have had to grapple with the apparently intractable problems posed by the differences in scale between the sweeping lines, gentle curves, and great widths of proposed highways, and the intricate, intimate, small scale landscapes of hedged fields, small copses, hidden valleys, and scattered farmsteads and cottages that have to be traversed.

## CYCLING

One can have a feast with cycling statistics.[24] The world has twice as many bicycles (around 800 million) as cars. Global production of cycles outnumbers car production by three to one. These figures, of course, include the less-developed countries where cycles play a very significant role in transport. But the British figures are higher than one might expect. There are over 13 million cycles, and over a third of all British households have at least one. About 11 million people use their cycles at least once a year; in an average week about 3.6 million are used. Over a million people use a bicycle as their main means of transport to work. These seemingly impressive figures have to been viewed in context. Only 4 per cent of total trips are made by cycle. The total distance travelled by cycles is between 5 and 6 million kilometres a year, compared with around 350 million kilometres for cars.

Despite this apparent abundance of statistics, it is difficult to obtain an accurate picture of cycle use (and still less of any potential increase). There is, in fact, a shortage of data: the National Travel Survey, for instance, ignores journeys of less than a mile, yet these account for over a third of all personal journeys (representing about a third of all cycle journeys); traffic counts are usually taken on main roads that are less used by cyclists. Despite the inadequacy of statistics, it is clear that there are great variations in the use of cycles in different developed countries (that is, ignoring the vastly different economic conditions in lesser-developed countries). Figures published in 1989 by the EEC show that 29 per cent of all trips in the Netherlands are made by cycle, as compared with 11 per cent in West Germany, and only 4 per cent in Britain.

It is on the basis of figures such as these that some argue that there is a significant potential for an increase in cycling – with benefits all round. In the words of the DoT 1981 Consultation Paper on cycling:

> Cycling is efficient and cheap, and can be healthy and enjoyable. It can help to save energy. Cycling is quiet and does not cause pollution. It provides personal transport for children and other people who cannot drive or do not have a car. Bicycles are relatively easy to park, and less subject to congestion than other vehicles.

Other figures can be used to reinforce the case for promoting more cycling. A leading advocate of cycling quantifies the case thus:

> A travelling car needs about eight times more space than a travelling bicycle whereas a parked car can require about twenty times as much as a parked bicycle. With average car occupancy in cities often only about 1.3 people per vehicle, a car requiring 18 sq m of space uses about 14 sq m per person, in contrast to the 4 sq m per person for a cyclist to move freely, and 2 sq m for a pedestrian.
>
> (McClintock 1992: 7)

Clearly there is much to be said for such a healthy and efficient mode of transport; but there are problems as well. Cyclists are exposed and vulnerable, and it is simply not possible to provide them with their own tracks on all roads. The DoT (which has traffic safety as a high priority) expresses great concern about cycle accidents – or, to be more precise, accidents to cyclists. In evidence to the HC Transport Committee (*Cycling* 1991: 54 – see 'Official Publications', Parliamentary Inquiries') the Head of the Traffic Policy Division warned that 'we need to be very careful about artificially boosting cycling as a means of transport'.

The Department of Transport's policy initially was that, though the cycle accident rate was of great concern to central government, most cycling was on local roads, and it was therefore considered that local authorities were best able to deal with the problems according to their local situations. However, the 1977 White Paper, *Transport Policy*, accepted the need for the provision of facilities for cyclists, and there followed increased study and promotion of experi-

mental schemes. The Department introduced an *Innovatory Projects Budget* which provided for contributions to the costs of local authority experimental cycling schemes. The success of the early schemes led to the *Statement of Cycling Policy* issued by the DoT in 1982 which extended the scope of financial assistance to *networks* of cycle routes. In fact, however, apart from Nottingham, the supported schemes consisted of a single route, with connecting spurs. In all, there have been around 80 schemes supported under this programme. The general assessment is that they have been reasonably successful, though there has not been the large increase in new cyclists which some optimists envisaged. Instead, existing cyclists have transferred to the more suitable routes provided. Other local authority schemes have included the conversion of disused railway lines to cycleways and, in London, the 50 projects planned and carried out by the Greater London Council's *Cycling Project Team* (McClintock 1992: 24).

Every field of public policy faces difficulties over the interpretation of statistics, and cycling (which is steadily becoming a field of public policy) is no exception. Indeed, arguments over the interpretation of accident statistics seem to consume an inordinate amount of energy. It is clear, however, that special cycle routes, though undoubtedly necessary, have only a limited impact on safety: most cycling will continue to be on ordinary roads. The safety problem of cyclists cannot be isolated from general traffic safety: accidents are often the result of the behaviour of non-cycle traffic. Safety is a matter involving all traffic, and is most effectively promoted by general traffic management measures. In urban areas, this means that policies in relation to cycles need to be set in the wider context of traffic calming.

## TRAFFIC CALMING

Traffic calming is an expressive term which, though used in different ways, essentially refers to measures for reducing the harmful effects of motor traffic. In its limited sense, it refers to speed reductions, parking restrictions, pedestrianisation schemes, and such like.

In a wider sense, it is synonymous with overall traffic policy, including car taxation and land-use measures designed to reduce the need for car journeys. Advocates of traffic calming can make some telling points in its support (FoE 1990a and 1992b; Devon CC 1991; Hass-Klau *et al*. 1992). For instance, a 50-kph speed limit (about 30 mph) in residential areas is 'acknowledged in many European countries' to be 'far too high'; at speeds of 30 kph or below additional road space is created since cars need less space; if traffic calming is restricted to a few streets, its benefits are reduced: traffic simply redistributes itself to neighbouring streets.

Hass-Klau *et al*. (1992) have noted that the British approach is focused on the reduction of accidents, whereas the objectives in other European countries are typically wider, and embrace environmental improvement and urban regeneration. Their manual contains detailed technical descriptions of well-established methods such as speed bumps, chicanes (kinks in a road to slow down traffic), pinch-points, as well as some less-well-known techniques. The book also presents an assessment of traffic calming experience in Germany, the Netherlands, Denmark, and Sweden. It describes and comments on some forty British traffic calming schemes. The term 'traffic calming' was introduced by Dr Hass-Klau as the translation of the German term *verkehrsberuhigung*.

The traditional approach has been to segregate traffic and pedestrians: with reductions in traffic speed, they can both be accommodated, but with the pedestrian instead of the car being master (Pharoah 1992). The Devon County Council calming guidelines (1991) describe nineteen different measures 'to moderate driver behaviour and to exploit the potential for safety and environmental improvement'.

Many of the measures now discussed under the heading of traffic calming have more traditionally been known as traffic management, though the concern is now with wide environmental and amenity issues as well as with traffic flow. This is becoming an increasingly sophisticated area of policy. Recent legislation is a testament to the importance now attached to it.

## TRAFFIC MANAGEMENT IN LONDON

The Road Traffic Act 1991 provides a new legislative framework for traffic management in London.[25] The Act empowers the Secretary of State to designate a network of priority routes (commonly known as *red routes* because of their distinctive red road markings and signs) which are subject to special parking and other traffic controls. They are aimed at reducing traffic congestion and improving traffic conditions on main routes, particularly for buses, without encouraging additional car commuting into central London. A pilot scheme in 1991 proved successful: overall journey times improved by 25 per cent, bus journey times were reduced by more than 10 per cent, and reliability increased by a third. More people used buses; and road casualties fell significantly. As a result, a permanent scheme was introduced in 1992: 320 miles of red routes have been designated throughout the capital. This network covers all trunk roads in London as well as local roads which are of strategic importance. It is thought that this network of specially controlled roads is 'coherent' and 'manageable for enforcement purposes', though consultations are taking place on additional routes where there is a need to assist bus movement. In addition to the red routes, other priority routes are being considered for central London. Here the aim will be to assist the movement of buses and local commercial traffic, rather than to serve longer distance movement.

The Road Traffic Act also provides for the appointment of a Traffic Director for London whose responsibility it is to coordinate the introduction and maintenance of traffic management measures in relation to designated priority routes. He has also been given the major objective of making the designated network operational in 1997. The Director's responsibilities include the preparation of a *Network Plan*. This will cover the overall objectives for the design and operation of the priority routes. The plan will provide a framework for detailed *Local Plans* which are to be approved by the Traffic Director. The red routes are to be given a distinctive 'theme' which 'will show drivers they are travelling on routes to which special controls apply and will provide a positive image to help foster self-enforcement'.

Central to this new system is a package of traffic management schemes and a reform of on-street parking in Greater London. Enforcement of parking controls on red routes is to be given priority by the police. Traffic management measures include increased priority for buses,[26] improved pedestrian crossings,and encouragement to cyclists to use alternative roads to red routes except where separate cycle tracks can be provided. A range of traffic calming measures are to be implemented on side roads which might be affected by the red-route traffic. These will regulate speed and deter motorists from using side roads as 'rat runs'. The DoT recommends the introduction of 20-mph zones to discourage through traffic. In such zones, there is the additional advantage that the road hump regulations are far more relaxed: for example, warning signs are not required. Doubts about the legality of traffic calming measures have been settled by the Traffic Calming Act 1992 which provides for the making of regulations governing them.

In addition to other parking restrictions, a new system of *Special Parking Areas* is being introduced. In these areas, which are to be designated by London local authorities, parking contraventions will no longer be criminal offences, and traffic wardens will be replaced by local authority *parking attendants*. The powers of these attendants include issuing *Penalty Charge Notices* and authorising wheelclamping and the removal of vehicles. A *Joint Parking Committee* has been appointed by the London local authorities (as required by the 1991 Act). This body has the duty of setting certain parking charges, and appointing *parking adjudicators* who will have a comparable role to magistrates' courts under the existing system of criminal parking controls. It is envisaged that the Joint Parking Committee will be used as a mechanism for coordinating London parking strategies.

These and similar provisions amount to an elaborate new system for traffic management in London (which can be extended to other areas in Britain). They constitute a new, and perhaps final, attempt to make

regulatory controls work. If they prove inadequate, some form of road pricing will probably be necessary. This has been resisted up to now, partly because of technical problems, but mainly because of the fear of a political backlash. The fear is that the public would be opposed to such a measure or, at least, the public is 'not yet ready' for it. This issue of public attitudes is worth examining further.

## PUBLIC ATTITUDES

Measures such as those outlined above would have been unacceptable without public support for stronger controls. This is a crucial factor in transport policy. It is also one that changes over time, particularly as the impacts of increased traffic are experienced. Yet there is a very real problem in reconciling private and public interests. Each car owner regards congestion problems as being created by *other* motorists; the individual's contribution to the total is negligible. This zero marginal cost for the individual imposes high costs on the collectivity of users, but car users have no incentive to economise in their use of road space: to them it is a free good.[27]

The car can be more than a means of transport. It can be an extension of a driver's personality, a symbol of affluence or power, an object to be loved as well as used. The 'love affair' with the car is, however, under strain: mass ownership and use has made it less appealing than it was (Goodwin *et al.* 1991: 144). Whether the disenchantment has gone far enough to warrant more penal methods of controlling its use is the basic political question. Recent surveys are helpful in showing the nature of public opinion and the scope that might exist for radical changes in policy.

In a 'poll of polls', P.M. Jones (1991b) summarises the major findings of ten surveys carried out between 1988 and 1990. First, there is no doubt about the general realisation of the seriousness of the problem of traffic congestion, but most people would be reluctant to significantly reduce their dependence on car use: despite the congestion, it still remains the favoured form of transport among car owners. Nevertheless, there seems to be an increasing willingness to consider switching to public transport for some types of journey *if public transport were better*. In looking at public transport as an alternative to the car, quality of service is much more important than the level of fares. (But the converse seems to be the case for car use: higher petrol prices are more significant than a doubling of journey times.) There is support for an increase in the range and quality of alternatives (or supplements) to car use, and for more effective parking restrictions, but little backing for road pricing. Londoners, however, are more favourably inclined towards road pricing, and Jones suggests that 'the Government is being unduly cautious in not proposing a road pricing scheme for London'.

Attitude surveys, of course, are not necessarily a good guide for policy-makers. A measure may be popular but ineffective: 'indeed its popularity may lie precisely in its ineffectiveness and lack of impact on car-based life styles. Some drivers may support better public transport, for example, because they believe that *other* drivers will use it, and so clear the roads for them.'

In another study commissioned by the Oxford Transport Studies Unit (not covered by Jones's review), Cullinane (1992) noted the extent of car-dependence: about a half of households in the survey perceived a car to be essential to their lifestyle and a further 13 per cent would not want to be without one. She also noted, however, that a quarter of households did not have a car and had no intention of getting one. The overall conclusion was that car dependence was increasing, and that, if things are allowed to continue as they are, it would become increasingly difficult to persuade owners to reduce their car usage.

Cullinane's study included that idiosyncratic British institution for the privileged: the company car. Company-assisted motoring increased dramatically during the 1970s, to the point where 60 per cent of new car registrations were attributable to companies and the self-employed (TEST 1984). The Government has recognised the importance of the issue in reducing the tax benefits of company cars.[28] Although a company car was perceived to be a necessity by three-quarters of those who had one, Cullinane suggests that 'there is some reason to believe that they are in some sense an unnecessary addition to the national park of cars'. Over a quarter of these drivers say that they would not replace their company car with a private one if it was withdrawn from them, and a third said they would reduce their mileage if they no longer had a company car.

Reflecting on the survey as a whole, Cullinane concludes that congestion seems likely to increase

> and that there will be some voluntary reduction in traffic as the problems intensify. However, the level of attachment of most people to their car is such that it will take some positive action from outside to force any real reduction in traffic, and this positive action will have the most impact if it hits people's purses.

A number of studies have pointed in the same direction. Cars are highly valued by those who can afford them, but the problems of congestion are becoming increasingly burdensome. There is support for better public transport and, though no massive changeover by car users is to be expected, 'all changes take place at the margin'. Goodwin *et al.* (1991: 147) suggest that 'policies that would have been very difficult to implement successfully only a few years ago, may now be more popular'. Though it is very apparent that motorists do not like the idea of road pricing, there is good evidence that they would accept it (reluctantly) if it were part of a package which provided them with some offsetting benefits, particularly in the form of good public transport. This is perhaps the most important finding of research both in Britain and abroad. Cervero has reviewed North American studies of transit pricing and concludes:

> For the most part, riders are insensitive to changes in either fare levels, structures, or forms of payments, though this varies considerably among user groups and operating environments. Since riders are approximately twice as sensitive to changes in travel time as they are to changes in fares, a compelling argument can be made for operating more premium quality transit services at higher prices. Such programs could be supplemented by vouchers and concessionary programs to reduce the burden on low-income users.
>
> (Cervero 1990: 117)

Goodwin (1989) underlines the point in his 'rule of three'. This useful article deals succinctly with a difficulty about road pricing which is frequently not addressed by its advocates. Though it is simple to demonstrate that road pricing increases total economic efficiency (since traffic will use the priced road only when the benefits are greater than the costs), it is also true that those who no longer use the road are losers. To make road pricing equitable and attractive, it is necessary to provide benefits to the non-users; and this can be done with the revenues that are collected from pricing. Goodwin divides these benefits into three groups: environmental improvement; traffic attracted to the less congested, faster, priced road; and the increased speed of all traffic on the priced road. The revenue raised by road pricing can be allocated in a similar threefold way: to general purposes (i.e. a tax), to new roads, and to the improvement of public transport. There is no magic in this threefold division (or the relative size of the individual parts, or even the purposes suggested); but such a scheme could be used to satisfy a range of legitimate claims and thus to increase support for road pricing. The essential point is that it provides a politically attractive approach, because it can satisfy a range of interests – which road pricing by itself does not.[29]

One further issue is selected for mention here: the effect of localised road pricing on land use. It is apparent that, if pricing were restricted to certain areas (e.g. within the area bounded by the M25) this could provide an incentive to relocation outside the priced area. It could also lead to a more dispersed pattern of origins and destinations (RTPI 1991b). An immediate response is that this is precisely what can be expected to happen with a high degree of congestion in a central urban area. But the implications are also the same in either case: first, transport policies should not be divorced from land-use planning policies. Transport is the linkage between land uses, and both should be planned in a coordinated way (to the extent that this is possible). At the least, policies in each area should take account of the context of, and the implications for, the other. An important land-use planning objective ought to be to minimise

the need to travel (as indicated in PPG 12).[30] Second, there is a case for road pricing to be extended over the whole road system, not merely the 'congested' parts.[31] If this were politically feasible, road taxes might replace some or all of current taxes. This, of course, raises some much wider issues than are being discussed here.

Even the most ardent supporter of road pricing admits that there are many unknowns in the matter. Theoretical studies may be suggestive, but many of the issues are empirical – or at least need empirical testing. Unfortunately, as May (1986: 120) has pointed out, it is one of the dilemmas of research on traffic restraint that though empirical evidence is needed, this is difficult to obtain since governmental authorities are unwilling to experiment without adequate predictions. This is a case where both academic and political considerations call for more research. In 1992, the Transport Secretary announced 'the biggest-ever study into whether motorists should be charged for driving into central London and other cities . . .'

## CENTRAL GOVERNMENT ORGANISATION FOR TRANSPORT

When the DoE was established it encompassed the former Ministry of Transport, and it was widely hoped that this would lead to a better coordination of transport and land-use policies. This did not happen and, indeed, the merger lasted for only a few years: the Department of Transport was re-established as a separate department in 1976. Though the reasons for this were largely political, there were differences between transport and planning officials within the DoE (Radcliffe 1991: 123). The independence of the Department of Transport facilitated its continuance as 'a well-oiled machine for producing roads' (Truelove 1992: 18). Among other things, this is leading to a growing conflict between central government policies for inter-urban traffic movement and 'many local authority policies that recognise a need to limit demand'.[32]

The overwhelming involvement of the Department

with roads has frequently been commented upon and, in recent years, there has been pressure for a reorganisation which would lead to less priority for roads. For example, both the National Economic Development Council and the CPRE have argued that executive responsibilities for trunk roads and motorways should be hived off. In the words of the CPRE 1992 report, *Where Motor Car is Master*, 'a streamlined Transport Department without direct responsibility for road building can become a true transport authority, taking an overview of the nation's requirement, both for transport and for meeting environmental objectives'. The National Economic Development Council 1992 report *A New Approach to Road Planning* endorses these ideas and additionally proposes that the reformed DoT should be responsible for a strategic plan which would be debated and approved by Parliament. Before trunk road proposals were included in a structure plan, the DoT would fund a feasibility study which would consider the need for the road 'and whether, in broad terms, a scheme is likely to be worthwhile in terms of the balance between the economy and the environment'. The study would be concerned only with the need for the road, not with its alignment. The merits of the proposal would be debated in a Select Committee of the House of Commons. If approved, the executive units would take on the responsibility for design and construction. The alignment, however, would be debated locally both by local politicians and all interested groups.

The NEDC proposal is an interesting one, though it would need considerable fleshing out before it represented a practicable operational scheme. But the narrower proposal to hive off the DoT's executive functions is very much in line with the government's *Next Step* policies which were discussed in Chapter 2. In 1993, it was announced that this was to be done. At the time of writing, the only information available was that a new agency, to be called Highway Command, is to be established.

## UPDATE

The metamorphosis of transport policy is taken a step further with the draft revised PPG 13, issued by DoE in April 1993. See also the DoE research report by ECOTEC Research and Consulting in association with Transportation Planning Associates, *Reducing Transport Emissions through Planning*, HMSO, 1993.

A volume in the CPRE *Campaigner's Guide* series deals with roads: W. Sheate and M. Sullivan, *Campaigners' Guide to Road Proposals*, CPRE (in conjunction with Transport 2000), 1993.

A green paper discusses options for *Paying for Better Motorways* (Cm 2200, HMSO, 1993). Views are sought on 'whether charging should be introduced to facilitate necessary improvements to the road network which could not otherwise be afforded and to make the most effective use of the network'.

The Traffic Policy Division of DoE has published a new edition of its *Cycling Bibliography* (DoE, 1993).

The House of Commons Transport Committee has reported on *The Government's Proposals for the Deregulation of Buses in London* (HC 623, Session 1992–93, HMSO, 1993).

## NOTES

1 Quoted in RTPI, *Traffic Growth and Planning Policy*, 1991b.
2 The measure used is the average daily flow: the number of vehicles passing a particular point on a road in a 24-hour period. This flow increased from 1,800 in 1971 to 3,100 in 1990. The largest increases were for trunk roads outside built-up areas and motorways. (See CSO, *Social Trends 22*, 1992: 1, Table 13.12.)
3 There was, however, an actual fall in the number of vehicles in 1991 (24,511,000 compared with 24,673,000 in the previous year). This is presumably a temporary result of the economic conditions in that year? *Annual Abstract of Statistics 1993*: Table 10.4.
4 The population of Great Britain was projected to increase to some 74 million by the year 2010. This huge increase led to considerable concern about population distribution (as well as to the establishment of several new towns of unprecedented size). See DoE, *Long Term Population Distribution in Great Britain – A Study*, which was published by DoE in 1971, after the

scare was over. The final chapter of this study is reproduced in Cullingworth 1973.

5 The figures are from Central Statistical Office, *Social Trends 22*, HMSO, 1992, Tables 13.8 and 13.10.

6 *Statistical Abstract of the United States 1992*, Washington, DC: US Government Printing Office, Table 1232.

7 There is an extensive literature on the Channel Tunnel. A particularly useful volume is Holliday *et al.* 1991 (which also has an excellent bibliography).

8 The following quotation from *National Road Traffic Forecasts (Great Britain) 1989* (p. 23) is instructive:

> The economy has changed markedly during the past 25 years, but there has been a near constant ratio between road tonne kilometres and GDP, with growth in one commodity making up for decline in others, and increased distances making up for near constancy in the quantity carried. There have also been changes in the location of industry and distribution points, the extent of part loaded and empty running, the proportions of line haul and delivery work and the relation between the road distance and the straight line distance, all of which will have had some influence on the tonne kms resulting from a given economic activity. Despite an apparent shift in final consumption to goods with a higher value per unit weight, the transport intensity of GDP has not fallen. Past experience therefore gives no basis for expecting the transport intensity of GDP to fall in the future.

9 'Road and rail by and large serve different markets, and for most traffic the one cannot readily be substituted for the other. Short freight movements are usually best suited to road; over 65% of loaded road freight journeys are of 50 miles or less. The different scale of road and rail activity are also important. Road transport is responsible for twelve times more passenger travel and ten times more freight movement than rail. A 50% increase in rail traffic would reduce road traffic by less than 5%. Rail has an important contribution to make, but it is not the panacea for congestion on inter-urban roads' (White Paper, *Roads for Prosperity*, 1989, para 12–13).

10 Note the comment of the DoE, in PPG 6, that major retail development is now a 'well-established form of retail development clearly meeting strong customer demand for convenient car-borne weekly household shopping'.

11 See Armitage Report 1980; Wardroper 1981; Hamer 1987; National Audit Office 1987.

12 Though the Buchanan Report is popularly remembered as a plea for taming the car, in fact its thrust was in favour of a massive increase in road building to cater

for the car. On this, see Goodwin *et al.* 1991, particularly pp. 66–9.

Mention should also be made of the now-forgotten Urban Motorways Committee, whose report *New Roads in Towns* (1972) recommended that 'the planning of new urban roads should form an integral part of planning the urban area as a whole; and that indirect costs and benefits of building urban roads should be looked at with the same care as the direct costs and movement benefits'. The first recommendation led to the 1972 White Paper *Development and Compensation – Putting People First* and the Land Compensation Act 1973. The second recommendation led to a new system of transport grants and the introduction of Transport Policies and Programmes (TPPs).

13 White Paper, *Transport Policy*, 1977. In Scotland, it was decided that the existing machinery was adequate without the necessity for additional statutory public transport plans. See SDD Circulars 19/1978 and 56/1978.

14 At the time of writing, the Government was planning to deregulate and privatise London's buses. Privatisation and its impacts are not discussed in this book. Useful short discussions are to be found in Banister 1990 and 1992. See also Bell and Cloke 1990.

15 Under s. 56 of the Transport Act 1968.

16 The lack of evidence about the impact of roads on economic growth is quite remarkable. A 1990 report from the House of Commons Transport Committee recommended that 'a thorough research exercise' was needed on the issue (HC Transport Committee, *Roads for the Future*, 1990: para. 17).

17 Adams (1990) comments that 'Although advertised as a "massive" addition to the existing road programme, the 4,300 kilometers of new or improved road . . . would add perhaps as much as 2% to the capacity of the country's road network.' The 1989 White Paper, *Roads for Prosperity*, concludes: 'A major expansion of the government's programme for road-building and improving inter-urban roads is being put in hand to meet the forecast needs of traffic into the next century. There is a logical void in the Government's case. The gross discrepancy between the government's forecast of the "needs of traffic" and the amount of new road-space they are proposing to build suggests that this void is likely to be filled with stationary motor vehicles.' This article contains the much-quoted calculation that the forecast increase in traffic could be accommodated by a new motorway from London to Edinburgh – if the traffic were stationary and the motorway was 257 lanes wide!

18 White Paper, *Trunk Roads England – Into the 1990s*, 1990: 1.

19 For a useful summary see Goodwin *et al.* 1991: chapter 7. See also FoE 1991b.

20  DoT Circular 5/92, *Traffic in London: Traffic Management and Parking Guidance*.

21  It was not until 1976 that a statutory code for highway inquiries was introduced. For an enlightening discussion of this murky area, see McAuslan 1980b: 55.

22  The SACTRA Report's dismissal of the argument that new roads spur new economic development has been ignored by successive governments.

23  *Annual Report of the Landscape Advisory Committee 1991*, DoE, 1992.

24  Figures are taken from various sources, including the DoT annual *Transport Statistics*. Useful secondary sources are McClintock 1992, and the HC Transport Committee's evidence on *Cycling* 1991.

25  Details are provided in the DoT's *Traffic in London: Traffic Management and Parking Guidance* (1992).

26  See DoT Local Transport Note 1/91, *Keeping Buses Moving*.

27  Hibbs (1991: 20) makes a telling point in comparing marginal costs for road usage, water supply and unmetered water:

> An extra kilometer of road moved over adds nothing to the vehicle-user's cost that is any way related to the decision to make the trip concerned. Zero marginal price, as with the case of non-metered water supply, provides no incentive to economise in the use of the scarce resource involved. The reader should contrast the complacency with which one regards a dripping tap with the known cost of the use of unnecessary electricity. The former has zero marginal price, while the latter is a unit-priced commodity.

28  The 1991b RTPI report *Traffic Growth and Planning Policy* comments:

> The company car problem is a peculiarly British phenomenon, distorting transport demand, in particular, encouraging greater use of the car, and encouraging the production and purchase of larger

cars, which feed through into the secondhand market, increasing pollution and the other adverse consequences . . . Government policy is to phase out those tax and other financial distortions which encourage the use of company cars though the implementation of the associated tax reforms has been protracted.

There are 3 million company cars; over 70,777 people have two or more company cars; one-third of cars commuting into central London are company cars, and another third are assisted in other ways such as free parking.

The benefits of the company car are being reduced by Exchequer action: see Inland Revenue 1992.

29  There are other factors which cannot be explored here. There is an extensive literature, including: Smeed Report 1964, May 1986, Mogridge 1986, Starkie 1986, Borins 1988, Chartered Institute of Transport 1990 and 1992, London Boroughs Association 1990, RTPI 1991b and Veld 1991. P. M. Jones 1991a and 1991b discusses the importance of relating the revenues from road pricing to a package of benefits.

30  See PPG 12, paras 6.10–6.16. For a more substantive discussion, see Cope *et al.* 1984; Owens 1984, 1985, 1986a and 1986b; Owens and Cope 1992.

31  'Unless road pricing is applied to *all* roads, irrespective of the sufficiency of road space, it will serve only to alleviate congestion in these areas and is likely to lead to re-location by the motoring public and commerce in order to avoid the inconvenience and extra transport costs' (Hillman 1992: 228).

32  Truelove 1992: 6. Truelove adds (p. 4) that the post-war nationalisation and denationalisation of the railways (the latter with a decentralised structure inimical to change, and an inappropriate modernisation plan) was an experience that the transport ministry did not remember with affection: 'The lasting legacy of this disastrous plan was a Ministry of Transport staffed with bureaucrats extremely suspicious of railway spending plans.'

# 11

# PLANNING AND THE PUBLIC

Publicity is the greatest and most effective check against arbitrary action.

Margaret Thatcher[1]

Democracy means that citizens have a significant influence over what happens, have equitable rights to exercise influence, and are entitled to know why policies have been adopted and that action taken is in line with these policies.

Patsy Healey, 1991b

## PLANNING AND POLITICS

Throughout the 1950s and 1960s, planning proposals were generally presented to the public as a *fait accompli*, and only rarely were they given a thorough public discussion.[2] Though there was machinery for objections and appeals, this quasi-judicial process was devised only for specified uses by a restricted range of interested parties. As will be shown later in this chapter, it was modified in its operation in response to increasing public pressures, but the general attitude to this system was (and remains) less favourable than to the normal judicial system with which it is frequently, though inappropriately, compared.

The lack of concern for public participation was a result partly of the political consensus of the post-war period, and partly of the trust that was accorded to 'experts' – which, by definition, included professionals. The time was perceived to be one of rapidly expanding scientific achievement, and the methods that had made such progress in the physical sciences were thought to be transferable to the problems of social and political organisation (Hague 1984). This,

together with the advent of new social security, health and other social and public services, led to a rapid growth in professions and the bureaucracies in which they worked. Town planners, though having identity problems which took many years to settle, had a good public image: they were to be the builders of the Better Britain which was to be won now that the military battle was over. In the same spirit as established professions, they sought to establish a strong, scientific and objective knowledge base. Armed with the right techniques in manipulating the physical environment, they were to address the physical problems of the nation and, at least by implication, the underlying social and economic forces. In retrospect, the approach implied a depoliticising of issues which were later appreciated to be of intense public concern. This was further obscured by professional techniques and language which the public could not be expected to understand.[3] Of course, planners were not alone in this: on the contrary, they simply took the same stance as other 'disabling professions' – to use Illich's term.[4] At the time, however, the lack of political debate and participation was not widely recognised as a problem.

Professionals were perceived as acting in everyone's interest – the general public interest.

It was in the 1960s that these ideas were effectively challenged in the UK, closely following experience in the USA.[5] By this time, the political consensus had broken down, and there was widespread dissatisfaction, both with the lack of access to decision making within government and to the way in which benefits were being distributed. Though it claimed to serve the public interest, the planning system began to be seen as an important agent in the distribution of resources – frequently with regressive effects.[6] The idea of an objective, neutral planning system was increasingly recognised to be false.

In particular, the physical bias of the planning system had failed to address social and economic problems: perhaps it even made them worse. There was growing concern for a new type of 'social planning' which would seek to redress the imbalance in the access to goods, services, opportunities, and power. To achieve this, some saw the need for 'advocacy planning', which would provide experts to work directly with disadvantaged groups.

This critique has had consequences for planning practice of greater permanence than that achieved by the intellectual arguments themselves. Changes were made in the statutory planning procedures, and consultation and participation gradually became an important feature of the planning process. The more open system was generally acclaimed by the profession, though there were critics who questioned underlying assumptions. Neo-Marxists drew attention to the more fundamental divisions of power in the political and economic structure of capitalist society. In practice, also, extensive participation exercises produced only limited gains, and some advocate planners were amongst the first to reject the approach for its weaknesses. The critics argued that, like all 'agents of the state', planners operate within a 'structural strait-jacket' and, irrespective of their own values, will inevitably serve the very interests which they are supposed to control. This was supported by research findings which demonstrated that planning had operated systematically in the interests of property owners.

There was also substantial theoretical work concerned with the role played by the planning system in the interests of capital.

These critiques were powerful but, by their very nature, they could offer little guidance to planners working in a professional, politically controlled system. Indeed, how could they respond to allegations that a fundamental purpose of planning in society is the legitimation of the existing order? If participation merely supports a charade of power sharing, leaving entrenched interests secure, what alternatives do planners have? They are, of course, used to unfair criticism for things that go wrong: the post-war housing estates that were built as quickly as possible (and with few resources left over for 'amenities'); the motorways that were belatedly built to cope with the great increase in traffic congestion, but which destroyed the social and physical fabric of towns; and the participation processes which raised hopes which were dashed by the outcomes. In Ambrose's words (1986), planning was the scapegoat.

More radical approaches have emerged. Popular planning aims

> to democratise decision making away from the state bureaucrats or company managers to include the workforce as a whole or people who live in a particular area . . . empowering groups and individuals to take control over decisions which affect their lives, and therefore to become active agents of change.
> (Montgomery and Thornley 1988: 5)

Not surprisingly, the few examples of such practice are to be found in the left-wing strongholds of the former GLC and a few of the other metropolitan district councils, and with only limited success.

Decentralisation of decision-making has only been effected (and perhaps only *can* be effected) on a very limited basis. In her study of *The People's Plan for the Royal Docks*, a major example of 'popular planning', Brownill identifies some of the contradictions.

> Although many of the ideas in the Plan do reflect the demands of local people, they are presented in a framework of overall GLC policy. We come back to the situation where there is an elected authority which has greater power than the community . . . The Plan was a very good example of the decentralisation of policy

implementation, but the fact that GLC policy was presented as a local people's plan shows dishonesty and a blurring of the edges between the state and civil society.

(Brownill 1988: 20)

Many planners find it difficult to come to terms with this type of analysis. They already have sufficient difficulties with their responsibilities for strategic planning concerns which go well beyond the particular locality in which they are employed. Interestingly, popular planning approaches have generally not been innovative in their methods of establishing community needs. They have generally involved the usual mixture of meetings, publicity and leaflets. They are thus subject to the same problems of achieving a positive and representative response that face all efforts to increase participation.

## THE PROFESSION

In 1993, there were 17,763 members of the Royal Town Planning Institute, of whom 13,153 (74 per cent) were corporate members. Three-quarters of the corporate membership work in the public sector (with about two-thirds in local government), and about a fifth in private consultancies and the development industry. Half of the local government members are in the non-metropolitan district councils (Nadin and Jones 1990: 18).

A 1992 survey of planners employed in local government shows that only about half of the professional staff employed in planning were members of the Institute (LGMB and RTPI 1993). The others will be professionals who are not eligible for membership, including other professionals such as architects who are working principally on planning matters, or students working for qualifications that lead to membership. If it were assumed that a similar balance of Institute members exists in the rest of the planning field, in the private and voluntary sectors and in education, the total 'professional body' in its widest sense is more than 35,000 strong. In addition, there are support staff who, in 1991, totalled over 8,000 in local government and an equal number

elsewhere. In total, therefore, there is a planning workforce of some 50,000.

A 1988 profile of the Institute membership showed its very homogeneous character (Nadin and Jones 1990). The overwhelming majority of the membership is young, white and male. Women and ethnic minorities are under-represented. Even in the younger age groups, women account for only about 30 per cent of members. At the higher levels, women are very poorly represented. For example, in the local government survey, only 1.6 per cent of chief planning officers are women. By contrast, women occupy two-fifths of junior posts and over four-fifths of part-time posts.

In the 1988 survey of Institute members, only 70 UK-based respondents fell outside the category of 'white European', with the highest proportions being in the London boroughs. The profession is also dominated by public sector employment: about two-thirds in local government, and a further tenth in central government and other public sector agencies. About a fifth work in consultancies or the development industry. Not surprisingly, the dominant activities undertaken by planners are in development control and development planning, though they are engaged in a very wide range of other jobs.

The planning profession is thus well established in Britain, and the RTPI is easily the largest professional planning body in Europe. How this position has been reached in the years since the Institute was established in 1913 is worthy of a note of explanation. Under the Royal Charter, the Institute is responsible for the education of prospective planners, and has the power 'to devise standards of knowledge and skills for persons seeking corporate membership of the Chartered Institute . . .' The Institute held its own examinations for membership until 1992 but, from the earliest days, specific courses were set up to train planners (the first being at Liverpool University in 1909).[7] By 1945, there were nine courses in town and country planning, all of which were postgraduate. By 1981, the number of courses had increased to 57, including 20 at the undergraduate level. These courses are accredited by the Institute: following two years' practical experience, graduates are able to apply for corporate membership. The Institute publishes guidelines for planning schools setting out the general policy on the education of planners, together with a core curriculum.

Student numbers in town and country planning increased sharply in the 1960s. They reached an early peak in 1978, when there were 959 enrolments and 919 graduates in 54 separate courses (Thomas 1990a and 1990b). During the 1980s, the Government reviewed the number of town planning courses being offered. This followed the Institute of Local Government Studies Report on *Manpower Requirements for Physical Planning* (Amos *et al.* 1982) which suggested that 'a plateau may have been reached and that further growth is unlikely'. Despite a spirited defence by the planning schools and the RTPI, some courses were forced to cease recruitment. However, the impact of the closures was reduced because of increased intakes in the other schools. In 1988, a total of 766 students were recruited into 31 courses.

Two factors have led to a dramatic increase in student numbers in the early 1990s. First, the 1988 Education Act changed the funding mechanism for higher education, with the result that the market in planning education was opened up, and larger numbers of students enrolled on planning courses. Second, the impact of previous course closures coincided with a sharp increase in demand for planning graduates which took place at the end of the 1980s. A shortfall in planning graduates led to a surge in recruitment of graduates from other related disciplines. These recruits to planning have sought professional qualification, and thereby swelled the numbers of part-time postgraduate students. In 1992, there were 1,119 students in the first year of RTPI accredited courses, and a total of 3,715 planning students in 24 schools.

Despite the pessimistic forecasts made in the early 1980s, and some apprehension about the Conservative Government's future policy in relation to the planning system, the demand for planning graduates increased significantly during the 1980s, and, by 1986, demand exceeded supply. The recession, however, led to a fall in demand and, at the time of writing, there is a shortage of posts for the number of available planners.[8]

## INTERESTS IN PLANNING

'Interests' in planning are usually thought of in terms of the organisations, groups, and individuals who are actively engaged in the planning arena: they are identified by their participation in the land development and planning processes. These include land and property owners, developers, special interest groups, national government and its agencies, and local authorities themselves (in both their landowning and regulatory capacities). Some organisations have become particularly skilled in presenting their views at both national and local levels. The House Builders' Federation, for example, is an important national organisation that regularly presents evidence at public inquiries in support of the interests of the house-building industry. It has a special place in the planning process by virtue of its role in the land availability studies discussed in Chapter 5. The Council for the Protection of Rural England (and its Scottish and Welsh counterparts) and the RSPB are examples of major conservation interests which are long-established, and which also have expanded greatly in membership.[9] National voluntary organisations obviously do not command the resources available to commercial interests, but they do employ experts and can be very effective in promoting their causes. Some of them have become increasingly sophisticated over the last decade or so,[10] and can appropriately be described as 'major elites' (Goldsmith 1980). There are innumerable 'minor elites' of small groups who become involved in an *ad hoc* way with particular issues. The evolution of participation and consultation in planning has favoured these self-defined interest groups, and given them a relatively privileged position in the planning process. It has long been appreciated that such groups are not necessarily representative of anything wider than the interests of their active supporters. Many people are not able or willing to take the time to engage in 'participation', and some groups who have a clear stake in planning outcomes (such as home buyers or job seekers) are too diffuse to have become effective participators, and 'rarely if ever emerge as definable actors in the development process'.[11]

Sometimes, however, an interest group emerges in an area where previously there was little or no effective articulation of views. Three of these are briefly discussed in the following pages: the interests of race, gender, and people with disabilities.

## Race and Planning

Questions of equal racial opportunities have figured prominently on the town planning agenda over the last fifteen years, though with questionable impact on practice. It was in 1978 that the RTPI established a joint working party with the Commission for Racial Equality (CRE) to investigate the multi-racial dimension of planning, and to make recommendations for any necessary changes in practice.[12] Its 1983 report, *Planning for a Multi-Racial Britain*, was a frank assessment of the inadequacies of the then current thinking on race and planning. It is perhaps only a little less relevant today.

The working party's deliberations were spurred by the deteriorating race relations in Britain's cities, and by numerous reports calling for more action from central government and other bodies.[13] These and other studies demonstrated that: 'Black people in Britain share all the problems of social malaise and multiple deprivation with their white neighbours. In addition, however, they experience the additional difficulties of racial discrimination and disadvantage, because of the colour of their skin' (CRE 1982: 9).

The 1983 RTPI/CRE report argued that, despite its record of innovation in participation, the profession had failed to address the issue of race. Indeed, the RTPI's own 1982 report on participation failed to explicitly consider the racial dimension. Ethnic minorities were mentioned only once, with reference to the need to provide interpretation at public meetings. *Planning for a Multi-Racial Britain* sought to improve sensitivity to racial issues 'and show how planning practice can be modified to avoid racial discrimination, promote equality of opportunity, and improve race relations for the benefit of the whole community'. It identified three elements in the racial dimension of planning:

1 reviewing the impact of current policies, practices and procedures upon different racial groups, with a view to ascertaining actual or potential racial discrimination;
2 building racial distinctions into surveys, analyses and monitoring with a view to identifying the special needs of different racial groups; allowing the impact of policies to be assessed, and providing a basis for any appropriate positive action;
3 positive action in planning policies, procedures, standards and decision-making, partly by directing positive non-racial policies and actions towards groups containing high proportions of black people, and partly by taking special steps to ensure that black people have equal access to the benefits offered by town planning.

The report also considered how the profession could be made more representative in terms of its membership, and the implications of this for the education of planners. It became an important guide for committed practitioners and teachers, and formed the basis for other more detailed guidance, foremost of which was the GLC's *Race and Planning Guidelines*. Publication of this was squeezed in just before abolition (when perhaps the most vigorous supporter of equal opportunities was lost).

The GLC report, however, has subsequently provided a rich source of material for guiding good practice in the London boroughs and elsewhere.[14] The main themes are: better knowledge of specific ethnic minority needs, more data on the nature of ethnic minority characteristics, monitoring of the impact of policies on particular groups, and an empathetic approach to cultural traditions and practices. Overall, the recommendations illustrate the inadequacy of the 'colour-blind' approach identified as commonplace in the RTPI/CRE report. Such an approach, though holding that all people should be treated equally, is insensitive to the cultural traditions and needs of particular ethnic groups. Unintentional discrimination can therefore result.[15] Though good practice has been noted in numerous areas, discrimination remains insidious and widespread.

## Planning and Gender

The absence of policy explicitly related to concerns of women has attracted little attention until recently.

One of the many reasons for this is the inadequacy of the classic texts on social theory and urban studies. In reviewing these, Greed writes:

> Women appear in studies of working class communities as a variety of oversimplified stereotypes, based on observing them as mono-dimensional residents tied to the area rather than as people with jobs, interests and aspirations beyond its boundaries. Young and Willmott give emphasis to women in their study, but their fondness for seeing them in the role of 'Mum', as virtually tea machines, and almost as wall paper to the main action of life, is open to question.
>
> (Greed 1993: 233)

Greed has elsewhere (1992) described the male domination of the profession as 'only a temporary intermission'. Women were primary contributors to the social movement which promoted town planning at the turn of the century. She argues that the professionalisation of planning, its institutionalisation within the government structure, and the limited access to qualifying courses has 'kept most women out'. The gender bias reflects, and in part perpetuates, the patriarchal structure of British society, and continues to influence the recruitment and education of planners. Women generally tend 'to under-achieve and under-aspire as regards a career', and they 'hesitate to embark upon a professional career'.[16]

An illustration of the gender bias is the way in which some issues are defined in land-use terms, whereas others are labelled 'social'. Thus, the provision of sporting facilities and the open-space standards applied to them are routinely regarded as legitimate land-use matters. These predominantly male activities are contrasted by Greed (1993: 237) with crèches, which are commonly regarded as social issues even though they 'may have major implications for central area office development' – a fact which is explicitly taken into account in some US cities.[17]

Awareness of gender issues has grown in recent years. Women's perspectives on planning have been addressed by several RTPI reports, by the GLC Development Plan, and by its successors.[18] It is less clear whether such efforts have had a significant impact. One difficulty (in addition to the power of traditional attitudes and ways of thinking and perceiving) is the general lack of explicit social policies in plans. There has long been argument about the extent to which land-use plans should incorporate social issues, but the Conservative Government has taken a strong line against this. Nevertheless, the Development Plan Regulations provide some leeway in that they require local authorities 'to have regard to social and economic considerations'.[19] Furthermore, although PPG 12 does not explicitly refer to 'women' or 'gender', it does advise that:

> Authorities will wish to consider the relationship of planning policies and proposals to social needs and problems, including their likely impact on different groups in the population, such as ethnic minorities, religious groups, elderly and disabled people, single parent families, students, and disadvantaged and deprived people in inner urban areas.

A survey of development plans found that a number of LPAs had had some success in incorporating the special needs of women in their development plans, even weathering DoE scrutiny (Davies 1993). However, this policy area is generally much less developed than those of race or disability, especially outside London. One likely reason is that, as in the case of the Wolverhampton UDP, local authorities 'didn't consider this an issue' (ibid.). This points to the importance in planning education and practice of the promotion of equal opportunities and sensitivity to women's perspectives.

## Planning and People with Disabilities

One group that has received more attention from the planning system is that of people with disabilities. The 1990 Planning Act requires local authorities to draw to the attention of planning applicants the need to consider the requirements of the Chronically Sick and Disabled Persons Act 1970, and the Building Regulations require 'access provision' in new buildings.[20]

Despite this explicit concern, the needs of people with disabilities have been considered largely in terms of the design of the built environment. Important though this is, it leads to an overly simplistic stereotyping of the problems faced by individuals with disabilities. Thomas gives a strong critique of current attitudes:

> The 'regs' can become a checklist which defines the needs of disabled people, ignoring, indeed disallowing, the possibility that individual professionals dealing with particular cases need to learn from the experience of disabled people themselves. The British legislation which relates specifically to planning with its references to practicality and reasonableness, reinforces a strand in planners' professional ideologies which emphasises the role of the planner in reaching optimum solutions in situations involving competing needs or interests. Thus might a fundamental right to an independent and dignified life be reduced to an 'interest' to be balanced against the 'requirements' of conservation or aesthetics.
> (Thomas 1992: 25)

Davies (1993) concludes that policies related to access for the disabled, and to women's special needs, are now finding their way into plans, especially in the London Boroughs. She is, however, critical of central government advice, which although often only very recently updated, fails to give the necessary impetus. The DoE *Good Practice Guide*, for example, is described as 'woefully lacking'. She also observes that, whereas negotiations between interest groups and planners have often strengthened plans on these matters, further objection by other interests and scrutiny by the DoE later in the process have resulted in a 'watering down of policies'.

## THE SKEFFINGTON REPORT

Concern with, and even interest in, public participation has not been a particularly obvious strength of British local government. With little experience to build on, it was perhaps inevitable that a committee should be appointed 'to consult and report on the best methods, including publicity, of securing the participation of the public at the formative stage in the making of development plans for their area'. The Committee was set up under the chairmanship of the late Arthur Skeffington (then Joint Parliamentary Secretary to the Minister of Housing and Local Government), and its report was published in 1969.

The Skeffington Report made a number of rather obvious recommendations which did not carry the issues much further, for example:

people should be kept informed throughout the preparation of a structure or local plan for their area;

local planning authorities should seek to publicise proposals in a way that informs people living in the area to which the plan relates;

the public should be told what their representations have achieved or why they have not been accepted;

people should be encouraged to participate in the preparation of plans by helping with surveys and other activities as well as by making comments.

The mundane nature of many of the recommendations is testimony to the distance which British local government had to go in making citizen participation a reality.

Unfortunately, the report did not discuss many of the crucial issues, though passing references suggest that the Committee was aware of some of them. For instance, it is rightly stated that 'planning' is only one service, 'and it would be unreasonable to expect the public to see it as an entity in itself'. The report continues: 'public participation would be little more than an artificial abstraction if it becomes identified solely with planning procedures rather than with the broadest interests of people'. This has major implications for the internal organisation and management of local authorities (which are not discussed). So have the proposals for the appointment of 'community development officers . . . to secure the involvement of those people who do not join organisations' and for 'community forums' which would 'provide local organisations with the opportunity to discuss collectively planning and other issues of importance to the area', and which 'might also have administrative functions, such as receiving and distributing information on planning matters and promoting the formation of neighbourhood groups'.

What was conspicuously lacking in this debate on public participation was an awareness of its political implications. The Skeffington Report noted that it was feared that a community forum might become the centre of political opposition: but the only comment made was: 'we hope that would not happen;

it seems unlikely that it would, as most local groups are not party political in their membership'. The issue is not, however, one of party politics: it is one of local concerns, pressures and interests. Public participation implies a transfer of some power from local councils to groups of electors. It is power which is the crucial issue – not in any sinister sense, but simply in terms of who is to decide local issues. The DoE does not want to be concerned with these (except where they have ramifications over a larger front). Curiously, it was not the Skeffington Committee but the Seebohm Committee (1968) which highlighted another related issue:

> The participants may wish to pursue policies directly at variance with the ideas of the local authorities, and there is certainly a difficult link to be forged between the concepts of popular participation and traditional representative democracy. The role of the social worker in this context is likely to give rise to problems of conflicting loyalties. The Council for Training in Social Work suggest in evidence that if community work is to be developed by the local authority, then the authority 'will need to recognise the fact that some of its staff may be involved in situations which lead to criticism of their services or with pressure groups about new needs. The workers themselves will need to be clear about their professional role and this will depend upon their training and the organisational structure within which they work' . . . Participation provides a means by which further consumer control can be exercised over professional and bureaucratic power.

A further problem in public participation is that of determining the representativeness of the views expressed by participating citizens. As the Skeffington Report implies, the views of 'the non-joiners and inarticulate' are as important as those of 'the actively interested and organised'. And, as American experience shows, public participation can lead to strong demands to keep an area 'white', to exclude social housing, and to safeguard local amenities at a high cost to the larger community.

Finally, reference needs to be made to the tricky problem of planning blight. The best way of avoiding this is to maintain the utmost secrecy until definite plans can be presented to the public as a *fait accompli*. Obviously, this is difficult to reconcile with a greater degree of public participation. There is no easy answer

to this. Indeed, the Skeffington Committee was probably right in saying that 'some increase in planning blight may have to be accepted if there is to be increased participation by the public'. Whether the compensation provisions for planning blight are adequate is another matter.

An essential ingredient of effective public participation is a concern on the part of elected members and professional staffs to make participation a reality. This cannot be effective unless it is organised, but this, of course, is one of the fundamental difficulties. Though a large number of people may feel vaguely disturbed in general about the operation of the planning machine (and particularly upset when they are individually affected), it is only a minority who are prepared to do anything other than grumble. The minority may be growing, and with the general rise in educational levels it can be expected to continue to do so. It has to be recognised, however, that as far as can be seen, public participation will always be restricted. In the words of Maurice Broady:

> the activity of responsible social criticism is not congenial to more than a minority. Most of us for most of the time are content to remain complacently acquiescent in our social niche . . . The activist, the social critic, the reformer, will always be a small section of any society. Their activities require not only an extra effort which few are willing to expend, but also the ability to criticise and organize which comparatively few possess.[21]

## LOCAL CHOICE

Chris Patten is often credited for an about-turn in policy on local participation during his short term of office in 1989. In fact, his predecessor, Nicholas Ridley, had already begun the shift to more local decision-making. It was during his time as Environment Secretary that a clearer national planning framework was instituted through PPGs, that local authorities were strongly encouraged to produce more plans, and that warnings were given that developers would have to bear costs if they pursued applications contrary to up-to-date statutory plans. On coming into office, Patten accelerated the rate of change. In the face of concerted opposition, much of it from within the ranks of the Conservative Party, he reversed the judgement on the proposal for a new settlement at Foxley Wood in Hampshire. His statement, under the banner *Planning and Local Choice* made much of the opportunity for local communities to make their own decisions.[22]

> While there is undoubtedly a continuing need for more houses, there are choices about the way we meet that need. One of the functions of the planning system is to help us identify those choices, and make them sensibly. What is more, many of the important choices are decisions which can and should be made locally, to reflect the values which local communities place on their surroundings. If the planning system works properly at the local level, there is less need for the central government decision taking – by me or by my Inspectors – which can so easily appear to the local community to attach too little weight to their views.

However, local autonomy was to be exercised only where it was within parameters laid down by the centre in national and regional policy statements. Plans and development control decisions still needed to be 'realistic about the overall level of provision'. This was supported soon afterwards with the publication of PPG 15 and the introduction of a firmer policy on the production of regional guidance. Nevertheless, the statement marks an important milestone in the relationship between central and local decision-making. It was a clear move away from the previous line of argument, so closely linked to Ridley's early term of office, that local concerns would have to be set aside in favour of a presumption in favour of new development.

## ACCESS TO INFORMATION

Information is power; so it is not surprising that undemocratic societies guard it jealously. It is surprising, however, that secrecy is so prevalent in Britain. The fiasco over the Crossman Diaries revealed the absurdities in striking detail. British secrecy is a legacy of old styles of government.[23] These persist in many ways, and the elitist origins are still apparent. Government is carried on in an elitist atmosphere of

determining what actions are in the public interest, as viewed through the eyes of the Government. Participation is limited, and information restricted.[24]

Ironically, though traditional attitudes still prevail at the centre, it is the central government which has forced local government to provide greater 'freedom of information'. A major milestone in this is the Local Government (Access to Information) Act 1985, which imposes a duty on local authorities 'to publish information . . . about the discharge of their functions and other matters'.[25] The underlying principle of this Act is that all meetings of local authorities, their committees and subcommittees should be open to the press and the public. There is a power to exclude only in narrowly defined circumstances. The Act also provides for public access to agendas, reports and minutes of all meetings, and opens for public inspection certain background papers which relate to the subject matter of reports to council, committee or subcommittee meetings.

One aspect of this 'freedom of information' issue which receives little attention is the cost of purchasing published material. Central government publications are now highly priced (presumably at market levels), as a result of which their cost is prohibitive to ordinary citizens. Only occasionally is an important paper published in summary form at modest cost (a notable example being the summary of *Our Common Inheritance*. There is a striking contrast with many US Government publications which the public can obtain free of charge through their representatives.

With local government, a bigger problem is the paucity of publications, but the cost of planning documents tends to be very high. Taken almost at random, a list of recently published plans, which appeared in *Planning*,[26] included the *Mid-Suffolk Local Plan – Consultation Draft* (£30, plus £6 postage); the *Hillingdon Unitary Development Plan* (£36, plus £3 postage); and the *Stratford-on-Avon District Local Plan – Deposit Draft* (£17, plus £3 postage). Topping them all for cost was the *North West Leicestershire Draft Local Plan* (£50), but this is accompanied by a *free* local plan guide. No doubt, the expensive reports are intended for a small high-price market, but high quality (or quantity) of plan production is not important in relation to the needs for public information and participation. One enterprising local authority in Canada (Peterborough, Ontario) printed a version of its town plan which was issued free in newspaper format. This is a model well worth copying.

A good example has been set by the Scottish Office which announced at the end of 1992 that it had decided to issue its planning guidance free of charge. This followed the responses to a Consultation Paper: 'most consultees opposed imposing a charge for better quality publications, arguing that information on government policy should be freely available'.[27]

A major new influence on the provision of information is the EC, particularly with its 1990 *Directive on Freedom of Access to Information on the Environment*.[28] This was a product of the commitment in the EC's Fourth Action Programme to enable groups and individuals to take a more effective part in protecting and promoting their interests.[29] The Directive was brought into force in the UK by the Environmental Information Regulations 1992. The objective of the Directive is 'to ensure freedom of access to, and dissemination of, information on the environment held by public authorities and to set out the basic terms and conditions on which such information should be made available'. This has potentially significant implications for a very wide range of bodies including central and local government departments; other organisations that have public administration responsibilities in relation to the environment; and any others, including private organisations, whose behaviour is subject to the 'decisive influence' of government or public authorities. (The latter category includes private firms which provide environmental services on contract to public bodies.)

The regulations, which came into force at the end of 1992, define environmental information as 'the state of any water or air, the state of any flora or fauna, the state of any soil, or the state of any natural site or other land', together with activities or measures adversely affecting, or designed to protect, these states. Organisations affected are given two months to respond to any requests for information, and

there are limited provisions for refusal to supply information where, for example, it is incomplete or subject to legal proceedings. An important provision in the regulations is the requirement for relevant organisations to produce a list of all information sources, and for this to be made publicly available. The Directive, however, does not address the two most important issues: 'knowing that there is someone to ask, and knowing that there is something to ask for' (Clabon and Chance 1992: 25).

The use that is to be made of the right to environmental information remains to be seen. Some evidence is available from research concerning the use of the public registers on the discharge of trade or sewage effluent under the Control of Pollution Act 1974 – a major anti-secrecy piece of legislation.[30] Since registers seem likely to be the main mechanism for providing public information, it is useful to examine the ways in which they have been working. From an analysis of enquiries made to three water authorities, Burton (1989: 193) concludes that 'interest to date has been disappointing, both in terms of the number of enquiries made and the range of people making those enquiries'. There are several difficulties facing the searcher for information. First, it must be known to exist, yet neither the water authorities nor the DoE made any significant effort to inform the public about the existence of the registers. Second, there is a problem of access: the convenience of the location of the information, and the hours when it can be seen. (The Act requires that access be provided at reasonable hours, which typically means the working hours of the water authorities; but potential inquirers may well work the same 'reasonable hours'.) Third, there are costs involved in providing and obtaining information: to cover the costs (at least in part) of copying information an authority may charge a fee which, though small to the authority, might be prohibitive to a small amenity group. Finally, the information should be comprehensible, but what is comprehensible to those administering the register may be far from such for a group with little technical expertise. All these problems can be met, but a positive attitude, some imagination, and modest resources are required. 'The bare legal requirement to maintain registers is not itself sufficient to increase public awareness of their existence and encourage their use' (Burton 1989: 206).

## THE CITIZEN'S CHARTER

The Citizen's Charter has four main themes: improvement in the quality of public services; the creation of greater choice between service providers; the setting of performance standards; and value for money.[31] A central aim is to furnish more information to the public about the performance of service providers. In this, it is closely linked to the extension of performance indicators, first established in 1982, emerging from the Audit Commission's Report on *Building in Quality*. Although often credited to the Citizen's Charter initiative of the Prime Minister, John Major, 'quality review' has been a steadily growing component of public, private and voluntary sector management practice. The general concept has been taken up with enthusiasm by many organisations. This is evidenced in the progress made in the production of charters for specific individual services. After one year, it was reported that 28 charters had been produced 'covering patents, parents, passengers, council tenants, benefits agency customers, job seekers, court users and others'.[32] Since then, applicants for planning permission have been added to the list, following the publication in 1993 of the Development Control Charter.[33] A *Planning Charter* for the entire service is on the agenda. In the meantime, local authorities, agencies, private companies, and even universities are preparing their own customer charters.[34] There is a further proposal for a *Local Environment Charter*, with separate versions for England, Scotland and Wales. This would cover all environmentally related local authority services. It would address three issues: the right of access to environmental information held by public authorities; the right to participate in decision-making on environmental issues; and the right to seek remedies in the event of shortcomings in environmental services.[35] Some progress has already been made

on this with the publication in 1992 of *Green Rights and Responsibilities: A Citizen's Guide to the Environment* (DoE 1992; also available in Welsh). The Environment Charter, as proposed, is very similar.

It is not clear whether these charters will make any difference to the relationship between the public and the planning and environmental protection systems. On this, there are two important questions to consider. The first is the long-standing debate on the problems of measuring quality in planning. Quality is an elusive concept, but some guidance and encouragement is provided by the British Standards Institution.[36] This has been one of the factors responsible for much of the increasing interest within management circles about quality, service delivery, and the customers' experience. (Interest has been prompted also by the Government's drive to introduce competition in the public sector.) The British Standard lays emphasis on extending control to the wide range of factors that might affect the quality of service for the customer. These include management, personnel, training, organisational objectives and resources. The thrust of the charters, however, is to focus on easily measurable facets of service delivery. In some cases, it is reduced to rather shallow measurements and setting of targets for responding to inquiries, making decisions and the like. The value of these is limited, and their impact will depend on how challenging they are.

The second question is the extent to which the charters extend the rights of the citizen in planning matters. The clear answer is 'very little'. The charters spell out existing rights and, in so far as this helps to increase understanding, they are to be welcomed. But the relationship between citizen and government is not fundamentally changed: indeed, it is defined in a one-dimensional way – the citizen as consumer.[37] Thus, attention is focused on aspects of information provision, consultation, complaint and redress, equal access, and even empowerment. But 'the ultimate power of decision must remain with those who have acquired legitimacy thanks to the ballot box'.[38] It is difficult to see how it could be otherwise in the provision of the planning 'service'. By its very nature, planning deals with an array of competing interests, and it involves difficult questions concerning the distribution of costs and benefits.

The RTPI has argued that the role of interest groups, and the existing provisions for managing public participation in the planning system, should be recognised. Indeed, it has been suggested that the statutory consultation in the planning system has provided a 'de facto Citizen's Charter for many years'. This is the subject of the next section.

## STATUTORY PROVISIONS

### Development Plans

A major landmark in the growth of public participation was the 1968 Planning Act (and its Scottish equivalent of 1969) which made public participation a statutory requirement in the preparation of development plans.

The main stimulus for this came not from the grass roots but from central government. Under the old development plan system, the Department was becoming crippled by what a former permanent secretary called 'a crushing burden of casework'. The concept of ministerial responsibility was clearly shown to be inapplicable over the total field of development plan approval and planning appeals. Not only was much of this work inappropriate to a central government department, its sheer weight prevented central government from fulfilling its essential function of establishing major planning policies. A new system was therefore required which would remove much of the detailed work of planning, including approval of local plans, from central to local government. This was provided by the 1968 Act, discussed in Chapter 3.

The 1991 Act extended the powers of local authorities for the adoption of plans: they are now responsible for both strategic and local land-use policy. As noted above, Ministers have expressed their desire to see local communities making their own decisions on planning matters but, in delegating this responsibility, a set of procedures has been put into place to ensure that local choice, however democratically arrived at, does not transgress 'the general public interest' (or other private interests which the centre deems to be important).

The procedures for adoption of plans ensure that local authorities stay within the parameters set down by central government and generally act responsibly. The procedural safeguards do this, however, at some cost of time and resources. The problem for government has been to balance the controls over local discretion with the need for a locally responsive and efficient development plan system. During the 1970s and 1980s, many local authorities avoided preparing statutory development plans, in part because they believed the costs of taking a plan through the formal procedures outweighed any benefits (Bruton and Nicholson 1983). Benefits were limited because the plan was only one consideration in development control, and might be overturned with relative ease. As a result, the legitimacy which plans provided to decision-making was limited. The failure of local authorities to keep plans up to date exacerbated this.

The perverse outcome of all this was an over-reliance on informal policy (or in some cases no policy at all), *ad hoc* decision-making, and consequently much less accountability. Much of the debate over 'the future of development plans' has turned on this issue. From the local authorities' point of view, it was argued that in order to facilitate the production of plans, the procedures should be streamlined, for example by removing the requirement for a public inquiry. But local authorities in general had demonstrated little commitment to plan production.

It is against this background that plans have been made mandatory, and their significance in development control increased. Furthermore, central government is now playing a more active role in setting limits to local discretion, and in determining the content of plans.

The full procedure for the adoption of development plans is set out in Chapter 3. The legislation has always provided only the bare bones of the system. Consultation and participation in practice have been much more than adherence to formal procedures. This is now even more so following the Planning and Compensation Act 1991. The general effect of the changes made by this Act has been to reduce the emphasis on public participation and consultation in the statutory procedure, whilst increasing the rights of those who have made formal objections later in the process. Local authorities now have discretion to decide the appropriate publicity for individual plans. The result of this is a rather illusory reduction in the procedural steps required by statute, whilst the imperative for local authorities to involve and consult local communities in plan preparation is in reality no less than before. In contrast, the rights of formal objection after deposit of the plan have been extended by including the provision for objections where the local authority has not accepted the Inspector's or Panel's recommendations.

In Scotland, advice on consultation follows similar lines, but lays greater stress on the benefits to be gained from early consultation with a wide range of interests.[39] PAN 37 notes the importance of 'developing policies in co-operation with other implementation agencies', giving special mention to the Local Enterprise Companies, which are having an increasing influence on planning policy.

In general, however, there is no doubt that over the last twenty years there has been a shift in emphasis away from early participation in the plan-making process, towards formal opportunities for objecting to plan policies in the post-deposit stages. This has been reinforced by the increasing pressure to produce plans within a reasonable time-scale, as well as the sheer size and complexity of plans. Inevitably, this means that the plan preparation process will focus more on the concerns of those whose interests are most directly affected and who also have the inclination, skills and resources to participate. Whilst the procedural safeguards are in principle open to all, it is only the better-organised and well-financed groups who are able to make most use of them.

## Planning Applications

Around a half of a million applications for planning permission are made each year to local planning authorities in Britain, of which over four-fifths are granted. This enormous spate of applications involves great strains on the local planning machinery which, generally speaking, is not adequately staffed to deal with them and at the same time undertake the necessary work involved in preparing and reviewing development plans. Yet full consideration by local planning staffs is needed if planning committees are to have the requisite information on which to base their decisions.

The importance of this is underlined by the fact that planning committees often have remarkably little time during a meeting in which to come to a decision. Agendas for meetings tend to be long: an average of five to six minutes for consideration of each application is nothing unusual, and in some cases the time may be as little as two minutes. It cannot, therefore, be surprising that in a large proportion of cases (in the bigger authorities at least) the recommendations of the planning officer are approved pro forma. This may, of course, result in part from the harmonious relationship which commonly exists between local authority representatives and their officers; and, in any case, lay members tend to accept the technical expertise of their officials, while, on the other hand, the officials well know the minds of their political masters. Yet the point remains that both elected representatives and planning officials are hard pressed to cope with the constant flood of applications.

Several important implications follow from this. First, and most obvious, is the danger that decisions will be given which are 'wrong' – that is, they do not accord with planning objectives. Second, good relationships with the public in general and unsuccessful applicants in particular are difficult to attain: there is simply not sufficient time. Third, this lack of time corroborates the view of many (unsuccessful) applicants that their case has never had adequate consideration: a view which is further supported by the manner in which refusals are commonly worded. Phrases such as 'detrimental to amenity' or 'not in accordance with the development plan', and so on, mean little or nothing to the individual applicant. He suspects that his case has been considered in general terms rather than in the particular detail which he naturally thinks is important in his case. And he may be right:

understaffed and overworked planning departments cannot give each case the individual attention which is desirable.

This, of course, is not the whole picture. For instance, individuals who may not wholly agree with a general planning principle will tend to see it in a different light when it is applied to their own applications:

> The man who has his home in one part of a green belt and owns what an estate agent would call 'fully ripe building land' in another part, is as vociferous in relying on green belt principles to oppose building near his home as he is in denouncing the extreme and ridiculous lengths to which those principles have been carried when he is refused planning permission on his other land, and frequently seems to achieve this without any conscious hypocrisy.
>
> (Grove 1963: 130)

This natural human failing is encouraged by the curious compromise situation which currently exists in relation to the control of land. On the one hand, it is accepted in principle (and law) that there is no right to develop land, unless the development is publicly acceptable (as determined by a political instead of a financial decision). On the other hand, though the allocation of land to particular uses is determined by a public decision, the motives for private development are financial, and the financial profits which result from the development constitute private gain. This unhappy circumstance (which is discussed at length in Chapter 5) involves a clash of principles which the unsuccessful applicant for planning permission experiences in a particularly sharp manner. It follows that local planning officials may have a peculiarly difficult task in explaining to a landowner why, for example, a particular field needs to be 'protected from development'.

Nevertheless, the success which attends this unenviable task does differ markedly among different local authorities. The question is not simply one of the great variations in potential land values in different parts of the country or in the relative adequacy of planning staffs. Though these are important factors, there remains the less-easily documented question of attitudes towards the public.

Some local authorities make a great effort to assist and explain matters to an applicant, while others give the impression of a bureaucratic machine which displays little patience or kindness towards the individual applicant who does not understand 'planning procedures'.

## DELEGATION OF PLANNING DECISIONS TO OFFICERS

The 1968 Planning Act made provision for the delegation to officers of planning decisions. The reason for this is that the majority of planning applications are of 'a simple nature'. A 1967 *Management Study on Development Control* (HMSO) found that a large proportion of these 'simple' applications were determined by a committee or by the council without presentation of details, without discussion, and in accordance with the recommendations of the officers. The conclusion was that many development control applications were already effectively delegated to officers for decision but were required to go through a formal procedure for ratification by a body of members. This created unnecessary work for the local authority and unnecessary delay for the applicant. The 1968 provisions enabled local authorities to delegate decisions on a wide range of planning applications. The power is entirely discretionary: it is for local authorities to decide which officers, if any, should be given delegated powers and for which kinds of application. A decision of an officer exercising delegated powers has the same standing as one given by the council itself.

> A common pattern is for decisions on householder and similar minor applications to be delegated completely, and other categories of application to be delegated subject to the power of veto by the committee. A committee may also wish to approve an application in principle but reserve some detail to be approved by the officers before permission is issued.
>
> (Grant 1982: 256)

Decisions of a council can be delegated to a committee of the council. The Widdicombe Committee (1986) found cases where (unlawfully) decisions were also being delegated to the committee chair. It recommended that this should be made lawful in order to accelerate decision-making. This was not acceptable to the Government since it would 'breach the principle of corporate decision making and the principle of *pro-rata* representation on decision making committees'.

## MALADMINISTRATION AND THE OMBUDSMAN

Most legislation is based on the assumption that the organs of government will operate efficiently and fairly. This is not always the case but, even if it were, provision has to be made for investigating complaints by citizens who feel aggrieved by some action (or inaction). As modern post-industrial society becomes more complex, and as the rights of electors and consumers are viewed as important, pressures for additional means of protest, appeal and restitution grow.

At the Parliamentary level, the case for an ombudsman was reluctantly conceded by the Government, and a Parliamentary Commissioner for Administration was appointed in 1967. The Commissioner is an independent statutory official whose function is to investigate complaints of maladministration referred to him through Members of Parliament.[40] Powers of investigation extend over all central government departments, and there is an important right of access to all departmental papers.

Only a small fraction of the Parliamentary Commissioner's cases relate to planning matters and, of course, the concern is with administrative procedures, not with the merits of planning decisions. The Commissioner's reports give full but anonymised texts of reports of selected cases which have been investigated. Illustrative cases include a complaint that the Secretary of State for the Environment failed to understand the grounds on which a request had been made for intervention in (that is, to use the default powers in relation to) a redevelopment scheme; a complaint by a Motorways Action Committee that, following a motorway inquiry, the Inspector called

for further evidence from the DoE (much of which, the Committee submitted, was 'highly dubious and contentious, and contained a number of misleading assumptions') on which it was not given the opportunity to cross-examine the Department's witness; a complaint by a group of local residents that an appeal decision to allow a gypsy caravan site paid little heed to local residents' objections, ignored important relevant facts, and was taken on the basis of inconsistent attitudes; and a complaint that an appeal refusal to allow the replacement of a coach house was unfair and improper in that the reasons given in the decision letter were not in accordance with the facts, and that the decision could not be reconciled with the policies followed by the local planning authority, or with planning permissions they had given for other development in their area. In all these cases, the Parliamentary Commissioner concluded that the complaint could not be upheld. This is not always the case, however; the Commissioner has had occasion to criticise some aspects of the Department's handling of particular cases and this has led to changes in internal administrative procedures.

The cases in which the Commissioner does find 'maladministration' are often of extraordinary complexity, if not real confusion. Indeed, complexity and confusion can be major factors in the failures in communication and the misunderstandings which result in 'maladministration'. Of the complaints dealt with in 1991, the Commissioner found 47 per cent to be wholly justified; in 43 per cent it was found necessary (while not upholding the main complaint) to criticise at least some aspects of the way in which the matter was handled by the department concerned; and in 10 per cent no justification for complaint was found.[41] Interestingly, the number of complaints against the DoE in 1992 was only 53, compared with 110 which were made in 1967 against the former MHLG. The Commissioner offers no explanation for the decline, though there is a comment on the vehement protests made by applicants who have had an appeal dismissed by an Inspector.[42]

The popularity of the Parliamentary Commissioner led to pressures for the establishment of a similar institution for local government. Finally, in the mid-1970s, *Commissioners for Local Administration* were set up for England, Scotland, and Wales. With good sense, they recently decided that they should be known as the *Local Government Ombudsmen*: this is not only their popular name, but it also makes explicit that their responsibilities are confined almost entirely to local government (though it is hardly gender-sensitive!).[43]

A high proportion of complaints concern planning matters: in 1992, about a third in Wales and a quarter in England, but only 15 per cent in Scotland. As with the Parliamentary Commissioner, complaints have to be referred via an elected member – a requirement on which there is considerable controversy.[44] There is also concern about the situation which arises when a local authority refuses to 'remedy' a case in which maladministration or injustice is found by a Commissioner. To date, however, only limited legislative changes have been made. These include a power for local authorities to incur expenditure to remedy injustice without specific authorisation by the Secretary of State; a requirement that local authorities must notify the Ombudsman of action taken in response to an adverse report; a power for the Ombudsman to publish in a local newspaper a statement concerning cases in which a local authority has refused to comply with the Ombudsman's recommendations; and a new responsibility for the Ombudsmen to provide local authorities with advice on good practice, based on the experience of their investigations.

The statutory provisions relating to publicity for planning applications and to the legal position of third parties (which are outlined on pp. 262–3) are limited, and local authorities have considerable freedom to devise their procedures according to their own views of what is appropriate. Not all have taken kindly to the 'interference' of the local Ombudsman, and the annual reports (while noting with satisfaction a general improvement in the handling of complaints by local authorities) often name authorities which have refused to remedy cases of maladministration and personal injustice.

The Ombudsmen have constantly noted that aggrieved objectors to planning permissions have little or no redress – unlike the aggrieved applicant who can appeal to the Secretary of State.[45] The Ombudsmen have no power to deal with the merits of planning decisions, but they have difficulty in explaining the difference between a planning decision which constitutes maladministration and one which is simply disputed.[46] It is, of course, not surprising that (for example) unsatisfied neighbours should take the view that their objections have been ignored, even though a local authority will usually have considered the objections and rejected them. (It would be extremely difficult to substantiate a claim that the objections had been disregarded.) Hopefully, the increased publicity for planning applications (discussed on p. 263) will lead to an improvement in this situation. In the meantime, the Ombudsmen can take pride in the impact they have had on encouraging local authorities to improve their planning procedures, and to go beyond minimum statutory requirements. In the words of the Scottish Ombudsman (CLAS *Annual Report* 1992: 15): 'The elimination of grounds for complaint is perhaps a greater achievement than the resolution of complaints. While the impact perhaps tends to be less apparent to the individual complainant, it is wider reaching and longer lasting.'

## PLANNING APPEALS

An unsuccessful applicant for planning permission can, of course, appeal to the Secretary of State and, as already noted, a large number do so. Each case is considered by the Department on its merits. This allows a great deal of flexibility, and permits cases of individual hardship to be sympathetically treated. At the same time, however, it can make the planning system seem arbitrary, at least to the unsuccessful appellant. Although broad policies are set out in such publications as the *Planning Policy Guidance Notes*, the general view in the central departments is that a reliance on precedent could easily give rise to undesirable rigidities.

Other issues relevant to this view are the flexibility

of the development plan, the wide area of discretion legally allowed to the planners in the operation of planning controls, and the very restricted jurisdiction of the courts. All these necessitate a judicial function for the Department. However, this function is only quasi-judicial: decisions are taken not on the basis of legal rules as in a court of law or in accordance with case-law, but on a judgement as to what course of action is, in the particular circumstances and in the context of ministerial policy, desirable, reasonable and equitable. By its very nature this must be elusive, and the unsuccessful appellant may well feel justified in believing that the dice are loaded. The very fact that public inquiries on planning appeals are heard by ministerial 'Inspectors' (and probably in the town hall of the authority whose decision is being appealed) does not make for confidence in a fair and objective hearing.

Of course, part of the expressed dissatisfaction comes from those who are compelled to forgo private gain for the sake of communal benefit: the criticisms are not really of procedures, and they are not likely to be assuaged by administrative reforms or good public relations. Fundamentally, they are criticisms of the public control of land use – in particular, if not in principle.

## THIRD PARTY INTERESTS

The rights of third parties – those affected by planning decisions but having no legal 'interest' in the land subject to decision – were highlighted in the so-called Chalk Pit case.[47] This, in brief, concerned an application to 'develop' certain land in Essex by digging chalk. On being refused planning permission, the applicants appealed to the Minister, and a local inquiry was held. Among those who appeared as objectors at the inquiry were some substantial landowners, including a Major Buxton, whose land was adjacent to the appeal site and was being used for agricultural and residential purposes. The Inspector's recommendation was that the appeal should be dismissed, mainly because there was a serious danger of chalk dust being deposited on the

land of Major Buxton and others in quantities which would be 'detrimental to the user of the land'; and that there was no present shortage of chalk in the locality. The Minister disagreed with the Inspector's recommendations and allowed the appeal.

Major Buxton then appealed to the High Court, partly on the ground that in rejecting his Inspector's findings of fact, the Minister had relied on certain subsequent advice and information given to him by the Minister of Agriculture without giving the objectors any opportunity of correcting or commenting upon this advice and information. But Major Buxton now found that he had no legal right of appeal to the courts: indeed he apparently had no legal right to appear at the inquiry. (He only had what the judge thought to be a 'very sensible' administrative privilege.) In short, Major Buxton was a 'third party': he was in no legal sense a 'person aggrieved'. Yet clearly in the wider sense of the phrase Major Buxton was very much aggrieved, and at first sight he had a moral right to object and to have his objection carefully weighed. But should the machinery of town and country planning be used for this purpose by an individual? Before the town and country planning legislation, any landowner could develop his land as he liked, provided he did not infringe the common law which was designed more to protect the right to develop rather than to restrain it. The law of nuisance and trespass was not a particularly strong constraint on the freedom to use land. However, as the judge stressed, the planning legislation was designed 'to restrict development for the benefit of the public at large and not to confer new rights on any individual member of the public'.

This, of course, is the essential point. It is the job of the local planning authority to assess the public advantage or disadvantage of a proposed development, subject to a review by the Secretary of State if those having a legal interest in the land in question object. Third parties cannot usurp these government functions. Nevertheless, it might be generally agreed that those affected by planning decisions should have the right to make representations for consideration by a planning committee. The present position is that third parties have an administrative privilege to appear at a public inquiry, but generally no similar privilege in relation to a planning application.[48]

Of course, those who object to a proposed development always have the traditional recourse to the political process, but this is of no relevance if a proposal is not known. In some areas, a small breed of energetic 'application watchers' will regularly consult the *Register of Planning Applications*, but these do not provide a general means of alerting the general public to applications (Sharman 1985). There have been wider arrangements for publicity in Scotland (and Northern Ireland) for some years, particularly for 'neighbour notification'.[49] In the Scottish system, notification is the responsibility of the applicant, who certifies to the local authority that neighbours, as well as owners and lessees, have been notified. This can be problematic for the applicant, and can lead to false certification (whether inadvertent or deliberate). One study has concluded that the system is burdensome to both the applicant and the local authority.[50] The Scottish procedures for neighbour notification are a constant source of complaint. The Ombudsman has commented that omissions are often inadvertent, but on other occasions there is at least a suspicion that they are deliberate. The onus to make the notification lies clearly with the applicant, and the local authority is entitled to rely on the certification. 'There is no doubt, however, that the public expect the authority to shoulder some responsibility for the proper implementation', and there must be some sympathy for this view (Renton 1992: 43).

In England and Wales, there is a similar requirement for notification of owners and other interests in land which is the subject of a planning application, but this does not necessarily extend to neighbours. Provision for notification of neighbours is dealt with under the provisions for publicity. Local authorities have the responsibility of deciding, on a case-by-case basis, what type of publicity to require. Major developments, as defined in the GDO,[51] require *either* site notices or neighbour notification, *and* a newspaper advertisement. This system was introduced in 1992, and replaces the former requirements in relation to specified 'bad neighbour' developments (such as sewage works, dance halls, and zoos). Thus,

the statutory requirements for publicity have been reduced rather than extended. Moreover, in its Circular on the matter (15/92), the DoE stresses that obligations to publicise applications should not jeopardise the target of deciding 80 per cent of applications within a period of eight weeks. Speed is thus apparently to have higher priority than public participation.

A Scottish commentator has expressed incredulity at 'how authorities can operate a discretionary system without incurring the wrath of neighbours, not to mention the local government ombudsman' (Watt 1992: 15).

## THE CHANGING NATURE OF PUBLIC INQUIRIES

Public inquiries into major planning appeals, and called-in planning applications have had a stormy passage for many years, particularly those held in connection with highways and major developments such as Stansted, Windscale and Sizewell. Similar difficulties are now being experienced with local plan inquiries, which, following the 1991 changes to the development plan regime, are bigger and more keenly contested affairs.

The planning inquiry is a microcosm of the land-use planning system, and it reflects many of its competing positions and underlying conflicts of interest. It is perhaps in the inquiry where the clash of ideologies is most easily seen. McAuslan has used the example of road inquiries:

> The disenchantment with public inquiries into road proposals is only the most public and publicised manifestation of a general disenchantment with the system of land use planning, to which the conflict of ideologies within and over the use of the law is an important contributor. This conflict is heightened in public inquiries into road proposals because the issues of substance give rise to such sharp divisions of opinion, and because participators are making such explicit use of the inquiry for the promotion of alternative policies and versions of the public interest. What this use of the inquiry has shown is that the reforms introduced as a result of the Franks Report twenty years ago based on

the principle of openness, fairness and impartiality, and concentrating on procedures did not change (perhaps were not designed to change) the overriding purpose of the public local inquiry which was and is to advance the administration's version of the public interest.

(McAuslan 1980b: 72)

Using McAuslan's terminology, this is a triumph of 'the public interest ideology' over 'the ideology of public participation'. The important point here is that the inquiry is not an extension of public participation, but 'a limited and carefully controlled and confined discussion of specific proposals . . . inimical to the kind of wide ranging discussion that participators are demanding'. This applies equally to major planning inquiries and even, as is discussed later (see next section), examinations in public.

A difficulty with many inquiries is determining where the boundaries of discussion are to be drawn: there is always the danger that argument will spill over into a broader policy framework. It is common at inquiries into particular matters for the most general questions of policy to arise. This is hardly surprising since typically the development being debated is, in fact, the application of one or more policies to a particular situation: this readily offers the opportunity for questioning whether the policy is intended to apply to the case at issue – or whether it should. Even wider issues arise, such as the desirability of supporting a particular way of generating nuclear power, or the need for more roads, or the role of the planning system in providing affordable housing. Pressure groups which, for example, may be opposed to the building of new roads or out-of-town shopping centres anywhere, irrespective of the merits (or otherwise) of particular projects, will want to use the inquiry as a platform on which to make their wider case.

This raises the question as to whether the provisions for national policy debate are adequate. It makes sense, of course, to argue that Parliament should be the arena for the national policy debate, and the local authority for debate on local policies. It also seems reasonable to maintain that it is quite inappropriate for major issues of principle to be raised when they

are simply being applied locally. But issues are not so easily packaged: for instance, some fall between national and local levels and need consideration at a regional tier of government which does not exist; some site-specific proposals raise acute issues of policy which have not been settled or adequately discussed; and sometimes government may avert proper discussion because of the complexity and sensitivity of the issues involved.

This may be the reason that one type of public inquiry, for which legislative provision was made in 1968, has never been used: the Planning Inquiry Commission (PIC). This was heralded in the 1967 White Paper which preceded the 1968 reforms of the planning system. It was argued that for planning cases which raised wide or novel issues of more than local significance 'the ordinary public local inquiry is not satisfactory either as a method of permitting the full issues to be thrashed out or as a basis for a decision which can take into account the whole range of practicable alternatives'. The proposed PIC, consisting of three to five members, would be appointed by the Secretary of State to examine major proposals. The types of proposal envisaged were those to which there had previously been fierce public opposition, such as the processing of natural gas at Bacton, Norfolk; the new London airport at Stansted, Essex; a hovercraft terminal at Pegwell Bay, Kent; and a gasholder at Abingdon, Berkshire. In terms of the statute, the proposals are those which raise 'considerations of national or regional importance' or where there are unfamiliar 'technical and scientific aspects'.[52] The Commission would have worked in two stages separating the broad policy issues, to be considered by a procedure akin to that of a Royal Commission. The second stage would be the inquiry to consider objections and cross-examine both promoters and objectors to test the evidence. The PIC procedure has never been used, mainly because the procedure is 'fundamentally flawed'. 'It is virtually impossible to distinguish between site specific issues, which need to be considered at an ordinary public local inquiry, and issues of general policy, which can be investigated by means of the first stage of a Planning Inquiry Commission.'[53] The reasons reflect the problems inherent in trying to separate strategic decision-making from site-specific issues.

The reality is that the policy framework for decisions on major planning issues that may be subject to an inquiry will be incomplete and subject to constant review. It will be imprecise or even ambiguous in the way that it applies to a specific proposal, and so it is inevitable that inquiry participants will want to explore and challenge the framework.

There have been several proposals for the funding of third parties at major public inquiries, though they differ on the form that this should take – and the difficulties to which it could give rise.[54] The Government has taken the narrow approach that 'most objectors participate in public inquiries to defend their own interests. This is a perfectly proper activity, but there is no reason why it should be financed out of public funds.'[55] In Canada, however, the Berger Commission on the Mackenzie Valley Pipeline Inquiry arranged for a funding programme which cost nearly 2 million dollars, for 'those groups that had an interest that ought to be represented, but whose means would not allow it'. The federal government has an 'intervenor funding programme' which was used in the Beaufort Sea environmental assessment review (Cullingworth 1987). On the basis of Canadian experience, Purdue and Kemp have advocated some limited state funding on the basis that some objectors 'genuinely contribute to the wider understanding of the issues involved' (1985: 685).

## EXAMINATIONS IN PUBLIC

In the case of development plan inquiries, the separation of broad strategic policy and detailed site-specific issues has been widely, if not completely, accepted. Whilst delegating the adoption of local plans to local authorities, the 1968 Act confirmed that the public local inquiry would continue to be used for all development plans, and that objectors would maintain the statutory right to have their objections heard. The maintenance of the rights of those affected to obtain an independent hearing was thought to be particularly important given concerns raised in debate about the empowerment of local authorities to adopt their own plans (Bridges 1979). But this argument quickly lost ground with the realisation of the practical consequences, evidenced in the inquiry into the Greater London Development Plan (GLDP). This inquiry considered 28,000 objections over 22 months in the years 1970 to 1972. The GLDP was not typical of the emerging notion of a structure plan and contained many detailed proposals, but the experience led to support for the introduction, in 1972, of the *examination in public* (EIP), a major departure from former practice. This involves a panel which considers only those matters which are selected for discussion. Objectors have no statutory right to be heard, 'effectively relieving the Secretary of State of any duty to inquire, in public, into objections made to a submitted development plan' (Dunlop 1976: 9). These changes produced a system which is the opposite of that intended by the Planning Advisory Group (PAG). The introduction of the EIP made the procedure for structure plans 'almost entirely administrative in character, being governed at almost every stage by discretion' exercised, until 1992, by central government (Bridges 1979: 246).

The rationale for EIPs, however, is far more than the negative one of avoiding lengthy, time-consuming and quasi-judicial public inquiries: it is related essentially to the basic purpose and character of the plan. A structure plan does not set out detailed proposals and, therefore, does not show how individual properties will be affected. It deals with broad policy issues: the examination in public focuses on these, and on alternatives to those set out in the plan. These include such matters as the future level and distribution of population and employment, transportation policies, and availability of resources for major proposals of the plan. Additionally, major inconsistencies within the plan, or issues on which there is unsettled controversy, may be the subject of examination.

An EIP is a required part of the adoption procedure for structure plans, unless the Secretary of State decides otherwise.[56] The issues selected are placed on deposit prior to the examination, together with a list of those selected to participate. There will usually be a preliminary meeting where the procedure and agenda can be discussed. This meeting, like the examination itself, is carried out by a panel with an independent chairman, supported by a panel secretary. The chairman has the discretion, both before and during an examination, to invite additional participants in addition to those selected by the authority, and to adjust the form of the proceedings if he considers this necessary. Though the Act made provision for regulations governing the conduct of the EIP, none have been made: instead the DoE published a Code of Practice.[57] This stressed that the proceedings should be organised so as to promote 'intensive discussion without formality'. For example, 'objections to the general policies and proposals of the plan may be heard by means of a round-table session of the inquiry, chaired by the Inspector'. It is not necessary for participants to be professionally represented, and they should not be made 'to feel at a disadvantage if they are not'.[58]

The experience of EIPs has sometimes been quite different from this ideal, with excessively formal hearings involving senior counsel acting for local authorities and others. The proceedings certainly do not lend themselves to involvement by ordinary members of the public, and in fact this is not encouraged at any stage in the structure planning process. The main participants tend to be representative interest groups, notably the House Builders' Federation, and the Council for the Protection of Rural England, as well as local authorities.

> The aim should be to select participants (whether statutory bodies, Government departments, interest groups or individuals) who between them represent a broad range of viewpoints and have a relevant contribution to make. Organisations and individuals who are likely to contribute to discussion of the topics concerned at the strategic level should be invited, as should constituent local planning authorities.[59]

This procedure clearly gives rise to difficulties, particularly since there is likely to be considerable criticism by any objectors who are excluded from participation in the examination. This is likely to become even more sensitive in England and Wales where the planning authority itself is now responsible for adopting the structure plan, holding and paying for the EIP, and selecting issues and participants. In this connection, it is important to stress that the examination is envisaged as only one part of the process by which the plan is adopted (or in Scotland, approved by the Secretary of State). Of crucial importance in this process is the extent to which effective citizen participation has taken place in the preparation of the plan, but here, as noted above, it can be argued that the 'safeguards' have been weakened.

## LOCAL AND UNITARY DEVELOPMENT PLAN INQUIRIES

The precise role of the local plan inquiry has long been a subject of debate.[60] Like the appeal inquiries, local plan inquiries involve the same balancing of private and public interests through a procedure which, although essentially administrative, has many of the hallmarks of judicial courtroom practice. However, the essential nature of the planning procedure is administrative. Final decisions are taken by government, at either the central or the local level. In making these decisions, the administration takes into account matters not discussed at the inquiry. As the Franks Report (1957: para. 272) noted, the process 'must allow for the exercise of a wide discretion in the balancing of public and private interests'. The legitimacy of the decisions rests with the political accountability of the decision-maker (Parliament or the local council) rather than on the weighing and testing of evidence as in a court of law.

Whilst the Secretary of State has ultimate discretion, the procedure also attempts to safeguard the rights of the individual citizen. Some aspects of the inquiry procedure are much more akin to a judicial process. Objectors have a statutory right to appear, and the evidence is tested through a process of adversarial questioning before an independent party. There is inherent ambiguity in a system which has as its main objective the gathering of evidence to assist in the making of a governmental decision, whilst at the same time operating in the manner of a judicial hearing (Wraith and Lamb 1971). The essential dilemma of this quasi-judicial process was described in the Franks Report:

> If the administrative view is dominant the public enquiry cannot play its full part in the total process, and there is a danger that the rights and interests of the individual citizen affected will not be sufficiently protected . . . If the judicial view is dominant there is a danger that people will regard the person before whom they state their case as a kind of judge provisionally deciding the matter, subject to an appeal to the Minister. What begins in many ways like an action at law, with two or more parties appearing before a judge-like Inspector and stating their case to him, usually in public is thereafter suddenly removed from public gaze until the ministerial decision is made. Often the main factors at the enquiry seem to have counted for little in the final decision. New factors − they may have been considerations of broad policy − have come in so that the final decision does not seem to flow from the proceedings at the enquiry.
>
> (Franks Report 1957: paras 273−5)

The difficulties have been increased by the 1991 reforms. In confirming the role of districts as the responsible authority for adopting local plans, and extending the same responsibility to counties for structure plans, the administrative role of the inquiry is reinforced. In introducing the provision which allows for objections where the local authority does not accept the recommendations of an Inspector or panel,[61] the changes lend weight to the judicial role. Thus, the central questions have changed little over the years following the Franks Committee, not least because whilst identifying the ambiguity in objectives, the Report found in favour of neither.

> The Franks Committee concluded its long deliberations on this issue inconclusively, referring to the need for 'balance' and the tendency for the matter to resolve itself in practice, so long as the inquiry is conducted with 'openness, fairness and impartiality'.
>
> (Bruton et al. 1980: 377)

To some extent Franks was right. The three principles of 'openness, fairness and impartiality' have guided Inspectors with some success, and the courts have played only a small part in the planning process.[62]

Nevertheless, each of the three principles requires some qualification. The Franks Report itself recognised that impartiality needed to be qualified since in some circumstances central government was both a party to the debate, perhaps putting forward a proposal, and at the same time the decision-maker. How, in this situation, can the procedure be impartial? This is the major complicating factor for local plan inquiries, EIPs and major call-in inquiries. Here, one of the parties to the dispute will make the final decision, giving at least the appearance of being the judge and jury in its own court.

With development plans, the findings of research (outlined in Chapter 3) show that local authorities make modest use of their power to reject Inspectors' recommendations (only in one out of ten cases). It is, however, the much smaller number of apparently inconsistent decisions which receive the most publicity. Such examples certainly lend weight to McAuslan's thesis that:

> The legal and administrative system as at present constructed and operated is such that the interests of maintaining and preserving the status quo and its institutional bases prevails, and will always prevail, over the interests of any fundamentally different or alternative point of view, be it a non-nuclear future for society or the giving of priority to social as opposed to property and economic considerations in clearance policies.
>
> (McAuslan 1980b: 236)

The openness and fairness of the inquiry also need to be qualified. First, there is widespread misunderstanding of the procedure, especially the respective roles of Inspector and local authority.[63] The adversarial nature of the inquiry, with the Inspector playing a passive role while objectors and the local authority exchange evidence and questions, has important implications for the way in which the agenda is structured; and it limits potential outcomes. In his case-study of the Belfast Urban Areas Plan inquiry, Blackman (1991) points out how an adversarial hearing focuses attention on the evidence brought forward to support the position of particular interests. The inquiry becomes moulded into a battle about which interest should prevail; and this precludes debate about alternative and potentially shared solutions, which may be in a 'common or generalisable social interest'.

All this has now to be considered in the context of the 'plan-led system'. More emphasis on statutory plans means that more development interests, neighbouring authorities and service providers will be concerned to influence the content of plans and thus the outcome of inquiries. Despite the recession, the number of objections to plans has increased dramatically over recent years. The Planning Inspectorate's work on local plan inquiries grew threefold between 1988 and 1991. This was largely due to an increase in the length of inquiries, from just over two weeks in 1988 to an estimated eight weeks in 1993.[64]

The question arises as to whether the system can cope with this burden, particularly since the biggest test is yet to come. A study of more complex London inquiries suggested that the most significant impact of the higher number of objections and the more contentious issues associated with these plans was likely to come in the later adoption stages (Bruton *et al.* 1985). It was found that the added complexity resulted in an increase of about a fifth in the time needed to process the plan from deposit to the receipt of the Inspector's report, but an increase of about three-quarters from then to plan adoption. These figures reflect the difficulties of coping with modifications to plans that have a broader scope.

Certainly, earlier findings demonstrated that the sheer number of objections was less of a problem than dealing with 'in-principle objections' to strategic policies that could have repercussions throughout the plan. Such policies are more commonly found in district-wide local plans and UDPs.[65]

One response to the increased scale of work at inquiries (and the burden on Inspectors) has been to emphasise the potential that pre-deposit consultation and post-deposit negotiation might have in reducing the number of objections. Local authorities are being encouraged to come forward with 'suggested changes' agreed with objectors before the inquiry. The proposed changes have to be widely advertised before the Inspector deals with the issue, so that the likely response can be assessed. The benefits of this are least questionable. The study by Bruton *et al.* (1982a) came to the clear conclusion that whilst participation will lend some credibility, it 'does not remove or significantly reduce the number of objections made to the plan'.[66]

All this demonstrates the important difference between participation before deposit of the plan and objections at the inquiry after deposit. The opportunity to formally object to a plan is not a general extension of 'participation'. It merely provides a limited opportunity for individuals and groups to air particular grievances. But, at this stage, the local authority will be committed to the plan, and any significant modifications will be effectively a challenge to the overall strategy.

Those who want to contribute to shaping the strategy will have to put considerable effort into the early stages of participation. This might now be more difficult in view of the increasing pressure on authorities to hasten plan preparation. This could be a recipe for conflict, frustration and perhaps less credible plans.

## IN CONCLUSION

The planning scene has been dominated for many years by a veritable orgy of institutional change. Though all this was intended as a means of facilitating better planning, it is possible that it has had the opposite effect of restraining the development of policies appropriate to changing conditions and perceptions. If the filing cabinets are being constantly moved, it is difficult to bring their contents up to date. Furthermore, some of the institutional changes (even if promising in the longer run) may have added to the confusion over the role of 'town and country planning' in relation to regional and national economic planning, to the management of the economy, to the increasingly strident demands for environmental protection, to the place of public participation in the planning process, and to even more intractable issues such as 'the energy question', the distribution of incomes and 'access to opportunity'. It is, however, a nice question as to whether a more stable institutional structure would have facilitated the formulation of more appropriate and effective policies in the context of the baffling economic and social problems of the time.

What does seem clear is that the faith in the efficacy of institutional change was misplaced. The reorganisation of local government (the term 'reform' has significantly fallen out of use) seems to have created as many problems as it solved, and another reorganisation is in progress. As the wag said, 'when in doubt reorganise'; or, in the words of Matthew Arnold, 'faith in machinery is our besetting danger'.

The basic problems lie deeper: they relate to the functions, scope and practicability of 'town and country planning'. The Greater London Development Plan Inquiry was perhaps the most dramatic illustration of the fact that many of the crucial issues with which 'planning' is concerned do not fall within the responsibility or competence of the planning authority, or even within that of local government — jobs and incomes being the two most obvious ones. Hence, central government wrestles with the political pressures to which problems in such areas give rise, though typically with disappointing results.

From a cynical viewpoint, much effort is wasted at both local and central levels in attempting to control the uncontrollable. The proclamations of politicians are given a credibility which is unwarranted. It also has unfortunate consequences, since the illusion that problems can be 'solved' turns easily into a delusion, and constant failure debases the political process and breeds cynicism. Illich (1977: 11) noted that the mid-twentieth century was 'the age of the disabling professions': an age when people had 'problems', experts had 'solutions', and scientists measured such imponderables as 'abilities' and 'needs'. The words have more than a suggestion of truth, though Illich was surely wrong in asserting that the age which he caricatures was ending.

More positively, there has been wider discussion of the limits, role and purpose of planning. A greater understanding of the operations of government has been provided by writings ranging from the Crossman Diaries to academic studies and reflections such as those of Heclo and Wildavsky, King, and Solesbury

(to mention but a few). More remarkable were the clear signs of some fundamental rethinking within the planning profession itself, which was heralded by the RTPI 1976 discussion paper on *Planning and the Future*. Many more such thoughtful and thought-provoking papers have followed.

It would be interesting to speculate why this untypically deep questioning started when it did. Perhaps it was a sign of the coming of age of planning. Two factors were of particular importance: an awakening of concern for making government more responsive (what was inadequately termed 'public participation'), and a sea change in the economy.

The first started with protests against unwanted developments, big and small, particular and generalised. Some of these protests led to gargantuan 'inquiries' — of which Roskill and Windscale were the epitome. Others were more modest and localised, but also much more numerous. With hindsight, the most important were those which in reality were protests not simply against a particular development (though that was the manifest objective), but against the policies which these represented. Typically, these were not the responsibility of planners, but of other professions and, above all, of politicians who forged the policies. Politicians, at both central and local levels, perceived problems (understandably) in the terms in which they were presented. Problems labelled as housing shortages, road congestion, slum clearance, and redevelopment portrayed the obvious solutions: build houses quickly; build more roads; clear the slums; redevelop the worn-out parts of the inner city. The political responses were to 'solve' these clearly articulated problems. But policies involve choices and, again with hindsight, some of the choices had undesirable results: more houses involved high densities and few amenities; new roads increased the attraction of private transport and the decline of public alternatives; slum clearance destroyed communities; and so on.

The perceived 'failures' of planning — high-rise development, difficult-to-let council housing schemes, urban motorways, inner-city decline, and the like — added to the mounting concern about the role and character of planning. Whether, or to what extent, these were 'failures', and, if so, the degree to which 'planning' was to blame, are questions which were seldom raised, let alone answered in their historical context. But they were seen to symbolise the inadequacy of planning.

An alternative interpretation would lay emphasis on the growth of real public participation. Public participation is not a subsidiary process which can be held in check: once it begins to work effectively it transforms the nature of the planning process. On occasion, it can get 'completely out of control', as it did in some well-publicised highway inquiries. Though disruptive, these led to a major reappraisal of both highway inquiry procedures and highway planning. Here the point is that the lesson was learned: it had become apparent that participation could work.

The professional acceptance of public participation (though by no means unanimous) was a remarkable feature of the 1970s. That it came first in planning, but not in other fields such as education or health, may be related to the transformed nature of planning education and the changed character of the 'intake' to the profession.[67] Indeed, it may be that it is this which above all explains the new humility, the introspective questioning and the new intellectualism which was so marked a feature of the time. In this respect, planners departed from the norms of professionalism, though not without internal strife.[68]

The profession's commitment to public participation continued into the 1980s, despite an increasingly hostile political framework. The growth of a participatory ethic, however, may have been of lesser importance than the impact of economic change. A new humility grew in response to a gradual realisation that changes in the economy were structural rather then cyclical. Policies based on the assumption that the task in hand was to channel the forces of economic growth were increasingly perceived to be misplaced. Planning was no longer to be preoccupied with controls over the location of growth: it was to be remoulded to assist in the actual promotion of growth.

Certainly, the 1980s saw a remarkable change in the political scene. A new and clear political philosophy emerged: the objective of planning now is to facilitate enterprise with the minimum of constraints. Planning controls have been reduced, most of the new town development corporations disbanded, the GLC and the metropolitan county councils have been abolished, and statutory requirements for public participation in the preparation of plans have been cut down. Local government has been increasingly bypassed in favour of *ad hoc* bodies designed to promote private sector involvement. Ironically, a major example of this is the urban development corporation, modelled on the new town development corporation but with the added responsibility for development control. Other initiatives include the Financial Institutions Group (FIG) consisting of 26 managers seconded for a year by leading financial institutions to develop new ideas for dealing with inner-city problems. Their recommendations led to the introduction of the urban development grant designed (like the American scheme on which it is modelled) to lever private sector investment into the inner cities.

Much of this dramatic change stems from the explicit political stance of the Thatcher government, and the belief that, somehow or other, planning itself was part of the problem – an attitude encapsulated by the remark that jobs were being locked up in the filing cabinets of planners. But there are also some deeper undercurrents. Above all, the poor state of the economy has raised the importance of the *promotion* of development in contrast to its *control*, while virtually zero population growth has reduced the apparent (though not necessarily the real) need for long-term developments of new town character. Successive public expenditure crises have also taken their toll. The problems of urban decay are seemingly of a growing intractability: or at least it looks as if traditional planning approaches are inadequate.

More widely, there is increased confusion about the role of planning. The promises held out by the 'new' structure plan system failed to materialise. It appeared to be no more effective, speedy, flexible, or satisfying than the system it was designed to replace. Whether the latest changes will prove to be more effective remains to be seen. When the needs for economic growth and for good planning clash, the former is likely to win.

It is always difficult to see current events in perspective, and there is abundant scope for debating whether the changes that have taken place are fundamental or not. More likely they will be overtaken by new problems, or by the redefinition of old problems which cannot readily be foreseen.

## UPDATE

For a discussion of the 1992 Environmental Information Regulations, see W. Birtles, 'A right to know: the Environmental Information Regulations 1992', *JPL* 1993: 615–26.

*Good Practice in Equal Opportunities*, by R. Gilroy (Avebury, Aldershot, 1993) is an important new book drawing together an explanation of discrimination (whether concerned with race, gender, sexuality, disability or age) with examination of the generally weak policy responses. It links equal opportunities to the current agenda of 'quality' and 'customer care' with the message that action is more important than policy and that planners must 'put people back at the centre of their practice'.

In 'Why we no longer need a town planning profession', (*Planning Practice and Research*, 8 (1): 9–15, 1993), B. Evans takes forward the arguments for de-professionalisation of planning, as previously argued by Reade (1987).

A review of current issues in public participation in planning and case studies is given in the *Report of the 1992 National Planning Aid Conference: Public Participation in Planning*, Planning Aid for London, December 1992.

A report on *Ethnic Minorities and the Planning System*, by V. Krishnarayan and H. Thomas, has been published by the RTPI. Also published by the RTPI in conjunction with the Access Committee for England is *Access Policies for Local Plans* which deals with the inadequacy of the provision of women's conveniences.

## NOTES

1 Mrs Thatcher's speech (as a new Member) introducing her Private Member's Bill 'championing the cause of local government freedom of information' (Tant 1990: 486).

2 There is an extensive literature on this; see, for example, Davies 1972, Dennis 1972, Wates 1977, Anson 1981.

3 Glass (1959) drew attention to the way in which planning jargon 'contributes to the mystique of planning'. Forester (1980 and 1982) discusses the problems of bureaucratic language and procedures, and the distortions which are created when political decisions are presented as technical matters. Kemp (1985) discusses the way in which distorted communication at public inquiries allows the domination of particular interests over 'more generalisable interests'.

4 Illich 1977. The reader will remember Shaw's earlier remark in the same vein, that all professions are a conspiracy against the laity.

5 Broady 1968, Levin and Donnison 1969, Ravetz 1980 and 1986. (See also the earlier article by Glass (1959) reprinted in Faludi 1973a.) American writings include Gans 1968, and Jacobs 1961. Despite the increasing amount of criticism, the pursuit of an objective and scientific theory of planning continued both in the USA (Davidoff and Reiner 1962) and Britain (McLoughlin 1969; Faludi 1973b).

6 Dennis 1970; Davies 1972; Pickvance 1982. The planner was described at the time as an 'urban gatekeeper' at the centre of the distribution of resources.

7 Batey 1985 and 1993. The course at University College, London followed in 1914 (Collins 1989). The first examination syllabus of the then TPI was produced in 1916. For a review of the development of planning education, see Healey 1985. For a review of recent changes to the core curriculum for accredited courses, see Healey 1991b.

8 Fidler 1987; K. Thomas 1989, 1990a and 1990b. For a separate discussion of the Scottish planning education scene, see Begg 1990b. The market for planners is analysed in Dickins's continuing study: see Dickins and Fidler 1984, and Dickins and Jones 1990. See also Dickins 1992.

9 There has been a major increase in the last two decades in the membership of many organisations concerned with planning. Between 1971 and 1991 the membership of the CPRE and its Scottish and Welsh equivalents increased from 21,000 to 45,000; that of the RSPB increased from 98,000 to 852,000; the National Trust from 278,000 to 2,152,000. The relative newcomer, Friends of the Earth, had only 1,000 members in 1971, but 111,000 in 1991 (England and Wales). These and

other similar figures are given in *Social Trends* 23 (1993: 126).

10  See Burton 1992 on the operations of the CPRE. The CPRE now publish comprehensive *Campaigners' Guides* to local plans and EC environmental law (CPRE 1992a and 1992b). The RSPB monitors development plans: see Bain *et al.* 1990a and 1990b; and Davies *et al.* 1992. The political activities of such groups are discussed in Chapter 6.

11  Healey *et al.* 1988, chapter 7.

12  The Race Relations Act 1976 sets the framework and imposes a duty on all local authorities 'to make appropriate arrangements with a view to securing that their various functions are carried out with due regard to the need to eliminate unlawful racial discrimination; and to promote equality of opportunity, and good relations between persons of different racial groups'. (The RTPI/CRE Report's recommendations, of course, apply to all planners wherever they work).

13  See *Racial Disadvantage*: Report of the HC Home Affairs Race Relations and Immigration Sub-committee, HMSO, 1981; Scarman 1981; and Commission for Racial Equality 1982.

14  The GLC's *Guidelines* (in reporting on earlier consultation) give an eloquent, succinct account of the confused and ill-informed state of thinking about race:

> At one end of the range there was a denial that any form of racism in planning existed; next came the view that planning should, as a matter of principle, be colour-blind and provide an 'equal service to all' (thus perpetuating a white male view of what was important and what was a priority); then there was the view that black and other ethnic minorities were in some way 'disadvantaged' and therefore needed special treatment (thus implying that disadvantage was inherent in being black, rather than being caused by racism and discrimination); a further view was that ethnic minorities were 'special' and should have a whole range of policies directed to their 'special needs' (thus tending to marginalise black and ethnic minorities or, at worst, perpetuating the view that black people deviate from the norm); finally, and more positively, there were views that saw the issues of racism and discrimination as the kernel of the problem.

15  An excellent overview of the literature on race relations in Britain and the relationship between ethnic minorities, government, and the planning system is given by Madden (1987). Thomas and Krishnarayan (1993a) have noted the almost complete absence of reference to racial matters in two major and influential recent reports: the Audit Commission's *Building in Quality*,

and the DoE's *Development Plans: A Good Practice Guide*, both published in 1992.

16  Fitzsimmons 1990. It is noteworthy that once embarked upon a planning course, women tend to out-perform men. For example, in 1987, 42 per cent of women obtained first class or upper second class degrees, compared to 30 per cent of men (Fitzsimmons 1990: 29). Women's membership of the RTPI is significantly higher than is the case in other professions concerned with the built environment. The proportions are RICS: 4 per cent; ICE: 0.7 per cent; and RIBA: 6 per cent. By contrast, the figure for the Institute of Housing is 33 per cent.

17  See the discussion in Cullingworth 1993, chapter 7.

18  RTPI, *Report and Recommendations of the Working Party on Women in Planning*, 1987; *Managing Equality: The Role of Senior Planners*, 1988; and *Choice and Opportunity in Planning*, 1989. The GLC Development Plan included a chapter devoted to 'Women in London', and further advice has now been produced for the London Boroughs (Foulsham 1990; London Women and Planning Group 1991).

19  Town and Country Planning (Development Plan) Regulations 1991, SI 2794: para 9(1).

20  The provisions of the Building Regulations (part M) were extended in 1992 to include people with sensory impairments. The British Standards Institute publish the *Code of Practice for Access for the Disabled to Buildings* (BS 5810) and *Code of Practice for Design for the Convenience of Disabled People* (BS 5619). DoE advice is given in Development Control Policy Note 16, 1985. This has been supplemented by the RTPI's Planning Advice Note, *Access for Disabled People* (1988c), and the London Boroughs Disability Resource Team's *Towards Integration: The Participation of Disabled People in Planning* (1991).

21  M. Broady, *Social Change and Town Development*, Paper given to the TCPA National Conference (mimeo) 1963. This was not published, but see his *Planning for People*, 1968.

22  The statement 'Planning and Local Choice' was reprinted in the *Municipal Journal*, 13 October 1989, pp. 18–19.

23  The following discussion borrows in part from the author's *The Political Culture of Planning* (1993: 191) where there is a fuller account of British secrecy in a comparative context. See particularly chapter 13, 'Cross-cultural perspectives'.

24  In Tant's words (1990: 480): 'Since government is not (directly) accountable to the people, there is little need for the people to be well-informed about the details of public policy; it is for parliament, not the unsophisticated public, to scrutinise government decision making. Indeed, law, order and stability might be threatened

by disclosure to those unschooled in responsible judgment . . . Thus the consistency between the basic nature of British government and official secrecy is quite apparent. Official information is "owned" by government "office", the proper custodians being the government of the day.'

25  See DoE Circular 6/86 (which is still operative). The DoE has published codes of practice on certain types of publication: *Explaining the Local Authority Rate Bill*, HMSO, 1980; and *Local Authority Annual Reports*, HMSO, 1981.

26  *Planning* 1016, 30 April 1993.

27  SOEnD *Planning Bulletin* 6 (November 1992): 1. It is noted, however, that 'in exceptional circumstances, depending on the quality and content of the documents, it may be appropriate to impose a charge for some PANs'.

In Scotland, NPPGs provide statements of government policy on nationally important planning matters, and include locational guidance where this is appropriate. Circulars also provide statements of government policy, but mainly in relation to legislative and other procedural changes. PANs provide advice on best practice.

28  Council Directive 90/313/EC of 7 June 1990 on the Freedom of Access to Information on the Environment, OJ No. L158, 23.6.90, pp. 56–58. See Birtles 1991.

29  The EC Treaty also provides a complaints procedure which enables any citizen to make a complaint to the Commission that an EC provision is not being applied. As Krämer (1991: 55) comments, this casts the EC in the role of an Ombudsman for the European environment. (Krämer cites figures showing that the number of complaints rose steadily in the 1980s, reaching 465 in 1989.)

30  Burton (1989: 192) comments that the Act 'reversed the trend of previous water pollution legislation, by removing the emphasis on secrecy, and replacing it by a regime designed to enable the public to obtain, especially through public registers, information about discharges of trade or sewage effluent, and to participate in decisions to regulate such discharges'.

31  White Paper, *The Citizen's Charter*, 1991. See also *The Citizen's Charter: First Report*, 1992. An anonymous article in *Scottish Planning Law and Practice* (No. 34, October 1991: 65) contends that the Citizen's Charter has a major omission: the standard of service provided for the citizen by Parliament. It is argued that the Parliamentary service needs major improvement in accordance with the aims of the Charter. There are several specific complaints: "Too often the publicly-debated provisions [of a bill] offer a poor guide to what is really intended, and vital issues are left for ministerial regulation or administrative arrangement . . . too often the initial version of a Bill appears merely a

statement of intent to do something in an area, and the final proposals are revealed only at a very late stage. . . . there can be long delays before non-controversial reforms find a place in the parliamentary timetable — for example, the government accepted in 1983 the need for the irrigation provisions in the Natural Heritage (Scotland) Act 1991, after consultations in the late 1970s. Moreover, too often such matters depend on the chance of finding an MP willing to adopt a measure as a Private Member's Bill.'

32  White Paper, *The Citizen's Charter: First Report 1992*.

33  National Planning Forum 1993. Free copies of the Charter are available from the ADC, ACC and AMA.

34  Local authority charters coming forward are based on the National Planning Forum model with local variations. See, for example, the reports in *Planning* of charters produced by Woking District Council (*Planning* 1011, 26 March 1993, p. 9) and Southampton City Council (*Planning* 1007, 26 February 1993, p. 11).

35  A draft outline of the *Local Environment Charter* was first issued by the DoE in November 1992 and a fully revised draft appeared in March 1993. In their response to the earlier paper in December 1992, the RTPI noted that the separation of the 'environment' and 'planning' charters reflected central government's continued distinction between these two policy areas, 'the latter being taken to be synonymous with pollution aspects of the environment'.

36  British Standards Institution (1991) British Standard 5750, Part 8: *Quality Systems*, London, BSI.

37  A discussion of the wider relationship between the citizen and government is to be found in Local Government Management Board 1992b: 17.

38  Ibid.

39  PAN 37: Structure Planning, and PAN 30: Local Planning.

40  A discussion of this contentious issue, within the context of a broad historical survey of the working of the Parliamentary Commissioner scheme, is to be found in Gregory and Pearson 1992.

41  Parliamentary Commissioner for Administration 1992: 36.

42  Ibid. p. 18.

43  Their remit includes police authorities and urban development corporations.

44  Though complaints to the local ombudsman normally must be channelled through a member of the authority, the Ombudsmen have the power, when satisfied that a member has failed to sponsor a complaint, to accept a complaint direct. This has been a matter of much debate, with the Ombudsmen pressing for direct access, and also for the power to undertake investigations on their own initiative. The 1986 Widdicombe Report

supported this and other extensions to the powers of the ombudsmen. Successive Governments have been unsympathetic to such proposals.

45 Many aggrieved objectors do complain to the Ombudsman who, typically, will carefully explain why such matters cannot be dealt with. However, on occasion the Ombudsman has challenged decisions on the ground that they involve a gross misinterpretation of established policy. There is an uncertain area here: see, for example, Hammersley 1987, and Macpherson 1987.

46 The Parliamentary Commissioner for Administration (1992: 18) makes the same point in relation to planning appeals: 'decisions taken on planning appeals by Inspectors appointed by the Secretary of State continue to engender strong feelings, both among those parties whose appeals have been dismissed and those who live close to a development which has been permitted. In many cases, the complainant disagrees vehemently with the decision reached by the Inspector and with my decision should I decline with reasons not to investigate; but such disagreement, however vehement, does not of itself provide a basis for my intervention. Only some evidence of maladministration in the way in which a decision has been reached and consequent injustice to the complainant can provide me with the basis for an investigation.'

47 *Buxton and Others* v. *Minister of Housing and Local Government*, 1960, 3 WLR 866. The account given here of the case is based on a summary contained in *Public Law*, Summer 1961, pp. 121–8. See also, 'The chalkpit case', in Griffith and Street 1964. A later examination of the status and rights of the public at public inquiries is to be found in Sharman 1985.

48 This oversimplifies a complex and confusing legal situation. For those who have the temerity to venture into this labyrinth, a useful discussion is in Hough 1992. Even heftier fare (on a broader plate) is provided by the Law Commission's Consultation Paper on judicial review and statutory appeals: Law Commission 1993.

49 Brand and Thompson 1982, and Thompson 1985. Gillett (1983: 71) explains the background to this in Scotland. (It had always been a requirement of the building regulations that neighbours were notified and allowed to make objections.)

50 'If planning permission is granted and it later emerges that a notifiable neighbour has not been notified, the local authority cannot revoke the planning permission. The only recourse open to the third party is a private action against the applicant. This is difficult for the aggrieved party to prove since it must be shown that failure to notify was not carried out by the applicant knowingly and with deceitful intention' (Berry *et al.* 1988: 806). In Northern Ireland, the central government is responsible for all planning matters including neighbour notification.

51 The categories of development which are defined as 'major' include the erection of ten or more dwellings, development on 1,000 sq. m or more, development on a site of one hectare or more, and all minerals and waste developments.

52 Now s. 101 of the 1990 Act. The Scottish provisions are ss. 44 to 47 of the Town and Country Planning (Scotland) Act 1972.

53 The phrase 'fundamentally flawed' is from Grant *Encyclopedia*, notes on s. 101.3. The longer quotation is from the *Government's Response* to the Environment Committee's Report on *Planning Appeals, Call-in and Major Public Inquiries*, 1986. The relevant passage is also reproduced in Grant *Encyclopedia*. For further discussion of the PIC, see Edwards and Rowan-Robinson 1980; and Pearce *et al.* 1979.

54 See, for example, Armstrong 1985a, and HC Environment Committee, *Planning Appeals, Call-in, and Major Public Inquiries*, 1986.

55 *Government's Response to the HC Environment Committee's Report on Planning Appeals, Call-in, and Major Public Inquiries* 1986: 18.

56 The principal sources for procedure and practice on EIPs are s. 35B of the 1990 Act, which sets out the requirement for an EIP; the 1991 Regulations, which prescribe periods for notification and deposit of the plan; Annex A to PPG 12: 'Code of Practice on Development Plans', which is the non-statutory code governing procedure; and Annex C to PPG 12: 'EIPs: A Guide for Local Planning Authorities', which considers how to prepare for the examination, the consideration of objections, selection of participants and other matters.

57 DoE and Welsh Office 1973, *Structure Plans: The Examination in Public*, which accompanied DoE Circular 36/73 (WO Circular 74/73). This was subsequently updated but, in 1992, the Code for EIPs was merged with that for local plan inquiries, and is published as Annex A to PPG 12 (1992), and reproduced in the DoE 1992 booklet *Development Plans: What You Need to Know*.

58 Annex A to PPG 12, 1992, paras 56–7.

59 Annex C to PPG 12, 1992, para 24.

60 The procedure is a long-standing feature of British government administration. Its origin lies in the Parliamentary Private Bill procedure which provided an opportunity for objections to government proposals to be heard by a Parliamentary Committee. Because of rapidly expanding government intervention in the nineteenth century, the responsibility for hearing objections was first delegated to Ministers. Later, from 1845, commissioners were engaged to 'hold a meeting or meetings to hear objections' (Wraith and Lamb 1971: 20). By 1876, the first set of procedures were introduced for notification of objectors, holding inquiries and

reporting, and the inquiry was included as a central feature of the development plan system from its inception in 1947. Over that time, the procedure has grown by accident as much as by design, but the twofold nature of its purpose has continued: to gather information for government and to provide a route for individual redress.

61 Introduced by the Town and Country Planning (Development Plans) Regulations 1991, SI 2794: 16.

62 The bench-mark research on inquiries is that conducted by Bruton and his colleagues in the early 1980s which concluded that in general they have been 'fair orderly and impartial . . . Inspectors have handled the proceedings appropriately with considerable skill, and clear impartiality' (Bruton, Crispin, Fidler and Hill 1982: 37).

63 In Bruton's study (1980a and 1980b), 45 per cent of objectors were unable to accurately define the decision-making roles of Inspector and local authority. The formality of proceedings, especially the use of counsel by both major objectors and the local authority, is widespread and can work to the detriment of small unrepresented objectors. Concern has been expressed about the ability of Inspectors to overcome this in more complex inquiries (Bruton et al. 1985: 41). According to Adams and Pawson (1991), only about 10 per cent of objections have the benefit of professional representation.

64 Local plan inquiries generally sit for between three and four days each week. A guideline of three days' writing-up time for each day of the inquiry is used.

65 One example of this is to be found in effect of the Inspector's report following the 1992 inquiry into the Solihull Unitary Development Plan. This found that the plan's general approach did not recognise the need to meet the requirements of strategic guidance in the amount of land allocated for housing. This one recommendation was enough to require a fundamental reappraisal of the Council's policy, and an inevitable lengthy delay to the plan process.

66 Bruton et al. 1982a: 28. More recent work by Webster and Lavers, on the first UDP inquiry at the London Borough of Barnet, comes to similar conclusions (1991: 808). Objectors noted the reluctance of the authority to consider other than minor changes, except, to an extent, in the case of the most 'powerful commercial interests'. In Adams and Pawson's (1991: 25) sample of 7,579 objections to 16 plans, 5.8 per cent led to a suggested change before the inquiry.

67 See Cherry 1974: 210, and Centre for Environmental Studies 1973.

68 See the references quoted in the previous note. For a striking illustration of the two extremes of planning philosophy, compare Eversley's *The Planner in Society* (1973) with Keeble's standard textbook *Principles and Practice of Town and Country Planning* (1969).

# BIBLIOGRAPHY

*Note*: Two frequently quoted journals are abbreviated: *Journal of Planning and Environment Law* (JPL), and *Town Planning Review* (TPR).

Abercrombie, P. (1945) *Greater London Plan 1944*, London: HMSO

Abraham, H.C. (1991) 'Control of advertisements – the power to issue enforcement and stop notices', *JPL* 1991: 312–15

Adair, A.S., Berry, J.N., and Mcgreal, W.S. (1991) 'Land availability, housing demand and the property market', *Journal of Property Research* 8: 59–69

Adams, B., Okely, J., Morgan, D., and Smith, D. (1976) *Gypsies and Government Policy in Britain*, London: Heinemann

Adams, C.D., Baum, A.E., and Macgregor, B.D. (1985) 'The influence of valuation practices upon the price of vacant inner city land', *Land Development Studies* 2: 157–73

Adams, C.D., Baum, A.E., and Macgregor, B.D. (1987a) 'Inner city land vacancy: the influence of the compensation code', *JPL* 1987: 253–70

Adams, C.D., Baum, A.E., and Macgregor, B.D. (1987b) 'Vacant urban land: the planners' responsibility?', *The Planner* 73: 31–8

Adams, D. (1992) 'The role of landowners in the preparation of statutory local plans', *TPR* 63: 297–323

Adams, D. and Pawson, G.P. (1991) *Representation and Influence in Local Planning*, Manchester: Department of Planning and Landscape, University of Manchester

Adams, D., May, H., and Pawson, G.P. (1990) 'The distribution of influence at local plan inquiries', *Planning Outlook* 33: 133–5

Adams, J.G.U. (1990) 'Car ownership forecasting: pull the ladder up, or climb back down?', *Traffic Engineering and Control* 31: 136–41

Adams, P.T. (1978) 'The medium and the message (or circular reasoning)', *JPL* 1978: 685–92

Adams, W.M. (1984) *Implementing the Act: A Study of Habitat Protection under Part II of the Wildlife and Countryside Act 1981*, London: British Association of Nature Conservationists and World Wildlife Fund

Adams, W.M. (1986) *Nature's Place: Conservation Sites and Countryside Change*, London: Allen and Unwin

Adcock, B. (1984) 'Regenerating Merseyside docklands: the Merseyside Development Corporation 1981–1984', *TPR* 55: 265–89

Adger, W.N. and Whitby, M.C. (1991) 'Environmental assessment in forestry: the initial experience', *Journal of Rural Studies* 7: 385–95

Advisory Committee on Business and the Environment (1993) *Report of the Financial Sector Working Group*, London: Department of Trade and Industry

Advisory Committee on Hazardous Substances (1992) *First Annual Report*, London: HMSO

Advisory Committee on the Safe Transport of Radioactive Materials (1988) *The Transport of Low Level Radioactive Waste in the UK*, London: HMSO

Advisory Council on Science and Technology (1990) *The Enterprise Challenge: Overcoming Barriers to Growth in Small Firms*, London: HMSO

Advisory Group on Neighbourhood Councils (1977) *A Voice for Your Neighbourhood: The Neighbourhood Council*, London: HMSO

Agriculture Economic Development Committee (1987) *Directions for Change: Land Use in the 1990s*, London: NEDO

Ahmed, Y. (1989) 'Planning and racial equality', *The Planner* 75, 32 (1 December): 18–20

Aitken, P. and Sparks, L. (1986) 'The Scottish Development Agency: a case for coordination?', *Regional Studies* 20: 476–80

Albrechts, L. (1991) 'Changing roles and positions of planners', *Urban Studies* 28: 123–37

Albrechts, L., Moulaert, F., Roberts, P., and Swyngedouw, E. (eds) (1989) *Regional Policy at the Crossroads: European Perspectives*, London: Jessica Kingsley

Alden, J. (1992) 'Strategic planning guidance in Wales', *TPR* 63: 429–32

Alder, J. (1989) 'The loss of existing use rights – what difference does planning permission make?', *JPL* 1989: 814–23

Alder, J. (1990) 'Planning agreements and planning powers', *JPL* 1990: 880–9

Aldous, A. (1975) *Goodbye Britain*, London: Sidgwick and Jackson

Aldous, T. (1989) *Inner City Urban Regeneration and Good Design*, London: HMSO

Aldridge, H.R. (1915) *The Case for Town Planning*, London: National Housing and Town Planning Council

Aldridge, M. (1979) *The British New Towns*, London: Routledge and Kegan Paul

Aldridge, M. and Brotherton, C.J. (1988) 'Being a programme authority: is it worthwhile?', *Journal of Social Policy* 16: 349–69

Alexander, A. (1982) *Local Government in Britain since Reorganisation*, London: Allen and Unwin

Alexander, E.R. (1981) 'If planning isn't everything, maybe it's something', *TPR* 52: 131–42

Allen, A.J.R. (1988) 'Established use certificates and illegality', *JPL* 1988: 239–42

Allen, J. and Hamnett, C. (eds) (1991) *Housing and Labour Markets: Building the Connections*, London: Unwin Hyman

Allen, K. (1986) *Regional Incentives and the Investment Decision of the Firm* (DTI), London: HMSO

Allison, L. and Benton, J. (1978) 'Public planning of private development: a review and appraisal of the report of the expenditure committee on planning procedures', *Public Administration* 56: 73–85

Alonso, W. (1971) 'Beyond the inter-disciplinary approach to planning', *Journal of the American Institute of Planners* 37: 169–73 (reprinted in Cullingworth 1973)

Alterman, R., Harris, D., and Hill, M. (1984) 'The impact of public participation on planning: the case of the Derbyshire structure plan', *TPR* 55: 177–96

Alty, R. and Darke, R. (1991) 'A city centre for the people: involving the community in planning for Sheffield's central area', in Nadin and Doak

Ambrose, P. (1974) *The Quiet Revolution: Social Change in a Sussex Village 1871 1971*, London: Chatto and Windus

Ambrose, P. (1986) *Whatever Happened to Planning?*, London: Methuen

Ambrose, P. (1992) 'Changing planning relations', in Cloke

Ambrose, P. and Colenutt, B. (1975) *The Property Machine*, Harmondsworth: Penguin

Amery, C. and Cruikshank, D. (1975) *The Rape of Britain*, London: Paul Elek

Amin, A. and Tomaney, J. (1991) 'Creating an enterprise culture in the North East? The impact of urban and regional policies of the 1980s', *Regional Studies* 25: 479–87

Amos, C. (1989) 'A testing time for new settlements?', *Town and Country Planning* 58: 314–19

Amos, C. (1991) 'Flexibility and variety: the key to new settlement policy', *Town and Country Planning* 60: 52–6

Amos, F.J.C. (1987) 'Twenty years after PAG – is the system still working?', *The Planner, TCPSS Proceedings* 73, 2: 19–23

Amos, F.J.C., Davies, D., Groves, R., and Niner, P. (1982) *Manpower Requirements for Physical Planning*, Birmingham: Institute of Local Government Studies

Amos, F.J.C., Smith, B.M.D., and Lomas, G.M. (1978) 'The inner area studies: a review', *TPR* 49: 195–208

Amundson, C. (1993) 'Sustainable aims and objectives – a planning framework', *Town and Country Planning* 62: 20–2

Ancient Monuments Board for Scotland (annual) *Annual Reports*, London: HMSO

Anderson, J. (1990) 'The "new right", enterprise zones, and urban development corporations', *International Journal of Urban and Regional Research* 14: 468–89

Anderson, M.A. (1981) 'Planning policies and development control in the Sussex Downs AONB', *TPR* 52: 5–25

Anderson, M.A. (1990) 'Areas of outstanding natural beauty and the 1949 National Parks Act', *TPR* 61: 311–39

Anon (1956) 'Ye olde English green belt', *Journal of the Town Planning Institute* 42: 68–9

Anson, B. (1981) *I'll Fight for You: Behind the Struggle for Covent Garden*, London: Cape

Anstis, G. (1985) *Redditch: The History of Redditch New Town*, London: Batsford

Archbishops' Commission on Rural Areas (1990) *Faith in the Countryside*, Stoneleigh Park, Warwickshire: ACORA Publishing

Archbishop of Canterbury's Commission on Urban Priority Areas (1985) *Faith in the City: A Call for Action by Church and Nation*, London: Church House Publishing

Archbishop of Canterbury's Commission on Urban Priority Areas (1990) *Living Faith in the City: A Progress Report*, London: General Synod of the Church of England

Armitage Report (1980) *Lorries, People and the Environment* (Report of the Inquiry), London: HMSO

Armstrong, H.W. (1986) 'The division of regional industrial policy powers in Britain: some implications of the 1984 policy reforms', *Environment and Planning C: Government and Policy* 4: 325–42

Armstrong, H.W. and Fildes, J. (1988) 'Industrial development initiatives in England and Wales: the role of the district councils', *Progress in Planning* 30: 85–156

Armstrong, J. (1983) 'Procedures at the Sizewell inquiry', *JPL* 1983: 508–10

Armstrong, J. (1985a) *Sizewell Report: A New Approach for Major Public Inquiries*, London: TCPA

Armstrong, J. (1985b) 'The Sizewell inquiry', *JPL* 1985: 686–9

Arnstein, S.R. (1969) 'A ladder of citizen participation', *Journal of the American Institute of Planners* 35: 216–24

Arton Wilson Report (1959) *Caravans as Homes*, Cmnd 872, London: HMSO

Arup Economic Consultants (1990) *Mineral Policies in Development Plans*, London: HMSO

Arup Economic Consultants (1991) *Simplified Planning Zones: Progress and Procedures* (DoE Planning Research Programme), London: HMSO

Ashby, E. (1978) *Reconciling Man with the Environment*, Stanford: Stanford University Press

Ashby, E. and Anderson, M. (1981) *The Politics of Clean Air*, Oxford: Clarendon Press

Ashford, D.E. (ed.) (1979) *The Politics of Urban Resources*, Chicago: Maaroufa

Ashworth, W. (1954) *The Genesis of Modern British Town Planning*, London: Routledge and Kegan Paul

Assembly of Welsh Counties (1992) *Strategic Planning Guidance in Wales*, Mold: Clwyd County Council

Association of British Chambers of Commerce (1985) *Reviving the Inner Cities: A Review of the Urban Programme in England*, London: The Association

Association of Conservation Officers (1992) *Listed Buildings Repair Notices*, The Association

Association of County Archaeological Officers (1993) *Archaeological Heritage*, London: Association of County Councils

Association of County Councils (1991) *Towards a Sustainable Transport Policy*, London: The Association

Association of County Councils (1992a) *National Parks – The New Partnership*, London: The Association

Association of County Councils (1992b) *Making the Most of Parish and Town Councils*, Review of Local Government Paper 8, London: The Association

Association of County Councils (1992c) *Making the Most of Parish and Town Councils*, Briefing Paper 5/92, London: The Association

Association of County Councils (1993) *The Enabling Authority and County Government*, London: The Association

Association of District Councils (1990) *Survey of Local Plan Progress and Intentions*, London: ADC

Association of District Councils (1991) *Survey of Local Plan Progress and Intentions*, London: ADC

Association of London Authorities and Docklands Consultative Committee (1991) *Ten Years of Docklands: How the Cake Was Cut*, London: DCC

Association of National Park Officers (1988) *National Parks: Environmentally Favoured Areas? A Proposal for a New Agricultural Policy to Achieve the Aims of National Park Designation*, Bovey Tracey: The Association

Aston University: *see* Public Sector Management Research Unit

Audit Commission: *see* Official Publications at end of this bibliography

Aves, A.M. (1991) 'Precedent in planning decision-making', *JPL* 1991: 923–9

Backwell, J. and Dickens, P. (1978) *Town Planning, Mass Loyalty and the Restructuring of Capital: The Origins of the 1947 Planning Legislation Revisited*, Brighton: Urban and Regional Studies Working Paper 11, University of Sussex

Bailey, N. and Barker, A. (eds) (1992) *City Challenge and Local Regeneration Partnerships: Conference Proceedings*, London: Polytechnic of Central London

Bailey, R. (1984) *Abolition of the Metropolitan Counties: A Denial of Civil Liberties*, London: Community Rights Project, London Planning Aid Service, TCPA

Bailey, S.J. (1990) 'Charges for local infrastructure', *TPR* 61: 427–53

Bain, C., Dodd, A., and Pritchard, D. (1990a) 'Nature conservation and structure plans', *The Planner* 76, 28 (20 July) 11–13

Bain, C., Dodd, A., and Pritchard, D. (1990b) *RSPB Planscan: A Study of Development Plans in England and Wales*, Conservation Topic 28, London: Royal Society for the Protection of Birds

Baldock, D., Cox, G., Lowe, P., and Winter, M. (1990) 'Environmentally sensitive areas: incrementalism or reform?', *Journal of Rural Studies* 6: 143–62

Ball, R.M. (1989) 'Vacant industrial premises and local development: a survey, analysis, and policy assessment of the problem in Stoke-on-Trent', *Land Development Studies* 6: 105–28

Ball, S.N. (1985) 'Sites of special scientific interest', *JPL* 1985: 767–77

Ball, S. and Bell, S. (1991) *Environmental Law*, London: Blackstone

Banham, R., Barker, P., Hall, P., and Price, C. (1969) 'Non-Plan: an experiment in freedom', *New Society* 26: 435–43

Banister, D. (1990) 'Privatisation in transport: from the company state to the contract state', in Simmie and King

Banister, D. (1992) 'Transport', in Cloke

Barker, A. and Cooper, M. (1984) 'The art of quasi-judicial administration: the planning appeal and inquiry systems in England', *Urban Law and Policy* 6: 363–476

Barker, T.C. and Savage, C.I. (1974) *An Economic History of Transport*, London: Hutchinson

Barkham, J.P., MacGuire, F.A.S., and Jones, S.J. (1992) *Sea-Level Rise and the UK*, London: Friends of the Earth

Barlow, J. (1982) 'Planning practice, housing supply and migration', in Champion and Fielding

Barlow, J. (1986) 'Landowners, property ownership, and the rural locality', *International Journal of Urban and Regional Research* 10: 309–29

Barlow, J. (1988) 'The politics of land into the 1990s: landowners, developers, and farmers in lowland Britain', *Policy and Politics* 16: 111–21

Barlow, J. and Chambers, D. (1992) *Planning Agreements and Affordable Housing Provision*, Brighton: Centre for Urban and Regional Research, University of Sussex

Barlow, J. and Duncan, S. (1992) 'Markets, states and housing provision: four European growth regions compared', *Progress in Planning* 38, 2: 93–177

Barlow, J. and King, A. (1992) 'The state, the market, and competitive strategy: the housebuilding industry in the United Kingdom, France, and Sweden', *Environment and Planning A* 24: 381–400

Barlow Report (1940) *Report of the Royal Commission on the Distribution of the Industrial Population*, Cmd 6153, London: HMSO

Barnekov, T., Boyle, R., and Rich, D. (1989) *Privatism and Urban Policy in Britain and the United States*, Oxford: Oxford University Press

Barnekov, T., Hart, D., and Benfer, W. (1990) *US Experience in Evaluating Urban Regeneration* (DoE Inner Cities Research Programme), London: HMSO

Barnes, I. and Preston, J. (1985) 'The Scunthorpe enterprise zone: an example of muddled interventionism', *Public Administration* 63: 171–81

Barras, R. and Broadbent, T.A. (1979) 'The analysis in English structure plans', *Urban Studies* 16: 1–18

Barrett, S. (1981) 'Local authorities and the community land scheme', in Barrett and Fudge

Barrett, S. and Fudge, C. (eds) (1981) *Policy and Action*, London: Methuen

Barrett, S. and Healey, P. (eds) (1985) *Land Policy: Problems and Alternatives*, Aldershot: Avebury

Barrett, S. and Whitting, G. (1983) *Local Authorities and Land Supply*, Bristol: School for Advanced Urban Studies, University of Bristol

Barrett, S., Boddy, M., and Stewart, M. (1979) *Implementation of the Community Land Scheme*, Bristol: School for Advanced Urban Studies, University of Bristol

Barrett, S., Stewart, M., and Underwood, J. (1978) *The Land Market and Development Process*, Bristol: School for Advanced Urban Studies, University of Bristol

Barron, J., Crawley, G., and Wood, T. (1991) *Councillors in Crisis: The Public and Private Worlds of Local Councillors*, London: Macmillan

Barty-King, H. (1985) *Expanding Northampton*, London: Secker and Warburg

Bateman, M. (1985) *Office Development: A Geographical Analysis*, New York: St Martin's Press

Batey, P. (1985) 'Postgraduate planning education in Britain', *TPR* 56: 407–20

Batey, P. (1993) 'Planning education as it was', *The Planner* 79, 4 (April): 25–6

Batho Report (1990) *Report of the Noise Review Working Party*, London: HMSO

Batley, R. (1989) 'London docklands: an analysis of power relations between UDCs and local government', *Public Administration* 67: 167–87

Batley, R. and Stoker, G. (eds) (1991) *Local Government in Europe: Trends and Development*, London: Macmillan

Batty, M. (1984) 'Urban policies in the 1980s: a review of the OECD proposals for managing urban change', *TPR* 55: 489–98

Batty, M. (1990) 'How can we best respond to changing fashions in urban and regional planning?', *Environment and Planning B: Planning and Design* 17: 1–7

Baxter, J.D. (1990) *State Security, Privacy and Information*, Hemel Hempstead: Harvester/Wheatsheaf

Beckerman, W. (1990) *Pricing for Pollution: Market Pricing, Government Regulation, Environmental Policy* (2nd edition), London: Institute of Economic Affairs

Beesley, M.E. and Kain, J.F. (1964) 'Urban form, car ownership and public policy: an appraisal of *Traffic in Towns*', *Urban Studies* 1: 174–203

Beevers, R. (1988) *The Garden City Utopia*, London: Macmillan

Begg, H.M. (1990a) 'Planning in Tayside', *Scottish Geographical Magazine* 106: 20–7

Begg, H.M. (1990b) 'Planning education in Scotland', *The Planner* 76, 14 (13 April): 15–21

Begg, H.M. and Pollock, S.H.A. (1991) 'Development plans in Scotland since 1975', *Scottish Geographical Magazine* 107: 4–11

Begg, I. (1991) 'High technology location and the urban areas of Great Britain: development in the 1980s', *Urban Studies* 28: 961–81

Begg, I. and Moore, B. (1986) *The New Roles of UK Cities*, Oxford: Clarendon Press

Begg, T. (1987) *Fifty Special Years: A Study in Scottish Housing*, London: Henry Melland

Belbin, R. (1985) 'Job creation programmes: a new analysis of their effectiveness', *People and Jobs International* 1: 13–17

Belcher, E.M. (1971) *Advocacy Planning for Urban Development*, New York: Praeger

Bell, C. and Bell, R. (1972) *City Fathers: Early History of Town Planning in Britain*, Harmondsworth: Penguin

Bell, P. and Cloke, P. (eds) (1991) *Deregulation and Transport: Market Forces in the Modern World*, London: David Fulton

Bell, S. (1992) *Out of Order: The 1987 Use Classes Order: Problems and Proposals*, London: London Boroughs Association

Bendixson, T. (1989) *Transport in the Nineties: The Shaping of Europe*, London: Royal Institution of Chartered Surveyors

Benington, J. (1986) 'Local economic strategies: paradigms for a planned economy', *Local Economy* 1: 7–24

Benson, J.F. and Willis, K.G. (1992) *Valuing Informal Recreation on the Forestry Commission Estate* (Forestry Commission Bulletin 104), London: HMSO

Bentham, C.G. (1985) 'Which areas have the worst urban problems?', *Urban Studies* 22: 119–31

Benyon, J. (ed.) (1984) *Scarman and After: Essays Reflecting on Lord Scarman's Report, the Riots, and their Aftermath*, Oxford: Pergamon

Berry, J.N., Fitzsimmons, D.F., and McGreal, W.S. (1988) 'Neighbour notification: the Scottish and Northern Ireland models', *JPL* 1988: 804–8

Best, J. and Bowser, L. (1986) 'A people's plan for central Newham', *The Planner* 27, 11 (November 1986): 21–5

Best, R. (1981) *Land Use and Living Space*, London: Methuen

Bettle, J. (1988) 'Noise: the problem of overlapping controls', *JPL* 1988: 79–83

Beveridge Report (1942) *Social Insurance and Allied Services*, Cmd 6404, London: HMSO

Bianchini, F. (1990) 'The crisis of urban public social life in Britain: Origins of the problem and possible responses', *Planning Practice and Research* 5, 3 (Winter): 4–8

Bibby, P.R. and Shepherd, J.W. (1991) *Rates of Urbanisation in England 1981–2001* (DoE Planning Research Programme), London: HMSO

Birkenshaw, P. (1990) *Government and Information*, London: Butterworths

Birtles, W. (1991) 'The European directive on freedom of access to information on the environment', *JPL* 1991: 607–10

Bishop, K. (1992) 'Assessing the benefits of community forests: an evaluation of the recreational use benefits of two urban fringe woodlands', *Journal of Environmental Management* 35: 63–76

Bishop, K. and Hooper, A. (1991) *Planning for Social Housing*, London: National Housing Forum (Association of District Councils)

Blackaby, D.H. and Manning, D.N. (1990) 'The north-south divide . . .' *Papers of the Regional Science Association* 69: 43–65

Blackman, T. (1991) 'People-sensitive planning: communication, property and social action', *Planning Practice and Research* 6, 3. 11–15

Blacksell, M. (1984) 'Government policy and the uplands in the late twentieth century', *TPR* 55: 102–9

Blacksell, M. and Gilg, A.W. (1981) *The Countryside: Planning and Change*, London: Allen and Unwin

Blacksell, M., Blowers, A., and Shaw, T. (1987) 'Celebration or wake? 40 years of British town and country planning', *Planning Outlook* 30: 1–3

Blakely, E.J. (1989) *Planning Local Economic Development*, Newbury Park, Calif.: Sage

Blau, J.R., Lagory, M.E., and Pipkin, J.S. (1983) *Professionals and Urban Form*, Albany, N.Y.: State University of New York Press

Blowers, A. (1980) *The Limits of Power: The Politics of Local Planning Policy*, Oxford: Pergamon

Blowers, A. (1983) 'Master of fate or victim of circumstance - the exercise of corporate power in environmental policy making', *Policy and Politics* 11: 375–91

Blowers, A. (1984) *Something in the Air: Corporate Power and the Environment*, London: Harper and Row

Blowers, A. (1986) 'Environmental politics and policy in the 1980s: a changing challenge', *Policy and Politics* 14: 11–18

Blowers, A. (1987) 'Transition or transformation? - environmental policy under Thatcher', *Public Administration* 65: 277–94

Blunden, J. and Curry, N. (1988) *A Future for our Countryside?*, Oxford: Blackwell

Blunden, J. and Curry, N. (1989) *A People's Charter? Forty Years of the National Parks and Access to the Countryside Act 1949*, London: HMSO

Blunkett, D. and Jackson, K. (1987) *Democracy in Crisis: The Town Halls Respond*, London: Hogarth

Boaden, N., Goldsmith, M., Hampton, W., and Stringer, P. (1979) 'Public participation in planning within a representative local democracy', *Policy and Politics* 7: 55–67

Boaden, N., Goldsmith, M., Hampton, W., and Stringer, P. (1980) 'Planning and participation in practice: a study of public participation in structure planning', *Progress in Planning* 13: 1–102

Boddy, M., Lovering, J., and Bassett, K. (1986) *Sunbelt City? A Study of Economic Change in Britain's M4 Growth Corridor*, Oxford: Oxford University Press

Body, R. (1982) *Agriculture: The Triumph and the Shame*, London: Maurice Temple Smith

Bolan, R.S. (1967) 'Emerging views of planning', *Journal of the American Institute of Planners* 33: 233–45

Bond, M. (1992) *Nuclear Juggernaut: The Transport of Radioactive Materials*, London: Earthscan

Bongers, P. (1990) *Local Government and 1992*, Harlow: Longman

Bonyhandy, T. (1987) *Law and the Countryside: The Rights of the Public*, Oxford: Professional Books

Booker, C. and Green, C.L. (1973) *Goodbye London: An Illustrated Guide to Threatened Buildings*, London: Fontana

Booth, P. and Beer, A.R. (1983) 'Development control and design quality', *TPR* 54: 265–84 and 383–404

Borins, S.F. (1988) 'Electronic road pricing: an idea whose time may never come', *Transportation Research A* 22A: 37–44

Boucher, S. and Whatmore, S. (1990) *Planning Gain and Conservation: A Literature Review*, Reading: Department of Geography, University of Reading

Bourne, F. (1992) *Enforcement of Planning Control* (2nd edition), London: Sweet and Maxwell

Bovaird, T. (1992) 'Local economic development and the city', *Urban Studies* 29: 343–68

Bovaird, T., Gregory, D., and Martin, S. (1991) 'Improved performance in local economic development: a warm embrace or an artful sidestep?', *Public Administration* 69: 103–19

Bovaird, T., Gregory, D., Martin, S., Pearce, G., and Tricker, M. (1990) *Evaluation of the Rural Development Programme Process*, London: HMSO

Bovaird, T., Tricker, M., Hems, L., and Martin, S. (1991) *Constraints on the Growth of Small Firms: A Report on a Survey of Small Firms* (Aston Business School), London: HMSO

Bovaird, T., Tricker, M., Martin, S.J., Gregory, D.G., and Pearce, G.R. (1990) *An Evaluation of the Rural Development Programme Process*, London: HMSO

Bowers, J. (1990) *Economics of the Environment: The Conservationists' Response to the Pearce Report*, Newbury: British Association of Nature Conservationists

Bowers, J. (1992) 'The economics of planning gain: a reappraisal, *Urban Studies* 29: 1329–39

Bowers, J. (ed.) (1990) *Agriculture and Rural Land Use*, Swindon: Economic and Social Research Council

Bowers, J.K. and Cheshire, P.C. (1983) *Agriculture, the Countryside and Land Use: An Economic Critique*, London: Methuen

Bowley, M. (1945) *Housing and the State 1919–1944*, London: Allen and Unwin

Bowman, J.C. (1992) 'Improving the quality of our water: the role of regulation by the National Rivers Authority', *Public Administration* 70: 565–75

Box, J.D. (1991) 'Local nature reserves: nature conservation and public enjoyment', *The Planner* 77, 25 (12 July): 5–7

Boydell, P. and Lewis, M. (1989) 'Applications to the High Court for the review of planning decisions', *JPL* 1989: 146–56

Boyle, R. (1993) 'Changing partners: the experience of urban economic policy in West Central Scotland, 1980–90', *Urban Studies* 30: 309–24

Boyle, R. (ed.) (1985) 'Leveraging urban development: a comparison of urban policy directions and programme impact in the United States and Britain', *Policy and Politics* 13: 175–210

Boynton, J. (1986) 'Judicial review of administrative decisions – a background paper', *Public Administration* 64: 147–61

Bracewell-Milnes, B. (1982) *Land and Heritage: The Public Interest in Personal Ownership*, London: Institute of Economic Affairs

Bracken, I. and Kingaby, J. (1987) 'An analysis of "stop notice" use in planning enforcement', *JPL* 1987: 538–51

Bramley, G. (1984) 'Local government in crisis', *Policy and Politics* 12: 311–24

Bramley, G. (1989) *Land Supply, Planning, and Private Householding*, Bristol: School for Advanced Urban Studies, University of Bristol

Bramley, G. (1993) 'Planning, the market and private house-building', *The Planner* 19,1 (January): 14–16

Brand, C.M. and Thompson, B. (1982) 'Third parties and development control – a better deal for Scottish neighbours?', *JPL* 1982: 743–62

Brand, C.M. and Williams, D.W. (1984) 'Circular 22/80: three years on', *Estates Gazette* 169 (18 February): 610–11 and 638

Brand, C.M. and Williams, D.W. (1985) 'Amusement centres: planning morals and planning practice', *JPL* 1985: 5–10

Brayshaw, P. (1990) 'Urban development corporations and enterprise boards revisited: a survey of current policies and practice', *Local Economy* 5: 214–24

Breach, I. (1978) *Windscale Fallout*, Harmondsworth: Penguin

Breakell, M. and Elson, M. (1983) *Development Control and Industry*, Oxford: Oxford Polytechnic

Breheny, M.J. (1983) 'A practical view of planning theory', *Environment and Planning B: Planning and Design* 10: 101–15

Breheny, M.J. (1990a) 'Chewing the cud or biting the bullet?', *Town and Country Planning* 59: 327–28

Breheny, M.J. (1990b) 'SERPLAN: A model for strategic planning?', *Town and Country Planning* 59: 77–80

Breheny, M.J. (1991) 'The renaissance of strategic planning', *Environment and Planning B: Planning and Design* 18: 233–49

Breheny, M.J. (1993) 'Fragile regional planning', *The Planner* 79, 1 (January): 10–12

Breheny, M.J. and Congdon, P. (eds) (1989) *Growth and Change in a Core Region: The Case of South East England*, London: Pion

Breheny, M.J. and Hall, P. (1984) 'The strange death of strategic planning and the victory of the know-nothing school', *Built Environment* 10: 95–9

Breheny, M.J. and Hooper, A. (1985) *Rationality in Planning: Critical Essays on the Role of Rationality in Urban and Regional Planning*, London: Pion

Bridges, L. (1978) 'The approval of structure plans – the Staffordshire case', *JPL* 1978: 599–609

Bridges, L. (1979) 'The structure plan examination in public as an instrument of intergovernmental decision making', *Urban Law and Policy* 2: 241–64

Briggs, A. (1952) *History of Birmingham* (2 vols), Oxford: Oxford University Press

Brindley, T. and Stoker, G. (1988) 'Partnership in inner city renewal – a critical analysis', *Local Government Policy Making* 15: 3–12

Brindley, T., Rydin, Y., and Stoker, G. (1989) *Remaking Planning*, London: Unwin Hyman

Bristow, R. (1985) 'Some questions on unitary development plans', *Regional Studies* 19: 263–8

British Property Federation (1986) *The Planning System: A Fresh Approach*, London: The Federation

British Road Federation (annual) *Basic Road Statistics*, London: BRF

British Road Federation (1986) *The Price of Congestion in Inner London*, London: BRF

British Waterways Board (annual) *Annual Report and Accounts*, Watford: The Board

British Waterways Board (1992) *British Waterways and Development Plans: Consultation Document*, Watford: The Board

Britton, D. (ed.) (1990) *Agriculture in Britain: Changing Pressures and Policies*, Wallingford: CAB International

Broads Authority (1982) *What Future for Broadland?*, Norwich: The Authority

Broads Authority (1993) *Functional Strategies 1992/94 to 1995/96*, Norwich: The Authority

Broads Consortium (1971) *Broadland Study and Plan*, Norwich: Norfolk County Council

Broady, M. (1968) *Planning for People*, London: Bedford Square Press

Bromley, M.P. (1990) *Countryside Management*, London: Spon

Bromley, M.P. and Morgan, R.H. (1985) 'The effects of enterprise zone policy: evidence from Swansea', *Regional Studies* 19: 403–13

Bromley, R.D.F. and Rees, J.C.M. (1988) 'The first five years of the Swansea enterprise zone: an assessment of change', *Regional Studies* 22: 263–75

Brooke, R. (1989a) *Managing the Enabling Authority*, Harlow: Longman

Brooke, R. (1989b) 'The enabling authority – practical consequences', *Local Government Studies* 15, 5 (Sept/Oct): 55–63

Brookes, J. (1989) 'Cardiff Bay renewal strategy: another hole in the democratic system', *The Planner* 75, 1 (January): 38–40

Brotherton, D.I. (1982) 'Development pressures and control in the national parks, 1966–1981', *TPR* 53: 439–59

Brotherton, D.I. (1985) 'Issues in national park administration', *Environment and Planning A* 17: 47–58

Brotherton, D.I. (1986) 'Party political approaches to rural conservation in Britain', *Environment and Planning A* 18: 151–60

Brotherton, D.I. (1989a) 'Arrangements for prior notification of agricultural operations in national parks', *TPR* 60: 71–87

Brotherton, D.I. (1989b) 'National parks south of the Border', *Planning Outlook* 32: 121–7

Brotherton, D.I. (1989c) 'The evolution and implications of mineral planning policy in the national parks of England and Wales', *Environment and Planning A* 21: 1229–40

Brotherton, D.I. (1992a) 'On the control of development by planning authorities', *Environment and Planning B: Planning and Design* 19: 465–78

Brotherton, D.I. (1992b) 'On the quantity and quality of planning applications', *Environment and Planning B: Planning and Design* 19: 337–57

Brown, A.J. (1972) *The Framework of Regional Economics in the United Kingdom*, Cambridge: Cambridge University Press

Brown, D.A.H. and Taylor, K. (1988) 'The future of Britain's rural land', *Geographical Journal* 154: 406–11

Brownill, S. (1988) 'The People's Plan for the Royal Docks: some contradictions in popular planning', *Planning Practice and Research* No. 4 (Spring): 15–21

Brownill, S. (1990) *Developing London's Docklands: Another Great Planning Disaster?*, London: Paul Chapman

Brundtland Report (1987) *Our Common Future* (World Commission on Environment and Development), Oxford: Oxford University Press

Brunivells, P. and Rodrigues, D. (1989) *Investing in Enterprise: A Comprehensive Guide to Inner City Regeneration and Urban Renewal*, Oxford: Blackwell

Brunskill, I. (1989) *The Regeneration Game: A Regional Approach to Regional Policy*, London: Institute for Public Policy Research

Bruton, M.J. (1980a) 'PAG revisited', *TPR* 48: 134–44

Bruton, M.J. (1980b) 'Public participation, local planning and conflicts of interest', *Policy and Politics* 8: 423–42

Bruton, M.J. (1982) 'The present-day role of the town planner in society', *Planning Outlook* 25: 81–8

Bruton, M.J. (1983) 'Local plans, local planning and development plan schemes in England, 1974–82', *TPR* 54: 4–23

Bruton, M.J. (1984) *The Spirit and Purpose of Planning*, London: Hutchinson

Bruton, M.J. (1985) *Introduction to Transportation Planning* (3rd edition), London: Hutchinson

Bruton, M.J. and Gore, A. (1981) 'Vacant urban land: South Wales survey questions some basic assumptions', *The Planner* 57: 34–5

Bruton, M.J. and Nicholson, D.J. (1983) 'Non-statutory local plans and supplementary planning guidance', *JPL* 1983: 432–43

Bruton, M.J. and Nicholson, D.J. (1984a) 'Local plans and planning in England', *Planning Outlook* 27, 1: 1–11

Bruton, M.J. and Nicholson, D.J. (1984b) 'The use of non-statutory local planning instruments in development control and section 36 appeals', *JPL* 1984: 552–65 and 633–8

Bruton, M.J. and Nicholson, D.J. (1985a) 'Local planning in practice: a review', *The Planner* 17, 12 (December): 14–17

Bruton, M.J. and Nicholson, D.J. (1985b) 'Supplementary planning guidance and local plans', *JPL* 1985: 837–44

Bruton, M.J. and Nicholson, D.J. (1985c) 'Strategic land use planning and the British development plan system', *TPR* 56: 21–41

Bruton, M.J. and Nicholson, D.J. (1987a) *Local Planning in Practice*, London: Hutchinson

Bruton, M.J. and Nicholson, D.J. (1987b) 'A future for development plans?', *JPL* 1987: 687–703

Bruton, M.J., Crispin, G., and Fidler, P.M. (1980) 'Local plans: public local inquiries', *JPL* 1980: 374–85

Bruton, M.J., Crispin, G., and Fidler, P.M. (1982a) *Local Plans: Public Local Inquiries: Final Report and Summary of Findings to the SSRC*, Birmingham: Department of Planning and Landscape, City of Birmingham Polytechnic

Bruton, M.J., Crispin, G., and Fidler, P.M. (1982b) 'Local plans: the role and status of the public local inquiry', *JPL* 1982: 276–86

Bruton, M.J., Crispin, G., and Fidler, P.M. (1983) 'The conduct and content of local plan inquiries', *JPL* 1983: 279–87

Bruton, M.J., Crispin, G., Fidler, P.M., and Firth, M. (1985) *Local Plans: Public Local Inquiries: A Supplementary Investigation of the London Experience: Final Report and Summary of Findings*, Birmingham: Department of Planning and Landscape, City of Birmingham Polytechnic

Bruton, M.J., Crispin, G., Fidler, P.M., and Hill, E.A. (1981–1982) *Local Plans, Public Local Inquiries: Research Reports* (8 vols), Birmingham: Department of Planning and Landscape, City of Birmingham Polytechnic

Bruton, M.J., Crispin, G., Fidler, P.M., and Hill, E.A. (1982) *Local Plans, Public Local Inquiries: Final Report and Summary of*

*Findings to the SSRC*, Birmingham: Department of Planning and Landscape, City of Birmingham Polytechnic

Buchanan, C.D. (1958) *Mixed Blessing: The Motor Car in Britain*, London: Leonard Hill

Buchanan, C.D. (1963) *Traffic in Towns* (Buchanan Report), London: HMSO

Budd, L. and Whimster, S. (eds) (1992) *Global Finance and Urban Living: A Study of Metropolitan Change*, London: Routledge

Budd, S. (1990) *The EEC – A Guide to the Maze* (3rd edition), London: Kogan Page

Bulpitt, J. (1983) *Territory and Power in the United Kingdom*, Manchester: Manchester University Press

Burbridge, V. (1990) *Review of Information on Rural Issues*, Central Research Unit Papers, Edinburgh: Scottish Office

Burns, W. (1983) *Personal Reflections of the Changing Planning System*, Cambridge: Department of Land Economy, University of Cambridge

Burton, A. and Johnson, R. (1976) *Public Participation in Planning: A Review of Experience in Scotland*, Glasgow: The Planning Exchange

Burton, T.P. (1989) 'Access to environmental information: the UK experience of water registers', *Journal of Environmental Law* 1: 192–208

Burton, T.P. (1992) 'The Council for the Protection of Rural England', *Planning Practice and Research* 7, 1 (Spring): 37–40

Business in the Community (1990) *Leadership in the Community: A Blueprint for Business Involvement in the 1990s*, London: Business in the Community

Business in the Community (1992a) *A Measure of Commitment: Guidelines for Measuring Environmental Performance*, London: Business in the Community

Business in the Community (1992b) *UK Waste Management: A Business in the Environment Working Party Report*, London: Business in the Community

Butler, S.M. (1981) *Enterprise Zones: Greening the Inner Cities*, London: Heinemann

Byrne, D. (1989) *Beyond the Inner City*, Milton Keynes: Open University Press

Byrne, D. (1992) 'The city', in Cloke

Byrne, S. (1989) *Planning Gain: An Overview – A Discussion Paper*, London: Royal Town Planning Institute

Cabinet Office (1988) *Action for Cities*, London: Cabinet Office

Cabinet Office (1989) *Progress on Cities*, London: Cabinet Office

Calder, A. (1971) *The People's War*, London: Panther

Callies, D.L. and Grant, M. (1991) 'Paying for growth and planning gain: an Anglo-American comparison of development conditions, impact fees and development agreements', *Urban Lawyer* 23: 221–48

Cameron, G.C. (1990) 'First steps in urban policy evaluation in the United Kingdom', *Urban Studies* 27: 475–95

Cameron, G.C., Monk, S., and Pearce, B.J. (1988) *Vacant Urban Land: A Literature Review*, London: DoE

Campbell, M. (ed.) (1990) *Local Economic Policy*, London: Cassell

Carley, M. (1990) 'Neighbourhood renewal in Glasgow: policy and practice', *Housing Review* 39 (March-April): 49–51

Carley, M. (1991) 'Business in urban regeneration partnerships: a case study in Birmingham', *Local Economy* 6: 100–15

Carlisle, G. (1987) 'Public involvement in the development control process', *The Planner* 73, 10 (October): 23–5

Carmichael, P. (1992) 'Is Scotland different? local government policy under Mrs Thatcher', *Local Government Policy Making* 18, 5 (May): 25–32

Carnwath Report (1989) *Enforcing Planning Control: Report by Robert Carnwath QC*, London: HMSO

Carnwath, R. (1991) 'The planning lawyer and the environment', *Journal of Environmental Law* 3: 57–67

Carnwath, R. (1992) 'Environmental enforcement: the need for a specialist court', *JPL* 1992: 799–808

Carson, R. (1951) *The Sea Around Us*, New York: Oxford University Press

Carson, R. (1962) *Silent Spring*, Harmondsworth: Penguin edition (1965)

Carter, C. and John, P. (1992) *A New Accord: Promoting Constructive Relations between Central and Local Government*, York: Joseph Rowntree Foundation

Carter, N., Brown, T., and Abbott, T. (1991) *The Relationship Between Expenditure-Based Plans and Development Plans*, Leicester: School of the Built Environment, Leicester Polytechnic

Carter, N., Brown, T., Abbott, T., and Robson, F. (1991) 'Local authorities as strategic enablers', *Planning Practice and Research* 6, 2 (Summer ): 25–30

Catalano, A. (1983) *A Review of Enterprise Zones*, London: CES Ltd

Catchpole, L. (1981) 'The Local Government, Planning and Land Act 1980 – The secretary of state may . . .', *JPL* 1981: 174–9

Caudle, D. (1987) 'Overcoming the inhibitors to inner city development', *JPL* 1987: 334–8

Central Housing Advisory Committee (1967) *The Needs of New Communities*, London: HMSO

Central Office of Information (1992a) *Planning (Aspects of Britain)*, London: HMSO

Central Office of Information (1992b) *Britain in the European Community (Aspects of Britain)*, London: HMSO

Central Policy Review Staff (1977) *Relations between Central Government and Local Authorities*, London: HMSO

Central Regional Council (1992) *All Change*, Stirling: The Council

Central Statistical Office (annual) *Annual Abstract of Statistics*, London: HMSO

Central Statistical Office (annual) *Regional Trends*, London: HMSO

Central Statistical Office (annual) *Social Trends*, London: HMSO

Centre for Environmental Studies (1970) *Observations on the Greater London Development Plan*, London: CES (reprinted in Cullingworth 1973)

Centre for Environmental Studies (1973) 'Education for planning', *Progress in Planning* 1: 1–100

Centre for Local Economic Strategies (1990) *Inner City Regeneration: A Local Authority Perspective*, Manchester: The Centre

Centre for Local Economic Strategies (1991) *City Centres, City Cultures: The Role of the Arts in the Revitalisation of Towns and Cities*, Manchester: The Centre

Centre for Local Economic Strategies (1992a) *Reforming the TECs: Towards a Strategy – Final Report of the CLES TEC/LEC Monitoring Project*, Manchester: The Centre

Centre for Local Economic Strategies (1992b) *Social Regeneration: Directions for Urban Policy in the 1990s*, Manchester: The Centre

Centre for Regional Economic and Social Research (1991) *City Challenge Working Paper: Some Preliminary Observations*, Sheffield: CRESR, Sheffield City Polytechnic

Cervero, R. (1990) 'Transit pricing research: a review and synthesis', *Transportation* 17: 117–39

Chalkley, B. (1992) 'Waterfront UDC – city lifeline or a drop in the ocean?', *Town and Country Planning* 61: 152–3

Champion, A.G. (1989) *Counterurbanisation: The Changing Pace and Nature of Population Deconcentration*, London: Edward Arnold

Champion, A.G. and Fielding, A.J. (eds) (1982) *Migration Processes and Patterns, Vol 1: Research Progress and Prospects*, London: Belhaven

Champion, A.G. and Green, A.E. (1992) 'Local economic performance in Britain during the late 1980s: the results of the third booming towns study', *Environment and Planning A*: 243–72

Champion, T. and Congdon, P. (1988) 'An analysis of the recovery of London's population change rate', *Built Environment* 13: 193–211

Champion, T. and Watkins, C. (1991) *People in the Countryside: Studies of Social Change in Rural Britain*, London: Paul Chapman

Chapman, D. and Larkham, P. (1992) *Discovering the Art of Relationship*, Birmingham: Faculty of the Built Environment, Birmingham Polytechnic

Chapman, R.A. and Greenway, J.R. (1980) *The Dynamics of Administrative Reform*, London: Croom Helm

Charles, HRH The Prince of Wales (1989) *A Vision of Britain – A Personal View of Architecture*, London: Doubleday

Chartered Institute of Transport (1990) *Paying for Progress: A Report on Congestion and Road Use Charges*, London: CIT

Chartered Institute of Transport (1991) *London's Transport: The Way Ahead*, London: CIT

Chartered Institute of Transport (1992) *Paying for Progress: A Report on Congestion and Road Use Charges: Supplementary Report*, London: CIT

Checkland, S.G. (1981) *The Upas Tree: Glasgow 1875–1975 and after 1975–1980*, Glasgow: University of Glasgow Press

Cherry, G.E. (1974) *The Evolution of British Town Planning*, London: Leonard Hill

Cherry, G.E. (1975) *National Parks and Access to the Countryside: Environmental Planning 1939–1969, Volume 2*, London: HMSO

Cherry, G.E. (1981) *Pioneers in British Planning*, London: Architectural Press

Cherry, G.E. (1982) *The Politics of Town Planning*, London: Longman

Cherry, G.E. (1984) 'Wilfred Burns, 1923–1984: a memorial note', *TPR* 55: 506–11

Cheshire, P. and Sheppard, S. (1989) 'British planning policy and access to housing: some empirical estimates', *Urban Studies* 26: 469–85

Chesman, G.R. (1991) 'Local authorities and the review of the definitive map under the Wildlife and Countryside Act 1981', *JPL* 1991: 611–14

Chief Planning Inspector (annual) *Annual Report*, London: HMSO

Chisholm, M. (1985) 'Better value for money? Britain's 1984 regional industrial package', *Environment and Planning C: Government and Planning* 3: 111–19

Chisholm, M. (1988) 'Regional development: the Reagan-Thatcher legacy', *Environment and Planning C: Government and Policy* 5: 197–218

Chisholm, M. and Kivell, P. (1987) *Inner City Waste Land: An Assessment of Government and Market Failure in Land Development*, London: Institute of Economic Affairs

Christensen, C. (1986) *The American Garden City*, Ann Arbor: UMI Research Press

Christensen, T. (1979) *Neighbourhood Survival*, Dorchester: Prism

Chubb, R.N. (1988) *Urban Land Markets in the United Kingdom*, London: HMSO

Church, A. (1988) 'Urban regeneration in London docklands: a five-year review', *Environment and Planning C: Government and Policy* 6: 187–208

Churchill, R., Warren, L.M., and Gibson, J. (eds) (1991) *Law, Policy and the Environment*, Oxford: Blackwell

Civic Trust (1974) *Pride of Place: A Manual for Those Wishing to Improve Their Surroundings*, London: The Trust

Civic Trust (1988) *Urban Wasteland Now*, London: The Trust

Civic Trust (1991) *Audit of the Environment*, London: The Trust

Clabon, S. and Chance, C. (1992) 'Legal profile: freedom of access to environmental information', *European Environment* 2, 3 (June): 24–5

Clark, D.M. (1992) *Rural Social Housing – Supply and Trends; A 1992 Survey of Affordable New Homes*, Cirencester: Association of Community Councils in Rural England

Clark, G. (1982) *Housing and Planning in the Countryside*, Taunton: Research Studies/Wiley

Clark, M. and Herington, J. (1988) *The Role of Environmental Impact Assessment in the Planning Process*, London: Mansell

Clark, M., Smith, D., and Blowers, A. (1992) *Waste Location: Spatial Aspects of Waste Management, Hazards, and Disposal*, London: Routledge

CLAS: *see* Commissioner for Local Administration in Scotland

Clawson, M. and Hall, P. (1973) *Land Planning and Urban Growth*, Baltimore: Johns Hopkins University Press

CLES: *see* Centre for Local Economic Strategies

Cloke, P. (1985) 'Counterurbanisation: a rural perspective', *Geography* 70: 13–23

Cloke, P. (ed.) (1988) *Policies and Plans for Rural People*, London: Allen and Unwin

Cloke, P. (ed.) (1992) *Policy and Change in Thatcher's Britain*, Oxford: Pergamon

Cloke, P. and Little, J. (1987) 'Officer-member relations in county-level policy making for rural areas: the case of the Gloucestershire structure plan', *Public Administration* 65: 25–43

Cloke, P. and Little, J. (1990) *The Rural State: Limits to Planning in Rural Society*, Oxford: Clarendon Press

Cloke, P. and Shaw, D. (1983) 'Rural settlement policies in structure plans', *TPR* 54: 338–54

Clout, H. and Wood, P. (eds) (1986) *London: Problems of Change*, London: Longman

Cochrane, A. (1991) 'The changing state of local government: restructuring for the 1990s', *Public Administration* 69: 281–302

Cochrane, A. and Clarke, A. (1990) 'Local enterprise boards: the short history of a radical initiative', *Public Administration* 68: 315–36

Cockburn, C. (1977) *The Local State*, London: Pluto

Cocks, R. (1991) 'First responses to the new "breach of condition" notice', *JPL* 1991: 409–18

Coleman, A. (1990) *Utopia on Trial* (2nd edition), London: Hilary Shipman (1st edition 1985)

Colenut, B. (1991) 'The London Docklands Development Corporation', in Keith and Rogers

Collins, M.P. (1989) 'A review of 75 years of planning education at UCL', *The Planner* 75, 6 (June): 18–22

Collins, M.P. and McConnell, S. (1988) *The Use of Local Plans for Effective Town and Country Planning: Report of a Research Project Funded by the Nuffield Foundation*, London: Bartlett School of Architecture and Planning, University College London

Collis, H. (1991) 'The pilot red route in London', *Traffic Engineering and Control* 32: 236–9

Commission for Local Administration in England (annual) *Annual Report*, London: The Commission

Commissioner for Local Administration in Scotland (annual) *Annual Report*, Edinburgh: HMSO

Commission for Local Adminstration in Wales (annual) *Annual Report*, Bridgend: The Commission

Commission for Racial Equality (1982) *Local Government and Racial Equality*, London: CRE

Commission of the European Communities (1990) *Green Paper on the Environment*, Brussels: EEC

Commission of the European Communities (1991a) *Europe 2000: Outlook for the Development of the Community's Territory*, Luxembourg: EEC

Commission of the European Communities (1991b) *Employment in Europe*, Luxembourg: EEC

Confederation of British Industry (1988) *Initiatives beyond Charity: Report of the CBI Task Force on Business and Urban Regeneration*, London: CBI

Confederation of British Industry (1989a) *The Capital at Risk: Transport in London Task Force Report*, London: CBI

Confederation of British Industry (1989b) *Trade Routes to the Future*, London: CBI

Consortium Developments (1985) *New Country Towns*, London: Consortium Developments

Coombes, M., Raybould, S., and Wong, C. (1992) *Developing Indicators to Assess the Potential for Urban Regeneration* (DoE Inner Cities Research Programme), London: HMSO

Coombes, T., Fidler, P., and Hathaway, A. (1992) 'South West regional planning review – towards a regional strategy', *TPR* 63: 426–9

Coon, A. (1981) *A Comparison of Rates of Development Plan Progress under the Old and New Planning Systems*, Glasgow: Glasgow School of Art

Coon, A. (1986) 'Local plan coverage in the UK', *The Planner* 72,1 (January): 28–30

Coon, A. (1988) 'Local plan provision: the record to date and prospects for the future', *The Planner* 74, 5 (May): 17–20

Coon, A. (1989) 'An assessment of Scottish development planning', *Planning Outlook* 32, 2: 77–85

Cooper, D.E. and Palmer, J.A. (eds) (1992) *The Environment in Question*, London: Routledge

Cooper, D.J. and Hopper, T.M. (1990) *Critical Accounts*, Basingstoke: Macmillan

Coopers & Lybrand (1984) *Streamlining the Cities: An Analysis of the Costs Involved in the Government's Proposal for Reorganising Local Government in the Six Metropolitan Counties*, London: Coopers & Lybrand

Coopers & Lybrand (1985) *Land Use Planning and the Housing Market: An Assessment*, London: Coopers & Lybrand

Coopers & Lybrand (1986) *The Accommodation Needs of Modern Industry: Key Findings and Policy Issues*, London: Coopers & Lybrand

Coopers & Lybrand (1987) *Land Use Planning and Indicators of Housing Demand*, London: Coopers & Lybrand

Cope, D.R., Hills, P., and James, P. (1984) *Energy Policy and Land Use Planning: An International Perspective*, Oxford: Pergamon

Corfield, F.V. (1959) *Compensation and the Town and Country Planning Act*, London: Solicitors Law Stationery Society

Cornford, J. and Gillespie, A. (1992) 'The coming of the wired city? the recent development of cable in Britain', *TPR* 63: 243–64

Costonis, J.J. (1989) *Icons and Aliens: Law, Aesthetics, and Environmental Change*, Urbana-Champaign Illin.: University of Illinois Press

Couch, C. (1990) *Urban Renewal: Theory and Practice*, London: Macmillan

Coulson, A. (1990) 'Evaluating local economic policy', in Campbell

Council of Europe (1989) *European Campaign for the Countryside: Conclusion and Declarations*, Strasbourg: The Council

Council of Europe (1991) *The Bern Convention of Nature Conservation*, Strasbourg: The Council

Council of Europe (1992) *The European Urban Charter*, Strasbourg: Council of Europe Standing Conference of Local and Regional Authorities of Europe

Countryside Commission (annual) *Annual Report*, Cheltenham: The Commission

Countryside Commission (1970a) *The Planning of the Coastline*, Cheltenham: The Commission

Countryside Commission (1970b) *The Coastal Heritage*, Cheltenham: The Commission

Countryside Commission (1976) *The Broads: A Consultation Paper*, Cheltenham: The Commission

Countryside Commission (1978) *Areas of Oustanding Natural Beauty: Report of a One Day Conference*, Cheltenham: The Commission

Countryside Commission (1984a) *A Better Future for the Uplands*, Cheltenham: The Commission

Countryside Commission (1984b) *The Broads: A Review – Conclusions and Recommendations*, Cheltenham: The Commission

Countryside Commission (1987) *Enjoying the Countryside: Priorities for Action*, Cheltenham: The Commission

Countryside Commission (1989) *Planning for a Greener Countryside*, Cheltenham: The Commission

Countryside Commission (1990a) *Areas of Outstanding Natural Beauty: A Policy Statement*, Cheltenham: The Commission

Countryside Commission (1990b) *Planning Tools: Implementing Countryside Planning Policies in Metropolitan Areas through the Planning System*, Cheltenham: The Commission

Countryside Commission (1991) *Heritage Coasts: Policies and Priorities*, Cheltenham: The Commission

Countryside Commission (1992) *Enjoying the Countryside: Policies for People*, Cheltenham: The Commission

Countryside Commission and Nature Conservancy Council (1990) *Countryside and Nature Conservation Issues in District Plans*, Cheltenham: The Commission

Countryside Commission for Scotland (annual) *Annual Report*, Redgorton, Perth: CCS

Countryside Commission for Scotland (1974) *A Park System for Scotland*, Redgorton, Perth: CCS

Countryside Commission for Scotland (1978) *Scotland's Scenic Heritage*, Redgorton, Perth: CCS

Countryside Commission for Scotland (1987) *A Park System and Scenic Conservation in Scotland*, Redgorton, Perth: CCS

Countryside Commission for Scotland (1990) *The Mountain Areas of Scotland*, Redgorton, Perth: CCS

County Planning Officers' Society (1985) *Improving the Development Plan System*, CPOS

County Planning Officers' Society (1986) *The Future of Development Plans: Response to the DoE Consultation Paper*, CPOS

County Planning Officers' Society (1990) *Regional Guidance and Regional Planning Conferences*, CPOS

County Planning Officers' Society (1991) *Regional Guidance and Regional Planning Conferences {Progress Report}*, CPOS

County Planning Officers' Society (1992a) *Opencast Coalmining Statistics*, CPOS (published annually by Durham County Council)

County Planning Officers' Society (1992b) Metropolitan Planning Officers' Society, and District Planning Officers' Society, *Planning in the Urban Fringe: Final Report of the Joint Special Advisory Group*, CPOS, Middlesbrough: Department of Environment, Development and Transportation, Cleveland County Council

County Planning Officers' Society (1993) *Planning for Sustainability*, CPOS, Winchester: County Planning Department, Hampshire County Council

Cousins Stephens Associates (1991) *Constraints on the Growth of Small Firms: A Report on a Survey of Small Firms by Aston Business School*, London: Department of Trade and Industry

Cowie, H. (1985) *The Phoenix Partnership: Urban Regeneration in the 21st Century*, London: National Council of Building Material Producers

Cox, A. (1980) 'Continuity and discontinuity in conservative urban policy', *Urban Law and Policy* 3: 269-92

Cox, A. (1992) 'The limits of central government intervention in the land and development market: the case of the Land Commission', *Policy and Politics* 8: 267-84

Cox, G. and Lowe, P. (1983a) 'Countryside politics: goodbye to goodwill?', *Political Quarterly* 54: 268-82

Cox, G. and Lowe, P. (1983b) 'A battle not a war', in Gilg

Cox, G., Lowe, P., and Winter, M. (1986) *Agriculture, People and Policies*, London: Allen and Unwin

Cox, G., Lowe, P., and Winter, M. (1990) *The Voluntary Principle in Conservation*, Chichester: Packard

Cox, K.R. and Mair, A. (1988) 'Locality and community in the politics of local economic development', *Annals of the Association of American Geographers* 78: 307-25

CPOS: *see* County Planning Officers' Society

CPRE (1988) *Welcome Homes: Housing Supply from Unallocated Land*, London: The Council

CPRE (1990a) *From White Paper to Green Future*, London: The Council

CPRE (1990b) *Our Finest Landscapes: CPRE Submission to the National Parks Review Panel*, London: The Council

CPRE (1991a) *South East Regional Planning Guidance: A Submission by the CPRE*, London: The Council

CPRE (1991b) *Development Plan Regulations: Comments on Government Proposals*, London: The Council

CPRE (1992a) *Campaigners' Guide to Using EC Environmental Law*, London: The Council

CPRE (1992b) *Campaigners' Guide to Local Plans*, London: The Council

CPRE (1992c) *Our Common Home – Housing Development and the South East's Environment*, London: The Council

CPRE (1992d) *Transport and the Environment: CPRE's Submission to the Royal Commission on Environmental Pollution*, London: The Council

CPRE (1992e) *Where Motor Car is Master*, London: The Council

CPRE (1993) *Index of National Planning Policies*, London: The Council

CPRW (1990) *How Green Was My Valley: The Case for Defining Wales' First Statutory Green Belts*, Welshpool: The Council

Crawford, C. (1989) 'Profitability and its role in planning decisions', *Journal of Environmental Law* 1: 221-44

CRE: *see* Commission for Racial Equality

Cripps, J. (1977) *Accommodation for Gypsies: A Report on the Working of the Caravan Sites Act 1968*, London: HMSO

Crispin, G., Fidler, P., and Nadin, V. (1985) *The Process of Local Plan Adoption and Inspectors' Recommendations on Local Plans, Final Report to the DoE, Vol 1: Main Findings; Vol 2: Case Studies*, Coventry: Coventry Polytechnic

Cross, D. (1992) 'Regional planning guidance for East Anglia', *TPR* 63: 419-22

Cross, D.C. and Bristow, R. (eds) (1983) *English Structure Planning*, London: Pion

Crossman, R. (1975-1977) *The Diaries of a Cabinet Minister* (3 vols), London: Hamilton/Cape

Crouch, C. and Marquand, D. (eds) (1989) *The New Centrism: Britain out of Step with Europe?*, Oxford: Blackwell

Cuddy, M. and Hollingsworth, M. (1985) 'The review process in land availability studies: bargaining positions for builders and planners', in Barrett and Healey

Cullinane, S. (1992) 'Attitudes towards the car in the UK: some implications for policies on congestion and the environment', *Transportation Research* 26A: 291-301

Cullingworth, J.B. (1960) *Housing Needs and Planning Policy: A Restatement of the Problems of Housing Need and 'Overspill' in England and Wales*, London: Routledge and Kegan Paul

Cullingworth, J.B. (1979) *New Towns Policy: Environmental Planning 1939-1969, Volume 3*, London: HMSO

Cullingworth, J.B. (1981) *Land Values, Compensation and Betterment: Environmental Planning 1939-1969, Volume 4*, London: HMSO

Cullingworth, J.B. (1986) 'Groping for a national urban policy: the case of Canada', *Planning Perspectives* 1: 96-106

Cullingworth, J.B. (1987) *Urban and Regional Planning in Canada*, New Brunswick, N.J.: Transaction

Cullingworth, J.B. (1993) *The Political Culture of Planning: American Land Use Planning in Comparative Perspective*, New York and London: Routledge

Cullingworth, J.B. (ed.) (1973) *Planning for Change* (vol. 3 of *Problems of an Urban Society*), London: Allen and Unwin

Cullingworth, J.B. (ed.) (1990) *Energy, Land, and Public Policy* (Energy Policy Studies vol. 5), New Brunswick, N.J.: Transaction

Cullingworth Report (1967) *Scotland's Older Houses* (Report of the Scottish Housing Advisory Committee, Subcommittee on Unfit Housing in Scotland), Edinburgh: HMSO

Cullingworth, J.B. and Karn, V.A. (1968) *The Ownership and Management of Housing in the New Towns*, London: HMSO

Cunningham, I. (1991) *Forestry Expansion – A Study of Technical, Economic, and Ecological Factors*, Edinburgh: Forestry Commission

Curl, J.S. (1977) *The Erosion of Oxford*, Oxford: Oxford Illustrated Press

Curry, N. (1985) 'Countryside recreation sites policy', *TPR* 56: 70-90

Curry, N. (1992a) 'Nature conservation, countryside strategies and strategic planning', *Journal of Environmental Management* 35: 79-91

Curry, N. (1992b) 'Controlling development in the national parks of England and Wales', *TPR* 63: 107-21

Curry, N. (1993) 'Negotiating gains for nature conservation in planning practice', *Planning Practice and Research* 8, 2 (April): 10–15

Dales, J.H. (1968) *Pollution, Property and Prices*, Toronto: University of Toronto Press

Dalziel, M. and Rowan-Robinson, J. (1986) 'Resurrecting the two-price system for land', *JPL* 1986: 409–15

Damer, S. and Hague, C. (1971) 'Public participation in planning: evolution and problems', *Town Planning Review* 42: 217–24

Damesick, P.J. (1986) 'The M25 – a new geography of development?', *Geographical Journal* 152: 155–60

Danson, M.W., Lloyd, M.G., and Newlands, D. (1989) 'Rural Scotland and the rise of Scottish Enterprise', *Planning Practice and Research* 4, 3 (Winter): 13–17

Danson, M.W., Lloyd, M.G., and Newlands, D. (1992) *The Role of Regional Development Agencies in Economic Regeneration*, London: Jessica Kingsley

Darke, R. (1979) 'Public participation and state power: the case of South Yorkshire', *Policy and Politics* 7: 337–55

Darke, R. (1981) 'Attitudes towards public participation', *Local Government Studies*, (May-June): 61–6

Darley, G., Hall, P., and Lock, D. (1991) *Tomorrow's New Communities*, York: Joseph Rowntree Foundation

Daunton, M.J. (1987) *A Property Owning Democracy?*, London: Faber

Davidoff, P. and Reiner, T.A. (1962) 'A choice theory of planning', *Journal of the American Institute of Planners* 28: 103–15 (also reprinted in Faludi 1973a)

Davies, C., Pritchard, D., and Austin, L. (1992) *Planscan Scotland: A Study of Development Plans in Scotland*, London: Royal Society for the Protection of Birds

Davies, H.W.E. (1992) 'Britain 2000: the impact of Europe for planning and practice', *The Planner, TCPSS Proceedings* 78, 21 (November): 21–2

Davies, H.W.E. and Edwards, D. (1989) *Planning Control in Western Europe*, London: HMSO

Davies, H.W.E., Edwards, D., and Rowley, A.R. (1984) 'The relevance of development control', *TPR* 51: 5–24

Davies, H.W.E., Edwards, D., and Rowley, A.R. (1986a) *The Relationship between Development Plans, Development Control, and Appeals*, Reading: Department of Land Management and Development, University of Reading

Davies, H.W.E., Edwards, D., and Rowley, A.R. (1986b) 'The relationship between development plans and development control', *The Planner* 72, 10: 11–15.

Davies, H.W.E., Edwards, D., and Rowley, A.R. (1989) *The Approval of Reserved Matters following Outline Planning Permission* (DoE Development Control Study Series), London: HMSO

Davies, H.W.E., Edwards, D., Roberts, C., Rosborough, L., and Sales, R. (1986) *The Relationship between Development Plans and Appeals*, Reading: Department of Land Management and Development, University of Reading

Davies, H.W.E., Rowley, A.R., Edwards, D., Blom-Cooper, A., Roberts, C., Rosborough, L., and Tilley, R. (1986) *The Relationship between Development Plans and Development Control*, Reading: Department of Land Management and Development, University of Reading

Davies, J.G. (1972) *The Evangelistic Bureaucrat: A Study of a Planning Exercise in Newcastle-upon-Tyne*, London: Tavistock

Davies, L. (1993) 'Aspects of quality', *The Planner* 79, 3: 14–16

Davies, R.L. and Campion, A.G. (1983) *The Future of the City Centre*, Institute of British Geographers, London: Academic Press

Davis, K.C. (1969) *Discretionary Justice: A Preliminary Inquiry*, Baton Rouge: Louisiana State University Press

Davison, I. (1990) *Good Design in Housing: A Discussion Paper*, London: House Builders Federation/Royal Institute of British Architects

Davison, R.C. (1938) *British Unemployment Policy: The Modern Phase since 1930*, London: Longman

Dawson, A.H. (1981) 'The idea of the region and the 1975 reorganization of Scottish local government', *Public Administration* 59: 279–93

Dawson, A.H. (1984) 'Local government and the idea of the region: a comment on the present situation in Scotland', *Scottish Geographical Magazine* 100: 113–22

Dawson, D. (1985) 'Economic change and the changing role of local government', in Loughlin, Gelfand, and Young

Dawson, J. (1992) 'European city networks: experiments in trans-national urban collaboration', *The Planner* 78, 1 (10 January): 7–9

Dawson, J. and Parkinson, M. (1991) 'Merseyside Development Corporation 1981–1989: physical regeneration, accountability, and economic challenge', in Keith and Rogers

Dawson, J. and Walker, C. (1990) 'Mitigating the social costs of private development: the experience of linkage programmes in the United States', *TPR* 61: 157–70

Day, G. and Hedger, M. (1990) 'Mid Wales: missing the point', *Urban Studies* 27: 283–90

Deakin, N. and Edwards, J. (1993) *The Enterprise Culture and the Inner City*, London: Routledge

Dear, M. and Scott, A.J. (eds) (1981) *Urbanization and Urban Planning in a Capitalist Society*, London: Methuen

Debenham, Tewson and Chinnocks (1988) *Planning Gain: Community Benefit or Commercial Bribe?*, London: Debenham, Tewson and Chinnocks

de Groot, L. (1992) 'City challenge: competing in the urban regeneration game', *Local Economy* 7: 196–209

Delafons, J. (1990a) *Development Impact Fees and Other Devices*, Berkeley, Calif.: Institute of Urban and Regional Development, University of California at Berkeley

Delafons, J. (1990b) *Aesthetic Control: A Report on Methods Used in the USA to Control the Design of Buildings*, Berkeley, Calif.: Institute of Urban and Regional Development, University of California at Berkeley

Delafons, J. (1991a) 'Planning in the USA – aesthetic control', *The Planner* 77, 16 (10 May): 7–8

Delafons, J. (1991b) 'Planning in the USA – paying for development', *The Planner* 77, 20 (7 June): 8–9

Denington Report (1966) *Our Older Homes: A Call for Action* (Central Housing Advisory Committee), London: HMSO

Dennington, V.N. and Chadwick, M.J. (1983) 'Derelict land and waste land: Britain's neglected land resource', *Journal of Environmental Management* 16: 229–39

Dennis, N. (1970) *People and Planning*, London: Faber

Dennis, N. (1972) *Public Participation and Planners' Blight*, London: Faber

Derby City Council (1989) *Sir Francis Ley Industrial Park – Simplified Planning Zoning: The First Twelve Months*, Derby: The Council

Derby City Council (1991) *Sir Francis Ley Industrial Park – Simplified Planning Zoning: The First Three Years*, Derby: The Council

De Soissons, M. (1988) *Welwyn Garden City*, Cambridge: Publications for Companies

Devon County Council (1991) *Traffic Calming Guidelines*, Exeter: The Council

Diamond, D. (1979) 'The uses of strategic planning: the example of the National Planning Guidelines in Scotland', *TPR* 50: 18–25

Diamond, D. and Spence, N. (1989) *Infrastructure and Industrial Costs in British Industry*, London: HMSO

Dickins, I. (1992) 'Junior jobs, planning graduates, and student recruitment', *The Planner* 78, 8: 17–18

Dickins, I. and Fidler, P. (1984) *Junior Employment in Town Planning*, Working Paper 16, Birmingham: Department of Town Planning, City of Birmingham Polytechnic

Dickins, I. and Jones, S. (1990) *Employment in Town Planning and Related Areas, and the Supply of Recognised Graduates in Town Planning* (Reports of the RTPI Study on Monitoring Supply, Demand and Employment Trends in the Town Planning Profession), London: RTPI

Disability Unit (annual) *Annual Report*, London: DoT

Distributive Trades Economic Development Committee (1988) *The Future of the High Street*, London: HMSO

District Planning Officers' Society (1982) *The Local Plan System: The Need for Radical Change*, DPOS

District Planning Officers' Society (1986) *The Future of the Planning System*, DPOS

District Planning Officers' Society (1992) *Affordable Housing*, DPOS

Dix, G. and Tarn, J.N. (1985) *Design and Conservation in the City*, Liverpool: Liverpool University Press

Dobry Report (1974a) *Control of Demolition*, London: HMSO

Dobry Report (1974b) *Review of the Development Control System: Interim Report*, London: HMSO

Dobry Report (1975) *Review of the Development Control System: Final Report*, London: HMSO

Dobson, A. (1990) *Green Political Thought: An Introduction*, London: Harper Collins

Docklands Consultative Committee (1985) *Four Year Review of the LDDC*, London: DCC

Docklands Consultative Committee (1990) *The Docklands Experiment: A Critical Review of Eight Years of the London Docklands Development Corporation*, London: DCC

Docklands Consultative Committee (1991) *Ten Years of Docklands: How the Cake Was Cut*, London: DCC

Docklands Consultative Committee (1992) *All That Glitters is Not Gold: A Critical Assessment of Canary Wharf*, London: DCC

Docklands: *see also* London Docklands

Doern, G.B. (1993) 'The UK citizen's charter: origins and implementation in three agencies', *Policy and Politics* 21: 17–29

Donnison, D. and Eversley, D.E.C. (1973) *London: Urban Patterns, Problems and Policies*, London: Sage

Donnison, D. and Middleton, A. (eds) (1987) *Regenerating the Inner City: Glasgow's Experience*, London: Routledge

Dower Report (1945) *National Parks in England and Wales*, Cmd 6628, London: HMSO

Downs, A. (1992) *Stuck in Traffic: Coping with Peak-Hour Traffic Congestion*, Washington, DC: Brookings Institution/Lincoln Institute of Land Policy

DPOS: *see* District Planning Officers' Society

Draper, P. (1977) *Creation of the DoE: A Study of the Merger of Three Departments to Form the Department of the Environment*, Civil Service Studies 4, London: HMSO

Drewry, G. (ed.) (1989) *The New Select Committees: A Study of the 1979 Reforms*, Oxford: Clarendon Press

Drewry, G. and Butcher, T. (1991) *The Civil Service Today* (2nd edition), Oxford: Blackwell

Drucker, H. *et al.* (eds) (1986) *Developments in British Politics 2*, London: Macmillan

Duncan, S. (1989) 'Development gains and housing provision in Britain and Sweden', *Transactions of the Institute of British Geographers* N.S. 14: 157–72

Duncan, S. and Goodwin, M. (1985) 'The local state and local economic policy: why the fuss?', *Policy and Politics* 13: 227–53

Duncan, S. and Goodwin, M. (1987) *The Local State and Uneven Development: Behind the Local Government Crisis*, New York: St Martin's Press

Dunleavy, P. and Rhodes, R.A.W. (1986) 'Government beyond Whitehall', in Drucker *et al.*

Dunlop, J. (1976) 'The examination in public of structure plans: an emerging procedure', *JPL* 1976: 8–17

Dunmore, K. (1992) *Planning for Affordable Housing*, London: Institute of Housing

Dyer, S. (1991) *Mobile Homes in England and Wales: Report of a Postal Survey of Local Authorities*, London: HMSO

East Midlands Regional Planning Forum (1992) *Regional Strategy for the East Midlands*, Nottingham: The Forum

Economic and Transport Planning Group (1989) *Telecommunications in Rural England*, Salisbury: Rural Development Commission

Economist Intelligence Unit (1975) *Housing Land Availability in the South East: Report to the DoE*, London: Economist Intelligence Unit

ECOTEC Research and Consulting Ltd (1987) 'Review of Data Sources for Urban Policy: Report to the DoE', London: DoE Library [unpublished, but available at the Library, 2 Marsham Street, London SW1]

ECOTEC Research and Consulting Ltd (1990) *Dynamics of the Rural Economy: Final Report to the DoE*, Birmingham: ECOTEC

Edwards, A. (1981) *The Design of Suburbia — A Critical Study in Environmental History*, London: Pembridge

Edwards, D. (1986) *Monitoring the Operation of the Planning System: Monitoring of the Planning System by Local Authorities*, Reading: Department of Land Management and Development, University of Reading

Edwards, J. and Batley, R. (1978) *The Politics of Positive Discrimination*, London: Tavistock

Edwards, J. and Deakin, N. (1992) 'Privatism and partnership in urban regeneration', *Public Administration* 70: 359–68

Edwards, L. and Rowan-Robinson, J. (1980) 'Whatever happened to the planning inquiry commission?', *JPL* 1980: 307–15

Edwards, M. (1990) 'What is needed from public policy?', in Healey and Nabarro

Edwards Report (1991) *Fit for the Future: Report of the National Parks Review Panel*, Cheltenham: Countryside Commission

Elcock, H. (1989) *Local Government* (2nd edition), London: Methuen

Elkin, S.L. (1974) *Politics and Land Use Planning: The London Experience*, Cambridge: Cambridge University Press

Elkin, T., McLaren, D., and Hillman, M. (1991) *Reviving the City: Towards Sustainable Development*, London: Policy Studies Institute

Elkington, J. (1990) *The Environmental Audit: A Green Filter for Company Policies, Plants, Processes and Products*, London: SustainAbility/WWF

Elliott, D. (1992) 'Yes, we have no policy', *Town and Country Planning* 61: 195–6

Elliott, S., Lomas, G., and Riddell, A. (1984) *Community Projects Review*, London: DoE

Elson, M.J. (1986) *Green Belts: Conflict Mediation in the Urban Fringe*, London: Heinemann

Elson, M.J. (1987) 'The urban fringe – will less farming mean more leisure?', *The Planner* 73, 10 (October): 19–22

Elson, M.J. (1990) *Negotiating the Future: Planning Gain in the 1990s*, Gloucester: ARC Ltd

Elsworth, S. (1984) *Acid Rain*, London: Pluto

Emmerich, M. and Peck, J. (1992) 'Strategy versus short-termism in the new training system: a tale of two TECs', *Local Government Policy Making* 19: 18–25

Emms, J.E. (1980) 'The Community Land Act: a requiem', *JPL* 1980: 78–86

Employment Department (1992) *People, Jobs and Opportunity*, Cm 1810, London: HMSO

Employment Department Group (1992) *The Government's Expenditure Plans 1992–1993 to 1994–1995*, Cm 1906, London: HMSO

English Heritage (annual) *Annual Report and Accounts*, London: HBMC

English Heritage (1990) *The Conservation Areas of England*, London: HBMC

English Heritage (1992a) *Development Plan Policies for Archaeology*, London: HBMC

English Heritage (1992b) *Managing England's Heritage: Setting our Priorities for the 1990s*, London: HBMC

English Heritage (1992c) *Consultation Paper on the Implementation of Changes in the Role of English Heritage in Greater London*, London: HBMC

English Heritage (1992d) *Buildings at Risk: A Sample Survey*, London: HBMC

English Historic Towns Forum (1992) *Townscape in Trouble: Conservation Areas – The Case for Change*, Bath: The Forum

English, J., Madigan, R., and Norman, P. (1976) *Slum Clearance: The Social and Administrative Context*, London: Croom Helm

English Nature (1992a) *Strategic Planning and Sustainable Development: An Informal Consultation Paper*, Peterborough: English Nature

English Nature (1992b) *Progress '92*, Peterborough: English Nature

English Tourist Board (annual) *English Heritage Monitor*, London: The Board

Erikson, R.A. and Syms, P.M. (1986) 'The effects of enterprise zones on local property markets', *Regional Studies* 20: 1–4

Esher, L. (1981) *A Broken Wave: The Rebuilding of England 1940–1980*, London: Allen Lane (Penguin edition 1983)

Essex County Council (1973) *Design Guide for Residential Areas*, Chelmsford: The Council

Etherington, D. (1987) 'Local economic strategies and area based initiatives – another view of improvement areas', *Local Economy* 2: 31–7

Evans, A.W. (1988) *No Room! No Room! The Costs of the British Town and Country Planning System*, London: Institute of Economic Affairs

Evans, A.W. (1991) 'Rabbit hutches on postage stamps: planning, development and political economy', *Urban Studies* 28: 853–70

Evans, A.W. and Eversley, D. (eds) (1980) *The Inner City: Employment and Industry*, London: Heinemann

Evans, B. (1985) *Public Involvement in the Planning Process: A Greater London Case Study*, London: Town and Country Planning Association

Evans, D. (1992) *A History of Nature Conservation*, London: Routledge

Evans, R. (1991) 'Training and enterprise councils – an initial assessment', *Regional Studies* 25: 173–84

Eve, Gerald, Chartered Surveyors (1992) *The Relationship between House Prices and Land Supply* (DoE Planning Research Programme), London: HMSO

Eve, Grimley J.R. (1992) *Use of Planning Agreements*, London: HMSO

Everest, D.A. (1990) 'The provision of expert advice to government on environmental matters: the role of advisory committees', *Science and Public Affairs* 4: 17–40

Eversley, D.E.C. (1973) *The Planner in Society*, London: Faber

Eversley, D.E.C. (1986) *Tillingham Hall Inquiry: Proof of Evidence Given on Behalf of the CPRE*, London: CPRE

Eversley, Lord (1910) *Commons, Forests and Footpaths: The Story of the Battle during the Past Forty-five Years for Public Rights over the Commons, Forests and Footpaths of England and Wales*, London: Cassell

Everton, A.R. and Hughes, D.J. (1987) 'Minerals subject plans in action', *JPL* 1987: 174–84

Eyre, E. (1987) 'Planning and the Local Government (Access to Information) Act 1985', *JPL* 1987: 311–23

Fagence, M. (1977) *Citizen Participation in Planning*, Oxford: Pergamon

Fainstein, S.S. and Fainstein, N.I. (1985) 'Citizen participation in local government', in Judd

Fairbrother, N. (1970) *New Lives, New Landscapes*, London: Architectural Press (Penguin edition, 1972)

Faludi, A. (1973a) *A Reader in Planning Theory*, Oxford: Pergamon

Faludi, A. (1973b) *Planning Theory*, Oxford: Pergamon

Faludi, A. (1986) 'Flexibility in US zoning: a European perspective', *Environment and Planning B: Planning and Design* 13: 255–78

Farquhar, J.Y. (1983) 'The policies of the European Community towards the environment – the "dangerous substances" directive', *JPL* 1983: 145–55

Fergusson, A. (1973) *The Sack of Bath: A Record and an Indictment*, Salisbury: Compton Russell

Fidler, P. (1987) 'Planning education and the demand for qualified planners', *The Planner* 73, 6: 46–7

Field, B. (1983) 'Local plans and local planning in Greater London', *TPR* 54: 24–40

Fielder, S. (1986) *Monitoring the Operation of the Planning System: The National Dimension*, Reading: Department of Land Management and Development, University of Reading

Fielding, T. and Halford, S. (1990) *Patterns and Processes of Urban Change in the United Kingdom* (DoE Reviews of Urban Research), London: HMSO

Fitzsimmons, D. (1990) 'Training for planning', *The Planner* 76, 14 (13 April): 29–30

Fladmark, J.M. (1988) *The Countryside around Towns: A Scottish Programme of Partnership and Action*, Redgorton, Perth: Countryside Commission for Scotland

Fleming, P.W. (1990) *Caring for Cities – Town Planning's Role*, London: RTPI

Fleming, S.C. (1984) *Housebuilders in an Area of Growth: Negotiating the Built Environment of Central Berkshire*, Reading: Department of Geography, University of Reading

Fleming, S.C. and Short, J.R. (1984) 'Committee rules OK? an examination of planning committee action on officer recommendations', *Environment and Planning A* 16: 965–73

Flowers Report (1981) *Coal and the Environment*, London: HMSO

Flynn, A., Gray, A., Jenkins, W., and Rutherford, B. (1988) 'Implementing the "next steps"', *Public Administration* 66: 439–45

Flynn, N., Leach, S., and Vielba, C. (1985) *Abolition or Reform? The GLC and the Metropolitan County Councils*, London: Allen and Unwin

Flynn, N. and Walsh, K. (1988) *Competitive Tendering*, Birmingham: Institute of Local Government Studies, University of Birmingham

FoE: *see* Friends of the Earth

Foley, D. (1963) *Controlling London's Growth: Planning the Great Wen 1940–1960*, Berkeley, Calif.: University of California Press

Foley, D. (1972) *Governing the London Region: Reorganisation and Planning in the 1960s*, Berkeley, Calif.: University of California Press

Foley, P. (1992) 'Local economic policy and job creation: a review of evaluation studies', *Urban Studies* 29: 557–98

Forbes, J. (1984) 'A view of planning in Scotland 1974 to 84', *Scottish Geographical Magazine* 100: 104–12

Fordham, R. (1989) 'Planning gain: towards its codification', *JPL* 1989: 577–84

Fordham, R. (1990) 'Planning consultancy: can it serve the public interest?', *Public Administration* 68: 243–8

Forester, J. (1980) 'Critical theory and planning practice', *Journal of the American Planning Association* 46: 275–86

Forester, J. (1982) 'Planning in the face of power', *Journal of the American Planning Association* 48: 67–80

Forester, J. (ed.) (1985) *Critical Theory and Public Life*, Cambridge, Mass.: MIT Press

Forestry Commission (annual) *Annual Report and Accounts*, London: HMSO

Forestry Commission (series) *Bulletins*, London: HMSO

Forestry Commission (1984) *Broadleaves in Britain: A Consultative Paper*, Edinburgh: The Commission

Forestry Commission (1986) *Forestry in the Environment*, Edinburgh: The Commission

Forestry Commission (1989) *Forest Nature Reserves*, Edinburgh: The Commission

Forestry Commission (1990a) *Forest Nature Conservation Guidelines*, London: HMSO

Forestry Commission (1990b) *The Future for the New Forest*, London: HMSO

Forestry Commission (1990c) *Scotland's Forest Heritage*, London: HMSO

Forrest, R. and Murie, A. (1990) 'A dissatisfied state: consumer preferences and council housing in Britain', *Urban Studies* 27: 617–35

Forrester, A., Lansley, S., and Pauley, R. (1985) *Beyond our Ken*, London: Fourth Estate

Forshaw, J.H. and Abercrombie, P. (1943) *County of London Plan*, London: Macmillan

Forsyth, J. (1992) 'Tower Hamlets: setting up a regeneration corporation in Bethnal Green', in Bailey and Barker

Fothergill, S. and Gudgin, G. (1982) *Unequal Growth: Urban and Regional Change in the UK*, London: Heinemann

Fothergill, S. and Guy, N. (1990) *Retreat from the Regions: Corporate Change and the Closure of Factories*, London: Jessica Kingsley/ Regional Studies Association

Fothergill, S., Kitson, M., and Monk, S. (1985) *Urban Industrial Change: The Causes of the Urban-Rural Contrast in Manufacturing Employment Change* (DoE), London: HMSO

Fothergill, S., Kitson, M., and Perry, M. (1987) *Property and Industrial Development*, London: Hutchinson

Foulsham, J. (1990) 'Women's needs and planning: a critical evaluation of recent local authority practice', in Montgomery and Thornley

Fowler, P.J. (1977) *Approaches to Archaeology*, London: Black

Francis Report (1971) *Report of the Committee on the Rent Acts*, Cmnd 4609, London: HMSO

Franks Report (1957) *Report of the Committee on Administrative Tribunals and Enquiries*, Cmnd 218, London: HMSO

Freestone, D. (1991) 'European Community environmental policy and law', in Churchill, Warren, and Gibson

Fried, M. (1969) 'Social differences in mental health', in Kosa, J., Antonovsky, A., and Zola, I.K., *Poverty and Health: a Sociological Analysis*, Cambridge, Mass.: Harvard University Press

Friedman, J. (1973) *Retracking America: A Theory of Transactive Planning*, New York: Doubleday

Friend, J.K. and Jessop, W.N. (1969) *Local Government and Strategic Choice*, London: Tavistock

Friends of the Earth (1990a) *An Illustrated Guide to Traffic Calming*, London: FoE

Friends of the Earth (1990b) *How Green is Britain: The Government's Environmental Record*, London: Hutchinson Radius

Friends of the Earth (1990c) *Stealing our Future: Friends of the Earth's Critique of 'This Common Inheritance'*, London: FoE

Friends of the Earth (1991a) *Disinheriting the Earth: Friends of the Earth's Progress Report on the Government's Inaction since the Publication of 'This Common Inheritance'*, London: FoE

Friends of the Earth (1991b) *Local Responses to 1989 Traffic Forecasts*, London: FoE

Friends of the Earth (1992a) *Dumping on our Countryside: A Survey of Damage to Key Designated Areas by Waste Disposal*, London: FoE

Friends of the Earth (1992b) *Less Traffic, Better Towns*, London: FoE

Frost, M. and Spence, N. (1993) 'Global city characteristics and Central London's employment', *Urban Studies* 30: 547–58

Fry, G.K. (1988) 'Outlining the next steps', *Public Administration* 66: 429–38

Fry, G.K., Flynn, A., Gray, A., Jenkins, W., and Rutherford, B. (1988) 'Symposium on improving management in government', *Public Administration* 66: 429–45

Fudge, C. (ed.) (1979) *Approaches to Local Planning*, Bristol: School for Advanced Urban Studies, University of Bristol

Fudge, C. (ed.) (1981) *Approaches to Local Planning (2)*, Bristol: School for Advanced Urban Studies, University of Bristol

Fudge, C., Lambert, C., and Underwood, J. (1982) 'Local plans; approaches, preparation and adoption', *The Planner* 68 (March/ April): 52–3

Fyson, A. (1992) 'Achieving quality', *The Planner* 78, 10 (15 May): 3

Fyson, A. (1993) 'A proper plan in prospect', *The Planner* 79, 4 (April 1993): 3

Gahagan, M. (1992) 'City challenge: a solution to regeneration through partnership?', in Bailey and Barker

Gans, H.J. (1968) *People and Plans: Essays on Urban Problems and Solutions*, New York: Basic Books

Garner, J. (1989) 'Rights of way: modifications to the definitive map', *Journal of Environmental Law* 1: 209–20

Garside, P.L. (1988) 'Unhealthy areas: town planning, eugenics and the slums, 1890–1945', *Planning Perspectives* 3: 24–46

Garside, P.L. and Hebbert, M. (eds) (1989) *British Regionalism 1900–2000*, London: Mansell

Gasson, R. (1990) 'Part-time farming and pluriactivity', in Britton

Gatenby, I. and Williams, C. (1992) 'Section 54A: the legal and practical implications', *JPL* 1992: 110–20

Geddes, P. (1915) *Cities in Evolution*, London: Benn

Gellner, E. (1975) 'A social contract in search of an idiom: the demise of the Danegeld state?', *Political Quarterly* 46: 127–52

Gentleman, H. (1993) *Counting Travellers in Scotland*, Edinburgh: Scottish Office

Gentleman, H. and Swift, S. (1971) *Scotland's Travelling People*, Edinburgh: HMSO

Georger, M. (1992) *The Land Use, Ecology, and Conservation of Broadland*, Chichester: Packard

Geraghty, P.J. (1992) 'Environmental assessment and the application of an expert systems approach', *TPR* 63: 123–42

Gibson, J. (1984) 'Marine nature reserves', *JPL* 1984: 699–706

Gibson, J. (1991) 'The integration of pollution control', in Churchill, Warren, and Gibson

Gibson, M.S. and Langstaff, M.J. (1982) *An Introduction to Urban Renewal*, London: Hutchinson

Gilbert, A. and Healey, P. (1985) *The Political Economy of Land: Urban Development in an Oil Economy*, Aldershot: Gower

Gilfoyle, I. (1978) 'Public participation: lessons from Cheshire', *Town and Country Planning* 48: 25–9

Gilg, A.W. (ed.) (1983) *Countryside Planning Yearbook 1983*, Norwich: Geo Books

Gilg, A.W. (ed.) (1986) *Countryside Planning Yearbook 1986*, Norwich: Geo Books

Gilg, A.W. (1988) *The International Year Book of Rural Planning*, London: Elsevier

Gilg, A.W., Briggs, D., Dilley, R., Furseth, O., and McDonald, G. (1991) *Progress in Rural Policy and Planning, Volume 1: 1991*, London: Belhaven

Gilg, A.W., Briggs, D., Dilley, R., Furseth, O., and McDonald, G. (1992) *Progress in Rural Policy and Planning, Volume 2: 1992*, London: Belhaven

Gillett, E. (1983) *Investment in the Environment: Planning and Transport Policies in Scotland*, Aberdeen: Aberdeen University Press

Gillingwater, D. (1992) 'Regional strategy for the East Midlands', *TPR* 63: 422–5

Ginsburg, L. (1956) 'Green belts in the Bible', *Journal of the Town Planning Institute* 42: 129–30

Glaister, S. (ed.) (1987) *Transport Subsidy*, Newbury: Policy Journals

Glaister, S. and Mulley, C. (1983) *Public Control of the British Bus Industry*, Aldershot: Gower

Glasgow Action (1991) *Towards a Great European City: A Final Progress Report*, Glasgow: Glasgow Action

Glass, R. (1959) 'The evaluation of planning: some sociological considerations', in Faludi 1973a

Glasson, B. and Booth, P. (1992) 'Negotiation and delay in the development control process', *TPR* 63: 63–78

Glasson, J. (1978) *An Introduction to Regional Planning* (2nd edition), London: Hutchinson

Glasson, J. (1992) 'The fall and rise of regional planning in the economically advanced nations', *Urban Studies* 29: 505–31

Gleave, S.D. (1992) *Financing Public Transport: How Does Britain Compare?*, (no publisher stated)

Glenny Consultants (1992) *Business Activity and Land Use Patterns in the North East Thames Corridor*, London: Department of Estate Management, University of East London

Goddard, J.B. and Champion, A.G. (1983) *The Urban and Regional Transformation of Britain*, London: Methuen

Goldsmith, M. (1980) *Politics, Planning and the City*, London: Hutchinson

Goldsmith, M. (1992) 'Local government', *Urban Studies* 29: 393–410

Goldsmith, M. and Newton, K. (1986) 'Central-local government relations: a bibliographical summary of the ESRC research initiative', *Public Administration* 64: 102–8

Goldsmith, W.W. (1982) 'Enterprise zones: if they work, we're in trouble', *International Journal of Urban and Regional Research* 6: 435–42

Goodchild, R.N. and Munton, R.J.C. (1985) *Development and the Landowner: An Analysis of the British Experience*, London: Allen and Unwin

Goodman, R. (1972) *After the Planners*, Harmondsworth: Penguin

Goodwin, M. (1991) 'Replacing a surplus population: the employment and housing policies of the London Docklands Development Corporation', in Allen and Hamnett

Goodwin, M. and Duncan, S. (1989) 'The crisis of local government: uneven development and the Thatcher administrations', in Mohan

Goodwin, P.B. (1989) 'The "rule of three" – a possible solution to the political problem of competing objectives for road pricing', *Traffic Engineering and Control* 30: 495–7

Goodwin, P., Hallett, S., Kenny, F., and Stokes, G. (1991) *Transport: The New Realism*, Oxford: Transport Studies Unit, University of Oxford

Gordon, G. (1986) *Regional Cities in the UK 1890–1980*, London: Harper and Row

Gosling Report (1968) *Report of the Footpaths Committee*, London: HMSO

Gottdiener, M. (1987) *The Decline of Urban Politics*, Newbury Park, Calif.: Sage

Gould, P.C. (1988) *Early Green Politics*, Sussex: Harvester Press

Gowers Report (1950) *Report of the Committee on Houses of Outstanding Historic and Architectural Interest*, London: HMSO

Graham, C. and Prosser, T. (eds) (1988) *Waiving the Rules: The Constitution under Thatcherism*, Milton Keynes: Open University Press

Graham, T. (1990) 'Planning Policy Guidance Note 1 and the presumption in favour of development', *JPL* 1990: 175–9

Graham, T. (1991) 'The interpretation of planning permissions and a matter of principle', *JPL* 1991: 104–12

Grant, J. (1977) *The Politics of Urban Transport Planning: An Analysis of Transportation Policy in Three UK County Boroughs between 1947 and 1974*, London: Earth Resources Research

Grant, J.S. (1987) 'Government agencies and the Highlands since 1945', *Scottish Geographical Magazine* 103: 95–9

Grant, M. (1975) 'Planning by agreement', *JPL* 1975: 501–8

Grant, M. (1978a) 'Developers' contributions and planning gains: ethics and legalities', *JPL* 1978: 8–15

Grant, M. (1978b) 'Planning, politics and the judges', *JPL* 1978: 512–23

Grant, M. (1979) 'Britain's Community Land Act: a post mortem', *Urban Law and Policy* 2: 359–73

Grant, M. (1982) *Urban Planning Law* (Supplement 1990), London: Sweet and Maxwell

Grant, M. (1989) *Permitted Development: The Use Classes Order 1987 and General Development Order 1988*, London: Sweet and Maxwell

Grant, M. (1992) 'Planning law and the British planning system', *TPR* 63: 3–12

Grant, M. (ed.) (1993) *Encyclopedia of Planning Law and Practice* (6 vols), London: Sweet and Maxwell (looseleaf; updated regularly)

Gray, C. (1982) 'The regional water authorities', in Hogwood and Keating

Grayson, L. (1990) *Green Belt, Green Fields and the Urban Fringe: The Pressure on Land in the 1980s: A Guide to Sources*, London: London Research Centre

Greater London Council (1974) *Supplementary Licensing*, London: GLC

Greater London Council (1979) *Area Control*, London: GLC

Greater London Group (1985) *The Future of London Government*, London: Greater London Group, London School of Economics

Greed, C. (1992) 'Women in planning', *The Planner* 78, 13 (3 July): 11–13

Greed, C. (1993) *Introducing Town Planning*, Harlow: Longman

Green, A., Hasluck, C., Owen, D., and Winnett, C. (1993) *Local Unemployment Change in Britain: Leaps and Lags in the Response to National Economic Cycles*, London: Jessica Kingsley

Green, B. (1981) *Countryside Conservation*, London: Allen and Unwin

Green Balance (1992) *Campaigners' Guide to Local Plans*, London: CPRE

Green, H. (1991) *Counting Gypsies* (DoE), London: HMSO

Green, R. and Holliday, J. (1991) *Country Planning: A Time for Action*, London: TCPA

Green, R.E. (ed.) (1991) *Enterprise Zones: New Directions in Economic Development*, Newbury Park, Calif.: Sage

Greenwood, B.J. (1987) 'The advertisement regulations – a brief airing', *JPL* 1987: 21–6

Greer, P. (1992) 'The next steps initiative: an examination of the agency framework documents', *Public Administration* 70: 89–98

Gregory, D. and Martin, S. (1988) 'Issues in the evaluation of inner city programmes', *Local Economy* 2: 237–50

Gregory, R. and Pearson, J. (1992) 'The parliamentary ombudsman after twenty-five years', *Public Administration* 70: 469–98

Griffith, J.A.G. and Street, H. (1964) *A Casebook on Administrative Law*, London: Pitman

Griffiths, R. (1986) 'Planning in retreat? town planning and the market in the eighties', *Planning Practice and Research* 1: 3–7

Griffiths, R. (1990) 'Planning in retreat? town planning and the market in the eighties', in Montgomery and Thornley

Griffiths, R. (1993) 'The politics of cultural policy in urban regeneration strategies', *Policy and Politics* 21: 39–46

Grove, G.A. (1963) 'Planning and the appellant', *Journal of the Town Planning Institute* 49: 128–33

Groves, P. (1992) 'A chairman's view of a TEC', *Local Government Policy Making* 19, 1 (July): 9–17

Grove-White, R. (1991) 'Land use law and the environment', in Churchill, Warren and Gibson

Gulliver, S. (1984) 'The area projects of the Scottish Development Agency', *TPR* 55: 322–34

Gunnell, J. (1990) 'Enterprise boards', in Campbell

Gunther, W.D. and Leathers, C.G. (1987) 'British enterprise zones; a critical assessment', *Review of Regional Studies* 17: 1–12

Gurr, T.R. and King, D.S. (1987) *The State and the City*, Chicago Illin.: University of Chicago Press

Gwilliam, K.M. (1988) 'Planning urban public transport', *The Planner, TCPSS Proceedings* 74, 2: 10–13

Gwilliam, K.M. (1991) 'Transport planning in a liberalised European Community', *The Planner, TCPSS Proceedings*, 13 December: 40–4

Gyford, J. (1990) 'The enabling authority – a third model', *Local Government Studies* 17, 1: 1–4

Gyford, J. (1991) *Citizens, Consumers and Councils: Local Government and the Public*, London: Macmillan

Haar, C.M. (1951) *Land Planning in a Free Society*, Cambridge, Mass.: Harvard University Press

Haar, C.M. (ed.) (1984) *Cities, Law, and Social Policy*, Lexington, Mass.: Lexington

Hadjilambrinos, C.J. (1993) 'Energy Regimes and the Development of the European Community', Ph.D. Dissertation, Newark, Del.: College of Urban Affairs and Public Policy, University of Delaware

Hagman, D.G. and Misczynski, D.J. (1978) *Windfalls for Wipeouts: Land Value Capture and Compensation*, St Paul, Minn.: West

Hague, C. (1982) 'Reflections on community planning', in Paris

Hague, C. (1984) *The Development of Planning Thought: A Critical Perspective*, London: Hutchinson

Haigh, N. (1987) 'Environmental assessment – the EC directive', *JPL* 1987: 4–20

Haigh, N. (1990) *EEC Environmental Policy* (2nd edition), Harlow: Longman,

Haigh, N. and Irwin, F. (1990) *Integrated Pollution Control in Europe and North America*, Bonn: Institute for European Environmental Policy; and Washington, DC: Conservation Foundation

Hain, P. (1980) *Neighbourhood Participation*, London: Temple Smith

Hain, P. (1982) 'The nationalisation of public participation', *Community Development Journal* 17: 36–40

Hall, A.C. (1990) 'Generating urban design objectives for local areas: a methodology and case study application to Chelmsford, Essex', *TPR* 61: 287–309

Hall, D. (1989) 'The case for new settlements', *Town and Country Planning* 58: 111–14

Hall, P. (1963) *London 2000*, London: Faber

Hall, P. (1980) *Great Planning Disasters*, London: Weidenfeld and Nicolson

Hall, P. (1981) *The Enterprise Zone Concept: British Origins, American Adaptations*, Berkeley, Calif.: Institute of Urban and Regional Development, University of California at Berkeley

Hall, P. (1982) 'Enterprise zones: a justification', *International Journal of Urban and Regional Research* 6: 415–21

Hall, P. (1983) 'The Anglo-American connection: rival rationalities in planning theory and practice, 1955–1980', *Environment and Planning B: Planning and Design* 10: 41–6

Hall, P. (1988) *Cities of Tomorrow*, Oxford: Blackwell

Hall, P. (1989) *London 2001*, London: Unwin Hyman

Hall, P. (1991) 'The British enterprise zones', in R.E. Green

Hall, P. (1992a) *Urban and Regional Planning*, London: Routledge

Hall, P. (1992b) 'A new agenda for government', *Proceedings of the*

*Town and Country Planning Summer School 1992, The Planner* 78, 21 (27 November): 30–4

Hall, P. (1993) 'Planning in the 1990s: an international agenda', *European Planning Studies* 1: 3–12

Hall, P. (ed.) (1981) *The Inner City in Context: The Final Report of the Social Science Research Council Inner Cites Working Party*, London: Heinemann (reprinted 1986 by Gower)

Hall, P. and Hass-Klau, C. (1985) *Can Rail Save the City?*, Aldershot: Gower

Hall, P., Breheny, M., McQuaid, R., and Hart, D. (1987) *Western Sunrise: Genesis and Growth of Britain's Major High Tech Corridor*, London: Unwin Hyman

Hall, P., Gracey, H., Drewett, R., and Thomas, R. (1973) *The Containment of Urban England*, London: Allen and Unwin

Hallett, G. (1980) 'Physical planning – beyond polemics to a new synthesis', *National Westminster Bank Quarterly Review*, February: 31–41

Hallett, G. (ed.) (1977) *Housing and Land Policies in West Germany and Britain*, London: Macmillan

Halsey, A.J. (ed.) (1972) *Educational Priority: Vol 1: EPA Problems and Policies*, London: HMSO

Hambleton, R. (1978) *Policy Planning and Local Government*, London: Hutchinson

Hambleton, R. (1981) 'Implementing inner city policy: reflections from experience', *Policy and Politics* 9: 51–71

Hambleton, R. (1986) *Rethinking Policy Making*, Bristol: School for Advanced Urban Studies, University of Bristol

Hambleton, R. (1990) *Urban Government in the 1990s: Lessons from the USA*, Bristol: School for Advanced Urban Studies, University of Bristol

Hambleton, R. (1991) 'The regeneration of U.S. and British cities', *Local Government Studies* 17, 5: 53–69

Hambleton, R. and Hoggett, P. (1990) *Beyond Excellence: Quality Government in the 1990s*, Bristol: School for Advanced Urban Studies, University of Bristol

Hambleton, R., Stewart, M., and Underwood, J. (1980) *Inner Cities: Management and Resources*, Bristol: School for Advanced Urban Studies, University of Bristol

Hamer, M. (1976) *Getting Nowhere Fast*, London: Friends of the Earth

Hamer, M. (1987) *Wheels within Wheels: A Study of the Road Lobby*, London: Routledge and Kegan Paul

Hammersley, R. (1987) 'Plans, policies and the local ombudsman: the Chellaston case', *JPL* 1987: 101–5

Handley, J.R. (1987) 'Industrial improvement areas – success or failure', *Land Development Studies* 4: 35–53

Handmer, J.W. and Parker, D.J. (1992) 'Hazard management in Britain: another disastrous decade?', *Area* 24: 113–22

Harding, A. (1989) 'Central control in British urban economic development programmes', in Crouch and Marquand

Harding, A. (1991) 'The rise of urban growth coalitions, UK-style?', *Environment and Planning C: Government and Policy* 9: 295–317

Hardy, D. (1979) *Alternative Communities in Nineteenth Century England*, London: Longman

Hardy, D. (1991a) *From Garden Cities to New Towns: Campaigning for Town and Country Planning*, Vol 1: 1899–1946, London: Spon

Hardy, D. (1991b) *From New Towns to Green Politics: Campaigning for Town and Country Planning*, Vol 2: 1899–1946, London: Spon

Harris, R. (1992a) 'The Environmental Protection Act 1990: penalising the polluter', *JPL* 1992: 515–24

Harris, R. (1992b) 'Integrated pollution control in practice', *JPL* 1992: 611–23

Harris, R.I.D. (1988) 'Market structure and external control in the regional economies of Great Britain', *Scottish Journal of Political Economy* 35: 334–60

Harrison, A. (1990) 'Planning, satellites and moving pictures', *JPL* 1990: 399–402

Harrison, A. (1992) 'What shall we do with the contaminated site?', *JPL* 1992: 809–16

Harrison, B. (1982) 'The politics and economics of the urban enterprise zone proposal: a critique', *International Journal of Urban and Regional Research* 6: 422–8

Harrison, J. (1984) 'Planning fees – right third time?', *JPL* 1984: 472–84

Harrison, M. (1992) 'A presumption in favour of planning permission?', *JPL* 1992: 121–9

Harrison, M.L. and Mordey, R. (eds) (1987) *Planning Control: Philosophies, Prospects and Practice*, London: Croom Helm

Harrison, P. (1983) *Inside the Inner City: Life under the Cutting Edge*, Harmondsworth: Penguin

Harrison, R.T. and Hart, M. (eds) (1992) *Spatial Policy in a Divided Nation*, London: Jessica Kingsley

Harrison, T. (1988) *Access to Information in Local Government*, London: Sweet and Maxwell

Hart, D.M. (1986) *A Review of Community Councils in Scotland*, Edinburgh: Scottish Development Department

Hart, T. (1992) 'Transport, the urban pattern and regional change, 1960–2010', *Urban Studies* 29: 483–503

Harte, J.D.C. (1985) 'Church v State in listed building control', *JPL* 1985: 611–21 and 690–7

Harte, J.D.C. (1989) 'The scope of protection resulting from the designation of Sites of Special Scientific Interest', *Journal of Environmental Law* 1: 245–54

Harte, J.D.C. (1990) 'The scheduling of ancient monuments and the role of interested members of the public in environmental law', *Journal of Environmental Law* 2: 224–49

Harvey, D. (1973) *Social Justice and the City*, London: Edward Arnold

Haslam, M. (1990) 'Green belts and the future – a view from the districts', *The Planner* 76, 34 (31 August): 14–16.

Hasluck, C. (1987) *Urban Unemployment: Local Labour Markets and Employment Initiatives*, London: Longman

Hass-Klau, C. (1990) *The Pedestrian and City Traffic*, London: Belhaven

Hass-Klau, C., Nold, I., Bocker, G., and Crampton, G. (1992) *Civilised Streets: A Guide to Traffic Calming*, Brighton: Environmental and Transport Planning

Haughton, G. (1990) 'Targeting jobs to local people: the British urban policy experience', *Urban Studies* 27: 185–98

Hausner, V.A. (1986) *Urban Economic Adjustment and the Future of British Cities: Directions for Urban Policy*, Oxford: Clarendon Press

Hausner, V.A. (ed.) (1987) *Critical Issues in Urban Economic Development* (2 vols), Oxford: Clarendon Press

Hausner, V.A. and Robson, B. (1986) *Changing Cities: An Introduction to the Economic and Social Research Council Inner Cities Research Programme*, Swindon: The Council

Hausner, Victor, & Associates (1990) *Leicester, Preston and*

*Wolverhampton Task Forces: An Assessment* (DTI Inner Cities Unit), London: DTI

Hawes, D. (1987) 'Gypsy site policy: a failure of both carrot and stick', *Policy and Politics* 15: 49–54

Hawke, J.N. (1980) 'Section 52 agreements and the fettering of planning powers', *JPL* 1980: 386–9

Hawke, J.N. (1981) 'Planning agreements in practice', *JPL* 1981: 5–14 and 86–97

Hawke, N. (1987) 'Contemporary issues in environmental policy implementation', *JPL* 1987: 241–53

Hawke, N. and Himan, J. (1988a) 'Noise pollution law enforcement', *JPL* 1988: 84–90

Hawke, N. and Himan, J. (1988b) 'Water pollution law: plugging the leaks', *JPL* 1988: 670–3

Hawkins, K. (1984) *Environment and Enforcement Regulation and the Social Definition of Pollution*, Oxford: Oxford University Press

Hawtree, M. (1981) 'The emergence of the town planning profession', in Sutcliffe (ed.)

Hays, Leslie, Consultants Ltd (1990) *Evaluation of Regional Enterprise Grants*, London: Department of Trade and Industry

Hayton, K. (1989) 'The future of local economic development', *Regional Studies* 23: 549–57

Hayton, K. (1990) *Getting People into Jobs* (DoE Case Studies of Good Practice in Urban Regeneration), London: HMSO

Hayton, K. (1991a) 'The future for local authority economic development companies', *Local Government Studies* 17, 3: 53–67

Hayton, K. (1991b) 'Planning and Scottish experience', *Scottish Planning Law and Practice*, No. 34: 69–70

Hayton, K. (1992) 'Scottish Enterprise: a challenge to local land use planning?', *TPR* 63: 265–78

Hayton, K. (1993) 'Scottish Enterprise: a challenge to local land use planning?', *Planning Practice and Research* 8, 2 (April): 5–9

Hayward, J. and Watson, M. (eds) (1975) *Planning, Politics and Public Policy*, Cambridge: Cambridge University Press

Healey, M.J. and Ibery, B.W. (1985) *The Industrialisation of the Countryside*, Norwich: Geo Books

Healey, P. (1979) *Statutory Local Plans – Their Evolution in Legislation and Administrative Interpretations*, Oxford: Department of Town Planning, Oxford Polytechnic

Healey, P. (1983) *Local Plans in British Land Use Planning*, Oxford: Pergamon

Healey, P. (1985) 'The professionalisation of planning in Britain', *TPR* 56: 492–507

Healey, P. (1986a) 'The role of development plans in the British planning system: an empirical assessment', *Urban Law and Policy* 8: 1–32

Healey, P. (1986b) 'Planning policies, policy implementation and development plans', *The Planner* 72, 9: 9–12

Healey, P. (1987) 'The future of local planning and development control', *Planning Outlook* 30: 30–40

Healey, P. (1988) 'The British planning system and managing the urban environment', *TPR* 59: 397–417

Healey, P. (1989) 'Directions for change in the British planning system', *TPR* 60: 125–49; 'Comments and response' (by Goodchild, R., Marwick, A., Grant, M., Jones, A., Lyddon, D., and Robinson, D.) *TPR* 60: 319–32

Healey, P. (1990a) 'Democracy in the planning system', *The Planner* 76, 19 (18 May): 14–15

Healey, P. (1990b) 'Places, people and politics: plan-making in the 1990s', *Local Government Policy Making* 17, 2: 29–39

Healey, P. (1991a) 'Urban regeneration and the development industry', *Regional Studies* 25: 97–110

Healey, P. (1991b) 'The content of planning education programmes: some comments from recent British experience', *Environment and Planning B: Planning and Design* 18: 177–89

Healey, P. (1992a) 'Development plans and markets', *Planning Practice and Research* 7, 2: 13–20

Healey, P. (1992b) 'The reorganisation of state and market in planning', *Urban Studies* 29: 411–34

Healey, P. (1992c) 'Planning through debate: the communicative turn in planning theory', *TPR* 63: 143–62

Healey, P. (1992d) 'Boards, caucuses and collaboration: the three way partnerships in City Challenge', Paper presented to the MPOS/RTPI seminar on *The Challenge for Cities*, Manchester, 27 November (mimeo)

Healey, P. and Nabarro, R. (1990) *Land and Property Development in a Changing Context*, Aldershot: Gower

Healey, P., Davoudi, S., O'Toole, M., Tavsanoglu, S., and Usher, D. (1992) *Rebuilding the City: Property-Led Urban Regeneration*, London: Spon

Healey, P., Doak, J., McNamara, P.F., and Elson, M. (1985) *The Implementation of Planning Policies and the Role of Development Plans: Report to the DoE* (2 vols), Oxford: Oxford Polytechnic

Healey, P., Ennis, F., and Purdue, M. (1992) 'Planning gain and the "new" local plans', *Town and Country Planning* 61: 39–43

Healey, P., McNamara, P., Elson, M., and Doak, A. (1988) *Land Use Planning and the Mediation of Change*, Cambridge: Cambridge University Press

Healey, P., Purdue, M., and Ennis, F. (1992) 'Rationales for planning gain', *Policy Studies* 13: 18–30

Heap, D. (1938) *Planning Law for Town and Country*, London: Sweet and Maxwell

Heap, D. (1955) 'Presidential address', *Journal of the Royal Town Planning Institute* 42: 6

Heap, D. (1989) 'Regina v Westminster City Council, ex parte Monahan', *JPL* 1989: 3–8

Heap, D. (1991) *An Outline of Planning Law*, London: Sweet and Maxwell

Hebbert, M. (1980) 'The British new towns: a review article', *TPR* 51: 414–20

Hebbert, M. (1983) 'The daring experiment – social scientists and land use planning in 1940s Britain', *Environment and Planning B: Planning and Design*: 10: 3–17

Hebbert, M. (1989) 'Britain in a Europe of regions', in Garside and Hebbert

Hebbert, M. (1992) 'The British garden city: metamorphosis', in Ward

Hebbert, M. and Travers, T. (1988) *The London Government Handbook*, London: Cassell

Heclo, H. and Wildavsky, A. (1974) *The Private Government of Public Money: Community and Policy Inside British Politics*, London: Macmillan

Heim, C. (1990) 'The Treasury as developer-capitalist? British new town building in the 1950s', *Journal of Economic History* 50: 903–24

Henderson, R.C. (1986a) *Planning Permission: A Guide for Homeowners*, Dundee: Hillside Publishing

Henderson, R.C. (1986b) *Urban Conservation in Scotland A Basic Guide*, Dundee: Park Place Publishing

Henderson, R.C. (1988) *Planning Appeals: A Guide for Homeowners*, Dundee: Hillside Publishing

Henderson, R.C. (1989) 'Aspects of planning in Scotland: an introductory paper', *Planning Outlook* 32, 2: 73–6

Hennessy, P. (1989) *Whitehall*, London: Secker and Warburg

Henry, D. (1982) *Planning by Agreement in a Berkshire District*, Oxford: Department of Town Planning, Oxford Polytechnic

Herington, J. (1984) *The Outer City*, London: Harper and Row

Heseltine, M. (1987) *Where There's a Will*, London: Hutchinson

Hewitt, P. (1989) *A Cleaner, Faster London: Road Pricing, Transport Policy and the Environment*, London: Institute for Public Policy Research

Heycock, M., (1991) 'Public policy, need and land use planning', in Nadin and Doak

Heywood, F. (1990) *Clearance: The View from the Street: A Study of Politics, Land and Housing*, Birmingham: Community Forum

Heywood, R. (1992) 'Planning and rail freight', *The Planner* 78, 11 (5 June): 7–9

Hibbs, J. (1989) *The History of the British Bus Services*, Newton Abbot: David and Charles

Hibbs, J. (1991) 'Freeing Europe's roads', *European Freedom Review* 2, 4: 19–26

Higgins, J., Deakin, N., Edwards, J., and Wicks, M. (1983) *Government and Urban Poverty: Inside the Policy-Making Process*, Oxford: Oxford University Press

Higgins, T.J. (1986) 'Road pricing attempts in the United States', *Transportation Research A*, 20A: 145–50

Highlands and Islands Development Board (1991) *Highlands and Islands Development Board 25th Annual Report 1990*, Inverness: The Board

Highlands and Islands Enterprise (1991) *A Strategy for Enterprise Development in the Highlands and Islands of Scotland*, Inverness: The Board

Highlands and Islands Enterprise (1992) *Highlands and Islands Enterprise First Report*, Inverness: The Board

Higman, Roger (1991) *Local Responses to 1989 Traffic Forecasts*, London: Friends of the Earth

Hill, L. (1991) 'Unitary development plans for the West Midlands: first stages in the statutory responses to a changing conurbation', in Nadin and Doak

Hill, M.P. (1987) 'Housing land availability — some observations of the process of housing development in contrasting urban locations', *Land Development Studies* 4: 209–19

Hillier, J. (1991) 'A theoretic view of the Bristol inner city project', in Nadin and Doak

Hillman, J. (1988) *A New Look for London*, Royal Fine Art Commission, London: HMSO

Hillman, J. (1990) *Planning for Beauty: The Case for Design Guidelines*, Royal Fine Art Commission, London: HMSO

Hillman, M. (1989) 'More daylight, less accidents', *Traffic Engineering and Control* 30: 191–3

Hillman, M. (1990) 'Planning for the green modes: a critique of public policy and practice', in Tolley

Hillman, M. (1992) 'Reconciling transport and environmental policy objectives: the way ahead at the end of the road', *Public Administration* 70: 225–34

Hillman, M. and Whalley, A. (1979) *Walking Is Transport*, London: Policy Studies Institute

Hillman, M. and Whalley, A. (1980) *The Social Consequences of Rail Closures*, London: Policy Studies Institute

Hillman, M. and Whalley, A. (1983) *Energy and Personal Travel: Obstacles to Conservation*, London: Policy Studies Institute

Hillman, M., Adams, J., and Whitelegg, J. (1991) *One False Move: A Study of Children's Independent Mobility*, London: Policy Studies Institute

Himsworth, K.S. (1980) *A Review of Areas of Outstanding Natural Beauty*, Cheltenham: Countryside Commission

Hinds, W. (1988) 'Third party objections to planning applications: an expectation of fairness?', *JPL* 1988: 742–8

Hinings, B. (1985) 'Policy planning solution', in Ranson, Jones and Walsh

H.M. Inspectorate of Pollution (1989) *Radioactive Waste Management and Radioactivity in the Environment*, London: HMSO

Hobhouse Report (1947) *Report of the National Parks Committee (England and Wales)*, Cmd 7121, London: HMSO

Hobley, B. (1987) 'Rescue archaeology and planning', *The Planner* 73: 25–7

Hodge, I. (1986) 'Rural development and the environment', *TPR* 57: 175–86

Hodge, I. (1989) 'Compensation for nature conservation', *Environment and Planning A* 21: 1027–36

Hodge, I. (1990a) 'Conflict or consensus over agricultural and countryside issues?', in Britton

Hodge, I. (1990b) 'The changing place of farming', in Britton

Hodge, I. (1990c) 'Land use by design', in Britton

Hodge, I. (1991) 'Incentive policies and the rural environment', *Journal of Rural Studies* 7: 373–84

Hodge, I. and Monk, S. (1991) *In Search of a Rural Economy: Patterns and Differentiation in Non-Metropolitan England*, Cambridge: Department of Land Economy

Hogwood, B.W. and Keating, M. (eds) (1982) *Regional Government in England*, Oxford: Clarendon Press

Holford, W.G. (1953) 'Design in city centres', part 3 of MHLG, *Design in Town and Village*, London: HMSO

Holliday, I., Marcou, G., and Vickerman, R. (1991) *The Channel Tunnel: Public Policy, Regional Development, and European Integration*, London: Belhaven

Hollox, R.E. and Biart, S.W. (1982) 'Local plan inquiries – a case study', *JPL* 1982: 17–23

Holman, R. and Hamilton, L. (1973) 'The British urban programme', *Policy and Politics* 2: 104

Holterman, S. (1975) 'Areas of urban deprivation in Great Britain: an analysis of 1971 census data', *Social Trends* 6: 33–47

Home, R. (1989) *Planning Use Classes: A Guide to the 1987 Order* (2nd edition), Oxford: BSP Professional

Home, R. (1992) 'The evolution of the use classes order', *TPR* 63: 187–201

Home, R.H. (1982) *Inner City Regeneration*, London: Spon

Home, R.K. (1987) 'Planning decision statistics and the use classes debate', *JPL* 1987: 167–73

Home, R.K. (1991) 'Deregulating UK planning control in the 1980s', *Cities* 8: 292–300

Home, R.K. (1993) 'Planning aspects of the government consultation paper on gypsies', *JPL* 1993: 13–18

Hooper, A. (1979) 'Land availability', *JPL* 1979: 752–6

Hooper, A. (1980) 'Land for private housebuilding', *JPL* 1980: 795–806

Hooper, A. (1982) 'Land availability in South East England', *JPL* 1982: 555–60

Hooper, A. (1985) 'Land availability studies and private house-building', in Barrett and Healey

Hooper, A., Pinch, P., and Rogers, S. (1988) 'Housing land availability: circular advice, circular arguments and circular methods', *JPL* 1988: 225–39

Hooper, A., Pinch, P., and Rogers, S. (1989) 'Housing land availability in the South East', in Breheny and Congdon

Hough, B. (1992) 'Standing in planning permission appeals', *JPL* 1992: 319–29

Houlder, M., Smith, A., and Williams, G. (1986) 'Community influences on local planning policy', *Progress in Planning* 25: 1–82

Houlder, V. (1993) 'Treading troubled waters', London: *Financial Times*, 14 May: 12

Houlihan, B. (1984) 'The regional offices of the DoE', *Public Administration* 62: 401–21

Houlihan, B. (1988) 'The professionalisation of public sector sport and leisure management', *Local Government Studies* 14: 69–81

House Builders' Federation (1987) *Private Housebuilding in the Inner Cities*, London: HBF

House Builders' Federation (1990) *Safeguarding Rural Social Housing through Section 52 Agreements: A Guidance Note*, London: HBF

Housing Choice (1991) *Planning: A Citizen's Charter*, London: Housing Choice

Howard, E. (1898) *Tomorrow: A Peaceful Path to Real Reform*, London: Swan Sonnenschein

Howard, E. (1902) *Garden Cities of Tomorrow*, London: Swan Sonnenschein (reprinted by Faber in 1946, with an introduction by F.J. Osborn, and an introductory essay by Lewis Mumford)

Howard, J.R. and Jennings, W.I. (1946) *The Law Relating to Town and Country Planning*, London: Charles Knight

Howes, C.K. (1984) 'The ownership of vacant land by public agencies', *Land Development Studies* 1: 23–33

Howes, C.K. (1988) 'Urban regeneration initiatives in England', *Land Development Studies* 5: 57–65

Howes, L. (1981) 'Community development projects', *The Planner* 67 (January-February): 24–8

Hudson, R. and Williams, A. (1986) *The United Kingdom*, London: Harper and Row

Hughes, D. (1992) *Environmental Law* (2nd edition), Oxford: Butterworth

Hughes, J.T. (1991) 'Evaluation of local economic development: a challenge for policy research', *Urban Studies* 28: 909–18

Humber, J.R. (1980) 'Land availability – another view', *JPL* 1980: 19–23

Humber, R. (1990) 'Prospects and problems for private housebuilders', *The Planner* 76, 7 (23 February): 15–19

Hunt, E.L.R. (1988) *Managing Growth's Impact on the Mid-South's Historic and Cultural Resources*, Washington, DC: National Trust for Historic Preservation

Hunt Report (1969) *The Intermediate Areas*, London: HMSO

Huppes, G. and Kagan, R.A. (1989) 'Market-oriented regulation of environmental problems in the Netherlands', *Law and Policy* 11: 215–39

Hutcheson, J.D. (1984) 'Citizen representation in neighborhood planning', *Journal of the American Planning Association* 50: 183–93

Hutter, B.M. (1989) 'Variations in regulatory enforcement styles', *Law and Policy* 11: 153–74

Hutton, N. (1986) *Lay Participation in a Public Inquiry: A Sociological Case Study*, Aldershot: Gower

Hutton, R.H. (1991) 'Local needs policy initiatives in rural areas: missing the target', *JPL* 1991: 303–11

Huxley Report (1947) *Conservation of Nature in England and Wales*, Cmd 7122, London: HMSO

Hyman, E.L. (1981) 'The valuation of extramarket benefits and costs in environmental impact assessment', *Environmental Impact Assessment Review* 2: 227–58

Ibbot, M. (1984) *Public Land Registers: An Assessment*, Reading: Department of Land Management and Development, University of Reading

Ilbery, B.W. (1991) 'Farm diversification as an adjustment strategy on the urban fringe of the West Midlands', *Journal of Rural Studies* 7: 207–18

Illich, I. (1971) *Deschooling Society*, New York: Harper and Row

Illich, I. (1977) *Disabling Professions*, London: Boyars

Ince, M. (1984) *Sizewell Report: What Happened at the Inquiry*, London: Pluto

Industry Department for Scotland (1988) *Scottish Enterprise: A New Approach to Training and Enterprise Creation*, Cm 534, London: HMSO

Industry Department for Scotland (1989) *The Scottish New Towns: The Way Ahead*, Cm 711, London: HMSO

Inland Revenue (1992) *Company Cars: Reform of Income Tax Treatment: A Consultative Document*, London: Inland Revenue

Insight Social Research (1989) *Local Attitudes to Central Advice*, London: ISR

International City Management Association (1986) *A Framework for Citizen Participation: Portland's Office of Neighbourhood Associations*, Washington, DC: ICMA Management Information Service

International Energy Agency (1989) *Energy and the Environment*, Paris: OECD

ITCU and Coventry Polytechnic (1992) *The Europe 1992 Directory*, London: HMSO

Jackson, A., Mair, D., and Nabarro, R. (1987) *Managing Workspaces* (DoE Case Studies of Good Practice in Urban Regeneration), London: HMSO

Jackson, F. (1985) *Sir Raymond Unwin: Architect, Planner and Visionary*, London: Zwemmer

Jacobs, B.D. (1992) *Fractured Cities: Capitalism, Community and Empowerment in Britain and America*, London: Routledge

Jacobs, J. (1961) *The Death and Life of Great American Cities*, London: Cape/Penguin

Jacobs, M. (1990) *Sustainable Development: Greening the Economy*, London: Fabian Society

Jacobs, M. (1991) *The Green Economy: Environment, Sustainable Development, and the Politics of the Future*, London: Pluto Press

Jacobs, S. (1976) *The Right to a Decent House*, London: Routledge and Kegan Paul

James, S. (1990) 'A streamlined city: the broken pattern of London government', *Public Administration* 68: 493–504

Jansen, A.J. and Hetsen, H. (1991) 'Agricultural development and spatial organization in Europe', *Journal of Rural Studies* 7: 143–51

Jenkins, K., Oates, G., and Stott, A. (1985) *Making Things Happen: A Report on the Implementation of Government Efficiency Scrutinies: Report to the Prime Minister*, London: HMSO

Jenkins, T.N. (1990) *Future Harvest: The Economics of Farming and the Environment – Proposals for Action*, London: CPRE and WWF

Jesper, L. and Grass, A. (1989) 'Saltley, Birmingham – a first for SPZs', *Property Management* 7: 324–30

Jewell, M. (1979) 'Is there an alternative to the public inquiry?', *JPL* 1979: 216–22

John, P. (1991) 'The restructuring of local government in England and Wales', in Batley and Stoker

Johnson, D. (1988) 'An evaluation of the urban development grant programme', *Local Economy* 2: 251–70

Johnson, D., Martin, S., Pearce, G., and Simmons, S. (1992) *The Strategic Approach to Derelict Land Reclamation* (DoE), London: HMSO

Johnson, S. (1970) *The Politics of the Environment and the British Experience*, London: Tom Stacey

Johnson, S.P. and Corcelle, G. (1989) *The Environmental Policy of the European Communities*, London: Graham and Trotman

Johnson, W.C. (1984) 'Citizen participation in local planning in the UK and USA', *Progress in Planning* 21: 149–99

Johnston, A. (1982) 'Metropolitan housing policy and strategic planning in the West Midlands', *TPR* 53: 179–99

Johnston, R.J. and Doornkamp, J.C. (1982) *The Changing Geography of the United Kingdom*, London: Methuen

Johnstone, D. (1988) *Developing Businesses* (DoE Case Studies of Good Practice in Urban Regeneration), London: HMSO

Joint Docklands Action Group (1983) *Docklands Fights Back: Eighteen Months of the LDDC*, London: JDAG

Jones, M. (1987) 'Chairman's action: the courts, the local ombudsman, and the Widdicombe committee', *JPL* 1987: 612–23

Jones, P. (1987) 'Urban fringe management projects in Scotland', *Scottish Geographical Magazine* 103: 166–70

Jones, P. (1990) *Traffic Quotes: Public Perception of Traffic Regulation in Urban Areas: Report of a Research Study* (DoT Traffic Advisory Unit), London: HMSO

Jones, P.M. (1991a) 'Gaining public support for road pricing through a package approach', *Traffic Engineering and Control* 32: 194–6

Jones, P.M. (1991b) 'UK public attitudes to urban traffic problems and possible countermeasures: a poll of polls', *Environment and Planning C: Government and Policy* 9: 245–56

Jordan, A.G. and Richardson, J.J. (1987) *British Politics and the Policy Process*, London: Allen and Unwin

Jordan, G. (1992) *Next Steps Agencies: From Managing by Command to Managing by Contract*, Aberdeen: Aberdeen Papers in Accountancy, Finance and Management, University of Aberdeen

Joseph, C. (1990) 'When is a chalet a caravan?', *JPL* 1990: 724–9

Jowell, J. (1969) 'The limits of the public hearing as a tool of urban planning', *Administrative Law Review* 21: 123–52

Jowell, J. (1975) 'Development control' (Review article on the Dobry Report), *Political Quarterly* 46: 340–4

Jowell, J. (1977a) 'Bargaining in development control', *JPL* 1977: 414–33

Jowell, J. (1977b) 'The limits of law in urban planning', *Current Legal Problems 1977* 30: 63–83

Jowell, J. (1983) 'Structure plans and social engineering', Journal of Planning and Environment Law Occasional Paper: *Structure Plans and Local Plans – Planning in Crisis*, London: Sweet and Maxwell

Jowell, J. and Grant, M. (1983) 'Guidelines for planning gain?', *JPL* 1983: 427–31

Jowell, J. and Millichap, D. (1983) 'The enforcement of planning control in London', *JPL* 1983: 644–54

Jowell, J. and Millichap, D. (1986) 'The enforcement of planning law: a report and some proposals', *JPL* 1986: 482–98

Jowell, J. and Millichap, D. (1987) 'Enforcement: the weakest link in the planning chain', in Harrison and Mordey

Jowell, J. and Noble, D. (1980) 'Planning as social engineering: notes on the first English structure plans', *Urban Law and Policy* 3: 293–317

Jowell, J. and Noble, D. (1981) 'Structure plans as instruments of social and economic policy', *JPL* 1981: 466–80

Jowell, M. (1979) 'Is there an alternative to the public inquiry?', *JPL* 1979: 216–21

Judd, D.R. (ed.) (1985) *Public Policy Across States and Communities*, Greenwich, Conn.: JAI Press

Judge, D. (1989) 'Urban development corporations: parliamentary pointers towards assessment', *Local Economy* 4: 57–66

JURUE (1986a) *Evaluation of Environmental Projects Funded under the Urban Programme* (DoE Inner Cities Research Programme), London: HMSO

JURUE (1986b) *An Evaluation of Industrial and Commercial Improvement Areas* (DoE Inner Cities Research Programme), London: HMSO

JURUE (1987) *Greening City Sites* (DoE Case Studies of Good Practice in Urban Regeneration), London: HMSO

JURUE (1988) *Improving Urban Areas* (DoE Case Studies of Good Practice in Urban Regeneration), London: HMSO

Kain, J.F. and Beesley, M.E. (1965) 'Forecasting car ownership and use', *Urban Studies* 2: 163–85

Kain, R. (ed.) (1981) *Planning for Conservation*, London: Mansell

Kay, P. and Evans, P. (1992) *Where Motor Car is Master*, London: CPRE

Keating, M. (1982) 'The debate on regional reform', in Hogwood and Keating

Keating, M. (1989) 'Regionalism, devolution and the state, 1969–1989', in Garside and Hebbert

Keating, M. and Boyle, R. (1986) *Remaking Urban Scotland: Strategies for Local Economic Development*, Edinburgh: Edinburgh University Press

Keating, M. and Jones, B. (1985) *Regions in the European Community*, Oxford: Oxford University Press

Keating, M., Midwinter, A., and Taylor, P. (1984) 'Enterprise zones: implementing the unworkable', *Political Quarterly* 55: 78–84

Keeble, D. (1976) *Industrial Location and Planning in the United Kingdom*, London: Methuen

Keeble, D. (1988) *The Economic Context for Information Technology and Telecommunications Strategy in the Rural Areas of the Northern European Community: Final Report to the European Commission*, Cambridge: Department of Geography, University of Cambridge

Keeble, D., Tyler, P., Broom, G., and Lewis, J. (1992) *Business Success in the Countryside: The Performance of Rural Enterprise* (DoE), London: HMSO

Keeble, L. (1969) *Principles and Practice of Town and Country Planning*, London: Estates Gazette

Keith, M. and Rogers, A. (eds) (1991) *Hollow Promises: Rhetoric and Reality in the Inner City*, London: Mansell

Kellett, J. (1990) 'The environmental impact of wind energy developments', *TPR* 61: 139–55

Kemp, R. (1985) 'Planning, public hearings, and the politics of discourse', in Forester

Kemp, R., O'Riordan, T., and Purdue, M. (1986) 'Environmental politics in the 1980s: the public examination of radioactive waste', *Policy and Politics* 14: 9–25

Kenny, P.H. (1983) 'The Mobile Homes Act 1983', *JPL* 1983: 524–9

Kenyon, R.C. (1991) 'Environmental assessment: an overview on behalf of the RICS', *JPL* 1991: 419–22

Keogh, G. (1985) 'The economics of planning gain', in Barrett and Healey

Keogh, G. and Evans, A.W. (1992) 'The private and social costs of planning delay', *Urban Studies* 29: 687–99

Kerry, M. (1986) 'Administrative law and judicial review: the practical effects of developments over the last 25 years on administration in central government', *Public Administration* 64: 163–72

Kidd, S. and Kumar, A. (1993) 'Development planning in the English metropolitan counties: a comparison of performance under two planning systems', *Regional Studies* 27: 65–73

Kilbrandon Report (1973) *Report of the Royal Commission on the Constitution* (Kilbrandon Report), Cmnd 5640, London: HMSO

King, A. (1975) 'Overload: problems of government in the 1970s', *Political Studies* 23: 284–96

King, A.D. (1990) *Global Cities: Post-imperialism and the Internationalisation of London*, London: Routledge

King, A.D. (ed.) (1980) *Buildings and Society: Essays on the Social Development of the Built Environment*, London: Routledge

King, J. (1990) *Regional Selective Assistance 1980–84: An Evaluation by DTI, IDS, and WOID*, London: HMSO

Kingdom, J. (1991) *Local Government and Politics in Britain*, London: Philip Allan

Kirby, A. (1985) 'Nine fallacies of local economic change', *Urban Affairs Quarterly* 21: 207–20

Kirk, G. (1980) *Urban Planning in a Capitalist Society*, Croom Helm

Kivell, P. (1993) *Land and the City: Patterns and Processes of Urban Change*, London: Routledge

Klein, R. (1974) 'The case for elitism: public opinion and public policy', *Political Quarterly* 45: 406–17

Klosterman, R.E. (1985) 'Arguments for and against planning', *TPR* 56: 5–20

Knox, P.L. (1988) 'Public-private cooperation: a review of experience in the US', *Cities* 5: 340–46

Knox, P.L. and Cullen, J.L. (1981) 'Planners as urban managers: an exploration of the attitudes and self-image of senior British planners', *Environment and Planning A* 13: 885–98

Kraan, R.J. and Veld, R.J. (eds) (1991) *Environmental Protection: Public or Private Choice?*, Dordrecht: Kluwer

Krämer, L. (1991) 'The implementation of Community environmental directives within member states: some implications of the direct effect doctrine', *Journal of Environmental Law* 3: 39–56

Krämer, L. (1992) *Focus on European Environmental Law*, London: Sweet and Maxwell

Kromarek, P. (1986) 'The single European Act and the environment', *European Environment Review* 1: 10–12

Labour Party (1978) *Local Government Reform in England*, London: National Executive of the Labour Party

Labour Party (1991) *Citizen's Charter: Labour's Better Deal for Consumers and Citizens*, London: Labour Party

Lambert, A.J. and Wood, C.M. (1990) 'UK implementation of the European directive on EIA', *TPR* 61: 247–62

Lambert, C.M. (1984) *Streamlining the Cities: A Selection of Material on the Government's Proposals to Abolish the Greater London Council and the Metropolitan Counties*, London: DoE Library, Bibliography 207

Land and Urban Analysis Ltd (1990) *Community Businesses* (DoE Case Studies of Good Practice in Urban Regeneration), London: HMSO

Land Authority for Wales (1992) *Annual Report 1991–1992*, Cardiff: LAW

Land Capability Consultants (1990) *Cost Effective Management of Reclaimed Derelict Sites*, London: HMSO

Land Use Consultants (1986) *Channel Fixed Link: Environmental Appraisal of Alternative Proposals* (DoT), London: HMSO

Land Use Consultants (1991) *Permitted Development Rights for Agriculture and Forestry* (DoE Planning Research Programme), London: HMSO

Lane, J. and Vaughan, S. (1992) *An Evaluation of the Impact of PPG 16 on Archaeology and Planning*, London: Pagoda Associates Ltd

Lannon, J. (1987) 'Planning law and the control of licensed premises', *JPL* 1987: 754–9

Lannon, J. (1988) 'Planning conditions: the main difficulty with Newbury', *JPL* 1988: 460–6

Larkham, P.J., (1990a) *Development Pressure and Development Delay: A Study of Two Aspects of the British Planning System*, Birmingham: School of Geography, University of Birmingham

Larkham, P.J. (1990b) 'The use and measurement of development pressure', *TPR* 61: 171–83

Larkham, P.J. (1990c) 'The concept of delay in development control', *Planning Outlook* 33: 101–7

Larkham, P.J. and Jones, A. (1993) 'Conservation and conservation areas in the UK: a growing problem', *Planning Practice and Research* 8, 2 (April 1993): 19–29

Lasok, D. and Bridge, J.W. (1991) *Law and Institutions of the European Communities*, London: Butterworths

Latham, R. (1982) 'Enterprise zones: monitoring the effects on the local economy', *West Midlands Regional Management Centre Review* 1: 94–100

Lavery, P. (1982) 'Countryside management schemes in the urban fringe', *Planning Outlook* 25: 52–9

LAW: *see* Land Authority for Wales

Law, C.M. (1982) *British Regional Development since World War I*, London: Methuen

Law, C.M. (1988) 'Public-private partnership in urban revitalisation in Britain', *Regional Studies* 22: 446–51

Law, C.M. (1992) 'Urban tourism and its contribution to economic regeneration', *Urban Studies* 29: 599–619

Law, C.M., Grime, E.K., Grundy, C.J., Senior, M.L., and Tuppen, J.N. (1988) *The Uncertain Future of the Urban Core*, London: Routledge

Law, S. (1977) 'Planning and the future: a commentary on the debate', *TPR* 48: 365–72

Law Commission (1993) *Administrative Law: Judicial Review and Statutory Appeals*, Law Commission Consultation Paper 126, London: HMSO

Lawless, P. (1979) *Urban Deprivation and Government Initiative*, London: Faber

Lawless, P. (1981) *Britain's Inner Cities: Problems and Policies*, London: Harper and Row

Lawless, P. (1986) *The Evolution of Spatial Policy: A Case Study of Inner Urban Policy in the United Kingdom 1968–1981*, London: Pion

Lawless, P. (1988a) 'British inner urban policy: a review', *Regional Studies* 22: 531–42

Lawless, P. (1988b) 'Enterprise boards: evolution and critique', *Planning Outlook* 31: 13–18

Lawless, P. (1988c) 'Urban development corporations and their alternatives', *Cities* 5: 277–89

Lawless, P. (1989) *Britain's Inner Cities* (2nd edition), London: Paul Chapman

Lawless, P. (1990) *The Economic and Physical Restructuring of the City: The Case of the English Urban Development Corporations*, Sheffield: Centre for Regional Economic and Social Research, Sheffield Polytechnic, Working Paper 9

Lawless, P. and Rabin, C. (1986) *The Contemporary British City*, London: Harper and Row

Laws, F.G. (1991) *Guide to the Local Government Ombudsman Service*, Harlow: Longman

Laws, P. (1955) 'Ribbon development: present trends', *Town and Country Plannng* 23: 167–9

Law Society (1982) 'Planning gain: the Law Society's observations', *JPL* 1982: 346–51

Lawton, R. and Pooley, C.G. (1992) *The New Geography of London*, London: Edward Arnold

Layfield, F. (1992) 'The Environmental Protection Act 1990: the system of integrated pollution control', *JPL* 1992: 3–13

Layfield, F. and Whybrow, C. (1973) 'The examination of structure plans', *JPL* 1973: 516–22

Leach, S. (1992) 'Strategic land use/transportation planning: the implications of post-abolition experience in the metropolitan counties for the current reorganisation debate', *Strategic Government* (Policy Journal of the Association of County Councils), Winter: 5–50

Leach, S. (1993) 'Strategic planning and the local government review', *Strategic Government*, Summer: 5–10

Leach, S. (ed.) (1984) *The Future of Metropolitan Government*, Birmingham: Institute of Local Government Studies, University of Birmingham

Leach, S. and Game, C. (1991) 'English metropolitan government since abolition: an evaluation of the abolition of the English metropolitan councils', *Public Administration* 69: 141–70

Leach, S. and Stoker, G. (1988) 'The transformation of central-local relationships', in Graham and Prosser

Leach, S., Davis, H., Game, C., and Skelcher, C. (1991) *After Abolition: The Operation of the Post-1986 Metropolitan Government System*, Birmingham: Institute of Local Government Studies, University of Birmingham

Leach, S., Hinings, C.R., Ranson, S., and Skelcher, C.K. (1983) 'The uses and abuses of policy planning systems', *Local Government Studies* 9: 23–8

Leach, S., Stewart, J., Spencer, K., Walsh, K., and Gibson, J. (1992) *The Heseltine Review of Local Government: A New Vision or Opportunities Missed?*, Birmingham: Institute of Local Government Studies, University of Birmingham

Leclerc, R. and Draffan, D. (1984) 'The Glasgow Eastern Area Renewal project', *TPR* 55: 335–51

Ledgerwood, G. (1985) *Urban Innovation: The Transformation of the London Docklands 1968–84*, Aldershot: Gower

Lee Valley Regional Park Authority (annual) *Annual Report*, Enfield: The Authority

Lee Valley Regional Park Authority (1985) *Lee Valley Park Plan*, Enfield: The Authority

Leitch Report (1977) *Report of the Advisory Committee on Trunk Road Assessment*, London: HMSO

Le-Las, W. (1983) 'The major public inquiry: politics and the rational verdict', *Urban Law and Policy* 6: 39

Le-Las, W. (1987) *Playing the Public Inquiry Game*, London: Osmosis Publishing Services

Leung, H.L. (1979) *Redistribution of Land Values: A Re-examination of the 1947 Scheme*, Cambridge: Department of Land Economy, University of Cambridge

Leung, H.L. (1987) 'Developer behaviour and development control', *Land Development Studies* 4: 17–34

Lever, W.F. (1991) 'Deindustrialisation and the reality of the post-industrial city', *Urban Studies* 28: 983–99

Lever, W.F. (1992) 'Local authority responses to economic change in West Central Scotland', *Urban Studies* 29: 935–48

Lever, W.F. (ed.) (1987) *Industrial Change in the UK*, London: Harper and Row

Lever, W.F. and Moore, C. (1986) *The City in Transition: Policies and Agencies for the Economic Regeneration of Clydeside*, Oxford: Oxford University Press

Levin, P.H. (1979) 'Highway inquiries: a study in government responsiveness', *Public Administration* 57: 21–49

Levin, P. and Donnison, D.V. (1969) 'People and planning', *Public Administration* 49: 473–79

Levine, M.C. (1987) 'Downtown redevelopment as an urban growth strategy: a critical appraisal of the Baltimore renaissance', *Journal of Urban Affairs* 9: 103–23

Levy, F., Meltsner, A.J., and Wildavsky, A.B. (1974) *Urban Outcomes: Schools, Streets, and Libraries*, Berkeley, Calif.: University of California Press

Lewis, J. and Townsend, A. (1989) *The North-South Divide: Regional Change in Britain in the 1980s*, London: Paul Chapman

Lewis, N. (1992) *Inner City Regeneration: The Demise of Regional and Local Government*, Buckingham: Open University Press

Lewis, R.P. (1992) 'The Environmental Protection Act 1990: waste management in the 1990s: waste regulation and disposal', *JPL* 1992: 303–12

Lichfield, N. (1989) 'From planning gain to community benefit', *JPL* 1989: 68–81

Lichfield, N. and Darin-Drabkin, H. (1980) *Land Policy in Planning*, London: Allen and Unwin

Lichfield, N., Kettle, P., and Whitbread, M. (1975) *Evaluation in the Planning Process*, Oxford: Pergamon

Likierman, A. (1982) 'Management information for ministers: the MINIS system in the Department of the Environment', *Public Administration* 60: 127–42

Linders, B.E.M. (1985) 'Strategic planning in South East England 1968–78: a case study', *Progress in Planning*, 23: 69–154

Lindley, P.D. (1982) 'The framework of regional planning 1964–1980', in Hogwood and Keating

Little, A.J. (1992) *Planning Controls and their Enforcement* (6th edition), Crayford, Kent: Shaw

Little, J., Peake, L., and Richardson, P. (eds) (1988) *Women in Cities*, New York: New York University Press

Lloyd, M.G. (1984) 'Enterprise zones: the evaluation of an experiment', *The Planner* 70, 6 (June): 23–5

Lloyd, M.G. (1985) 'Privatisation, liberalisation and simplification of statutory land use controls', *Planning Outlook* 28: 46–9

Lloyd, M.G. (1987) 'Simplified planning zones: the privatisation of land use controls in the U.K.?', *Land Use Policy* 4: 51–61

Lloyd, M.G. (1990) 'Simplified planning zones in Scotland: government failure or the failure of government?', *Planning Outlook* 33: 128–32

Lloyd, M.G. (1992a) 'Industrial closure, land development and the Lanarkshire EZ', *Town and Country Planning* 61: 322–5

Lloyd, M.G. (1992b) 'Simplified planning zones, land development, and planning policy in Scotland', *Land Use Policy* 9: 249–58

Lloyd, M.G. and Botham, R.W. (1985) 'The ideology and implementation of enterprise zones in Britain', *Urban Law and Policy* 7: 33–55

Lloyd, M.G. and Danson, M.W. (1991) 'The Inverclyde enterprise zone: a continuing experiment in regeneration', *Scottish Geographical Magazine* 107: 58–62

Lloyd, M.G. and Livingstone, L.H. (1991) 'Marine fish farming in Scotland: proprietorial behaviour and the public interest', *Journal of Rural Studies* 7: 253–63

Lloyd, M.G. and Rowan-Robinson, J. (1988) 'Regional reports or structure plans? Opportunities for strategic planning in England and Wales', *Planning Outlook* 31: 47–51

Lloyd, M.G. and Rowan-Robinson, J. (1992) 'Review of strategic planning guidance in Scotland', *Journal of Environmental Planning and Management* 35: 93–9

Lloyd, M.G., Rowan-Robinson, J., and Dawson, J. (1989) 'Policy adaption in Scotland: national planning guidelines and agricultural land resources', *Scottish Geographical Magazine* 105: 19–24

Local Government Management Board (1992a) *Competing for Professional Services: An Outline of the Issues*, Luton: LGMB

Local Government Management Board (1992b) *Citizens and Local Democracy: Charting a New Relationship*, Luton: LGMB

Local Government Management Board and RTPI (1993) *Planning Staffs Survey 1992*, Luton: LGMB and RTPI

Lock, D. (1989) *Riding the Tiger: Planning the South of England*, London: TCPA

Logan, J.R. and Swanstrom, T. (eds) (1990) *Beyond the City Limits*, Philadelphia: Temple University Press

Logan, T. (1976) 'The Americanization of German zoning', *Journal of the American Institute of Planners* 42: 377–85

London and South East Regional Planning Conference: see *SERPLAN*

London Boroughs Association (1990) *Road Pricing for London*, London: The Association

London Boroughs Association (1992a) *Out of Order: The 1987 Use Classes Order: Problems and Proposals*, London: The Association

London Boroughs Association (1992b) *The Scope for Bus Park and Ride Schemes in London*, London: The Association

London Boroughs Disability Resource Team (1991) *Towards Integration: The Participation of Disabled People in Planning*, London: London Boroughs Association

London Docklands Development Corporation (annual) *Annual Report and Financial Statements*, London: LDDC

London Economics (1992) *The Potential Role of Market Mechanisms in the Control of Acid Rain* (DoE Environmental Economics Research Series), London: HMSO

London Planning Advisory Committee (1991) *London: World City Moving into the 21st Century*, London: HMSO

London Research Centre (1991) *Much Ado About Nothing: An Examination of the Potential for the Planning System to Secure Affordable Housing with Special Reference to Planning Agreements*, London: The Centre

London Women and Planning Group (1991) *Shaping our Borough: Women and Unitary Development Plans*, London: Planning Aid for London

Loney, M. (1983) *Community Against Government: The British Community Development Project 1968–78*, London: Heinemann

Long, A.R. (1976) *Participation and the Community*, Oxford: Pergamon

Longley, P., Batty, M., Shepherd, J., and Sadler, G. (1992) 'Do green belts change the shape of urban areas? A preliminary analysis of the settlement geography of South East England', *Regional Studies* 26: 437–52

Loughlin, M. (1978) 'Bargaining as a tool of development control: a case of all gain and no loss?', *JPL* 1978: 290–5

Loughlin, M. (1980a) 'Planning control and the property market', *Urban Law and Policy* 3: 1–22

Loughlin, M. (1980b) 'The scope and importance of material considerations', *Urban Law and Policy* 3: 171–92

Loughlin, M. (1982) 'Planning gain: another viewpoint', *JPL* 1982: 352–8

Loughlin, M. (1984) *Local Needs Policies and Development Control Strategies*, Bristol: School for Advanced Urban Studies, University of Bristol

Loughlin, M. (1986) *Local Government in the Modern State*, London: Sweet and Maxwell

Loughlin, M., Gelfand, M.D., and Young, K. (eds) (1985) *Half a Century of Municipal Decline*, London: Allen and Unwin

Low, N. (1991) *Planning, Politics and the State: Political Foundations of Planning Thought*, London: Unwin Hyman

Lowe, P. and Flynn, A. (1989) 'Environmental politics and policy in the 1980s', in Mohan

Lowe, P. and Goyder, J. (1983) *Environmental Groups in Politics*, London: Allen and Unwin

Lowe, P., Cox, G., MacEwen, M., O'Riordan, T., and Winter, M. (1986) *Countryside Conflicts: The Politics of Farming, Forestry and Conservation*, Aldershot: Gower/Temple Smith

Lowry, I.S. and Ferguson, B.W. (1992) *Development Regulation and Housing Affordability*, Washington, DC: Urban Land Institute

Lutyens, E. and Abercrombie, P. (1945) *A Plan for the City and County of Kingston upon Hull*, Hull: Brown

Lyddon, D. (1985) 'Planning and recovery: an alternative route 1975–1985', *The Planner, TCPSS Proceedings* 71, 2 (February): 26–30

McArthur, A.A. (1986) 'An unconventional approach to economic development', *TPR* 57: 87–100

McAuslan, J.P.W.B. (1971) 'The plan, the planners, and the lawyers', *Public Law* 1971: 247–75

McAuslan, J.P.W.B. (1975) *Land, Law and Planning*, London: Weidenfeld and Nicolson

McAuslan, J.P.W.B. (1980a) 'Local government and resource allocation in England: changing ideology, unchanging law', *Urban Law and Policy* 4: 215–68

McAuslan, J.P.W.B. (1980b) *The Ideologies of Planning Law*, Oxford: Pergamon

McAuslan, J.P.W.B. (1991) 'The role of courts and other judicial type bodies in environmental management', *Journal of Environmental Law* 3: 195–208

McBride, D. (1979) 'Planning delays and development control – a proposal for reform', *Urban Law and Policy* 2: 47–64

McBride, J. (1973) 'The urban aid programme: is it running out of cash?', *Quest* (16 March)

McClenaghan, J. and Blatchford, C. (1993) 'Development plan slippage', *The Planner* 79, 2 (February): 29–30

McClintock, H. (1982) 'Planning for the cycling revival', *TPR* 53: 383–402

McClintock, H. (ed.) (1992) *The Bicycle and City Traffic*, London: Belhaven Press

McConaghy, D. (1972) *SNAP 1969–72: Another Chance for Cities*, London: Shelter

McConaghy, D. (1978) 'Setting up six towns: an urban strategy gap', *TPR* 46: 184–94

McConnell, R.S. (1987) 'The implementation and the future of development plans', *Land Development Studies* 4: 79–107

McCormick, J. (1991) *British Politics and the Environment*, London: Earthscan

McCrone, G. (1969) *Regional Policy in Britain*, London: Allen and Unwin

McCrone, G. (1991) 'Urban renewal: the Scottish experience', *Urban Studies* 28: 919–38

Macdonald, G. (1993) 'Planning gain a must for economic development', *Planning* No. 1005 (12 February): 12–13

McDonald, S.T. (1977) 'The regional report in Scotland', *TPR* 48: 215–32

McDonald, S.T. (1984) 'The Scottish Development Agency and the Scottish townscape', *TPR* 55: 352–67

McEldowney, J.J. (1991) 'Evaluation and European regional policy', *Regional Studies* 25: 261–5

MacEwen, A. and MacEwen, M. (1982a) 'An unprincipled Act', *The Planner* 68: 69–91

MacEwen, A. and MacEwen, M. (1982b) *National Parks: Conservation or Cosmetics?*, London: Allen and Unwin

MacEwen, A. and MacEwen, M. (1987) *Greenprints for the Countryside? The Story of Britain's National Parks*, London: Allen and Unwin

MacEwen, M. (1973) *Crisis in Architecture*, London: Royal Institute of British Architects

MacEwen, M. and Sinclair, G. (1983) *New Life for the Hills*, London: Council for National Parks

MacGregor, S. and Pimlott, B. (1990) *Tackling the Inner Cities: The 1980s Revisited, Prospects for the 1990s*, Oxford: Clarendon Press

McKay, D.H. and Cox, A.W. (1979) *The Politics of Urban Change*, London: Croom Helm

Mackie, P.J. (1980) 'The new grant system for local transport - the first five years', *Public Administration* 59: 187–206

MacKinnon, J. (1992) 'Planning appeals in Scotland', in Planning Exchange

Mackintosh, M. (1992) 'Partnership: issues of policy and negotiation', *Local Economy* 7: 210–24

McLaren, D. (1989) '*Action for Cities* and the urban environment', *Local Economy* 4: 99–111

Maclennan, D. (1986) *The Demand for Housing: Economic Perspectives and Planning Practices*, Edinburgh: Scottish Development Department

Maclennan, D. (1987) 'Rehabilitating older housing', in Donnison and Middleton

Maclennan, D. (1989) 'Housing in Scotland 1977–1987', in M.E.H. Smith

Maclennan, D. and Parr, J.B. (1979) *Regional Policy: Past Experience and New Directions*, London: Martin Robertson

McLoughlin, J.B. (1969) *Urban and Regional Planning: A Systems Analysis*, Oxford: Pergamon

McNamara, P. and Healey, P. (1984) 'The limitations of development control data in planning research: a comment on Ian Brotherton's recent study', *TPR* 55: 91–101

McNamara, P., Jackson, A., and Mathrani, S. (1985) *Appellants' Perceptions of the Planning Appeal System: Final Report to DoE*, Oxford: Departments of Town Planning and Estate Management, Oxford Polytechnic

Macpherson, M. (1987) 'Local ombudsman or the courts?', *JPL* 1987: 92–101

Macrory, R. (1990) 'The privatisation and regulation of the water industry', *Modern Law Review* 53: 78–87

Macrory, R. (1992) *Campaigners' Guide to Using EC Environmental Law*, London: CPRE

Macrory, R. and Lafontiane, M. (1982) *Public Inquiry and Enquête Publique: Forms of Public Participation in England and France*, Institute for European Environmental Policy and International Institute for Environment and Development

Madden, M. (1987) 'Planning and ethnic minorities; an elusive literature', *Planning Practice and Research*, No. 2 (March): 29–32

MAFF (1986) *Farm and Countryside Initiative: A Guide to a Community Programme for Rural Areas*, London: The Ministry

MAFF (1989) *Environmentally Sensitive Areas*, London: HMSO

MAFF (1992) *The Digest of Agricultural Census Statistics, United Kingdom 1991*, London: HMSO

Maitland, R., Newman, P., and Slater, M. (1991) 'The use of consultants by local planning authorities', *The Planner* 77, 28: 9

Manchester, C. (1982) 'Much ado about the location of sex shops', *JPL* 1982: 89–95

Manley, J. (1987) 'Archaeology and planning: a Welsh perspective', *JPL* 1987: 466–84 and 552–63

Manning, P.K. (1989) 'Managing risk: managing uncertainty in the British nuclear installations inspectorate', *Law and Policy* 11: 350–69

Marcuse, P. (1985) 'Professional ethics and beyond: values in planning', in Wachs

Markowski, S. (1978) *A Study of Vacant Land in Urban Areas*, London: Centre for Environmental Studies

Marriott, O. (1967) *The Property Boom*, London: Hamilton

Marris, P. (1982) *Community Planning and Conceptions of Change*, London: Routledge and Kegan Paul

Marsh, G. (1983) 'The local plan inquiry: its role in local plan preparation', *Progress in Planning* 19: 91–167

Marshall, R. (1988) 'Agricultural policy development in Britain', *TPR* 59: 419–35

Marshall, T. (1991) *Regional Planning in England and Germany*, Oxford: School of Planning, Oxford Polytechnic

Martin, L.R.G. (1989) 'The important published literature of British planners', *TPR* 60: 441–57

Martin, R.L. (1985) 'Monetarism masquerading as regional policy? the government's new system of regional aid', *Regional Studies* 19: 379–88

Martin, R.L. and Hodge, J.S.C. (1983a) 'The reconstruction of British regional policy: 1. The crisis of conventional practice', *Environment and Planning C: Government and Policy* 1: 133–52

Martin, R.L. and Hodge, J.S.C. (1983b) 'The reconstruction of British regional policy: 2. Towards a new agenda', *Environment and Planning C: Government and Policy* 1: 317–40

Martin, S. (1989) 'New jobs in the inner city: the employment impacts of projects assisted under the urban development grant programme', *Urban Studies* 26: 627–38

Martin, S. (1990) 'City grants, urban development grants, and urban regeneration grants', in Campbell

Martin, S. and Pearce, G. (1992) 'The internationalisation of local authority economic development strategies: Birmingham in the 1980s', *Regional Studies* 26: 499–509

Martin, S.J., Ticker, M.J., and Bovaird, A.G. (1990) 'Rural development programmes in theory and practice', *Regional Studies* 24: 268–76

Masser, I. (1983) *Evaluating Urban Planning Efforts*, Aldershot: Gower

Massey, D. (1982) 'Enterprise zones: a political issue', *International Journal of Urban and Regional Research* 6: 429–34

Massey, D. and Catalano, A. (1978) *Capital and Land: Landownership by Capital in Great Britain*, London: Edward Arnold

Mather, A.S. (1991) 'The changing role of planning in rural land use: the example of afforestation in Scotland', *Journal of Rural Studies* 7: 299–309

Mather, G. (1988) *Paying for Planning*, London: Institute of Economic Affairs

Mawson, J. and Skelcher, C. (1980) 'Updating the West Midlands regional strategy: a review of inter-authority relationships', *TPR* 51: 152–70

May, A.D. (1986) 'Traffic restraint: a review of the alternatives', *Transportation Research* A, 20A: 109–21

May, A.D. and Gardner, K.E. (1990) 'Transport policy for London in 2001: the case for an integrated approach', *Transportation* 16: 257–77

Meager, N. (1991) 'TECs: a revolution in training and enterprise, or old wine in new bottles?', *Local Economy* 6: 4–20

Mellors, C. and Copperthwaite, N. (1990) *Regional Policy*, London: Routledge

Memon, P.A. (1988) 'Public policy in an ethnically plural society: approaches of London boroughs towards black business development', *TPR* 59: 45–64

Men of the Trees (1991) *Trees: Journal and Yearbook 1991*, Crawley: Men of the Trees

Mercer, E. (1988) 'Dishes of the day: planning and the new media', *Law* 1988: 75–9

Mcrlin, P. (1971) *New Towns*, London: Methuen

Mertz, S.W. (1989) 'The European Economic Community directive on environmental assessments: how will it affect United Kingdom developers?', *JPL* 1989: 483–98

Metcalf, H., Pearson, R., and Martin, R. (1990) 'The charitable role of companies in job creation', *Regional Studies* 24: 261–76

Metropolitan Planning Officers' Society (1992) *Economic Development and the Green Factor*, London: The Society

Meyer, P. (1986) 'Assessing improvement area policy', *Local Economy* 1: 35–43

Meyer, P.B. and Boyle, R. (1990) 'Lessons from the USA and directions for British local economic development efforts', *Local Economy* 4: 317–20

Meynell, A. (1959) 'Location of industry', *Public Administration* 37: 9

Midwinter, A., Keating, M., and Mitchell, J. (1991) *Politics and Public Policy in Scotland*, London: Macmillan

Miller, B. (1957) 'Citadels of local power', *The Twentieth Century* 162: 325–30

Miller, C. and Wood, C. (1983) *Planning and Pollution: An Examination of the Role of Land Use Planning in the Protection of the Environment*, Oxford: Clarendon Press

Miller, C.E. (1990) 'Development control as an instrument of environmental management', *TPR* 61: 231–45

Millichap, D. (1988) 'Enforcing advertising control', *JPL* 1988: 382–9

Millichap, D. (1989) 'Conservation areas – Steinberg and after', *JPL* 1989: 233–40

Milner Holland Report (1965) *Report of the Committee on Housing in Greater London*, Cmnd 2605, London: HMSO

Milroy, B.M. (1991) 'Taking stock of planning, space, and gender', *Journal of Planning Literature* 6: 3–15

Milton, K. (1991) 'Interpreting environmental policy: a social scientific approach', in Churchill, Warren, and Gibson

Minay, C.L.W. (1992a) 'Developing regional planning guidance in England and Wales: a review symposium', *TPR* 63: 415–19 and 432–4

Minay, C.L.W. (1992b) *Regional Frameworks for Development Plans: A Process Initiated*, Oxford: School of Planning, Oxford Polytechnic

Mishan, E.J. (1976) *Elements of Cost-Benefit Analysis*, London: Allen and Unwin

Mitchell Report (1991) *Railway Noise and the Insulation of Dwellings: Report of the Committee to Recommend a National Noise Insulation Standard for New Railway Lines*, London: HMSO

Mogridge, M.J.H. (1986) 'Road pricing, the right solution for the right problem?', *Transportation Research A* 20A: 157–67

Mogridge, M.J.H. (1990) *Travel in Towns*, London: Macmillan

Mohan, J. (ed.) (1989) *The Political Geography of Contemporary Britain*, London: Macmillan

Moir, J. (1991) 'National parks: north of the Border', *Planning Outlook* 34: 61–7

Molotch, H. (1976) 'The city as a growth machine: towards a political economy of place', *American Journal of Sociology* 82: 309–31

Molotch, H. (1984) 'Tensions in the growth machine: overcoming resistance to value-free development', *Social Problems* 31: 483–99

Moltke, K. von (1988) 'The *vorsorgerprinzip* in West German environmental policy', Printed as an appendix to the 12th Report of the Royal Commission on Environmental Pollution, *Best Practicable Environmental Option*, London: HMSO

Monk, J. and Hanson, J. (1982) 'On not excluding half of the human in geography', *Professional Geographer* 34: 11–23

Montgomery, J. (1990) 'Cities and the art of cultural planning', *Planning Practice and Research* 5: 17–22

Montgomery, J. and Thornley, A. (1988) 'Phoenix ascending: radical planning institutions for the 1980s', *Planning Practice and Research*, No. 4 (Spring): 3–7

Montgomery, J. and Thornley, A. (eds) (1990) *Radical Planning Initiatives: New Directions for Urban Planning in the 1990s*, Aldershot: Gower

Montgomery Report (1984) *Report of the Committee of Inquiry into the Functions and Powers of the Islands Councils of Scotland*, Cmnd 9216, Edinburgh: HMSO

Montgomeryshire District Council (1990) *Village Workshop Programme: The First Ten Years*, Welshpool: The Council

Moon, C. (1986) 'Rural community development in action: the Leominster Marches', in Gilg

Moon, J. and Richardson, J.J. (1985) *Unemployment in the UK*, Aldershot: Gower

Moor, N. (1983) *The Planner and the Market*, London: Godwin

Moore, B. and Rhodes, J. (1973) 'Evaluating the effect of British regional policy', *Economic Journal* 83: 87–110

Moore, B. and Townroe, P. (1990) *Urban Labour Markets: Reviews of Urban Research* (DoE Inner Cities Research Programme), London: HMSO

Moore, B., Rhodes, J., and Tyler, P. (1986) *The Effects of Government Regional Economic Policy* (DTI), London: HMSO

Moore, C. (1988) 'Enterprise agencies: privatisation or partnership?', *Local Economy* 3: 21–30

Moore, C. and Booth, S. (1986) 'Urban policy contradictions: the market versus redistributive approaches', *Policy and Politics* 14: 361–87

Moore, V. (1977) 'The public control of land use: an anglophile's view', *Urban Lawyer* 10: 130–44

Moore, V. (1987) *A Practical Approach to Planning Law*, London: Financial Training Publications

Mordey, R. (1987) 'Development control, public participation and the need for planning aid', in Harrison and Mordey

Morgan, K. (1985) 'Regional regeneration in Britain: the territorial imperative and the conservative state', *Political Studies* 33: 560–77

Morgan, P. and Nott, S. (1988) *Development Control: Policy into Practice*, London: Butterworth

Morison, H. (1987) *The Regeneration of Local Economies*, Oxford: Clarendon Press

Morris, J. (1991) 'Expanding improvement areas', *Housing* (June/July): 41–7

Morrison, S.A. (1986) 'A survey of road pricing', *Transportation Research A* 20A: 87–97

Morton, D. (1991) 'Conservation areas – has saturation point been reached?', *The Planner* 7,17 (17 May): 5–8

Moss, G. (1981) *Britain's Wasting Acres*, London: Architectural Press

Mowie, A. (1986) *Nature Conservation in Rural Development*, Peterborough: Nature Conservancy Council

Muchnick, D.M. (1970) *Urban Renewal in Liverpool*, Occasional Papers on Social Administration 33, London: Bell

Munby, D.L. (1954) 'Development charge and the compensation-betterment problem', *Economic Journal* 64: 87–97

Munton, R.J.C. (1983) *London's Green Belt: Containment in Practice*, London: Allen and Unwin

Murie, A. (1985) 'The nationalisation of housing policy', in Loughlin, Gelfand, and Young

MVA Consultancy (1985) *Development Control Performance in Scotland*, Edinburgh: Scottish Office

Mynors, C. (1984) 'Conservation areas: protecting the familiar and cherished scene', *JPL* 1984: 144–57 and 235–47

Mynors, C. (1985) 'Render unto Caesar . . . the ecclesiastical exemption from listed building control', *JPL* 1985: 599–610

Mynors, C. (1988) 'Property in need of maintenance: section 65 notices', *Journal of Planning and Property Law* 1988: 154–61

Mynors, C. (1992) *Planning Control and the Display of Advertisements*, London: Sweet and Maxwell

Mynors, C. (1993) 'The extent of listing', *JPL* 1993: 99–111

Nadin, V. (1992) 'Consultation by consultants', *Town and Country Planning* 61: 272–4

Nadin, V. and Daniels, R. (1992) 'Consultants and development plans', *The Planner* 78, 15: 10–12

Nadin, V. and Doak, J. (eds) (1991) *Town Planning Responses to City Change*, Aldershot: Gower

Nadin, V. and Jones, S. (1990) 'A profile of the profession', *The Planner*, 76, 3 (January): 13–24

Nadin, V. and Wood, C. (1988) 'More questions than answers on UDPs', *Planning* 782 (15 August): 6–7

Nadin, V., Crispin, G., and Fidler, P. (1985) 'The adoption of local plans', *The Planner* 71, 12: 23–25

Nairn, I. (1955) *Outrage*, London: Architectural Press

Nairn, I. (1957) *Counter Attack Against Utopia*, London: Longman

National Audit Office: *see* Official Publications (p. 327)

National Committee for Commonwealth Immigrants (1967) *Areas of Special Housing Need*, London: NCCI

National Consumer Council (1987) *What's Wrong with Walking?*, London: The Council

National Heritage Memorial Fund (1992) *Accounts 1991–92*, HC 139 (1991–92), London: HMSO

National Housing Forum (1991) *Planning for Social Housing*, London: Association of District Councils

National Planning Forum (1990) *The Management of the Planning Application Process*, Advice Note 1, London: NPF

National Planning Forum (1993) *Development Control: A Charter Guide*, London: NPF

National Rivers Authority (annual) *Annual Report*, Bristol: NRA

National Rivers Authority (1992) *Corporate Plan 1992/93*, Bristol: NRA

Nature Conservancy Council (annual) *Annual Report*, Peterborough: NCC [English Nature since 1991]

Nature Conservancy Council (1965) *Report on Broadland*, Peterborough: NCC

Nature Conservancy Council (1990) *Protecting Internationally Important Bird Sites: A Review of the EEC Special Protection Areas Network in Great Britain*, Peterborough: NCC

Nettlefold, J.S. (1914) *Practical Town Planning*, London: St Catherine's Press

Newby, H. (1979) *Green and Pleasant Land: Social Change in Rural England*, Harmondsworth: Penguin Books

Newby, H. (1985) *Green and Pleasant Land: Social Change in Rural England* (2nd edition), London: Wildwood House

Newby, H. (1986) 'Locality and rurality: the restructuring of rural social relations', *Regional Studies* 20: 209–16

Newby, H. (1990) 'Ecology, amenity, and society', *Town Planning Review* 61: 3–20

Newby, H. (1991) 'The Future of Rural Society', Swindon: Economic and Social Research Council (unpublished mimeo)

Newman, P.W.G. and Kenworthy, J.R. (1989) *Cities and Automobile Dependence: A Sourcebook*, Aldershot: Gower

Newsom, G.H. (1988) *Faculty Jurisdiction of the Church of England*, London: Sweet and Maxwell

Nicholson, D.J. (1984) 'The public ownership of vacant urban land', *The Planner* 70: 18–20

Noise Review Working Party (1990) *Report of the Noise Review Working Party*, London: HMSO

Noortman, H.J. (1988) 'The changing context of transport and infrastructure policy', *Environment and Planning C: Government and Policy* 6: 131–44

Norcliffe, G.B. and Hoare, A.G. (1982) 'Enterprise zone policy for the inner city: a review and preliminary assessment', *Area* 14: 265–74

Norton, A. (1983) *The Government and Administration of Metropolitan Areas in Western Democracies: A Survey of Approaches to the Administrative Problems of Major Conurbations in Europe and*

*Canada*, Birmingham: Institute of Local Government Studies, University of Birmingham

Norton, A. (1988) *Notes on Local and Regional Government in Advanced Western Democracies*, Birmingham: Institute of Local Government Studies, University of Birmingham

Norton, D.M. (1993) 'Conservation areas in an era of plan led planning', *JPL* 1993: 211–13

Nott, S.M. and Morgan, P.H. (1984) 'The significance of Department of the Environment circulars in the planning process', *JPL* 1984: 623–32

Nott, S.M. and Morgan, P.H. (1986) 'Development plans: what role for the law?', *JPL* 1986: 875–90

Nuffield Report (1986) *Town and Country Planning*, London: The Foundation

Nugent, N. (1989) *The Government and Politics of the European Community*, London: Macmillan

Nutley, S.D. (1990) *Unconventional and Community Transport in the United Kingdom*, New York: Gordon and Breach

Oatley, N. (1989) 'Evaluation and urban development corporations', *Planning Practice and Research* 4, 3 (Winter): 6–12

Oc, T. (1991) 'Planning natural surveillance back into city streets', *Town and Country Planning* 60: 237–9

Oc, T. and Tiesdell, S. (1991) 'The London Docklands Development Corporation 1981–1991: a perspective on the management of urban regeneration', *TPR* 62: 311–30

O'Connor, J. (1973) *The Fiscal Crisis of the State*, New York: St Martin's Press

O'Leary, B. (1987a) 'British farce, French drama, and tales of two cities: reorganizations of Paris and London governments 1957–86', *Public Administration* 65: 369–89

O'Leary, B. (1987b) 'Why was the GLC abolished?', *International Journal of Urban and Regional Research* 11: 193–217

Oliver, D. and Waite, A. (1989) 'Controlling neighbourhood noise – a new approach', *Journal of Environment Law* 1: 173–91

Organisation for Economic Cooperation and Development (1983) *Managing Urban Change: Vol 1: Policies and Finance; Vol 2: The Role of Government in Urban Affairs*, Paris: OECD

Organisation for Economic Cooperation and Development (1992) *Cities and New Technologies*, Paris: OECD

O'Riordan, T. (1979) 'The role of environmental quality objectives: the politics of pollution control', in O'Riordan and D'Arge

O'Riordan, T. (1990) 'On the "greening" of major projects', *Geographical Journal* 156: 141–8

O'Riordan, T. (1992) 'The environment', in Cloke

O'Riordan, T. and D'Arge, R.C. (1979) *Progress in Resource Management and Environmental Planning*, New York: Wiley

O'Riordan, T. and Weale, A. (1989) 'Administrative re-organization and policy change: the case of Her Majesty's Inspectorate of Pollution', *Public Administration* 67: 277–94

Osborn, F.J. (1950) 'Sir Ebenezer Howard: the evolution of his ideas', *TPR* 21: 221–35

Osborn, F.J. (1969) *Green Belt Cities*, London: Evelyn, Adams and Mackay

Osborn, F.J. and Whittick, A. (1977) *The New Towns: The Answer to Megalopolis* (3rd edition), London: Leonard Hill

Osborne, D. and Gaebler, T. (1992) *Reinventing Government: How the Entrepreneurial Spirit is Transforming the Public Sector*, New York: Addison-Wesley

Ottaway, J. (1980) 'Costs and the local authority in enforcement notice appeals', *JPL* 1980: 452–5

Outer Circle Policy Unit, Council for Science and Society, and Council of Justice (1979) *The Big Public Inquiry: A Proposed New Procedure for the Impartial Investigation of Projects with Major National Implications*, London: Outer Circle Policy Unit

Owens, S. (1984) 'Energy and spatial structure: a rural example', *Environment and Planning A* 16: 1319–37

Owens, S. (1985) 'Potential energy planning conflicts in the UK', *Energy Policy* 13: 546–58

Owens, S. (1986a) 'Strategic planning and energy conservation', *TPR* 57: 69–86

Owens, S. (1986b) *Energy, Planning and Urban Form*, London: Pion

Owens, S. (1989) 'Integrated pollution control in the United Kingdom: prospects and problems', *Environment and Planning C: Government and Policy* 7: 81–91

Owens, S. (1990) 'The unified pollution inspectorate and best practicable environmental option in the United Kingdom', in Haigh and Irwin

Owens, S. (1991) *Energy Conscious Planning*, London: CPRE

Owens, S. and Cope, D. (1992) *Land Use Planning Policy and Climate Change*, London: HMSO

PA Cambridge Economic Consultants (1987) *An Evaluation of the Enterprise Zone Experiment* (DoE Inner Cities Research Programme), London: HMSO

PA Cambridge Economic Consultants (1990a) *Indicators of Comparative Regional-Local Economic Performance and Prospects* (DoE) London, HMSO

PA Cambridge Economic Consultants (1990b) *An Evaluation of Garden Festivals* (DoE Inner Cities Research Programme), London: HMSO

Pacione, M. (1990) 'Development pressure in the metropolitan fringe', *Land Development Studies* 7: 69–82

Pacione, M. (1991) 'Development pressure and the production of the built environment in the urban fringe', *Scottish Geographical Magazine* 107: 162–9

Pack, C. and Glyptis, S. (1989) *Developing Sport and Leisure* (DoE Case Studies of Good Practice in Urban Management), London: HMSO

Paddison, R., Money, J., and Lever, B. (eds) (1992) *International Perspectives in Urban Studies*, London: Jessica Kingsley

Page, E. (1978) 'Why should central-local relations in Scotland be different to those in England?' *Public Administration Bulletin* 28: 51–72

Pahl, R.E. (1970) *Whose City? and Other Essays in Sociology and Planning*, Harlow: Longmans

Painter, J. (1991) 'Compulsive competitive tendering in local government: the first round', *Public Administration* 69: 191–210

Painter, M. (1980a) 'Whitehall and roads: a case of sectoral politics', *Policy and Politics* 8: 163–86

Painter, M. (1980b) 'Policy coordination in the Department of the Environment, 1970–1976', *Public Administration* 59: 135–54

Paris, C. (ed.) (1982) *Critical Readings in Planning Theory*, Oxford: Pergamon

Parker, D. (1990) 'The 1988 Local Government Act and compulsory competitive tendering', *Urban Studies* 27: 653–68

Parker, G. and Oatley, N. (1989) 'The case against the proposed development corporation for Bristol', *The Planner* 75, 1 (January): 32–5

Parker, H.R. (1954) 'The financial aspects of planning legislation', *Economic Journal* 64: 82–6

Parkes, W. (1978) 'Remedies of third parties in planning law', *JPL* 1978: 739–47

Parkes, W. (1989) 'Fresh obstacles to planning enforcement', *JPL* 1989: 246–51

Parkinson, M. (1985) *Liverpool on the Brink*, Hermitage, Berkshire: Policy Journals Publishers

Parkinson, M. (1989) 'The Thatcher Government's urban policy 1979–1989', *TPR* 60: 421–40

Parkinson, M. and Evans, R. (1990) 'Urban development corporations', in Campbell

Parliamentary Commissioner for Administration (1992) *Annual Report for 1991*, HC 347 (1991–92), London: HMSO

Parry, M. and Slater, T.R. (1980) *The Making of the Scottish Countryside*, London: Croom Helm

Pateman, C. (1970) *Participation and Democratic Theory*, Cambridge: Cambridge University Press

Paterson Report (1973) *The New Scottish Local Authorities: Organisation and Management Structures*, Edinburgh: HMSO

Pavitt, J.H. (1990) 'Urban renewal in Wales', *The Planner, TCPSS Proceedings* 76, 49 (14 December): 70–74

Pearce, B.J. (1981a) 'An emerging style of planning', *Planning Outlook* 23: 7–13

Pearce, B.J. (1981b) 'Property rights vs development control', *TPR* 52: 47–60

Pearce, B.J. (1984) 'Development control: a neighbour protection service?', *The Planner* 70, 5 (May): 8–11

Pearce, B.J. (1992) 'The effectiveness of the British land use planning system', *TPR* 63: 13–28

Pearce, D. and Turner, R.K. (1992) 'Packaging waste and the polluter pays principle: a taxation solution', *Journal of Environmental Planning and Management* 35: 5–15

Pearce, D., Edwards, L., and Beuret, G. (1979) *Decision-Making for Energy Futures: A Case Study of the Windscale Inquiry*, London: Macmillan

Pearce, D., Markandya, A., and Barbier, E.B. (1989) *Blueprint for a Green Economy: Report for the UK Department of the Environment*, London: Earthscan

Pearce, G. (1988) 'City grants: lessons from the urban development grant programme', *The Planner* 74, 4: 15–19

Pearce, G., Hems, L., and Hennessy, B. (1990) *The Conservation Areas of England*, London: Historic Buildings and Monuments Commission (English Heritage)

Pearce, P. (1984) 'Officers and gentlemen: a study of confidentiality of information received by local government officers from civil servants in relation to structure plans', *JPL* 1984: 306–16

Peart, J.D. and Rutherford, L.A. (1986) 'Opencast coal guidelines', *TPR* 57: 285–302

Perry, M., Bruton, M.J., Crispin, G., and Fidler, P.M. (1985) 'Local plans: the process of adoption after an inquiry', *JPL* 1985: 521–9

Peterson, A. (1966) 'Regional economic planning councils and boards', *Public Administration* 44: 29–41

Peterson, P.E. (1981) *City Limits*, Chicago, Ill.: University of Chicago Press

Peterson, P.E. and Kantor, P. (1977) 'Political parties and citizen participation in English city politics', *Comparative Politics* 9: 197–217

Petherbridge, D. (1987) *Art for Architecture: A Handbook on Commissioning* (DoE), London: HMSO

Pharoah, T. (1992) *Less Traffic, Better Towns*, London: FoE

Pharoah, T. (1993) 'Traffic calming in Europe', *Planning Practice and Research* 8, 1: 20–8

Pickvance, C. (1982) 'Physical forces and market forces in urban development', in Paris

PIEDA (1987a) *Land Supply and House Prices in Scotland*, Edinburgh: Scottish Development Department

PIEDA (1987b) *GEAR Project Evaluation: Final Report*, Glasgow: Scottish Enterprise

PIEDA (1990) *Five Year Review of the Bolton, Middlesbrough and Nottingham Programme Authorities* (DoE Inner Cities Research Programme), London: HMSO

Pilcher Report (1975) *Commercial Property Development: First Report of the Advisory Group on Commercial Property Development*, London: HMSO

Plan Local (1992) *The Character of Conservation Areas*, London: RTPI

Planning Advisory Group (1965) *The Future of Development Plans*, London: HMSO

Planning Aid for London (1986) *Planning for Women*, London: Planning Aid for London

Planning, Economic and Development Consultants: *see* PIEDA

Planning Exchange (1992) *Scottish Planning Law and Practice Conference 1992*, Glasgow: The Planning Exchange

Planning Inspectorate (1992a) *Chief Planning Inspector's Report, April 1991 to March 1992*, London: HMSO

Planning Inspectorate (1992b) *The Planning Inspectorate Executive Agency Business Plan 1992–93*, Bristol: The Planning Inspectorate

Planning Inspectorate (1992c) *The Planning Inspectorate Corporate Plan 1993/94–1995/96*, Bristol: The Planning Inspectorate

Pliatsky Report (1980) *Report on Non-Departmental Bodies*, Cmnd 7797, London: HMSO

Plowden Report (1967) *Children and their Primary Schools* (Central Advisory Committee for Education), London: HMSO

Plowden, S. (1988) *A Case for Traffic Restraint in London*, London: Centre for Transport Planning

Plowden, S. and Hillman, M. (1984) *Danger on the Road: The Needless Scourge – A Study of Obstacles to Progress in Road Safety*, London: Policy Studies Institute

Plowden, W. (1971) *The Motor Car and Politics 1896–1970*, London: The Bodley Head

Political and Economic Planning (1939) *Location of Industry*, London: PEP

Pollitt, C. (1984) *Manipulating the Machine: Changing the Pattern of Ministerial Departments 1960–83*, London: Allen and Unwin

Polytechnic of Central London, School of Planning; Leisure Works; and DRV Research (1990) *Tourism and the Inner City: An Evaluation of the Impact of Grant Assisted Tourism Projects* (DoE Inner Cities Directorate), London: HMSO

Ponting, C. (1990) *Secrecy in Britain* (Historical Association Studies), Oxford: Blackwell

Porter, M. (1990) *The Competitive Advantage of Nations*, New York: Free Press

Potter, S. (1986) 'New towns in the real world', *Town and Country Planning* 55: 304–9

Potter, S. (1992) 'New town legacies', *Town and Country Planning* 61: 298–302

Pountney, M.T. and Kingsbury, P.W. (1983) 'Aspects of development control', *TPR* 54: 139–54 and 285–303

Powell, A.G. (1978) 'Strategies for the English regions: ten years of evolution', *TPR* 49: 5–13

Pratt, G. and Hanson, S. (1988) 'Gender, class, and space', *Environment and Planning D: Society and Space* 6: 15–35

Preece, R. (1990) 'Development control studies: scientific method and policy analysis', *TPR* 61: 59–74

Pressman, J.L. and Wildavsky, A.B. (1984) *Implementation: How Great Expectations in Washington are Dashed in Oakland; or Why It's Amazing that Federal Programs Work At All, This Being a Saga of the Economic Development Administration as Told by Two Sympathetic Observers who Seek to Build Morals on a Foundation of Ruined Hopes*, Berkeley, Calif.: University of California Press

Property Advisory Group (1980) *Structure and Activity of the Development Industry*, London: HMSO

Property Advisory Group (1981) *Planning Gain*, London: HMSO

Property Advisory Group (1983) *The Climate for Public and Private Partnerships in Property Development*, London: HMSO

Property Advisory Group (1985) *Report on Town and Country Planning (Use Classes) Order 1972*, London: DoE

Public Sector Management Research Unit (1988a) *An Evaluation of the Urban Development Grant Programme* (DoE Inner Cities Research Programme), Aston University, London: HMSO

Public Sector Management Research Unit (1988b) *Improving Inner City Shopping Centres: An Evaluation of Urban Programme Funded Schemes in the West Midlands* (DoE Inner Cities Research Programme), London: IIMSO

Public Sector Management Research Centre (1992) *Parish Councils in England: A Survey*, London: HMSO

Pugh-Smith, J. (1992) 'The local authority as a regulator of pollution in the 1990s', *JPL* 1992: 103–9

Pugh-Smith, J. and Samuels, J. (1993) 'PPG 16: two years on', *JPL* 1993: 203–10

Punter, J.V. (1985) *Office Development in the Borough of Reading 1951–1984: A Case Study of the Role of Aesthetic Control*, Reading: Department of Land Management, University of Reading

Punter, J.V. (1986–7) 'A history of aesthetic control: the control of the external appearance of development in England and Wales' (parts 1 and 2), *TPR* 57: 351–81, and 58: 29–62

Punter, J.V. (1990) *Design Control in Bristol, 1940–1990: The Impact of Planning in the Design of Office Development in the City Centre*, Bristol: Redcliffe

Punter, J.V. (1992) 'Design control and the regeneration of dock-lands: the example of Bristol', *Journal of Property Research* 9: 49–78

Purdom, C.B. (1913) *The Garden City: A Study in the Development of a Modern New Town*, Letchworth: Temple Press

Purdom, C.B. (1925) *The Building of Satellite Towns*, London: Dent

Purdue, M. (1981) 'The complexities of enforcing the development control system and the Mansi rule', *JPL* 1981: 154–64

Purdue, M. (1984) 'The right to revert to earlier uses of land', *JPL* 1984: 6–12

Purdue, M. (1986) 'The flexibility of North American zoning as an instrument of land use planning', *JPL* 1986: 84–91

Purdue, M. (1989) 'Material considerations: an ever expanding concept?', *JPL* 1989: 156–61

Purdue, M. (1991) 'Green belts and the presumption in favour of development', *Journal of Environmental Law* 3: 93–121

Purdue, M. and Kemp, R. (1985) 'A case for funding objectors at public inquiries? A comparison of the position in Canada as opposed to the United Kingdom', *JPL* 1985: 675–85

Purdue, M., Healey, P., and Ennis, F. (1992) 'Planning gain and the grant of planning permission: is the United States' test of the "rational nexus" the appropriate solution?', *JPL* 1992: 1012–24

Pye-Smith, C. and North, R. (1984) *Working the Land: A New Plan for a Healthy Agriculture*, Aldershot: Gower

Queen, D. (1990) 'Neighbourhood renewal: impact and implications of the Local Government and Housing Act', *Housing Review* 39, 1 (January): 9–10

Rackham, O. (1985) *The History of the Countryside*, London: Dent

Radcliffe, J. (1991) *The Reorganisation of British Central Government*, Aldershot: Dartmouth

Radioactive Waste Management Advisory Committee (1991) *Twelfth Annual Report*, London: HMSO

Rahtz, P.A. (1974) *Rescue Archaeology*, Harmondsworth: Penguin

Ramsar Convention (1976) *Convention on Wetlands of International Importance*, Cmnd 6465, London: HMSO

Ramsay Report [1] (1945) *Report of the Scottish National Parks Survey Committee*, Cmd 6631, Edinburgh: HMSO

Ramsay Report [2] (1947) *National Parks and the Conservation of Nature in Scotland*, Cmd 7235, Edinburgh: HMSO

Ranson, S., Jones, G., and Walsh, K. (eds) (1985) *Between Centre and Locality: The Politics of Public Policy*, London: Allen and Unwin

Rao, N. (1990) *The Changing Face of Housing Authorities*, London: Policy Studies Institute

Ravetz, A. (1980) *Remaking Cities*, London: Croom Helm

Ravetz, A. (1986) *The Government of Space: Town Planning in Modern Society*, London: Faber

Rawlings, H.F. (1986) 'Judicial review and the control of government', *Public Administration* 64: 135–45

Ray, T. (1991) 'Europe and economic development', *The Planner* 77, 24 (5 July): 9–10

Rayner, D. (1984) *Rayner Review of the Nature Conservancy Council*, London: DoE

Reade, E.J. (1982a) 'Section 52 and corporatism in planning', *JPL* 1982: 8–16

Reade, E.J. (1982b) 'If planning isn't everything . . .' *TPR* 53: 65–78

Reade, E.J. (1983) 'If planning is anything, maybe it can be identified', *Urban Studies* 20: 159–71

Reade, E.J. (1985) 'Planning's usurpation of political choice', *Town and Country Planning* 54: 184–6

Reade, E.J. (1987) *British Town and Country Planning*, Milton Keynes: Open University Press

Reade, E.J. (1992) 'The little world of Upper Bangor', part 1: 'How many conservation areas are slums?'; part 2: 'Professionally prestigious projects or routine public administration'; part 3: 'What is planning for anyway?', *Town and Country Planning* 61: 11–12, 25–7, and 44–7

Redcliffe-Maud Report (1969) *Report of the Royal Commission on Local Government in England*, Cmnd 4040, London: HMSO

Redman, M. (1988) *Change of Use*, London: Estates Gazette

Redman, M. (1989) 'Simplifying the system', *JPL* 1989: 563–76

Redman, M. (1990) 'Archaeology and development', *JPL* 1990: 87–98

Redman, M. (1991) 'Planning gain and obligations', *JPL* 1991: 203–18

Redmond, J. and Barrett, G. (1988) 'The European regional development fund and local government', *Local Government Studies*, September/October: 19–33

Redundant Churches Fund (1990) *Churches in Retirement: A Gazeteer*, London: HMSO

Rees, G. and Lambert, J. (1985) *Cities in Crisis: The Political*

*Economy of Urban Development in Postwar Britain*, London: Edward Arnold

Rees, W.E. (1990) 'Sustainable development as capitalism with a green face: a review article' [Review of Pearce, Markandya, and Barber], *TPR* 61: 91–4

Regan, D.E. (1978) 'The pathology of British land use planning', *Local Government Studies* 4, 2: 3–23

Regional Studies Association (1983) *Report of an Inquiry into Regional Problems in the United Kingdom*, Norwich: Geo Books

Regional Studies Association (1990) *Beyond Green Belts*, London: Jessica Kingsley

Rehbinder, E. and Stewart, R. (1985) *Environmental Protection Policy* (*Integration through Law* series, vol. 2), Berlin and New York: Walter de Gruyter

Reid, C.T. (1988) 'Afforestation: controls and controversies', *JPL* 1988: 610–14

Reith Reports (1946) *Interim Report of the New Towns Committee*, Cmd 6759; *Second Interim Report*, Cmd 6794; and *Final Report*, Cmd 6876, London: HMSO

Renton, J. (1992) 'The ombudsman and planning', in Planning Exchange

Reynolds, J.P. (1975) 'Heritage year in Britain: the aims and objectives of conservation', *TPR* 46: 355–64

Rhodes, G. (1981) *Inspectorates in British Government: Law Enforcement and Standards of Efficiency*, London: Allen and Unwin

Rhodes, R.A.W. (1981) *Control and Power in Central–Local Relations*, Aldershot: Gower

Rhodes, R.A.W. (1986) *The National World of Local Government*, London: Allen and Unwin

Rhodes, R.A.W. (1988) *Beyond Westminster and Whitehall: The Sub-Central Governments of Britain*, London: Unwin Hyman

Rhodes, R.A.W. (1992) 'Changing intergovernmental relations', in Cloke

Richards, P.G. (1973) *The Reformed Local Government System*, London: Allen and Unwin

Richardson, A. (1983) *Participation*, London: Routledge and Kegan Paul

Richardson, G., Ogus, A., and Burrows, A. (1982) *Policing Pollution: A Study of Regulation and Enforcement*, Oxford: Oxford University Press

RICS (1974) *The Land Problem: A Fresh Approach*, London: The Institution

RICS (1990) *A Place to Live: Housing in the Rural Community*, London: The Institution

RICS (1991) *Britain's Environmental Strategy: A Response by the Royal Institution of Chartered Surveyors to the White Paper 'This Common Inheritance'*, London: The Institution

Riddle, P. (1991) *The Thatcher Era*, Oxford: Blackwell

Ridley, F. (1986) 'Liverpool is different: political struggles in context', *Political Quarterly* 57: 125–36

Rietveld, P. and Wissen, L. van (1991) 'Transport policies and the environment: regulation and taxation', in Kraan and Veld

Rittel, H.W.J. and Webber, M.M. (1973) 'Dilemmas in a general theory of planning', *Policy Sciences* 4: 155–69

Ritzdorf, M. (1993) 'The fairy's tale: teaching planning and public policy in a different voice', *Journal of Planning Education and Research* 12: 99–106

Roberts, J., Cleary, J., Hamilton, K., and Hanna, J. (1992) *Travel Sickness: The Need for a Sustainable Transport Policy for Britain*, London: Lawrence and Wishart

Roberts, N.A. (1976) *The Reform of Planning Law*, London: Macmillan

Roberts, N.A. (ed.) (1977) *The Government Land Developers*, Lexington, Mass.: Heath

Roberts, P. (1991) 'Environmental priorities and the challenges of environmental management', *TPR* 62: 447–69

Robertson, G. (1989) *Freedom, the Individual and the Law* (6th edition), Harmondsworth: Penguin

Robins, N. (1991) *A European Environment Charter*, London: Fabian Society

Robinson, M. (1992) *The Greening of British Party Politics*, Manchester: Manchester University Press

Robinson, P.C. (1990) 'Tree preservation orders: felling a dangerous tree', *JPL* 1990: 720–3

Roche, F.L. (1986) 'New communities for a new generation', *Town and Country Planning* 55: 312–13

Rodger, J.J. (1978) 'Inauthentic politics and the public inquiry system: a discussion based on the Moss Morran controversy', *Scottish Journal of Sociology* 3: 103–27

Rodriguez-Bachiller, A., Thomas, M., and Walker, S. (1992) 'The English planning lottery: some insights from a more regulated system', *TPR* 63: 387–402

Rogers, A. (1985) 'Local claims on rural housing', *TPR* 56: 367–80

Roome, N.J. (1986) 'New directions in rural policy: recent administrative changes in response to conflict between rural policies', *TPR* 57: 253–63

Rose, C. (1990) *The Dirty Man of Europe: The Great British Pollution Scandal*, London: Simon and Schuster

Rose, D. (1992) 'The impact of the European Community on land use planning: expressions of interest invited on the next RTPI commissioned study', *The Planner* 78, 14 (17 July): 8

Rose, E. (1986) 'Urban development grants: policy and managerial aspects', *TPR* 57: 440–57

Rose, E. (ed.) (1986) *New Roles for Old Cities*, Aldershot: Gower

Rosenbloom, S. (1992) 'Why working families need a car', in Wachs and Crawford

Rosener, J.B. (1978) 'Citizen participation: can we measure its effectiveness?', *Public Administration Review* 38: 457–63

Ross, M. (1990) 'Listing historic buildings', *JPL* 1990: 551–61

Ross, M. (1991) *Planning and the Heritage*, London: Spon

Ross, S. (1988) 'SPZs in practice', *Estates Gazette*, July: 20–21 and 102

Ross, S. (1991) 'Planning and the public interest', *The Planner, TCPSS Proceedings* 77: 55–7

Rossi, P.H., Freeman, H.E., and Wright, S.R. (1979) *Evaluation: A Systematic Approach*, London: Sage

Roth, G.J. (1966a) *A Self-Financing Road System*, London: Institute of Economic Affairs

Roth, G.J. (1966b) 'An economic approach to traffic congestion', *TPR* 37: 49–74

Rowan-Robinson, J. (1981) 'The big public inquiry', *TPR* 57: 440–57

Rowan-Robinson, J. and Durman, R. (1992a) *Section 50 Agreements*, Central Research Unit Papers, Edinburgh: Scottish Office

Rowan-Robinson, J. and Durman, R. (1992b) 'Conditions or agreements', *JPL* 1992: 1003–11

Rowan-Robinson, J. and Durman, R. (1992c) 'Planning agreements and the spirit of enterprise', *Scottish Geographical Magazine* 108: 157–63

Rowan-Robinson, J. and Lloyd, M.G. (1986) 'Lifting the burden of planning: a means or an end?', *Local Government Studies* 12: 51–64

Rowan-Robinson, J. and Lloyd, M.G. (1988) *Land Development and the Infrastructure Lottery*, Edinburgh: T.& T. Clark

Rowan-Robinson, J. and Lloyd, M.G. (1991) 'National planning guidelines: a strategic opportunity wasting', *Planning Practice and Research* 6, 3: 16–19

Rowan-Robinson, J. and Young, E. (1987) 'Enforcement – the weakest link in the Scottish planning control system', *Urban Law and Policy* 8: 255–88

Rowan-Robinson, J. and Young, E. (1989) *Planning by Agreement in Scotland*, Glasgow: The Planning Exchange/Edinburgh: Green

Rowan-Robinson, J., Lloyd, M.G., and Elliott, R.G. (1987) 'National planning guidelines and strategic planning', *TPR* 58: 369–81

Rowan-Robinson, J., Young, E., and McLarty, I. (1984) *The Enforcement of Planning Control in Scotland*, Edinburgh: SDD

Royal Commission on Environmental Pollution; *see* Official Publications (p. 319)

Royal Fine Art Commission (annual) *Annual Reports*, London: HMSO

Royal Fine Art Commission for Scotland (annual) *Annual Reports*, London: HMSO

RTPI (1976) *Planning and the Future*, London: The Institute

RTPI (1982) *The Public and Planning: Means to Better Participation*, London: The Institute

RTPI (1983) *Public Transport in London: Report by the Transport Working Party*, London: The Institute

RTPI (1985) *Planners and Environmental Education*, London: The Institute

RTPI (1987a) *The Future of Development Plans: Memorandum of Observations to the DoE and the Welsh Office on their Consultation Paper*, London: The Institute

RTPI (1987b) *Report and Recommendations of the Working Party on Women in Planning*, London: The Institute

RTPI (1988a) *Local Plans Draft Planning Policy Guidance Note: Memorandum of Observations to the DoE*, London: The Institute

RTPI (1988b) *Managing Equality: The Role of the Senior Planners*, London: The Institute

RTPI (1988c) *Access for Disabled People* (Practice Advice Note 3), London: The Institute

RTPI (1989) *Choice and Opportunity in Planning*, London: The Institute

RTPI (1990) *The Pressing Case for Strategic Planning*, RTPI North West Branch

RTPI (1991a) *Planning – Is it a Service, and How Can it be Effective? A Study Commissioned from Elsworth Sykes Planning* (2 vols), London: The Institute

RTPI (1991b) *Traffic Growth and Planning Policy: A Report Commissioned from the London Research Centre*, London: The Institute

RTPI (1992a) *Planning Policy and Social Housing*, London: The Institute

RTPI (1992b) *The Regional Planning Process*, London: The Institute

RTPI (1993) *The Character of Conservation Areas*, London: The Institute

RTPI/CRE (1983) *Planning for a Multi-Racial Britain*, London: The Institute

Rural Development Commission (annual) *Annual Report*, Salisbury: The Commission

Rural Development Commission (1990) *An Evaluation of the Rural Development Programme Process*, Salisbury: The Commission

Rural Voice (1990) *Employment of the Land*, Cirencester: Rural Voice

Rush, M. (1990) *Parliament and Pressure Politics*, Oxford: Clarendon Press

Rutherford, L.A. and Peart, J.D. (1989) 'Opencast guidance – opportunities for green policies', *JPL* 1989: 402–10

Ryder, A.A. (1987) 'The Dounreay inquiry: public participation in practice', *Scottish Geographical Magazine* 103: 54–7

Rydin, Y. (1984) 'The struggle for housing land: a case of confused interests', *Policy and Politics* 12: 431–46

Rydin, Y. (1986) *Housing Land Policy*, Aldershot: Gower

Rydin, Y. (1992) 'Environmental dimensions of residential development and the implications for local planning practice', *Journal of Environmental Planning and Management* 35: 43–61

Rydin, Y., Home, R., and Taylor, K. (1990) *Making the Most of the Planning Appeals System: Report to the Association of District Councils*, London: Association of District Councils

SACTRA (1979) *Trunk Road Proposals: A Comprehensive Framework for Appraisal*, London: HMSO

SACTRA (1986) *Urban Road Appraisal*, London: HMSO

SACTRA (1992) *Assessing the Environmental Impact of Road Schemes*, London: HMSO

Salter, J.R. (1992a) 'Environmental assessment: the challenge from Brussels', *JPL* 1992: 14–20

Salter, J.R. (1992b) 'Environmental assessment – the need for transparency', *JPL* 1992: 214–21

Salter, J.R. (1992c) 'Environmental assessment – the question of implementation', *JPL* 1992: 313–18

Salter, M. and Newman, P. (1992) 'Minding their own business in the planning department', *Municipal Journal* 50 (11–17 December): 28–9

Samuels, A. (1980) 'Prostitution and planning law', *JPL* 1980: 578–82

Samuels, A. (1981) 'New roads: the assessment of need, usefulness and desirability', *JPL* 1981: 15–25

Samuels, A. (1985) 'Enforcement: why is it so weak?', *JPL* 1985: 233–42

Samuels, A. (1986) 'The Wildlife and Countryside (Amendment) Act 1985', *JPL* 1986: 174–6

Sandbach, F. (1980) *Environment, Ideology and Public Policy*, Oxford: Blackwell

Sandford Report (1974) *Report of the National Park Policies Review Committee*, London: HMSO

Sassen, S. (1991) *The Global City: New York, London, Tokyo*, Princeton: Princeton University Press

Saunders, P. (1979) *Urban Politics: A Sociological Interpretation*, Harmondsworth: Penguin

Saunders, P. (1981) *Social Theory and the Urban Question*, London: Hutchinson

Scarman Report (1981) *The Brixton Disorders 10–12 April 1981*, Cmnd 8427, London: HMSO

Schackleton, J.R. (1992) *Training Too Much? A Sceptical Look at the Economics of Skill Provision in the UK*, London: Institute of Economic Affairs

Schaffer, F. (1970) *The New Town Story*, London: MacGibbon and Kee

Schofield, J. (1987) *Cost–Benefit Analysis in Urban and Regional Planning*, London: Allen and Unwin

Scholefield, G.P. (1990) 'Transport and society: the Rees Jeffreys discussion papers', *TPR* 61: 487–93

Schon, D.A. (1971) *Beyond the Stable State*, London: Temple Smith

Schuster Report (1950) *Report of the Committee on the Qualifications of Planners*, Cmd 8059, London: HMSO

Scott, A.J. (1980) *The Urban Land Nexus*, London: Pion

Scott, M.G. (1990) 'Parliamentary private bill procedure and our built heritage', *JPL* 1990: 635–43

Scott Report (1942) *Report of the Committee on Land Utilisation in Rural Areas*, Cmd 6378, London: HMSO

Scottish Homes (1991) *Planning Agreements and Low Cost Housing in Scotland's Rural Areas*, Edinburgh: Scottish Homes

Scrase, A.J. (1987) 'Planning conditions – the law and the policy context', *JPL* 1987: 323–34

Scrase, A.J. (1988) 'Agriculture – 1980s industry and 1947 definition', *JPL* 1988: 447–60

Scrase, T. (1991) 'Archaeology and planning – a case for full integration', *JPL* 1991: 1103–12

Seebohm Report (1968) *Report of the Committee on Local Authority and Allied Personal Social Services*, Cmnd 3703, London: HMSO

Segal Quince Wicksteed (1988) *Encouraging Small Business Start-up and Growth* (Department of Employment), London: HMSO

Segal Quince Wicksteed (1992) *Evaluation of Regional Enterprise Grants; Third Stage*, London: Department of Trade and Industry

Self, P. (1961a) *Cities in Flood: The Problems of Urban Growth* (2nd edition), London: Faber

Self, P. (1961b) *The Wythall Inquiry*, London: Estates Gazette

Self, P. (1975) *Econocrats and the Policy Process*, London: Macmillan

Self, P. (1982) *Planning the Urban Region: A Comparative Study of Policies and Organisations*, London: Allen and Unwin

Sellgren, J. (1990) 'Development control data for planning research: the use of aggregated development control records', *Environment and Planning B: Planning and Design* 17: 23–7

Selman, P.H. (1976) 'Wildlife conservation in structure plans', *Journal of Environmental Management* 4: 149–59

Selman, P.H. (1982) 'The use of ecological evaluations by local planning authorities', *Journal of Environmental Management* 15: 1–13

Selman, P.H. (1987) 'Nature conservation and local plans', *Planning Outlook* 30: 78–83

Selman, P.H. (1988a) *Countryside Planning in Practice: The Scottish Experience*, Stirling: Stirling University Press

Selman, P.H. (1988b) 'Rural land-use planning – resolving the British paradox', *Journal of Rural Studies* 4: 277–94

Selman, P.H. (1989) 'Conservation, development and land use planning: Scotland leads the way', *Scottish Geographical Magazine* 105: 142–8

Senior, D. (1965) 'The city region as an administrative unit', *Political Quarterly* 36: 82–91

SERPLAN (1990a) *Access to Affordable Housing in the South East*, London: London and South East Regional Conference

SERPLAN (1990b) *A New Strategy for the South East*, London: London and South East Regional Conference

SERPLAN (1992a) *Housing Land Supply and Structure Plan Provisions in the South East*, London: London and South East Regional Conference

SERPLAN (1992b) *SERPLAN: Thirty Years of Regional Planning 1962–1992*, London: London and South East Regional Planning Conference

Sharman, F.A. (1985) 'Public attendance at planning inquiries', *JPL* 1985: 152–8

Sharp, E. (1969) *The Ministry of Housing and Local Government*, London: Allen and Unwin

Sharp, T. (1947) *Exeter Phoenix*, London: Architectural Press

Sharpe, L.J. (1981) 'The failure of local government modernisation in Britain: a critique of functionalism', *Canadian Public Administration* 24: 92–115

Sharpe, L.J. and Newton, K. (1984) *Does Politics Matter?: The Determinants of Public Policy*, Oxford: Clarendon Press

Shaw, M. (1989) 'The Broads Act 1988: a framework for environmental planning and management', *JPL* 1989: 241–6

Shaw, T. (1992) 'Regional planning guidance for the North East – advice to the secretary of state for the environment', *TPR* 63: 425–6

Sheail, J. (1983) 'Deserts of the moon – the Mineral Workings Act and the restoration of ironstone workings in Northamptonshire, England, 1936–1951', *TPR* 54: 405–24

Shelbourn, C. (1989) 'Development control and hazardous substances', *JPL* 1989: 323–30

Shelter (1972) *Another Chance for Cities: Shelter Neighbourhood Action Project*, London: Shelter

Shelton, A. (1991) 'The well informed optimist's view', in Nadin and Doak

Shepherd, J. and Abakuks, A. (1992) *The National Survey of Vacant Land in Urban Areas of England 1990* (DoE Planning Research Programme), London: HMSO

Shepley, C. and Fryer, D. (1991) 'A planner's guide to Europe', *The Planner* 77, 6 (15 February): 5–8

Sherlock, H. (1991) *Cities Are Good for Us*, London: Paladin

Sherr, A. (1985) 'The Scarman report on *The Brixton Disorders 10–12 April 1981* – a retrospective view', *Urban Law and Policy* 7: 227–41

Shiva, V. (1992) 'Recovering the meaning of sustainability', in Cooper and Palmer

Shoard, M. (1980) *The Theft of the Countryside*, London: Maurice Temple Smith

Shoard, M. (1987) *This Land is our Land*, London: Paladin

Shoesmith, R. and Scrase, A.J. (1987) 'The repair and recording of listed buildings', *JPL* 1987: 85–92

Short, J.R. and Kirby, A. (eds) (1984) *The Human Geography of Contemporary Britain*, London: Macmillan

Short, J.R., Fleming, S., and Witt, S. (1986) *Housebuilding, Planning and Community Action*, London: Routledge and Kegan Paul

Shucksmith, M. (1983) 'Second homes: a framework for policy', *TPR* 54: 174–93

Shucksmith, M. (1988a) 'Current rural land-use issues in Scotland', *Scottish Geographical Magazine* 104: 176–80

Shucksmith, M. (1988b) 'Policy aspects of housebuilding on farmland in Britain', *Land Development Studies* 5: 129–38

Shucksmith, M. and Lloyd, M. (1983) 'Rural planning in Scotland', in Gilg

Shucksmith, M. and Watkins, L. (1991) 'Housebuilding on farmland: the distributional effects in rural areas', *Journal of Rural Studies* 7: 153–68

Sillence, J.A.A. (1986) 'Why did Warwickshire key settlement policy change in 1982? An assessment of the political implications of cuts in rural services', *Geographical Journal* 152: 176–92

Simmie, J. (1974) *Citizens in Conflict*, London: Hutchinson

Simmie, J. (1981) *Power, Property and Corporatism*, London: Macmillan

Simmie, J. and French, S. (1989) 'Corporatism, participation and planning: the case of London', *Progress in Planning* 31

Simmie, J. and King, R. (eds) (1990) *The State in Action: Public Policy and Politics*, London: Pinter

Simmonds, D. (1990) *The Impact of the Channel Tunnel on the Regions*, London: RTPI

Simpson, I. (1987) 'Planning gain: an aid to positive planning', in Harrison and Mordey

Sinclair, G. (1983) *Uplands Landscapes Study*, Norwich: Environmental Information Services

Sinclair, G. (1992) *The Lost Land: Land Use Change in England 1945–1990*, London: CPRE

Sinfield, A. (1973) 'Poverty rediscovered', in Cullingworth

Sizewell Report (1987) *Sizewell B Public Inquiry: Report by Sir Frank Layfield: Summary*, London: HMSO

Skeffington Report (1969) *Report of the Committee on Public Participation in Planning*, London: HMSO

Skelcher, C. (1985) 'Transportation', in Ranson, Jones, and Walsh

Smallbone, D. (1991) 'Partnership in economic development: the case of U.K. local enterprise agencies', *Policy Studies Review* 10: 87–98

Smart, G. and Anderson, M. (1990) *Planning and Management of Areas of Outstanding Natural Beauty*, Cheltenham: Countryside Commission

Smeed Report (1964) *Road Pricing: The Economic and Technical Possibilities*, London: HMSO

Smith, A.G., Williams, G., and Houlder, M. (1986) 'Community influence on local planning policy', *Progress in Planning* 25: 1–82

Smith, D. (1989) *North and South: Britain's Economic, Social, and Political Divide*, Harmondsworth: Penguin

Smith, D.L. (1974) *Amenity and Urban Planning*, London: Crosby Lockwood and Staples

Smith, G. (1985) 'Policy making in London's transport planning', *Land Use Policy* 2: 299–308

Smith, K. (1983) 'Planning decisions: the application of green belt policy', *JPL* 1983: 777–85

Smith, K. (1986) 'The agricultural condition of occupancy revisited', *JPL* 1986: 416–21

Smith, M.E.H. (1989) *Guide to Housing*, London: The Housing Centre

Smith, M.P. (1980) *The City and Social Theory*, Oxford: Basil Blackwell

Smith, N. and Williams, P. (1986) *Gentrification of the City*, London: Allen and Unwin

Smith, R. (1979) *East Kilbride: The Biography of a New Town 1947–1973*, Edinburgh: HMSO

Smith, R. and Wannop, U. (1985) *Strategic Planning in Action: The Impact of the Clyde Valley Regional Plan 1946–82*, Aldershot: Gower

Smyth, H. (1984) *Land Supply, Housebuilders and Government Policies*, Bristol: School for Advanced Urban Studies, University of Bristol

Sneddon, D. (1988) 'Privacy in residential areas: a development control dilemma', *JPL* 1988: 3–11

Solesbury, W. (1974) *Policy in Urban Planning: Structure Plans, Programmes and Local Plans*, Oxford: Pergamon

Solesbury, W. (1975) 'Ideas about structure plans: past, present and future', *TPR* 46: 245–54

Solesbury, W. (1976) 'The environmental agenda: an illustration of how situations may become political issues and issues may demand responses from government: or how they may not', *Public Administration* 54: 379–97

Solesbury, W. (1981) 'Strategic planning: metaphor or method?', *Policy and Politics* 9: 419–37

Solesbury, W. (1983) 'Structure plans: underlying intentions and overriding influences', in Cross and Bristow

Solesbury, W. (1986) 'The dilemmas of inner city policy', *Public Administration* 64: 389–400

Solesbury, W. (1987) 'Urban policy in the 1980s: the issues and arguments', *The Planner* 73, 6 (June): 18–22

Solesbury, W. (1993) 'Reframing urban policy', *Policy and Politics* 21: 31–8

Somsen, H. (1990) 'EC water directives', *Water Law* 1: 93–8

Sorafu, F.J. (1957) 'The public interest reconsidered', *Journal of Politics* 19: 616–39

Sorensen, A.D. and Day, R.A. (1981) 'Libertarian planning', *TPR* 52: 390–402

Sparks, L. (1987) 'Retailing in enterprise zones: the example of Swansea', *Regional Studies* 21: 37–42

Spencer, K., Taylor, A., Smith, B., Mawson, J., Flynn, N., and Batley, R. (1986) *Crisis in the Heartland: A Study of the West Midlands*, Oxford: Clarendon Press

Spooner, D., Arnett, R., and Justice, M. (1992) 'Building a geographical base for integrated pollution control: some problems', *Area* 24: 105–12

Sports Council (1991) *Planning Policy Guidance Note: Sport and Recreation: The Sports Council Initial Response*, London: The Council

Standing Advisory Committee on Trunk Road Assessment: *see* SACTRA

Stanley, N. (1991) 'The Bath Society case – a Pandora's box', *JPL* 1991: 1014–15

Starkie, D.N.M. (1982) *The Motorway Age: Road and Traffic Policies in Postwar Britain*, Oxford: Pergamon

Starkie, D.N.M. (1986) 'Efficient and politic congestion tolls', *Transportation Research A* 20A: 169–73

*Steinberg and Sykes v. Secretary of State for the Environment and Camden L.B.C.* (1988) 'Notes of cases', *JPL* 1989: 258–63

Stephen, F.H. and Young, E. (1985) 'An economic insight on the judicial control of planning authorities' discretion', *Urban Law and Policy* 7: 133–64

Stevens Report (1976) *Report of the Committee on Planning Control over Mineral Working*, London: HMSO

Stewart, J.D. (1991) 'The changing organisation and management of local authorities', in Stewart and Stoker

Stewart, J.D. and Stoker, G. (eds) (1991) *The Future of Local Government*, London: Macmillan

Stewart, J.D., Leach, S., and Skelcher, C.K. (1978) *Organic Change: A Report on Constitutional, Management and Financial Problems*, London: Association of County Councils

Stewart, J.D., Spencer, K., and Webster, B. (1976) *Local Government: Approaches to Urban Deprivation*, Home Office Urban Deprivation Unit, London: Home Office

Stewart, J.M.W. (1973) 'Markets, choice and planning', *TPR* 44: 203–20

Stewart, J.M.W. (1983) 'The inner area planning system', *Policy and Politics* 11: 203–14

Stewart, J.M.W. (1990a) *Regional Development Prospects*, Bristol: School for Advanced Urban Studies, University of Bristol

Stewart, J.M.W. (1990b) *Urban Policy in Thatcher's England*, Bristol: School for Advanced Urban Studies, University of Bristol

Stocks, N. (1989) 'The Greater Manchester shopping inquiry: a case study of strategic retail planning', *Land Development Studies* 6: 57–83

Stodart Report (1981) *Report of the Committee of Inquiry into Local Government in Scotland*, Cmnd 8115, Edinburgh: HMSO

Stoker, G. (1989) 'Urban development corporations: a review', *Regional Studies* 23: 159–67

Stoker, G. (1991) *The Politics of Local Government*, London: Macmillan

Stokes, G., Goodwin, P., and Kenny, F. (1992) *Trends in Transport and the Countryside*, Cheltenham: Countryside Commission

Storey, D.J. (1990) 'Evaluation of policies and measures to create local employment', *Urban Studies* 27: 669–84

Stott, M. and Taylor, P. (1980) *The Nuclear Controversy: A Guide to the Issues of the Windscale Inquiry*, London: TCPA

Street, E.A. (1986) 'Land restoration after minerals extraction', *TPR* 57: 382–403

Stubbs, M. and Lavers, A. (1991) 'Steinberg and after: decision making and development control in conservation areas', *JPL* 1991: 9–19

Suddards, R.W. (1979) 'Section 52 agreements: a case for new legislation?', *JPL* 1979: 661–7

Suddards, R.W. (1988) 'Listed buildings: have we listed too far?', *JPL* 1988: 523–8

Suddards, R.W. and Morton, D.M. (1991) 'The character of conservation areas', *JPL* 1991: 1011–13

Sutcliffe, A. (1981a) *Towards the Planned City*, Oxford: Blackwell

Sutcliffe, A. (ed.) (1981b) *British Town Planning: The Formative Years*, Leicester: Leicester University Press

Sutcliffe, A. (ed.) (1984) *Metropolis 1890–1940*, London: Mansell

Sutcliffe, A. and Smith, R. (1974) *History of Birmingham*, Oxford: Oxford University Press

Switzer, J.F.Q. (1978) 'Managing the urban fabric', *JPL* 1978: 423–36

Switzer, J.F.Q. (1984) 'The duty of the Secretary of State for the Environment' (with a commentary by Sir Desmond Heap), *JPL* 1984: 72–6

Sylvester-Evans, A. (1980) *Urban Renaissance: A Better Life in Towns*, London: HMSO

Tait, J. (1990) 'The impact of biotechnology on the rural environment', in Bowers

Talbot, J. (1988) 'Have enterprise zones encouraged enterprise? Some empirical evidence from Tyneside', *Regional Studies* 22: 507–14

Tanner, J.C. (1967) *Revised Forecasts of Vehicles and Traffic in Great Britain*, Crowthorne: Transport and Road Research Laboratory

Tanner, J.C. (1974) *Forecasts of Vehicles and Traffic in Great Britain*, Crowthorne: Transport and Road Research Laboratory

Tanner, J.C. (1977) *Car Ownership Trends and Forecasts*, Crowthorne: Transport and Road Research Laboratory

Tanner, J.C. (1983) *Car Ownership Trends and Forecasts*, Crowthorne: Transport and Road Research Laboratory

Tanner, J.C. (1984) *Some Aspects of New Car Registrations*, Crowthorne: Transport and Road Research Laboratory

Tant, A.P. (1990) 'The campaign for freedom of information: a participatory challenge to elitist British government', *Public Administration* 68: 477–91

Taussik, J. (1992) 'Pre-application enquiries', *JPL* 1992: 414–19

Taylor, A. (1984) 'The planning implications of new technology in retailing and distribution', *TPR* 55: 161–76

Taylor, A. (1992) *Choosing our Future: A Practical Politics of the Environment*, London: Routledge

Taylor, B. (1984) 'Decentralisation in Walsall', *Local Government Policy Making*, November: 91–5

Taylor, J. (1991) *Reviving the Regions*, London: Fabian Society

Taylor, M.C. (1985) 'Concurrent inquiries: the programme officer's role', *JPL* 1985: 161–4

Taylor, S. (1981) 'The politics of enterprise zones', *Public Administration* 59: 421–39

TCPA (1955) *Dispersal: A Call for Action*, London: The Association

TCPA (1979) *Inner Cities*, London: The Association

TCPA (1986) *Whose Responsibility? Reclaiming the Inner Cities*, London: The Association

TCPA (1989) *Bridging the North–South Divide*, London: The Association

TCPA (1991a) *Europe 2000: A Response by the Town and Country Planning Association*, London: The Association

TCPA (1991b) *TCPA Campaign for Strategic Planning: Improving Regional Guidance*, London: The Association

TCPA (1992) *New Settlements: Planning Policy Guidance* (spoof PPG), London: The Association

TCPA (1993) *Strategic Planning for Regional Development*, London: The Association

TEST (1984) *The Company Car Factor*, London: TEST

TEST (1986a) *Changing to Green*, London: TEST

TEST (1986b) *Jobs on the Move: The Employment Potential of an Alternative Transport Policy*, London: TEST

TEST (1986c) *London: The Most Civilised City*, London: TEST

TEST (1991) *Wrong Side of the Tracks? Impacts of Road and Rail Transport on the Environment – A Basis for Discussion*, London: TEST

TEST (1992) *An Environmental Approach to Transport and Planning in Cardiff*, London: TEST

Thew, D. and Watson, P. (1988) 'The future of strategic planning', *The Planner* 74, 11: 19–23

Thomas, C.J. and Bromley, R.D.F. (1987) 'The growth and functioning of an unplanned retail park: the Swansea Enterprise Zone', *Regional Studies* 21: 287–300

Thomas, D. (1970) *London's Green Belt*, London: Faber

Thomas, D., Minett, J., Hopkins, J., Hamnett, S., Faludi, A., and Barrell, D. (1983) *Flexibility and Commitment in Planning*, The Hague: Martinus Nijhoff

Thomas, H. (1989) 'Evaluating CBDC's effectiveness', *The Planner* 75, 1 (January): 36–7

Thomas, H. (1991) *Dilemmas of Planning Practice: Ethics, Legitimacy and the Validation of Knowledge*, Aldershot: Avebury

Thomas, H. (1992) 'Disability, politics and the built environment', *Planning Practice and Research* 7, 1: 22–6

Thomas, H. and Healey, P. (1991) *Dilemmas of Planning Practice: Ethics, Legitimacy, and the Validation of Knowledge*, Aldershot: Avebury

Thomas, H. and Krishnarayan, V. (1993a) 'Planning aid and black and ethnic minorities – a story of unrealised potential', *Town and Country Planning* 61: 276–7

Thomas, H. and Krishnarayan, V. (1993b) 'Race, equality and planning', *The Planner* 79, 3: 17–20

Thomas, K. (1989) 'Jobs new planning graduates take: first career destinations of town planning graduates 1981–88', *The Planner* 75, 6 (23 June): 12–14

Thomas, K. (1990a) 'Planning students and careers: the enrolment of planning students and career destinations of new planning graduates 1977 to 1989', *The Planner* 76, 36 (14 September): 13–16

Thomas, K. (1990b) 'Enrolment of students and output of UK planning schools 1977 to 1988', *Education for Planning Association Newsletter*, February: 17–49

Thomas, R. (1969) *London's New Towns – A Study of Self Contained and Balanced Communities*, London: Political and Economic Planning

Thomas, R. (1981) 'New town obituaries', *Urban Law and Policy* 4: 285–96

Thomas, R. and Thomas, H. (1991) 'Local planning policies, the Use Classes Order, and hot food take aways', *JPL* 1991: 711–13

Thompson, B. (1983) 'Relevance in the determination of planning applications', *JPL* 1983: 97–101

Thompson, B. (1985) 'Neighbour notification: recent developments in Scotland and Northern Ireland', *JPL* 1985: 530–5

Thompson, B. (1989) 'Administrative justice in planning', *JPL* 1989: 8–13

Thompson, H. (1992) 'Contaminated land: the implications for property transactions and the property market', *National Westminster Bank Quarterly Review*, November: 20–33

Thompson, R. (1987) 'Is fastest best? – the case of development control', *The Planner* 73, 9 (September): 11–15

Thomson, J.M. (1971) 'Halfway to a motorized society', *Lloyds Bank Review*, October: 16–34 (reprinted in Cullingworth 1973)

Thomson, S. (1985) *Local Plans Preparation: Review of Scottish Experience*, Paper presented to the Research in Land Use Planning Seminar, Oxford: Oxford Polytechnic

Thornley, A. (1977) 'Theoretical perspectives on planning participation', *Progress in Planning* 7: 1–57

Thornley, A. (1986) 'Thatcherism and simplified planning zones', *Planning Practice and Research* 1: 19–22

Thornley, A. (1991) *Urban Planning under Thatcherism: The Challenge of the Market*, London: Routledge

Thrift, N.J. (1985) 'Taking the rest of the world seriously: the state of British urban and regional research in a time of economic crisis', *Environment and Planning A* 17: 7–24

Tibbs, N. (1991) 'The objectives and implementation of the Bristol inner city project', in Nadin and Doak

Titmuss, R.M. (1950) *Problems of Social Policy*, London: HMSO and Longman

Titmuss, R.M. (1958) 'War and social policy', in his *Essays on 'The Welfare State'*, London: Allen and Unwin

Todd, D. and Clark, G. (1991a) *Gypsy Site Provision and Policy* (DoE Research Report), London: HMSO

Todd, D. and Clark, G. (1991b) *Good Practice Guidelines for Gypsy Provision by Local Authorities* (DoE), London: HMSO

Todd, J.E. and Walker, A. (1980) *People as Pedestrians* (Office of Population Censuses and Surveys, Social Survey Division), London: HMSO

Tolley, R. (ed.) (1990) *The Greening of Urban Transport: Planning for Walking and Cycling in Western Cities*, London: Belhaven

Tomlinson, P. (1982) 'The environmental impact of opencast coal mining', *TPR* 53: 5–28

Tomlinson, P. (1986) 'Environmental assessment in the UK: implementation of the EEC directive', *TPR* 57: 458–86

Tompkins, S.C. (1986) *The Theft of the Hills: Afforestation in Scotland*, London: Ramblers Association/WWF

Totterdill, P. (1989) 'Local economic strategies as industrial policy: a critical review of British developments in the 1980s', *Economy and Society* 18: 478–526

Tourism Recreation Research Unit (1981) *The Economy of Rural Communities in the National Parks of England and Wales*, Edinburgh: Edinburgh University

Town and Country Planning Association: *see* TCPA

Town Planning Review (1977) 'Planning and the future: a review symposium', *TPR* 48: 233–46

Town Planning Review (1980) 'Forum: the relevance of development control', *TPR* 51: 5–24

Town Planning Review (1992) 'Developing regional planning guidance in England and Wales: a review symposium', *TPR* 63: 415–34

Townroe, P. and Martin, R. (1992) *Regional Development in the 1990s: The British Isles in Transition*, London: Jessica Kingsley

Townsend, P. (1976) 'Area deprivation policies', *New Statesman*, 6 August: 168–71

Transport and Environment Studies: *see* TEST

Travers, T. (1986) *The Politics of Local Government Finance*, London: Allen and Unwin

Travers, T., Jones, G., Hebbert, M., and Burnham, J. (1991) *The Government of London*, York: Joseph Rowntree Foundation

Treasury (1991) *Competing for Quality: Buying Better Public Services*, London: HMSO

Trench, S. (1991) 'Reclaiming the night', *Town and Country Planning* 60: 235–7

Tricker, M. and Martin, S. (1984) 'The Development Commission: the developing role of the Commission', *Regional Studies* 18: 507–14

Tromans, S. (1991) 'Roads to prosperity or roads to ruin? Transport and the environment in England and Wales', *Journal of Environmental Law* 3: 1–37

Tromans, S. and Clarkson, M. (1991) 'The Environmental Protection Act 1990: its relevance to planning controls', *JPL* 1991: 507–15

Truelove, P. (1992) *Decision Making in Transport Planning*, Harlow: Longman

Tucker, L.R. (1978) 'Planning agreements: the twilight zone of *ultra vires*', *JPL* 1978: 806–9

Tudor Walters Report (1918) *Report of the Committee on Questions of Building Construction in Connection with the Provision of Dwellings for the Working Classes*, Cd 9191, London: HMSO

Tugnutt, A. (1991) 'Design – the wider aspects of townscapes', *Town and Country Planning Summer School 1991: Report of Proceedings*: 19–22

Turner, T. (1992) 'Open space planning in London: from standards per 1000 to green strategy', *TPR* 63: 365–86

Turok, I. (1988) 'The limits of financial assistance: an evaluation of local authority aid to industry', *Local Economy* 2: 286–97

Turok, I. (1989) 'Evaluation and understanding in local economic policy', *Urban Studies* 26: 587–606

Turok, I. (1990a) 'Public investment and privatisation in the new towns: a financial assessment of Bracknell', *Environment and Planning A* 22: 1323–36

Turok, I. (1990b) *Targeting Urban Employment Initiatives* (DoE Inner Cities Research Programme), London: HMSO

Turok, I. (1992) 'Property-led urban regeneration: panacea or placebo?', *Environment and Planning A* 24: 361–79

Turok, I. and Wannop, U. (1990) *Targeting Urban Employment Initiatives* (DoE Inner Cities Research Programme), London: HMSO

Turrall-Clarke, R.T.F. (1983) 'The compulsory purchase of listed buildings', *JPL* 1983: 655–8

Turrall-Clarke, R.T.F. (1988) 'Planning control and Dutch blinds', *JPL* 1988: 151–3

Turvey, R. (1957) *The Economics of Real Property*, London: Allen and Unwin

Tyler, P., Moore, B., and Rhodes, J. (1988) *Geographical Variations in Costs and Productivity*, London: HMSO

Tym, Roger & Partners (1982–84) *Monitoring Enterprise Zones: Year One Report* (1982); *Year Two Report* (1983); and *Year Three Report* (1984), London: Roger Tym & Partners

Tym, Roger & Partners (1984) *Land Supply for Housing in Urban Areas*, London: Housing Research Foundation

Tym, Roger & Partners (in association with Land Use Consultants) (1987) *Evaluation of Derelict Land Grant Schemes* (DoE Inner Cities Research Programme), London: HMSO

Tym, Roger & Partners (1988) *An Evaluation of the Stockbridge Village Trust Initiative* (DoE), London: HMSO

Tym, Roger & Partners (1989a) *The Effect on Small Firms of Refusal of Planning Permission* (DoE Development Control Study Series), London: HMSO

Tym, Roger & Partners (1989b) *The Incidence and Effects of Planning Conditions* (DoE Development Control Study Series), London: HMSO

Tym, Roger & Partners (1990) *Development Control Performance*, London: National Planning Forum

Tym, Roger & Partners (1991) *Housing Land Availability* (DoE Planning Research Programme), London: HMSO

Tyme, J. (1978) *Motorways versus Democracy*, London: Macmillan

Tyson, W.J. (1976) 'Transport and planning: the rationale of public transport subsidies', *TPR* 47: 315–23

Underwood, J. (1980) *Town Planners in Search of a Role*, Bristol: School for Advanced Urban Studies, University of Bristol

Underwood, J. (1981) 'Development control: a review of research and current issues', *Progress in Planning* 16, 3: 175–242

Unger, S.E. (1982) 'Enterprise zones: some perspectives on Anglo-American development', *Urban Law and Policy* 5: 129–47

Ungerson, C. (1971) *Moving Home*, Occasional Papers on Social Administration 44, London: Bell

United Nations (1992) *Environmental Accounting: Current Issues, Abstracts and Bibliography*, New York: Department of Economic and Social Development, United Nations

University of Liverpool, Environmental Advisory Unit (1986) *Transforming our Waste Land: The Way Forward* (DoE), London: HMSO

Untermann, R.K. (1984) *Accommodating the Pedestrian: Adapting Towns and Neighborhoods for Walking and Bicycling*, New York: Van Nostrand Reinhold

Unwin, R. (1909) *Town Planning in Practice: An Introduction to the Art of Designing Cities and Suburbs*, London: T. Fisher Unwin

Urban and Economic Development Ltd (1987) *Re-using Redundant Buildings* (DoE Case Studies of Good Practice in Urban Regeneration), London: HMSO

Urban and Economic Development Ltd (1988) *Managing Urban Change: A Report on the Management Training Needs of Urban Programme Project Managers* (DoE Inner Cities Research Programme), London: HMSO

Urban Villages Group (1992) *Urban Villages: A Concept for Creating Mixed-use Urban Developments on a Sustainable Scale*, London: Urban Villages Group

Uthwatt Report (1942) *Final Report of the Expert Committee on Compensation and Betterment*, Cmd 6386, London: HMSO

Veld, R.J. (1991) 'Road pricing: a logical failure', in Kraan and Veld

Verney Report (1976) *The Way Ahead – Report of the Advisory Committee on Aggregates*, London: HMSO

Vickerman, R.W. (1989) 'The private provision of infrastructure: the Channel Tunnel project', *Local Economy* 4: 132–42

Vickerman, R.W. (1991) *Infrastructure and Regional Development*, London: Pion

Vine, C. (1993) 'Part I of the Transport and Works Act 1992', *JPL* 1993: 3–12

Vogel, D. (1986) *National Styles of Regulation: Environmental Policy in Great Britain and the United States*, Ithaca, N.Y.: Cornell University Press

Wachs, M. (ed.) (1985) *Ethics in Planning*, New Brunswick, N.J.: Center for Urban Policy Research

Wachs, M. and Crawford, M. (eds) (1992) *The Car and the City*, Ann Arbor: University of Michigan Press

Waddilove Report (1984) *The Repair and Compensation System for Coal Mining and Subsidence Damage*, London: HMSO

Wägenbaur, R. (1991) 'The European Community's policy on implementation of environmental directives', *Fordham International Law Journal* 14: 455–77

Wakeford, R. (1990) *American Development Control: Parallels and Paradoxes from an English Perspective*, London: HMSO

Wakeford, R. and Heywood, R. (1986) *Speeding Planning Appeals: A Review of the Handling of Transferred Written Representation Planning Appeals: Report of an Efficiency Scrutiny* (DoE), London: HMSO

Waldegrave, W., Byng, J., Paterson, T., and Pye, G. (1986) *Distant Views of William Waldegrave's Speech*, London: Centre for Policy Studies

Walker, G.P. (1989) 'Risks, rights and secrets: public access to information on industrial major hazards', *Policy and Politics* 17: 255–71

Walker, M. (1988) 'The award of costs in planning proceedings', *JPL* 1988: 598–610

Walker, M. and Reynard, M.V. (1990) *Costs in Planning Proceedings*, London: Longman

Waller, R.A. (1981) 'Expert witnesses at planning inquiries', *JPL* 1981: 394–404

Walmsley, D.A. and Perrett, K.E. (1992) *The Effects of Rapid Transport on Public Transport and Urban Development*, Transport Research Laboratory, State of the Art Review 6, London: HMSO

Walsh, K. (1991) 'Competition and service in local government', in Stewart and Stoker

Walters, A.A. (1968) *The Economics of Road User Charges*, Baltimor, Md.: Johns Hopkins University Press

Wannop, U. (1984a) 'Clydeside in transition: three questions on the significance of metropolitan strategic planning', *TPR* 55: 34–54

Wannop, U. (1984b) 'The evolution and roles of the Scottish Development Agency', *TPR* 55: 313–21

Wannop, U. (1986) 'Strategic planning in the 1980s: not moribund but a case for rehabilitation', in Willis

Wannop, U. (1988) 'Do we need regional government and is the Scottish model relevant?', *Regional Studies* 22: 439–46

Wannop, U. (1990) 'The Glasgow Eastern Area Renewal (GEAR) project: a perspective on the management of urban regeneration', *TPR* 61: 455–74

Warburton, D. (1988) *Creating Development Trusts* (DoE Case

Studies of Good Practice in Urban Regeneration), London: HMSO

Ward, A.J. (1981) 'Planning agreements and the march of time: removing obsolete restrictions', *JPL* 1981: 557–66

Ward, A.J. (1982) 'Planning bargaining: where do we stand?', *JPL* 1982: 74–84

Ward, R. (1986) 'Public–private partnerships', in Rose

Ward, R. (1987) 'London: the emerging docklands city', *Built Environment* 12: 117–27

Ward, S. (ed.) (1992) *The Garden City: Past, Present and Future*, London: Spon

Wardroper, J. (1981) *Juggernaut*, London: Temple Smith

Warren, H. and Davidge, W.R. (eds) (1930) *Decentralisation of Population and Industry: A New Principle in Town Planning*, London: King

Watchman, P.Q., Barker, C.R., and Rowan-Robinson, J. (1988) 'River pollution: a case for a pragmatic approach to enforcement', *JPL* 1988: 674–9

Wates, N. (1977) *The Battle for Tolmers Square*, London: Routledge and Kegan Paul

Wathern, P. (ed.) (1988) *Environmental Impact Assessment: Theory and Practice*, London: Unwin Hyman

Watkins, C. (1983) 'The public control of woodland management', *TPR* 54: 437–59

Watt, P. (1992) 'Publicity for planning applications', *Scottish Planning Law and Practice* 38. 15–16.

Watts, H.D. (1991) 'Plant closures in urban areas: towards a local policy response', *Urban Studies* 28: 803–17

Weale, A. (1992) *The New Politics of Pollution*, Manchester: Manchester University Press

Weale, A., O'Riordan, T., and Kramme, L. (1991) *Controlling Pollution in the Round: Change and Choice in Environmental Regulation in Britain and West Germany*, London: Anglo-German Foundation for the Study of Industrial Society

Weber, M.M. (1968–69) 'Planning in an environment of change', *TPR* 39: 179–95 and 277–95 (reprinted in Cullingworth 1973)

Webman, J.A. (1982) *Reviving the Industrial City: The Politics of Urban Renewal in Lyon and Birmingham*, London: Croom Helm

Webster, B. and Lavers, A. (1991) 'The effectiveness of public local inquiries as a vehicle for public participation in the plan making process: a case study of the Barnet unitary development plan inquiry', *JPL* 1991: 803–13

Wells, H.G. (1905) *A Modern Utopia*, London: Collins

Welsh Office (1992) *Roads in Wales: The Government Response to the Welsh Affairs Committee Report on Roads in Wales*, Cm 1851, London: HMSO

Wenban-Smith, A. (1991) 'Birmingham's response to change in the UDP', in Nadin and Doak

Wenban-Smith, A. and Meeston, J. (1990) *Negotiating with Planning Authorities*, London: Estates Gazette

West Midlands Regional Forum of Local Authorities (1991) *The West Midlands: Your Region, Your Future: Asking the Right Questions*, Regional Planning Guidance Consultation Paper No. 1, Stafford: The Forum

West Midlands Regional Forum of Local Authorities (1992) *The West Midlands: Your Region, Your Future: Making the Right Choices*, Regional Planning Guidance Consultation Paper No. 2, Stafford: The Forum

Wetstone, G.S. and Rosencranz, A. (1983a) 'Transboundary air pollution in Europe: a survey of national responses', *Columbia Journal of Environmental Law* 9: 1–62

Wetstone, G.S. and Rosencranz, A. (1983b) *Acid Rain in Europe and North America*, Washington, DC: Environmental Law Institute

Whatmore, S., Munton, R., and Marsden, T. (1990) 'The rural restructuring process: emerging divisions of agricultural property rights', *Regional Studies* 24: 235–45

Wheatley Report (1969) *Report of the Royal Commission on Local Government in Scotland*, Cmnd 4150, Edinburgh: HMSO

Wheen, F. (1985) *The Battle for London*, London: Pluto Press

Whitbread, M. and Marsay, A. (1992) *Coastal Superquarries to Supply South-East England Aggregate Requirements* (DoE Geological and Minerals Planning Research Programme), London: HMSO

Whitbread, M., Mayne, D., and Wickens, D. (1991) *Tackling Vacant Land: An Evaluation of Policy Instruments for Tackling Land Vacancy* (DoE Inner Cities Research Programme), London: HMSO

White, P. (1986a) *Planning for Public Transport*, London: Hutchinson

White, P. (1986b) 'Land availability, land banking and the price of land for housing: a review of recent debates', *Land Development Studies* 3: 101–11

Whitehand, J.W.R. (1989) 'Development pressure, development control, and suburban townscape change', *TPR* 60: 403–20

Whitehand, J.W.R. and Larkham, P.J. (1991) 'Suburban cramming and development control', *Journal of Property Research* 8: 147–59

Whitehead, P.T. (1976) 'Public participation in structure planning', *TPR* 47: 374–82

Whitelegg, J. (1988) *Transport Policy in the EEC*, London: Routledge

Whitelegg, J. (1989) 'Transport policy: off the rails?', in Mohan

Whitting, G. (1986) *The Urban Programme and the Unemployed* (DoE Inner Cities Research Programme), London: HMSO

Widdicombe Report (1986) *The Conduct of Local Authority Business: Report*, Cmnd 9797; *Research Volumes*, Cmnd 9798, 9799, 9800, and 9801; London: HMSO 1986. *Government Response to the Report*, Cm 433, London: HMSO, 1988

Wildavsky, A.B. (1973) 'If planning is everything, maybe it's nothing', *Policy Sciences* 4: 127–53

Wildavsky, A.B. (1979) *Speaking Truth to Power: The Art and Craft of Policy Analysis*, Boston, Mass.: Little Brown

Wilding, R. (1990) *The Care of Redundant Churches: A Review of the Operation and Financing of the Redundant Churches Fund*, London: HMSO

Wilkinson, D. (1992) *Maastricht and the Environment: The Implications for the EC's Environmental Policy of the Treaty on European Union Signed at Maastricht on 7 February 1992*, London: Institute for European Environmental Policy

Wilkinson, D. and Waterton, J. (1991) *Public Attitudes to the Environment in Scotland*, Edinburgh: Scottish Office

Williams, A. (1984) *Planning Law Casebook*, London: Laureate-Thomson Press

Williams, C. (1993a) 'Planners carry capacity for sustainable development', *Planning* No. 1012 (2 April): 18–19

Williams, C. (1993b) 'Pushing back policy barriers to reduce unsustainability', *Planning* No. 1013 (9 April): 18–19

Williams, G. (1983) *Inner City Policy: A Partnership with the Voluntary Sector?*, London: Bedford Square Press

Williams, G., Bell, P., and Russell, L. (1991) *Evaluating the Low Cost Rural Housing Initiative* (DoE Planning Research Programme), London: HMSO

Williams, G., Strange, I., Bintley, M., and Bristow, R. (1992) *Metropolitan Planning in the 1990s: The Role of Unitary Development Plans*, Manchester: Department of Planning and Landscape, University of Manchester

Williams, K., Williams, J., and Haslam, C. (1991) 'What kind of EC regional policy?', *Local Economy* 5: 331–46

Williams, M.R. (1989) 'Footpaths and bridleways affected by development – potential problems and possible reforms', *JPL* 1989: 651–61

Williams, M.R. (1990) 'The validity of occupancy conditions – a review', *JPL* 1990: 319–31

Williams, M.V. (1985) 'National park policy 1942–1984', *JPL* 1985: 359–77

Williams, P. (1992) 'Housing', in Cloke

Williams, R. (1973) *The Country and the City*, London: Chatto and Windus

Williams, R. (1978) 'Statutory local plans: progress and problems', *Planning Outlook* 21, 2: 22–7

Williams, R.H. (1984) *Planning in Europe*, London: Allen and Unwin

Williams, R.H. (1986) 'EC environmental policy, land use planning and pollution control', *Policy and Politics* 14: 93–106

Williamson, C.E. (1992) 'Development control: what is quality?', *The Planner* 78, 13 (3 July): 18

Willis, K.G. (ed.) (1986) *Contemporary Issues in Town Planning*, Aldershot: Gower

Willis, K.G. (1990) 'Mid-Wales: choosing the right perspective', *Urban Studies* 27: 449–54

Wilmers, P. and Bourdillon, B. (1985) *Managing the Local Economy: Planning for Employment and Economic Development*, Norwich: Geo Books

Wilson, D. (1983) *The Lead Scandal: The Fight to Save Children from Damage by Lead in Petrol*, London: Heinemann

Wilson, G.K. (1983) 'Planning lessons from the ports', *Public Administration* 61: 265–81

Wilson, G.K. (1985) *The Politics of Safety and Health*, Oxford: Clarendon Press

Wilson, M. (1993) 'What the HAT is and how it works', *Housing Review* 42, 2 (March/April): 25–6

Wilson Report (1963) *Committee on the Problems of Noise: Final Report*, Cmnd 2056, London: HMSO

Wiltshaw, D.G. (1984) 'Planning gain: a theoretical note', *Urban Studies* 21: 183–7

Winter, J. (1989) 'Is local plan review now under way?', *The Planner* 75, 1: 22–7

Winter, M. (1990) 'Land use policy in the UK: the politics of control', *Land Development Studies* 7: 3–14

Winter, M. (1991) 'Agriculture and the environment: the integration of policy?', in Churchill, Warren, and Gibson

Wistrich, E. (1983) *The Politics of Transport*, Harlow: Longman

Witt, S.J.G. (1984) *Planning Councillors in an Area of Growth: Little Power but all the Blame?*, Reading: Department of Geography, University of Reading

Wolfe, L. (1945) *The Reilly Plan*, London: Nicholson

Wood, C. (1986) 'Local planning authority controls over pollution', *Policy and Politics* 14: 107–23

Wood, C. (1988) 'E.I.A. and B.P.E.O. – acronyms for good environmental planning', *JPL* 1988: 310–12

Wood, C. (1989a) *Planning Pollution Prevention: A Comparison of Siting Controls Over Air Pollution Sources in Great Britain and the USA*, Oxford: Heinemann Newnes

Wood, C. (1989b) 'The utility of the UK pollution panels in achieving integrated pollution control', *Environment and Planning C: Government and Policy* 7: 1–12

Wood, C. (1991) 'Urban renewal: the British experience', in R. Alterman and G. Cars, *Neighbourhood Regeneration: An International Evaluation*, London: Mansell

Wood, C. and Hooper, P. (1989) 'The effects of the relaxation of planning controls in enterprise zones on industrial pollution', *Environment and Planning A* 21: 1157–67

Wood, C. and Jones, C. (1991) *Monitoring Environmental Assessment and Planning* (DoE Planning Research Programme), London: HMSO

Wood, C. and McDonic, G. (1989) 'Environmental assessment: challenge and opportunity', *The Planner* 75, 11 (7 July): 12–18

Wood, W. (1949) *Planning and the Law*, London: Marshall

World Commission on Environment and Development: Brundland Report (1987) *Our Common Future*, Oxford: Oxford University Press

Worskett, R. (1969) *The Character of Towns*, London: Architectural Press

Wraith, R.E. and Hutchesson, P.G. (1973) *Administrative Tribunals*, London: Allen and Unwin

Wraith, R.E. and Lamb, G.B. (1971) *Public Inquiries as an Instrument of Government*, London: Allen and Unwin

Wren, C. (1989) 'The revised regional development grant scheme: a case study in Cleveland County of a marginal employment subsidy', *Regional Studies* 23: 127–37

Wright, M. and Young, S. (1975) 'Regional planning in Britain', in Hayward and Watson

Wye College (1991) *Rural Society: Issues for the Nineties*, Wye, Kent: Wye College

Wynne, B. (1983) *Rationality and Ritual: The Windscale Inquiry and Nuclear Decisions in Britain*, London: British Society for the History of Science

Young, E. (1978) *The Law of Planning in Scotland*, Glasgow: Hodge

Young, E. (1979) 'Call-in of planning applications by regional planning authorities', *JPL* 1979: 358–70

Young, E. (1983) 'Is an unnecessary condition *ultra vires*?', *JPL* 1983: 357–62

Young, E. (1989) 'Shop canopies and advertisements', *JPL* 1989: 319–22

Young, E. (1991) *Scottish Planning Appeals*, Edinburgh: Green/Sweet and Maxwell

Young, E. and Rowan-Robinson, J. (1982) 'Section 52 agreements and the fettering of powers', *JPL* 1982: 673–85

Young, E. and Rowan-Robinson, J. (1985) *Scottish Planning Law and Practice*, Glasgow: Hodge

Young, (Sir) George (1992) Address to the Town and Country Planning Summer School 1992, *The Planner, TCPSS Proceedings* 78, 21 (November): 3–6

Young, J. (1981) 'The inner city', London: *The Times*, 10 March

Young, K. (1979) 'Implementing an urban strategy: the case of public housing in metropolitan London', in Ashford

Young, K. (1984) 'Metropolitan government: the development of the concept of reality', in Leach

Young, K. (1986a) 'Economic development in Britain: a vacuum in central–local government relations', *Environment and Planning C: Government and Policy* 4: 439–50

Young, K. (1986b) 'Metropolis, R.I.P.', *Political Quarterly* 57: 36–46

Young, K. and Davies, M. (1990) *The Politics of Local Government since Widdicombe*, York: Joseph Rowntree Foundation

Young, K. and Mason, C. (1983) *Urban Economic Development: New Roles and Relationships*, Basingstoke: Macmillan

Young, M. and Willmott, P. (1957) *Family and Kinship in East London*: Harmondsworth: Penguin

Young, R. (1988) *Taking the Initiative: Some Impressions and Examples of Urban Regeneration in the United States*, Glasgow: Strathclyde Regional Council

Yuille, R.J. and Howells, N. (1990) 'Section 17 of the Land Compensation Act – adventures in a land of make believe', *JPL* 1990: 3–7

# OFFICIAL PUBLICATIONS

# A NOTE ON OFFICIAL PUBLICATIONS

The student of Town and Country Planning now has a very rich library of official publications to consult. This has grown considerably over the last decade, partly because of the large research programme sponsored by the DoE. This section, though not comprehensive, lists the more important relevant publications.

A few words of explanation about the mysteries of government publications may be helpful. *White Papers* are technically *Command Papers*, i.e. they are 'presented to Parliament by Command of Her Majesty'. The reference to colour was at one time meaningful: a White Paper was a slim paper (often being a policy statement or report) which had a white cover. It was therefore easily distinguishable from the more substantial Blue Books (which had blue covers). The Victorian Royal Commission reports were perhaps the best known of these.

Command papers are numbered sequentially and have a short prefix which varies, but which (so far) is always an abbreviation of the word 'command'. The earliest papers were prefixed C, but this was changed to Cd at the turn of the century. This prefix lasted until 1918–19 when, on approaching the number 10,000, it was changed to Cmd. This served its purpose until 1956, in which year the prefix was changed again – and for the same reason – to Cmnd. The last (but presumably not the final) change was made in 1986, when the prefix became Cm. At the time of writing, the last number to be used was Cm 2207 – for the DoE *Annual Report* (of which more anon). Why the Queen's Printer is unable to go beyond 9,999 in its numbering is not clear. What *is* clear is that authors and publishers alike have difficulty in getting the prefix correct every time.

Though still used to denote a statement of government policy, the term 'White Paper' now has no precise meaning. Coloured covers are used extensively and, in recent years the amount of 'artwork' has increased. A white paper no longer necessarily looks like one. Colourful and graphic presentation has become common, and some White Papers bear a strong resemblance to company reports.

Until relatively recently, it was reasonable to assume that, if a White Paper was a policy document, it represented the government's view, or its fairly firm proposals. This distinguished it from a 'green paper' which was of the nature of a preliminary draft White Paper. Such papers began to appear in the late 1960s, and were popular for a time.

The distinction between white and green is now blurred and it is not uncommon to hear that a White Paper has a 'green tinge' (i.e. some of the proposals are still open for discussion). Similarly, green papers may have a 'white tinge' (i.e. certain issues have been firmly decided and are not open for further debate). Of course, circumstances change, and so do the minds of governments. (The White Paper on *The Future of Development Plans* announced the abolition of structure plans, but in fact they have been retained.)

Green Papers have now largely been superseded by Consultation Papers which, ironically, are often not published by HMSO but are 'available' from the Department concerned. The one advantage of this is that they are free. In recent years, there have been large numbers of these. Those concerned with planning are frequently printed in the monthly update to Grant's *Encyclopedia*.

Another recent innovation is the publication of annual reports of departments. Again these are Command Papers (with a range of colours). But they are both more and less than annual reports. They are more in the sense that they present details of recent and planned expenditure on the services which are covered by the budget of the department(s) concerned. In this, they are parts of *The Government's Expenditure Plans* (which is their subtitle). But they are less than a full annual report in that they do not enter into discussion of the policies to which the figures relate. They merely state what these policies are (which is useful, but limited). As increasing sections of the executive parts of departments are hived off to '*Next Steps*' Agencies, the reports become of an even more summary nature.

Most government publications are published by HMSO, but the market for Scottish and Welsh publications apparently does not justify the same treatment. As a consequence, many of the planning documents issued by the Scottish Office and the Welsh Office have to be obtained direct (as with most DoE Consultation Papers). Some publications of a number of English departments (such as Agriculture, Industry, and Transport) are also obtainable only from the departments concerned. In the following lists, the publisher is HMSO unless otherwise indicated.

## COMMAND PAPERS

1940 *Report of the Royal Commission on the Distribution of the Industrial Population* (Barlow Report), Cmd 6153
1944 *Employment Policy*, Cmd 6527
1944 *The Control of Land Use*, Cmd 6537
1947 *Town and Country Planning Bill 1947: Explanatory Memorandum*, Cmd 7006
1952 *Town and Country Planning Act, 1947: Amendment of Financial Provisions*, Cmd 8699
1957 *Report of the Committee on Administrative Tribunals and Enquiries* (Franks Report), Cmnd 218
1963 *London – Employment: Housing: Land*, Cmnd 1952
1965 *Report of the Committee on Housing in Greater London* (Milner Holland Report), Cmnd 2605
1965 *The Land Commission*, Cmnd 2771

1966 *Leisure in the Countryside*, Cmnd 2928
1966 *Transport Policy*, Cmnd 3057
1967 *Town and Country Planning*, Cmnd 3333
1967 *Public Transport and Traffic*, Cmnd 3481
1968 *The Older Houses in Scotland: A Plan for Action*, Cmnd 3598
1968 *Old Houses into New Homes*, Cmnd 3602
1968 *Transport in London*, Cmnd 3686
1968 *Report of the Committee on Local Authority and Allied Personal Social Services* (Seebohm Report), Cmnd 3703
1969 *Information and the Public Interest*, Cmnd 4089
1970 *The Protection of the Environment: The Fight Against Pollution*, Cmnd 4373
1970 *The Reorganisation of Central Government*, Cmnd 4506
1970 *Investment Incentives*, Cmnd 4516
1971 *Report of the Committee on the Rent Acts* (Francis Report), Cmnd 4609
1972 *Industrial and Regional Development*, Cmnd 4942
1972 *Development and Compensation: Putting People First*, Cmnd 5124
1973 *Land Resource Use in Scotland: The Government's Observations on the Report of the Select Committee on Scottish Affairs*, Cmnd 5248
1973 *Homes for People: Scottish Housing Policy in the 1970s*, Cmnd 5272
1973 *Widening the Choice: The Next Steps in Housing*, Cmnd 5280
1973 *Towards Better Homes: Proposals for Dealing with Scotland's Older Housing*, Cmnd 5338
1973 *Better Homes: The Next Priorities*, Cmnd 5339
1973 *Report of the Royal Commission on the Constitution* (Kilbrandon Report), Cmnd 5640
1974 *Land*, Cmnd 5730
1975 *Development Land Tax*, Cmnd 6195
1975 *Sport and Recreation*, Cmnd 6200
1975 *An Approach to Industrial Strategy*, Cmnd 6315
1977 *Nuclear Power and the Environment*, Cmnd 6820
1977 *Transport Policy*, Cmnd 6836
1977 *Statement on the Non-Statutory Inquiry by the Baroness Sharp into the Continued Use of Dartmoor for Military Training*, Cmnd 6837
1977 *Policy for the Inner Cities*, Cmnd 6845
1977 *The Water Industry in England and Wales: The Next Steps*, Cmnd 6876
1978 *Planning Procedures: The Government's Response to the Eighth Report from the Expenditure Committee, Session 1976–77*, Cmnd 7056
1978 *Airports Policy*, Cmnd 7084
1978 *Policy for Roads: England*, Cmnd 7132
1978 *Report on the Review of Highway Inquiry Procedures*, Cmnd 7133
1978 *The Challenge of North Sea Oil*, Cmnd 7143
1979 *A National Heritage Fund*, Cmnd 7428
1979 *Organic Change in Local Government*, Cmnd 7457
1979 *Farming and the Nation*, Cmnd 7458
1979 *Report of the Committee of Inquiry on Acquisition and Occupancy of Agricultural Land*, Cmnd 7599
1979 *Central Government Controls over Local Authorities*, Cmnd 7634
1980 *Proposals for a Code of Civic Government in Scotland: A Consultation Paper*, Cmnd 7958
1981 *Committee of Inquiry into Local Government in Scotland* (Stodart Report), Cmnd 8115
1981 *Lorries, People and the Environment*, Cmnd 8439
1982 *Policy for Roads: England 1981*, Cmnd 8496
1982 *Radioactive Waste Management*, Cmnd 8607
1982 *Public Transport Subsidy in Cities*, Cmnd 8735
1983 *Coal and the Environment: The Government's Response to the Commission on Energy and the Environment's Report*, Cmnd 8877
1983 *Public Transport in London*, Cmnd 9004
1983 *Rates: Proposals for Rate Limitation and Reform of the Rating System*, Cmnd 9008
1983 *Roads in Scotland: Report for 1982*, Cmnd 9010
1983 *Financial Management in Government Departments*, Cmnd 9058
1983 *Policy for Roads in England: 1983*, Cmnd 9059
1983 *Streamlining the Cities: Government Proposals for Reorganising Local Government in Greater London and the Metropolitan Counties*, Cmnd 9063
1983 *Regional Industrial Development*, Cmnd 9111
1984 *Training for Jobs*, Cmnd 9135
1984 *Report of the Committee of Inquiry into the Functions and Powers of the Islands Councils of Scotland* (Montgomery Report), Cmnd 9216
1984 *Progress in Financial Management in Government Departments*, Cmnd 9297
1984 *Buses*, Cmnd 9300
1984 *Acid Rain: The Government's Reply to the Fourth Report from the Environment Committee, Session 1983–84*, Cmnd 9397
1985 *Home Improvement: A New Approach: Government Proposals for Encouraging the Repair and Improvement of Private Sector Housing in England and Wales*, Cmnd 9513
1985 *Airports Policy*, Cmnd 9542
1985 *Home Improvement in Scotland: A New Approach: Government Proposals for Encouraging the Repair and Improvement of Private Sector Housing in Scotland*, Cmnd 9677
1986 *Paying for Local Government*, Cmnd 9714
1986 *Privatisation of the Water Authorities in England and Wales*, Cmnd 9734
1986 *The Channel Fixed Link*, Cmnd 9735
1986 *Building Businesses . . . Not Barriers*, Cmnd 9794
1986 *The Conduct of Local Authority Business: Report of the Committee of Inquiry* (Widdicombe Report), Cmnd 9797

1986  *Planning Appeals, Call-In and Major Public Inquiries: The Government's Response to the Fifth Report from the Environment Committee, Session 1985–86*, Cm 43
1987  *Annual Review of Agriculture 1987*, Cm 67
1987  *Policy for Roads in England: 1987*, Cm 125
1988  *DTI – The Department for Enterprise*, Cm 278
1988  *Training for Employment*, Cm 316
1988  *Releasing Enterprise*, Cm 512
1988  *Civil Service Management Reform: The Next Steps* (Government Reply to the Report from the Treasury and Civil Service Committee), Cm 524
1988  *Scottish Enterprise: A New Approach to Training and Enterprise Creation*, Cm 534
1988  *Employment in the 1990s*, Cm 540
1989  *The Future of Development Plans*, Cm 569
1989  *The Scottish New Towns: The Way Ahead*, Cm 711
1990  *This Common Inheritance: Britain's Environmental Strategy*, Cm 1200
1990  *Improving Management in Government: The Next Steps Agencies: Review 1990*, Cm 1261
1991  *Competition and Choice: Telecommunications Policy for the 1990s*, Cm 1461
1991  *Access and Opportunity: A Strategy for Education and Training* (Scottish Office), Cm 1530
1991  *The Citizen's Charter: Raising the Standard*, Cm 1599
1991  *This Common Inheritance: The First Year Report*, Cm 1655
1991  *Competing for Quality: Buying Better Public Services*, Cm 1730
1991  *Improving Management in Government: The Next Steps Agencies: Review 1991*, Cm 1760
1992  *People, Jobs and Opportunity*, Cm 1810
1992  *The Department of the Environment, Annual Report 1992: The Government's Expenditure Plans 1992–93 to 1994–95*, Cm 1908
1992  *This Common Inheritance: The Second Year Report*, Cm 2068
1992  *The Citizen's Charter: First Report*, Cm 2101
1993  *Local Government in Wales: A Charter for the Future*, Cm 2155
1993  *The Department of the Environment, Annual Report 1993: The Government's Expenditure Plans 1993–94 to 1995–96*, Cm 2207

# ROYAL COMMISSION ON ENVIRONMENTAL POLLUTION (HMSO)

*First Report*, Cmnd 4585, 1972
*Second Report: Three Issues in Industrial Pollution*, Cmnd 4894, 1972
*Third Report: Pollution in Some British Estuaries and Coastal Waters*, Cmnd 5054, 1972
*Fourth Report: Pollution Control – Progress and Problems*, Cmnd 5780, 1974
*Fifth Report: Air Pollution Control: An Integrated Approach*, Cmnd 6371, 1976
*Sixth Report: Nuclear Power and the Environment*, Cmnd 6618, 1976
*Seventh Report: Agriculture and Pollution*, Cmnd 7644, 1979
*Eighth Report: Oil Pollution of the Sea*, Cmnd 8358, 1981
*Ninth Report: Lead in the Environment*, Cmnd 8852, 1983
*Tenth Report: Tackling Pollution – Experience and Prospects*, Cmnd 9149, 1984
*Eleventh Report: Managing Waste: The Duty of Care*, Cmnd 9675, 1985
*Twelfth Report: Best Practicable Environmental Option*, Cm 310, 1988
*Thirteenth Report: The Release of Genetically Engineered Organisms to the Environment*, Cm 720, 1989
*Fourteenth Report: GENHAZ: A System for the Critical Appraisal of Proposals to Release Genetically Modified Organisms into the Environment*, Cm 1557, 1991
*Fifteenth Report: Emissions from Heavy Duty Diesel Vehicles*, Cm 1631, 1991
(*Emissions from Heavy Duty Diesel Engined Vehicles: The Government's Response to the 15th Report of the Royal Commission on Environmental Pollution*)
*Sixteenth Report: Freshwater Quality*, Cm 1966, 1992

# DEPARTMENT OF THE ENVIRONMENT

## DoE Circulars

42/55  *Green Belts*
50/57  *Green Belts*
48/59  *Town and Country Planning Act, 1959, with Explanatory Memorandum*
58/63  *Recovery of Planning Compensation*
12/68  *Grants to Local Authorities: Comprehensive Redevelopment and Public Open Space*
29/68  *Planning Control of Radio Masts*
67/68  *Planning Inquiry Commissions*
56/71  *Historic Towns and Roads*
60/71  *Town and Country Planning (Minerals) Regulations 1971*
12/72  *The Planning of the Undeveloped Coast*
10/73  *Planning and Noise*
63/73  *Local Government Act 1972: Administration of National Parks*
24/75  *Housing – Needs and Action*
4/76  *Report of the National Parks Policies Review Committee*
16/76  *National Land Use Classification*
34/76  *Consultation and Consents for New Electricity Generating Stations and Overhead Lines*

89/76    *Town and Country Planning General Regulations*
17/77    *Derelict Land*
28/77    *Gypsy Caravan Sites*
73/77    *Guidelines for Regional Recreational Strategies*
94/77    *New Streets*
109/77   *Enforcement of Planning Control — Established Use Certificates*
125/77   *Roads and Traffic: National Parks*
12/78    *Report of the Mobile Homes Review*
29/78    *Control of Pollution Act 1974: Waste on Land*
36/78    *Trees and Forestry*
57/78    *Accommodation for Gypsies: Report by Sir John Cripps*
58/78    *Report of the Committee on Planning Control over Mineral Working*
13/79    *Local Government and the Development of Tourism*
22/80    *Development Control — Policy and Practice*
2/81     *Development Control Functions: Act of 1980*
8/81     *Local Government, Planning and Land Act 1980 — Various Provisions*
26/81    *Local Government and Planning (Amendment) Act 1981*
32/81    *Wildlife and Countryside Act 1981*
10/82    *Disabled Persons Act 1981*
17/82    *Development in Flood Risk Areas — Liaison Between Planning Authorities and Water Authorities*
1/83     *Public Rights of Way*
4/83     *Wildlife and Countryside Act: Financial Guidelines for Management Agreements*
13/83    *Purchase Notices*
23/83    *Caravan Sites and Control of Development Act 1960*
28/83    *Publication by Local Authorities of Information About the Handling of Planning Applications*
1/84     *Crime Prevention*
9/84     *Planning Controls over Hazardous Development*
14/84    *Green Belts*
15/84    *Land for Housing*
18/84    *Crown Land and Crown Development*
22/84    *Memorandum on Structure and Local Plans: The Town and Country Planning Act 1971: Part II (as amended by the Town and Country Planning (Amendment) Act 1972, The Local Government Act 1972, and the Local Government, Planning and Land Act 1980)*
1/85     *The Use of Conditions in Planning Permissions*
2/85     *Planning Control over Oil and Gas Operations*
6/85     *Compulsory Purchase Orders: Procedures*
15/85    *Town and Country Planning (Compensation) Act 1985*
20/85    *Town and Country Planning Act 1971: Enforcement Appeals and Advertisement Appeals*
24/85    *Guidelines for the Provision of Silica Sand in England and Wales*
25/85    *Mineral Workings — Legal Aspects Relating to Restoration of Sites with a High Water Table*
28/85    *Reclamation and Re-use of Derelict Land*

29/85    *Planning Development Grant*
30/85    *Local Government Act 1985: Sections 3, 4 and 5: Schedule 1 Town and Country Planning: Transitional Matters*
6/86     *Local Government (Access to Information) Act 1985*
18/86    *Planning Appeals Decided by Written Representations*
19/86    *Housing and Planning Act 1986: Planning Provisions*
2/87     *Awards of Costs Incurred in Planning and Compulsory Purchase Order Proceedings*
8/87     *Historic Buildings and Conservation Areas — Policy and Procedures*
11/87    *Town and Country Planning (Appeals) (Written Representations Procedure) Regulations 1987*
13/87    *Change of Use of Buildings and Other Land: Town and Country Planning (Use Classes) Order 1987*
15/87    *Disposal of Colliery Spoil*
20/87    *Use of Waste Material for Road Fill*
21/87    *Development of Contaminated Land*
24/87    *Housing and Planning Act 1986: Town and Country Planning: Local Plans*
25/87    *Housing and Planning Act 1986: Town and Country Planning: Simplified Planning Zones (SPZs)*
27/87    *Nature Conservation*
28/87    *Opencast Coal Mining*
1/88     *Planning Policy Guidance and Mineral Planning Guidance*
3/88     *Local Government Act 1985: Unitary Development Plans*
10/88    *Town and Country Planning (Inquiries Procedure) Rules 1988, Town and Country Planning Appeals (Determination by Inspectors) (Inquiries Procedure) Rules 1988*
15/88    *Town and Country Planning (Assessment of Environmental Effects) Regulations*
22/88    *General Development Order Consolidation*
23/88    *Compulsory Purchase Orders by Urban Development Corporations*
24/88    *Environmental Assessment of Projects in Simplified Planning Zones and Enterprise Zones*
5/89     *Town and Country Planning (Fees for Applications and Deemed Applications) Regulations 1989*
14/89    *Caravan Sites and Control of Development Act 1960 — Model Standards*
15/89    *Town and Country Planning (Control of Advertisements) Regulations 1989*
17/89    *Landfill Sites Development Control*
18/89    *Publication of Information about Unused and Under-used Land*
20/89    *Water Act 1989*
1/90     *Compulsory Purchase by Non-Ministerial Acquiring Authorities (Inquiries Procedure) Rules 1990 (S.I. 1990 No. 512)*
14/90    *Electricity Generating Stations and Overhead Lines*

18/90    *Modifications to the Definitive Map: Wildlife and Countryside Act 1981*

4/91    *Part VII of the Environmental Protection Act 1990: Establishment of the Nature Conservancy Council for England*

7/91    *Planning and Affordable Housing*

12/91    *Redundant Hospital Sites in Green Belts: Planning Guidelines*

14/91    *Planning and Compensation Act 1991*

15/91    *Planning and Compensation Act 1991: Land Compensation and Compulsory Purchase*

16/91    *Planning and Compensation Act 1991: Planning Obligations*

17/91    *Water Industry Investment: Planning Considerations*

18/91    *Planning and Compensation Act 1991: New Development Plans System: Transitional Arrangements (England and Wales)*

20/91    *Town and Country Planning (Fees for Applications and Deemed Applications) (Amendment) Regulations 1991*

21/91    *Planning and Compensation Act 1991: Implementation of the Main Enforcement Provisions*

22/91    *Travelling Showpeople*

23/91    *Awards of Costs in Planning Proceedings, Following Late Cancellation of an Inquiry or Hearing*

1/92    *Planning Controls over Sites of Special Scientific Interest*

2/92    *Safeguarding Aerodromes, Technical Sites and Explosive Storage Areas: Town and Country Planning (Aerodromes and Technical Sites) Direction 1992*

5/92    *Town and Country Planning (Control of Advertisements) Regulations 1992*

11/92    *Planning Controls for Hazardous Substances*

14/92    *The Environmental Protection Act 1990 – Parts II and IV: The Controlled Waste Regulations 1992*

15/92    *Publicity for Planning Applications*

16/92    *Planning Controls over Demolition (withdrawn and replaced by 26/92)*

17/92    *Planning and Compensation Act 1991 – Implementation of the Remaining Enforcement Provisions*

19/92    *The Town and Country Planning Regulations 1992: The Town and Country Planning (Development Plans and Consultation) Directions 1992*

20/92    *Responsibilities for Conservation Policy and Casework*

23/92    *Motorway Service Areas*

24/92    *The Town and Country Planning (Inquiries Procedure) Rules 1992 (S.I. 1992 No. 2038); The Town and Country Planning Appeals (Determination by Inspectors) (Inquiries Procedure) Rules 1992 (S.I. 1992 No. 2039)*

26/92    *Planning Controls over Demolition*

27/92    *Town and Country Planning General Development Order 1988: Level Crossing Safety and the Planning System*

28/92    *Planning and Compensation Act 1991: Modification and Discharge of Planning Obligations*

29/92    *Indicative Forestry Strategies*

30/92    *Development and Flood Risk*

31/92    *The Town and Country Planning (Fees for Applications and Deemed Applications) (Amendment) (No 2) Regulations 1992*

4/93    *Environmental Protection (Control of Injurious Substances) Regulations 1993*

8/93    *Awards of Costs Incurred in Planning and Other (Including Compulsory Purchase Order) Proceedings*

## Development Control Policy Notes

5    *Development in Town Centres*
8    *Caravan Sites*
11    *Service Uses in Shopping Areas*
12    *Hotels and Motels*
16    *Access for the Disabled*

## Planning Policy Guidance Notes

(PPGs are usually issued jointly by the DoE and the Welsh Office. However, a small number are issued separately by the Welsh Office, and these are listed under Welsh Office Publications)

PPG 1    *General Policy and Principles*, 1992 (superseding 1988 version)

PPG 2    *Green Belts*, 1988

PPG 3    *Housing*, 1992 (superseding *Land for Housing*, 1988)

PPG 4    *Industrial and Commercial Development and Small Firms*, 1992 (revised)

PPG 5    *Simplified Planning Zones*, 1992 (revised)

PPG 6    *Major Retail Development*, 1988

PPG 7    *The Countryside and the Rural Economy*, 1992 (superseding *Rural Enterprise and Development*, 1988)

PPG 8    *Telecommunications*, 1992 (revised)

PPG 9    *Regional Guidance for the South East*, 1988

PPG 10    *Strategic Guidance for the West Midlands*, 1988

PPG 11    *Strategic Guidance for Merseyside*, 1988

PPG 12    *Development Plans and Regional Planning Guidance*, 1992 (superseding *Local Plans*, 1988)

PPG 13    *Highways Considerations in Development Control*, 1988

PPG 14    *Development on Unstable Land*, 1990

PPG 15    *Regional Planning Guidance, Structure Plans, and the Content of Development Plans* (cancelled by revised PPG 12)

PPG 16    *Archaeology and Planning*, 1990

PPG 17    *Sport and Recreation*, 1991

PPG 18    *Enforcing Planning Control*, 1991

PPG 19    *Outdoor Advertising Control*, 1992
PPG 20    *Coastal Planning*, 1992
PPG 21    *Tourism*, 1992
PPG 22    *Renewable Energy*, 1993

## Minerals Policy Guidance Notes

MPG 1     *General Considerations and the Development Plan System*, 1988
MPG 2     *Applications, Permissions and Conditions*, 1988
MPG 3     *Opencast Coal Mining*, 1988
MPG 4     *The Review of Mineral Working Sites*, 1988
MPG 5     *Minerals Planning and the General Development Order*, 1988
MPG 6     *Guidelines for Aggregates Provision in England and Wales*, 1989
MPG 7     *The Reclamation of Mineral Workings*, 1989
MPG 8     *Planning and Compensation Act 1991: Interim Development Order Permissions (IDOS) – Statutory Provisions and Proceedings*, 1991
MPG 9     *Planning and Compensation Act 1991: Interim Development Orders*, 1992
MPG 10    *Provision of Raw Material for the Cement Industry*, 1991

## Regional Planning Guidance Notes

RPG 1     *Strategic Guidance for Tyne & Wear*, 1989
RPG 2     *Strategic Guidance for West Yorkshire*, 1989
RPG 3     *Strategic Guidance for London*, 1991
RPG 3
(Annex)   *Supplementary Guidance for London on the Protection of Strategic Views*, 1991
RPG 4     *Strategic Guidance for Greater Manchester*, 1989
RPG 5     *Strategic Guidance for South Yorkshire*, 1989
RPG 6     *Regional Planning Guidance for East Anglia*, 1991

## Derelict Land Grant Advice Notes

DLGA 1    *Derelict Land Grant Policy*, 1991

## Case Studies of Good Practice in Urban Regeneration (HMSO)

*Community Businesses* (Land and Urban Analysis Ltd), 1990
*Creating Development Trusts* (D. Warburton), 1988
*Developing Businesses* (D. Johnstone), 1988
*Getting People into Jobs* (K. Hayton), 1990
*Greening City Sites* (JURUE: ECOTEC Research and Consultancy Ltd), 1987

*Improving Urban Areas* (JURUE: ECOTEC Research and Consultancy Ltd), 1988
*Managing Workspaces* (A. Jackson, D. Mair, and R. Nabarro), 1987
*Re-Using Redundant Buildings* (Urban and Economic Development Ltd), 1987

## DoE Research Reports (HMSO unless otherwise stated)

*Business Success in the Countryside: The Performance of Rural Enterprise* (D. Keeble, P. Tyler, G. Broom, and J. Lewis), 1992
*Coastal Superquarries to Supply South-East England Aggregate Requirements* (M. Whitbread and A. Marsay), 1992
*Cost Effective Management of Reclaimed Derelict Sites* (Land Capability Consultants), 1990
*Developing Indicators to Assess the Potential for Urban Regeneration* (M. Coombes, S. Raybould, and C. Wong), 1992
*Dynamics of the Rural Economy* (ECOTEC Research and Consulting Ltd), published by the DoE, 1990
*Evaluation of Derelict Land Grant Schemes* (Roger Tym & Partners in association with Land Use Consultants), 1987
*Evaluation of Environmental Projects Funded under the Urban Programme* (JURUE), 1986a
*Evaluation of the Enterprise Zone Experiment* (PA Cambridge Economic Consultants, 1987)
*Evaluation of Garden Festivals* (PA Cambridge Economic Consultants), 1990b
*Evaluation of Industrial and Commercial Improvement Areas* (JURUE), 1986b
*Evaluation of the Stockbridge Village Trust Initiative* (Roger Tym & Partners), 1988
*Evaluating the Effectiveness of Land Use Planning* (PIEDA in association with CUDEM, Leeds Polytechnic, and Professor Derek Diamond), 1992
*Evaluation of the Urban Development Grant Programme* (Public Sector Management Research Unit, Aston University), 1988a
*Five Year Review of the Bolton, Middlesbrough and Nottingham Programme Authorities* (PIEDA) 1990
*Housing Land Availability* (Roger Tym & Partners), 1991
*Improving Inner City Shopping Centres: An Evaluation of Urban Programme Funded Schemes in the West Midlands* (Public Sector Management Research Centre, Aston University), 1988b
*Indicators of Comparative Regional–Local Economic Performance and Prospects* (PA Cambridge Economic Consultants), 1990a
*Land Use Planning and Indicators of Housing Demand* (Coopers & Lybrand), published by Coopers & Lybrand 1987
*Land Use Planning and the Housing Market: An Assessment* (Coopers & Lybrand), published by Coopers & Lybrand, 1985

*Land Use Planning Policy and Climate Change* (S. Owens and D. Cope), 1992

*Managing Urban Change: A Report on the Management Training Needs of Urban Programme Project Managers* (Urban and Economic Development Ltd), 1988

*Mineral Policies in Development Plans* (Arup Economic Consultants), 1990

*Monitoring Environmental Assessment and Planning* (C. Wood and C. Jones), 1991

*National Survey of Vacant Land in Urban Areas of England 1990* (J. Shepherd and A. Abakuks), 1992

*Patterns and Processes of Urban Change in the United Kingdom* (T. Fielding and S. Halford, University of Sussex Centre for Urban and Regional Research), 1990

*Permitted Development Rights for Agriculture and Forestry* (Land Use Consultants), 1991

*Planning, Pollution and Waste Management* (Environmental Resources Ltd in association with Oxford Polytechnic School of Planning), 1992

*Potential Effects of Climate Change in the United Kingdom* (UK Climate Change Impacts Review Group, 1st Report), 1991

*Potential Role of Market Mechanisms in the Control of Acid Rain* (London Economics), 1992

*Process of Local Plan Adoption and Inspectors' Recommendations on Local Plans: Final Report to the DoE, Vol 1: Main Findings; Vol 2: Case Studies* (G. Crispin, P. Fidler, and V. Nadin), published by Coventry Polytechnic, 1985

*Rates of Urbanization in England 1981–2001* (P.R. Bibby and J.W. Shepherd), 1991

*Review of Data Sources for Urban Policy* (ECOTEC Research and Consulting Ltd), 1987

*Relationship between House Prices and Land Supply* (Gerald Eve with the Department of Land Economy, University of Cambridge), 1992

*Simplified Planning Zones: Progress and Procedures* (Arup Economic Consultants), 1991

*Strategic Approach to Derelict Land Reclamation* (Public Sector Management Research Centre, Aston University), 1992

*Tackling Vacant Land: An Evaluation of Policy Instruments for Tackling Urban Land Vacancy* (M. Whitbread, D. Mayne, and D. Wickens, Arup Economic Consultants), 1991

*Targeting Urban Employment Initiatives* (I. Turok and U. Wannop), 1990

*Tourism and the Inner City: An Evaluation of the Impact of Grant Assisted Tourism Projects* (Polytechnic of Central London School of Planning, Leisureworks, and DRV Research), 1990

*Transforming our Waste Land: The Way Forward* (University of Liverpool, Environmental Advisory Unit), 1986

*Urban Industrial Change: The Causes of the Urban-Rural Contrast in Manufacturing Employment Trends* (S. Fothergill, M. Kitson, and S. Monk) 1985

*Urban Labour Markets: Reviews of Urban Research* (B. Moore and P. Townroe), 1990

*Urban Programme and the Young Unemployed* (G. Whitting), 1986

*Use of Planning Agreements* (Grimley J.R. Eve incorporating Vigers in association with Thames Polytechnic School of Land and Construction Management and Alsop Wilkinson), 1992

*US Experience in Evaluating Urban Regeneration: Reviews of Urban Research* (T. Barnekov, D. Hart, and W. Benfer), 1990

*Vacant Urban Land: A Literature Review* (G.E. Cameron, S. Monk, and B.J. Pearce), published by the DoE, 1988

## DoE – Other Publications

*Action for the Countryside*, DoE, 1992

*Climate Change – Our National Programme for Carbon Dioxide Emissions*, DoE, 1992

*Climate Change: Report on United Kingdom National Programme for Limiting Carbon Dioxide Emissions*, DoE, 1992

*Community Projects Review* (S. Elliott, G. Lomas, and A. Riddell), DoE, 1984

*Cost Effective Management of Reclaimed Derelict Sites*, HMSO, 1989

*Development Control Statistics: England*, DoE (annual)

*Development Plans: A Good Practice Guide*, HMSO, 1992

*Development Plans: What You Need to Know*, DoE, 1992

*Digest of Environmental Protection and Water Statistics*, HMSO (annual)

*Environmental Assessment: A Guide to Procedures*, HMSO, 1989

*Estate Action: Annual Report 1991–92*, DoE, 1992

*Estate Action: New Life for Local Authority Estates: Guidelines for Local Authorities on Estate Action and Housing Action Trusts, and Links with Related Programmes*, DoE, 1992

*Functions of Local Authorities in England* (Local Government Review), HMSO, 1992

*Green Rights and Responsibilities: A Citizen's Guide to the Environment*, DoE, 1992

*Guidance on Safeguarding the Quality of Public Water Supplies*, HMSO, 1989

*Housing and Construction Statistics*, HMSO, annual

*Improving Environmental Quality: The Government's Proposals for a New Independent Environment Agency*, DoE, 1991

*Integrated Pollution Control: A Practical Guide*, DoE, 1992

*Land Use Change in England No 7* (Statistical Bulletin (92) 4), DoE, 1992

*Policy Appraisal and the Environment: A Guide for Government Departments*, HMSO, 1991

*Potential Effects of Climate Change in the United Kingdom* (First Report of the Climate Change Impacts Review Group), HMSO, 1991

*Priority Estates Project 1981: Improving Problem Council Estates*, HMSO, 1981

*Report of the Noise Review Working Party* (Batho Report), HMSO, 1990

*Speeding Planning Appeals: A Review of the Handling of Transferred Written Representation Planning Appeals: Report of an Efficiency Scrutiny* (R. Wakeford and R. Heywood), HMSO, 1986

*Speeding Planning Appeals: The Handling of Inquiries Planning Appeals: Action Plan and Review,* HMSO, 1987

*Transport and the Environment Study* (Joint Memorandum by the Departments of Environment and Transport to the Royal Commission on Environmental Pollution), DoE, 1992

*Urban Programme 1985: A Report on its Operation and Achievements in England,* DoE, 1986

*UK Environment,* HMSO, 1992

*Urban Air Quality in the United Kingdom* (First Report of the Quality of Urban Air Review Group), DoE, 1993

*Urban Programme: Annual Programme Guidance 1993/94,* DoE, 1993

*Waste Management: The Duty of Care: A Code of Practice,* HMSO, 1991

## MINISTRY OF AGRICULTURE, FISHERIES AND FOOD

*Agriculture and England's Environment: A Consultation Paper on Environmental Schemes under the Common Agricultural Policy,* MAFF, 1993

*Code of Good Agricultural Practice for the Protection of Air,* MAFF, 1992

*Digest of Agricultural Census Statistics,* HMSO (annual)

*Environmentally Sensitive Areas,* HMSO, 1989

*Farming UK,* MAFF, 1987

*Our Farming Future,* MAFF, 1991

## DEPARTMENT OF TRADE AND INDUSTRY

*Constraints on the Growth of Small Firms* (T. Bovaird, M. Tricker, L. Hems, and S. Martin, Aston Business School), HMSO, 1991

*Effects of Government Regional Economic Policy* (B. Moore, J. Rhodes, and P. Tyler), HMSO, 1986

*Evaluation of the Government's Inner Cities Task Force Initiative: Summary Report* (PA Cambridge Economic Consultants), DTI, 1991

*Geographical Variations in Costs and Productivity* (P. Tyler, B. Moore, and J. Rhodes), HMSO, 1988

*Regional Incentives and the Investment Decision of the Firm* (K. Allen), HMSO, 1986

*Task Forces: Leicester, Preston, and Wolverhampton: An Assessment,* DTI, 1990

*Task Forces in Action,* DTI, 1990

## DEPARTMENT OF TRANSPORT

*Channel Fixed Link: Environmental Appraisal of Alternative Proposals* (Land Use Consultants), HMSO, 1986

*Developers' Contributions to Highway Works: Efficiency Scrutiny Report and the Department's Response,* DoT, 1992

*Developers' Contributions to Highway Works: Consultation Document,* DoT, 1992

*Development in the Vicinity of Trunk Roads,* DoT Circular Roads 6/91, DoT, 1991

*Disability Unit Annual Report,* DoT (annual)

*Emissions from Heavy Duty Diesel Engined Vehicles,* HMSO, 1992

*Interdepartmental Review of Road Safety Policy: Report by the Department of Transport,* DoT, 1987

*National Road Traffic Forecasts (Great Britain) 1989,* HMSO, 1989

*Railway Noise and the Insulation of Dwellings: Report of the Committee to Recommend a National Noise Insulation Standard for New Railway Lines,* (Mitchell Report), HMSO, 1991

*Road Traffic Act 1991,* DoT Local Authority Circular 4/91, HMSO, 1991

*Role of Investment Appraisal in Road and Rail Transport,* DoT, 1992

*Section 56 Grant for Public Transport,* DoT Circular 3/89, HMSO, 1989

*Traffic in London: Traffic Management and Parking Guidance,* DoT Circular 5/92, HMSO, 1992

*Traffic Management and Parking Guidance,* Local Authority Circular 5/92, DoT, 1992

*Traffic Quotes: Public Perception of Traffic Regulation in Urban Areas: Report of a Research Study* (P. Jones), HMSO, 1990

*Transport – A Guide to the Department,* DoT, 1989

*Transport and the Environment,* DoT, 1988

*Transport and the Environment Study: Joint Memorandum by the Departments of the Environment and Transport* (Prepared for the Royal Commission on Environmental Pollution), DoE/DoT, 1992

*Transport Policies and Programme Submission for 1993/94,* DoT Local Authority Circular 3/92, HMSO, 1992

*Transport Statistics, Great Britain, 1992,* HMSO, 1992

## SCOTTISH OFFICE

(Published by the Scottish Office unless otherwise stated.)

### SDD Circulars

19/77   *National Planning Guidelines*
46/80   *Local Government, Planning and Land Act 1980*

24/81   Development Control

29/81   Provision of Public Buildings: Consideration of the Needs of the Disabled

5/82    Town and Country Planning (Minerals) Act 1981

16/82   Safeguarding of Aerodromes, Technical Sites and Explosive Storage Area: Town and Country Planning (Aerodromes)(Scotland) Direction 1982

29/82   Local Government and Planning (Scotland) Act: Planning Provisions

21/83   Private House Building Land Supply: Joint Venture Schemes

32/83   Structure and Local Plans

7/84    Town and Country (Tree Preservation Order and Trees in Conservation Areas) (Scotland) Amendment Regulations 1984

9/84    Planning Controls over Hazardous Development

10/84   Town and Country Planning (Control of Advertisements) (Scotland) Regulations 1984

21/84   Crown Land and Crown Development

22/84   Town and Country Planning (Scotland) Act 1972: Section 50 Agreements

26/84   Town and Country Planning (Scotland) Act 1972: Planning Appeals

6/85    Code of Practice for the Examination in Public of Structure Plans

7/85    Code of Practice for Local Plan Inquiries and Hearings

9/85    Single User Sites for High Technology Activities

17/85   Development Control Priorities and Procedures

18/85   Town and Country Planning (Scotland) Act 1972: Developments by Statutory Undertakers – Consultation with Planning Authorities

19/85   Town and Country Planning (Compensation) Act 1985

24/85   Development in the Countryside and Green Belts

25/85   Telecommunications Development

9/86    Changes to the General Development Order

12/86   Planning Control over Onshore Oil and Gas Operations

18/86   The Use of Conditions in Planning Permissions

22/86   Directional Advertising Signs for Tourist Attractions and Facilities

24/86   Consultation with the Royal Fine Art Commission for Scotland

37/86   Housing and Planning Act 1986

38/86   Location of Major Retail Developments

9/87    Development Control in National Scenic Areas

16/87   Housing and Planning Act 1986: Simplified Planning Zones

17/87   New Provisions and Revised Guidance Relating to Listed Buildings and Conservation Areas

18/87   Development Involving Agricultural Land

22/87   Town and Country Planning (Minerals) Act 1981

23/87   Opencast Coal Mining

1/88    EC Directive on the Conservation of Wild Birds (Directive 70/409/EEC)

13/88   Environmental Assessment: Implementation of EC Directive

26/88   Environmental Assessment of Projects in Simplified Planning Zones and Enterprise Zones

28/88   Caravan Sites

29/88   Notification of Applications

2/89    Administration of Planning Appeals

5/89    Scotland's Travelling People

6/89    The Town and Country Planning (Use Classes) (Scotland) Regulations 1989

13/89   Housing (Scotland) Act 1988: Scottish Homes

14/89   Advertisements: Delegation of Appeals

16/89   Housing Plans

17/89   The Road Humps (Scotland) Regulations 1989

6/90    Award of Expenses in Appeals and other Planning Proceedings and in Compulsory Purchase Order Inquiries

7/90    The Town and Country Planning (Appeals) (Written Submissions Procedure) (Scotland) Regulations 1990; The Town and Country Planning (General Development) (Scotland) Amendment Order 1990

8/90    Changes to the General Development Order

10/90   The Town and Country Planning (Fees for Applications and Deemed Applications) (Scotland) Regulations 1990

3/91    Electricity Generating Stations and Overhead Lines Permitted Development for Electricity Undertakings

13/91   Indicative Forestry Strategies

17/91   Caravan Sites and Control of Development Act 1960: Model Standards

21/91   Planning and Compensation Act 1991: Land Compensation and Compulsory Purchase

22/91   Planning and Compensation Act 1991

26/91   Environmental Assessment and Private Legislation Procedures

## SOEnD Circulars

27/91   Town and Country Planning (Fees for Applications and Deemed Applications) (Scotland) Amendment Regulations 1991

1/92    Planning and Compensation Act 1991: Agreements Relating to Crown Land

2/92    Planning and Compensation Act 1991: Mineral Provisions

5/92    Town and Country Planning (General Permitted Development) (Scotland) Order 1992

6/92    Town and Country Planning (General Development Procedure) (Scotland) Order 1992

8/92    Enforcing Planning Control

9/92    Planning and Compensation Act 1991: Enforcement of Tree Preservation Orders

10/92   Planning and Compensation Act 1991: Control of 'Fly Posting'

26/92   Planning and Compensation Act 1991: Interim Development Order Permissions

31/92   Control over Advertisements and Fish Farming

36/92   *Lawful Development and Enforcement*
38/92   *Disposal of Surplus Government Land – 'The Crichel Down' Rules*

## Planning Advice Notes

24   *Design Guidance*
26   *Disposal of Land and the Use of the Developer's Brief*
27   *Structure Planning* (superseded by 37)
28   *Local Plans* (superseded by 30)
29   *Planning and Small Businesses*
30   *Local Planning*
31   *Simplified Planning Zones*
32   *Development Opportunities and Local Plans*
33   *Development of Contaminated Land*
34   *Local Plan Presentation*
35   *Town Centre Improvement*
36   *Siting and Design of New Housing in the Countryside*
37   *Structure Planning*
38   *Structure Plans: Housing Land Requirements*
39   *Farm and Forestry Buildings*

## National Planning Guidelines

1.   *North Sea Oil and Gas: Coastal Planning Guidelines 1974*
2.   *National Planning Guidelines for Aggregate Working 1977*
3.   *National Planning Guidelines 1981: Priorities for Development Planning*
       – *Land for Housing*
       – *Land for Large Industry*
       – *Land for Petrochemical Development*
       – *Rural Planning Priorities*
       – *National Scenic Areas*
       – *Nature Conservation*
       – *Forestry*
4.   *National Planning Guidelines 1984: Skiing Developments*
5.   *National Planning Guidelines 1985: High Technology; Individual High Amenity Sites*
6.   *National Planning Guidelines 1986: Location of Major Retail Development*
7.   *National Planning Guidelines 1987: Agricultural Land*

## Other Scottish Office Publications (published by the Scottish Office unless otherwise indicated)

*Access and Opportunity: A Strategy for Education and Training*, Cm 1530, HMSO, 1991
*Counting Travellers in Scotland: The 1992 Picture* (H. Gentleman), 1993
*Development Control Performance in Scotland* (MVA Consultancy), 1985

*Environmentally Sensitive Areas in Scotland* (Department of Agriculture and Fisheries for Scotland), 1989
*Football Stadia – Policy Guidance* (Scottish Office Education Department, Circular 10/91), 1991
*Historic Buildings and Monuments: Guide for Grant Applicants*, 1988
*House Price Monitoring Systems and Housing Planning in Scotland* (Report by the Centre for Housing Research, University of Glasgow), 1989
*Improving Scotland's Environment: Consultation Paper on the Scottish Environmental Protection Agency* (SOEnD), 1992
*Industrial Strategy: Contribution of the Local Authorities* (Scottish Economic Planning Department, Circular 1978/2), 1978
*Land Supply and House Prices in Scotland* (PIEDA), 1987
*Listed Buildings and Conservation Areas – Memorandum of Guidance* (1987; Amended 1988), 1988
*New Life for Urban Scotland*, 1988
*Planning and Compensation Act 1991: Enforcement of Listed Building and Conservation Area Control* (Historic Scotland Circular 1/1992), 1992
*Public Attitudes to the Environment in Scotland* (D. Wilkinson and J. Waterton), 1991
*Review of Information on Rural Issues* (Consultant's Report by V. Burbridge), 1990
*Rural Framework*, 1992
*Scotland's Travelling People* (H. Gentleman and S. Swift), HMSO, 1971
*Scottish New Towns: The Way Ahead*, Cm 711, HMSO, 1989
*Scottish Enterprise: A New Approach to Training and Enterprise Creation*, Cm 534, HMSO, 1988
*Scottish Environment – Statistics*, No. 3, 1991
*Simplified Planning Zones – Streamlining of Procedures*, 1990
*Scottish Environment Protection Agency, A Consultation Paper*, 1992
*The Demand for Housing: Economic Perspectives and Planning Practices* (D. MacLennan), 1986
*The Enforcement of Planning Control in Scotland* (Consultants' Report by J. Rowan-Robinson, E. Young, and I. McLarty) (Scottish Development Department), 1984
*Urban Scotland into the 90s: New Life – Two Years On*, 1990
*Urban Scotland into the 90s: Report of the Conference held in Glasgow, May 1990*, 1990

## WELSH OFFICE

(Published directly by the Welsh Office; not available from HMSO; obtainable from the Map Library, Welsh Office, Crown Building, Cathays Park, Cardiff CF1 3NQ.)

Circular 61/81   *Historic Buildings and Conservation Areas – Policy and Procedure*
Circular 47/84   *Land for Housing in Wales*

Circular 53/88   *The Welsh Language: Development Plans and Planning Control*, 1988
Circular 31/91   *Planning and Affordable Housing*
PPG 3 (Wales)   *Land for Housing in Wales*, 1992
PPG 12 (Wales) *Development Plans and Strategic Guidance in Wales*, 1992
PPG 16 (Wales) *Archaeology and Planning*, 1991
*The Welsh Environment: A Guide to Your Rights and Responsibilities*, 1992

## COUNTRYSIDE COMMISSION: SELECTED PUBLICATIONS 1991–1992 (published by the Commission)

*Annual Report 1990–91* (CCP 350), 1991
*Areas of Outstanding Natural Beauty: A Policy Statement* (CCP 356), 1991
*Caring for the Countryside* (CCP 351), 1991
*Countryside Stewardship: An Outline* (CCP 346), 1991
*East Hampshire Landscape: An Assessment of the Area of Outstanding Natural Beauty* (CCP 358), 1991
*Environmental Assessment: The Treatment of Landscape and Countryside Recreation Issues* (CCP 326), 1991
*Fit for the Future: Report of the National Parks Review Panel* (CCP 323), 1991 [An *Executive Summary* is also available: CCP 335, 1991]
*Fit for the Future: The Countryside Commission's Response to the National Parks Review Panel* (CCP 337), 1991
*Forests for the Community* (CCP 340), 1991
*Green Capital: Planning for London's Greenspace* (CCP 344), 1991
*Heritage Coasts: Policies and Priorities 1991* (CCP 305), 1991
*Landscape Change in the National Parks* (CCP 359), 1991
*National Parks in Focus: A Report for 1990/91 – Omnibus Annual Report of the National Parks of England and Wales* (CCP 353), 1991
*Planning Tools: Implementing Countryside Planning Policies in Metropolitan Areas through the Planning System* (CCP 325), 1991
*Protected Landscapes in the United Kingdom* (CCP 362), 1992
*Tamar Valley Landscape* (CCP 364), 1992
*Wind Energy Development and the Landscape* (CCP 357), 1991

## NATIONAL AUDIT OFFICE (HMSO)

*Arrangements for Regional Industrial Incentives*, HC 346 (1987–88), 1988
*Coastal Defences in England*, HC 9 ((1992–93), 1992
*Control and Monitoring of Pollution*, HC 637 (1990–91), 1991
*Derelict Land Grant*, HC 689 (1987–88), 1988
*Enterprise Zones*, HC 209 (1985–86), 1986
*Investment Activities of the Scottish Development Agency, Welsh Development Agency, and the Highlands and Islands Development Board*, HC 230 (1984–85), 1985
*Expenditure on Motorways and Trunk Roads*, HC 571 (1984–85), 1985
*Protecting and Managing England's Heritage Property*, HC 132 (1992–93), 1992
*Regenerating the Inner Cities*, HC 169 (1989–90), 1990
*Regulation of Heavy Lorries*, HC 92 (1987–88), 1987
*Review of Forestry Commission Objectives and Achievements*, HC 75 (1985–86), 1986
*Road Planning*, HC 688 (1988–89), 1988
*Trunk Roads*, HC 571 (1984–85), 1985
*Urban Development Corporations*, HC 492 (1987–88), 1988
*Urban Programme*, HC 513 (1984–85), 1985

## AUDIT COMMISSION FOR LOCAL AUTHORITIES AND THE NATIONAL HEALTH SERVICE IN ENGLAND AND WALES (HMSO unless otherwise stated)

*Building in Quality: A Study of Development Control*, 1992
*Citizen's Charter Performance Indicators*, 1992 (published by the Commission)
*Putting Quality on the Map: Measuring and Appraising Quality in the Public Service*, 1993
*Urban Regeneration and Economic Development: The Local Government Dimension*, 1989
*Urban Regeneration and Economic Development: The European Community Dimension*, 1991

## PARLIAMENTARY INQUIRIES (HMSO)

*Acid Rain*, HC Environment Committee, 4th Report, Session 1983–84, HC 446 (1984)
*Air Pollution*, HC Environment Committee, 1st Report, Session 1987–88, HC 270 (1988)
*Air Pollution from Municipal Waste Incineration Plants*, HL Select Committee on the European Communities, 2nd Report, Session 1988–89, HL 17 (1989)
*British Waterways Board*, HC Environment Committee, 5th Report, Session 1988–89, HC 237 (1989)
*British Waterways Board: Government Response*, Cm 967 (1990)
*Cardiff Bay Barrage Bill*, HL Special Report from the Select

Committee on the Cardiff Bay Barrage Bill, Session 1988–89, HL 57 (1989)

*Coastal Zone Protection and Planning*, HC Environment Committee, 2nd Report, Session 1991–92, HC 17 (1992)

*Coastal Zone Protection and Planning: The Government's Response*, Cm 2011 (1992)

*Compliance with Public Procurement Directives*, HL Select Committee on the European Communities, 12th Report, Session 1987–88, HL 72 (1988)

*Condition and Repair of Privately Owned Housing*, HC Welsh Affairs Committee, 2nd Report, Session 1986–87, HC 230 (1987)

*Contaminated Land*, HC Employment Committee, 1st Report, Session 1989–90, HC 170 (1990)

*Contaminated Land: The Government's Response to the 1st Report from the House of Commons Select Committee on the Environment*, Cm 1161 (1990)

*Control and Monitoring of Pollution: Review of the Pollution Inspectorate*, HC Public Accounts Committee, 16th Report, Session 1991–92, HC 50 (1992)

*Cost of Nuclear Power*, HC Energy Committee, 4th Report, Session 1989–90, HC 205 (1990)

*Cycling*, HC Transport Committee, Minutes of Evidence, 8 May 1991, Session 1990–91, HC 423–i (1991)

*Derelict Land Grant*, HC Public Accounts Committee, 17th Report, Session 1988–89, HC 27 (1989)

*EC Draft Directive on the Landfill of Waste*, HC Environment Committee, 7th Report, Session 1990–91, HC 263 (1991)

*EC Draft Directive on the Landfill of Waste: The Government's Reply to the Seventh Report from the House of Commons Select Committee on the Environment*, Cm 1821 (1992)

*Employment Effects of Urban Development Corporations*, HC Employment Committee, 3rd Report, Session 1987–88, HC 327 (1988)

*Enterprise Zones*, HC Public Accounts Committee, 34th Report, Session 1985–86, HC 293 (1986)

*Environmental Issues in Northern Ireland*, HC Environment Committee, 1st Report, Session 1990–91, HC 39 (1990)

*Environment White Paper: This Common Inheritance*, HC Environment Committee, Session 1990–91, Minutes of Evidence, Department of the Environment, HC 48–i (1991)

*European Community Environmental Policy*, HC Environment Committee, 2nd Report, Session 1989–90, HC 372 (1990)

*Fifth Environmental Action Programme: Integration of Community Policies*, HL Select Committee on the European Communities, 8th Report, Session 1992–93, HL 27 (1992)

*Financing of Public Transport Services: The 'Buses' White Paper*, HC Transport Committee, Session 1984–85, HC 38 (1985)

*Financing of Rail Services*, HC Transport Committee, 3rd Report, Session 1986–87, HC 383 (1987)

*Fish Farming in the UK*, HC Agriculture Committee, 4th Report, Session 1989–90, HC 141 (1990)

*Fourth Environmental Action Programme*, HL Select Committee on the European Communities, 8th Report, Session 1986–87, HL 135 (1987)

*Freedom of Access to Information on the Environment*, HL Select Committee on the European Communities, 1st Report, Session 1989–90, HL 2 (1989)

*Government's Proposals for an Environment Agency*, HC Environment Committee, 1st Report, Session 1991–92, HC 55 (1992)

*Green Belt and Land for Housing*, HC Environment Committee, 1st Report, Session 1983–84, HC 275 (1984)

*Greenhouse Effect*, HL Select Committee on Science and Technology, 6th Report, Session 1988–89 (1989)

*Habitat and Species Protection*, HL Select Committee on the European Communities, 15th Report, Session 1988–89, HL 72 (1989)

*Hazardous Waste Disposal*, HL Select Committee on Science and Technology, 4th Report, Session 1988–89, HL 40 (1989)

*Hazardous Waste: The Government's Response to the Fourth Report from the House of Lords Select Committee on Science and Technology*, Cm 763 (1989)

*Highlands and Islands Development Board*, HC Scottish Affairs Committee, 2nd Report, Session 1984–85, HC 22 (1985)

*Historic Buildings and Ancient Monuments*, HC Environment Committee, 1st Report, Session 1986–87, HC 146 (1987)

*Historic Buildings and Ancient Monuments: Observations on the First Report of the Committee in Session 1986–87 (HC 146)*, HC Environment Committee, 1st Special Report, Session 1987–88, HC 268 (1988)

*Implementation and Enforcement of Environmental Legislation*, HL Select Committee on the European Communities, 9th Report, Session 1991–92, HL 53 (1992)

*Implementation of the Reform of the Common Agricultural Policy*, Select Committee on the European Communities, 9th Report, Session 1992–93, HL 28 (1992)

*Indoor Pollution*, HC Environment Committee, 6th Report, Session 1990–91, HC Environment Committee, 6th Report, Session 1990–91, HC 61 (1991)

*Indoor Pollution: The Government's Response to the Sixth Report from the House of Commons Select Committee on the Environment*, Cm 1633 (1991)

*Industrial Change: Retraining and Redeployment*, HC Employment Committee, 2nd Report, Session 1991–92, HC 71 (1992)

*Nature Conservancy Council*, HL Select Committee on Science and Technology, 2nd Report, Session 1989–90, HL 33 (1990)

*Nature Conservancy Council: Government Response*, HL Select Committee on Science and Technology, 6th Report, Session 1989–90, HL 60 (1990)

*Nitrate in Water*, HL Select Committee on the European Communities, 16th Report, Session 1988–89, HL 73 (1989)

*Operation and Effectiveness of Part II of the Wildlife and Countryside Act*, HC Environment Committee, 1st Report, Session 1984–85, HC 6 (1985)

*Paying for Pollution – Civil Liability for Damage Caused by Waste*, HL Select Committee on the European Communities, 25th Report, Session 1989–90, HL 84 (1990)

*Planning Appeals, Call-in, and Major Public Inquiries*, HC Environment Committee, 5th Report, Session 1985–86, HC 181 (1986)

*Planning Appeals, Call-in, and Major Public Inquiries: The Government's Response*, Cm 43 (1986)

*Planning Procedures*, HC Expenditure Committee, 8th Report, Session 1976–77, HC 395 (1977)

*Pollution of Beaches*, HC Environment Committee, 4th Report, Session 1989–90, HC 12 (1990)

*Pollution of Beaches: The Government's Response to the 4th Report from the House of Commons Committee on the Environment*, Cm 1363 (1990)

*Pollution of Rivers and Estuaries*, HC Environment Committee, 3rd Report, Session 1986–87, HC 183 (1987)

*Pollution of Rivers and Estuaries: Observations by the Government on the 3rd Report of the Committee*, Environment Committee, 3rd Special Report, Session 1987–88, HC 543 (1988)

*Problems of Management of Urban Renewal*, Environment Committee, Session 1982–83, HC 18 (1983)

*Proposed European Environment Agency*, HC Environment Committee, 7th Report, Session 1988–89, HC 612 (1989)

*Protecting and Managing England's Heritage Property*, Public Accounts Committee, Session 1992–93, Minutes of Evidence, 2 November 1992, HC 252–i (1992)

*Public Transport in Wales*, HC Welsh Affairs Committee, 1st Report, Session 1984–85, HC 35 (1985)

*Regenerating the Inner Cities*, HC Public Accounts Committee, 33rd Report, Session 1989–90, HC 216 (1990)

*Roads for the Future*, HC Transport Committee, 1st Report, Session 1989–90, HC 198 (1990)

*Tourism,* HC Employment Committee, 4th Report, Session 1989–90, HC 18 (1990)

*Tourism: Government Reply*, HC Employment Committee, 4th Special Report, Session 1989–90, HC 668 (1990)

*Toxic Waste*, HC Environment Committee, 2nd Report, Session 1988–89, HC 22 (1989)

*Toxic Waste: The Government's Reply to the Second Report from the Environment Committee*, Cm 679 (1989)

*Toxic Waste Disposal in Wales*, HC Welsh Affairs Committee, 1st Report, Session 1989–90, HC 34 (1990)

*Training and Enterprise Councils and Vocational Training*, HC Employment Committee, 5th Report, Session 1990–91, HC 285 (1991)

*Urban Public Transport: The Light Rail Option*, HC Transport Committee, 4th Report, Session 1990–91, HC 14 (1991)

*Water Quality Objectives for Chromium*, HL Select Committee on the European Communities, 2nd Report, 1986–87, HL 37 (1987)

*White Paper: People, Jobs and Opportunity, Cm 1810*, HC Employment Committee, Session 1991–92, Minutes of Evidence 3 March 1992, HC 322 (1992)

## OTHER OFFICIAL PUBLICATIONS

*Chief Planning Inspector's Report April 1991 to March 1992*, HMSO, 1992

*Civil Service Year Book 1992*, Cabinet Office, HMSO, 1992

*Civil Service Management Reform: The Next Steps* (Government reply to the Report from the HC Treasury and Civil Service Committee) Cm 524, HMSO, 1988

*Efficiency Report: Improving Management in Government: The Next Steps* (Report by K. Jenkins, K. Caines, and A. Jackson), HMSO, 1988

Departmental Annual Reports: published jointly by the Department concerned and the Treasury, e.g. *DoE Annual Report 1993: The Government's Expenditure Plans 1993–94 to 1995–96*, Cm 2207, 1993

# INDEX OF STATUTES

# GENERAL INDEX